The Routledge Companion to Mergers and Acquisitions

Mergers and acquisitions (M&As) are events that attract considerable interest from academics and practitioners, and much research has been conducted into their impact on individuals, organizations and societies. Yet, despite all the existing research and the varied theoretical and methodological approaches employed, there remains more to learn about M&As.

The Routledge Companion to Mergers and Acquisitions takes a detailed look at this multi-facted subject using a novel framework of four domains – substantive issues, contextual issues, methodological issues and conceptual issues. Drawing on the expertise of its international team of contributors, the volume surveys the state of the field, including emerging and cutting-edge areas such as social network analysis and corporate branding.

This Companion will be a rich resource for students, researchers and practitioners involved in the study of M&As, and organizational and strategic studies more widely.

Annette Risberg is Associate Professor at the Copenhagen Business School, Denmark.

David R. King is Associate Professor at Iowa State University, USA.

Olimpia Meglio is Associate Professor at University of Sannio, Italy.

This book provides a deep and rich compendium of knowledge about mergers and acquisitions. Because of the breadth of topics examined and the depth of the analyses provided, all scholars interested in this important strategy should make this required reading.

Michael A. Hitt, *University Distinguished Professor, Texas A&M University, USA*

This is a great book, one which manages to effectively traverse the contextual, methodological and practical facets to M&As. The book integrates a variety of views and in doing so offers coherent coverage of this salient and pervasive phenomenon. The Companion is an insightful read for anyone interested in exploring and understanding the substantive, methodological and conceptual domains of M&As which makes it relevant to both researching and teaching this important topic.

Sally Riad, *Victoria University of Wellington, New Zealand*

Mergers and acquisitions are strategic movements and researchers in this field need to open their minds to new approaches, theories and visions. This is exactly what this timely book does: its reading is sure to inspire new research in this complex field.

Philippe Very, *Professor of Strategy, Edhec Business School, France*

In today's high velocity and globalized world, mergers and acquisitions are common place in the arsenal of corporate strategy. *The Routledge Companion to Mergers and Acquisitions* provides invaluable insights into the complexities of M&As, relevant for academics and practitioners alike.

Frank T. Rothaermel, *The Russell and Nancy McDonough Chair, Professor & Sloan Industry Studies Fellow, Georgia Institute of Technology, USA*

Researchers and practitioners alike need novel perspectives to better understand the complex social and organizational dynamics of M&As, and this book provides just that. Leading scholars of the field provide insightful and inspiring reflections on merger dynamics as well as practically valuable conceptual and methodological tools.

Eero Vaara, *Professor of Organization and Management, Aalto University School of Business, Finland*

Anyone interested in exploring mergers and acquisitions from a multidisciplinary perspective will treasure this book. Besides focusing on specific merger issues and problems, it also offers an excellent section on methodology making it a must read for academics and practitioners.

Steffen Giessner, *Associate Professor in Organizational Behavior, Erasmus University, the Netherlands*

This book is a must-have companion for all strategy researchers and advanced M&A practitioners. The book provides a great cross-section of contemporary thinking and a glimpse into the latest research of the top scholars of our field.

Tomi Laamanen, *Professor, University of St. Gallen, Switzerland*

This book provides a timely and comprehensive view on mergers and acquisitions. Read this book and you will understand more of the complexity and challenges in merger and acquisition processes.

Virpi Havila, *Professsor of Business Studies, Uppsala University, Sweden*

The Routledge Companion to Mergers and Acquisitions

Edited by Annette Risberg,
David R. King and Olimpia Meglio

Routledge
Taylor & Francis Group

LONDON AND NEW YORK

First published 2016
by Routledge
4 Park Square, Milton Park, Abingdon, Oxon OX14 4RN

and by Routledge
605 Third Avenue, New York, NY 10017

First issued in paperback 2022

Routledge is an imprint of the Taylor & Francis Group, an informa business

British Library Cataloguing in Publication Data
A catalogue record for this book is available from the British Library

Library of Congress Cataloging-in-Publication Data
The Routledge companion to mergers and acquisitions / edited by Annette Risberg,
    David R. King and Olimpia Meglio.
        pages cm. — (Routledge companions in business, management and accounting)
    Includes bibliographical references and index.
    1. Consolidation and merger of corporations. I. Risberg, Annette.
    HD2746.5.R686 2015
    658.1'62—dc23
    2014046907

ISBN 13: 978-1-03-247730-5 (pbk)
ISBN 13: 978-0-415-70466-3 (hbk)
ISBN 13: 978-0-203-76188-5 (ebk)

DOI: 10.4324/9780203761885

Typeset in Bembo
by Apex CoVantage, LLC

To Léa
A.R.

To Zack
D.R.K.

To Carlo
O.M.

Contents

Figures

Tables

Contributors

Anjali Bansal earned her PhD in Human Resource Management (HRM) from the Faculty of Management Studies (FMS), University of Delhi. Anjali has also served the University of Delhi as Assistant Professor, where she taught courses related to HRM strategy in business. Anjali's research focuses on areas like HR as strategic partner to organizations, change management, mergers and acquisitions (M&As), post-M&A integration strategy and employees' psychological phenomena during change. Apart from teaching management subjects and writing for leading HRM and strategy journals Anjali also serves society while collaborating with a couple of NGOs (non-governmental organizations) which work for child and women welfare in India.

Florian Bauer is a Senior Lecturer at MCI Management Center Innsbruck and Director of the SMA Research Lab. After studying management and law (diploma) he finished his PhD at Innsbruck University in 2011. His main research focus is in the field of strategy, mergers and acquisitions and the effects of decision making. His research has been published in leading management journals and books.

Stefano Breschi is Professor of Applied Economics and Deputy Director of the Center for Research on Innovation, Organization and Strategy (CRIOS) at Bocconi University, Milan (Italy). His main research interests are in the economics of technical change, industrial dynamics, social networks, economics of science, economics of the patent system, economic geography and regional economics. He is author of numerous articles in journals like *Economic Journal, Research Policy, Industrial and Corporate Change, Regional Studies* and *Journal of Economic Geography*, among others. He is Associate Editor of *Industrial and Corporate Change*.

Laurence Capron is Professor of Strategy at INSEAD, Paris where she holds the Paul Desmarais Chair in Partnership and Active Ownership and is Director of the Executive Education Programme on M&As and Corporate Strategy. She is a leading expert on M&As, alliances and business portfolio strategy. She is co-author of *Build, Borrow, or Buy: Solving the Growth Dilemma*, which examines how companies should select and balance their different modes of growth: organic growth (*build*), licensing and alliances (*borrow*) and M&As (*buy*). She earned her PhD in strategy from HEC Paris.

Kaitlyn DeGhetto is an Assistant Professor of Management at the University of Colorado at Colorado Springs. Kaitlyn received her PhD from Florida State University (FSU) and her MBA and BA in Business Administration from the University of Florida. Her research interests include global strategy, corporate governance, entrepreneurship and acquisition processes. Prior to entering the doctoral programme at FSU, Kaitlyn worked in the health care and wholesale/distribution industries, as both a business development manager and product manager.

Lars Frimanson is Senior Lecturer in Business at Uppsala University. His research centres around the role of management control technologies in organizational change processes, including their consequences for stress and health.

Michael Grant is a PhD student at Uppsala University. His research interest is about M&A processes and what takes place within them. He has extensive experience from working internationally with M&A for more than 20 years.

Joseph S. Harrison is a PhD student at Mays Business School, Texas A&M University. Prior to entering the PhD programme, he received a BS in business administration from the Robins School of Business, University of Richmond and worked for several years in finance and consulting. His major research interests include corporate governance, upper echelons and corporate-level strategies such as mergers and acquisitions, alliances and innovation strategies.

Melanie Hassett is a postdoctoral Researcher in International Business at the Turku School of Economics, Finland. Her doctoral thesis on 'Key persons' organisational commitment in cross-border acquisitions' received the Emerald/EMFD Outstanding Doctoral Research Award in the Human Resource Management category. Her position as a project coordinator for three M&A-related research projects provides a solid basis for her research. She is currently a visiting researcher at Oxford Brookes University, UK. Melanie's research interest lies in mergers and acquisitions, cross-border acquisitions, M&A performance, value creation in acquisitions, human resource and cultural integration.

Güldem Karamustafa received her PhD in Management from Geneva School of Economics and Management (formerly HEC Geneva), University of Geneva. After completing her undergraduate degree in Environmental Engineering she worked as an HR professional at a multinational and obtained a Masters degree in HRM. Güldem's research focuses on the process of adaptation with the aim of understanding how individuals, groups and organizations can learn and grow through diverse experience. Her research interests include organizational learning, group dynamics, M&As, HRM and sustainability.

David R. King earned his PhD from Indiana University in 2002, as part of his military career, and he joined Iowa State University as an Associate Professor in 2013. His research appears in leading journals and focuses on M&A integration and performance, technology innovation and defence procurement.

David P. Kroon is an Assistant Professor of Strategic Management at the Faculty of Economics and Business Administration of VU University Amsterdam, the Netherlands. He received his PhD from Tilburg University. He teaches courses on strategy, international collaboration and research methodology at undergraduate, graduate and MBA level. His current research focuses on inter-organizational collaboration, organizational change and post-M&A integration, with a particular emphasis on identity/identification, justice, culture, communication and trust.

Bruce T. Lamont is the Thomas L. Williams Eminent Scholar in Strategy in the College of Business at Florida State University. He formerly served as the Chair of the Management Department and Associate Dean of Graduate Programs in the College of Business at Florida State. Professor Lamont received his PhD from the University of North Carolina at Chapel Hill. His research has been published in such outlets as the *Academy of Management Journal, Academy of Management Review, Journal of International Business Studies, Journal of Management* and *Strategic Management Journal*. He currently serves on the editorial review boards for the *Journal of Management Studies* and *Strategic Management Journal* and as Senior Associate Editor of the *Africa Journal* *of Management.* He has also served on the editorial review boards of the *Academy of Management Journal* and the *Journal of Management*, the Executive and Research Committees of the Business Policy and Strategy Division of the Academy of Management, as a Representative-At-Large for both the Strategy Process Interest Group and the Corporate Strategy Interest Group of the Strategic Management Society, and the Board of Governors of the Southern Management Association. His current research addresses the effective management of acquisition integration processes, knowledge investments and novel applications of theory to the African context.

Rebecca Lund is a PhD candidate in Organization and Management at Aalto University, Finland. Her doctoral research interests include institutional ethnography, feminist epistemologies and ontologies, gendered social relations, academic work and higher educational organizations. Her teaching has been on gender and diversity in organizations, and ethics in a global economy.

Anna A. Lupina-Wegener is Professor in Management at the University of Applied Sciences and Arts – Western Switzerland (HES-SO; HEIG-VD). Previously she was a postdoctoral fellow at the University of Geneva and she obtained her doctorate at the Warsaw School of Economics. Her research and teaching focus on organizational behaviour and international management, with a further research focus on socio-cultural integration processes in cross-border mergers and acquisitions, particularly those involving organizations in emerging economies.

Olimpia Meglio earned a PhD in Management from the University of Naples 'Federico II'. She is currently an Associate Professor at the University of Sannio. Her work has appeared in international journals and handbooks and focuses on M&A performance measurement and methodological issues in the study of M&As.

Nicola Mirc is Associate Professor at the Toulouse School of Management (University of Toulouse, France), Researcher at the Center for Research in Management (CRM) at the University of Toulouse and Associated Researcher at the Centre de Recherche en Gestion (CRG) at the Ecole Polytechnique, France. In her research, she studies organizational and human issues of post-acquisition integration. Her work addresses the dynamics of social structures and relations between acquirer and target, with a special focus on the evolution of work collaboration and knowledge transfer. Using social network analysis coupled with qualitative methods, her research aims at approaching post-acquisition integration on multiple levels, discussing the interdependence of factors and phenomena at the organizational, the group and the individual level. Her research has been published in journals such as the *Scandinavian Journal of Management, Advances in Mergers and Acquisitions* and *Thunderbird International Business Review*.

Fredrik Nilsson is Professor of Business Studies, especially Accounting, at Uppsala University. His research focuses on how information systems (e.g. management control systems, financial accounting systems and production control systems) are designed and used to formulate and implement strategies. He is currently studying the relationship between strategies, management control and financial accounting in banks. Fredrik has published in such journals as *Accounting & Finance, British Journal of Management, European Management Journal, Management Accounting Research* and *Scandinavian Journal of Management.* Two recent books co-authored by him are *Mergers and Acquisitions: The Critical Role of Stakeholders* (Routledge, together with Helén Anderson and Virpi Havila) and *Strategy, Control and Competitive Advantage: Case Study Evidence* (together with Erik Jannesson and Birger Rapp).

Niina Nummela is a Professor of International Business at the Turku School of Economics at the University of Turku. Her areas of expertise include international entrepreneurship, cross-border acquisitions and research methods. She has published widely in academic journals, including *International Business Review, Journal of World Business, Management International Review, European Journal of Marketing* and *International Small Business Journal*, among others. She has also contributed to several internationally published books and edited *International Growth of Small and Medium Enterprises* (Routledge, 2010).

Christina Öberg is the Chair in Marketing at Örebro University, Sweden. She is a Visiting Professor at Leeds University and Honorary Associate Professor at the University of Exeter. She has a background as an Associate Professor at Lund University and Assistant Professor at Linköping University. Her research interests are mergers and acquisitions, customer relationships and innovation management. Her research is published in such journals as *Journal of Business Research, Construction Management and Economics, International Journal of Innovation Management, European Journal of Marketing, The Service Industries Journal, Journal of Business-to-Business Marketing, Scandinavian Journal of Management, International Marketing Review* and *Industrial Marketing Management*.

Amy L. Pablo earned her PhD in Organization Studies from the University of Texas at Austin. After retiring from a position at Amoco Corporation, she joined academia and since 1991 has been an Associate Professor at the Haskayne School of Business at the University of Calgary, Alberta, Canada. Amy's research focuses on corporate mergers and acquisitions and the organizational decision making and changes that accompany being involved with such transactions. Due to her MS condition, she is currently on long-term disability from teaching, but continues with her research and publishing. An award-winning researcher, her research appears in leading management journals.

Kathleen Park earned her PhD degree at the MIT Sloan School of Management. After completing her postdoctoral research specialization in global leadership development and internationalization from emerging markets, she presently holds a dual appointment as Research Fellow at the MIT Sloan School of Management and International Faculty Fellow and Assistant Professor of Strategic and International Management at the Gulf University for Science and Technology in Kuwait. Her research has been published in business journals and book chapters and has received awards from the Academy of Management.

Pankaj C. Patel is an Associate Professor of management at the Miller College of Business at Ball State University, IN. His research interests focus on entrepreneurship, family business and innovation.

Lucia Piscitello is Professor of International Business at Politecnico di Milano. Her research interests cover the economics and management of multinational enterprises (MNEs), the international aspects of technological change and the geography of innovation. Her recent studies focus on agglomeration and MNEs' location strategies, globalization of R&D and technology development in the global network of MNEs, offshoring and global sourcing, and MNEs from emerging countries. She has published in international journals such as *Economic Geography, Journal of Economic Geography, Journal of International Business Studies, Global Strategy Journal, Strategic Entrepreneurship Journal, Industrial and Corporate Change, Research Policy*, among others. She is Associate Editor of the *Global Strategy Journal*, and serves on the editorial review boards of several journals. She has taught extensively in undergraduate and graduate programmes, customized executive education, and MBA and executive MBA programmes.

Roberta Rabellotti is Professor of Economics in the Department of Political and Social Sciences at the Università di Pavia in Italy. She has a Master of Science in Development Economics from the University of Oxford and a Doctor of Philosophy from the Institute of Development

Studies, University of Sussex. Her areas of expertise are the economics of innovation, economic development and regional economics. Her publications include books as well as numerous articles published in top academic journals. Prof. Rabellotti regularly advises international organizations such as UNIDO, UNCTAD, IADB, OECD and the European Commission on questions related to economic development (http://robertarabellotti.it).

Annette L. Ranft is the Associate Dean for Academic Affairs and the Reagan Professor of Business at the University of Tennessee Knoxville. She received her PhD in Business Administration from the University of North Carolina at Chapel Hill. She is also an active member of the Strategic Management Society, the Academy of Management and the Southern Management Association. She currently serves as an Associate Editor of the *Journal of Management* and is on the editorial review boards of the *Academy of Management Review* and the *Strategic Management Journal*. Her research interests are primarily in the areas of knowledge management, strategic leadership and innovation, particularly in the context of corporate acquisitions. Her research has been published in top journals, including the *Academy of Management Review, Academy of Management Journal, Organization Science*, the *Journal of International Business Studies* and the *Journal of Management*.

Annette Risberg holds a PhD from Lund University. She is currently working at Copenhagen Business School. Some of her latest publications on M&A can be found in the *Scandinavian Journal of Management, Handbook of Research on Mergers and Acquisition, Mergers and Acquisitions: The Critical Role of Stakeholders* and *Advances in Mergers and Acquisitions*.

Sangbum Ro earned his PhD in strategic management from Florida State University and MBA from Binghamton University, NY. Before joining higher education, he oversaw business operations for an architectural and engineering firm. He is currently a visiting clinical Assistant Professor at Georgia State University where he teaches business strategy. His research focuses on legitimacy of multinational corporations, merger and acquisition integration, and organizational learning and innovation.

Marcella Rothermel is a PhD student at Innsbruck University School of Management: Business. Her research focuses on brand and marketing management in mergers and acquisitions.

Audrey Rouzies is Associate Professor and Head of the Masters in International Management (1st year) at Toulouse School of Management (University of Toulouse, France). Her research deals with the human side of mergers and acquisitions. Her research interests focus on employees' reactions in post-merger integration. She studies employees' identification and re-identification processes after a merger and the impact of identity transition on employees' commitment in implementing the integration process. She uses mixed-methods designs to analyse international deals such as the merger between Air France and KLM or the acquisition of Tinfos by Eramet.

Vittoria Giada Scalera (PhD) is a post-doc research fellow at Politecnico di Milano, Italy. From October 2013 to September 2014 she was also visiting scholar at the Department of Strategic Management, Fox Business School, Temple University, PA. Her research focuses on internationalization strategies of MNEs, especially from emerging economies, knowledge-intensive acquisitions, innovation management and globalization of R&D in global networks. She has been involved in several international projects and she is currently part of the 'iBEGIN: The Temple Knowledge Maps Project. Global connectivity as the basis for local innovation' coordinated by Prof. Ram Mudambi (Temple University). At Politecnico di Milano Vittoria also teaches in graduate programmes.

Mario Schijven is an Assistant Professor of Business Administration at the University of Illinois at Urbana-Champaign. He received his PhD from Tilburg University in the Netherlands. In his primary line of research, he builds on perspectives from strategy and organization theory to study organizational learning, capability development and evolution in complex strategic settings, such as those of acquisitions and organizational restructuring. His work has appeared in the *Academy of Management Journal*, the *Strategic Management Journal*, and the *Journal of Management*, among others.

Susan C. Schneider is Professor Emeritus of the University of Geneva. Her teaching and research interests focus on cross-cultural management, diversity and social responsibility. Her book, *Managing Across Cultures*, was written with J.L Barsoux (translated into French, Dutch and Chinese) and G. Stahl (3rd edn, 2014). Previously Professor of Organizational Behavior at INSEAD, she has also been visiting professor at Zhejiang University (China), Nova University (Portugal) and ESSEC (France). She has a doctorate in clinical psychology and worked for several years in psychiatric hospitals in New York City. She then did a postdoctoral study of organizational analysis at New York University.

Svante Schriber earned his PhD in strategy and management from the Stockholm School of Economics. With a background in consulting, he joined academia and is currently a Researcher at Stockholm Business School. Svante's research focuses on merger and acquisition strategy and integration, strategic management and the development and use of organizational capabilities. He teaches M&A, strategy, and management and organization at executive, graduate and undergraduate levels.

Jennifer C. Sexton is Assistant Professor of Management at West Virginia University. She received a PhD in Business Administration from Florida State University. Her research interests include organizational learning, knowledge-based and resource-based perspectives, innovation, top management teams and mergers and acquisitions. She is especially interested in examining how firms develop, control and change their innovation processes. She has presented her research at the Strategic Management Society, the Babson College Entrepreneurship Research Conference and the Southern Management Association, and her work has appeared in several scholarly journals and anthologies, including *Organizational Research Methods*.

Satu Teerikangas is Senior Lecturer in management at University College London. Her research centres on the management of mergers and acquisitions, focusing on the human, cultural and emotional dimensions thereof. She is co-editor of the *Handbook of Mergers and Acquisitions* (2012), the first initiative to combine strategic, financial and sociocultural perspectives in the approach to M&As. Her work has been published in leading academic journals, such as *Journal of Management* and *British Journal of Management*. Before her academic career, she worked in telecommunications and oil and gas in Finland, the Netherlands and the UK.

Marco Testoni is a PhD student in Strategy at UCLA Anderson School of Management. He holds a double degree MSc in Economics and Management of Innovation and Technology from Bocconi University and Copenhagen Business School. Marco has worked as a research assistant at Bruegel – the Brussels-based think tank specialized in economic policy – in the area of economics of innovation. Previously, he worked at Roland Berger Strategy Consultants in Milan and as Research Assistant at the Institute of Management of USI in Switzerland.

Mahima Thakur earned her doctorate from the Indian Institute of Technology Delhi, India, in Organizational Psychology. Currently she is working as Assistant Professor at the Faculty of Management Studies, University of Delhi, where she teaches courses in the area of change management, industrial relations, organizational behaviour and business communication. She has presented her research at various international conferences in a number of countries and her work has been published in various international journals. Her research interests are primarily in the area of mergers and acquisitions, industrial relations, empowerment and leadership,

Janne Tienari is Professor of Organization and Management at Aalto University, School of Business, Finland. Tienari's research and teaching interests include managing multinational corporations, mergers and acquisitions, strategy work, gender and diversity, and cross-cultural management and communication. His latest passion is to understand management, new generations and the future. His work has been published in leading organization and management journals.

Giovanni Valentini is Associate Professor of Strategy and a fellow of CRIOS at Bocconi University, Milan (Italy). He received his PhD from IESE Business School. His research focuses on the organization of the innovation process, the relationship between technological innovation and export and the effect of M&A on technological performance.

Liisa Välikangas is Professor of Innovation Management at Hanken School of Economics and Aalto University. Previously, she has been affiliated with Stanford University, London Business School, Keio University in Japan and IMD in Switzerland. Her research on innovation, strategy and organizing has been published in *Harvard Business Review, MIT Sloan Management Review* and *Wall Street Journal*, among other leading journals, and presented to various executive audiences. She is the author of *The Resilient Organization, How Adaptive Cultures Thrive Even When Strategy Fails* (2010). She is currently studying the importance of vanguard companies for strategic discovery, to be published in 2015.

Acknowledgements

We thank our families and our colleagues, both past and present, who made this book possible. We recognize that the value of our book reflects research efforts that preceded us and we wish that our book's shadow influences future research.

We appreciate the contributions of the authors of the different chapters to the book, as it would not be what it is without your thoughts and time. We also thank the efforts of anonymous reviewers who helped to develop the chapters: you know who you are. A warm thank you to the research assistant Sofie Skovbo Gottlieb for her invaluable job checking all the small details in the manuscript. Last, but not least, we thank the people of Routledge for making this book a reality.

Malmö, Ames and Castellammare di Stabia
June 2015

Introduction

A widespread number of mergers and acquisitions (also M&As) are shaping industries across continents. Consequently, companies, as well as the people who work in them, are frequently affected by acquisitions one or more times during their lifetimes. The impact on companies' and peoples' lives, together with the pervasiveness of acquisitions, explains the continued and renewed interest from the academic community in investigating this phenomenon. Acquisitions are no longer extraordinary events for corporations. They have become a context where old and new management and organizational issues unfold, and the importance of these issues is magnified due to the seemingly simple circumstance that two companies become one. For example, all firms bring in new hires with established routines and processes. This rather simple act becomes complicated because a firm's managers and its processes are often unprepared to bring in thousands of established employees following an acquisition. Moreover, acquisitions tend to spread their effects not only within the boundaries of the companies involved but also outside their boundaries to include other stakeholders, such as consumers, suppliers, competitors, investors, and governments to name a few. These considerations illustrate that acquisitions are complex processes taking place at many levels of an organization, and across many organizational dimensions and boundaries at the same time. All these issues explain the continued attention that M&A scholars give to such a complex phenomenon.

Since the first study by Dewing (1921), mergers and acquisitions have catalyzed the attention of scholars from several disciplines, ranging from management and organization to financial economics, to grasp the complexity. So far, the common recipe to capture and render this complexity has been to integrate different theoretical lenses into models that are then empirically tested. Existing reviews of M&A research provide a detailed assessment of what we know already and what there is still to learn (e.g. Haleblian et al. 2009).

A common way to assess the current state of M&A literature is to point to inconsistency in research findings, particularly regarding how acquisitions perform. In order to solve such inconsistency, scholars seek to find different possible explanations. Some point to the fragmentation of M&A literature (e.g. King et al. 2004; Schweizer 2005). Others suggest an existence of substantive gaps in existing literature (e.g. Barkema and Schijven 2008; Haleblian et al. 2009) or a need for integrative frameworks to grasp such a complex, multifaceted, and multi-temporal phenomenon (e.g. Larsson and Finklestein 1999; Pablo and Javidan 2004). In the light of these inconsistencies, Bower (2004) and Javidan et al. (2004) posit that researchers aiming to explain M&A outcomes in general have not yet been able to successfully develop and test a grand theory about M&As. Unsatisfied with the current research results, scholars continue to pursue explanations of the complex processes in and around M&As.

The current situation in M&A research results in what Alvesson and Sandberg (2013) refer to as "gap-spotting" research, which is a focus on gaps in existing research that tends to reproduce current knowledge and often falls short of bringing forth novel and interesting ideas (Davis 1971). Understanding current M&A research as "gap-spotting" may explain the dissatisfaction that many M&A scholars express regarding the ability to grasp the complexity of this phenomenon. Given the complexity of M&As, there is a need for greater acceptance of multiple perspectives and interplay of paradigms to appreciate underlying nuances.

In this companion, we contribute novel and interesting ideas to the exploration of acquisitions. We believe that an improved understanding of M&A emerges by exploring lower-level contexts along with different methodological approaches. We approach the substantive field of mergers and acquisitions from a multiple disciplinary view and an examination of issues, or important matters that arise within and between organizations during M&A processes. Instead of elaborating and proposing even more complex frameworks, we focus on issues, topics, and problems that are important to practitioners conducting M&As, as well as the academics studying them. This book therefore presents a range of contributions by researchers who have explored a variety of M&A issues using diverse research methods in different research settings across the globe. In our view, this approach offers the potential for a more comprehensive view of M&A studies by considering both areas of difference and agreement.

What we propose to the reader is a journey in and around mergers and acquisitions, through classic and new substantive issues, concepts, and methods. The transit stops within this companion are represented by the four sections around which it is organized. The first section, or stop, intends to investigate substantive issues, whereas the second aims at analyzing M&As as a research context within which to investigate management and organizational topics. The third section is concerned with the methodological challenges and their implications in the use of different research designs when one studies M&As, while the fourth section draws scholarly attention to the definitions and meanings of popular concepts within the M&A domain. This structure extends Brinberg and McGrath's (1985) framework of marketing research that depicts three distinct, yet interrelated domains—the substantive, methodological, and conceptual. These elements are present in any research endeavor, yet their relative importance depends on where researchers start from and the aim they intend to achieve. This framework serves as a useful device to rejuvenate the inconsistency debate referred to earlier. To add to the framework, we introduce the idea of a contextual domain to further our understanding of how contexts influence acquisitions and how acquisitions differ depending on contextual factors, such as the industry or the countries where the merging companies operate. The companion sections are based on these domains.

The companion itself is the result of a journey initiated in 2012 when we submitted our proposal to Routledge and continued with the call for chapters which, once received, went through several rounds of blind peer reviews. The journey spans across continents, institutions, and disciplinary backgrounds. Scholars from different countries, from North America to India, from northern Europe to southern, joined us on the journey, offering their perspectives and backgrounds, contributing conceptual and empirical works to our companion. The chapters cover a broad range of topics, employ and discuss a variety of methods, and build upon a variety of academic foundations. To help the reader to get an overview of what the chapters are about, we summarize descriptive and relevant details in Table I.1. For each chapter, following the

Table I.1 An overview of the contributing chapters

Authors	Section/domain	Research purpose	Chapter type	Literature encompassed	Main findings
Sexton	Substantive	To examine the role of acquisitions as both a strategy for and a hindrance to organizational adaptation	Conceptual	Knowledge-based view Learning and innovation literature	Acquisitions help long-term survival. They can be successfully implemented as an adaptation strategy when they are combined with organizational learning
Öberg	Substantive	To explain how one acquisition follows after another, or how acquisitions respond to change	Empirical/Qualitative	Network theory	Pressures from customers, suppliers and competitors provide external explanations for why acquisitions occur and occur in waves
Thakur & Bansal	Substantive	To build on research and learning from practitioners and identify the enablers of integration success	Empirical/Qualitative	Practitioner-oriented literature HR-related M&A literature	Hard and soft enablers of integration play a key role in the success of acquisitions
Patel & King	Substantive	To understand motives that push family firms to acquire	Empirical/Quantitative	Socio-emotional wealth theory	Medium-sized family firms show a propensity to acquire and tend to acquire related companies
Nummela & Hassett	Substantive	To explore micro-foundations for acquisition capability	Empirical/Qualitative	Knowledge-based literature Dynamic capabilities literature Organizational learning literature	Sensing, seizing, and reconfiguring are second-order capabilities in acquisition capabilities. Micro-foundations are found in several organizational processes (e.g. knowledge transfer)
Testoni, Breschi, & Valentini	Contextual	To investigate how the network of strategic alliances' influence leads to an acquisition	Empirical/Quantitative	Acquisition motives literature Alliance literature	Two firms have higher chances to engage in an M&A if they are directly or indirectly linked in the strategic alliances' network, are centrally located within this structure, have dissimilar sizes, have experienced more acquisitions in the past, and are competing in close geographical markets

(Continued)

Table I.1 Continued

Authors	Section/domain	Research purpose	Chapter type	Literature encompassed	Main findings
Piscitello, Rabellotti, & Scalera	Contextual	To investigate ownership choices by emerging countries' multinational enterprises when acquiring European companies	Empirical/Quantitative	Ownership choices literature Motives and ownership choices	Chinese and Indian MNEs prefer less control if the goal of the acquisition is technological competences rather than a customer base or established brand name. Also, firm-level and industry-level characteristics have different impacts on the ownership decision depending on an acquisition's goal
Teerikangas & Valikangas	Contextual	To investigate employees' reactions from an engagement lens	Conceptual	Engagement literature	Typology of different engagement scenarios and dynamics pre- and post-deal
Capron	Contextual	To investigate M&As within the broader set of resource-sourcing decisions	Conceptual	Corporate development portfolio literature Growth modes literature	Trade-offs among different growth modes are analyzed and effects on resources and learning are discussed
Meglio	Contextual	To analyze the multidimensionality of acquisition performance from a stakeholder approach	Conceptual	Acquisition performance literature Stakeholder theory	Acquisition performance is portrayed as a game played by several stakeholders, internal and external to the merging companies, whose relative power influences outcomes
Park	Contextual	To explore leadership issues in cross-border acquisitions	Empirical/Qualitative	Leadership literature Family business literature Market for corporate control literature	Several conflict areas between firms can be resolved with a multifaceted collaborative framework that can encompass dissension, while also providing outlets for integrative decision making and actions

Author	Type	Purpose	Type	Literature	Finding
Kroon & Rouzies	Methodological	To discuss opportunities and challenges of mixed method research in M&As	Conceptual	Mixed method research literature	Mixed method research can further the understanding of M&A. An example from Air France-KLM study is provided
Harrison & Schijven	Methodological	To provide a critique of event study method in an M&A context	Conceptual	Financial economics literature; Behavioral finance literature; Economic sociology literature; Social psychology literature	Recommend refining the construct of acquisition performance and a reorientation in the use of event studies
Lund & Tienari	Methodological	To offer institutional ethnography as a new method for inquiring into M&As	Conceptual	Institutional ethnography; Culture literature; Identity literature	Institutional ethnography may overcome problems of objectification in research
Mirc	Methodological	To introduce social network analysis to investigate M&As from a relational perspective	Conceptual	Social network analysis	Social network analysis can enhance our understanding of M&As as merging networks of interpersonal and inter-organizational relationships
Risberg	Methodological	To discuss how the variety of qualitative research approaches enables a more nuanced understanding of M&As	Conceptual	Qualitative research methodology literature	Qualitative research is theory-generating research which enables the researcher to add new theory through new knowledge, and new perspectives to existing merger and acquisition theory
Grant, Frimanson, & Nilsson	Conceptual	To identify M&A processes in empirical research	Conceptual	Process literature	M&As involve environmental, coordination, leadership, employee, and identity processes
DeGhetto, Ro, Lamont, & Ranft	Conceptual	To explore the role of anticipatory justice in integration process	Conceptual	Organizational justice literature; Organizational sense-making literature	Pre-deal process affects anticipatory justice perceptions among target firm employees and their receptivity and support of the changes to follow after the deal is consummated

(Continued)

Table I.1 Continued

Authors	Section/ domain	Research purpose	Chapter type	Literature encompassed	Main findings
Schriber	Conceptual	To introduce a competitive dynamic perspective on value potential in M&As	Conceptual	Competitive dynamics literature Value creation literature	While *ex ante* comparisons of similarities or complementarities are likely to remain central for value potential assessments, lack of attention to changes in the environment risk makes such predictions incomplete, or even obsolete
Bauer	Conceptual	To dig deeper into the speed of integration construct	Conceptual	Speed of integration literature Acquisition performance literature	Review of integration speed and a proposal for how to measure this construct
Lupina-Wegener, Karamustafa, & Schneider	Conceptual	To investigate identity threats and employees' reactions to threats	Conceptual	Acculturation theory Social identity theory	A typology of identity threat and a process model of employees' reactions to different identity threats during sociocultural integration
Rothermel & Bauer	Conceptual	To explore the corporate brand in acquisitions	Conceptual	Branding literature	Challenges related to redeployment of corporate brands during the integration process

order of the table of contents, we have provided the authors' surnames, the section/domain that the chapter has been placed into, the chapter's purpose, the chapter type (labeled as either conceptual or empirical, either qualitative or quantitative), the literature encompassed, and the main findings. Taken together, this information allows the reader to get an initial and overall picture of the structure of the companion.

In closing, we would also like to take the opportunity to mention what this companion does not do. Our intent is not to provide any conclusive answer to research questions or practical concerns. In other words, this companion is not intended as a final stop in the continuing journey to understand M&As. Rather, we intend to offer an account of mergers and acquisitions that helps the reader to get a more comprehensive picture of this phenomenon and to open up future avenues for inquiry by blending alternate perspectives.

References

Alvesson, M. and Sandberg, J. (2013) "Has management studies lost its way? Ideas for more imaginative and innovative research," *Journal of Management Studies*, 50(1): 128–152.

Barkema, H. and Schijven, M. (2008). "Toward unlocking the full potential of acquisitions: The role of organizational restructuring," *Academy of Management Journal*, 51: 696–722.

Bower, J.L. (2004). When we study M&A, what are we learning. In Pablo, A. and Javidan, M. 2004. *Mergers and acquisitions: Creating integrative knowledge*. Blackwell Publishing: New York.

Brinberg, D. and McGrath, J.E. (1985) *Validity and the research process*. Sage Publications, Inc: Beverly Hills, CA.

Davis, M.S. (1971). "That's interesting! Towards a phenomenology of sociology and a sociology of phenomenology," *Philosophy of Social Sciences*, 1: 309–344.

Dewing, A. (1921) "A statistical test of the success of consolidations," *Journal of Economics*, 36(1): 84–101.

Haleblian, J., Devers, C., McNamara, G., Carpenter, M., and Davison, R. (2009) "Taking stock of what we know about mergers and acquisitions: A review and research agenda," *Journal of Management*: 35: 469–502.

Javidan, M., Pablo, A., Singh, H., Hitt, M., and Jemison, D. (2004). Where we've been and where we're going. In Pablo, A., Javidan, M. 2004. *Mergers and acquisitions: Creating integrative knowledge*. 245–261, Blackwell Publishing: New York.

King, D.R, Dalton, D., Daily, C., and Covin, J. (2004) "Meta-analyses of post-acquisition performance: Indications of unidentified moderators," *Strategic Management Journal*, 25(2): 187–200.

Larsson, R., and Finkelstein, S. (1999) "Integrating strategic, organizational, and human resource perspectives on mergers and acquisitions: A case survey of synergy realization," *Organization Science*, 10(1): 1–26.

Pablo, A. and Javidan, M. (2004) *Mergers and acquisitions: Creating integrative knowledge*. Blackwell Publishing: New York.

Schweizer, L. (2005) "Organizational integration of acquired biotechnology companies into pharmaceutical companies: The need for a hybrid approach," *Academy of Management Journal*, 48: 1051–1074.

Part I

Substantive domain of M&A research

The first section of the book focuses on substantive or important considerations in merger and acquisition (M&A) research. M&A research is analogous to the story of blind men feeling an elephant. Although the larger animal is the same, M&A also has distinct parts that contribute to the difficulty of understanding the whole. This has been recognized previously by Bower (2001); however, he largely distinguishes between industry consolidation within an industry or region, extension to new products or markets, and technology acquisitions. In considering observed M&As and developing how to explain or improve their performance, additional similarities and differences need to be considered. Using a variety of approaches and topics, this section begins to develop differences in M&A that researchers and managers need to consider.

A similarity across acquisitions is that they involve strategic change for the firms involved. This is the focus of the first two chapters. The first chapter by Jennifer Sexton expands on recognition that technology M&As are often unique. In her chapter, she develops theory to outline how learning from acquisitions can help organizations adapt to technological change. However, she also identifies the risk that organizations may simply reinforce existing tendencies with acquisitions that hinder adaptation. Conditions associated with each outcome are developed. In the second chapter, the theme of adaptation is also explored by Christina Öberg. She conducts case studies revealing that novel motives for acquisitions involve responding to changes in a firm's customer, supplier, and competitor network. As a result, firms may use acquisitions to mirror the strategies of others or to cope with competitive challenges. The cases also highlight conditions that impacted the resulting performance. The chapters suggest that the viewing of M&As from either technology or competitive dynamics perspectives can shift what is viewed, similar to viewing an elephant from different angles.

Beyond different views and perspectives, differences are also important, as M&As can serve alternate purposes or depend on different aspects of an organization or its experience. The other three chapters in this section explore these themes, beginning with the third chapter by Mahima Thakur and Anjali Bansal. They focus on the role of Human Resources (HR) in successful M&A integration. While integration is recognized as playing an important role in creating value from acquisitions (Cording *et al.* 2008), research needs to develop a more systematic approach to the human side of integration (Seo and Hill 2005). This chapter begins this process by pulling lessons from case studies to develop the importance of involving HR and providing tailored training during M&As. Meanwhile, the fourth chapter by Pankaj Patel and David King theoretically develops and then empirically tests how family ownership may influence acquisition behavior. The chapter outlines how maintaining a family's socio-emotional wealth as an acquisition motive may not be aimed at creating financial wealth. Additionally, this motive likely depends on the size of a family firm, with the middle-sized firm being more likely to use acquisitions. Considering a motive beyond financial performance in acquisitions by family firms has the potential to explain why not all M&As lead to improved financial performance. In the final chapter of the this section, Niina Nummela and Mélanie Hassett use a case study of Finnish firms to explore acquisition capability microfoundations. The chapter builds on one of the most studied acquisition variables—acquisition experience—to develop the idea that research considering this variable alone is not sufficient for creating and maintaining an acquisition capability. The overall M&A process is considered in identifying the four categories of acquisition capability: microfoundations of managerial capability, organizational structure, experiential learning, and knowledge transfer.

In summary, progress in M&A research likely requires understanding both underlying similarities and differences among acquisitions. A commonality is that acquisitions involve change, but the type and motivation of adaptations can differ. This drives the consideration that acquisitions can achieve different goals, for example, technology change, competitive pressures, or maintaining family socio-emotional wealth. Further, conditions within an acquirer, such as HR and experience with past acquisitions, can either hinder or facilitate reaching desired outcomes. An additional area where acquisitions may hinder goals is whether they reinforce existing approaches or create inertia. Achieving acquisition goals may be facilitated by developing an acquisition capability that requires going beyond simply completing the M&A.

In total, the chapters included in this section begin to explore similarities and differences in the substantive domain of M&A research and offer insights for management practice and future research.

References

Bower, J. (2001) 'Not all M&As are alike—and that matters,' *Harvard Business Review*, 79(3): 93–101.

Cording, M., Christmann, P., and King, D. (2008) 'Reducing causal ambiguity in acquisition integration: intermediate goals as mediators of integration decisions and acquisition performance,' *Academy of Management Journal*, 51: 744–67.

Seo, M. and Hill, S. (2005) 'Understanding the human side of merger and acquisition,' *Journal of Applied Behavioral Science*, 41: 422–43.

1

Acquisitions as an instrument of organizational adaptation through innovation

Jennifer C. Sexton

Introduction

Mergers and acquisitions (hereafter referred to as *acquisitions*) continue to be an important firm strategy and have received a significant degree of attention in the management field. Firms are motivated to acquire other firms for a variety of reasons; acquisitions can be used to increase market power, overcome barriers to entry, enter new markets quickly, and acquire new knowledge and resources (Vermeulen and Barkema 2001). Acquisitions have been examined in terms of their ability to both create and destroy firm value (Haleblian *et al.* 2009). At their most basic, acquisitions allow firms to grow larger in size, complementing or duplicating existing resources and capabilities. At the other end of this spectrum, acquisitions allow firms to add knowledge, increase their capabilities, enter into entirely new industries and markets, and serve an entirely new group of customers.

By their very definition, acquisitions have great potential to alter firms. Acquisitions, even those considered small or routine in nature, can have a large impact on the acquiring firm. Many studies on the impact of acquisitions on the firm have focused on value creation and performance, and the results are not rosy. These studies—focused on the "dark side" of acquisitions—highlight the negative impact on value creation (Seth *et al.* 2002), emphasize managerial hubris that leads to overvaluation of the acquired firm (Jensen 1993; Zhu 2013), and reveal the negative effects on firm innovation (Hitt *et al.* 1996; Lei and Hitt 1995).

While the outcomes of acquisitions are potentially negative, firms pursue acquisitions because the benefits may outweigh the risks. Acquisitions can expose firms to new knowledge, routines, and capabilities; the introduction of knowledge into the firm through acquisitions can be a source of innovation within the firm (Ahuja and Katila 2001) and lead to organizational learning (Ghoshal 1987; Hitt *et al.* 1996; Vermeulen and Barkema 2001). Exposure to new knowledge may stave off competency traps (Leonard 1995) and allow firms to adapt to rapidly changing competitive environments (Brown and Eisenhardt 1998; Vermeulen and Barkema 2001). Research has shown that firms learn from acquisitions (Vermeulen and Barkema 2001). In their study of 25 large Dutch firms, Vermeulen and Barkema (2001) found that acquisitions may improve the realization of a firm's later expansions. This improvement stems from both the procurement of the target firm's knowledge base and the recombination of new and existing knowledge within the acquiring firm. Although organizational learning may not be the primary motivation for the acquisition, the introduction of new knowledge may break inertia and subsequently revitalize the firm (Vermeulen and Barkema 2001). Firms can also learn from the process of pursuing an acquisition (Muehlfeld et al. 2012). Experience-based learning can affect both knowledge creation and transfer, subsequently inducing changes to organizational practices, strategies, and structures (Cyert and March 1963; Levitt and March 1988). Muehlfeld et al. (2012) examined whether firms were able to learn from success and failure experiences in different acquisition contexts. Their study of 4,973 acquisition attempts in the newspaper industry revealed that context moderates the effects of success and failure on subsequent acquisition performance. Both success and failure may shape the firm's organizational routines, resulting in adaptation.

Acquisitions whose explicit purpose is to gain access to new knowledge and new technologies have become an important and accepted strategic occurrence (Makri et al. 2010; Uhlenbruck et al. 2006). Previous scholars have asserted that technology acquisitions represent a way for firms to successfully innovate in dynamic changing environments. Technological resources of the potential target increase the likelihood that a firm would choose acquisitions over other forms of collaboration (Villalonga and McGahan 2005). In a study of 9,276 acquisitions, alliances, and divestitures between 1990 and 2000, a target firm's technological resources were significantly associated with the choice of acquisitions over alliances and divestitures (Villalonga and McGahan 2005). In their study of acquisition targets, Heeley et al. (2006) found that a target firm's investments in R&D led to a higher likelihood of being acquired under conditions of high environmental munificence and dynamism. Additionally, acquisitions can be used by firms to effectively access technological resources (King et al. 2008). These technological resources can be seen as an embodiment of organizational knowledge, and the acquisition of technologically rich targets may provide opportunities for organizational learning by exposing acquirers to new and diverse knowledge (Hitt et al. 1996). Thus, acquisitions represent a method used by firms to manage their resource profiles, and in the case of technological resources, their knowledge domains (Ahuja and Katila 2001; Capron, 1999; Capron and Pistre 2002; Sirmon et al. 2007).

Organizational innovation results from the combination of existing and new knowledge (Kogut and Zander 1992), and acquisitions represent a way for firms to both source and integrate knowledge (Almeida et al. 2011). Through the acquisition of knowledge, firms can further develop and enhance their innovative performance (Ahuja and Katila 2001), ultimately leading to organizational adaptation.

Studies have also focused on how the type of knowledge acquired can impact innovation. Characteristics such as knowledge complementarities, knowledge similarities, and the absolute versus relative size of the acquired knowledge base have been examined and found to impact innovation within firms (e.g. Ahuja and Katila 2001; Cassiman et al. 2005; Cloodt et al. 2006; Makri et al. 2010; Vermeulen and Barkema 2001). While the type of knowledge acquired has become a staple in studies examining the impact of acquisitions on innovation performance, additional work is needed to more deeply examine innovation in this context. Two aspects likely to play a role in how this area develops are relatedness of knowledge and absorptive capacity, as research recognizes that organization innovation is dependent upon both the relatedness of the knowledge acquired and the firm's ability to transfer, assimilate, and exploit it (Cohen and Levinthal 1990).

The impact of related knowledge is revealed in the type of resulting innovation. Related knowledge may lead to incremental innovations that reinforce existing practices, technologies, and capabilities (Chandy and Tellis 1998; Dewar and Dutton 1986; Henderson and Clark 1990). In this case, overall innovation has increased due to acquired knowledge, but the opportunity for organizational adaptation is limited but not negative. On the other hand, if newly acquired knowledge is distant from established knowledge domains within the firm, the opportunity for radical innovation increases. Innovation benefits from search in areas distinct from what firms already know. Li and co-authors (2013) found that unfamiliar, distant, and diverse search leads to an increase in new product introductions. Radical innovation pushes the firm towards new markets, new technologies, and new capabilities, aiding in organizational adaptation (Chandy and Tellis 1998; Dewar and Dutton 1986; Henderson and Clark 1990; Schumpeter 1934). Although both of these cases result in increased innovation, the type of innovation impacts the ability of the firm to adapt to changing circumstances. This distinction becomes important when applied to the context of acquisitions and organizational adaptation.

The purpose of this book chapter is to examine the role of acquisitions as both a strategy for organizational adaptation and a potential hindrance to organizational adaptation. First, this chapter examines in detail how innovation facilitates the process of organizational adaptation. Second, literature is reviewed that examines how the relatedness of knowledge can both enhance the firm's ability to adapt through innovation or hinder the firm's ability to adapt through innovation. Absorptive capacity is also further explored as a mechanism that underlies the firm's ability to transfer and apply newly acquired knowledge. Third, a 2x2 model and propositions are developed examining the interactions between the knowledge relatedness and absorptive capacity and the resulting types of innovation produced. The contribution of each type of innovation to organizational adaptation or organizational inertia is also discussed. To summarize, this chapter will address the following research question: How do acquisitions impact organizational innovation and, ultimately, organizational adaptation?

Acquisitions as organizational adaptation

Acquisitions play a direct role in the process of organizational adaptation through innovation and have been labeled as a potentially difficult and painful process. Acquired companies come with a pre-existing set of routines, processes, and knowledge, and the process of incorporating, synergizing, and transferring these acquired resources may lead to tension and confrontation. However, this conflict may be necessary to break the rigidities in the acquiring firm (Hambrick et al. 1996). Acquisitions may represent a "shock" to the acquiring firm that challenge what they know. Research has shown that these shocks can stave off organizational inertia and enhance adaptation to new and changing circumstances (Brown and Eisenhardt 1998). In fact, firms that regularly challenge themselves may experience short-term negative effects that ultimately lead to enhanced innovation and adaptation capabilities (Agarwal and Helfat 2009; Eisenhardt and Martin 2000). Although the process of integrating acquired businesses can lead to immediate problems relating to culture clashes and reduced performance, the insertion of new knowledge into the firm begins the process of adaptation (Haspeslagh and Jemison 1991; Vermeulen and Barkema 2001). In their study of acquisitions that took place within the semiconductor industry, Phene et al. (2012) found that exploratory innovation was enhanced when the target firm's technology base was different from the acquirer. The uniqueness of knowledge acquired may allow firms to adapt beyond their current capabilities. Experience processing and incorporating new knowledge from acquisitions may also promote the development of capabilities associated with adaptation. More frequent acquirers may be more likely to and better able to adapt as a result of their understanding of both acquisitions and adaption. For example, differential studies (e.g. Finkelstein and Haleblian, 2002; Haleblian and Finkelstein, 1999) indicate that firms can learn from past acquisitions and apply this knowledge to current acquisitions.

Acquisitions are often strategically used to grow the firm's knowledge base and obtain technological capabilities (Gerpott 1995; Granstrand and Sjolander 1990; Huber 1991; Uhlenbruck *et al.* 2006; Vermeulen and Barkema 2001). Acquisitions represent exposure to new situations and knowledge that can break through rigidity and inertia; this exposure may also lead to new knowledge that can renew firms and their internal processes (Vermeulen and Barkema 2001). Firms may especially benefit from acquisitions when their knowledge base is deteriorating or becoming obsolete (Vermeulen and Barkema 2001). Firms can use acquisitions as a way to gain access to technology resources (King *et al.* 2008). For example, research has shown that acquirers spend significantly less on R&D than industry peers, suggesting that acquisitions may take the place of internal knowledge development (King *et al.* 2008).

Because acquisitions are a deliberate act by the leaders of the firm, in a way, managers are able to impact and control the process of innovation within their firms. In their study of corporate renewal through innovation, Mezias and Glynn (1993) examine innovation as a managerial process rather than a purely technological process. Successful innovation within firms relies on management to recognize and pursue opportunities for change (Mezias and Glynn 1993). While acquisitions are often motivated by the need for new or greater depth of knowledge, research has shown that acquirers differ in their ability to capture value from acquisitions (King *et al.* 2008). For example, managers can apply their knowledge in ways that hurt the firm's ability to create value from acquisitions. Haleblian and Finkelstein (1999) found that when firms apply routines associated with acquisitions in a particular industry to a different industry, the performance of the acquisition worsened. Another factor that may impact the value captured from acquisitions is the relatedness of the acquisition to the acquirer's existing knowledge base. Firms that pursue knowledge-based acquisitions in domains closely related to their existing knowledge domains may find it easier to evaluate and exchange R&D resources (Cohen and Levinthal 1990); however, these acquisitions tend to be associated with exploitative, or incremental, innovation (Phene *et al.* 2012). Exploitative innovation builds upon and reinforces the firm's existing capabilities. Acquisitions that involve targets with unique resources or capabilities enhance exploratory innovation, although these acquisitions are more difficult to integrate (Phene *et al.* 2012). Exploratory innovation is associated with departures from existing practice and represents newness and change within the firm. Research has shown that exploitative innovation is associated with higher levels of performance in competitive environments, while explorative innovation is more effective in dynamic environments (Jansen *et al.* 2006). So, while acquisitions are an important source of both new knowledge and related knowledge that the firm can use in its innovation processes, the relatedness of the knowledge acquired coupled with the context of the acquisition can impact both the performance of the acquisition and the degree of change to the acquiring firm (Makri *et al.* 2010).

These firms develop competencies associated with making that particular type of acquisition; each subsequent acquisition enhances and fine tunes these capabilities and routines. In this context, acquisitions become a source of organizational inertia rather than a source of organizational adaptation. As research on acquisitions begins to investigate the firm's history of acquisitions (Barkema and Schijven 2008) and sequence of acquisitions (Ellis *et al.* 2011) from an organizational learning perspective, the impact of acquisitions on strategic inertia deserves attention.

Knowledge and innovation

Related knowledge, or knowledge that overlaps or complements existing firm knowledge domains, is generally considered to have a positive impact on innovation. Vermeulen and Barkema (2001) found support for their assertion that firms are better able to learn from acquisitions pursued in related domains. Another study has shown that acquisitions lead to higher levels of research and development (R&D) when complementary technologies were acquired in acquisitions between former partners rather than substitutive technologies (Cassiman *et al.* 2005). Both efficiency and effectiveness of the firm's R&D processes were improved when complementary technologies were acquired.

Prior research also suggests that, in addition to similarity and complementarity, size of the acquired knowledge base also impacts post-acquisition innovation performance (Ahuja and Katila 2001). In a study of 72 firms from the global chemicals industry, absolute size of the acquired knowledge base had a positive impact on subsequent innovation performance. As a result, both the relatedness of the acquired and acquiring knowledge bases coupled with the absolute and relative size of the acquired knowledge base impacts innovation performance (Ahuja and Katila 2001).

Knowledge that complements but does not substitute for existing firm knowledge provides an opportunity for the firm to expand beyond its current expertise, capabilities, and routines (Makri *et al.* 2010). For example, Makri and co-authors found that higher quality and more novel innovations resulted from complementary scientific and technology knowledge. Complementary knowledge may add value by enhancing the firm's innovation capabilities through novelty while allowing firms to more easily transfer and integrate the knowledge due to some relatedness to existing knowledge bases (King *et al.* 2008).

The acquisition of unrelated knowledge may provide the most potential for contributing to organizational adaptation. Discontinuous strategic transformations are more likely when acquirers seek out targets that have drastically different skills and knowledge (Capron and Mitchell 2009; Makri *et al.* 2010) and represent an opportunity for strategic renewal (Agarwal and Helfat 2009). The discontinuous transformations may take the form of radical innovations and represent clear departures from existing practice (Dewar and Dutton 1986). However, unrelated knowledge may be difficult for acquirers to integrate and use. Lane and Lubatkin (1998) suggest that, when firms acquire targets with similar knowledge, high relative absorptive capacity facilitates the process of integration. Unrelated knowledge is more difficult for firms to use due to a lack of a common knowledge base that precludes the firm from making use of its new knowledge (Cohen and Levinthal 1990; Lane *et al.* 2006; Zahra and George 2002). While unrelated knowledge may have more potential value for the innovating firm, the ability of the firm to innovate may be impacted negatively because the firm lacks the ability to integrate and use this new knowledge. Therefore, pursuing targets with unrelated knowledge bases may represent a risk for acquiring firms due to uncertainty associated with being able to use this newly acquired knowledge.

Firms acquiring unrelated knowledge related to technology may also not have immediate uses for preserving this knowledge. Because the knowledge is not immediately valuable to existing firm processes, routines, and other knowledge needs, these resources are often discarded before their value to the firm is ever discovered. For example, Ranft and Lord (2000) found that the retention of key employees in the acquired firm is positively associated with the transfer of technological capabilities from the acquired firm to the acquirer. In fact, the motivation for many of the acquisitions in their study was to gain access and control over technological capabilities and knowledge. This reinforces that relatedness between an acquirer and the acquired firm's knowledge base is a predictor of post-acquisition innovation performance (Hagedoorn and Schakenraad 1994). An important mechanism underlying the acquiring firm's ability to see a positive effect on innovation performance is absorptive capacity.

Absorptive capacity and innovation

Absorptive capacity refers to a firm's ability to recognize the value of new knowledge, assimilate or transfer this new knowledge, and apply it to its existing processes and capabilities (Cohen and Levinthal 1990; Lane *et al.* 2006; Zahra and George 2002). Absorptive capacity often is considered to be a critical link between knowledge and innovation, as knowledge is frequently cited as both an important input and output of the process of innovation (e.g. Chandy and Tellis 1998; Dewar and Dutton 1986; Grant 1996a, 1996b; Henderson and Clark 1990; Plowman *et al.* 2007). Thus, a firm's ability to gather, transfer, and use new knowledge is crucial to developing a firm's innovative capabilities (Cohen and Levinthal 1990) and ultimately impacts organizational adaptation.

The acquiring firm's knowledge base is an important component in determining the firm's absorptive capacity (e.g. Ahuja and Katila 2001; Arikan 2009; Kim 1998; Lavie and Miller 2008; McGaughey 2002). For example, Ahuja and Katila (2001) state that absorptive capacity underlies the firm's ability to innovate. The ability to use new knowledge to solve problems is boosted when the new knowledge is related to the firm's existing knowledge. Because there is overlap and complementarities between the new and existing knowledge within the firm, the ability to communicate, integrate, and apply new knowledge is facilitated through what the firm already knows (Cohen and Levinthal 1990; Grant 1996a; Lane *et al.* 2001). Greater levels of integration with existing firm knowledge means that the newly acquired can be used in the firm's innovative activities, thus increasing the level of innovation within the firm.

Still, acquired knowledge that is too related to existing firm knowledge can contribute to a lack of innovation. Existing firm knowledge can limit the firm's search for acquisition targets to related technological domains (Stuart and Podolny 1996). When acquired knowledge is too closely related to existing firm knowledge, the ability to benefit from addressing old problems with new approaches or by gleaning extra information from the external environment is limited (Ahuja and Katila 2001). In their study of 133 publicly traded, high-technology firms that were acquired, King *et al.* (2008) found that a target firm's technology resources can act as a substitute for an acquirer's technology resources. The authors suggest that these acquirers spent significantly less than their industry peers and may be using acquisitions as a strategy for accessing R&D capabilities instead of developing them internally. These acquirers may pursue internal R&D at a minimum level in order to maintain absorptive capacity, subsequently overcoming information asymmetry and facilitating easier integration of acquisitions.

The preceding review shows firm innovation is impacted both by the relatedness of knowledge acquired and the absorptive capacity of the acquiring firm. However, existing research does not distinguish between the types of innovation that result from these acquisitions. Incremental innovation builds upon existing knowledge, contributing to organizational adaptation in a gradual way. Radical innovation destroys existing competencies and creates new competencies (Tushman and Anderson 2004), potentially resulting in larger-scale organizational adaptation. The following section explores the interaction between the acquiring firm's absorptive capacity and the relatedness of the acquired knowledge and the resulting type of innovation. In addition, propositions associated with the impact of different types of innovation on organizational adaptation are developed and discussed. These relationships are illustrated in Figure 1.1 and related propositions are developed in the following subsections.

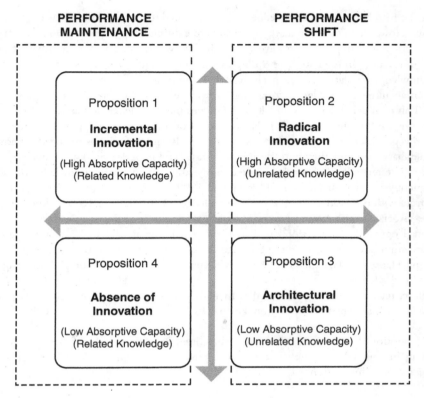

PERFORMANCE MAINTENANCE | **PERFORMANCE SHIFT**

Proposition 1

Incremental Innovation

(High Absorptive Capacity)
(Related Knowledge)

Proposition 2

Radical Innovation

(High Absorptive Capacity)
(Unrelated Knowledge)

Proposition 4

Absence of Innovation

(Low Absorptive Capacity)
(Related Knowledge)

Proposition 3

Architectural Innovation

(Low Absorptive Capacity)
(Unrelated Knowledge)

Figure 1.1   2 x 2 conceptual model

Incremental innovation and organizational inertia

Research has often categorized innovation based on the magnitude of change associated with a particular innovation. *Incremental innovation* and *radical innovation* are two types of innovation that are commonly found in the literature that reflect the magnitude of change.

While incremental innovation refers to minor improvements or simple changes to current firm technology, radical innovation results in a clear departure from existing practice (Dewar and Dutton 1986). The small changes that are present in incremental innovations reinforce the firm's processes and the capabilities of established firms; often this type of innovation leads to small changes in customer benefits per dollar (Chandy and Tellis 1998; Henderson and Clark 1990; Tushman and Smith 2002). As a result of improvements in processes, technology, and product offerings, incremental innovation has been found to reinforce prevailing knowledge within the firm (Subramaniam and Youndt 2005).

The depth and relatedness of the firm's knowledge domains has been found to impact innovation (Hitt *et al.* 2001). As stated above, incremental innovation enhances and improves existing processes, technology, and product offerings in the firm. As a result, when an acquired knowledge base contains knowledge that overlaps and complements existing firm knowledge, reinforcement of the existing knowledge base occurs (Cohen and Levinthal 1990). Acquired knowledge that overlaps with existing firm knowledge is easy to incorporate and assimilate within the firm because this knowledge is directly related to and fits within existing knowledge domains. However, knowledge that is too related to existing knowledge domains hampers novel innovations. For example, studies have shown that knowledge similarity is negatively related to radical innovation. In their study of 95 high-technology acquisitions, Makri *et al.* (2010) found that knowledge similarity is negatively related to invention novelty. High levels of similarity between acquired knowledge and existing knowledge were also found to create path dependency. This path dependency essentially fortifies existing knowledge domains.

Although innovation novelty is reduced in cases of similar or overlapping knowledge, there is still the possibility that innovation can take place. In order for firms to use the knowledge that they have acquired, they must be able to transfer and integrate the knowledge throughout the firm. The relatedness of newly acquired knowledge can encourage knowledge transfer and subsequently innovation (Cohen and Levinthal 1990). Deep knowledge domains can impart employees with the motivation to transfer knowledge within the firm. Related knowledge may also be associated with lower costs of knowledge transfer resulting from a shared knowledge domain (Kogut and Zander 1992). A shared knowledge domain will make transferring knowledge less arduous due to common knowledge stocks and greater absorptive capacity (Coff 1999; Haas and Hansen 2005; Szulanski 1996). Firm environments that encourage knowledge sharing lead to higher levels of incremental innovation (Ritala and Hurmelinna-Laukkanen 2013). Therefore, related knowledge coupled with higher levels of absorptive capacity is positively associated with incremental innovation. Formally stated,

> Proposition 1a: Acquired knowledge that duplicates the acquirer's existing knowledge domain coupled with high levels of absorptive capacity will result in increased levels of incremental innovation.

Because the firm's ability to gain knowledge from a knowledge acquisition is dependent upon the firm's absorptive capacity, related acquisitions allow firms to more easily and rapidly acquire, assimilate, transfer, and exploit new knowledge (Cohen and Levinthal 1990; Lane *et al.* 2006). As a firm repeats a task over time, the search and integration process triggered by that task becomes increasingly routinized (Barkema and Schijven 2008; Levitt and March 1988). Firms that pursue multiple acquisitions develop routines that homogenize the type of acquisition pursued and the integration of these acquisitions. The homogeneity of acquisitions may lead to the acquisition of knowledge related to the acquirer's existing domains which reinforces existing knowledge within the firm (Haspeslagh and Jemison 1991). These increased levels of incremental innovation are more likely to lead to organizational inertia and maintenance of existing firm performance (Burgelman 2002). Formally stated,

> Proposition 1b: Increased levels of incremental innovation lead to organizational inertia and maintenance of current firm performance.

Radical innovation and organizational adaptation

Radical innovation moves the firm beyond its current technology and capabilities (Dewar and Dutton 1986). Firms that pursue or experience radical innovations often begin to ask new sets of questions, address new problems in novel ways, and employ new problem-solving approaches (Henderson and Clark 1990). The results of pursuit of this type of innovation often involve new technology and greater customer value in product or service offerings (Chandy and Tellis 1998). While incremental innovation serves to reinforce the knowledge that the firm possesses, radical innovation destroys or makes obsolete the existing knowledge base of the firm (Subramaniam and Venkatraman 2001). Radical innovation transforms, changes, and creates new knowledge within the firm, leading to organizational adaptation.

Knowledge diversity has been shown to enhance innovation within firms. For example, firms rich in scientific diversity develop knowledge environments that are more conducive to innovation. Scientific diversity encourages creativity within the firm and aids in brainstorming processes (Cardinal 2001). A diversity of backgrounds, training, perspectives, and knowledge facilitates the generation of new ideas and the creation of knowledge, thus leading to innovation (Bantel and Jackson 1989; Wiersema and Bantel 1992).

Greater knowledge diversity within the firm can also aid firms competing in multiple industries, serving various groups of consumers, and offering multiple and varied products. Firms facing a diversity of challenges and problems require a diversity of knowledge to facilitate complex problem solving. For example, industries such as pharmaceuticals and high technology are dependent on a broad array of scientific disciplines ranging from chemistry, physiology, biology, and physics, to engineering. Knowledge diversity promotes innovation within the firm and can potentially maintain the firm's competitive advantages.

The availability of multiple areas of expertise can also aid R&D professionals in developing new knowledge and expanding existing knowledge through the cross-fertilization of ideas (Amason et al. 1995; Bantel and Jackson 1989). For example, Cardinal (2001) found that increased levels of knowledge diversity within pharmaceutical firms led to an increased likelihood of radical innovations.

The more unrelated that acquired knowledge is, relative to the firm's existing knowledge domains, the more difficult it becomes to assimilate and apply the acquired knowledge (Haspeslagh and Jemison 1991). Therefore, knowledge acquired by the firm must be similar enough to facilitate learning and use, but different enough to provide opportunities for exploration. Knowledge complementarities, or knowledge that supplements existing knowledge domains or is tangentially related to existing knowledge domains, impact both innovation quantity and quality. Makri et al. (2010) found that, when complementarities between technology and scientific knowledge domains were at their highest levels, the highest levels of invention novelty were also achieved. Firms acquiring complementary, or non-overlapping, knowledge domains can produce higher-quality and more novel innovations.

Knowledge diversity within the firm is a necessary condition to aid in innovation because it requires the transfer and recombination of different types of knowledge. A diversity of knowledge domains within the firm can increase knowledge available to the firm by exposing the firm to a multitude of perspectives, educational backgrounds, and disciplines. A rich and diverse knowledge environment within the firm creates an organizational context that sustains and supports knowledge transfer. Because employees have been exposed to a wide variety of knowledge, they are better able to assess the value of new knowledge within the firm and possess the capabilities to transfer it throughout the firm (Cohen and Levinthal 1990). This organizational context may also motivate firm employees to share knowledge within the firm, thus leading to greater knowledge transfer (Szulanski 1996). Formally stated,

Proposition 2a: Acquired knowledge that complements acquirer's existing firm knowledge coupled with high levels of absorptive capacity will result in increased levels of radical innovation.

Higher levels of knowledge diversity in conjunction with acquired complementary knowledge will lead to radical innovation. Acquired knowledge that is unrelated (or non-overlapping) with existing firm knowledge domains is more likely to destroy or render obsolete existing knowledge rather than reinforce or build upon existing knowledge, potentially leading to organizational adaptation. Additionally, radical innovation is often associated with large-scale organizational change, a risky prospect for firms, which can create uncertainty in performance (Amburgey *et al.* 1993). Firms that experience radical innovation find themselves exploring new markets, serving new customers, offering new products, or creating new organizational routines and capabilities that make obsolete their existing knowledge. As a result, firms may also experience greater variance in their performance (Burgelman 2002).

> Proposition 2b: Increased levels of radical innovation will lead to organizational adaptation and shifts in firm performance (positive or negative).

Architectural innovation and organizational adaptation

Other types of innovation that focus on the linkages between components and systems within an organization are also present in the literature. Tushman and Smith (2002) describe these types of innovations as architectural. *Architectural innovations* involve shifts in subsystems and linking mechanisms in the firm's processes. These types of innovations change the way in which the components of a product are linked together (Henderson and Clark 1990). The core design concepts remain the same; the innovation occurs in organizational structure, markets pursued, and production processes (Tushman and Smith 2002).

The acquisition of complementary knowledge coupled with low levels of absorptive capacity may facilitate architectural innovation. In architectural innovation, the change in knowledge occurs between knowledge domains. Linkages are altered in architectural innovation, and the acquisition of complementary knowledge can help firms find new ways to link and manipulate existing knowledge within the firm.

Low levels of absorptive capacity inhibit the ability of the firm to transfer and integrate new knowledge. When absorptive capacity is low, the newly acquired knowledge may not be fully transferred or integrated throughout the firm. This lack of integration may not allow firms to efficiently or effectively use new knowledge, but lack of integration helps preserve the firm's existing knowledge domains. Formally stated,

> Proposition 3a: Acquired knowledge that is complementary to the acquirer's existing knowledge domains coupled with low levels of absorptive capacity will result in architectural innovation.

Like incremental innovations, the basic knowledge underlying the components remains untouched in architectural innovations; however, this kind of innovation destroys the usefulness of the firm's architectural knowledge, or knowledge about the linkages of the components (Henderson and Clark 1990). Because this architectural knowledge is embedded within the structure and information-processing procedures of established firms, this destruction is difficult to recognize and correct (Henderson and Clark 1990). Therefore, architectural innovations present firms with significant consequences and ultimately impact the structure and functioning of the firm. These consequences are likely to lead to organizational adaptation in the firm.

> Proposition 3b: Increased levels of architectural innovation lead to organizational adaptation and shifts in firm performance (positive or negative).

Absence of innovation and organizational inertia

Repeated use of the firm's existing knowledge bases can lead to a tendency for organizations to become stagnant and rigid (Leonard 1995; Levinthal and March 1993; Miller 1994). As firms become more stagnant and rigid, their ability to adapt to changing circumstances, their capacity to respond to new challenges within their external environments, and ultimately their chances for survival are threatened. While acquisitions have traditionally been thought of as a means to enhance firm growth and competitiveness (Johnson 1996), the acquisition of related knowledge overlapping existing knowledge domains can lead to an absence of innovation.

Low levels of absorptive capacity also reinforce the absence of innovation. Even if the acquired knowledge is closely related to existing knowledge domains, transfer and assimilation must occur in order for it to be applied to the firm's processes. Without absorptive capacity, the acquiring firm will not gain what little additional value could be gleaned from the acquisition. However, acquisitions that are too related potentially reduce the value of the acquired knowledge and the ability of the acquiring firm to learn. As a result, knowledge will be more likely to be used and retained once it is transferred. Thus, low levels of absorptive capacity coupled with the acquisition of related knowledge will negatively impact the innovation output of the firm. In the absence of innovation, organizational inertia will occur. Formally stated,

> Proposition 4a: Acquired knowledge that is related to the acquirer's existing knowledge domains coupled with low levels of absorptive capacity will result in an absence of innovation.

> Proposition 4b: An absence of innovation will lead to organizational inertia and maintenance of current firm performance.

Discussion

The chapter set out to examine the relationships among relatedness of acquired knowledge, absorptive capacity, and organizational adaptation in the context of innovation. Access to new customers, technologies, and markets are common motivations for pursuing acquisitions (Uhlenbruck *et al.* 2006), and acquisitions can enhance the acquirer's innovativeness (Ahuja and Katila 2001).

Organizational acquisitions can be successfully implemented as an adaptation strategy when they are combined with organizational learning. Acquisitions may renew the acquiring organizations and help in long-term survival (Vermeulen and Barkema 2001). Given the rapid rate of change in today's competitive environment, organizational adaptation becomes increasingly important as firms seek to innovate and out-compete their rivals. Organizations that remain focused on perfecting their present capabilities may find it difficult or even impossible to change, leading to what Levitt and March call a "competency trap" (1988).

The ability to learn from acquisitions may give firms an edge in adapting to rapidly shifting environments and changing technologies. Globalization, innovation, and increasing competition contribute to continuous change in firms' competitive environments. As a result, acquisitions may provide firms with the processes to adapt to change and to create change within the firm. Therefore, the motive of maintaining performance in a changing landscape and not improved performance may represent a viable acquisition motive.

By regularly accessing new knowledge through acquisitions, firms are able to respond appropriately to changing external environments, thus ultimately aiding in firm survival.

Successful adaptation relies upon the fit of knowledge resources within the innovating firm (Armenakis and Bedeian 1999; Damanpour 1991). Because related and unrelated knowledge have differing degrees of fit with the firm's pre-existing domains, each type of knowledge influences organizational adaptation to varying degrees (or in some cases, promotes organizational inertia).

For example, the acquisition of similar knowledge can lead to competency traps in which pre-existing knowledge domains become a source of cognitive inertia, subsequently halting innovation (Levinthal and March 1993; Levitt and March 1988). While the acquisition of knowledge can be used by firms as an impetus for organizational adaptation, it can also be used to create organizational inertia. Amburgey and Miner (1992) identify that strategic momentum that can carry firms down the same paths, resulting in strategic inertia. Strategic momentum is the tendency to maintain or expand the emphasis and direction of prior strategic actions in current strategic behavior (Amburgey and Miner 1992). In the context of knowledge-acquisitions, firms that continue to acquire knowledge closely related to existing capabilities and knowledge domains create momentum through reinforcement.

By their very definition, acquisitions have great potential to alter firms. Acquisitions, even those considered small or routine in nature, can have a large impact on the acquiring firm. While the literature has found that knowledge acquired by the firm can impact organizational innovation, little work has extended beyond the acknowledgement that new knowledge leads to higher levels of innovation. Subsequent work that delves into the relationship between acquired knowledge and innovation output highlights a more complicated relationship. Ahuja and Katila (2001) studied 72 leading firms from the global chemicals industry and found that non-technological acquisitions had an insignificant impact on subsequent innovation output. They also find that characteristics of the acquisition can impact innovation output in different ways. The results of their study indicate that managers wanting to enhance innovation output should pursue targets with a moderately related knowledge base (Ahuja and Katila 2001). Other characteristics, including the absolute and relative size of the acquired knowledge base, can also impact innovation output, and not always for the better. As a result, acquisitions can be tools that both enhance organizational innovation and hinder organizational innovation.

Along these same lines, many different types of innovation are identified in the literature, and each type of innovation requires different types of knowledge. While some innovations, such as incremental, reinforce existing knowledge within the firm, other innovations, such as architectural and radical, evoke large-scale change in firms that can manifest in completely new processes, new technologies, and new capabilities. While innovations associated with large-scale firm change are more likely to lead to organizational adaptation, innovations that reinforce existing knowledge within the firm are more likely to create momentum that leads to organizational inertia.

In summary, there are several implications of this research. First, the creation and management of temporary competitive advantages has emerged as an alternative to sustainable models of competitive advantage in the strategy literature (D'Aveni et al. 2010). As competitive environments have grown in size and complexity, and as the pace of business continues to increase, achieving and sustaining competitive advantages is difficult, if not impossible (D'Aveni et al. 2010). As a result, firms are turning to innovation as a way to create temporary competitive advantages (Adner and Kapoor 2010). In many environments, firms must continue to innovate in order to compete with other firms in their industry or market (Adner and Kapoor 2010). This suggests the need for research to develop and examine explanations for acquisitions beyond performance improvement. This chapter also develops how innovation can lead to both organizational adaptation and organizational inertia. While previous research has proposed that the firm's strategic decision makers can deliberately choose both organizational adaptation and organizational inertia for their firms (Schwarz 2012), this chapter begins to examine innovation as a specific mechanism by which these choices are made. Finally, firms may have more control over innovation within their firm than previously realized. Innovation is often thought to be a serendipitous process that is difficult to control or manage. However, because acquisitions are a deliberate act by the leaders of the firm, in a way, managers are able to impact and control the process of innovation within their firms. Adding a layer of complexity, it is not simply enough to choose to pursue acquisitions. Firms and their strategic leaders can potentially impact the types of innovation produced by their firms. As a result, firms can strategically orient themselves to pursue specific knowledge acquisitions in the hopes of adapting to changing circumstances or reinforcing their core capabilities.

References

Adner, R. and Kapoor, R. (2010) "Value creation in innovation ecosystems: how the structure of techno-logical interdependence affects firm performance in new technology generations," *Strategic Management Journal*, 31: 306–33.

Agarwal, R., and Helfat, C. (2009) "Strategic renewal of organizations," *Organization Science*, 20: 281–93.

Ahuja, G., and Katila, R. (2001) "Technological acquisitions and the innovation performance of acquiring firms: a longitudinal study," *Strategic Management Journal*, 22: 197–220.

Almeida, P., Hohberger, J., and Parada, P. (2011) "Informal knowledge and innovation," in M. Easterby-Smith and M.A. Lyles (eds.), *Handbook of Organizational Learning and Knowledge Management*, 2nd edn, Hoboken, NJ: Wiley.

Amason, A.C., Thompson, K.R., Hochwarter, W.A., and Harrison, A.W. (1995) "Conflict—an important dimension in successful management teams," *Organizational Dynamics*, 24: 20–35.

Amburgey, T.L. and Miner, A.S. (1992) "Strategic momentum: the effects of repetitive, positional, and con-textual momentum on merger activity," *Strategic Management Journal*, 13: 335–48.

Amburgey, T.L., Kelly, D., and Barnett, W. (1993) "Resetting the clock: the dynamics of organizational change and failure," *Administrative Science Quarterly*, 38: 57–73.

Arikan, A.T. (2009) "Interfirm knowledge exchanges and the knowledge creation capability of clusters," *Academy of Management Review*, 34: 658–76.

Armenakis, A.A., and Bedeian, A.G. (1999) "Organizational change: a review of theory and research in the 1990s," *Journal of Management*, 25: 293–315.

Bantel, K.A., and Jackson, S.E. (1989) "Top management and innovations in banking—does the composi-tion of the top team make a difference?," *Strategic Management Journal*, 10: 107–24.

Barkema, H.G., and Schijven, M. (2008) "Toward unlocking the full potential of acquisitions: the role of organizational restructuring," *Academy of Management Journal*, 51: 696–22.

Brown, S., and Eisenhardt, K.M. (1998) *Competing on the Edge*, Boston, MA: Harvard Business School Press.

Burgelman, R.A. (2002) "Strategy as vector and the inertia of coevolutionalry lock-in," *Administrative Science Quarterly*, 47: 325–57.

Capron, L. (1999) "The long-term performance of horizontal acquisitions," *Strategic Management Journal*, 20: 987–1018.

Capron L., and Mitchell, W. (2009) "Selection capability: how capability gaps and internal social frictions affect internal and external strategic renewal," *Organization Science*, 20: 294–312.

Capron, L., and Pistre, N. (2002) "When do acquirers earn abnormal returns?," *Strategic Management Journal*, 23: 781–94.

Cardinal, L.B. (2001) "Technological innovation in the pharmaceutical industry: the use of organizational control in managing research and development," *Organization Science*, 12: 19–36.

Cassiman, B., Colombo, M.G., Garrone, P., and Veugelers, R. (2005) "The impact of M&A on the R&D pro-cess: an empirical analysis of the role of technological- and market-relatedness," *Research Policy*, 34: 195–220.

Chandy, R.K., and Tellis, G.J. (1998) "Organizing for radical product innovation: the overlooked role of willingness to cannibalize," *Journal of Marketing Research*, 35: 474–87.

Cloodt, M., Hagedoorn, J., and Van Kranenburg, H. (2006) "Mergers and acquisitions: their effect on the innovative performance of companies in high-tech industries," *Research Policy*, 35: 642–54.

Coff, R.W. (1999) "How buyers cope with uncertainty when acquiring firms in knowledge-intensive industries: caveat emptor," *Organization Science*, 10: 144–61.

Cohen, W., and Levinthal, D.A. (1990) "Absorptive capacity: a new perspective on learning and innovation," *Administrative Science Quarterly*, 35: 128–52.

Cyert, R.M., and March, J.G. (1963) *A Behavioral Theory of the Firm*, Oxford: Blackwell Publishers Ltd.

D'Aveni, R.A., Dagnino, G.B., and Smith, K.G. (2010) "The age of temporary advantage," *Strategic Management Journal*, 31: 1371–85.

Damanpour, F. (1991) "Organizational innovation: a meta-analysis of effects of determinants and moderators," *Academy of Management Journal*, 34: 555–90.

Dewar, R.D., and Dutton, J.E. (1986) "The adoption of radical and incremental innovations: an empirical analysis," *Management Science*, 32: 1422–33.

Eisenhardt, K.M., and Martin, J.A. (2000) "Dynamic capabilities: what are they?," *Strategic Management Journal*, 21: 1105–21.

Ellis, K.M., Reus, T.H., Lamont, B.T., and Ranft, A.L. (2011) "Transfer effects in large acquisitions: how size-specific experience matters," *Academy of Management Journal*, 54: 1261–76.

Finkelstein, S., and Haleblian, J. (2002) "Understanding acquisition performance: the role of transfer effects," *Organization Science*, 13: 36–47.

Gerpott, T. (1995) "Successful integration of R&D functions after acquisitions: an exploratory empirical study," *R&D Management*, 25: 161–78.

Ghoshal, S. (1987). "Global strategy: an organizing framework," *Strategic Management Journal*, 8: 425–40.

Granstrand, O., and Sjolander, S. (1990) "The acquisition of technology and small firms by large firms," *Journal of Economic Behavior & Organization*, 13: 367–86.

Grant, R.M. (1996a) "Prospering in dynamically-competitive environments: organizational capability as knowledge integration," *Organization Science*, 7: 375–87.

Grant, R.M. (1996b) "Toward a knowledge-based view of the firm," *Strategic Management Journal*, 17 (Winter Special Issue): 109–22.

Haas, M.R., and Hansen, M.T. (2005), "When using knowledge can hurt performance: the value of organizational capabilities in a management consulting company," *Strategic Management Journal*, 26: 1–24.

Hagedoorn, J., and Schakenraad, J. (1994) "The effect of strategic technology alliances on company performance," *Strategic Management Journal*, 15: 291–309.

Haleblian, J., and Finkelstein, S. (1999). "The influence of organizational acquisition experience on acquisition performance: a behavioral learning perspective," *Administrative Science Quarterly*, 44: 29–56.

Haleblian, J., Devers, C.E., McNamara, G., Carpenter, M.A., and Davison, R.B. (2009) "Taking stock of what we know about mergers and acquisitions: a review and research agenda," *Journal of Management*, 35: 469–502.

Hambrick, D.C., Cho, T.S., and Chen, M.J. (1996) "The influence of top management team heterogeneity on firms' competitive moves," *Administrative Science Quarterly*, 41: 659–84.

Haspeslagh, G., and Jemison, D.B. (1991), *Managing Acquisitions: Creating Value through Corporate Renewal*, New York: Free Press.

Heeley, M.B., King, D.R., and Covin, J.G. (2006) "Effects of firm R&D investment and environment on acquisition likelihood," *Journal of Management Studies*, 43: 1513–35.

Henderson, R.M., and Clark, K.B. (1990) "Architectural innovation—the reconfiguration of existing product technologies and the failure of established firms," *Administrative Science Quarterly*, 35: 9–30.

Hitt, M.A., Hoskisson, R.E., Johnson, R.A., and Moesel, D.D. (1996) "The market for corporate control and firm innovation," *Academy of Management Journal*, 39: 1084–119.

Hitt, M.A., Bierman, L., Shimizu, K., and Kochhar, R. (2001) "Direct and moderating effects of human capital on strategy and performance in professional service firms: a resource-based perspective," *Academy of Management Journal*, 44: 13–28.

Huber, G.P. (1991) "Organizational learning: the contributing processes and the literatures," *Organization Science*, 2: 88–115.

Jansen, J.J.P., Van Den Bosch, F.A.J., and Volberda, H.W. (2006) "Exploratory innovation, exploitative innovation, and performance: effects of organizational antecedents and environmental moderators," *Management Science*, 52: 1661–74.

Jensen, M.C. (1993) "The modern industrial-revolution, exit, and the failure of internal control-systems," *Journal of Finance*, 48: 831–80.

Johnson, R.A. (1996) "Antecedents and outcomes of corporate refocusing," *Journal of Management*, 22: 439–83.

Kim, L. (1998) "Crisis construction and organizational learning: capability building in catching-up at Hyundai Motor," *Organization Science*, 9: 506–21.

King, D.R., Slotegraaf, R.J., and Kesner, I. (2008) "Performance implications of firm resource interactions in the acquisition of R&D-intensive firms," *Organization Science*, 19: 327–40.

Kogut, B., and Zander, U. (1992) "Knowledge of the firm, combinative capabilities and the replication of technology," *Organization Studies*, 3: 383–97.

Lane, P.J., and Lubatkin, M. (1998) "Relative absorptive capacity and interorganizational learning," *Strategic Management Journal*, 19: 461–77.

Lane, P.J., Salk, J.E., and Lyles, M.A. (2001) "Absorptive capacity, learning, and performance in international joint ventures," *Strategic Management Journal*, 22: 1139–61.

Lane, P.J., Koka, B.R., and Pathak, S. (2006) "The reification of absorptive capacity: a critical review and rejuvenation of the construct," *Academy of Management Review*, 31: 833–63.

Lavie, D., and Miller, S.R. (2008) "Alliance portfolio internationalization and firm performance," *Organization Science*, 19: 623–46.

Lei, D., and Hitt, M.A. (1995) "Strategic restructuring and outsourcing: the effect of mergers and acquisitions and LBOs on building firm skills and capabilities," *Journal of Management*, 21: 835–59.

Leonard, D. (1995) *Wellsprings of Knowledge: Building and Sustaining the Sources of Innovation*, Boston, MA: Harvard Business School Press.

Levinthal, D.A., and March, J.G. (1993) "The myopia of learning," *Strategic Management Journal*, 14: 319–33.

Levitt, B., and March, J.G. (1988) "Organizational learning," *American Review of Sociology*, 14: 319–40.

Li, Q., Maggitti, P.G., Smith, K.G., Tesluk, P.E., and Katila, R. (2013) "Top management attention to innovation: the role of search selection and intensity in new product introductions," *Academy of Management Journal*, 56: 893–916.

Makri, M., Hitt, M.A., and Lane, P.J. (2010) "Complementary technologies, knowledge relatedness, and invention outcomes in high technology mergers and acquisitions," *Strategic Management Journal*, 31: 602–28.

McGaughey, S.L. (2002) "Strategic interventions in intellectual asset flows," *Academy of Management Review*, 27: 248–74.

Mezias, S.J., and Glynn, M.A. (1993) "The three faces of corporate renewal: institution, revolution, and evolution," *Strategic Management Journal*, 14: 77–101.

Miller, D. (1994) "What happens after success: the perils of excellence," *Journal of Management Studies*, 31: 325–58.

Muehlfeld, K., Sahib, P.R., and Van Witteloostuijn, A. (2012) "A contextual theory of organizational learning from failures and successes: a study of acquisition completion in the global newspaper industry, 1981–2008," *Strategic Management Journal*, 33: 938–64.

Phene, A., Tallman, S., and Almeida, P. 2012. "When do acquisitions facilitate technological exploration and exploitation?," *Journal of Management*, 38: 753–83.

Plowman, D.A., Baker, L.T., Beck, T.E., Kulkarni, M., Solansky, S.T., and Travis, D.V. (2007) "Radical change accidentally: the emergence and amplification of small change," *Academy of Management Journal*, 50: 515–43.

Ranft, A.L., and Lord, M.D. (2000) "Acquiring new knowledge: the role of retaining human capital in acquisitions of high-tech firms," *The Journal of High Technology Management Research*, 11: 295–319.

Ritala, P., and Hurmelinna-Laukkanen, P. (2013) "Incremental and radical innovation in coopetition—the role of absorptive capacity and appropriability," *Journal of Product Innovation Management*, 30: 154–69.

Schwarz, G.M. (2012) "The logic of deliberate structural inertia," *Journal of Management*, 38: 547–72.

Seth, A., Song, K.P., and Pettit, R.R. (2002) "Value creation and destruction in cross-border acquisitions: an empirical analysis of foreign acquisitions of U.S. firms," *Strategic Management Journal*, 23: 921–40.

Schumpeter, J. (1934) *Capitalism, socialism, and democracy*. New York: Harper & Row.

Sirmon, D.G., Hitt, M.A., and Ireland, R.D. (2007) "Managing firm resources in dynamic environments to create value: Looking inside the black box," *Academy of Management Review*, 32: 273–92.

Stuart, T.E., and Podolny, J.M. (1996) "Local search and the evolution of technological capabilities," *Strategic Management Journal*, 17: 21–38.

Subramaniam, M., and Venkatraman, N. (2001) "Determinants of transnational new product development capability: testing the influence of transferring and deploying tacit overseas knowledge," *Strategic Management Journal*, 22: 359–78.

Subramaniam, M., and Youndt, M.A. (2005) "The influence of intellectual capital on the types of innovative capabilities," *Academy of Management Journal*, 48: 450–63.

Szulanski, G. (1996) "Exploring internal stickiness: impediments to the transfer of best practice within the firm," *Strategic Management Journal*, 17: 27–43.

Tushman, M.L., and Smith, W.K. (2002) "Organizational technology," in J.A.C. Baum (ed.), *The Blackwell Companion to Organizations*, Oxford: Blackwell Publishers Ltd.

Tushman, M.L., and Anderson, P. (2004) "Preface," in M.L. Tushman, and P. Anderson (eds.), *Managing Strategic Innovation and Change*, 2nd edn., New York: Oxford University Press.

Uhlenbruck, K., Hitt, M.A., and Semadeni, M. (2006) "Market value effects of acquisitions involving internet firms: a resource-based analysis," *Strategic Management Journal*, 27: 899–913.

Vermeulen, F., and Barkema, H. (2001) "Learning through acquisitions," *Academy of Management Journal*, 44: 457–76.

Villalonga, B., and McGahan, A.M. (2005) "The choice among acquisitions, alliances, and divestitures," *Strategic Management Journal*, 26: 1183–208.

Wiersema, M.F., and Bantel, K.A. (1992) "Top management team demography and corporate strategic change," *Academy of Management Journal*, 35: 91–121.

Zahra, S.A., and George, G. (2002) "Absorptive capacity: a review, reconceptualization, and extension," *Academy of Management Review*, 27: 185–203.

Zhu, D.H. (2013) "Group polarization on corporate boards: theory and evidence on board decisions about acquisition premiums," *Strategic Management Journal*, 34: 800–22.

2

Acquisitions as an adaptation strategy

Christina Öberg

Introduction

Why do companies engage in acquisitions? Research frequently discusses mergers and acquisitions (henceforth, acquisitions) as a means to reach new markets and to develop new products and competences (Kaul 2012; Trautwein 1990; Walter and Barney 1990). Alternatively, acquisition motives include managers trying to gain personal or career-related benefits (Gomez-Mejia and Wiseman 1997; Grinstein and Hribar 2004). These motives indicate that acquisition research largely takes a company-centric perspective (cf. Kelly et al. 2003) focused on planning or risk taking (e.g. Chaffee 1985; Mintzberg 1973). Meanwhile, adaptation motives focus on environmental reasons for an acquisition (cf. Haleblian et al. 2009) that includes a company's context in making decisions. This suggests a need to consider acquisitions as a strategic tool to respond to and adjust to changes in a company's network, where adaptation refers to how a company's strategy reconciles its ambition with contextual changes (Mintzberg 1973; Ronchi 1980). A network refers to groups of companies directly or indirectly connected by means of business arrangements (Anderson et al. 1994). The network approach constitutes a theoretical point of view that describes company interconnections as an influence on individual company decisions and outcomes (Ford and Håkansson 2006; Håkansson 1982). In focusing on acquisitions as an adaptation strategy that considers a company's network, the chapter seeks to explain how one acquisition follows after another, or how acquisitions respond to change. Advantages of applying a network approach include explaining mutual adaptation and the spread of acquisitions to additional parties (Hallén et al. 1991; Havila and Salmi 2000).

The chapter contributes to previous research by developing an alternative explanation for why companies acquire. In general, studies that examine environmental reasons for acquisitions focus on how business connections between companies or individuals affect the choice of target (e.g. Finkelstein 1997; Pfeffer 1972) or refer to macro-economic changes as explanations for acquisition frequencies (e.g. Haleblian et al. 2009; Heeley et al. 2006). By comparison, this chapter focuses on customers, suppliers, and competitors that may also provide external explanations for acquisitions. It also contributes to research on adaptation by providing observed examples and alternative explanations to why acquisitions occur in waves (cf. Harford 2005).

Theory

A large stream of acquisition research has focused on motives. Depending on the theoretical lens and the perspective taken, explanations for acquisitions include market imperfection, hubris of managers, and revenue enhancement/cost reduction (Seth et al. 2000; Trautwein 1990). Efficiency goals to lower costs or market expansion to increase revenue by entering new markets are among the most frequently mentioned motives when an acquisition is announced (Kelly et al. 2003; Öberg 2004), and these motives are consistent with horizontal acquisitions of firms in the same or similar industries. Motives described by Carpenter and Sanders (2007) cover risk reduction from diversification, increased market power, and other synergy-related motives that reinforce an assumption of rationality underlying most acquisition motives. Meanwhile, hubris and empire-building motives suggest that managers plan acquisitions for their own benefit (Grinstein and Hribar 2004; Trautwein 1990).

Various motives have been linked to different trends (Weston and Weaver 2001) and also to different types of acquisitions. Prior to and during the 1970s, many firms used acquisitions to diversify. More recently, technology acquisitions offer access to unique resources or knowledge (Chen 2008; Graebner et al. 2010; Hennart and Park 1993; Prabhu, Chandy and Ellis 2005; Puranam et al. 2006). Additionally, an increase in international acquisitions suggests market-entry motives. Vertical acquisitions involve upstream acquisition to ensure the supply of raw materials and their quality, or downstream acquisitions to access customers or ensure the quality of a company's distribution and service (Argyres 1996; Díez-Vial 2007). Table 2.1 summarizes different acquisition motives.

Again, a shared feature of the acquisition motives mentioned in most research is that they are company-centric, with limited attention paid to the context of the firm. Literature that refers to environmental reasons for acquisitions focus on two main areas: 1) how the choice of acquired party results from connections at a company level or contacts between individuals (Haunschild 1993; Pfeffer 1972), and 2) descriptions of macro-economic factors that affect the acquisition frequency (Matsusaka 1996). Neither of these environmental explanations considers adaptation to changes in a company's network as a motive for acquisition.

Table 2.1 Summary of acquisition motives

Motives	Explanation	Theoretical lens
Efficiency gains (cost reduction); market expansion (revenue enhancement); new competences	Rationalistic from company's point of view: the acquisition is performed to increase scale or scope of the business	Strategic management
Diversification/risk reduction	The acquisition is performed to spread risk and thereby reduce owners' exposure to certain industries.	Finance/strategy
Market power; market imperfections; wealth transfer	Acquisitions are performed to gain competitive advantage and offset the free market forces	Economic theory/ Neo-classical theory
Hubris/empire-building	Rationalistic from managers' point of view: they are to gain personal or career-related benefits	Organizational theory
Emerging and multiple motives	Motives are constructed as the acquisition evolves, or several motives are combined	Strategy and related

Strategy as adaptation

The strategic management field has gone through several cycles of development (Baden-Fuller and Volberda 1997; Floyd and Wooldridge 1999) with a recent focus on the impact of networks (Castells 2000). This change within strategic management as a field reflects how strategy is embedded in company structures and context (Granovetter 1985). For example, strategic decisions are not made in isolation, but their formulation and implementation considers internal and external stakeholders of the firm (Freeman 1984; Mintzberg 1978).

In considering approaches to strategy, Mintzberg (1973) distinguishes between entrepreneurial, planning, and adaptive modes. The entrepreneurial mode indicates strategy-making based on risk-taking and visionary ideas. Meanwhile, the planning mode refers to a future-oriented view for achieving goals. These approaches are similar to Chaffee's (1985) strategies of linear (planning), and adaptive and interpretive strategies, where the interpretive strategy relates to how frames rather than directives are given to the organization. Adaptation describes how a firm reacts, acts, and copes, rather than attempts to master its environmental context (Cyert and March 1963; Lindblom 1959). Chaffee (1985) also identifies adaptation as a mode that considers stakeholders (cf. Freeman 1984). In stakeholder theory (Freeman 1984), a firm's context is understood as other companies; customers, suppliers, and competitors that comprise a network that influences strategy implementation (cf. Håkansson and Ford 2002; Håkansson and Snehota 1989).

Alternate strategies involve either confronting a firm's network to create opportunities (Mintzberg 1973) or conforming to it with adaptation (Håkansson and Ford 2002). Literature has suggested that adaptation is an inferior approach to strategy, but that perception is changing. For example, Ronchi (1980) describes adaptation as the intersection between the company's capabilities and changes in the environment to uphold a firm's position (cf. Hallén et al. 1991; Johanson and Mattsson 1992) and recent research suggests a possible rejuvenation of adaptation (Hammer et al. 2012). Viewing organizations as an open system with a focus on coordination and co-evolution between firms, emphasizes the embeddedness of social, political, cultural, and institutional influences on firms (Gavetti et al. 2007; Granovetter 1985), and it offers insights into adaptation.

Acquisitions as an adaptation strategy

Acquisition research has just begun to consider stakeholders' influence (Anderson et al. 2012) and how an acquisition impacts customers and suppliers (Havila and Salmi 2000). While it is recognized that acquisitions can trigger change (Anderson et al. 2001; Halinen, Salmi and Havila 1999; Havila and Salmi 2000), this research has not focused on how firms adapt to their network with acquisitions. An exception involves research treating acquisitions as patterns of change (cf. Dahlin et al. 2005; Hertz 1998), studies using resource dependency to explain acquisition as reflecting changes in resource exchange patterns, and research examining patterns of change in a sequence of acquisitions (Shi and Prescott 2011). Still, existing research remains focused on an acquirer (company-centric) and not how different companies adapt to one another.

Acquisitions as an adaptation strategy would mean that an acquisition is carried out to meet with contextual changes. The changes become the triggers, and the acquisition the response to such triggers, or the reverse to how it has been described in most network studies on acquisitions. In addressing the context as consisting of stakeholders or network parties (Ford and Håkansson 2006; Freeman 1984), the adaptation becomes translated into how explicit activities of other firms lead the company to acquire. Compared to the arguments in research on

Christina Öberg

dependence (Finkelstein 1997; Pfeffer and Salancik 1978), it involves acquiring parties other than the one upon which the company is dependent. It also contrasts with explanations of waves in that firms and not necessarily macro-economic factors trigger acquisitions. Acquisitions as an adaptation strategy introduce new insights into why acquisitions are performed and also connect acquisition studies with network studies, stakeholder theory, and the adaptive strategic mode.

Method

A case study methodology was used to examine an adaptation explanation for acquisitions based on changes in a firm's network. A case study allows for capturing acquisitions and their context to consider connections between the different activities (Yin 1994). The chapter uses multiple cases with the intention to provide additional dimensions and comparison among the cases (Eisenhardt 1991). Three acquisition cases were selected based on how they describe adaptation to customers, suppliers, and competitors. They were taken from previous research conducted by the author over the past ten years in different projects on acquisitions, where the selection criteria were to find cases that illustrated adaptations to different parties. Conversational interviews were the main data-capturing method in the study. The interviews were performed with representatives of the acquirer, acquired party, and customers and suppliers to the focal firms. The interviewees included CEOs and financial, marketing, sales, and procurement managers, or they worked as users or maintenance staff of the companies.

Between 2003 and 2012 a total of 58 interviews were conducted (see Table 2.2). To provide a longitudinal perspective, some interviewees were approached again with a time lapse between the first and second interview. Based on the interviews' informal character (McCracken 1988), they were adjusted for each interviewee and also involved the follow up of aspects mentioned during the interviews. Interviews covered, but were not limited to the following areas: general descriptions of the acquisition; why and when it was performed; integration and the outcome of it; and descriptions of different companies surrounding the firm and their mutual impact on the acquisition and its outcome. Interviews were complemented with secondary data, including: annual reports, newspaper items, and internal documentation (cf. Welch 2000). Secondary data provided a timeline of events for each acquisition, the verification of details, and a comparison of motives provided in press releases and those shared by interviewees (cf. Öberg 2004).

Table 2.2 Case interviews

	EuroLifter acquiring USLifter	AutoInternational acquiring Solution	EuroLifter acquiring MediterraneanTruck
Acquirer	CEO, CFO, sales managers, sales and marketing staff (25 interviews)		Overlapping with Case 1
Acquired party		CEO, development manager (3 interviews)	CEO, procurement manager, etc. (3 interviews)
Customers	Procurement, production managers and maintenance staff from 15 different customer companies	R&D manager, procurement manager, etc. (11 interviews)	
Suppliers	Sales manager for 1 supplier company		

30

In the analysis procedure, the interviews and secondary data were used to produce case descriptions that were also approved and corrected by the interviewees. Direct quotations in the final case descriptions intend to highlight central items of the cases (Eisenhardt and Graebner 2007). Next, the interview material was searched for descriptions consistent with an adaptation strategy. These occurrences were coded and compared on a within-case basis (Pratt 2009). The codes represented how the adaptation was described, what parties it involved, and how it linked to the overall acquisition. This part of the analysis was performed in several cycles, moving between the empirical material and previous research, and also included the search for explanations of the adaptation and their relation to present theory (Dubois and Gadde 2002). Conflicting findings were either seen as results of differences in perspectives, or approached to find an explanation. As a final step, the different cases were compared to see whether the explanations of adaptation were linked to different stakeholders, or if shared reasons could be found. Adaptation was also challenged in this stage by other explanations of the acquisitions, in order to test its explanation value. This last point is discussed in the discussion section in terms of whether other motives may explain the acquisitions, and it is concluded how adaptation adds understanding beyond such motives.

Case studies

This section presents three case studies, each illustrating adaptation to customers, suppliers, and competitors, respectively.

Case I: Adapting to customers—EuroLifter acquiring USLifter

In the late 1990s, EuroLifter acquired USLifter. The acquirer and its target were both manufacturers of a specific type of material-handling equipment. At the time of the acquisition, EuroLifter was the third largest player on the European market and USLifter was the market leader in the US. The two companies were of similar size, and EuroLifter had for several years looked into how to strengthen its position in the US. EuroLifter saw its customers increasingly globalizing their business, and a trend of US companies moving into Europe using either greenfield investments or acquisitions.

> We experienced globalization, meaning that some customers started crossing the Atlantic; whether it was USShopping moving outside the US, or EuroFurniture to North America or EuroFood to South America. Here we experienced trends that would make a global presence an advantage.
>
> *(CFO, EuroLifter)*

The intention was that USLifter would represent the US market and South American customers, while EuroLifter would do the same for the customers' European presence. Hence, USLifter would also become a regional supplier to EuroLifter's customers, and vice versa. The acquisition created the world's largest lifter manufacturer in the specific type of material-handling equipment, and it increased EuroLifter's US market presence. As such, the acquisition responded to how customers internationalized their businesses.

Following the acquisition, some global deals were negotiated with customers, but customers had different aspirations, and USLifter was kept largely independent of EuroLifter. There were differences in preferences for the two main markets that divided customers into two different categories. Customers that expanded through organic growth tended to use the same equipment, regardless of geographical region. If the company originated from Europe, European variants were also requested in the US, and conversely for companies having the US as their starting point. If the customers had grown through acquisitions, there was the trend that they required US variants in the US, and European variants in Europe, and this created the best fit with EuroLifter's way of thinking about the market. However, those customers that expanded with acquisitions often found it more difficult to actually negotiate global deals, and suppliers rarely changed. This meant that EuroLifter did not gain many new customers following the acquisition.

Case II: Adapting to suppliers—AutoInternational acquiring Solution

At the beginning of the new millennium, AutoInternational acquired Solution. AutoInternational was a car manufacturer based in Europe, and Solution was a young firm producing software for cars. The acquisition would allow for AutoInternational to have access to that technology and earn revenues from it, if the software was used by other car manufacturers. The acquisition coincided with several acquisitions in the car industry and among its suppliers driven by an outsourcing trend among car manufacturers. To meet the associated demands, suppliers made horizontal acquisitions. For example car manufacturing suppliers sought acquisitions to gain needed technology and negotiation power, and to have the size and capacity to meet customer needs. As part of this trend, suppliers took on increasingly more of the manufacturing and development, increasing their power relative to car manufacturers. As a result, car manufacturers lost knowledge, or did not stay up to date on current manufacturing techniques.

> 80–90 percent of their [the car manufactures'] employees have a mechanical background. But already today, electronics account for one third to 40 percent of the value of the car. The software is almost five to ten percent. And if you calculate it that way, 40 percent of the engineers should be within electronics. But this is not the case, and it will take them ten years to adjust. That is why they [the car manufacturers] have been forced to outsource much of this development to their suppliers. And they themselves are only integrators. They are only project managers. They say: "We develop a new car," but they do not. They are in charge of the time table and allocate money to others, who do the job. This has in turn resulted in suppliers growing and becoming very dominating.
>
> *(Founder I, Solution)*

The car manufacturers increasingly realized their loss of power in comparison with the suppliers. As a consequence, they started to take on making more of the cars themselves. This included placing orders at suppliers for parts rather than entire modules. Acquiring companies that developed components was another step toward regaining power and control. AutoInternational's acquisition of Solution was aimed at making it less dependent on suppliers. While the target was not a powerful party, it meant that the acquirer, in addition to other acquisitions, could provide solutions that it had previously outsourced to suppliers. It also meant that AutoInternational integrated new knowledge.

Following the acquisition, Solution was largely kept independent to allow the small firm to develop its technology and enable the potential for it to sell to other car manufacturers. However, Solution was increasingly regarded as a competitor to other car manufacturers. Solution also found it difficult to integrate its offerings with hardware produced by suppliers. In the end, suppliers developed competing solutions and marketed them to car manufacturers.

Case III: Adapting to competitors—EuroLifter acquiring MediterraneanTruck

When EuroLifter (same company as in Case I) acquired MediterraneanTruck, EuroLifter had moved to become the largest manufacturer of its material-handling equipment. MediterraneanTruck was the dominant player in its domestic market and produced a different variant of equipment. Customers were largely segmented by industry, with food producers and logistics firms using products manufactured by such companies as EuroLifter, while the manufacturing industry used equipment produced by companies such as MediterraneanTruck. Acquisitions were used by industry participants to enable offering both variants of equipment.

> GermanLifter has had [since the mid-1980s] a full product range consisting of both variants. MidEuropeTruck, being obsessed with what GermanLifter does, copied GermanLifter's strategy and made acquisitions in Germany and the UK, of GermanTruck and UKTruck, which provided them with the other variant than the one the company itself provided so they could become as full-ranged as GermanLifter.
>
> *(Deputy CEO, EuroLifter)*

The reason was to enable cross-selling and meet customer needs. For example, manufacturing industry customers on occasion need the variant generally used by logistics firms and food producers, and vice versa. This had the consequence that customers started to do business with manufacturers offering the rival variant of equipment. As long as the variants were manufactured by different companies, this was a marginal issue. However, as soon as competitors in the same product niche were able to provide both variants, this meant lost sales from customers buying from competitors. EuroLifter acquired MediterraneanTruck to become a full-range supplier. Additionally, MediterraneanTruck had acted as a sales representative for EuroLifter in its domestic market. The trend among competitors to acquire such material-handling companies meant that EuroLifter saw the risk that it would lose its sales representation on that market if a competitor acquired MediterraneanTruck.

> And at the same time, we realized that MediterraneanTruck might slip through our fingers, as there were others striving for a similar goal: to consolidate and find a market for their products. And as I see it, if MediterraneanTruck had been acquired by a competitor, we would have had to say good-bye to the beautiful distribution position we had built on MediterraneanTruck's domestic market, and would have returned to a very weak position.
>
> *(Former CEO, EuroLifter International)*

Following the acquisition, MediterraneanTruck started to produce its variants for EuroLifter. In addition to MediterraneanTruck's domestic market, EuroLifter largely owned its distribution network, enabling sales organizations throughout Europe to start selling EuroLifter-branded equipment manufactured by MediterraneanTruck. Meanwhile, MediterraneanTruck continued to represent both brands in its domestic market. Although the acquisition meant that MediterraneanTruck increased its unit sales from 2,000 to 5,000 annually, MediterraneanTruck's products were considered inferior to competitors' and the gains did not entirely reach expectations.

Discussion

As shown in Table 2.3, the case studies support viewing acquisitions as a strategic tool to adapt to customers, suppliers, and competitors. Instead of completing acquisitions to meet changes for a single actor, the actions of customers, suppliers, or competitors contributed to an acquisition being made to respond to changes among networks of customers, suppliers, or competitors. In the case of EuroLifter's acquisition of USLifter, several customers internationalized their businesses. AutoInternational's acquisition was the consequence of how suppliers had increased their power through increased modularization and technological development. EuroLifter's acquisition of MediterraneanTruck resulted from how EuroLifter's main competitors in the European market had diversified into related product niches. Rather than seeing the acquisition as adaptation in a specific relationship (Hallén et al.1991), adaption through acquisition resulted from changes on a network level.

The cases also suggest that acquisitions resulted from trends in each party's industry. For example, customers internationalized their business as other customers did; suppliers acquired other firms to acquire technology and scale, and manufacturers of material-handling acquired firms to offer competing products. Previously, acquisition trends have been described as acquisition waves (Harford 2005; Weston and Weaver 2001), indicating how acquisitions with a specific orientation appear.in groups of several such acquisitions. However, acquisition waves have rarely considered the industry level (Haleblian et al. 2012). Research has also not considered acquisitions as leading to acquisitions among customers and suppliers. This suggests that adaptation to a firm's network may provide a better understanding of observed acquisitions. To explore this idea, several questions are considered.

Could the studied acquisitions be explained by traditional company-centric motives? Looking at the three case studies, the motives coincide with company-centric explanations. EuroLifter's acquisition of USLifter meant a geographical expansion and the strengthening of a market position (Chen 2008; Trautwein 1990). AutoInternational's acquisition of Solution explains how new capabilities were sought by the acquirer (Ahuja and Katila 2001; Prabhu et al. 2005).

Table 2.3 Case summaries

	EuroLifter acquiring USLifter	AutoInternational acquiring Solution	EuroLifter acquiring MediterraneanTruck
Horizontal/vertical acquisition	Horizontal	Vertical (acquisition of party in a position between acquirer and suppliers)	Horizontal (complementary product)
Adaptation to	Customers' globalization	Suppliers' increased power and suppliers holding the knowledge needed to manufacture cars	Competitors' acquisitions
Reason for adaptation	Opportunity to expand to new customers and add sales among current ones	Regaining power and knowledge (consequence of outsourcing strategy)	Imitating competitors
Indirect adaptation to	–	(Competitors)	Customers
Reason for indirect adaptation	–	Imitating competitors	Coping with customer losses

EuroLifter's acquisition of MediterraneanTruck indicates diversification as a motive (Chatterjee and Lubatkin 1990; Limmack 2003; Markides and Ittner 1994). In the associated press releases, reference was made to traditional motives (cf. Kelly et al. 2003; Öberg 2004), suggesting that the acquirers wanted to portray themselves as driving the acquisitions rather than simply adapting to change. This reinforces the importance of methodological choices in acquisition research (Meglio and Risberg 2010) and the advantage here of using case studies to identify adaptation as a motive.

What is behind acquisitions as an adaptive strategy? The cases describe adaptation as adjustments to respond to activities by customers, suppliers, and competitors. Instead of making adjustments based on their requests (cf. Hallén et al. 1991), acquisitions represent a way to deal with external change. However, acquisitions are not the only mode of change used (Öberg and Holtström 2006), and organic growth can also involve adaptation. Still, an adaptation corresponds to imitating a strategic intention of another party (cf. DiMaggio and Powell 1983; Ordanini et al. 2008). For example, meeting geographical expansion of customers with geographical expansion, as illustrated by EuroLifter's acquisition of USLifter (cf. Meyer 2006) technological development and the need for new competences being met with the acquisition of new knowledge as illustrated by AutoInternational's acquisition of Solution, and diversification into a related product niche being met with similar diversification by the acquirer, as illustrated in EuroLifter's acquisition of MediterraneanTruck.

What does adaptation add to current research? Adaption indicates how acquisitions are embedded in the context of other firms (Granovetter 1985). A company acts as described by Lindblom (1959) in a complex context and reacts to occurring issues rather than masters the context. Adaptation creates a link to different strategic actions that go beyond company-centric explanations or planning modes (Chaffee 1985; Mintzberg 1973) and it reflects recent developments in strategy research (Castells 2000; Furrer et al. 2008; Gavetti et al. 2007; Hammer et al. 2012). By integrating a network approach, the complex context of a firm and choices to pursue acquisitions can be explained by considering other stakeholder activities (cf. Chaffee 1985). In summary, adaptation helps to explain why individual acquisitions occur and also why they frequently occur among companies in an industry.

What patterns of adaptation are seen? Previous research has described the spread of change among business partners (Havila and Salmi 2000), using supply chain (Hertz 1998) or random patterns (Dahlin et al. 2005), and sequences of acquisitions (Shi and Prescott 2011). The cases studied indicate adaptation to upstream (EuroLifter's acquisition of USLifter), downstream (AutoInternational's acquisition of Solution), or competing parties (EuroLifter's acquisition of MediterraneanTruck), and they represent supply-chain rather than random patterns (cf. Dahlin et al. 2005). In comparison to Hertz (1998) and Havila and Salmi (2000), the firms in the case do not continue to add new parties upstream or downstream in the supply chain. Instead, the cases suggest acquisition according to the following patterns: 1) previous activities by the acquiring firm or companies at the same supply chain position lead to strategic changes among suppliers or customers that the acquiring firm adapts to, or 2) activities by firms in either an upstream or downstream supply chain position that parallels parties at the same supply chain position explain the acquisition. Adaptation as a response to competitors is illustrated in Euro-Lifter's acquisition of MediterraneanTruck, while it also included adaptation to customers. The case of AutoInternational's acquisition responded to growing supplier power due to outsourcing and points to how companies may have created the situation they later adapt to.

How can the adaption be explained? Though there are multiple explanations, the cases suggest that the strategic intention (reach a new geographical market, add knowledge, or diversify) involved *imitation* by the acquirer, which may involve grasping opportunities or defending current positions (copying or coping). EuroLifter's acquisition of USLifter indicates that it copied its customers' globalization as a voluntary, strategic movement, where adaptation reflects a firm regarding itself as a follower rather than a leader of strategic activities (Haleblian et al. 2012; Mintzberg 1973). The other two cases suggest how the acquirer performed the acquisition to defend its position (Johanson and Mattsson 1992), either driven by how the party that was adapted to challenged it, or based on the indirect adaptation. This suggests that adaptation involves *coping* strategy, or responding to threats to a firm's continuity; of customer losses; of competitors' actions; of supplier power; and anticipated threats to access to resources.

Conclusion

This chapter describes and discusses acquisitions as an adaptation strategy, with a focus on adaptation to changes in a firm's network. The chapter extends literature on sequences of acquisitions and patterns of change (Shi and Prescott 2011) through seeking their explanation and describing adaptation to network parties, and it offers implications for management research and practice.

Research implications

Foremost, an adaptation perspective offers an improved explanation for acquisitions by placing acquirers in the context that impact them (Granovetter 1985; Haleblian et al. 2012). Acquisition as adaptation also enables viewing acquiring firms as responding to other parties through copying or coping. Coping reflects challenges based on restrictions on resources or the defense of a network position. Meanwhile, adaptation to customers can be seen as a more voluntary copying of strategies.

Most companies are followers (Haleblian et al. 2012) and they are dependent on other parties for resources, outputs, development, and ideas. This applies both in their strategy formulation and its realization (Levitt 1966). Studying acquisitions as an adaptation strategy provides new explanations for why acquisitions occur and it connects ideas from adaptation, network, and acquisition research. Compared to other studies on environmental reasons for acquisitions (Haleblian et al. 2009), this chapter focuses on the activities by actors within a firm's network to explain acquisition activity. Acquisitions as an adaptation strategy indicates that acquisitions respond to changes in network relationships.

Managerial implications

Adaptation signals the need to analyze the context of the firm and consider its consequences for the company. For managers, viewing acquisitions as adaptation can provide better outcomes. This likely requires managers apply to stakeholder analyses to determine how external actions (currently and in the near future) will impact the firm (Freeman 1984). In other words, adaptation means a company cannot make company-centric decisions without calculating the consequences for other parties and their subsequent response. In the planning for an acquisition, the following questions should be addressed:

1   What parties do we need to consider in accomplishing our goal?
2   How will this be received by customers, suppliers, and competitors?
3   What are the implications of acquisition goals, and responses for target integration?

Limitations and further research

It would be interesting to study what external events drive firm adaptation with acquisitions and compare the frequency of company-centric and adaptation motives behind acquisitions. Drawing on Mintzberg (1973) and Chaffee (1985), the three modes of strategy could be used to frame different acquisition motives and to compare features of acquirers and acquired parties, to see whether certain acquirers or acquisitions are based on adaptation. The implication of different acquisition motives on outcomes could also be examined. This may enable identifying when employing an adaptation strategy would be advantageous. Another opportunity involves recognizing that acquisitions consist of several phases (Calipha et al. 2010), with value creation largely determined in the integration phase (Haspeslagh and Jemison 1987). It would be interesting to study adaptation in the integration phase so as to see how companies adjust to customers and suppliers (cf. Spedale et al. 2007; Öberg 2008).

A limitation of the chapter is that it only examines three case studies. In contrast to the cases presented here, the need for adaptation may be greater for small firms, and this represents an opportunity for future research. Research can also verify findings and handle contextual limitations from the cases presented here. Research could also focus on capturing patterns of acquisitions (Shi and Prescott 2011) on the network level. In closing, viewing acquisitions as adapting to external change offers the potential for greater insights than the company-centric approach traditionally used.

References

Ahuja, G. and Katila, R. (2001) "Technological acquisitions and the innovation performance of acquiring firms: A longitudinal study," *Strategic Management Journal*, 22: 197–219.

Anderson, H., Havila, V., and Nilsson, F., (eds.) (2012) *Mergers and Acquisitions: The Critical Role of Stakeholders*. Routledge Advances in Management and Business Studies. New York: Routledge.

Anderson, H., Havila, V., and Salmi, A. (2001) "Can you buy a business relationship?: On the importance of customer and supplier relationships in acquisitions," *Industrial Marketing Management*, 30: 575–86.

Anderson, J.C., Håkansson, H., and Johanson, J. (1994) "Dyadic business relationships within a business network context," *Journal of Marketing*, 58: 1–15.

Argyres, N. (1996) "Evidence on the role of firm capabilities in vertical integration decisions," *Strategic Management Journal*, 17: 129–50.

Baden-Fuller, C. and Volberda, H.W. (1997) "Strategic renewal," *International Studies of Management & Organization*, 27: 95–120.

Calipha, R., Tarba, S. and Brock, D. (2010) "Mergers and acquisitions: A review of phases, motives, and success factors," *Advances in Mergers and Acquisitions*, 9: 1–24.

Carpenter, M.A. and Sanders, W.G. (2007) *Strategic Management: A Dynamic Perspective*. Upper Saddle River, NJ: Pearson Prentice Hall.

Castells, M. (2000) *The Rise of the Network Society*. Malden: Blackwell.

Chaffee, E.E. (1985) "Three models of strategy," *Academy of Management Review*, 10: 89–98.

Chatterjee, S. and Lubatkin, M. (1990) "Corporate mergers, stockholder diversification, and changes in systematic risk," *Strategic Management Journal*, 11: 255–68.

Chen, S.-F. (2008) "The motives for international acquisitions: Capability procurement, strategic considerations, and the role of ownership structure," *Journal of International Business Studies*, 39: 454–71.

Cyert, R.M. and March, J.G. (1963) *A Behavioral Theory of the Firm*. Englewood Cliffs, NJ: Prentice-Hall.

Dahlin, P., Fors, J., Havila, V., and Thilenius, P. (2005) *Netquakes: Describing Effects of Ending Business Relationships on Business Networks*. 21st IMP Conference, Rotterdam, RSM Erasmus University.

Díez-Vial, I. (2007) "Explaining vertical integration strategies: Market power, transactional attributes and capabilities," *Journal of Management Studies*, 44: 1017–40.

DiMaggio, P.J. and Powell, W.W. (1983) "The iron cage revisited: Institutional isomorphism and collective rationality in organizational fields," *American Sociological Review*, 48: 147–60.

Dubois, A. and Gadde, L.-E. (2002) "Systematic combining: An abductive approach to case research," *Journal of Business Research*, 55: 553–60.

Eisenhardt, K.M. (1991) "Better stories and better constructs: The case for rigor and comparative logic," *Academy of Management Review*, 16: 620–27.

Eisenhardt, K.M. and Graebner, M.E. (2007) "Theory building from cases: Opportunities and challenges," *Academy of Management Journal*, 50: 25–32.

Finkelstein, S. (1997) "Interindustry merger patterns and resource dependence: A replication and extension of Pfeffer (1972)," *Strategic Management Journal*, 18: 787–810.

Floyd, S.W. and Wooldridge, B. (1999) "Knowledge creation and social networks in corporate entrepreneurship: The renewal of organizational capability," *Entrepreneurship: Theory & Practice*, 23: 123–43.

Ford, D. and Håkansson, H. (2006) "The idea of interaction," *The IMP Journal*, 1(1): 4–27.

Freeman, R.E. (1984) *Strategic Management: A Stakeholder Approach*. Boston, MA: Pitman.

Furrer, O., Thomas, H., and Goussevskaia, A. (2008) "The structure and evolution of the strategic management field: A content analysis of 26 years of strategic management research," *International Journal of Management Reviews*, 1: 1–23.

Gavetti, G., Levinthal, D., and Ocasio, W. (2007) "Neo-Carnegie: The Carnegie School's past, present, and reconstructing for the future," *Organization Science*, 18: 523–36.

Gomez-Mejia, L. and Wiseman, R.M. (1997) "Reframing executive compensations: An assessment and outlook," *Journal of Management*, 23: 291–374.

Graebner, M.E., Eisenhardt, K.M., and Roundy, P.T. (2010) "Success and failure in technology acquisitions: Lessons for buyers and sellers," *Academy of Management Perspectives*, 24(3): 73–92.

Granovetter, M. (1985) "Economic action and social structure: The problem of embeddedness," *The American Journal of Sociology*, 91: 481–510.

Grinstein, Y. and Hribar, P. (2004) "CEO compensation and incentives: Evidence from M&A bonuses," *Journal of Financial Economics*, 73: 119–43.

Håkansson, H., (ed.) (1982) *International Marketing and Purchasing of Industrial Goods: An Interaction Approach*. London: John Wiley & Sons.

Håkansson, H. and Ford, D. (2002) "How should companies interact in business networks?," *Journal of Business Research*, 55: 133–39.

Håkansson, H. and Snehota, I. (1989) "No business is an island: The network concept of business strategy," *Scandinavian Journal of Management*, 5: 187–200.

Haleblian, J., McNamara, G., Kolev, K., and Dykes, B.J. (2012) "Exploring firm characteristics that differentiate leaders from followers in industry merger waves: A competitive dynamics perspective," *Strategic Management Journal*, 33: 1037–52.

Haleblian, J., Devers, C.E., McNamara, G., Carpenter, M.A., and Davison, R.B. (2009) "Taking stock of what we know about mergers and acquisitions: A review and research agenda," *Journal of Management*, 35: 469–502.

Halinen, A., Salmi, A., and Havila, V. (1999) "From dyadic change to changing business networks: An analytical framework," *Journal of Management Studies*, 36: 779–94.

Hallén, L., Johanson, J., and Seyed-Mohamed, N. (1991) "Interfirm adaptation in business relationships," *Journal of Marketing*, 55: 29–37.

Hammer, R.J., Edwards, J.S., and Taponis, E. (2012) "Examining the strategy development process through the lens of complex adaptive systems theory," *Journal of Operational Research Society*, 63: 909–19.

Harford, J. (2005) "What drives merger waves?," *Journal of Financial Economics*, 77: 529–60.

Haspeslagh, P.C. and Jemison, D. (1987) "Acquisitions: Myths and reality," *Sloan Management Review*, 28: 53–58.

Haunschild, P.R. (1993) "Interorganizational imitation: The impact of interlocks on corporate acquisition activity," *Administrative Science Quarterly*, 38: 564–92.

Havila, V. and Salmi, A. (2000) "Spread of change in business networks: An empirical study of mergers and acquisitions in the graphic industry," *Journal of Strategic Marketing*, 8: 105–19.

Heeley, M., King D., and Covin, J. (2006) "R&D investment level and environment as predictors of firm acquisition," *Journal of Management Studies*, 43: 1513–36.

Hennart, J.F. and Park, Y.R. (1993) "Greenfield vs. acquisition: The strategy of Japanese investors in the United States," *Management Science*, 39: 1054–70.

Hertz, S. (1998) "Domino effects in international networks," *Journal of Business-to-Business Marketing*, 5: 3–31.

Johanson, J. and Mattsson, L.-G. (1992) "Network positions and strategic action: An analytical framework," in D. Ford *Understanding Business Marketing and Purchasing*. London: Thompson Learning: 205–17.

Kaul, A. (2012) "Technology and corporate scope: Firm and rival innovation as antecedents of corporate transactions," *Strategic Management Journal*, 33: 347–67.

Kelly, J., Cook, C., and Spitzer, D. (2003) *Unlocking Shareholder Value: The Keys to Success: Mergers and Acquisitions: A Global Research Report*. Annapolis, MD: KPMG.

Levitt, T. (1966) "Innovative imitation," *Harvard Business Review*, 44: 63–70.

Limmack, R. (2003) "Shareholder wealth effects of diversification strategies: A review of recent literature," *Advances in Mergers and Acquisitions*, 2: 177–205.

Lindblom, C.E. (1959) "The science of 'muddling through,'" *Public Administration Review*, 19: 79–88.

McCracken, G. (1988) *The Long Interview*. Newbury Park, CA: Sage Publications.

Markides, C.C. and Ittner, C.D. (1994) "Shareholder benefits from corporate international diversification: Evidence from U.S. international acquisitions," *Journal of International Business Studies*, 25: 343–66.

Matsusaka, J.G. (1996) "Did tough antitrust enforcement cause the diversification of American corporations?," *Journal of Financial and Quantitative Analysis*, 31: 283–94.

Meglio, O. and Risberg, A. (2010) "Mergers and acquisitions: Time for a methodological rejuvenation of the field?," *Scandinavian Journal of Management*, 26: 87–95.

Meyer, K.E. (2006) "Globalfocusing: From domestic conglomerates to global specialists," *Journal of Management Studies*, 43: 1109–44.

Mintzberg, H. (1978) "Patterns in strategy formation," *Management Science*, 24: 934–48.

Mintzberg, H. (1973) "Strategy-making in three modes," *California Management Review*, 16(2): 44–53.

Öberg, C. (2008) *The Importance of Customers in Mergers and Acquisitions*. Department of Management and Engineering, Linköping: Linköping University.

Öberg, C. (2004) *On Customers in Mergers and Acquisitions*. Department of Management and Economics, Linköping: Linköping University.

Öberg, C. and Holtström, J. (2006) "Are mergers and acquisitions contagious?," *Journal of Business Research*, 59: 1267–75.

Ordanini, A., Rubera, G., and DeFillippi, R. (2008) "The many moods of inter-organizational imitation: A critical review," *International Journal of Management Reviews*, 10: 375–98.

Pfeffer, J. (1972) "Merger as a response to organizational interdependence," *Administrative Science Quarterly*, 17: 382–94.

Pfeffer, J. and Salancik, G.R. (1978) *The External Control of Organizations: A Resource Dependence Perspective*. New York: Harper & Row.

Prabhu, J., Chandy, R.K., and Ellis, M.E. (2005) "The impact of acquisitions on innovation: Poison pill, placebo or tonic?," *Journal of Marketing*, 69: 114–30.

Pratt, M.G. (2009) "From the editors: For the lack of boilerplate: tips on writing up (and reviewing) qualitative research," *Academy of Management Journal*, 52: 856–62.

Puranam, P., Singh, H., and Zollo, M. (2006) "Organizing for innovation: Managing the coordination-autonomy dilemma in technology acquisitions," *Academy of Management Journal*, 49: 263–80.

Ronchi, L. (1980) "The decision-making process for strategic adaptation," *Long Range Planning*, 13: 48–54.

Seth, A., Song, K.P., and Pettit, R.R. (2000) "Synergy, managerialism or hubris? An empirical examination of motives for foreign acquisitions of U.S. Firms," *Journal of International Business Studies*, 31: 387–405.

Shi, W. and Prescott, J.E. (2011) "Sequence patterns of firms' acquisitions and alliance behaviour and their performance implications," *Journal of Management Studies*, 48: 1044–70.

Spedale, S., Van den Bosch, F.A.J., and Volberda, H.W. (2007) "Preservation and dissolution of the target firm's embedded ties in acquisitions," *Organization Studies*, 28: 1169–96.

Trautwein, F. (1990) "Merger motives and merger prescriptions," *Strategic Management Journal*, 11: 283–95.

Walter, G. and Barney, J. (1990) "Research notes and communications: Management objectives in mergers and acquisitions," *Strategic Management Journal*, 11: 79–86.

Welch, C. (2000) "The archaeology of business networks: The use of archival records in case study research," *Journal of Strategic Marketing*, 8: 197–208.

Weston, J. and Weaver, S. (2001) *Mergers and Acquisitions*. The McGraw-Hill Executive MBA Series. New York: McGraw-Hill.

Yin, R.K. (1994) *Case Study Research: Design and Methods*. Thousand Oaks, CA: Sage Publications, Inc.

3

A framework of HR enablers for successful M&A integration

A study of three transactions

Mahima Thakur and Anjali Bansal[1]

Introduction

Mergers and acquisitions (M&As) have become a popular strategy for companies to expand and grow, yet the success rate of M&As remains low (King *et al.* 2004). Many researches attribute the high rate of M&A failure to "employee related problems" (Davy *et al.* 1988; Dass 2008), due to insufficient pre- and post-acquisition integration strategies—especially integration of cultures, systems and technologies (Bragg 2001; Carleton and Lineberry 2004; Gallos 2006).

Most organizations jump the gun once the decision for the merger is made. They do not fully prepare during due diligence and have ill-conceived plans of action. Organizations that know how to minimize post-merger drift are the ones that succeed in integration initiatives (Giffords and Dina 2003), giving credence to the adage—the more you sweat in peace, the less you bleed in war. Still, each M&A transaction is unique, so the strategies and processes followed should be well suited to the given context. Companies need to consider multiple concerns, as outlined in Table 3.1. Research has pointed toward various enablers of integration success: human resource management (Dass 2008), training (Schweiger and Goulet 2005), leadership (Thach and Nyman 2001), communication (Seo and Hill 2005) and knowledge management (Empson 2001). This chapter builds on research and learning from practitioners, and attempts to identify and study the enablers of integration success.

The first section of this chapter discusses the conceptual framework of integration while stressing post-acquisition integration. This lays the foundation of the second section of the paper, which draws attention to various integration capability factors while providing a thorough discussion of integration models developed by different researchers, and lessons for training and communication. Section three pertains to the extensive investigation of three cases representing mergers or acquisitions in the Asian context. In this section, qualitative interviews were discussed and further content-analyzed to arrive at conclusions. Section four presents the findings of the study. The concluding section five presents an overview of the research, the inferences of the study and its implication for corporations.

Table 3.1 Questions to answer before entering into M&A deal

1. What is the purpose of this merger/ acquisition?
2. What would be the preferred roadmap to reaching the goal?
3. What is the vision for the future organization?
4. Do we intend to preserve the old culture, transfer one culture onto the other, or create a new culture by transforming the organizations?
5. What are the key processes that can help us to achieve task and cultural synergies?
6. What should be the communication strategy to the employees? Should it be limited to "spray and pray" strategy, or should it be a more detailed and customized exercise?
7. What are the anticipated potential restraining forces towards the achievement of this merger? What would be the respective strategies to be used to manage these forces?

Integration during M&As

While stressing the importance of a pre-acquisition integration plan, Tetenbaum (1999) reviews two studies conducted by Mercer Management and Boston Consulting Group. Mercer Management found that success or failure, three years after a deal, could be explained by the presence or absence of an integration plan following the merger. Companies with strong integration plans created above-average value in their industries. Mercer found that effective post-merger management policies can improve the odds of success by as much as 50 percent. Unfortunately, most companies do not effectively manage integration, so this value is lost. For example, the Boston Consulting Group found that, prior to acquisition, fewer than 20 percent of the companies had considered the steps necessary to integrate the acquired company into their own organization. While integration pertains to all aspects of an organization (i.e. technologies, policies, systems, culture), failures in consolidation are attributed primarily to the lack of an integration plan focused on people and human resource (HR) issues.

The integration of two organizations is an interactive and gradual process where individuals on both sides learn to work together and cooperate in the transfer of resources and capabilities (Haspeslagh and Jemison 1991). The success of this process depends on cooperation, and it requires the organization's ability to address conflicts and various HR challenges. Transferring and integrating resources is difficult because of cultural differences that create conflicts, communication problems, employee resistance, and the turnover of acquired talent and executives (Lubatkin *et al.* 1998;). While discussing this issue, Ashkenas *et al.* remark:

> The tendency to see integration as a unique event in an organization's life is magnified by the fact that acquisition and mergers are often painful and anxiety-producing experiences. They involve job loss, restructured responsibilities, derailed careers, diminished power and much else that is stressful. No wonder most managers think about how to get them over with—not how to do them better the next time.
>
> *(1998, p. 166)*

Post-merger integration is a complicated, touchy, and multi-faceted function that combines change management, task management, and people integration (Maire and Collerette 2011). Acquisition integration is defined by Pablo:

> Integration involves the changes in the functional activities, organizational structures, and cultures of the acquiring and acquired firm (or merging entities) that facilitates their

consolidation into a functioning whole. Unless the acquisition is motivated by purely financial reasons—to lower the cost of capital—post-acquisition integration plays an important role in determining the acquisition results.

(Pablo 1994, p. 803)

This definition can be broken into four separate management challenges: 1) handling organizational issues to manage change and stay on track, 2) facing administrative, technological, financial, geographical, and socio-cultural issues, 3) managing perceptions of social justice and equity, and 4) bringing together the talent of different companies to build a new and stronger entity (Maire and Collerette 2011). In handling these challenges, research has developed different suggestions that are captured in integration models.

Models of integration

This section summarizes five different models of integration with the goal of summarizing the common elements that organizations can apply. Most of the models of integration focus on the management of different processes along different phases of a merger or acquisition.

In the Path Finder model (Ashkenas *et al.* 1998), four phases of acquisition are developed with different sets of activities. Initially this model was developed for GE Capital, a company that assimilated more than 100 acquisitions in a few years (Ashkenas *et al.* 1998). The model outlines an integration game plan for: 1) pre-acquisition, which covers due diligence through closing of the deal, when a leader and communication plan are identified, 2) foundation building, which launches integration, and assigns resources and responsibilities, 3) rapid integration, which focuses on executing developed plans, including feedback to improve organizational processes, and 4) assimilation, which crystallizes routines and culture into a new system.

A more recent model, the FIDESS model, was developed by Vester (2002) after a case study of Xerox's acquisition of Tektronix's Printer Division. FIDESS stands for: "Focus, Innovation, Discipline, Excellence, Speed, and Simplicity" (Vester 2002, p. 33). The FIDESS model includes six lessons-learned categories and 26 related integration best practices. In brief, Focus ensures the rationale, timeline, and ownership for change initiative; Innovation involves sharing best practices to enable creative destruction of existing processes; Discipline requires both planning to take stock of situation and communication to develop a sense of urgency; Excellence covers management of human capital and using both internal and external talent; Speed propels integration by appointing an integration team and top management; and Simplicity provides the corner stone of this model. It advocates keeping in touch with grassroots efforts and direct involvement of senior executives.

The human capital model (Nalbantian *et al.* 2005) proposes a framework of the degree and speed of integration. In this model, the strategic intent can span degree of integration from: 1) total absorption of the other entity's culture (e.g. Sun Microsystems and smaller entities), 2) best of both the cultures (EADS) (Barmeyer and Mayrhofer 2008), 3) no integration at all (remote subsidies of many multinational corporations—MNCs), or 4) transformation to a totally new entity (Marks and Mirvis 2001). Different strategic intent dictates different action plans. The model suggests that full integration is not always needed and may also be potentially destructive (Marlin *et al.* 2004). It also identifies the restraining barriers and the facilitative forces related to the integration process. Barriers reflect several factors, including: 1) demographics, 2) cultural dissimilarities, 3) skill variances, 4) degree of autonomy, 5) employee selection and training processes, (6) differences in governance, and 7) compensation incompatibilities, and they could be rated as high or low. The forces of integration cover strategic intent, human capital requirements, core business process requirements, or any combination that are rated as high or low.

The Merger Management Model (M3) was developed by Lynch and Lynd (2002) as a result of a study of 25 acquisitions between 1980 and 1999 that ranged in size from $5 million to multi-billion dollars in value. The resulting model is based on disparity and goodwill. Disparity refers to the degree of similarity between combining companies, while goodwill is the excess amount above book value paid for a company. Therefore, goodwill represents the expected added value of a merger or an acquisition. Crossing these two dimensions produced four acquisition types that form the core of the M3. Surrounding this core are two additional layers representing acquisition goals and key integration actions, respectively.

The 4S Integration Model was developed by Ashkenas and Francis (2000) at Harvard, and it suggests that integration managers contribute to integration success in four ways: 1) injecting "speed," 2) creating new "structures," 3) forging "social" connections, and 4) creating short-term "success" that leads to long-term goals. The specific methods and potential trade-offs in this model are less clear.

Summary of integration models

A comparison of the integration models shows a diversity of perspectives in approaching integration. While the labels of what is important differ, common elements suggest that the integration has multiple phases or levels and that integration is a process. Processes vary in their effectiveness across organizations, making it worthwhile to consider elements that comprise integration capability.

Organizational initiatives toward developing integration capability

What is amazing after nearly five decades of research into M&As and robust models of integration developed by researchers is that companies do not appear to value these models. Most of the scientific models of integration point toward a well planned, cogent approach to integration based on a strategic intent and a vision for the future entity. Whether it is the Path Finder model or the human capital model, all advocate identifying the strategic intent of degree of integration and aligning change initiatives along these strategic intents. Training, performance management, and communication play a vital role in achieving this strategic intent. The FIDESS model and the 4S model also suggest that certain key HR factors like planning, linking innovation to appraisals, and communication between the top management and grassroots should be taken into consideration for effective and fruitful integration. When these competencies and capabilities are developed along the length and breadth of the organization, it helps develop integration capability.

To produce a sustainable competitive advantage and a sustained integrative capability the acquirer must transfer assets, people, and knowledge between combined units. Firms that do this better than competitors will more likely gain from making acquisitions. Achieving integration is difficult without gaining cooperation from both an acquirer and target. Employees from both the organizations who are involved in the merger must learn about the other company and its assets, people, structure, culture, and HR practices, as well as understand their role in transferring and coordinating resources (Weber and Tarba 2010). If the knowledge stocks of the acquiring and the acquired firms are different, they are likely to be less duplicative and more complementary and therefore offer increased potential for synergies and knowledge transfer (Bjorkman et al. 2007; Larsson and Finkelstein 1999; Shenkar 2001). No matter how attractive a business opportunity, an acquisition will not create value until capabilities are transferred and collaboration begins to create the expected benefits. The need for collaboration highlights the need for HR involvement, which research has correlated with M&A success (Schmidt 2002; Dass 2008; Froese *et al.* 2008).

Organizational effectiveness, innovation, and survival require "respect for and attention to the human side of enterprise" (Gallos 2006, p. 130). The role of the HR department resembles a conductor of a large orchestra where, to achieve harmony, all the musicians need to follow the conductor's guidance. Failure to involve HR professionals especially in the initial stages of M&As (pre-deal and due-diligence) can overlook or ignore people-related issues (Schmidt, 2002) throughout the integration process. Thus, research finds that HR involvement during integration is a possible contributing factor to the success or failure of M&As. The following subsections outline specific HR considerations that facilitate the development of an integration capability.

Human resource initiatives as enablers of integration

Early involvement of HR in the integration planning can avoid overlooking people issues in an acquisition. Success stories of integrations (e.g. the deal between Arcelor and Mittal, 2006; another deal between Vodafone and Essar, 2001; and the formation of EADS group, 2005) pave the way for future M&As. In most of these cases, it has been found that HR played an extensive role. Specific issues that HR can help to address during integration planning and identified by Dass and Way (2005) include:

1   determining organizational blueprint;
2   identifying top management teams, middle-level management teams, and change agents;
3   identifying the core competence and job profile needed in the new context;
4   developing job description, job families, and new roles;
5   determining talent management and retention strategies;
6   providing relevant training at different stages;
7   determining the new organizational culture;
8   developing communications strategy and plan; and
9   reconciling disparate HR policies, compensation, and benefits programs of the two merging entities.

Training: cornerstone of a successful integration program

An element worth expanding on is HR's role in training for M&A success. Training is important throughout integration so that employees can meet the expectations of the new job as well as they adapt to the new environment. Integration needs to be done both at the task level as well as at the human level. Birkinshaw *et al.* (2000) point out that integration should start at the human level (e.g. stress training, counseling, and behavioral training) and then go on to task integration (e.g. knowledge management training and technical training). We propose a training map for the different psychological contours faced by the integration team (refer to Figure 3.1). During the initial shock and denial stage, training forms should cater to behavioral issues that may graduate to more technical forms of training once the employees accept the situation. More specifically, Birkinshaw *et al.* (2000) propose that eventual acquisition success is a function of the parallel processes of task integration and human integration. Task integration is defined as the identification and realization of operational synergies, and human integration is defined as the creation of

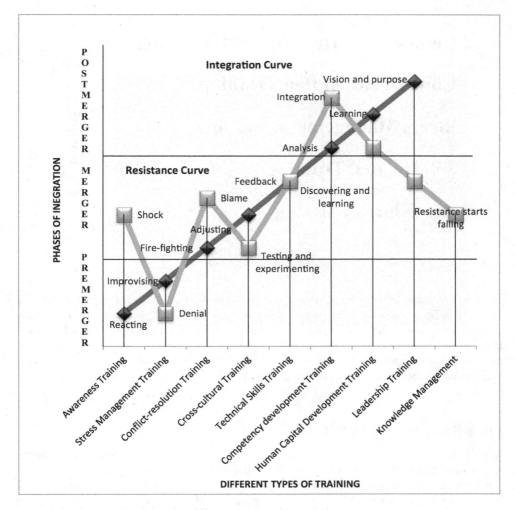

Figure 3.1 Proposed training for different stages of integration

positive attitudes toward integration among employees on both sides. Overall acquisition success is thus contingent on the effective management of both sub-processes.

Thus, integration initiatives begin with the combining organizations understanding the know-how of the other company's assets, people, structure, culture, their HR practices, and their own role in the merged entity. This can help identify specific training needs.

Different types of training for integration

To face the cross-cultural challenges during an interface of two different cultures, researchers suggest that employees need to be made aware of their own thinking processes, as well as the perspectives and perceptions of others. They should be able to identify and assuage their own emotions and others' emotions and thus be able to monitor their own behavior and understand other people's behavior. Intense psychological training has been proposed over the years to cater

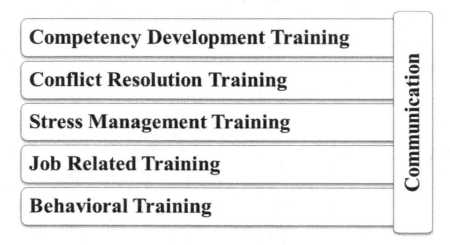

Figure 3.2   Categorization of training during M&A

to the emotional, cognitive, and behavioral aspects of M&As (Landis and Bhagat 1996). Training may also differ at different levels in the organization. Marks (1997) pointed out that human resource professionals should take an active role in educating senior executives about HR issues that can interfere with the success of the merger and with meeting key business objectives, indicating that training at all levels is crucial for effective integration. Different types of training that can play a role in M&A success are discussed in the following subsections, and presented in Figure 3.2.

Competency development training

The competency approach to human resource management focuses on identifying, defining, and measuring individual differences in terms of specific work-related constructs, especially the KSA (knowledge, skills and abilities) that are critical to successful job performance. The competency approach provides a basis for integrating key HR activities such as selection and assessment, performance management, training, development, and reward management, thus developing a coherent approach to the management of people in organizations (Lucia and Lepsinger 1999). Once the merger takes place, new requirements from market expansion, product diversification, and technology upgrades drive an assessment of the training needs of all the employees to move the new merged organization with a new energy, confidence, and positivity infused in every employee. Competence-based training focuses on making employees feel more adept, secure, and motivated.

Conflict resolution training

One of the most important challenges during integration is addressing grievances, whether real or imaginary, expressed or unexpressed. It is these grievances that can pile up and snowball later until they are out of control. O'Connor (1993) categorizes various types of resisters to change, ranging from overt resistance to covert resistance, and unconscious resistance to conscious resistance. He suggests that managers of change need to identify the unconscious and conscious resistance and deal with the intra-personality and inter-personality conflict. This resulted in four categories of resistors-protestors (overt and conscious resistors), saboteurs (covert and conscious resistance), survivors (covert and unconscious resistance), and zombies (overt and unconscious resistance). Conflict resolution training would help managers to identify different types of resistors and conflicts and to use appropriate strategies to manage them. There might be other kinds of conflict (e.g. inter-departmental conflict and role conflict) that managers also need to address.

Stress management training

Elizabeth Kubler-Ross (1969) vividly depicted the range of emotions experienced during any kind of change in life, starting from "shock" and "denial" and finally evolving into "acceptance." Management researchers and practitioners have extensively borrowed from her model and developed transition curve/ psychological curve during M&As (Devine 2002). Confusion and uncertainty caused during the merger announcement contributes to the employee's stress levels. During the early phases of shock, denial, anger, and experimentation, organizations need to provide intense stress-handling training to managers as well as to other employees which would help them to manage their own emotions as well as others' emotions. As depicted in Figure 3.1, appropriate training along the different phases of the resistance curve would help the employees cope with the challenges of the change. Educational seminars should be developed and delivered to curtail stress and uncertainty in the organization during the change process (Seo and Hill 2005). For example, employee assistance programs and "town meetings," where employees can voice their views openly, listen to others, and take solace in the fact that others are experiencing the same emotions (Fugate *et al.* 2002) help release stress.

Job-related training

The roles and responsibilities of employees tend to change during an acquisition. This causes employees to feel less competent for their present job role. Managers need to consider job-related training, as employees' behavioral and psychological processes that are linked with different roles have a great impact on integration outcomes. A substantial effort expended in teaching, training, and communication, and effective HR processes could help in reducing ambiguity and culture clashes and to lower perceptions of inequity in the organization (King *et al.* 2004; Stahl *et al.* 2011).

Managers need to identify new roles, do a detailed job analysis of all roles, and relate job descriptions and then design training programs related to the new roles. This training also needs to consider the alignment with the new roles of others. Additional training that can be subsumed under job-related training include: 1) expert training for knowledge and information related to roles, 2) processes training related to coordinating mechanisms, and 3) knowledge management training.

Behavioral training

Training related to new expected behaviors and cultural norms assist in understanding each groups' behavior. Successful mergers have banked on intense behavioral training to mitigate the impact of wide cross-cultural gaps. The Daimler and Chrysler (DCX) merger, underestimating the potential impact of cross-cultural challenges, led to steep losses. The meticulous Germans found the attitudes of the Americans unnerving, and the Americans found the behavior of Germans to be regimented (Hollmann *et al.* 2010). Further, thousands of workers in India went on strike when a Japanese supervisor "playfully" kicked a worker and upset his sacred head gear, thus hurting relations with workers (Saini 2005). A thorough behavioral training of both entities will help them respect and accept differences.

Training summary

Effective training programs can help fight acculturation blues. Most M&As are plagued by multiple cultural clashes which snowball into huge integration challenges. One of the best examples of such a flawed M&A planning and execution was that of the Daimler-Chrysler merger. In May, 1998, Daimler-Benz and Chrysler Corporation, two of the world's leading car manufacturers, agreed to combine their businesses in what they claimed to be a "merger of equals." The merger resulted in a large automobile company, ranked third in the world in terms of revenues, market capitalization, and earnings, and fifth in the number of units (passenger-cars and commercial vehicles combined). Chrysler was the very symbol of American adaptability and resilience, valuing efficiency, empowerment, and fairly egalitarian relations among staff, whereas Daimler-Benz was the epitome of German respect for authority, bureaucratic precision, and centralized decision-making. Another key issue at DCX was the differences in pay structures between the two pre-merger entities. Germans disliked huge pay disparities and were unlikely to accept any steep revision of top management salaries. But American CEOs were rewarded handsomely, and Chrysler's CEO Eaton earned a total of $10.9 million in 1997. When faced with cultural clashes, both managements got into intense training programs, but the damage had been done. The chasm was too wide to be bridged, and the dividing lines were dug deeper over time. Had these training programs been conceived earlier, anticipating the cultural clashes, they would have been more effective. Eaton's address to Germans was not taken well, as they did not appreciate an open display of emotion (tears) by a leader. This case also throws light on the designing of communication: communicators should consider 1) the strategic goal in mind, 2) customizing the message to address the needs and fears of the various target groups, and 3) frequency to reinforce desired messages. Senior management cannot "spray and pray" and simply hope that all will end well. Instead, communication needs to be consistent to drive some important messages and create bonds; relevant observations on communication are summarized next.

Role of communication in integration success

A Wyatt company study of CEOs in 531 U.S. firms found that, if they had another chance to go through a major restructuring, they would have focused more on communication with their employees (Larkin and Larkin 1996). This is consistent with a KPMG survey of managers in 131 of Canada's top corporations, which found that managers viewed communication as the most important factor in achieving successful organizational change (Barrett and Luedecke 1996). Implementing an acquisition requires that communication be consistent, content rich, and customized.

This implies a need to consider communication early. M&As take place in an environment of uncertainty and gossip, where employees often operate in a state of bewilderment. The mere announcement of an acquisition creates a great deal of uncertainty and speculation with the "all-too-pervasive" rumor mill or proverbial office grapevine potentially sabotaging an otherwise effective corporate communication program. To address the importance of communication, the concept of "Merger Syndrome" was proposed by Marks and Mirvis (1985). This situation is characterized by increased centralization and decreased communication by management with employees. For example, one survey found that 58 percent of respondents felt that "undercommunication" in acquisitions was more problematic than "financial synergy" and "not meeting promises" (Appelbaum *et al.* 2007). This has detrimental consequences for an atmosphere of trust and equity in the organizations.

Trust is an important behavioral aspect in the integration process. Sorting out grievances at the incipient stage would help arrest the development of feelings of inequity, injustice, and lack of managerial empathy. Most M&As do not give due consideration to the issue of conflict resolution and grievance handling. When the organization institutionalizes a proper grievance handling mechanism, such as suggestion boxes, it can help manage integration.

In considering how to overcome perceived communication shortfalls and their implications, Daly (1995) identifies that employees are more likely to be successfully integrated when: 1) they are provided with accurate information and feedback, 2) changes are explained adequately to frame decisions, and 3) communication enables an exchange of ideas. These factors highlight the importance of not just the content of information but also its tone, frequency, and timeliness. Thus, timing is significant, and a good communication plan should be developed before an acquisition is finalized (Balmer and Dinnie 1999). In developing a communication plan, Davy *et al.* (1988) propose some guidelines to increase the effectiveness of communication:

1   timely distribution of information;
2   comprehensiveness of information;
3   frequency of distribution of information through different media;
4   communications that are perceived as credible by employees;
5   communication of the rationale for organizational changes; and
6   effective planning of the communication program across the stages of transition.

Consistent with these ideas, Ashkenas *et al.* (1998) suggest four considerations in any communication plan—audience, timing, mode, and message. For example, GE Capital's Private Label Credit Cards business identified several distinct audiences, including the senior management of both the companies, the integration team, the employees of both organizations, the customers, clients, and vendors of the combined unit, the affected communities, and the media. Before the deal was closed, the details were conveyed to each audience through the appropriate mode of communication to facilitate success. Next, we examine how developed ideas apply in three relevant cases.

Exploration of three M&As

A case study using a qualitative design attempted to study the correlates of successful integration from three mergers (Yin 1994). The three M&As chosen were selected using convenience sampling to examine organizations ranging from the public sector, to the private sector, to multinationals in Asia. Organizations selected were in their post-merger period (six months to two years). Transaction 1 chosen was the acquisition of a "government-owned IT service firm" (entity B) by another "government-owned electrical equipment industry firm" (entity A). Transaction 2 was the merger of a "government-owned aviation sector firm" (entity C) with another "government-owned aviation sector firm" (entity D), while Transaction 3 involved a merger of a private telecom giant of India (entity E) with another Indian "private telecom sector firm" (entity F).

Research methodology

This scientific investigation adopted a dual approach of studying qualitative data from interviews and developing cases. The sample size was of 117 engineering managers from the three organizations. The sampling was multi-stage, with organizations chosen on a purposive basis, but the respondents were chosen randomly. All the respondents were engineers from the lower and middle rung in the organization. It was imperative to study the perception of the middle and lower rung because most of the resistance comes from these levels and they are separate from the decision-making process.

An interview schedule was prepared with open-ended questions related to proposed enablers of integration (independent variables) and the dependent variables of satisfaction with the integration process, integration outcomes, and organizational commitment. A pilot study of 49 managers helped in identifying questions on role ambiguity and role isolation that related to the dimension of role stress. The independent variable of training had nine questions about their perception of training initiatives related to the dimensions of awareness training, cross-cultural training, and human capital development (competency) training. HR conducted training programs, as most of the people in the IT department were from a different cultural background with varying competencies. Additional measures included:

1   Communication: measured along three dimensions—relevance of information provided, frequency of communication to employees, and customized communication to target groups, keeping in mind their apprehensions and fears. Questions were also asked about communication in case of grievances or queries of employees.
2   HR initiatives: questions were related to the various areas like training, talent management, work force planning and distribution, role stress, career growth planning, performance appraisal systems (structure and objectivity), and reward structure.
3   Cultural convergence: measured by asking questions related to three dimensions of culture—style of decision making, routine institutionalization, and value institutionalization practices.
4   Task integration initiatives: these include the placement of resources required for successful task outcomes (e.g. alignment of task routines, resource sharing, clarification of role identities, and identification of job descriptions).
5   Perception of integration process: determined by measuring the level of satisfaction of employees with the integration process.

Results

The results indicated a high correlation between HR initiatives and perception of integration success. In both Transactions 1 and 2, HR planning for integration was limited, and employees reported role isolation and role ambiguity. The employees of the acquired organization felt that the new roles given to them were less important and clear. In Transaction 3, the organizations were trying to preserve the work routines as the two entities were managing their own spheres of work. Table 3.2 summarizes the transactions and integration intentions.

Transaction 1 depicts the impact of poor cultural integration on M&A outcomes despite thorough HR planning, training initiatives, and resources for both the entities. In Transaction 1, the acquiring organization, a public sector company (entity A) let the acquired IT organization (entity B) continue operations as an extension of the company. The major conflict which emerged was related more to the human/ cultural integration than the task integration. Entity B was primarily made up of young engineers from the IT sector with international exposure, while entity A was a typical monolithic bureaucratic government sector organization doing fairly well. Though the qualitative data revealed that the member of the IT group (entity B) felt that the government organization conducted extensive training programs for them, the main source of dissatisfaction was the cultural difference. The employees of entity B felt that it was

Table 3.2 Summary of initiatives to achieve integration

Transactions	Organizations	HR initiatives	Training	Communication	Cultural integration	Task integration
Transaction 1	**Entity A** (government-owned company) **Entity B** (government-owned IT service firm)	Career growth plans were determined; performance appraisal procedures of only entity A were followed; no recognition system	Task integration training; competency development training	Nothing was communicated before deal took place; work norms were communicated once merger was done	No participation of workers in decision-making; entity A routines and practices were circulated; (absorption)	Preservation of routines; clearly stated job description and task distribution
Transaction 2	**Entity C** (government-owned aviation sector firm) **Entity D** (government-owned aviation sector firm)	No career growth plans were determined; old performance appraisal procedures were followed	Cross-cultural training; behavioral training	No clarity of processes; minimal efforts were put into communicating about the processes; no communication with the unions; unions went on strike	Integration of values; cross-cultural training; procedures integration; (midway of absorption and preservation)	Duplication of tasks; parallel development of processes
Transaction 3	**Entity E** (private telecom sector giant) **Entity F** (private telecom sector organization)	HR processes were integrated to set harmony	Human capital training; job role training; knowledge management training	Communication was done before, during, and after the acquisition; communication by leader; customized according to various target groups; suggestion boxes and gripe boxes	Preservation of cultures; communicated leadership vision; interaction with targets; inter-organizational cross postings (preservation)	Clear-cut processes; joint committees; conflict resolution committees; integration managers

like going "back to school" as they (entity A) issued a list of do's and don'ts—for their younger counterparts. For example, having coffee in the winter sun in the parking lot with friends was considered inappropriate and disallowed. When interviewed, the members of entity A felt that the members of entity B were "immature" and needed to be trained into senior management's values and credo. When asked if this was dissatisfying, the younger employees reported that, though it was irritating, the learning was worthwhile. What was most irking for these IT engineers of entity B was the fact that they had separate canteens for the two organizations. "Needless to say that the canteen of the government organization (mostly senior officials) was better in service quality and in product range than that of the employees of the IT firm (mostly young and junior IT engineers). It is a reflection of their mindsets, remarked one of the younger engineers who were experiencing a high level of power distance. A senior HR executive who was involved in Transaction 1 stated: "We established our basic rules. We would provide them career growth opportunities but we will not compromise on discipline and performance." This was in sharp contrast with the open working style of the young engineers.

The responses for Transaction 1 clearly show that a "them and us" divide served as the main reason of dissatisfaction. They also said that their communication was neither clear nor frequent. We conclude that cultural alignment is even more crucial than task alignment as it involves human issues such as satisfaction, anger, frustration, and belongingness. The findings of this research are in tandem with the conclusions posited by Birkinshaw *et al.* (2000) that cultural alignment (human integration) is of vital significance and should precede task alignment (task integration) as it involves human issues like satisfaction, anger, frustration, and belongingness.

Transaction 2 depicts the impact of poor HR planning initiatives on M&A outcomes. Transaction 2 was a merger of a government-owned aviation sector organization with another smaller organization in the same sector. The major issue was related to task integration as there was reported role duplication, role ambiguity, and perceived injustice. Culturally the two organizations were similar, but HR did not seem to have done its work. One of the respondents pointed out in an exasperated tone: "they give all the plum tasks to their 'own' people and soon they would promote them on that basis. I am planning to quit and open my own courier business." HR had failed to do workforce planning, and role descriptions were not charted out for various job families. As a result, people felt lost and wasted. Thus, as pointed out in the human capital management model, the managers in Transaction 2 could not address the issues related to human capital management for redefining the role, clarity of career pathway, and inter-departmental conflicts which resulted in entropy and overwhelming feelings of alienation and dejection. People were ready to leave their lucrative government jobs in a developing economy.

Organizations often go into a heightened drive of cultural integration, as seen by the cultural convergence institutionalization practices in Transaction 2. Training budgets were allocated and the organizations went into a thorough training program related to culture and competence. What was interesting is that, despite such thorough HR involvement, HR planning was not perceived favorably by the employees. The HR initiatives were seen as "half-baked" policies. One of the managers reported that the presence of unions was a major obstacle to HR planning. The unions were resisting major reshuffles and job cuts and often threatened an organization-wide strike if even one job was touched. The HR department worked extensively around cultural integration, but it did not touch task integration. HR conducted an orientation program for the employees of entity D, the smaller of two merging entities, wherein entity C's vision and HR processes were communicated to them. The HR managers failed to address the key concerns of a typical M&A employee experiencing merger syndrome, with feelings of uncertainty, loss of power, fear of the unknown, and survivors' anxiety rampant. Most of the employees feared losing their current roles and lacked meaning to associate with their roles in the new scenario.

Transaction 3 is a depiction of a well planned M&A process with a proper focus on task integration, cultural integration, and communication. Transaction 3 was a merger of a private telecom giant in India (entity E) with a mid-sized private telecom firm (entity F). Job-related training was provided to employees to make them better understand the expectations of their new job roles. One of the participants in Transaction 3 said: "training helped in clear understanding of procedures and processes that helped employees to acclimatize during integration." The results support the contention of Weber and Tarba (2010), who state that the training for a specific situation such as a merger is perceived by managers and employees as a good development and career opportunity that helps them both on the job and in future hiring and retention. Inputs from qualitative interviews in Transaction 3 also corroborated this conclusion. For example, respondent comments indicated: "the good part about this merger is that we got to learn new skills and competencies," and "I was not very happy in the beginning but now I feel good about it as we have been given training on many new technologies."

In Transaction 3, the emphasis on communication was given at all the stages of the M&A where mid-level managers communicated about the processes and organizational structure. The acquiring organization held frequent meetings to answer questions and help allay fears of the acquired company employees by communicating that every employee would be retained on their current positions and no lay-offs or retrenchment would be done. This transaction shows that, though the previous two entities had different organizational cultures, mutual respect between the strategies, cultures, structures, participative leadership style, and HR processes can lead to success.

Discussion

This investigation makes a contribution to the existing literatures of both human resource management (HRM) and M&A. The results suggest a significant role for HR in the M&A process. It is clear from the evidence that HR plays a variety of roles during the M&A process depending on the phase. In the pre-deal phase, HR professionals are researchers, analyzers, planners, and negotiators. They collect data of the partner organization and examine HR implications from the information they gather. Later in the post-merger phase, HR professionals identify integration levels and reconcile compensation and job descriptions. This is then used in the training of employees to facilitate integration and cultural convergence in this phase. Our findings are strengthened from using multiple sources of data that increase the confidence of our results. Additional implications for management research and practice are discussed below.

Research implications

The results of this study corroborate findings of previous research stressing the role of hard enablers (e.g. task integration practices) and soft enablers (e.g. cultural convergence institutionalization practices, communication, and HR practices) (Birkinshaw et al. 2000; Schuler and Jackson 2001). Specifically, Birkinshaw et al. (2000) divide integration into two equally important processes, task integration and human integration. Our results support their contention that M&A success depends on both processes being effective. For example, an emphasis on human integration may result in satisfied and committed employees without operational synergies, while an emphasis on task integration can lead to the achievement of synergies without employee commitment and satisfaction.

Our research also has implications for research on trust. Perceptions of fairness and honesty are dependent upon the relationship between the trustor and trustee (Bhattacharya et al. 1998;

Butler 1991; Jones and George 1998). Unless employees feel that the newly merged organization is working for their well-being, they won't trust it. We find that training helps to alleviate feelings of distrust and ambiguity. The use of training for supervisors, shop floor training, and training on appraisal systems provides clarity and sends important signals to employees. As a result, training leads to the metamorphosis of feelings from apprehension, to excitement, and acceptance. This suggests that training may provide an important foundation for trust.

Managerial implications

M&As involve labor pains, but well planned and chalked out integration strategies can help ease that pain. The results of the study identify enablers associated with integration capability that managers can strengthen. Continuous and customized communication, grievance resolution, and multifaceted training programs hold center stage positions in the road map to integration. Still, they tend to be ignored the most. Once distrust is established, it will be difficult to recapture employee commitment and satisfaction. For example, the study also highlights the importance of managing unions, which may be overlooked in M&A research.

Limitations and future research

Performing our study involved trade-offs and areas that we incompletely explore and require additional research. For example, the examination of the cases highlighted the importance of managing unions, which we do not examine in depth. Future research can attend to this issue, as it is a key reason for the failure of a merger involving two major airlines in India. The use of surveys has its own limitations such as social desirability factors and issues related to self-report surveys and interviews. The addition of archival data to validate our findings is needed. Additionally, it would have been ideal to have observed the organizations in a longitudinal design over the integration period. Nevertheless, the study points to unique socio-cultural issues and offers solutions and suggestions for future research.

Note

1 Anjali Bansal is the corresponding author for the chapter.

References

Appelbaum, S.H., Lefrancois, F., Tonna, R. and Shapiro, B.T. (2007) "Mergers 101 (part one): training managers for communications and leadership challenges," *Industrial and Commercial Training*, 39: 128–36.

Ashkenas, R.N. and Francis, S. (2000) "Integration managers: special leaders for special times," *Harvard Business Review*, 78: 108–16.

Ashkenas, R.N., DeMonaco, L.J., and Francis, S.C. (1998) "Making the deal real: how GE Capital integrates acquisitions," *Harvard Business Review*, 76(1): 149–80.

Balmer, J.M.T. and Dinnie, K. (1999) "Corporate identity and corporate communications," *Corporate Communications: An International Journal*, 4: 182–92.

Barmeyer, C. and Mayrhofer, U. (2008) "The contribution of intercultural management to the success of international mergers and acquisitions," *International Business Review*, 17: 28–38.

Barrett, M., and Luedecke, B. (1996) "What management says it wants in communicating change," *Communication World – San Francisco*, 13: 29–32.

Bhattacharya, R., Devinney, T.M., and Pillutla, M.M. (1998) "A formal model of trust based on outcomes," *Academy of Management Review*, 23: 459–73.

Birkinshaw, J., Bresman, H., and Hakanson, L. (2000) "Managing the post-acquisition integration process: how the human integration and task integration processes interact to foster value creation," *Journal of Management Studies*, 37: 395–425.

Bjorkman, I., Stahl, G., and Vaara, E. (2007) "Impact of cultural differences on capability transfer in acquisitions: the mediating roles of capability complementarity, absorptive capacity, and social integration," *Journal of International Business Studies*, 38: 658–72.

Bragg, T. (2001) "Lessons from a mismanaged merger," *Industrial Management*, 43(2): 6–8.

Butler Jr., J.K. (1991) "Toward understanding and measuring conditions of trust: evolution of a trust inventory (OTI)," *Journal of Management*, 17: 643–63.

Carleton, J.R. and Lineberry, C. (2004) *Achieving post-merger success: a stakeholder's guide to cultural due diligence, assessment, and integration*. San Francisco, CA: John Wiley & Sons.

Daly, J.P. (1995) "Explaining changes to employees: the influence of justifications and change outcomes on employees' fairness judgments," *Journal of Applied Behavioral Sciences*, 31: 415–28.

Dass, T.K. (2008) "Human resource processes and the role of the human resources function during mergers and acquisitions in the electricity industry," PhD dissertation. University of Cincinnati: UMI 3340321.

Dass, T.K. and Way, P.K. (2005) "Management education and M&As: are managers acquiring critical HR knowledge?," presentation. Academy of Management meeting, Honolulu, Hawaii, August.

Davy, J.A., Kinicki, A., Kilroy, J., and Scheck, C. (1988) "After the merger: dealing with people's uncertainty," *Training and Development Journal*, 42: 57–61.

Devine, M. (2002) *Successful mergers: getting the people issues right*, London: *The Economist*.

Empson, L. (2001) "Fear of exploitation and fear of contamination: impediments to knowledge transfer in mergers between professional service firms," *Human relations*, 54: 839–62.

Froese, F.J., Pak, Y.S., and Chong, L.C. (2008) "Managing the human side of cross-border acquisitions in South Korea," *Journal of World Business*, 43: 97–108.

Fugate, M., Kinicki, A.J., and Scheck, C.L. (2002) "Coping with an organizational merger over four stages," *Personnel Psychology*, 55: 905–28.

Gallos, J.V. (2006) "The OD core: understanding and managing planned change, part 2," in Gallos, J.V. (ed.), *Organizational development: a Jossey-Bass reader*. San Francisco, CA: Jossey-Bass, 129–31.

Giffords, E.D. and Dina, R.P.(2003) "Changing organizational cultures: the challenge in forging successful mergers," *Administration in Social Work*, 27: 69–81.

Haspeslagh, P.C. and Jemison, D.B. (1991) "The challenge of renewal through acquisitions," *Planning Review*, 19: 27–32.

Hollmann, J., de MouraCarpes, A., and Beuron, T.A. (2010) "The DaimlerChrysler merger—a cultural mismatch?," *Revista de Administração da UFSM*, 3: 431–40.

Jones, G.R. and George, J.M. (1998) "The experience and evolution of trust: implications for co-operation and teamwork," *Academy of Management Review*, 23: 531–46.

King, D.R., Dalton, D.R., Daily, C.M., and Covin, J.G. (2004) "Meta-analyses of post-acquisition performance: indications of unidentified moderators," *Strategic Management Journal*, 25: 187–200.

Kubler-Ross, E. (1969), *On death and dying*. Collier, NY: Scribner's.

Landis, D. and Bhagat, R. (eds.), (1996) *Handbook of intercultural training*. London: Sage Publications.

Larkin, T.J. and Larkin, S. (1996) "Reaching and changing frontline employees," *Harvard Business Review*, 74(3): 95–104.

Larsson, R. and Finkelstein, S. (1999) "Integrating strategic, organizational, and human resource perspectives on mergers and acquisitions: a case survey of synergy realization," *Organization Science*, 10: 1–26.

Lubatkin, M., Calori, R., Very, P., and Veiga, J.F. (1998) "Managing mergers across borders: a two-nation exploration of a nationally bound administrative heritage," *Organization Science*, 9: 670–84.

Lucia, A. and Lepsinger, R. (1999) *The art and science of competency models*. San Francisco, CA: Jossey-Bass/ Pfeiffer.

Lynch, J.G. and Lind, B. (2002) "Escaping merger and acquisition madness," *Strategy & Leadership*, 30: 5–12.

Maire, S. and Collerette, P. (2011) "International post-merger integration: lessons from an integration project in the private banking sector," *International Journal of Project Management*, 29: 279–94.

Marks, M.L. (1997) Let's make a deal, *HR Magazine*, 42: 125–31.

Marks, M.L. and Mirvis, P.H. (2001) "Making mergers and acquisitions work: strategic and psychological preparation," *Academy of Management Executive*, 15(2): 80–92.

Marks, M.L. and Mirvis, P.H. (1985) "Merger syndrome: stress and uncertainty," *Mergers & Acquisitions*, 20: 50–55.

Marlin, D., Lamont, B.T., and Geiger, S.W. (2004) "Diversification strategy and top management team fit," *Journal of Managerial Issues*, 16: 361–81.

Nalbantian, H.R., Guzzo, R.A., Kieffer, D., and Doherty, J. (2005) "Making acquisitions work," *Journal of Organizational Excellence*, 24: 45–52.

O'Connor, C.A. (1993) "Resistance: the repercussions of change," *Leadership & Organization Development Journal*, 14: 30–36.

Pablo, A.L. (1994) "Determinants of acquisition integration level: a decision-making perspective," *Academy of Management Journal*, 37: 803–36.

Pritchett, P., Robinson, D., and Clarkson, R. (1997) *After the merger: the authoritative guide for integration success*, 2nd edn. New York: McGraw-Hill.

Saini, D.S. (2005) "Honda Motorcycles and Scooters India Limited (Hmsi)," *Vision: The Journal of Business Perspective*, 9(4): 71–81.

Schmidt, A.J. (2002) *Making mergers work: the strategic importance of people*. Alexandria, VA: Towers Perrin and Society for Human Resource Management.

Schuler, R. and Jackson, S. (2001) "HR issues and activities in mergers and acquisitions," *European Management Journal*, 19: 239–53.

Schweiger, D.M. and Goulet, P.K. (2005) "Facilitating acquisition integration through deep-level cultural learning interventions: a longitudinal field experiment," *Organization Studies*, 26: 1477–99.

Seo, M.G. and Hill, N.S. (2005) "Understanding the human side of merger and acquisition: an integrative framework," *The Journal of Applied Behavioral Science*, 41: 422–43.

Shenkar, O. (2001) "Cultural distance revisited: towards a more rigorous conceptualization and measurement of cultural differences," *Journal of International Business Studies*, 32: 519–35.

Stahl, G.K., Larsson, R., Kremershof, I., and Sitkin, S.B. (2011) "Trust dynamics in acquisitions: a case survey," *Human Resource Management*, 50: 575–603.

Tetenbaum, T.J. (1999) "Seven key practices that improve the chance for expected integration and synergies," *Organizational Dynamics*, 28: 22–36.

Thach, L. and Nyman, M. (2001) "Leading in limbo land: the role of a leader during merger and acquisition transition," *Leadership & Organization Development Journal*, 22: 146–50.

Vester, J. (2002) "Lessons learned about integrating acquisitions," *Research Technology Management*, 45: 33–41.

Weber, Y. and Tarba, S.Y. (2010) "Human resource practices and performance of mergers and acquisitions in Israel," *Human Resource Management Review*, 20: 203–11.

Yin, R. (1994) *Case Study Research: Design and Methods*, Thousand Oaks, CA: Sage Publications.

4

Acquire or get acquired

Defensive acquisitions in medium-sized family firms

Pankaj C. Patel and David R. King

Introduction

Beyond economic and non-economic motives for acquisitions (Gorton *et al.* 2009; Haleblian *et al.* 2009), family firm research consistently shows that family firms engage in lower levels of diversification (Anderson and Reeb 2003b; Basu *et al.* 2009; Caprio *et al.* 2011; Gomez-Mejía *et al.* 2010; Miller *et al.* 2010; Sraer and Thesmar 2007). While acquisitions are complex events, according to Miller *et al.* (2010: 208), family firms' unique social priorities and risk preferences lead to fewer acquisitions, such that "at 20 percent of family ownership, the average number of acquisitions is 1.55 with a value of $788MM; at 60 percent of family ownership these numbers decline to 1.03 and $28MM, respectively." Research demonstrates limited consensus on the impact of family ownership on firms (O'Boyle *et al.* 2012). However, recent work on 777 large continental European firms confirms that family control is negatively related with acquisition propensity (Caprio *et al.* 2011). In the quest for preserving socioemotional wealth, family firms exhibit lower acquisition activity than non-family firms (Bauguess and Stegemoller 2008; Sraer and Thesmar 2007). Socioemotional wealth refers to "non-financial aspects of the firm that meet the family's affective needs, such as identity, the ability to exercise family influence, and the perpetuation of the family dynasty" (Gomez-Mejía *et al.* 2007: 106).

As family firms possess additional social, affective, and emotional endowments, their utility functions for acquisition decisions are different from those of non-family firm managers who are typically driven by economic motives (Daily *et al.* 2003). Compared to non-family firms, family firms engage in economic, social, and emotional calculus of maintaining socioemotional wealth, sometimes at the expense of financial gains (Gomez-Mejía *et al.* 2007). As acquisitions dilute control and often require non-family human and financial capital to create post-acquisition synergies, risk-averse family firms prefer fewer acquisitions than non-family firms (Gomez-Mejía *et al.* 2011). However, research has only scratched the surface in explaining observed differences between family and non-family firm acquisition activity.

Acquisition literature on family firms has largely focused on the differences in "demand" between family and non-family acquirers for target firms in the market for corporate control (Gomez-Mejía *et al.* 2007, 2010, 2011). From a "supply side" for acquisitions, we examine whether the prospect of being acquired motivates family firm acquisition activity. As potential acquisition targets, family firms are motivated to take steps that mitigate this threat to socioemotional wealth (Gomez-Mejía *et al.* 2007). As a result, we contend that family firms are more likely to engage in defensive acquisitions with the non-financial motive of preserving socioemotional wealth. This is consistent with the "eat or be eaten" hypothesis that maintains that managers of mid-sized firms may undertake defensive acquisitions to lower threat of future takeover (cf. Gorton *et al.* 2009). Under the behavioral agency model (Wiseman and Gomez-Mejía 1998), socioemotional wealth is proportional to firm size—as firm size increases, so does the affective endowment from owning the firm. Therefore, varying levels of socioemotional wealth for family firms of different sizes would lead to different levels of perceived threat of acquisition. Owners of larger family firms would perceive greater loss of endowment than owners of smaller family firms. Therefore, sensitivity to loss of endowment would be greater for larger family firms.

Research consistently finds that firm size is inversely related to the likelihood of acquisition (Heeley *et al.* 2006; Moeller *et al.* 2004; Offenberg 2009; Palepu 1986). Larger targets are more difficult to integrate and require greater financial resources to cover the cost of acquisition, which in turn decreases the acquisition likelihood of larger firms. In combining this insight to family firm acquisition behavior, we expect the following: 1) larger family firms perceive a lower threat to socioemotional wealth from a lower probability of being acquired, and 2) smaller family firms have a higher likelihood of being acquired, but the socioemotional wealth endowment may determine whether being acquired is viewed as a threat. Family firms of low socioemotional wealth could be more open to acquisitions as perceived socioemotional wealth losses are offset by average acquisition premiums that range between 30 and 50 percent of a target's purchase price (Laamanen 2007). However, greater information asymmetries in acquiring smaller firms suggest that there is a greater risk of overpayment, which reduces the attractiveness of smaller firms as acquisition targets (Kusewitt 1985; Officer *et al.* 2009).

Meanwhile, family firm size is proportional to socioemotional wealth endowment (Gomez-Mejía *et al.* 2011), so small and large-sized family firms likely perceive fewer takeover risks that threaten the loss of socioemotional wealth. This holds true as large firms perceive a lower acquisition risk and small firms have a smaller socioemotional wealth endowment, or loss, compared to gains from an acquisition premium. Meanwhile, mid-size family firms are more likely to focus on loss of socioemotional wealth and engage in defensive acquisitions to maintain it. To test a greater likelihood of acquisition by medium-sized family firms than non-family firms, we draw on a sample of 1,837 acquisitions from 738 firms representing 8,372 firm-year observations in 1993–2007.

Theoretical development and hypotheses

Family firms offer a unique opportunity for comparison in that they exhibit important differences from managerial decisions in other firms (Gomez-Mejía *et al.* 2011). With respect to acquisition motives, a stronger tendency for defensive acquisitions by family firms can be explained by the behavioral agency model that combines agency theory with prospect theory to develop an improved model of corporate governance (Gomez-Mejía *et al.* 2010; Miller and Chen 2004; Wiseman and Gomez-Mejía 1998). Combining elements of agency theory on corporate governance with prospect theory explanations of framing, the behavioral agency model compares outcomes against a reference point. When outcomes are below expected reference point, loss aversion is activated, and when performance is above aspirations, then risk aversion is activated (Wiseman and Gomez-Mejía 1998). In family firms, the primary reference point is the loss of socioemotional wealth, and family firms will accept options with lower financial performance to mitigate loss of socioemotional wealth (Gomez-Mejía *et al.* 2007). Consistent with prospect theory, the focus in family firms is on the final state of maintaining socioemotional wealth and not changes in financial wealth (Gomez-Mejía *et al.* 2007; cf. Kahneman and Tversky 1979). We further develop this logic in building hypothesized relationships for family firm acquisitions for family firm size and acquisition relatedness.

Family firm size and acquisition activity

The perceived risk of getting acquired, or reference point for loss of socioemotional wealth, likely depends on firm size, and we define firm size as firm assets relative to assets of firms in the industry. In their "eat or be eaten" hypothesis, Gorton and others (2009) state that medium-sized firms are more likely to be the targets of acquisition. If there are private benefits to maintaining control of a firm, medium-sized firms may engage in defensive acquisitions. Both larger and smaller family firms perceive lower threat of being acquired and, therefore, do not perceive their relative asset size as a threat to socioemotional wealth. Maintaining socioemotional wealth represents a private benefit that is unique to family firms. However, acquisition activity is likely impacted by family firm size as it approximates socioemotional wealth at risk in family firms (Gomez-Mejía *et al.* 2011), and we discuss the perspective of small, large, and medium-sized family firms.

With respect to smaller family firms, the perceived threat of takeovers is lower because they are less attractive targets, have less socioemotional wealth at risk (Gomez-Mejía *et al.* 2011), and lack resources for defensive acquisitions. Acquirers are less likely to acquire smaller firms (King *et al.* 2008), and one reason offered is an increased risk of overpayment from information asymmetries (Humphery-Jenner and Powell 2011; Kusewitt 1985). Increased information asymmetry in acquiring smaller targets also increases valuation difficulties and an acquirer's overpayment risk (Bargeron *et al.* 2008). Further, smaller firms also lack needed managerial and financial resources to create synergies in the post-acquisition phase (King *et al.* 2003). The combined implication is that small family firms are less concerned about takeovers.

For different reasons, large family firms are also less likely to be acquired. Research has already established a demand side explanation that acquisitions dilute family ownership (Gomez-Mejía *et al.* 2010, 2011). However, there are additional reasons why large family firms will be less likely to be pursued as acquisition targets: greater integration challenges, availability of managerial resources from family executives, limited synergy from non-productive assets that are embedded in family legacy, and possibly prolonged takeover battles and reviews (Haspeslagh and Jemison 1991; Palepu 1986; Lubatkin 1983; Seth 1990; Shrivastava 1986). Research consistently finds that large firms have a lower likelihood of being acquired (Ambrose and Megginson 1992; Billett 1996; Cremers *et al.* 2009; Heeley *et al.* 2006; Heron and Lie 2010; Moeller *et al.* 2004; Powell and Yawson 2007; Song and Walkling 1993). Additionally, firms that acquire targets with higher family socioemotional wealth have lower value creation (Basu *et al.* 2009), further suggesting that large family firms are less desirable targets.

Meanwhile, based on the "eat or be eaten" hypothesis (Gorton *et al.* 2009), mid-sized firms are strategically attractive acquisition targets in that they balance synergies and transaction costs. Additionally, mid-size family firms have more socioemotional wealth at stake. This suggests that, compared to non-family firms, medium-sized family firms with socioemotional wealth at stake are more likely to engage in defensive acquisitions to make them less attractive targets. As a result, defensive acquisitions provide a means to preserve socioemotional wealth for mid-size family firms. The non-financial benefits of defensive acquisitions for mid-size firms would then offset financial repercussions, as defensive motives lead to decline in shareholder wealth (Kaplan *et al.* 2000; Seth *et al.* 2002). Medium-sized family firms through acquisitions increase their relative industry size, providing managerial benefits and maintaining socioemotional wealth. Therefore, we predict the following:

> Hypothesis 1 (H1): The likelihood that family firms make acquisitions has an inverted-U relationship with size. In other words, medium-sized (relative to the size of other firms in the industry) family firms are more likely to acquire than non-family firms.

Family firms and related acquisitions

Gomez-Mejía *et al.* (2010: 224) state that family firms are pulled in two opposite directions of deciding to "opt for less diversification in order to preserve socioemotional wealth or choose greater diversification . . . in order to dilute or spread concentrated business risk but at the expense of family socioemotional wealth." While gains from unrelated acquisitions have less potential to improve financial performance (Lee and Madhavan 2010; Singh and Montgomery 1987) and can dilute socioemotional wealth by including managerial talent outside the family (Gomez-Mejía *et al.* 2010), unrelated diversification is often pursued by family firms to smooth cash flow, lower portfolio risk, and increase firm survival (Anderson and Reeb 2003b; Faccio *et al.* 2001; Salter and Weinhold 1978; Shleifer and Vishny 1997). While portfolio theory would suggest that family firms are more likely to acquire unrelated firms to lower firm risk, on average family firms are less diversified (Gomez-Mejía *et al.* 2010) and medium-sized family firms are more likely to acquire related targets for at least two reasons.

First, for a mid-size family firm, acquiring unrelated firms provides a lower defensive benefit to a possible takeover. The primary reason is that diversified assets are less likely to be integrated within the complex social structure of a family firm (Eddleston *et al.* 2008; Habbershon and Williams 1999; Pearson *et al.* 2008; Sirmon and Hitt 2003). This means that the asset base of an unrelated target is more likely to remain distinct, making it easier for a prospective acquirer to divest unrelated assets. For example, Porter (1987) suggests that over 70 percent of unrelated acquisitions are later divested. This suggests that a mid-sized family firm, by acquiring an unrelated target does not mitigate threat of takeover, because undesired assets can later simply be spun off by an acquirer and socioemotional wealth can still be destroyed. Meanwhile, by acquiring a related target, a family firm increases the benefits of defensive acquisitions as future acquirers might find the combined firm less attractive due to increased integration complexity and lower chances to divest non-performing assets. The implication is that an acquirer may require greater restructuring of a family firm with larger related operations to unlock a resulting acquisition's potential (e.g. Barkema and Schijven 2008b).

Second, continuing earlier arguments, medium-sized family firms frame threat of being acquired as a loss of socioemotional wealth and therefore are more likely to increase social complexity by integrating related targets. In the post-acquisition integration process, family firms exhibit stewardship to reconfigure a target's resources within a complex social structure under family governance (Arregle *et al.* 2007; Carney 2005; Miller and Le Breton-Miller 2006). Such integration increases the combination of new resources with prior resources, or provides a greater benefit of size by integrating a related target into the socioemotional wealth of a family firm. Integration of a related target also preserves socioemotional wealth by continuing to leverage socioemotional resources and allows stakeholders to maintain a coherent organizational identity (Stavrou *et al.* 2007; Zellweger and Nason 2008). This complicates integration costs for a prospective acquirer which must consider the costs of integrating socially complex stakeholder resources (Capron and Guillén 2009; Hitt *et al.* 2001). The combined implication is that medium-sized family firms are more likely to acquire related targets to provide a greater defensive benefit. Therefore, we propose:

> Hypothesis 2 (H2): The likelihood that family firms make related acquisitions has an inverted-U relationship with size. In other words, medium-sized (relative to size of other firms in the industry) family firms are more likely to acquire related targets than non-family firms.

Methodology

Dependent variables

We identified acquisition events from *Thomson Financial*'s Securities Data Company (SDC Platinum) database. Next, we matched acquirers in the manufacturing sector who acquired targets in the manufacturing sector with firms in CRSP, COMPUSTAT, ExecuComp, Hoover's Company records, yearly proxy statements, and Investor Responsibility Research Center. To derive additional information on stock market reaction and firm characteristics, we used the following additional filters: a) at least five-years of continuous financial information is available; b) at least 100 days of stock market trading data is available; c) information on top management team is available. Based on these criteria, between 1993 and 2007, 1,837 acquisitions by 738 US acquirers were identified.

We applied multiple definitions of family firms to distinguish them from non-family firms, using blockholder information (Anderson and Reeb 2003a, 2003b; Gomez-Mejía *et al.* 2011; López de Silanes *et al.* 1999). We classify firm as a family firm if family blockholders own 10 percent or more equity and at least one family member is involved in the top management team (defined as executives in Tier 1 of the firm). Family members in the top management team are identified from the pool of executives listed in ExecuComp, annual reports (particularly Item 404 or Regulation S-K that identifies transactions with related persons, promoters, and certain control persons) and Ancestry.com. Of the 1,837 acquisition events by 738 firms between 1993 and 2007, 617 acquisitions were by 341 family firms representing 4,037 family-firm-years.

Likelihood of acquisition

The dependent variable is the likelihood of acquisition. If a firm acquires one or more targets in a given year, "1" is coded and, if it did not make an acquisition, "0" is coded. Acquisition information was obtained from the SDC Platinum database.

Relatedness of acquisitions

Relatedness is operationalized as follows: if the four digits of target and acquirer are the same, we code relatedness as "1"; if only the first three digits are the same, we code relatedness as "0.75"; if only the first two digits match, we code relatedness as "0.5"; if only the first digit is common, we code relatedness as "0.25"; otherwise, we code relatedness as "0" (Hoskisson *et al.* 1993). Therefore, higher values indicate increased relatedness. If a firm acquired more than one firm in a period of observation, we code it as 1 for the first outcome measure. For the second outcome measure, we take the target with lowest relatedness. Additionally, only 2.9 percent of firm-year observations included a firm that acquired more than one target.

Independent variables

Firm size

Based on prior work by Palepu (1986), Powell and Yawson (2007), Ambrose and Meggison (1992), and Dietrich and Sorenson (1984), firm size was measured by firm assets. We used natural log of book value of total assets adjusted for median book value of total assets at the four-digit SIC code level as a proxy for firm size.

Family ownership

We distinguished family firms from non-family firms based on ownership and family involvement in governance and management (e.g. Allen and Sharon 1982; Anderson and Reeb 2003a; Gomez-Mejía *et al.* 2010; Villalonga and Amit 2006). Specifically, family firms are those firms where founders or other family members related by blood or by marriage have significant shareholdings and are executives or directors. Specifically, continuing from earlier discussion, we use four definitions of a family firm: 1) percentage family ownership (≥10 percent + at least 1 top management team member); 2) percentage founding CEO ownership (≥10 percent + at least 1 top management team member); 3) percentage later generation ownership (≥10 percent + at least 1 top management team member); or 4) family involvement (percentage of family top management team members). Firms were treated as a family firm for meeting one or more of the individual definitions.

Control variables

We applied multiple controls to limit the influence of other variables on examined relationships. First, we included relative size, as the relative distribution of firm size in an industry could affect acquisition dynamics (Gorton *et al.* 2009), using Palepu's (1986) application of the Theil Index to measure entropy in distribution of assets. We also control for anti-takeover provisions using the Gompers-Ishii-Metrick (GIM) index developed by Gompers *et al.* (2003) from 24 anti-takeover provisions reported in the Investor Responsibility Research Center database. We also control for organizational slack, where absorbed slack is the ratio of selling, general, and administrative expenses to sales; unabsorbed slack is the ratio of current assets to current liabilities; potential slack is the debt to equity ratio (Bourgeois 1981). To account for bankruptcy risk, we controlled for Altman's Z, where higher values indicate increasing distance from bankruptcy (Altman 1968). Resource investments by firms can influence acquisition likelihood (Heeley *et al.* 2006; Iyer and Miller 2008), so we controlled for R&D intensity (ln[R&D]/ln[Sales]), advertising intensity (ln[Advertising expenses]/ln[Sales]), and capital intensity (ln[Capital expenditures]/ln[Sales]). We also controlled for total number of prior acquisitions and value of prior acquisitions (in 2,000 US dollars) in the previous five years of the respective acquisition (Barkema and Schijven 2008a). Finally, we incorporated multiple financial controls, including Tobin's Q, or the ratio of market to book value of assets; free cash flows (Jensen 1986); unsystematic risk using the standard deviation of errors in the regression of market returns (daily market returns in S&P 1500 firms), and firm stock market returns over 252 trading days in a year (Bansal and Clelland 2004).

Analysis

To test our hypotheses we used random effects logit to predict the likelihood of acquisition. The relatedness of acquisition is a latent variable where the degree of commonality between a target and acquirer cannot be observed beyond the matching of four-digit SIC codes. In other words, the data exhibits truncation on right and left side for acquisition relatedness, suggesting a two-limit random effects model. Furthermore, as there is a self-selection effect among firms choosing to acquire, for relatedness of the outcome we include inverse-Mill's ratio using Heckman's two-stage self-selection model. In step 1, using the control variables we predict whether firm acquires a target (=1, or = 0 otherwise). The resulting inverse-Mill's ratio from the probit regression is used as a control in the main analysis predicting relatedness of acquisition.

Table 4.1 lists the mean, standard deviation, and correlations. The highest VIF value is 6.784, or below the recommended cut-off of 10 (O'Brien 2007). The mean value for likelihood of acquisition suggests that firms have a 25 percent chance on average of making an acquisition in a given year. Additionally, the mean value of relatedness averages between a match at the 1 or 2 digit level, suggesting a low level of relatedness between an acquirer and target on average. We also included measures of acquisition performance to examine whether family firm acquisitions destroyed value. Consistent with prior research, acquirer returns in our sample, while positive, are essentially zero on average across multiple measures of performance (King *et al.* 2004).

The results are presented in Table 4.2. Hypothesis 1 proposed that mid-sized family firms are more likely to undertake acquisitions. Results of our random effects logit models support a positive relationship between family firm size and acquisition likelihood across different definitions of family firms (percentage family ownership: $\beta = 0.021$, p<0.05; percentage founding CEO ownership: $\beta = 0.022$, p<0.05; percentage later generation ownership: $\beta = 0.023$, p<0.05; and family involvement: $\beta = 0.025$, p<0.05). Still, the underlying nature of the anticipated relationship between acquisition likelihood and family firm size was an inverted-U relationship with likelihood of acquisition increasing with firm size up to a certain level, and then declining as firms get larger. Hypothesis 2 proposed that mid-sized family firms are more likely to undertake related acquisitions. Results of our random effects two-limit Tobit models support a positive relationship between family firm size and related acquisitions (percentage family ownership: $\beta = 0.042$, p<0.05; percentage founding CEO ownership: $\beta = 0.045$, p<0.05; percentage later generation ownership: $\beta = 0.044$, p<0.05; and family involvement: $\beta = 0.043$, p<0.05). Still, the underlying relationship suggested an inverted-U relationship where mid-sized firms were more likely to engage in related acquisitions.

Using Cox regression with results presented in Table 4.3, the hazard of acquisition in the post-acquisition period for mid-sized family firms is significantly lower (Size^2×family firm acquired another firm in the past: percentage family ownership: $\beta = -0.169$, p<0.05; percentage founding CEO ownership: $\beta = -0.118$, p<0.05; percentage later generation ownership: $\beta = -0.159$, p<0.05; and family involvement: $\beta = -0.173$, p<0.05). Further, medium-sized family firms that acquire related firms are also less likely to be acquired in the future (Size^2×relatedness of target acquired by family firm: percentage family ownership: $\beta = -0.147$, p<0.05; percentage founding CEO ownership: $\beta = -0.182$, p<0.05; percentage later generation ownership: $\beta = -0.116$, p<0.05; and family involvement: $\beta = -0.174$, p<0.05). Significant financial loss from acquiring related targets by medium-sized family firms indirectly supports preference towards

Table 4.1 Mean, SD, correlations

	Mean	SD	1	2	3	4	5	6	7	8	9	10	11	12	13	14	15	16	17	18	19	20	21	22	23	24	25
1. Relative industry size distribution	22.759	9.07	0.109																								
2. GIM index	9.747	3.512	0.080	1																							
3. Absorbed slack	0.596	1.812	0.072	0.097	1																						
4. Unabsorbed slack	2.117	1.961	0.036	0.056	0.162	1																					
5. Potential slack	0.495	3.627	0.109	0.124	0.105	0.101	1																				
6. Distance from bankruptcy	2.393	8.672	0.021	0.100	0.125	0.169	0.094	1																			
7. R&D intensity	5.224	2.091	0.102	0.131	0.094	0.134	0.054	0.061	1																		
8. Advertising intensity	0.117	0.539	0.077	0.144	0.087	0.165	0.098	0.073	0.140	1																	
9. Capital intensity	0.075	0.084	0.062	0.163	0.077	0.145	0.095	0.067	0.163	0.111	1																
10. Number of prior acquisitions	2.101	1.123	0.096	0.157	0.066	0.138	0.113	0.166	0.168	0.119	0.115	1															
11. Value of prior acquisitions	8.215	11.406	0.089	0.085	0.073	0.083	0.089	0.133	0.111	0.149	0.143	0.164	1														
12. Tobin's Q	1.565	0.915	0.094	0.087	0.056	0.095	0.084	0.154	0.151	0.145	0.155	0.071	0.126	1													
13. ln (free cash flow)	9.004	6.304	0.031	0.132	0.153	0.133	0.139	0.077	0.135	0.055	0.134	0.124	0.079	0.114	1												
14. Unsystematic risk	1.185	4.738	0.085	0.150	0.126	0.138	0.159	0.166	0.114	0.101	0.130	0.147	0.115	0.073	0.095	1											
15. Unsystematic return	0.057	0.081	0.087	0.058	0.075	0.148	0.104	0.086	0.075	0.154	0.146	0.118	0.052	0.060	0.107	0.131	1										
16. Debt ratio	0.549	0.241	0.073	0.074	0.126	0.130	0.060	0.105	0.163	0.111	0.068	0.143	0.065	0.122	0.070	0.105	0.122	1									
17. Size ln (asset millions)	11.576	18.359	0.025	0.069	0.141	0.157	0.076	0.157	0.078	0.147	0.159	0.109	0.058	0.105	0.155	0.107	0.094	0.133	1									

18.	Percentage family ownership	0.303	0.197	0.077	0.145	0.160	0.099	0.135	0.127	0.155	0.134	0.081	0.145	0.123	0.065	0.169	0.150	0.152	0.146	0.089	1							
19.	Percentage founding CEO ownership	0.244	0.268	0.056	0.074	0.151	0.091	0.117	0.126	0.144	0.134	0.152	0.118	0.087	0.085	0.137	0.122	0.075	0.076	0.085	0.079	1						
20.	Percentage later generation ownership	0.208	0.208	0.065	0.105	0.118	0.162	0.132	0.141	0.065	0.098	0.098	0.096	0.133	0.137	0.068	0.155	0.156	0.096	0.103	0.093	0.065	1					
21.	Family involvement	2.216	0.824	0.112	0.104	0.065	0.073	0.154	0.071	0.099	0.062	0.089	0.088	0.137	0.120	0.158	0.069	0.079	0.150	0.108	0.133	0.086	0.161	1				
22.	Likelihood of acquisition	0.254	–	0.032	0.102	0.064	0.155	0.164	0.106	0.112	0.116	0.089	0.143	0.075	0.160	0.091	0.154	0.084	0.123	0.131	-0.082	-0.092	-0.150	-0.065	1			
23.	Relatedness of acquisition	0.309	0.146	0.048	-0.265	0.030	0.119	0.099	0.047	0.087	-0.056	0.092	0.106	0.034	0.023	0.116	-0.157	0.085	0.081	-0.088	-0.106	-0.091	-0.064	-0.084	0.210	1		
24.	3-day CAR	0.087	0.155	-0.244	0.097	0.112	0.093	0.164	0.117	0.156	0.098	0.090	0.128	0.117	0.061	0.159	0.100	0.139	0.081	0.122	-0.085	-0.153	-0.123	-0.057	0.136	0.243	1	
25.	1-year BHAR	0.046	0.191	-0.245	0.056	0.162	0.160	0.072	0.128	0.056	0.088	0.157	0.058	0.125	0.147	0.056	0.160	0.105	0.065	0.072	-0.125	-0.135	-0.083	-0.123	0.075	0.327	0.087	1
26.	3-year BHAR	0.077	0.307	-0.199	0.124	0.105	0.101	0.065	0.146	0.133	0.102	0.159	0.090	0.089	0.113	0.120	0.100	0.161	0.167	-0.133	-0.156	-0.163	-0.116	0.163	0.193	0.161	0.099

Notes:
1,837 from 738 firms representing 8,372 firm-year observations in 1993–2007
All correlations above |0.086| are significant at 0.05 or below (two-tailed)
All correlations above |0.133| are significant at 0.01 or below (two-tailed)

Table 4.2 Likelihood and relatedness of acquisition

	Random effects logit				Two-limit random effects Tobit			
	DV = Likelihood of acquisition				DV = Relatedness of acquisition			
	Percentage family ownership	Percentage founding CEO ownership	Percentage later generation ownership	Family involvement	Percentage family ownership	Percentage founding CEO ownership	Percentage later generation ownership	Family involvement
Size	0.008***	0.009***	0.011***	0.012***	-0.113**	-0.112***	-0.124***	-0.124***
Size-square	-0.003***	-0.004***	-0.005***	-0.007***	-0.104*	-0.107***	-0.113***	-0.113***
Size-cube	0.003	0.005	0.007	0.008	0.101	0.102	0.102	0.102
Family firm	-0.015***	-0.014***	-0.012***	-0.011***	-0.112***	-0.114***	-0.114***	-0.114***
Size × family firm	-0.032*	-0.031*	-0.029*	-0.027*	-0.112*	-0.112*	-0.111*	-0.111*
Size-square × family firm	0.021*	0.022*	0.023*	0.025*	0.042*	0.045*	0.044*	0.043*
Size-cubed × family firm	0.000	0.001	0.001	0.001	0.000	0.001	0.001	0.000
Relative industry size distribution	0.019*	0.021*	0.023*	0.024*	-0.034*	-0.024*	-0.027*	-0.032*
GIM index	0.076*	0.078*	0.079*	0.080*	-0.172***	-0.170***	-0.141***	-0.171***
Absorbed slack$_{t-1}$	0.057	0.058	0.060	0.061	0.014	0.023	0.024	0.024
Unabsorbed slack$_{t-1}$	0.059*	0.061*	0.062*	0.064*	0.017	0.024	0.03	0.031
Potential slack$_{t-1}$	0.066	0.067	0.069	0.070	0.044*	0.041*	0.042*	0.042*
Distance from bankruptcy$_{t-1}$	-0.045*	-0.044*	-0.042*	-0.041*	0.042*	0.043*	0.033	0.034
R&D intensity$_{t-1}$	-0.007	-0.005	-0.004	-0.003	0.004	0.012	0.012	0.004
Advertising intensity$_{t-1}$	-0.008	-0.007	-0.006	-0.004	0.004	-0.002	-0.01	-0.02
Capital intensity$_{t-1}$	-0.006	-0.004	-0.003	-0.001	0.004	-0.002	-0.004	-0.012

Number of prior acquisitions$_{t-1}$	0.067*	0.068*	0.070*	0.072*	0.044*	0.042*	0.043*	0.042*
Value of prior acquisitions$_{t-1}$	0.063*	0.064*	0.066*	0.067*	0.042*	0.042*	0.044*	0.043*
Tobin's Q$_{t-1}$	0.061***	0.062***	0.063***	0.065***	0.044	0.042	0.042	0.044
ln (free cash flow$_{t-1}$)	0.023***	0.025***	0.026***	0.028***	0.044	0.027	0.044	0.024
Unsystematic risk	0.073***	0.074***	0.076***	0.078***	-0.204***	-0.205***	-0.212***	-0.234***
Unsystematic return	0.103***	0.105***	0.106***	0.108***	0.214***	0.212***	0.202**	0.222***
Debt ratio	-0.108*	-0.106*	-0.105*	-0.103*	-0.107*	-0.114*	-0.107*	-0.104*
Inverse-Mills ratio					0.307***	0.244***	0.237***	0.244***
Intercept	1.590***	1.592***	1.593***	1.595***	0.234***	0.244***	0.141***	0.147***
Industry dummies [reference category: 39]	Yes	Yes	Yes	Yes	Yes	Yes	Yes	Yes
Likelihood ratio χ^2	181.364***	136.268***	107.807***	104.335***	71.324***	76.268***	84.619***	67.658***

Notes:
1,837 from 738 firms representing 8,372 firm-year observations in 1993–2007

***$p<0.001$, ** $p<0.01$, **$p<0.05$

Table 4.3 Hazard of getting acquired after acquisition in the main sample—Cox regression

	DV = Hazard of getting acquired after acquisition in the main sample (1993–2011)			
	Percentage family ownership	Percentage founding CEO ownership	Percentage later generation ownership	Family involvement
Size[1]	-0.378**	-0.397***	-0.315*	-0.281*
Size-square	0.448***	0.432***	0.352***	0.333*
Size-cube	0.074	0.085	0.024	0.079
Family firm[2]	-0.205*	-0.194*	-0.185*	-0.163*
Family firm relatedness of acquisition[3]	-0.196**	0.147*	0.134*	0.148*
Size × family firm	0.132*	0.112*	0.117*	0.128*
Size-square × family firm	-0.169*	-0.118*	-0.159*	-0.173*
Size-cubed × family firm	0.043	0.019	0.034	0.037
Size × family firm relatedness of acquisition	-0.169*	-0.197*	-0.185*	-0.136*
Size-square × family firm relatedness of acquisition	-0.147*	-0.182*	-0.116*	-0.174*
Size-cubed × family firm relatedness of acquisition	0.006	0.007	0.003	0.005
Controls	Yes	Yes	Yes	Yes
Intercept	0.890***	0.792***	0.693***	0.795***
Industry [reference category: 39]	Yes	Yes	Yes	Yes
Likelihood ratio χ^2	85.410***	168.763***	89.882***	137.501***

Notes:
[1] Size at the time of acquisition in the main sample.
[2] =1 if a family firm acquired a firm in the main sample [n=341]; =0 if a non-family firm acquired a firm in the main sample [n=397].
[3] =1 if a family firm acquired a firm in the main sample multiplied by relatedness of acquisition; =0 if a non-family firm acquired a firm in the main sample multiplied by relatedness of acquisition
1,837 acquisitions followed for 738 firms in 1993–2011; we followed 341 family firms who acquired 2,254 firms and 397 non-family firms acquiring 3,118, to test whether they were themselves acquired following acquisition. Of the 341 family firms, 58 were acquired and of the 397 non-family firms, 84 were acquired
***p<0.001, ** p<0.01, *p<0.05.

preserving socioemotional wealth over financial gains. Overall, mid-sized family firms who acquired another firm are less likely to be acquired, providing further support to H1 and H2 by validating the underlying theory of defensive acquisitions.

Discussion

By examining the socioemotional wealth at risk in family firms based on firm size, we develop and validate a framework that explains why medium-sized family firms are more likely to acquire and why they focus on related firms. Applying a "supply side" perspective suggests that mid-sized family firms are more likely to be acquired and have more socioemotional wealth at risk, creating a motivation to make defensive acquisitions. This validates Gorton *et al.*'s (2009) "eat or be eaten" explanation for defensive acquisitions by applying it to the context of family firms. Due to perceived risk to socioemotional wealth under the behavioral agency model, mid-sized family firms have private motives that justify defensive acquisitions that offset potential wealth losses. Post-hoc analysis confirmed that defensive acquisitions by mid-sized family firms destroyed financial value at the same time that they reduced the likelihood of being acquired. Our findings have important contributions for research and managers.

Implications for research

One implication for research involves extending acquisition research into family firms that suggests reasons for both an increased and decreased propensity to acquire. On one hand, Miller *et al.* (2010) find that family firms engage in fewer acquisitions (in number of acquisitions and dollar value), because of dilution of control, increased firm risk resulting from post-acquisition debt, and lower managerial capital. Meanwhile, Gomez-Mejía and others (2010) find that family firms engage in acquisitions as risk increases. A contingency framework that considers firm size and perceived threat to socioemotional wealth can reconcile these results. For example, family firms in general are less likely to engage in acquisitions unless they perceive takeovers as a threat to socioemotional wealth.

We find mid-size family firms face the greatest threat of acquisition and loss of socioemotional wealth and are the most likely to engage in acquisitions. Further, they are more likely to pursue related acquisitions as they require integration into the social complexity of family firms, which provides the benefit of making them more complicated to integrate by a potential acquirer. Defensive motives after such acquisitions lead to decline in firm value (lower short- and long-term stock market reaction) but increase the benefits of private control (lower likelihood of acquisitions). The context of value-destroying acquisitions supports the view that family firms are rational, but use different criteria (Gomez-Mejía *et al.* 2011). This is significant in that a more aggregated look at family firm acquisitions suggests that family firms exhibit better acquisition performance (Ben-Amar and Andre 2006).

Coincidently, our research also offers contributions to acquisition research. A significant contribution is that it helps explain a rational motive for value-destroying acquisitions, when acquisitions on average have no impact on performance (King *et al.* 2004), and most research focuses on identifying drivers of higher acquisition performance. However, identifying value destruction in acquisitions is equally important in solving the "puzzle" of why managers continue to pursue acquisitions in the face of evidence that they do not create value (Agrawal and Jaffe 2000), and our post-hoc analysis corroborates the value-destroying nature of acquisitions by medium-sized, family firms. Family firms are the most common form of business, and supplying a rationale for value-destroying acquisitions supports the view that family businesses have a different perspective (Gomez-Mejía *et al.* 2011; Miller *et al.* 2010). Additionally, the most commonly researched variable in acquisition research involves relatedness, yet research results remain equivocal (Hitt *et al.* 2009; King *et al.* 2004). Our research suggests that relatedness takes on meaning when it is considered in an interaction with another variable. This meets and validates a long-standing need to examine interactions in acquisition research (Hoskisson and Hitt 1990; King *et al.* 2004). Further, while broader acquisition research on relative size and acquisitions has focused on transfer of resources, routines and capabilities (e.g. Capron and Mitchell 1998; Capron and Pistre 2002; King *et al.* 2008), our research suggests that firm governance structures play a role in acquisition attractiveness. For example, in socially complex family firms, part of the value may be intrinsically linked to family relationships that could be removed if key family members depart following a takeover. This would question the attractiveness of family firms as targets, and it would also be worth examining reasons why family firms decide to sell.

Implications for managers

The primary implication for managers is that carrying out an acquisition represents a viable takeover defense, as firms undertaking acquisitions experienced significantly lower risk of acquisition themselves. Further, the decrease in acquisition likelihood was greater for related acquisitions that largely require integration or increase the complexity of a firm. However, while it is a successful defensive strategy, the market appears to perceive non-financial motives and that financial performance is lower over short- and long-term stock performance. A specific implication for family firms is that an important consideration is how to manage firm growth. Getting acquired by another firm could be detrimental to socioemotional wealth, so an added complexity for family firm managers is the need to consider their attractiveness as a takeover target.

Limitations and future research

Our results must be interpreted in light of several limitations. First, we only use a surrogate measure of socioemotional wealth, and additional research using firm size and more direct measures and additional controls can validate our findings. While we control for several factors, examining family dynamics could provide additional explanations as to why some medium-sized family firms engage in acquisitions and others do not. A possible limitation is that the family ownership level displays weak variation across yearly observations. This is consistent with socioeconomic wealth motivations in family firms, but limits observed variance. Again, we used a random effect estimator to control for fixed effects. Additional research with a larger sample across countries could examine the consistency of our findings. Research could also focus on whether family firms make inherently less attractive takeover targets due to their social complexity. Due to complex social and relational factors, potential acquirers may "discount" the net present value of family firms. This is likely more true for small firms that are more difficult to value, but may be ambivalent to takeover. Future research could explore additional signals for how family firms could influence takeover attractiveness, and how small family firms manage growth. For example, an important question is: How do small family firms grow and maneuver in the markets for corporate control?

References

Agrawal, A. and Jaffe, J. (2000) "The post-merger performance puzzle." In C. Cooper and A. Gregory (eds.), *Advances in Mergers and Acquisitions*, New York: Elsevier Science, pp. 7–42.

Allen M.P. and Sharon K.P. (1982) "Power, performance, and succession in the large corporation," *Administrative Science Quarterly*, 27: 538–47.

Altman E.I. (1968) "Financial ratios, discriminant analysis and the prediction of corporate bankruptcy," *Journal of Finance*, 23: 589–609.

Ambrose B.W. and Megginson W.L. (1992) "The role of asset structure, ownership structure, and takeover defenses in determining acquisition likelihood," *Journal of Financial and Quantitative Analysis*, 27: 575–89.

Anderson R.C. and Reeb D.M. (2003a) "Founding-family ownership and firm performance: Evidence from the S&P 500," *Journal of Finance*, 58: 1301–28.

Anderson R.C. and Reeb D.M. (2003b) "Founding-family ownership, corporate diversification, and firm leverage," *Journal of Law and Economics*, 46: 653–84.

Arregle, J.L., Hitt, M.A., Sirmon, D.G., and Very P. (2007) "The development of organizational social capital: Attributes of family firms," *Journal of Management Studies*, 44: 73–95.

Bansal, P. and Clelland, I. (2004) "Talking trash: Legitimacy, impression management, and unsystematic risk in the context of the natural environment," *Academy of Management Journal*, 47: 93–103.

Bargeron, L.L., Schlingemann, F.P., Stulz, R.M., and Zutter, C.J. (2008) "Why do private acquirers pay so little compared to public acquirers?," *Journal of Financial Economics*, 89: 375–90.

Barkema, H.G. and Schijven, M. (2008a) "How do firms learn to make acquisitions? A review of past research and an agenda for the future," *Journal of Management*, 34: 594–634.

Barkema, H.G. and Schijven, M. (2008b) "Toward unlocking the full potential of acquisitions: The role of organizational restructuring," *Academy of Management Journal*, 51: 696–722.

Basu, N., Dimitrova, L., and Paeglis, I. (2009) "Family control and dilution in mergers," *Journal of Banking & Finance*, 33: 829–41.

Bauguess, S. and Stegemoller, M. (2008) "Protective governance choices and the value of acquisition activity," *Journal of Corporate Finance*, 14: 550–66.

Ben-Amar, W. and Andre, P. (2006) "Separation of ownership from control and acquiring firm performance: The case of family ownership in Canada," *Journal of Business Finance & Accounting*, 33: 517–43.

Billett, M.T. (1996) "Targeting capital structure: The relationship between risky debt and the firm's likelihood of being acquired," *Journal of Business*, 69: 173–92.

Bourgeois, L.J. (1981) "On the measurement of organizational slack," *Academy of Management Review*, 16: 29–39.

Caprio L., Croci, E., and Del Giudice A. (2011) "Ownership structure, family control, and acquisition decisions," *Journal of Corporate Finance*, 17: 1636–57.

Capron, L. and Mitchell, W. (1998) "Bilateral resource redeployment and capabilities improvement following horizontal acquisitions," *Industrial and Corporate Change*, 7: 453–84.

Capron, L., and Pistre, N. (2002) "When do acquirers earn abnormal returns?," *Strategic Management Journal*, 23: 781–94.

Capron, L. and Guillén, M. (2009) "National corporate governance institutions and post-acquisition target reorganization," *Strategic Management Journal*, 30: 803–33.

Carney, M. (2005) "Corporate governance and competitive advantage in family controlled firms," *Entrepreneurship Theory and Practice*, 29: 249–65.

Cremers, K.J.M., Nair, V.B., and John, K. (2009) "Takeovers and the cross-section of returns," *Review of Financial Studies*, 22: 1409–45.

Daily, C.M., Dalton, D.R., and Rajagopalan, N. (2003) "Governance through ownership: Centuries of practice, decades of research," *Academy of Management Journal*, 46: 151–58.

Dietrich, J.K. and Sorensen, E. 1984. "An application of logit analysis to prediction of merger targets," *Journal of Business Research*, 12: 393–402.

Eddleston, K.A., Kellermanns, F.W., and Sarathy, R. (2008) "Resource configuration in family firms: Linking resources, strategic planning and technological opportunities to performance," *Journal of Management Studies*, 45: 26–50.

Faccio, M., Lang, L., and Young, L. (2001) "Dividends and expropriation," *American Economic Review*, 91: 54–78.

Gomez-Mejía, L.R., Makri, M., and Larraza-Kintana, M. (2010) "Diversification decisions in family-controlled firms," *Journal of Management Studies*, 47: 223–52.

Gomez-Mejía, L.R., Cruz, C., Berrone, P., and De Castro, J. (2011) "The bind that ties: Socioemotional wealth preservation in family firms," *Academy of Management Annals*, 5: 653–707.

Gomez-Mejía L.R., Haynes, K.T., Núñez-Nickel, M., Jacobson, K.J.L., and Moyano-Fuentes, J. (2007) "Socioemotional wealth and business risks in family-controlled firms: Evidence from Spanish olive oil mills," *Administrative Science Quarterly*, 52: 106–37.

Gompers, P., Ishii, J., and Metrick, A. (2003) "Corporate governance and equity prices," *Quarterly Journal of Economics*, 118: 107–56.

Gorton, G., Kahl, M., and Rosen, R.J. (2009) "Eat or be eaten: A theory of mergers and firm size," *Journal of Finance*, 64: 1291–344.

Habbershon, T.G. and Williams, M.L. (1999) "A resource-based framework for assessing the strategic advantages of family firms," *Family Business Review*, 12: 1–25.

Haleblian, J., Devers, C.E., McNamara, G., Carpenter, M.A., and Davison, R.B. (2009) "Taking stock of what we know about mergers and acquisitions: A review and research agenda," *Journal of Management*, 35: 469–502.

Haspeslagh, P.C. and Jemison, D.B. (1991) *Managing Acquisitions: Creating Value through Corporate Renewal*, New York: The Free Press.

Heeley, M.B., King, D.R., and Covin, J.G. (2006) "R&D investment level and environment as predictors of firm acquisition," *Journal of Management Studies*, 43: 1513–36.

Heron, R.A. and Lie, E. (2010) "What fraction of stock option grants to top executives have been back-dated or manipulated?," *Management Science*, 55: 513–25.

Hitt, M., Harrison, J.S., and Ireland, R.D. (2001) *Mergers and Acquisitions: A Guide to Creating Value for Stakeholders*, New York: Oxford University Press.

Hitt, M., King, D.R., Krishnan, H., Makri, M., Schijven, M., Shimizu, K., and Zhu, H. (2009) "Mergers and acquisitions: Overcoming pitfalls, building synergy and creating value," *Business Horizons*, 52: 523–29.

Hoskisson, R. and Hitt, M.A. (1990) "Antecedents and performance outcomes of diversification: A review and critique of theoretical perspectives," *Journal of Management*, 16: 461–509.

Hoskisson, R., Hitt, M.A., Johnson, R.A., and Moesel, D.D. (1993) "Construct validity of an objective (entropy) categorical measure of diversification strategy," *Strategic Management Journal*, 14: 215–35.

Humphery-Jenner, M.L. and Powell R.G. (2011) "Firm size, takeover profitability, and the effectiveness of the market for corporate control: Does the absence of anti-takeover provisions make a difference?," *Journal of Corporate Finance*, 17: 418–37.

Iyer, D.N. and Miller, K.D. (2008) "Performance feedback, slack, and the timing of acquisitions," *Academy of Management Journal*, 51: 808–22.

Jensen, M.C. (1986) "Agency costs of free cash flow, corporate finance, and takeovers," *American Economic Review*, 76: 323–29.

Kahneman, D. and Tversky, A. (1979) "Prospect theory: An analysis of decision under risk," *Econometrica*, 47: 263–91.

Kaplan, S.N., Mitchell, M., and Wruck, K. (2000) *A Clinical Exploration of Value Creation and Destruction in Acquisitions, Organizational Design, Incentives, and Internal Capital Markets*, Chicago, IL: University of Chicago Press.

King, D.R., Covin, J.G., and Hegarty, W.H. (2003) "Complementary resources and the exploitation of technological innovations," *Journal of Management*, 29: 589–606.

King, D.R., Dalton, D. Daily, C., and Covin, J.G. (2004) "Meta-analyses of post-acquisition performance: Indications of unidentified moderators," *Strategic Management Journal*, 25: 187–200.

King, D.R., Slotegraaf, R., and Kesner, I. (2008) "Performance implications of firm resource interactions in the acquisition of R&D-intensive firms," *Organization Science*, 19: 327–40.

Kusewitt, J.B. (1985) "An exploratory study of strategic acquisition factors relating to performance," *Strategic Management Journal*, 6: 151–69.

Laamanen, T. 2007. "On the role of acquisition premium in acquisition research," *Strategic Management Journal*, 28: 1359–69.

Lee, D., and Madhavan, R. (2010) "Divestiture and firm performance: A meta-analysis," *Journal of Management*, 36: 1345–71.

López de Silanes, F., La Porta, R., and Shleifer, A. (1999) "Corporate ownership around the world," *Journal of Finance*, 54: 471–517.

Lubatkin, M. (1983) "Mergers and the performance of the acquiring firm," *Academy of Management Review*, 8: 218–25.

Miller, D. and Le Breton-Miller, I. (2006) "Family governance and firm performance: Agency, stewardship, and capabilities," *Family Business Review*, 19: 73–87.

Miller, D., Le Breton-Miller, I., and Lester, R.H. (2010) "Family ownership and acquisition behavior in publicly-traded companies," *Strategic Management Journal*, 31: 201–23.

Miller, K.D. and Chen, W.R. (2004) "Variable organizational risk preferences: Tests of the March-Shapira model," *Academy of Management Journal*, 47: 105–15.

Moeller. S.B., Schlingemann. F.P., and Stulz. R.M. 2004. "Firm size and the gains from acquisitions," *Journal of Financial Economics*, 73: 201–28.

O'Boyle, E., Pollack, J., and Rutherford, M. (2012) "Exploring the relation between family involvement and firms' financial performance: A meta-analysis of main and moderator effects," *Journal of Business Venturing*, 27: 1–18.

O'Brien, R. (2007) "A caution regarding rules of thumb for variance inflation factor," *Quality & Quantity*, 41: 673–90.

Offenberg, D. (2009) "Firm size and the effectiveness of the market for corporate control," *Journal of Corporate Finance*, 15: 66–79.

Officer, M.S., Poulsen, A.B., and Stegemoller, M. (2009) "Target-firm information asymmetry and acquirer returns," *Review of Finance*, 13: 467–93.

Palepu, K.G. (1986) "Predicting takeover targets: A methodological and empirical analysis," *Journal of Accounting and Economics*, 8: 3–35.

Pearson, A. W., Carr, J. C., and Shaw, J. C. (2008) "Toward a theory of familiness: A social capital perspective," *Entrepreneurship Theory and Practice*, 32: 949–69.

Porter, M. E. (1987) "From competitive advantage to corporate strategy," *Harvard Business Review*, 65: 43–59.

Powell, R. and Yawson, A. (2007) "Are corporate restructuring events driven by common factors? Implications for takeover prediction," *Journal of Business Finance & Accounting*, 34: 1169–92.

Salter, M. S. and Weinhold, W. A. (1978) "Diversification via acquisition: Creating value," *Harvard Business Review*, 56(4): 166–76.

Seth, A. (1990) "Sources of value creation in acquisitions: An empirical investigation," *Strategic Management Journal*, 11: 431–46.

Seth, A., Song, K. P., and Pettit, R. R. (2002) "Value creation and destruction in cross-border acquisitions: An empirical analysis of foreign acquisitions of US firms," *Strategic Management Journal*, 23: 921–40.

Shleifer, A. and Vishny, R. (1997). "A survey of corporate governance," *Journal of Finance*, 52: 737–83.

Shrivastava, P. (1986) "Postmerger integration," *Journal of Business Strategy*, 7: 65–76.

Singh, H. and Montgomery, C. A. (1987) "Corporate acquisition strategies and economic performance," *Strategic Management Journal*, 8: 377–86.

Sirmon, D. G. and Hitt, M. A. (2003) "Managing resources: Linking unique resources, management, and wealth creation in family firms," *Entrepreneurship Theory and Practice*, 27: 339–58.

Song, M. H. and Walkling, R. A. (1993) "The impact of managerial ownership on acquisition attempts and target shareholder wealth," *Journal of Financial and Quantitative Analysis*, 28: 439–57.

Sraer, D. and Thesmar, D. (2007) "Performance and behavior of family firms: Evidence from the French stock market," *Journal of the European Economic Association*, 5: 709–51.

Stavrou, E., Kassinis, G. and Filotheou A. (2007) "Downsizing and stakeholder orientation among the Fortune 500: Does family ownership matter?," *Journal of Business Ethics*, 72: 149–62.

Villalonga, B. and Amit, R. (2006) "How do family ownership, control and management affect firm value?," *Journal of Financial Economics*, 80: 385–417.

Wiseman, R. M. and Gomez-Mejía, L. R. (1998) "A behavioral agency model of managerial risk taking," *Academy of Management Review*, 23: 133–53.

Zellweger, T. M. and Nason, R. S. (2008) "A stakeholder perspective on family firm performance," *Family Business Review*, 21: 203–16.

5

Opening the black box of acquisition capabilities

Niina Nummela and Mélanie Hassett

Introduction

Firms differ in their abilities to manage mergers and acquisitions (M&As) (Jemison and Sitkin 1986a), and this notion has encouraged M&A researchers to highlight the role of experience, knowledge, and learning in acquisitions (Empson 2007; Bower 2001, Ranft and Lord 2000). Theories on organizational learning suggest that acquisition capability will improve over time with accumulated experience. However, findings from empirical studies on the linkage between acquisition experience and performance remain contradictory (Barkema and Schijven 2008). In response, a number of researchers have claimed that expertise developed through experiential learning is inherently more complex, with considerable time and effort needed for experience to develop into *acquisition capability* (e.g. Barkema and Schijven 2008; Haleblian *et al.* 2006; Hébert *et al.* 2005; Zollo and Singh 2004).

Acquisition capability refers here to an organization's ability to execute acquisitions (cf. Keil *et al.* 2012), which is particularly significant for the growing number of serial acquirers (Laamanen and Keil 2008; Smit and Moraitis 2010). However, to date, studies focusing on acquisition capability remain scarce, findings inconsistent, and empirical studies almost non-existent. Therefore, this chapter aims to refine our knowledge on the concept and also provides new empirical evidence on these capabilities. The chapter takes a dynamic-capabilities perspective on the phenomenon and focuses particularly on the microfoundations of acquisition capability (cf. Teece 2007). As such, we contribute to the literature on M&As and offer an interesting, less investigated context for dynamic capability research.

The chapter also has managerial implications. The key questions from the perspective of sustainable competitive advantage through acquisitions are: 1) How can individual capabilities become organizational capabilities? and 2) How can the organization enhance the development and maintenance of these capabilities? A literature review accompanied by empirical data from Finnish multinational companies provides some answers to these questions.

The multi-layered concept of acquisition capability

Acquisition capability deconstructed

Acquisitions are long-term processes of organizational renewal combined with complex series of decisions. They are often accompanied by a high level of uncertainty and also have a direct link to company performance. Thus, the M&A process is a strategic organizational process where a company alters its resource base (cf. Eisenhardt and Martin 2000; Teece and Pisano 1994; Teece 2007) and, therefore, acquisition capability has been defined as a dynamic capability (Capron and Anand 2007; Zollo 2009; Zollo and Winter 2002).

Dynamic capabilities are embedded in processes (Wang and Ahmed 2007) such as sensing, seizing, and reconfiguring (Teece 2007). In the case of acquisition capability, these underlying microprocesses refer to the sensing of acquisition-related opportunities, seizing of identified opportunities, and the resulting business reconfiguration (see Figure 5.1).

The M&A process begins with recognition that acquisitions represent a suitable growth strategy from identifying suitable targets (i.e. sensing), followed by an information search, negotiations and due diligence (i.e. seizing), and the process concludes with integration of business activities (i.e. reconfiguration). Completion of this process requires a number of skills, procedures, processes, structures, routines, and rules within an organization to provide the microfoundations of an acquisition capability.

What do we know about acquisition capability so far?

In the M&A literature, it has been emphasized that the concept of acquisition capability does not refer to a single capability but that there are diverse acquisition capabilities (e.g. Keil *et al.* 2012; Capron and Anand 2007; Haspeslagh and Jemison 1991). This thought is very much in line

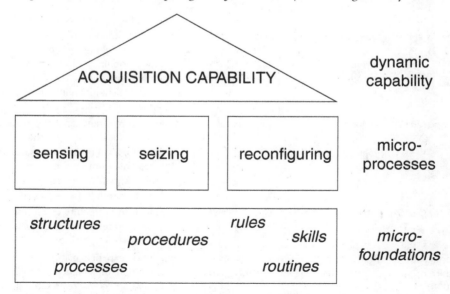

Figure 5.1 Acquisition capability as a dynamic capability (cf. Teece 2007)

with the dynamic capabilities literature where broader capabilities are termed meta-capabilities (Ambrosini and Bowman 2009), or third-order capabilities that enable a company's continuous renewal (Wang and Ahmed 2007; Collis 1994).

Thus, acquisition capability is a third-order meta-capability that comprises a number of second-order elements or capabilities including, for example, acquisition selection, identification, negotiation, integration, or reconfiguration, and acquisition program capability (Amiryany *et al.* 2012; Keil *et al.* 2012, Capron and Anand 2007; Zollo and Singh 2004; Haspeslagh and Jemison 1991). There are few existing studies on acquisition capabilities and they are quite difficult to compare because most have concentrated only on one second-order capability or a small number of them (see Table 5.1). Further, there remains some inconsistency in the use and definitions of the key terms and concepts. For example, although integration capability most often refers to a company's ability to reconfigure its overall resource base after an acquisition, Mitchell and Shaver (2003) focus only on the integration of product lines after the acquisition.

As Table 5.1 shows, our knowledge on acquisition capability and related second-order capabilities remains limited and scattered. The majority of studies have focused on the capability required for reconfiguring the resource base after an acquisition and ignored other parts of the M&A process. Further, the exceptional studies that have taken a broader perspective have been

Table 5.1 A summary of previous research on acquisition-related capabilities

Author	Focus	Type of study	Key findings
Amiryany *et al.* (2012)	Acquisition reconfiguration capability	Conceptual	Acquisition experience, acquisition-specific and knowledge management tools and functions enhance post-acquisition knowledge sharing.
Heimeriks *et al.* (2012)	Integration capability and routine codification	Mixed-method study (interviews and survey)	Integration capability requires both zero- and higher-order routine codification. In particular, developing higher-order routine codification improves acquisition integration performance.
Keil *et al.* (2012)	Acquisition capability and acquisition program capability	Conceptual	Acquisition program capability includes the capabilities 1) to pace the program, 2) to optimize its scope, 3) to acquire optimally sized and fitting targets, and 4) to manage multiple simultaneous integration processes.
Oladottir (2010)	Integrative capacity	Qualitative case study	A strategic infrastructure and resources are needed to support the integrative capacity.
Barkema and Schijven (2008)	Restructuring capability	Quantitative study (panel)	Acquisition experience improves acquisition implementation and decreases need for restructuring. Restructuring experience provides synergistic benefits when there is need for restructuring.

Table 5.1 Continued

Author	Focus	Type of study	Key findings
Capron and Anand (2007)	Acquisition selection, identification and resource reconfiguration capabilities	Quantitative study (survey)	Acquisition capability is a relational dynamic capability that has a positive effect on acquisition performance if the target is a multinational corporation (MNC).
Capasso and Meglio (2005)	Integration capability	Qualitative case study	Integration capability is influenced not only by learning from past acquisitions, but also by the characteristics of the deals, experience spillover from interfirm collaboration, and the context.
Zollo and Singh (2004)	Integration capability and acquisition performance	Quantitative study (survey)	Knowledge codification has a positive influence on acquisition performance, whereas experience accumulation does not.
Mitchell and Shaver (2003)	Integration capability	Quantitative study (database)	Integration capability increases with product line scope.
Zollo and Winter (2002)	Development of integration capability	Conceptual	Integration capability is a dynamic capability that develops through experiential learning and is supported by organizational routines, such as knowledge codification.

conceptual studies without any empirical evidence. In our opinion, it is important to recognize that acquisition capability is a dynamic capability capturing the whole M&A process from identification of opportunities to the completion of integration. This holistic approach is also in line with the dynamic capabilities perspective, including the sensing, seizing, and reconfiguration processes.

In addition to refining the existing knowledge and adopting a more holistic perspective, we see a need to go deeper and extend the discussion from second-order capabilities to the underlying microfoundations of acquisition capability that, to date, have been neglected.

Building a theoretical framework for the study

In this chapter, we examine the microfoundations of acquisition capability from two perspectives: skills and structures, and routines and processes. In terms of skills and structure, the microfoundations are analyzed at the managerial and organizational levels. In terms of routines and processes, our focus is on two separate but tightly intertwined processes: experiential learning of individuals and knowledge transfer within the newly formed organization. We adopt a narrow definition of routines (cf. Becker 2004) with a focus on organizational, acquisition-specific patterns and processes that can be codified to improve acquisition performance (cf. Heimeriks *et al.* 2012). To this end, we focus on four areas beginning with managerial skills.

Managerial skills

Managerial skills refer to the skills of an individual (e.g. an M&A director or an integration manager) that have been gained through imprinting, learning, and/or experience. Previous M&A research has pointed out that some persons are particularly relevant for the success of the M&A process (cf. Ranft and Lord 2002; Very 2004; Kiessling and Harvey 2006). It is important to note that, while the M&A literature often refers to key persons in the acquired organization, that is, persons who are important to retain in the organization due to their knowledge, know-how, and experience (e.g. cf. Ranft and Lord 2002; Very 2004; Kiessling and Harvey 2006), from a capability perspective, there are a number of key persons in the *acquiring company* who are involved in the M&A process. This chapter focuses on the latter.

The key persons involved during the M&A process can be roughly divided into the deal-makers (i.e. those who negotiate the deal) and deal-executors (i.e. those who integrate) (cf. Jemison and Sitkin 1986b; Heimeriks *et al.* 2012). During the pre-M&A phase (i.e. the preparatory phase), the process usually involves a team of people including top management, supported by experts from the business development group, managers from the business units concerned, and, in some cases, by external consultants (Meckl 2004). However, the Board often gives the ultimate approval to the acquisition (Jemison and Sitkin 1986a). Further, the core team of the M&A project is preferably headed by employees from the M&A department while, later, the integration process is usually the responsibility of the integration manager and the integration team made up of different functional teams (Meckl 2004). Consequently, the necessary managerial skills can be possessed by different people over the M&A process.

Previous research has paid particular attention to one group among the key persons, with a budding stream of the literature focusing on integration managers, their characteristics, and behavior. The term "integration manager" refers to the project manager appointed to coordinate activities relating to the integration of the acquired firm into the acquiring firm (Teerikangas *et al.* 2011). Integration managers act on behalf of top management and, in many cases, take full responsibility—and accountability—for making the integration work (Marks and Mirvis 2000). This person is expected to have management skills and functional knowledge that enable him/her to lead the integration process and act as a change agent within the organization (Seo and Hill 2005). An integration manager's role is significant over the whole integration process; however, it is particularly highlighted in its early stages (Ashkenas and Francis 2000). Integration managers are clearly expected to be capable of multi-tasking as they are supposed to possess the characteristics of integration planner, change agent, relationship builder, staff mobiliser, know-how promoter, cultural carrier, knowledge transferor and staff mobiliser, know-how respecter and promoter. At best, integration managers are engaged in capturing value from a) the pre-acquisition phase, b) the acquiring firm, and c) the acquired firm (Teerikangas *et al.* 2011).

In sum, a number of managerial skills are needed during the M&A process. In the pre-acquisition phase it is crucial to have a good, capable negotiator(s) and also reliable support groups assisting during the due diligence phase (cf. Jemison and Sitkin 1986a, 1986b; Meckl 2004). During the post-acquisition phase, the integration manager's change management skills cannot be overemphasized (cf. Teerikangas *et al.* 2011), although, at least in larger acquisitions, the integration manager should also receive support from an integration team (e.g. Meckl 2004). Consequently, the completion of a successful M&A process requires multiple managerial skills delivered by a number of individuals.

Organizational structure

Organizational structure refers to the characteristics and processes that improve an organization's ability to execute acquisitions that can vary across M&As and phases of the process. Although no generally accepted stage model of M&As exists, researchers agree that the great majority are conducted over a similar process. It begins with *sensing* opportunities: choosing M&A as a growth strategy, determining objectives for the deal, searching for potential candidates, selecting the target company, negotiating, conducting due diligence, and planning (e.g. Buono and Bowditch 1989; Haspeslagh and Jemison 1991; Hubbard 1999; Seo and Hill 2005). This *pre-acquisition phase* ends with closing the deal. Typically, this phase is relatively complex due to considerable time pressure, especially over the negotiation process. No person can single-handedly execute the process; executing an acquisition is always group work. Consequently, in this phase, the organization needs to be able to combine the different skills required to complete the phase: (international) negotiation skills, the ability to read financial and legal documents, the ability to assess and evaluate the target company and, finally, the capability to close the deal or, if necessary, walk away (cf. Cullinan *et al.* 2004).

However, the time following the announcement of the deal is also critical; it is the time for *seizing* opportunities. Seo and Hill (2005) have termed the stage following the announcement of an M&A until it is legally completed the *initial planning and formal combination phase*. This stage comprises the creation of a new vision and goals, joint committees and teams to make decisions regarding management changes, staffing plans and a new organizational structure (Seo and Hill 2005: 433). Again, a combination of multiple skills is required for assessing the fit of the target and evaluating required changes, while, simultaneously, under considerable time pressure, the organization needs to create a structure to support the process and form a strategic vision and objectives for the newly combined entity. Furthermore, organizational skills are needed to manage uncertainty and personnel in the midst of rumors (cf. Kusstatscher and Cooper 2005), especially if the details of the deal have not been disclosed due to pending approval from the competition authorities.

Reconfiguring the business (i.e. the *post-acquisition phase*) begins when the deal is closed; it involves the takeover of the acquired company and the actual integration of organizational functions and operations. During the operational combination stage, the budget, space, work assignments, and reporting responsibilities are reorganized (cf. Seo and Hill 2005). Integration is the most critical second-order capability during the post-acquisition phase (cf. Capasso and Meglio 2005). However, developing and maintaining such a capability is very challenging because motives for acquisitions differ, as do the needs of integration. For example, if the motive is merely to increase the size of the company, a simple accounting integration might be sufficient; however, deeper integration is probably necessary if the motive is to acquire resources, knowledge, and/or capabilities. Consequently, while the procedural and physical integration of the parties can require understanding on accounting systems, production line, or production technologies (cf. Shrivastava 1986), the managerial and socio-cultural integration of entities requires capabilities with which to address employees' emotions, stress, anxiety, change resistances, and cultural clashes (cf. Cartwright and Cooper 1993; Kusstatscher and Cooper 2005; Seo and Hill 2005).

In sum, from the organizational perspective, orchestrating an M&A process requires more generic and analytical skills, typically possessed by top management, and also the ability to create a support structure rapidly and delegate operational responsibilities to the correct people in the organization over the M&A process.

Experiential learning

Organizational learning in the context of M&As has generated a great amount of interest, although the research results have been mixed and inconclusive (Barkema and Schijven 2008). One reason for the contradictory findings is probably the huge variety of M&A deals. Traditionally, in management research, researchers have emphasized the importance of experiential learning; that is, the process over which "knowledge is created through the transformation of experience" (Kolb 1984: 38). However, if no two deals are the same (Barkema and Schijven 2008; Bower 2001), what is the value of the collected experience?

Another challenge with the previous research is that it has usually adopted the traditional learning curve perspective, which assumes that experience always has a positive impact, thus failing to acknowledge that experience can be detrimental when transferred to a setting in which previous lessons do not apply (Barkema and Schijven 2008). It also fails to take into account the possibility of superstitious learning (Zollo 2009) and the possibility of learning from others (cf. Barkema and Schijven 2008; Keil et al. 2012).

Earlier research has demonstrated the complexity of learning over the M&A process (Vermeulen and Barkema 2001; Very and Schweiger 2001) and the importance of having organizational mechanisms in place to facilitate learning (e.g. Zollo and Winter 2002; Barkema and Schijven 2008). Deliberate learning mechanisms refer to, for example, utilization of expatriates, conduits of information, experience codification, training programs, and dedicated departments. Nevertheless, in reality, developing these mechanisms takes time, if the firm is able to develop them at all. Moreover, the risk increases for negative experience transfer (Barkema and Schijven 2008; Zollo and Singh 2004).

In sum, while research results on experiential learning remain inconclusive (cf. Zollo and Singh 2004; Barkema and Schijven 2008), there is a need to obtain deeper understanding on how organizations learn to acquire successfully. From a capability perspective, the main challenges lie in the complexity of acquisitions that require just-in-time coordination of a number of diverse capabilities, both in-house and in the company's external network. Research on international acquisitions suggests that not all provide the same opportunity to learn (see Collins et al. 2009), which makes it very challenging to build acquisition capability based on experiential learning. Moreover, it has been argued that effective knowledge management and, in particular, routine codification are essential elements of experiential learning (cf. Zollo and Winter 2002; Keil 2004; Barkema and Schijven 2008; Heimeriks et al. 2012).

Knowledge transfer

An acquisition can be described as a process of knowledge transfer, involving a combination of know-what and know-how, between the parties (Bresman et al. 1999). Over this process, the parties learn about each other, the business, and markets, and also management of the acquisition process, which results in an accumulated practical skill or expertise relating to management of the acquisition (cf. Kogut and Zander 1992). Thus, knowledge transfer in acquisitions can be either intra-organization knowledge transfer (i.e. within the acquiring company) or inter-organizational knowledge transfer (i.e. between the acquirer and the acquired firm). M&A research has focused a great deal on inter-organization knowledge and capability transfer (e.g. Ranft and Lord 2000, 2002; Zollo and Singh 2004; Björkman et al. 2007; Sarala and Vaara 2010). However, there is less research on intra-organization knowledge transfer and capability building.

While knowledge transfer in acquisitions entails the transfer of various knowledge (e.g. Ranft and Lord 2002; Amiryany et al. 2012), the transfer of acquisition-specific knowledge can result in the improvement of a firm's acquisition capability (Heimeriks *et al.* 2012; Nummela 2011). Previous research on acquisition capabilities suggests that experiential learning and development of integration capability is supported by knowledge codification (Zollo and Winter 2002). However, codification of tacit knowledge and acquisition-related routines has both benefits and disadvantages: reduced ambiguity can be accompanied by increased organizational inertia and rigidity. To maximize the advantages and minimize the drawbacks, knowledge codification needs to include both zero- and higher-order routines (Heimeriks *et al.* 2012).

The development of acquisition capabilities also requires that the codified knowledge is transferred within the organization. Knowledge transfer can occur though a number of concrete tools, such as manuals or checklists; however, transfer practices should also include social interaction among key persons through training, meetings, and other personal contacts (Heimeriks *et al.* 2012; Björkman *et al.* 2007). Although top management can introduce a number of such practices, individuals (e.g. M&A team members and integration managers) decide on whether the tools are employed and practices are followed. Thus, their role is pivotal in building the capability (Amiryany *et al.* 2012).

Summary of acquisition capability microfoundations

It is noteworthy that each M&A process is unique and, as such, there are always a number of contingency factors that also impact the required acquisition capability. The context in which the company operates, the size and value of the deal, and the degree of integration needed are all issues of importance. Nevertheless, we propose that it is also possible to identify some generic microfoundations for acquisition capability that are significant in all cases.

We argue that microfoundations can be found both at individual and organizational levels and individual-level microfoundations become those at the organizational level through experiential learning and knowledge transfer. By maintaining and nurturing the microfoundations, it is possible for an organization to develop an acquisition capability that will provide sustainable competitive advantage.

Methodology

Due to the exploratory nature of the study, a qualitative approach was chosen. As the focus of the study is on the identification of multiple types of acquisition capabilities as "naturally occurring, ordinary events in natural settings" (cf. Miles and Huberman 2004), it was necessary to adopt a qualitative research strategy. However, due to the sensitive and strategic nature of acquisitions, access to the companies required that informants would be able to discuss M&A strategies, acquisition capabilities, and capability building at a general level, not referring to any specific deal or case. As this study mainly aims at conceptual development, this was not considered a problem.

The data were collected by face-to-face interviews with M&A experts from Finnish multinational companies (Table 5.2). To obtain as broad a perspective on acquisition capabilities as possible, we searched for companies that are both experienced acquirers and also represent a number of different industries, as the spread of industries would enable us to determine whether identified acquisition capabilities were context-dependent. The researchers contacted numerous companies in spring 2010 and 14 companies participated in the study; all but one were listed companies.

The collected data set comprises 17 interviews, mainly with M&A directors. Only one interviewee was an integration manager. At the time of the interviews, all informants had considerable

Table 5.2 The companies interviewed for the research

Company	Industry	Personnel 2009	Turnover 2009 (billion EUR)	Ownership	M&A experience (deals 2000–10)[1]
Cargotec	Cargo handling	9,500	2.6	listed	18
Elisa	Telecommunications	3,200	1.4	listed	14
Itella	Information services	30,000	1.8	state-owned	10
Karl Fazer	Food and catering services	17,000	1.4	family-owned	5
Kemira	Chemicals	85,000	2.5	listed	31
Kone	Machinery	34,000	4.7	listed	50
Metso	Pulp and paper	27,000	5.0	listed	21
NSN[2]	Telecommunications	63,900	12.6[3]	Nokia-Siemens	3
Orion	Pharmaceutical	3,200	0.8	listed	1
Outokumpu	Metal	7,600	2.6	listed	10
Rautaruukki	Metal	11,500	2.0	listed	12
Tieto	Information technology	17,000	1.7	listed	76
Yara International	Chemicals	8,000	7.7	listed	N/A

Notes:
[1] Based on information from Talouselämä database
[2] Formed through a joint venture in 2007
[3] Consolidated with Nokia

experience on cross-border acquisitions and were able to reflect on acquisition capabilities and capability development from a broad perspective. The interviews were semi-structured and covered the entire M&A process from strategic decision-making to the closing and evaluation of the integration process. In line with the recommendations of Welch *et al.* (2002), the majority of the interviews were conducted in the mother tongue of both the interviewer and the interviewees. The interviews were tape-recorded with the consent of each interviewee. To ensure a comfortable environment for the interviews (cf. Hart 1991), most of the interviews were conducted at the organizations where the respective interviewees work, either in a conference room or the interviewee's office. The duration of the interviews varied from 45 to 90 minutes. To protect the identity of the interviewees, it was agreed that they remain anonymous in the study (cf. Kvale 1996).

Data analysis and the trustworthiness of the study

The qualitative data analysis was conducted in several steps. First, the interviews were transcribed verbatim and then analyzed qualitatively. To facilitate the analysis, the researchers employed Nvivo10 software to code and arrange the data (Bazeley 2007). The coding proceeded in two phases. First, all transcriptions were coded utilizing the four key concepts developed in our theoretical framework: managerial skills, organizational structure, experiential learning, and knowledge transfer. Second, issues and themes from these four categories were then coded inductively to identify microfoundations of an acquisition capability. The analysis began when the data had been arranged, coded, and reduced (cf. Kvale 1996).

The trustworthiness of the research has been evaluated utilizing four criteria: credibility, transferability, dependability, and confirmability (cf. Lincoln and Guba 1985). To improve the credibility of the study's findings, they were carefully compared by the researchers across informants and also with previous research on acquisition capabilities. The fact that the findings received support from a considerable number of informants representing diverse industries and with varying experiences of acquisitions gave confidence of the validity of the findings. According to Lincoln and Guba (1985), transferability of the findings requires a thick description of the study to the readers. To make the interpretation of the findings as transparent as possible, the authors include a number of quotations from the interviews and also provide a detailed description of the research process. Confirmability refers to a qualitative definition of objectivity and relates to the characteristics of the data. To increase confirmability, the researchers have been as detailed as possible in data description and in providing data sources. In addition, it has been argued that the use of computer-assisted qualitative analysis software, such as Nvivo, enhances the trustworthiness of the research (Sinkovics and Alfoldi 2012).

Discussion

Results of the interviews from the first phase of coding are discussed here. We then use this information to draw conclusions about acquisition capability microfoundations.

Managerial skills

Managerial skills refer to the skills of persons such as the M&A director or integration manager. Our interviews confirmed that multiple skills are needed to manage the M&A process. Foremost, the interviewees emphasized the fact that the key persons should be knowledgeable on the acquisition process, how it evolves, and the potential pitfalls. This knowledge enables them to manage the process better. This expertise on acquisitions was mostly based on the informants' previous experience of acquisitions, which could have been collected either within their current companies or in previous positions, as illustrated by the following quotation:

> Working for several years with acquisitions as an external advisor, I obviously formed an opinion on how the process should be managed, where the risks lie, especially legal risks and identifying corporate governance issues. Then, I received an offer from this company, where my current job is tailored around my background and experience; a reason why I wanted to come to work for this company.
>
> *(Director, M&A Group Administration)*

The interviews also indicated that acquisition capability can be improved if the key persons are knowledgeable about their own organizations. Organizational tenure would enable them both to sense and seize opportunities better and, in particular, it would facilitate the integration of the new unit to the existing one.

Besides having acquisition-specific and organizational expertise, the managerial skills needed were related to cross-cultural competence, project management, and the capability to understand legal and business documents. Here, cross-cultural competence refers to the managers' ability to understand and manage cultural clashes caused by differences in national and organizational culture in cross-border deals. In addition, many informants perceived acquisitions as projects and, therefore, emphasized the importance of good project management skills. From the perspective of continuity in the M&A process, it was considered significant that all key persons involved over the process should understand legal and business documents. This expertise can be obtained through formal education—most of the informants had an M.Sc. degree, either in law or business—or though utilizing in-house expertise.

The spread of managerial skills within the organizations was highlighted in the interviews. The informants, who were M&A experts, particularly emphasized the importance of in-house experts in the sensing phase before the acquisition takes place and in seizing, particularly when conducting due diligence. These experts where often referred to as a key function or department during the interviews: for example, "the HR [human resources] department" or "Finance." While these functions hide individuals with various experience and capabilities, interestingly, the position or function was regarded as more critical than the individual doing the actual work. The next quotation illustrates this well:

> I can just give "HR" the assignment . . . I don't have to guide them. I know that they will handle all the relevant questions. Of course, we have told them about the case, they know the case environment, what we are looking for, but we won't give them [HR] any advice because they know what they are doing so damn well.
>
> (Corporate M&A Director)

In sum, our findings confirm that managerial skills needed for building an acquisition capability are close to the characteristics expected of an integration manager (cf. Teerikangas et al. 2011). Nevertheless, the interviews highlight the fact that these skills are not possessed by a single person but by a "virtual team" comprising multiple members within the organization and its network. However, it seems that the team gets smaller as the responsibility for managing the process is given to the integration manager and the receiving business unit towards the end of the M&A process.

Organizational structure

Organizational structure refers to the processes that improve an organization's ability to execute acquisitions. Based on our results and in line with previous research (cf. Zollo and Winter 2002; Zollo and Singh 2004), codified routines that have been institutionalized in the organization can be considered organizational skills embedded in acquisition capability. In the interviews, they were often referenced as the M&A strategy, M&A process design, and M&A resources.

M&A strategy is a company's acquisition strategy as part of the company's overall strategy. Following the financial crisis in 2007 and 2008, many interviewees stated that their M&A strategy became more focused and that, increasingly, acquisitions needed top management approval. Many companies have structured procedures and policies regarding acquisition propositions and approval at the Board of Directors or Executive Group levels. Accordingly, a more structured M&A process design, together with M&A tools and manuals to support it, has become increasingly important. Most of the interviewed companies have a very structured and well-defined pre-acquisition process. However, the end of the M&A process, such as the integration process and its closure, together with feedback loops and evaluation sessions, is often less structured and proceeds more on a case-by-case basis. In many companies, the M&A directors/teams were further developing their processes and working on manuals to share the knowledge. The following quotation illustrates the importance of aligning M&A strategy with corporate strategy:

The M&A strategy has to link with the corporate strategy. It has to be a means with which to implement the corporate strategy. Actually, we have an M&A strategy template, things that need to be considered. It is very simple, it is one A4 sheet . . . you have to consider the strategic drivers for next year . . . you have to give arguments on why you think you can achieve them with acquisitions.

(Director M&A Group Administration)

M&A resources are a very critical element in organizational skills and structure as the term describes the M&A resource base within the organization. M&A resources are understood here more broadly than the concept "acquisition-specific functions" that can be found in the literature (e.g. Amiryany *et al.* 2012). Based on our results, they comprise a large number of key persons from across the organization. M&As were an integral part of the business activity in all interviewed companies, which had dedicated M&A directors or M&A teams, typically comprising one to three members. Some companies also have dedicated integration managers, although, most often, the integration manager is chosen based on who is available to manage the integration project. M&A resources also entail a number of internal and external experts. Internal experts refer usually to corporate-level support functions such as the legal, financial, HR and information technology (IT) departments. Usually, the interviewed companies rely greatly on internal experts with their accumulated knowledge and process experience. The following quotation describes well the team formation process:

For each case we gather the team . . . we evaluate first whether it belongs to the XXX division or the YYY division. Then we decide who is going to manage, who is the business owner. We always need to find a business owner; in practice I am in charge here, but the business owner has to be found [in the division] and he/she has to take responsibility for the project and its progress. . . . And then we include other people from the business [division]. . . . Of course, we include lawyers from the support functions, controllers, but it is very important to include people from the business; that is their thing not the support function's thing.

(Vice President Corporate Planning, Mergers and Acquisitions)

External experts were typically utilized for legal and financial due diligence. Many companies have trusted partners with which they have long-term collaboration, but some chose their external partners case by case.

Experiential learning

In terms of experience, all except three of the interviewed companies had considerable acquisition experience (Table 5.2). Interviewees referred to good and bad experiences and, according to many interviewees, there were attempts to employ deliberate learning mechanisms (cf. Barkema and Schijven 2008) and codify previous M&A experience (cf. Heimeriks *et al.* 2012). The aim of experiential learning comes out well in the following quotation:

We try to learn lessons from each case, where we look back and see how the integration project went. Did we achieve the targets we needed to achieve? We compare them with what we expected.

(Vice President Corporate Planning, Mergers and Acquisitions)

Experiential learning was not only acquisition-specific, and the interviewees also connected learning with organizational tenure and project management. Experiential learning occurred at all organizational levels, ranging from top management to the integration managers, as the following quotations indicate:

> Due to the XX integration process, we have obtained quite a lot of experience on integration projects for a relatively large number of people, and now we have even more know-how for projects. We try to spread the know-how we have across the organization.
>
> *(Head of Strategy and Business Development)*

> There have been so many projects, and as the Executive Group has remained pretty much the same throughout the years, they are beginning to have quite a bit of accumulated knowledge and understanding on different projects and different situations.
>
> *(M&A Director)*

Thus, although all the deals have been different, the informants felt that there was some generic experience which was valuable also in later cases. Interestingly, our interviews did not include any examples of negative experience transfer or learning from imitation or vicarious learning (cf. Barkema and Schijven 2008). However, the interviewees themselves expressed their interest in learning from others who had participated in a project when the study's findings became available.

Knowledge transfer

Codification of routines and knowledge transfer is needed to turn managerial skills and experience into organizational capabilities (Heimeriks *et al.* 2012). Companies have a number of methods to support internally the development of acquisition capabilities. The most common acquisition-specific tools (cf. Amiryany *et al.* 2012) were different intranet platforms and M&A manuals that contain codified knowledge on routines, as the following quotation demonstrates:

> We have an intranet portal, from where you can find the templates etcetera. In it, you can find a lot of tools, project templates; basic stuff to initiate the project, run and support it. One thing that is good, which doesn't relate to the templates, is that we learn a lesson, a description, from each project.
>
> *(Head of Strategy and Business Development)*

Other methods included documentation during the M&A process in the form of different weekly, monthly, and final reports, personal involvement in the process, involving the same persons in the pre- and post-acquisition phase, and (informal) discussions. One interviewee mentioned that they previously had a virtual support group from which integration managers could receive peer support. The following quotation describes well how this virtual support group works:

> We created this, it was called the Integration Network, a voluntary network of people who, in key roles, had managed or participated in the integration process. In the beginning, it had virtual meetings every now and then. At some point, we had many more ongoing projects

and, especially then, the network met because it was a sort of peer group environment where you could get support from others managing similar types of project. It has since faded into a more ad-hoc activity.

(Head of Strategy and Business Development)

In general, the informants agreed that social interaction was required for knowledge transfer and felt that the knowledge embedded in experienced individuals needed to be shared. Thus, the feelings towards routine codification and different kinds of code of conduct were positive and were not interpreted as a means of control (cf. Heimeriks *et al.* 2012). However, the aspect of control was raised as a side issue when discussing knowledge transfer and the role of integration managers. Some interviewees felt that, concerning knowledge transfer, the integration managers also had a controlling function, as the following quotation illustrates:

In the future, if we acquire a bigger company, we will always send our people. You just can't manage them from a distance and observe, you have to be there, breathe the company's air, see the atmosphere inside and know how to react to it. . . . It isn't just that we send someone to control and monitor, their role is also to talk and explain the complexity because, as we include 15 countries, it can't be easy to look at us from one country.

(Division Director M&A and Business Development)

To conclude, the interviews supported our literature-based assumption that developing acquisition capability requires individual skills to be turned into organizational-level skills and structures with the help of experiential learning and knowledge transfer. The identified microfoundations of acquisition capability in the form of skills, structures, routines, and processes hopefully form the basis of future research in the area.

Conclusions

Our chapter begins to open the black box of acquisition capabilities, refine the existing knowledge on the concept and also provide some additional microfoundations. While acquisition capability has attracted increasing academic interest (e.g. Zollo and Singh 2004; Amiryany *et al.* 2012; Keil *et al.* 2012), what acquisition capabilities truly entail has remained vague and unclear. The findings of our study are interesting, particularly from the perspective of the microfoundations underlying the concept.

This research extends the work of Keil *et al.* (2012) by taking into account the multiple layers of the acquisition capability concept and adding more flesh to it. First, our study shows that acquisition capability is a truly multi-layered meta-capability that comprises a number of important second-order capabilities. Thus, we can speak of acquisition capabilities in the plural, while remembering the hierarchy (see Figure 5.2).

Second, acquisition capability is an embedded capability, based on a number of microfoundations (i.e. skills, structures, and processes in the organization). As our analysis confirms, these microfoundations can be further divided into our framework of managerial skills, organizational structure, experiential learning, and knowledge transfer. Maintaining and nurturing all of these microfoundations is fundamental to the development of acquisition capability. However, this task is not a simple one as the skills, structures, and processes involve a number of individuals throughout a long and complex M&A process.

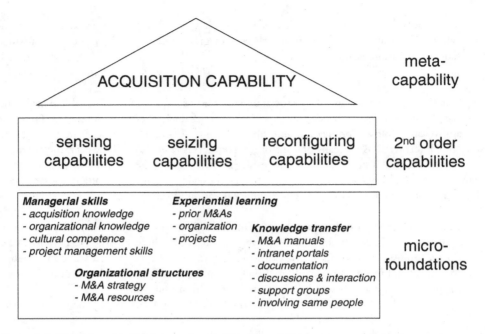

Figure 5.2 Opening the black box of acquisition capabilities

Third, our study refined our knowledge on some concepts often employed in the context of acquisition capability. At least, in the interviews it seemed natural to talk about M&A resources when referring to all the people who were involved in the M&A process. Interestingly, possibly due to the Finnish context where the data were collected, all of the companies involved seemed to prefer centralization of learning mechanisms at the corporate level (cf. Barkema and Schijven 2008), and a variety of methods to support both deliberate and vicarious learning and knowledge transfer were used. The negative side of experiential learning did not appear to be significant. This is clearly an area that deserves more investigation in the future.

From a managerial perspective, this research provides a better understanding of what underlies an acquisition capability. In fact, this research clearly demonstrates that acquisition capabilities comprise a number of capabilities relating to different aspects of the M&A process (cf. Zollo and Singh 2004). More importantly, it discusses ways to acquire, maintain, and develop acquisition capabilities. In order to enhance knowledge transfer within an organization, management needs to ensure that the responsibilities of headquarters, the M&A team, and strategic business units are clear and explicit. Although the M&A function is often centralized to a few people within an organization, acquisition capabilities can be found widely within it. One of the key challenges is to somehow capture this knowledge and experience, so that it can be effectively employed in subsequent M&A projects. This would support Barkema and Schijven's (2008) suggestion that it might be best to centralize learning mechanisms at the corporate level; however, this increases the knowledge gap between the codifiers and implementers of knowledge (cf. Heimeriks *et al.* 2012). Therefore, the process of codifying experience should be done with great care.

The knowledge gap identified by Heimeriks *et al.* (2012) draws our attention also to the continuity aspect of the process. To nurture the development of acquisition capability in the acquiring company, particular attention should be given to the development of knowledge transfer. All individuals involved in acquisitions should be able to participate in the codification of knowledge and assessment of the M&A process. Only this kind of involvement enables capability development to benefit future acquisitions. In other words, the process is like passing on the baton in a relay—the exchange is planned, exercised, and completed smoothly.

Finally, this study has a number of limitations. First, because of the sensitivity and strategic importance of acquisitions, the informants only discussed acquisition capabilities at a general level and did not connect their experiences with any concrete cases or deals. The possibility to link capability development with an M&A process would have been an informative and interesting approach, but unfortunately that was not possible in this study. Second, our data set is biased towards large and experienced acquirers who have already developed best practices within their organization. It is probable that studying the acquisition capabilities of smaller and less experienced acquirers would provide a different perspective that can be explored in future research. In sum, while we have opened the black box of acquisition capabilities, we are only able to offer an incomplete picture of associated processes. Figure 5.2 and our conclusions are not intended to be exhaustive, and we hope that this chapter will inspire other researchers to continue to study acquisition capabilities.

References

Ambrosini, V. and Bowman, C. (2009) "What are dynamic capabilities and are they a useful construct in strategic management?," *International Journal of Management Reviews*, 11: 29–49.

Amiryany, N., Huysman, M., de Man A-P., and Cloodt, M. (2012) "Acquisition reconfiguration capability," *European Journal of Innovation Management*, 15: 177–91.

Ashkenas, R.N. and Francis, S.C. (2000) "Integration managers: special leaders for special times," *Harvard Business Review*, 78(6): 108–116.

Barkema, H.G. and M. Schijven (2008) "How do firms learn to make acquisitions? A review of past research and an agenda for the future," *Journal of Management*, 34: 594–634.

Bazeley, P. (2007) *Qualitative data analysis with NVivo*. London: Sage Publications.

Becker, M.C. (2004) "Organizational routines: a review of the literature," *Industrial and Corporate Change*, 14: 643–77.

Björkman, I., Stahl, G.K., and Vaara, E. (2007) "Cultural differences and capability transfer in cross-border acquisitions: the mediating roles of capability complementarity, absorptive capacity, and social integration," *Journal of International Business Studies*, 38: 658–72.

Bresman, H., Birkinshaw, J., and Nobel, R. (1999) "Knowledge transfer in international acquisitions," *Journal of International Business Studies*, 30: 439–62.

Bower, J.L. (2001) "Not all M&As are alike—and that matters," *Harvard Business Review*, 79(3): 92–101.

Buono, A.F. and Bowditch, J.L. (1989) *The human side of mergers and acquisitions: Managing collisions between people, cultures, and organizations*. San Francisco, CA: Jossey-Bass.

Capasso, A. and Meglio, O. (2005) "Knowledge transfer in mergers and acquisitions: how frequent acquirers learn to manage the integration process," in A. Capasso, G.B. Dagnino, and A. Lanza (eds.) *Strategic capabilities and knowledge transfer within and between organizations*. Cheltenham: Edward Elgar Publishing, pp. 199–225.

Capron, L. and Anand, J. (2007) "Acquisition-based dynamic capabilities," in C.E. Helfat, S. Finkelstein, W. Mitchell, M. Peteraf, H. Singh, D. Teece, and S. Winter (eds.) *Dynamic capabilities: Understanding strategic change in organizations*, Malden, MA: Blackwell Publishing, pp. 80–99.

Cartwright, S. and Cooper, C.L. (1993) "The role of culture compatibility in successful organizational marriage," *Academy of Management Executive*, 7(2): 57–70.

Collins, J.D., Holcomb, T.R., Certo, S.T., Hitt, M.A., and Lester, R.H. (2009) "Learning by doing: cross-border mergers and acquisitions," *Journal of Business Research*, 62: 1329–34.

Collis, D.J. (1994) "Research note: How valuable are organizational capabilities?," *Strategic Management Journal*, 15: 143–52.

Cullinan, G., Le Roux, J-M., and Weddigen, R-M (2004) "When to walk away from the deal," *Harvard Business Review*, 82(4): 96–104.

Eisenhardt, K.M. and Martin, J.A. (2000) "Dynamic capabilities: what are they?," *Strategic Management Journal*, 21: 1105–21.

Empson, L. (2007) "M&As as knowledge," in Duncan Angwin (ed.), *Mergers and acquisitions*, Malden, MA: Blackwell Publishing, pp. 229–55.

Haleblian, J., Kim, J.Y., and Rajagopalan, N. (2006) "The influence of acquisition experience and performance on acquisition behaviour: evidence from the U.S. commercial banking industry," *Academy of Management Journal*, 49: 357–70.

Hart, S.J. (1991) "A first-time user's guide to the collection and analysis of interview data from senior managers," in N.C. Smith and P. Dainty (eds.) *The management research handbook*. London: Routledge, pp. 190–203.

Haspeslagh, P.C. and Jemison, D.B. (1991) *Managing acquisitions: Creating value through corporate renewal*, New York: Free Press.

Hébert, L., Very, P., and Beamish, P.W. (2005) "Expatriation as a bridge over troubled water: a knowledge-based perspective applied to cross-border acquisitions," *Organization Studies*, 26: 1455–76.

Heimeriks, K.H., Schijven, M., and Gates, S. (2012) "Manifestations of higher-order routines: the underlying mechanisms of deliberate learning in the context of postacquisition integration," *Academy of Management Journal*, 55: 703–26.

Hubbard, Nancy (1999) *Acquisition strategy and implementation*. London: Macmillan Press.

Jemison, D.B. and Sitkin, S.B. (1986a) "Corporate acquisitions: a process perspective," *Academy of Management Review*, 11: 145–63.

Jemison, D.B. and Sitkin, S.B. (1986b) "Acquisitions: the process can be a problem," *Harvard Business Review*, 64(2): 107–16.

Keil, T. (2004) "Building external corporate venturing capability," *Journal of Management Studies*, 41: 799–825.

Keil, T., Laamanen, T. and A. Mäkisalo (2012) "Acquisitions, acquisition programs, and acquisition capabilities," in D. Faulkner, S. Teerikangas, and R.J. Joseph (eds.) *The handbook of mergers and acquisitions*. Oxford, UK: Oxford University Press, pp. 148–67.

Kiessling, T. and Harvey, M. (2006) "The human resource management issues during an acquisition, the target firm's top management team and key managers," *International Journal of Human Resource Management*, 17: 1307–20.

Kogut, B. and Zander, U. (1992) "Knowledge of the firm, combinative capabilities, and the replication of technology," *Organization Science*, 3: 383–97.

Kolb, D.A. (1984) *Experiental learning: Experience as the source of learning and development*. Englewood Cliffs, NJ: Prentice-Hall.

Kvale, Steinar (1996) *InterViews: An introduction to qualitative research interviewing*. Thousand Oaks, CA: Sage Publications.

Kusstatscher, V. and Cooper, C.L. (2005) *Managing emotions in mergers and acquisitions*. Cheltenham: Edward Elgar Publishing.

Laamanen, T. and Keil, T. (2008) "Performance of serial acquirers: toward an acquisition program perspective," *Strategic Management Journal*, 29: 663–72.

Lincoln, Y.S. and Guba, E.G. (1985) *Naturalistic inquiry*. Beverly Hills, CA: Sage Publications.

Marks, M.L. and Mirvis, P.H. (2000) "Managing mergers, acquisitions and alliances, creating an effective transition structure," *Organizational Dynamics*, 28: 35–47.

Meckl, R. (2004) "Organizing and leading M&A projects," *International Journal of Project Management*, 22: 455–62.

Miles, M.B. and Huberman, A.M. (2004) *An expanded sourcebook: Qualitative data analysis*, 2nd edn. Thousand Oaks, CA: Sage Publications.

Mitchell, W. and Shaver, J.M. (2003) "Who buys what? How integration capability affects acquisition incidence and target choice," *Strategic Organization*, 1: 171–201.

Nummela, N. (2011) "Knowledge management in cross-border acquisitions," in M. Hassett, M. Räikkönen, and T. Rantala (eds.) *M&A as a strategy: From opportunities to new business creation*, Tampere, Finland: Teknologiainfo Teknova Oy.

Oladottir, A.D. (2010) "Integrative capacity as a moving force in newly formed Icelandic multinational enterprises," *Review of Market Integration*, 2: 135–72.

Ranft, A.L. and Lord, M.D. (2002) "Acquiring new technologies and capabilities: a grounded model of acquisition implementation," *Organization Science*, 13: 420–41.

Ranft, A.L. and Lord, M.D. (2000) "Acquiring new knowledge: the role of retaining human capital in acquisitions of high-tech firms," *Journal of High Technology Management Research*, 11: 295–319.

Sarala, R.M., and Vaara, E. (2010) "Cultural differences, convergence, and cross-convergence as explanations of knowledge transfer in international acquisitions," *Journal of International Business Studies*, 41: 1365–90.

Seo, M-G. and Hill, N.S. (2005) "Understanding the human side of merger and acquisition: an integrative framework," *Journal of Applied Behavioral Science*, 41: 422–443.

Shrivastava, Paul (1986) "Post-merger integration," *Journal of Business Strategy*, 7: 65–76.

Sinkovics, R. and E. Alfoldi (2012) "Progressive focusing and trustworthiness in qualitative research. The enabling role of computer-assisted qualitative data analysis software (CAQDAS)," *Management International Review*, 52: 817–45.

Smit, H. and T. Moraitis (2010) "Playing at serial acquisitions," *California Management Review*, 53(1): 56–89.

Teece, D. (2007) "Explicating dynamic capabilities: the nature and microfoundations of (sustainable) enterprise performance," *Strategic Management Journal*, 28: 1319–50.

Teece, D. and Pisano, G. (1994) "Dynamic capabilities of a firm: an introduction," *Industrial and Corporate Change*, 18: 509–33.

Teerikangas, S., Very, P., and Pisano, V. (2011) "Integration managers' value-capturing roles and acquisition performance," *Human Resource Management*, 50: 651–83.

Vermeulen, F. and Barkema, H. (2001) "Learning through acquisitions," *Academy of Management Journal*, 44: 457–76.

Very, P. (2004) *The management of mergers and acquisitions*. Chichester: John Wiley & Sons.

Very, P. and Schweiger, D.M. (2001) "The acquisition process as a learning process: evidence from a study of critical problems and solutions in domestic and cross-border deals," *Journal of World Business*, 36: 11–31.

Wang, C. and Ahmed, P. (2007) "Dynamic capabilities: a review and research agenda," *International Journal of Management Reviews*, 9: 31–51.

Welch, C., Marschan-Piekkari, R., Penttinen, H., and Tahvanainen, M. (2002) "Corporate elites as informants in qualitative international business research," *International Business Review*, 11: 611–28.

Zollo, M. (2009) "Superstitious learning with rare strategic decisions: theory and evidence from corporate acquisitions," *Organization Science*, 20: 894–908.

Zollo, M. and Singh, H. (2004) "Deliberate learning in corporate acquisitions," *Strategic Management Journal*, 25: 1233–56.

Zollo, M. and Winter, S.G. (2002) "Deliberate learning and the evolution of dynamic capabilities," *Organization Science*, 13: 339–51.

Part II

Contextual domain of M&A research

The second part of the companion focuses on "the contextual domain" and hosts six chapters. In this section, there are three conceptual and three empirical chapters covering an array of issues and employing a variety of field methods. Taken together, these chapters provide different ways in which the "contextual perspective" can be approached and understood.

One approach to the contextual domain covers classic topics in the context of mergers and acquisitions (M&As) such as leadership or employee engagement. Mergers and acquisitions are not extraordinary or isolated events in a company's life and represent a frequent means to pursue strategies for growth. In addition, their effects span over time, from a few months to many years, and these effects vary a great deal according to the phase or stage of the deal. Our intent is to understand how an acquisition influences enduring themes in organization and management studies.

Two chapters in this section follow this perspective. Kathleen Park investigates leadership issues in international mergers involving privatized or family companies from Arabic countries. She contends that these deals demand a particular finesse on the part of the leadership to coordinate the purchase and integration of companies across national and organizational cultural boundaries. She explores issues related to conflict and resolution in cross-border combinations. Her field research highlights that leadership conflict occurs within an individual leader as well as between leaders and followers. In the second chapter, Satu Teerikangas and Lisa Valikangas propose a conceptual analysis of employees' reactions using engagement. This leads them to propose a typology of engagement scenarios in an acquisition context, whether by nurturing individual action or by means of organizational support. They also provide an overview of how differing audiences' engagement dynamics differ in pre- and post-transaction phases.

A second approach to the contextual domain arises from enlarging the domain of analysis in acquisition research. This approach is followed in separate chapters by Laurence Capron and Olimpia Meglio. In her chapter, Laurence Capron focuses on the importance of investigating acquisitions as events belonging to the broader set of growth strategies that companies pursue over time. In so doing, she enlarges the domain of acquisition's decision-making process and includes other means to grow such as joint ventures or alliances. Acquisitions are viewed as one way to grow among many others that entails trade-offs related to resource and learning requirements. This enables a more nuanced view of how companies can both achieve their exploitation–exploration balance and reach their optimal configuration of growth modes. Meanwhile, Olimpia Meglio enlarges the domain of analysis of acquisition performance. Specifically, she investigates the multidimensionality of acquisition performance through a stakeholder lens. The underlying idea is that the merging companies are not monoliths; rather, they host several stakeholders inside and outside their boundaries. These stakes are put at risk by an acquisition and exert an influence on acquisition performance over time. Acquisition performance is portrayed as a game played by several stakeholders, whose relative power influences outcomes.

A third approach to the contextual domain arises from the widespread idea that no two acquisitions are alike and that differences include social, geographical, and industry factors. Again, two chapters in this section investigate acquisitions in different contexts, thus contributing to fine-tuning our understanding of differences among acquisitions. Marco Testoni, Stefano Breschi, and Giovanni Valentini analyze the social context surrounding an organization that, in their view, may significantly influence the opportunity set that it perceives for acquisitions. Specifically, the chapter focuses on the effects of the network of strategic alliances on subsequent M&A decisions. They empirically test two competing hypotheses in the US semiconductor industry. The argument underlying these alternative hypotheses is that M&As and alliances are substitute inter-firm governance modes. In the other chapter, Lucia Piscitello, Roberta Rabellotti, and Vittoria Giada Scalera investigate the ownership choices by emerging market multinational enterprises (EMNEs) when they invest in Europe through M&As. They also consider the influence of motivations underlying EMNE international expansion. The deals under investigation focus on Chinese and Indian MNEs in high- and medium-tech industries. They conclude that EMNEs are less interested in acquiring control and prefer to keep the local partner for the sake of gaining knowledge. Additionally, EMNEs choose partial acquisitions in cases where there is high dissimilarity in terms of culture, industry, and knowledge base.

At the end of this transit stop in our journey in and around M&A, we have illustrated that mergers and acquisitions can no longer be seen as isolated events in a company's life. They need to be analyzed as a single step in the broader context of a corporate development portfolio. Each and every acquisition is in turn affected by several constraints or opportunities that arise from where the company is based or where the industry competes. These factors are some that shape an acquisition process. We still have much to learn before we start grasping all possible factors affecting acquisitions. An additional message that stands out in this section is the pervasiveness of acquisition on organizations. Seeing companies as constellations of relationships with external and internal stakeholders helps us to get a more nuanced understanding of several classic and new issues surrounding the phenomenon of acquisition.

6

Assessing the effects of the network of strategic alliances on M&A decisions

Some empirical evidence from the US semiconductor industry

Marco Testoni, Stefano Breschi, and Giovanni Valentini

Introduction

Literature has increasingly recognized that firms are deeply embedded in networks of social and economic relations. These include client–supplier relationships, trade association memberships, relationships among individual employees, interlocking directorates, and prior strategic alliances (e.g. Gulati 1998). Importantly, this network of relationships can considerably influence firms' behavior (Uzzi 1996). The hypotheses developed in this chapter contend that this is true also for firms' acquisition strategy, and in particular that the opportunity set perceived by firms active in the market for corporate control is affected in important ways by their bundle of social relations. More specifically, in this study we will focus on the network of strategic alliances. Two competing hypotheses concerning the effect of the network of alliances on merger and acquisition (M&A) decisions are developed and tested. First, we argue that proximity within the alliance network structure increases the probability that two firms will engage in a merger or acquisition because of the informational advantages provided by network proximity. Second, we contend that two firms that are closer in the network have a lower probability of merging compared to more distant or disconnected firms. The argument underlying this alternative prediction is that M&As and alliances are substitute inter-firm governance modes. It follows that the presence of a network of alliances may make an M&A unnecessary. We test these competing hypotheses on a sample of firms from the US semiconductor industry and find support for the informational advantage hypothesis.

Literature review

Several studies have examined the relationship between strategic alliances and M&As. Inter alia, Reuer and Ragozzino (2008) found that an M&A between prior partners is more likely to be paid in cash, while an acquisition between firms without a prior collaborative relationship is more likely to be made with a payment contingent on the post-acquisition performance of the target (i.e. using stock as payment). They interpret this result as a symptom of the fact that alliances can significantly reduce the information asymmetry between acquirer and target, thus reducing the risk of the transaction. Other researchers found that M&As between previously allied firms can perform better than other transactions. Indeed, alliances provide firms with "experiential capital" about the partner and can increase the merging firms' awareness of their compatibility or about potential problem areas (Dyer and Singh 1998; Porrini 2004; Zaheer *et al.* 2010). Thus, they are less likely to experience the post-acquisition problems that are detrimental to value creation (Porrini 2004). Overall, these studies provide arguments supporting the idea that an acquirer should have a preference for a target that has been a direct partner in the past.

Other scholars have studied directly the effect of alliances on the propensity to acquire. Yang *et al.* (2011) investigated whether some types of alliances have higher probability to lead to the acquisition of the partner than others. They found that *exploration* alliances (such as R&D agreements) are more likely to lead to the acquisition of the partner than *exploitation* alliances (such as marketing or licensing agreements). They argue that exploration alliances require close and continuous interaction that better exposes firms to partners' tacit knowledge base and enables a better understanding of the true value of the partner firm's resources. On the contrary, exploitation alliances have less need for deep interaction on knowledge creation and transfer. Moreover, exploration alliances are more dynamic than exploitation alliances and can generate more opportunities for future expansion that can be facilitated by the acquisition of the partner. Their result is in contrast with the study of Hagedoorn and Sadowski (1999), who analyzed technology alliances (R&D and technology transfer agreements) involving firms from several industries and found that the transition from partnership to acquisition hardly ever takes place. These studies, however, considered only M&As between firms that are or were partners in an alliance, and did not take into account the whole network of firms in an industry.

Lin *et al.* (2009) also contribute to this stream of literature by studying whether the position within the alliances' network structure may affect the propensity of a firm to acquire. They found evidence that in a developed institutional environment—such as the USA—the tendency to acquire is negatively associated with a firm's centrality in the alliances network and positively associated with its structural hole positioning, while in a less developed institutional setting—such as China—an opposite pattern is observed. This chapter builds on this study and complements it by shifting the analysis from a single firm focus—i.e. from the question "Who acquires?"—to a dyadic perspective—i.e. to the question "Who acquires whom?"

Highly relevant to our theory is the framework developed by Gulati (1995, 1998, and 1999) to study the dynamics of alliance formation. As the author illustrates, faced with uncertainty about a potential partner's capabilities and reliability, companies tend to resort to existing networks to discover information that lowers search costs and alleviates the risk of opportunism. Accordingly, Gulati (1995) shows that previously unconnected firms are more likely to enter into alliances if they have common partners or are less distant from each other in the alliances network. An interesting insight of Gulati's analysis is that the conditions of mutual economic advantage and of strategic interdependence are necessary but non-sufficient conditions for the creation of a partnership between two organizations. Indeed, while considerations about complementarities of resources are important, a firm's social connections are what allow it to identify new alliance opportunities and choose specific partners that possess such complementary assets. Coherently, Chakrabarti and Mitchell (2013) argued that. because distance reduces the information that the acquirer can collect about the potential target, acquirers prefer targets that are geographically proximate relative to the whole set of potential targets. In other words, this work evidenced that information availability significantly biases decision making in M&A. While Chakrabarti and

Mitchell (2013) measure information availability through geographical distance, our study tries to capture information availability by considering the network of strategic alliances.

Hypotheses

Informational advantage

M&As are complex events in a firm's life, and they may easily turn into a failure if not well managed. Their success depends upon several different factors, such as the characteristics of the acquirer, those of the target, and the features of their combination. Target-specific information such as internal strengths, weaknesses, knowledge base, and culture can help the acquirer in evaluating the target's resources and the realizable benefits of the M&A. The failure to rightly evaluate these characteristics can easily lead managers to formulate wrong expectations about the M&A outcomes and result in a value-decreasing operation (Chatterjee et al. 1992). Unfortunately, markets convey less (reliable) information concerning a firm's intangible and knowledge-related assets than about its physical capital. Indeed, while the latter is adequately represented in financial statements, knowledge is under-represented in publicly available information. "It is almost as if balance sheets are provided for some industries but not for others (since the primary assets of knowledge-intensive industries are systematically excluded)" (Coff 1999: 146). The main issue is that several of the qualitative aspects of a target are difficult to measure as an external observer. This is due to the tacit and contextual nature of knowledge that resides in individual employees' minds, organizational processes and routines. Coff (1999) identifies three different kinds of uncertainty about the target's knowledge-related assets: 1) uncertainty regarding the *quality of assets*, since these may include considerable tacit elements; 2) uncertainty about *what can be transferred*, since the transfer of knowledge and human capital is less predictable than tangible assets (for example, an acquisition may break implicit contracts and cause a voluntary turnover of key employees); and 3) uncertainty about the *prospects for synergy*, since the combined capabilities cannot be observed a priori. These informational problems are likely to be exacerbated in knowledge-intensive sectors where knowledge is complex and represents the main asset of a firm (Coff 1999; Zaheer et al. 2010). Our hypothesis is that these informational problems can affect first of all the selection of the target firm. In other words, a bidder may prefer to choose targets for which the informational problems are less severe.

Prior interaction experience with potential targets in alliances may offer a valuable mechanism through which information on the intrinsic characteristics of targets can be transmitted. Indeed, partnerships allow firms to share and combine their resources and capabilities and enable them to learn from each other. Thus, by exposing companies to internal processes of partners, alliances increase firms' awareness of targets' value in tacit resources and capabilities (Gulati 1995, 1998 and 1999; Dyer and Singh 1998; Porrini 2004; Reuer and Ragozzino 2008; Zaheer et al. 2010; Yang et al. 2011). The underlying logic is that alliances facilitate the creation of inter-personal links that allow an improved understanding of *who knows what* and *where critical expertise resides* within each firm (Dyer and Singh 1998). This mechanism may operate *directly*—i.e. firms have access to information about others with whom they have a partnership—but also *indirectly*. Indeed, a company embedded in a network may have access to information about a potential target—even though it is not directly linked to it—by asking other players in its network. The potential for information exchange through the network decreases as the distance between the two focal firms increases, and it is maximal when the social distance is equal to one—i.e. when the two firms are partners in an alliance. This is a reasonable assumption given the costs associated with indirect information access (Gulati 1995; Singh 2005; Sorenson et al. 2006). This line of reasoning implies that, *ceteris paribus*, a bidder will be more likely to select a target that is closer in the network of alliances, because more information is available about it than about more distant firms. Thus, by selecting a closer firm, the acquirer attempts to reduce the information asymmetry and its associated risk.

Moreover, the information transmission channels of the network may also facilitate the discovery of favorable deals at the right time. Indeed, a firm embedded in a network is better positioned to take advantage of acquisition opportunities (such as the development of promising new technologies or the discovery of an undervalued target) that may arise in its immediate surroundings (Gulati 1999). This also increases the probability that a firm acquires a target in its surroundings. These effects are summarized in the *informational advantage* hypothesis.

> Hypothesis 1.a (H1.a): The closer firms are in the network of prior alliances, the higher the probability that they will engage in a merger or in an acquisition.

Given the heterogeneity in the types of alliances, it is straightforward to question if all types of alliances really drive the effect described in Hypothesis 1.a. In fact, alliances may be distinguished empirically according to their scope, such as: R&D, marketing, manufacturing, technology transfer, supply agreement, licensing, etc. Some researchers illustrated that not all typologies of collaborations are expected to have the same potential for knowledge exchange and learning (Anand and Khanna 2000a and 2000b; Porrini 2004; Lin *et al.* 2009; Zaheer *et al.* 2010; Yang *et al.* 2011). Some alliances—such as R&D, marketing,[1] manufacturing, and technology transfer agreements—require close and continuous interaction which better exposes firms to partners' tacit knowledge base and engenders more trust between the parties. It follows that such partnerships are more powerful knowledge transmission channels and are better suited for understanding intrinsic characteristics of targets than other types of cooperative agreements such as licensing, supply, and other types of agreements. Given this argumentation, it is predicted that these kinds of alliances are the actual driver of the *informational advantage* effect described in the previous hypothesis. Meanwhile, other types of partnerships that have less need for intensive interaction should have less power as devices for reducing the informational asymmetry. The literature includes among this second kind of collaborations: licensing agreements (Porrini 2004; Lin *et al.* 2009; Zaheer *et al.* 2010; Yang *et al.* 2011), supply alliances (Lin *et al.* 2009; Zaheer *et al.* 2010), equity only partnerships (Zaheer *et al.* 2010), and other less specific types of contracts (Lin *et al.* 2009).

> Hypothesis 1.b (H1.b): The effect predicted in Hypothesis 1.a will be more pronounced in a network defined by alliances that require close and continuous interaction between parties.

Substitution effect

There is an alternative and opposite effect that could influence the M&A decision of a firm. The underlying logic is that alliances can be considered substitutes to acquisitions as a way to get access to other firms' assets (Williamson 1991; Besanko *et al.* 2000). It follows that it might be superfluous for a firm embedded in a network to acquire other players in its surroundings. Moreover, through a partnership a company can gain access just to the resources that are actually needed, while excluding other unnecessary assets. By contrast, acquisitions do not allow disentangling desirable assets from unwanted ones (so-called "indigestible" assets) (Hennart and Reddy 1997; de Man and Duysters 2005). Therefore, not only might acquiring a partner be superfluous, but it could also be harmful. Under this view, the presence of a network will actually decrease the probability that an acquirer will select a close target.

It is conceivable that this negative effect could operate between direct partners (i.e. a firm is less likely to acquire a direct partner since it already has access to some of its assets). However, it might also operate for indirect relationships. For example, a firm willing to have access to some assets of an indirect partner may find it less costly to be referenced by their common partner and sign a direct alliance with the other firm. Gulati (1995) documents that firms closer in the network have higher probability of signing an alliance. If alliances and M&As are substitutes, whatever makes an alliance more likely decreases the probability that an M&A occurs. Thus, if network proximity increases the likelihood of an alliance between two firms, it should also reduce the probability of a merger.[2] Given the decreasing value of indirect referrals and of knowledge transmission, the indirect effect linked with the *substitution effect*—as in the case of Hypothesis 1—is also expected to decrease its potential as the dyad is further apart in the network. We thus predict the following hypothesis:

> Hypothesis 2 (H2): The closer are firms in the network of prior alliances, the lower the probability that they will engage in a merger or in an acquisition.

Methods

In order to avoid cross-country and cross-sector heterogeneity, the hypotheses were tested by focusing on a single industry in one country: the US semiconductor industry was selected for the empirical investigation. The study considered M&As that occurred between 2003 and 2007; 2007 was selected as the final year in order to avoid including in the data the post-2008 financial crisis and its consequences on the M&A market.

The data collection started by selecting all the firms with primary SIC code 3674 (semiconductor industry), operating in the US and active during the period 2003–2007.[3] Data on companies' SIC codes and locations were obtained from *Orbis*. Additional information was found in *Thomson One Banker* and *Lexis-Nexis*. Financial data were retrieved from *Thomson Financial*. Data on alliances were obtained from *Thomson SDC Platinum*. For each period of analysis, the main explanatory variables were constructed from the network present at time *t-1*. Unfortunately, *Thomson SDC* provides information on the date of creation of the alliance, but the termination date is usually unavailable. According to Kogut (1988) the average duration of an alliance is no more than five years. Therefore, the network was drawn using a lagged five-year moving window for each year of analysis.[4] Data on M&As were obtained from *Zephyr* and from the *Thomson One Banker—Deals* database. We chose to focus on announcement dates instead of the dates in which the transactions effectively started since this study investigates the motives behind the M&A decision (Luypaert and Huyghebaert 2006). Therefore, we included all the M&As that were announced among the firms in the sample during the period 2003–2007.[5] Finally, patents data were obtained from the *NBER Patent Data Project* (Hall *et al*. 2001). We collected data on 267 firms and 103 M&As[6] during the period 2003–2007. The network included a total of 462 dyadic ties (arising from 347 alliances[7]) for the whole period 1998–2006. Table 6.1 shows the main characteristics of the alliances in the sample.

Manufacturing agreements are the most common type of alliances, followed respectively by R&D, licensing, marketing, and technology transfer agreements. Instead, supply agreement is a quite rare form of collaboration. A given alliance may be aimed at various purposes. This is the reason why the first section of Table 6.1 does not sum up to 100 percent. Moreover, one-quarter of the agreements cannot be labeled according to these categories. This evidence suggests that

Table 6.1 Characteristics of alliances

Scope	
Manufacturing agreement	34%
R&D agreement	21%
Licensing agreement	21%
Marketing agreement	14%
Technology transfer agreement	12%
Supply agreement	3%
Other	25%
Governance	
Joint ventures	6%
Strategic alliances (non-JV)	94%
Number of participants	
Two partners	80%
Three partners or more	20%

alliances are an extremely flexible form of inter-firm relationship, whose objective can vary greatly. Concerning the governance structure, the sample shows that 94 percent of the alliances are contractual agreements, while joint ventures involve just 6 percent of the sample.[8] Finally, Table 6.1 shows that alliances are predominantly a dyadic phenomenon: only one-fifth of the sampled collaborations involved more than two participants.

Since the unit of analysis is the dyads of firms, all the possible combinations of companies were considered. Reverse-ordered dyads were not included (i.e. if dyad $i+j$ was included, dyad $j+i$ was excluded).[9] By excluding missing values, we ended up having a total of 35,352 complete dyadic observations in the dataset.

Dependent variable

The dependent variable *M&A* is a dummy variable which equals one if the dyad announced a merger or an acquisition in that year and zero otherwise.

Independent variables

Unrestricted network distances

The main independent variable of this model is the distance between the two firms in the network of prior alliances. For each year of analysis, the network was drawn using the partnerships that were signed in the previous five years. In order to test hypotheses 1.a and 2, the networks were created without restrictions on the typology of alliances. The social distance between firms was calculated using an interactive matrix language (IML) procedure in *SAS®* and it is defined as the smallest number of nodes separating two firms.[10] For example, firms that have a direct partnership have a distance of 1, while firms that are separated from a common partner have a distance of 2. Four dummy variables were generated for each year: *distance_1, distance_2, distance_3*, and *distance_4* which were set equal to one if the distance was respectively 1, 2, 3, or 4 and zero otherwise. Since the aim of this research is to investigate whether social proximity has an effect on M&A decisions, the base group is identified in distances greater than 4 and in the absence of connections between firms.

Hypothesis 1.a would be supported if the dummy variables indicating a short distance between firms exert a positive effect on the probability of a merger. Conversely, Hypothesis 2 predicts a negative effect. Moreover, according to both the hypotheses, the coefficients of the dummy variables should decrease in their magnitude moving from *distance_1* to *distance_4*.

Restricted network distances

In order to test Hypothesis 1.b, *restricted* networks were generated by filtering the types of alliances. In particular, this specification of the model included just alliances that were coded as R&D, marketing, manufacturing, or technology transfer agreement. This reduced the total number of ties to 299. As in the case of the unrestricted network, four dummy variables were generated indicating the social distance calculated in the restricted networks.

Hypothesis 1.b predicts that the distance variables should increase in magnitude and significance when moving from the unrestricted to the restricted network. Moreover, the coefficients of the four dummy variables should be positive and their magnitude should progressively decrease when moving from the first to the last one.

Control variables

Asymmetry in firm size

This variable accounts for the fact that, if two firms are of equal size, it might be harder for one to acquire the other (e.g. Yang *et al.* 2011). Therefore, asymmetry is expected to exert a positive effect on the probability of an M&A. The variable *asymmetry in firm size* was calculated as the logarithm of the absolute value of the difference in total assets (in million USD) of the two firms.

Market relatedness

Market relatedness may affect the decision to acquire in different ways. For example, two firms competing in the same product markets may have more incentives to merge compared to non-competing firms, since they could more easily transfer routines across units, create economies of scale (Baum *et al.* 2000), and gain market power. Also, when two companies are direct competitors, other forms of collaboration are less likely to work because they are more likely to suffer from opportunistic behavior and because they are at higher risk of involuntary spillovers to partners (Miotti and Sachwald 2003; Lavie 2007). Finally, a company that acquires a target that operates in similar businesses may better evaluate the target's resources and capabilities. This may also affect acquisition integration and performance (Porrini 2004). Given these argumentations, the level of market relatedness is expected to be positively associated with the probability of an M&A. The variable *market relatedness* was calculated as the number of four-digit SIC codes that the two firms have in common, divided by the total number of codes covered by them together (Porrini 2004). It follows that, the closer the ratio is to one, firms are competing in a higher number of product markets.

Geographical proximity

Geographical proximity is another factor likely to affect the selection of the target. Firms may have a preference for close targets because of lower transportation and integration costs, easier transfer of routines, and higher potential for economies of scale (Baum *et al.* 2000; Grote and Umber 2007). Distance contributes also to increasing the costs that the acquirer must bear in order to monitor the newly acquired entity (Grote and Umber 2007). Finally, proximity enables interaction between individuals, which could facilitate the acquirer's evaluation of the tacit knowledge and the internal strengths and weaknesses of the target (Baum *et al.* 2000; Grote and Umber 2007; Lahiri 2010; Chakrabarti and Mitchell 2013). Previous studies analyzing the effect of geographical distance on M&As usually consider the distance separating the headquarters of the two firms (e.g. Grote and Umber 2007). Nevertheless, companies may have several different locations if one considers also branches and subsidiaries. For these firms, headquarter locations give just scant information about their geographical positioning. Therefore, we considered the whole geographical distribution of companies. The variable *geographical proximity* is calculated as the number of overlapping locations prior to the merger divided by the total number of locations covered by the two firms together. Firms' locations are defined by the headquarter city plus the cities in which the company had branches[11] prior to the merger (if this occurred).

Joint M&A experience

This variable controls for the number of M&As that the firms experienced in the past and accounts for two effects. First, it controls for the fact that firms may develop M&A capabilities through experience. For example, Hayward (2002) shows that organizations (provided that they are exposed to a variety of acquisition experiences) may learn from their past acquisitions. The development of these skills enables companies to obtain superior M&A performance in subsequent transactions. Applying this principle to our framework, we expect that greater M&A capabilities positively affect the propensity to engage in these transactions. Second, the number of past M&As may account for a tendency of the firm. On the acquirer side, a high number of past acquisitions may indicate that the company is pursuing a strategy of aggressive external growth. On the target side, it may indicate that the firm is divesting its activities. In both cases, the number of past M&As should be positively associated with the probability of an acquisition. The variable *joint M&A experience* was created for each year by summing the number of M&As that involved the two firms of the dyad in the previous five years. In particular, while the focus of the analysis is on M&As that occurred between US semiconductor firms, companies' *M&A experience* was calculated without imposing any restriction on the sector or country of origin of the companies involved.

Technological proximity

Technological distance between firms is another important factor that should be taken into account. For each company and for each year of analysis one vector was created representing the distribution of patents across the 37 technological categories defined by the US Patent and Trademark Office (USPTO). The vectors were created by considering the patents assigned in the previous five years. *Technological proximity* was then calculated by considering the angular separation of the vectors (see Jaffe 1989). This measure equals one if the two companies have identical patent distributions, and zero if they have no overlap in the classification of their patents. Several studies analyzed the effects of M&As on the subsequent innovative performance of firms. This literature generally found that the relatedness of merging firms' knowledge bases is curvilinearly (inverted-U) related to the post-merger innovation output (measured in terms of number of patents). This non-linear relationship is due to the overlap of two contrasting effects. On the one hand, the closer the knowledge bases, the easier it is to absorb and integrate them into a single unit. Technical communication and learning is facilitated by the existence of shared languages, similar cognitive structures, and common skills (Ahuja and Katila 2001; Cloodt *et al.* 2006). If firms are technologically distant from each other, integration may be difficult and innovation performance is likely to decrease. On the other hand, if firms have very similar knowledge bases, they have less opportunity to learn something new from each other. Conversely, more diverse knowledge bases increase the potential to combine different knowledge elements: this improves the quality of the innovation process (Fleming 2007). It follows that a moderate level of knowledge relatedness should be optimal, since it provides the benefits of enhancing the variety of possible combinations, while maintaining the preconditions for a smooth integration (Ahuja and Katila 2001; Cloodt *et al.* 2006; Valentini and Dawson 2010). Given this curvilinear relationship between technological proximity and innovation performance, an acquirer willing to maximize its patent output should select targets moderately distant in the technological space. To account for this effect the variable *technological proximity* and its squared term are introduced in the model. We expect to observe the signs of an inverted parabola.

Total cash available

Most acquisitions rely on cash as a means of payment (Lin *et al.* 2009; Yang *et al.* 2011). Hence, a lack of cash may constraint the firm's ability to acquire. Consequently, the variable *total cash available* was included in the model. It was calculated as the sum of cash and equivalents (in million USD) of the two firms.

Year dummies

To control for unobserved heterogeneity across years, year dummies were also included in the model.

Additional network variables

Joint network centrality

The network variables considered so far focused on the effects of the social distance between firms on the probability of an M&A. However, other elements of the companies' positioning within the network might be relevant. For example, a high level of centrality in the network is usually associated with higher social visibility and prestige (Gulati 1998 and 1999; Ahuja *et al.* 2009). This may have a separate effect to that of distance on the probability of an M&A. Given that we are dealing with dyads of firms, the level of their joint centrality should be considered. Different effects may be expected on the likelihood of an acquisition. On the one hand, since centrality is associated with higher reputation, perceived trust, and visibility, high network embeddedness can decrease the informational asymmetry between two firms. This effect is independent from the fact that firms may be directly or indirectly connected between them. Also, network centrality may provide a signal of the quality of targets. This follows from the fact that it may be more costly for companies with poor quality resources to develop and sign such alliances (Spence 1974; Reuer and Ragozzino 2008). In a sense, joint network centrality might be considered a thermometer measuring the level of information asymmetry of the dyad. Moreover, given the importance of the network of alliances (Lavie 2007), the firms' portfolio of connections may constitute a valuable asset to acquire. It follows that a high level of centrality could increase the value of the target. Finally, an acquirer which is centrally located in the network is more likely to obtain valuable information on M&A opportunities at the right time. These effects all point to a positive relation between the joint network centrality and the likelihood of an M&A. On the other hand, a high centrality may also decrease the probability of an M&A. Indeed, a company deeply embedded in a network may have access to the resources of all the firms that are in its surroundings. This may reduce the need to pursue an acquisition (Lin *et al.* 2009). In addition, the high level of prestige and trust facilitates the creation of subsequent alliances (Gulati 1998 and 1999; Ahuja *et al.* 2009). It follows that two centrally located firms may find it easier and less costly to sign an alliance instead of a merger in order to get access to the other firm's resources. In order to test these predictions, the variable *joint network centrality* was created. Each firm's centrality in the network of alliances signed in the previous five years was measured using Bonacich's (1987) eigenvector measure.[12] The *joint network centrality* variable was then calculated as the geometric mean[13] of the centrality scores of the two firms in the dyad (Ahuja *et al.* 2009).

Socially asymmetric dyad

Along with firms' joint centrality, the asymmetry in their level of embeddedness may also be relevant. Some studies illustrated that a high level of centrality is associated with higher status and bargaining power (e.g. Ahuja *et al.* 2009). This suggests that, if firms have similar centrality scores, they might have more power struggles during negotiations. On the other hand, dissimilar social status may lead to smoother transactions (Yang *et al.* 2011). To test this hypothesis, the variable *socially asymmetric dyad* was introduced. This is a dummy variable that equals one if one of the firms in the dyad has a centrality score higher than the mean score in the observation year while the other has a score lower than the mean (Ahuja *et al.* 2009).

Statistical approach

By considering the whole set of dyads, a very large amount of non-merging dyads are included in the sample, and just a few dyads actually engaged in a merger or in an acquisition. King and Zeng (2001) show that performing a normal logistic regression with rare event data can produce biased results and sharply underestimate the probability of rare events. Accordingly, we estimated our model using the rare events logistic regression procedure (Tomz *et al.* 1999; King and Zeng 1999, 2001).

Results

Tables 6.2 and 6.3 show the descriptive statistics, while Table 6.4 illustrates the main results of the regressions. Model 1 includes just the control variables, Model 2 introduces the distance dummies calculated from the unrestricted network, and Model 3 includes the distance variables calculated from the restricted network.

By observing the three models, we notice that the control variables have the expected signs and their significance is largely unchanged across the different specifications. Model 2 provides supporting evidence for the informational advantage hypothesis (H1.a). The coefficients of the dummy variables indicating the network distance are positive. Moreover, the likelihood

Table 6.2 Correlation matrix

		1	2	3	4	5	6	7	8
1	M&A	1							
2	Distance_1	0.0271	1						
3	Distance_2	0.0206	-0.005	1					
4	Distance_3	0.013	-0.007	-0.017	1				
5	Distance_4	0.0044	-0.007	-0.017	-0.024	1			
6	Joint network centrality	0.0302	0.2596	0.5386	0.437	0.2139	1		
7	Socially asymmetric dyad	0.0168	0.0119	0.1054	0.1792	0.115	0.1834	1	
8	Asymmetry in firm size	0.0208	0.052	0.12	0.1444	0.1001	0.2063	0.4667	1
9	Market relatedness	0.0005	-0.006	0.0156	-0.011	0.0005	-0.005	0.0103	-0.003
10	Geographical proximity	0.001	0.0076	0.0163	0.0106	0.0056	0.0208	-0.005	-0.053
11	Joint M&A experience	0.0222	0.0666	0.1045	0.1178	0.1077	0.1935	0.2344	0.4763
12	Technological proximity	-0.005	-0.016	-0.037	-0.073	-0.038	-0.076	-0.207	-0.297
13	Sq. technological proximity	-0.006	-0.016	-0.038	-0.07	-0.04	-0.078	-0.184	-0.261
14	Total cash	0.0179	0.1163	0.1865	0.1471	0.0715	0.3241	0.4653	0.5865

		9	10	11	12	13	14
9	Market relatedness	1					
10	Geographical proximity	0.0674	1				
11	Joint M&A experience	-0.162	-0.021	1			
12	Technological proximity	0.0297	0.024	-0.1	1		
13	Sq. technological proximity	0.0322	0.0256	-0.1	0.9592	1	
14	Total cash	-0.041	-0.008	0.5695	-0.177	-0.166	1

Table 6.3 Descriptive statistics

Variable	Obs.	Mean	Std. Dev.	Min.	Max.
M&A	152385	0.0006759	0.0259898	0	1
Distance_1	177555	0.0082589	0.0905026	0	1
Distance_2	177555	0.0314845	0.1746234	0	1
Distance_3	177555	0.0660305	0.248336	0	1
Distance_4	177555	0.0699773	0.2551092	0	1
Joint network centrality	177555	0.1670297	1.200093	0	42.63272
Socially asymmetric dyad	177555	0.1155248	0.3196551	0	1
Asymmetry in firm size	55622	6.321174	2.112652	-4.60517	10.78475
Market relatedness	164100	0.4727148	0.299437	0	1
Geographical proximity	177555	0.0173201	0.085074	0	1
Joint M&A experience	172265	4.536882	6.126038	0	69
Technological proximity	91792	0.3611336	0.3029926	0	1
Squared technological proximity	91792	0.222221	0.2913637	0	1
Total cash	54598	1090.258	2350.081	0	27880

Table 6.4 Factors affecting the probability of an M&A between two firms

Variables	Model 1	Model 2 (unrestricted network)	Model 3 (restricted network)
Distance_1		3.07**	3.31***
		(2.47)	(2.63)
Distance_2		1.75**	1.64
		(2.06)	(1.47)
Distance_3		1.16	1.33
		(1.47)	(1.23)
Distance_4		0.71	1.31
		(0.69)	(1.28)
Asymmetry in firm size	0.40**	0.38***	0.39**
	(2.54)	(2.61)	(2.54)
Market relatedness	1.09*	1.03	1.03
	(1.68)	(1.63)	(1.59)
Geographical proximity	3.47***	3.46***	3.49***
	(3.43)	(3.20)	(3.34)
Joint M&A experience	0.07*	0.07*	0.07*
	(1.83)	(1.72)	(1.81)
Technological proximity	2.01	1.71	1.79
	(0.64)	(0.54)	(0.56)
Squared technological proximity	-2.20	-1.79	-1.89
	(-0.59)	(-0.48)	(-0.51)
Total cash	-0.00	-0.00	-0.00
	(-0.92)	(-1.21)	(-1.21)
Year 2007	-0.15	-0.10	-0.16
	(-0.24)	(-0.15)	(-0.25)
Year 2006	-0.38	-0.31	-0.35
	(-0.56)	(-0.46)	(-0.51)
Year 2005	-0.63	-0.55	-0.58
	(-0.83)	(-0.72)	(-0.76)
Year 2004	-0.07	-0.06	-0.06
	(-0.11)	(-0.10)	(-0.10)
Constant	-11.02***	-10.87***	-10.91***
	(-7.93)	(-8.03)	(-7.91)
N	35352	35352	35352

Notes: Dependent variable is a dummy variable which equals 1 if the dyad merged in that year and 0 otherwise
Z-values are in parenthesis
Two-tailed p-values: *** $p \leq 0.01$; ** $0.01 < p \leq 0.05$; * $0.05 < p \leq 0.1$

of acquisition progressively decreases in magnitude moving from *distance_1* to *distance_4*. The variables indicating a distance of one or two are positive and they are statistically significant at the 5 percent level, while *distance_3* becomes significant at the 15 percent level. Overall, these findings support the prediction that proximity in the network of alliances actually increases the likelihood of a merger or acquisition.[14]

In Model 3, the distance variables are built from the network of R&D, marketing, technology transfer, and manufacturing agreements. In this specification the variable *distance_1* increases in magnitude and significance. Nevertheless, by testing the equality of the coefficients across specifications (Paternoster *et al.* 1998), we see that this increase is not statistically significant (z=0.14). Moreover, the other distance variables become non-significant. Overall, these findings do not support Hypothesis 1.b and indicate that both "strong" and "weak" alliances are relevant for transmitting information. In other words, once the intrinsic characteristics of the target have been observed and codified in transmittable information (Nonaka *et al.* 1996 call this process *externalization*), the information flows through the network regardless of the typology of ties.

As expected, *asymmetry in firm size* exerts a positive effect on the probability of an M&A and this effect is statistically significant across the three models. *Market relatedness* shows the expected sign but is statistically significant only in the first model. This result provides rather weak support for the prediction that the greater the overlaps in the product markets, the higher the probability of an M&A. The significance of *geographical proximity* shows that firms have higher chances of merging if they have similar geographical distributions (considering both headquarters and branch locations). Indeed, geographical proximity is likely to be associated with lower integration and monitoring costs, easier target screening and higher potential for economies of scale (Baum *et al.* 2000; Grote and Umber 2007; Lahiri 2010; Chakrabarti and Mitchell 2013). As predicted, the coefficient of *joint M&A experience* is also positive and statistically significant in the three models. This effect can be interpreted by considering that firms can develop acquisition capabilities through experience (Hayward 2002). Moreover, this variable controls for companies' possible strategies of external growth (for acquirers) and divestitures (for sellers). *Technological proximity* and its squared term assume the signs of an inverted parabola as expected; however, these variables are never significant. Given that we are considering a high-tech sector, technological factors are likely to be relevant for M&A decisions and the lack of significance of the *technological proximity* variable seems surprising. One possible way to interpret this result is to assert that our measure of technology is not able to adequately represent firms in the knowledge space (at least in this context). Another possibility could be that the informational opacity of firms in this industry makes it hard for acquiring firms to observe the knowledge base of all the possible firms in the industry and select the optimal one with respect to the technological parameter. Finally, *total cash* and the year dummies are never significant.

Table 6.5 introduces into the model the additional network variables. Models 4 and 5 add to the control variables, respectively, *joint network centrality* and *socially asymmetric dyad*. Model 6 introduces them simultaneously. Model 7 adds also the distance dummy variables.

In the four models, the signs and significance of the control variables remain substantially consistent with the base specification. In Models 4 and 5, we notice that the coefficients of *joint network centrality* are positive and significant. This evidence suggests that an acquisition between two centrally located firms is less likely to experience problems of information asymmetry. In addition, on the one hand a centrally located acquirer is more likely to obtain valuable information about M&A opportunities at the right time. On the other hand, a target's embeddedness into the network may be a valuable asset to acquire for a bidder. In Model 7, *distance_2* and *joint network centrality* both become non-significant. This is likely to be due to a problem of multicollinearity, as the two variables are correlated. This suggests that, if two firms are centrally located in the network, they have also good chances of being indirectly linked to each other. A joint test of these two variables shows that they are jointly significant at the 10 percent level. Given this correlation, we are not able to completely disentangle the effects operated by network centrality to that of indirect referrals. However, these two effects are likely to be deeply interlinked. Moreover, they all point to the informational advantages provided by the network. Finally, the variable *socially asymmetric dyad* is positive as expected, but it is never statistically significant.

Table 6.5 Adding the joint network centrality and socially asymmetric dyad variables

Variables	Model 4 (unrestricted network)	Model 5 (unrestricted network)	Model 6 (unrestricted network)	Model 7 (unrestricted network)
Distance_1				2.60***
				(3.76)
Distance_2				1.22
				(1.02)
Distance_3				0.74
				(0.7)
Distance_4				0.47
				(0.46)
Joint network centrality	0.13*		0.14**	0.07
	(1.93)		(2.03)	(0.72)
Socially asymmetric dyad		0.34	0.42	0.33
		(0.66)	(0.90)	(0.72)
Asymmetry in firm size	0.41**	0.37**	0.36**	0.36**
	(2.53)	(2.53)	(2.54)	(2.56)
Market relatedness	1.08*	1.07*	1.06*	1.02
	(1.71)	(1.66)	(1.66)	(1.63)
Geographical proximity	3.48***	3.48***	3.48***	3.47***
	(3.27)	(3.41)	(3.26)	(3.18)
Joint M&A experience	0.07*	0.07*	0.07**	0.07*
	(1.90)	(1.91)	(2.05)	(1.87)
Technological proximity	1.74	2.05	1.79	1.76
	(0.55)	(0.64)	(0.55)	(0.55)
Squared technological proximity	-1.85	-2.22	-1.86	-1.80
	(-0.50)	(-0.59)	(-0.50)	(-0.48)
Total cash	-0.00	-0.00	-0.00	-0.00
	(-1.13)	(-1.02)	(-1.26)	(-1.17)
Year 2007	-0.28	-0.14	-0.28	-0.16
	(-0.43)	(-0.21)	(-0.42)	(-0.25)
Year 2006	-0.45	-0.39	-0.47	-0.37
	(-0.64)	(-0.56)	(-0.65)	(-0.51)
Year 2005	-0.65	-0.63	-0.65	-0.57
	(-0.84)	(-0.82)	(-0.84)	(-0.75)
Year 2004	-0.07	-0.06	-0.06	-0.05
	(-0.11)	(-0.10)	(-0.10)	(-0.08)
Constant	-10.99***	-10.86***	-10.74***	-10.77***
	(-7.77)	(-8.29)	(-8.21)	(-8.22)
N	35352	35352	35352	35352

Notes: Dependent variable is a dummy variable which equals 1 if the dyad merged in that year and 0 otherwise
Z-values are in parenthesis.
Two-tailed p-values: *** $p \leq 0.01$; ** $0.01 < p \leq 0.05$; * $0.05 < p \leq 0.1$

Conclusions

This research found that two firms have higher chances to engage in an M&A if they are directly or indirectly linked in the strategic alliances' network, centrally located within this structure, have dissimilar sizes, experienced more acquisitions in the past, and are competing in close geographical markets. Moreover, it was highlighted that all the typologies of alliances are relevant for transmitting information.

This study contributes to the extant literature by showing that relational drivers may partly account for the selection of targets in the context of a corporate acquisition. These drivers add to the traditional economic and financial explanations for improving our understanding of the market for corporate control. One of the implications of this research is that economic and strategic motives constitute necessary but non-sufficient conditions for the occurrence of an M&A between two companies (Gulati 1995). By influencing the extent to which firms have access to information about potential targets, social networks can alter the opportunity set that firms perceive for acquisitions. In particular, by providing additional information on the target's intrinsic characteristics, the network helps to reduce the information asymmetry that a traditional due diligence process cannot solve. Moreover, alliances may also be the conduits for precious information about new acquisition opportunities. Similar to previous studies (e.g. Gulati 1995; Baum *et al.* 2000), this chapter shows that firms rely on past experiences and leverage previous knowledge to plan their actions. When facing the risks associated with an acquisition, the firm resorts to the knowledge accumulated through prior alliances in order to make decisions (Gulati 1995). Overall, this study shows that firms follow path-dependent trajectories: a company's M&A decision is affected by its previous collaboration decisions.

A caveat should be made concerning the generality of these results. The analysis tested two competing hypotheses. The *informational advantage* view predicts that proximity within the network of alliances increases the likelihood of an M&A. The *substitution effect* view instead predicts an opposite effect. The results show that the first hypothesis prevails. However, the prevalence of one pattern over the other may depend on the sector chosen for the analysis. In a high-tech sector—such as the semiconductor industry—where knowledge represents the main asset of firms, problems of informational asymmetry are exacerbated (see Coff 1999) and the value of network links as knowledge-transmission mechanisms are maximal. Moreover, in a knowledge-intensive sector characterized by turbulence and constant innovation, alliances may communicate information regarding new technological discoveries and consequently information about new acquisition opportunities. Instead, in a less knowledge-intensive industry in a late stage of its life cycle, these effects may be lowered and a different pattern may be observed. This distinction helps to reconcile the results of this study to those of Lin *et al.* (2009). As was illustrated in the literature review, these authors found that, in the USA, the higher the centrality of a firm in the network of collaborations, the lower the probability that it will choose to acquire. Their evidence seems to be more consistent with our substitution effect hypothesis. Despite the difference in the empirical approach (i.e. Lin *et al.* 2009 assume a single-firm focus while we adopted a dyadic perspective), the contrast in the findings may also be driven by differences in the empirical setting chosen for the analysis, with the other sample using data encompassing the whole electronic and electric equipment macro-industry (SIC code 36), while we focused just on the semiconductor industry (SIC code 3674). Their sample is quite heterogeneous and it includes sectors at different stages in their life cycle. The prevalence of a substitution effect in their sample might be due to an over-representation of firms in low-growth industries, where innovation is less frequent and knowledge is more codified.

Also the observed patterns captured by the other control variables may be specific to the semiconductor industry. For example, we found that geographical proximity increases the probability of an M&A, while we found only partial support for the prediction that overlaps in product markets increase this probability. In other empirical settings different patterns may be observed: for instance, a tendency to exploit M&As to diversify geographically or with respect to product markets may be observed. Overall, repeating our analysis in different sectors could shed additional light on the factors that determine the prevalence of one pattern over the other and considerably improve our understanding of the M&A market.

Finally, this study presents some limitations that pose the basis for further research. For instance, the analysis focused on the probability of a merger or an acquisition between the dyad *i-j*, without distinguishing between the possibility of *i* acquiring *j*, *j* acquiring *i*, or *i* and *j* merging. This represents just a first approximation of the reality. Despite the simplicity of this symmetric approach, the model produced significant results consistent with the predictions. Further research should develop a methodology to empirically distinguish between the case of a merger and an acquisition and adopt a directional approach for the case of an acquisition. However, the most relevant limitation of a study that tries to explain the probability of an acquisition as a function of past alliance links is the possibility of endogeneity. As far as unobserved factors affect both firms' preferences for collaboration partners (at time *t-1*) and acquisition targets (at time *t*), a spurious result can be obtained.[15] In order to reduce this concern, we tried to include all the factors that are likely to affect both acquisitions and partnerships. Such factors include geographical, product market, and technological proximity, as well as firm size. Despite these efforts, endogeneity could still be a concern for this study and further research should attempt to overcome this limitation.

Acknowledgements

The authors gratefully acknowledge the helpful comments of Thomas Rønde, the editor, and the reviewers on earlier versions of this article.

Notes

1 As described in the literature review, Yang *et al.* (2011) include marketing agreements among the "weak" types of partnerships, which they call *exploitation* alliances. Conversely, in our main model we include marketing agreements among the "strong" types of alliances (i.e. those that imply close interaction between partners). This is in line with other previous studies (e.g. Porrini 2004; Lin *et al.* 2009; Zaheer *et al.* 2010). Excluding marketing agreements from the cluster of "strong" alliances leaves our results substantially unchanged.
2 If the specific asset needed from an indirect partner concerns knowledge or some specific capabilities, an additional possibility arises. Let us say that firm A needs to gain access to some know-how possessed by C, and firm A is connected to B, while B to C. Since alliances allow firms to learn from their partners (Anand and Khanna 2000a), through time B may have learned the needed capabilities from C. It follows that eventually A can directly obtain them from B. This also reduces the incentives of the focal firm to acquire (or sign a direct alliance with) the third one.
3 Conglomerate companies were included in the initial sample if they satisfied simultaneously the following two criteria: they had at least 3674 as the secondary SIC code; and they had a subsidiary with 3674 as the primary SIC code. Similarly, foreign companies were included if they had a subsidiary in the US with primary SIC code 3674. Financial and patent data for these companies were included only if data specific to the semiconductor subsidiary were available.
4 Given that some firms engaged in an M&A during the years analyzed, their corresponding nodes in the network were merged into a single node if the target was completely acquired.

5 None of the announced deals in the final sample was eventually withdrawn.
6 The sample includes also acquisitions of single business units or divisions of another company (while the parent remained independent).
7 Some alliances involved more than two parties. In these cases it was assumed that each participant had a direct relation with all the other partners. Hence, multiple alliances were converted into dyadic relationships.
8 These data are in line with the findings of Hagedoorn and Sadowski (1999): These authors reported that joint-ventures are less likely than other contractual agreements in knowledge-intensive sectors characterized by rapid technological change. Indeed, industries characterized by a high rate of innovation are expected to require more organizational flexibility leading to a general preference for contractual agreements.
9 The risk set was adjusted for each year in order to take into account the companies that were completely acquired by others: dyads including these firms were excluded in the years following the acquisition as they were non-feasible combinations.
10 Implicit in this model is the assumption that information flow takes the shortest path between two agents. This assumption seems reasonable given the decreasing potential of indirect information transmission and the costs associated with indirect information access (Gulati 1995; Singh 2005; Sorenson et al. 2006).
11 While branches—as defined by Orbis—generally are direct extensions of the business of the headquarters, subsidiaries are sometimes operating in different businesses. For this reason we opted to exclude the subsidiaries' locations for computing the geographical proximity.
12 For each period of analysis and for each firm, this measure was calculated using UCINET 6 software package (Borgatti et al. 2002). We considered the normalized centrality measures.
13 Alternatively, the arithmetic mean was also computed. This produced similar results.
14 An assumption underlying the dyadic analysis is that observations in each year are independent from each other (Gulati 1995). This assumption is questionable since the presence of the same company in various dyads in the same year can lead to interdependence. This problem is also known as "common-actor effect" (Lincoln 1984) and can lead to inefficient parameter estimates. In order to test this concern, additional models have been estimated using the cluster option provided by the Relogit procedure in Stata®. This allows the estimation of a model when observations are interdependent within a cluster, but independent between clusters. These additional regressions present minimal changes in the statistics. This can be a sign that results are robust for interdependence across dyads.
15 For example, some authors proposed that, when deciding to acquire, firms can choose a more conservative strategy and use an alliance as a first step towards an M&A in order to pre-test the potential fit between the two firms (Mitchell and Singh 1992; Bowman and Hurry 1993; Mody 1993; Porrini 2004). If we consider alliances as a first step for M&As, we are assuming that the decision to acquire a given firm logically precedes the acquisition announcement. In this case, the selection of the target would occur when the alliance is signed and not at the time of the acquisition. Specifically, these authors provide supporting arguments for being concerned about endogeneity when considering M&As between firms that signed a direct partnership (i.e. dyads of firms with a network distance of one). Indeed, that alliance might be a "test" for a subsequent acquisition.

References

Ahuja, G. and Katila, R. (2001) "Technological acquisitions and the innovation performance of acquiring firms: a longitudinal study," Strategic Management Journal, 22: 197–220.
Ahuja, G., Polidoro, F., and Mitchell, W. (2009) "Structural homophily or social asymmetry? The formation of alliances by poorly embedded firms," Strategic Management Journal, 30: 941–58.
Anand, B.N. and Khanna, T. (2000a) "Do firms learn to create value? The case of alliances," Strategic Management Journal, 21: 295–315.
Anand, B.N. and Khanna, T. (2000b) "The structure of licensing contracts," Journal of Industrial Economics, 48: 103–35.
Baum, J.A.C., Li, S.X., and Usher, J.M. (2000) "Making the next move: how experiential and vicarious learning shape the locations of chains' acquisitions," Administrative Science Quarterly, 45: 766–801.
Besanko, D., Dranove, D., and Shanley, M. (2000) Economics of Strategy, 2nd edn., New York: John Wiley & Sons.

Bonacich, P. (1987) "Power and centrality: a family of measures," *American Journal of Sociology*, 92: 1170–82.

Borgatti, S.P., Everett, M.G., and Freeman, L.C. (2002) *Ucinet for Windows: Software for Social Network Analysis*, Harvard, MA: Analytic Technologies.

Bowman, E.H. and Hurry, D. (1993) "Strategy through the option lens: an integrated view of resource investments and the incremental-choice process," *Academy of Management Review*, 18: 760–82.

Chakrabarti, A. and Mitchell, W. (2013) "The persistent effect of geographic distance in acquisition target selection," *Organization Science*, Articles in Advance: 1–22.

Chatterjee, S., Lubatkin, M.H., Schweiger, D.M., and Weber, Y. (1992) "Cultural differences and shareholder value in related mergers: linking equity and human capital," *Strategic Management Journal*, 13: 319–34.

Cloodt, M., Hagedoorn, J., and Van Kranenburg, H. (2006) "Mergers and acquisitions: their effect on the innovative performance of companies in high-tech industries," *Research Policy*, 35: 642–54.

Coff, R.W. (1999) "How buyers cope with uncertainty when acquiring firms in knowledge-intensive industries: caveat emptor," *Organization Science*, 10: 144–61.

de Man, A.P. and Duysters, G. (2005) "Collaboration and innovation: a review of the effects of mergers, acquisitions and alliances on innovation," *Technovation*, 25: 1377–87.

Dyer, J.H. and Singh, H. (1998) "The relational view: cooperative strategy and sources of interorganizational competitive advantage," *The Academy of Management Review*, 23: 660–79.

Fleming, L. (2007) "Breakthroughs and the long tail of innovation," *MIT Sloan Management Review*, 49: 69–74.

Grote, M.H. and Umber, M.P. (2007) "Home biased? A spatial analysis of the domestic merging behavior of US firms," paper presented at the Financial Management Association Annual Meeting, Orlando, October 2007.

Gulati, R. (1995) "Social structure and alliance formation patterns: a longitudinal analysis," *Administrative Science Quarterly*, 40: 619–52.

Gulati, R. (1998) "Alliances and networks," *Strategic Management Journal*, 19: 293–317.

Gulati, R. (1999) "Network location and learning: the influence of network resources and firm capabilities on alliance formation," *Strategic Management Journal*, 20: 397–420.

Hagedoorn, J. and Sadowski, B. (1999) "The transition from strategic technology alliance to mergers and acquisitions: an exploratory study," *Journal of Management Studies*, 36: 87–106.

Hall, B.H., Jaffe, A.B., and Trajtenberg, M. (2001) "The NBER patent citation data file: lessons, insights and methodological tools," NBER Working Paper 8498.

Hayward, M.L.A. (2002) "When do firms learn from their acquisition experience? Evidence from 1990–1995," *Strategic Management Journal*, 23: 21–39.

Hennart, J.F. and Reddy, S. (1997) "The choice between mergers/acquisitions and joint ventures: the case of Japanese investors in the United States," *Strategic Management Journal*, 18: 1–12.

Jaffe, A.B. (1989) "Characterizing the 'technological position' of firms, with application to quantifying technological opportunity and research spillovers," *Research Policy*, 18: 87–97.

King, G. and Zeng, L. (1999) "Estimating absolute, relative, and attributable risks in case-control studies," Department of Government, Harvard University.

King, G. and Zeng, L. (2001) "Logistic regression in rare events data," *Political Analysis*, 9: 137–63.

Kogut, B. (1988) "A study of the life cycle of joint ventures," in F. Contractor and P. Lorange (eds.) *Cooperative Strategies in International Business*, Lexington, MA: Lexington Books.

Lahiri, N. (2010) "Geographic distribution of R&D activity: how does it affect innovation quality?," *Academy of Management Journal*, 53 (5): 1194–1209.

Lavie, D. (2007) "Alliance portfolios and firm performance: a study of value creation and appropriation in the U.S. software industry," *Strategic Management Journal*, 28: 1187–212.

Lin, Z.J., Peng, M.W., Yang, H., and Sun, S.L. (2009) "How do networks and learning drive M&As? An institutional comparison between China and the United States," *Strategic Management Journal*, 30: 1113–32.

Lincoln, J.R. (1984) "Analyzing relations in dyads," *Sociological Methods and Research*, 13: 45–76.

Luypaert, M. and Huyghebaert, N. (2006) "Determinants of growth through mergers and acquisitions: an empirical analysis," Working Paper. Department of Accountancy, Finance and Insurance, Katholieke Universiteit Leuven, European University College Brussels (EHSAL).

Miotti, L. and Sachwald, F. (2003) "Co-operative R&D: Why and with whom? An integrated framework of analysis," *Research Policy*, 32: 1481–99.

Mitchell, W. and Singh, K. (1992) "Incumbents' use of pre-entry alliances before expansion into new technical subfields of an industry," *Journal of Economic Behavior and Organization*, 18: 347–72.

Mody, A. (1993) "Learning through alliances," *Journal of Economic Behavior and Organization*, 20: 151–70.

Nonaka, I., Takeuchi, H., and Umemoto, K. (1996) "A theory of organizational knowledge creation," *International Journal of Technology Management*, 11: 833–84.

Paternoster, R., Brame, R., Mazerolle, P., and Piquero, A. (1998) "Using the correct statistical test for the equality of regression coefficients," *Criminology*, 36: 859–66.

Porrini, P. (2004) "Can a previous alliance between an acquirer and a target affect acquisition performance?," *Journal of Management*, 30: 545–62.

Reuer, J.J. and Ragozzino, R. (2008) "Adverse selection and M&A design: the roles of alliances and IPOs," *Journal of Economic Behavior & Organization*, 66: 195–212.

Singh, J. (2005) "Collaborative networks as determinants of knowledge diffusion patterns," *Management Science*, 51: 756–70.

Sorenson, O., Rivkin, J.W. and Fleming, L. (2006) "Complexity, networks and knowledge flow," *Research Policy*, 35: 994–1017.

Spence, A.M. (1974) *Market Signaling: Informational Transfer in Hiring and Related Screening Processes*, Cambridge, MA: Harvard University Press.

Tomz, M., King, G., and Zeng, L. (1999) *RELOGIT: Rare Events Logistic Regression*, Version 1.1, Cambridge, MA: Harvard University, Available at: http://gking.harvard.edu (accessed 1 November 2011).

Uzzi, B. (1996) "The sources and consequences of embeddedness for economic performance of organizations: the network effect," *American Sociological Review*, 61: 674–98.

Valentini, G. and Dawson, A. (2010) "Beyond knowledge bases: towards a better understanding of the effects of M&A on technological performance," in C. Cooper and S. Finkelstein (eds.) *Advances in Mergers and Acquisitions*, vol. 9: 177–97, Oxford: Elsevier.

Williamson, O.E. (1991) "Comparative economic organization: the analysis of discrete structural alternatives," *Administrative Science Quarterly*, 36: 269–96.

Yang, H., Lin, Z.J. and Peng, M.W. (2011) "Behind acquisitions of alliance partners: exploratory learning and network embeddedness," *Academy of Management Journal*, 54: 1069–80.

Zaheer, A., Hernandez, E., and Banerjee, S. (2010) "Prior alliances with targets and acquisition performance in knowledge-intensive industries," *Organization Science*, 21: 1072–91.

7

Chinese and Indian M&As in Europe

The relationship between motive and ownership choice

Lucia Piscitello, Roberta Rabellotti, and Vittoria Giada Scalera

Introduction[1]

Emerging country multinational enterprises (EMNEs) are increasingly involved in a process of international expansion in Europe through foreign direct investment (FDI), in the form of greenfield investments and mergers and acquisitions (M&As). Although EMNEs suffer late-comer disadvantages and lag behind incumbent multinational enterprises (MNEs) (Child and Rodrigues 2005), they become global players within a very short space of time. For example, since the mid-2000s they have been influential actors in the international scenario, challenging advanced country MNEs (AMNEs) in many different industries (Awate *et al.* 2012; Narula 2012; UNCTAD 2012).

This rapid and peculiar evolution has led to a flourishing literature focused on the characteristics and strategies of the EMNE internationalization process (among many others, see Ramamurti 2008, 2012). EMNEs have few accumulated firm-specific advantages and their strengths rely mainly on their specific home country advantages (e.g. low factor costs, state support). Therefore, their expansion abroad, especially in advanced countries, is likely to be driven by the search for technology, management and strategic skills, brands and commercial knowledge, which often are lacking in their home countries (Rugman 2009). In fact, their internationalization can be considered mainly as a strategy aimed at accumulating resources (see among others: Awate *et al.* 2012; Child and Rodrigues 2005; Li *et al.* 2012; Makino *et al.* 2002) and appropriating strategic assets (Dunning 1993). Cross-border acquisition of companies in advanced countries is considered the fastest and most effective means of accessing strategic assets and key capabilities (Chung and Alcacer 2002).

EMNEs investing in more advanced economies face technological and commercial competitive disadvantages (Deng 2009; Gammeltoft *et al.* 2010). In addition, they also suffer from the *liability of emergingness* due to lack of reputation and legitimacy (Madhok and Keyhani 2012; Yildiz 2013) and the disadvantage with respect to advanced country firms of a knowledge gap which may severely limit their absorptive capacity to acquire and incorporate external knowledge (Cohen and Levinthal 1990).

Within this context, a crucial trade-off in EMNEs' acquisition of foreign companies is the extent of equity ownership, which has major implications for resource commitments, performance and risk (Anderson and Gatignon 1986; De Beule *et al.* 2014). The resource-based view (RBV) and transaction cost economics (TCE) approaches suggest that complete acquisition of the target company provides access to embedded knowledge and competences and minimizes transaction costs through full control over the foreign activities (Barney 1991; Williamson 1975). However, partial acquisition may be preferable because takeover implies radical organizational change and may result in the dispersion of the core competences developed by local managers and key employees (Cannella and Hambrick 1993). In this case, EMNEs may prefer to maintain a local partner, particularly if the main motive for the investment is the acquisition of knowledge and competences.

In this chapter, we develop an empirical analysis of EMNEs' ownership choices in M&As undertaken in Europe and investigate the relationship with the underlying motives. We investigate the relationship between the ownership choices of EMNEs acquiring firms in advanced countries and the motivation for their investment. The analysis is focused on Chinese and Indian acquisitions in Europe between 2003 and 2011. In particular, we relate ownership choice, that is, the level of commitment of Chinese and Indian MNEs to the target companies, to the motives underlying their investments. Data on M&As come from a newly created database, EMENDATA (Emerging Multinationals Events and Networks DATAbase) that combines data from BvD Zephyr and SDC Platinum. Information on motives is based on companies' public announcements published in Lexis-Nexis. We conduct qualitative content analysis which shows that Chinese and Indian acquisitions in Europe are motivated by the search for knowledge, market and legitimacy. We propose an econometric model to investigate the relationship between motive and ownership choice in order to provide new quantitative evidence on the technological upgrading strategies pursued by EMNEs in Europe.

Conceptual framework and research hypotheses

Ownership choices

A difference between EMNEs' and AMNEs' international expansion is that in the former case it is aimed not at exploiting existing ownership advantages (Dunning 1993), but rather at building sustainable global competitive capacity by extending their networks of relationships and boosting their home country advantages (Buckley *et al.* 2007; Mathews 2006; Ramamurti 2008; Rugman and Li 2007). EMNE investment in more advanced countries is usually market- and/or strategic asset-seeking FDI (Deng 2009; Luo and Tung 2007). Acquisition is often chosen in order to access technological knowledge and other strategic resources in advanced market companies. It can enable direct access to sophisticated competences and skilled labour, and allow exploitation of local knowledge and development of formal and/or informal collaborations and networks with local actors such as suppliers, customers, universities and research centres (Cantwell and Mudambi 2011; Li *et al.* 2012).

When acquiring a company, a critical consideration is the level of equity ownership in the acquired company. The level of ownership in the target firm represents the level of commitment to the foreign activity (Chari and Chang 2009). Degree of ownership affects several factors such as the effective transfer of tacit and tangible assets, risk sharing between the acquiring and target firms, resource commitment and control over activities (Anderson and Gatignon 1986; Barkema and Vermeulen 1998; Brouthers and Hennart 2007).

According to the RBV (e.g. Barney 1991), full acquisition of the local target company allows the investing firm to access the knowledge and competences embedded in the company

(Barkema and Vermeulen 1998). Similarly, TCE theorizes that a higher level of control is needed to reduce the transaction costs involved (Madhok 1997). Based on these arguments, foreign investors generally should prefer a high level of control to achieve complete access to the knowledge and technological competences rooted in the acquired company.

However, MNEs often choose low levels of equity ownership, and there are theoretical and empirical explanations for shared ownership (Chari and Chang 2009; Mariotti *et al.* 2014). Complete acquisition of the target firm implies radical organizational changes and can disrupt its embedded core competences and result in huge losses for the acquirer (Jemison and Sitkin 1986). In the case of full acquisition, the acquiring firm may find it difficult to motivate the acquired firm's managers and employees, who may underinvest in new competences, behave opportunistically and hold up the transfer of critical tacit assets such as technological knowledge, or even leave their jobs (Chen and Hennart 2004). There is a large literature (e.g. Cannella and Hambrick 1993) showing that turnover rate in acquired top management teams is significantly higher than the normal turnover rate and that exit of managers after an M&A involves loss of critical knowledge resources, thus lowering the performance of the target firm. Alternatively, partial ownership gives the acquiring company the opportunity to share investments and risks (Anderson and Gatignon 1986; Kogut and Zander 1993). This is likely to be more relevant in the case of EMNEs investing in advanced countries where *liability of emergingness* represents an additional disadvantage that hinders the acquisition of legitimacy and capabilities (De Beule *et al.* 2014; Madhok and Keyhani 2012). The different host country environment, limited absorptive capacity and lack of reputation increase the EMNEs' need to rely on local employees and managers who embody competences and know-how which may be tacit and difficult to acquire. Hence, our first hypothesis is:

> Hypothesis 1: EMNEs are more likely to acquire a lower equity share in cross-border M&As motivated by knowledge seeking.

However, the chosen level of ownership in the target company depends also on the characteristics of the target firms. In particular, the degree of uncertainty in cross-border acquisitions may be higher if the dissimilarity (in terms of culture, knowledge base, managerial style and labour skills) among the partners is high. Specifically, the literature highlights three types of dissimilarity between target and acquiring company (Barkema and Vermeulen 1998; Chari and Chang 2009).

The first is cultural distance, and evidence on its relationship with level of ownership commitment in the target company is mixed. On the one hand, a culturally distant environment can hinder the transfer of intra-organizational practices, thus, encouraging full ownership and greater control of the parent company. On the other hand, in unfamiliar environments, MNEs may prefer shared equity with local partners to ease their adaptation to the local context (Barkema and Vermeulen 1998; Hennart and Larimo 1998). In the case of EMNEs acquiring firms in advanced countries and facing high uncertainty due to high cultural distance, we expect that they will recognize the importance of local resources and choose a lower level of equity ownership to retain the local partner.

The second is dissimilar knowledge bases, which may influence the acquirer's equity ownership decision. It is well known that the transfer of routines and knowledge can be difficult in a new environment (Cohen and Bacdayan 1994), and firms expanding into unrelated businesses may encounter several problems related to absorption of acquired technological capabilities (Harrison *et al.* 1991; Ranft and Lord 2002). The transfer of competences and capabilities may require very close cooperation with the acquired company to achieve learning by the acquiring firm. When EMNEs invest in unrelated sectors, partial ownership may mitigate knowledge transfer problems.

The third type of dissimilarity is related to the external business environment. A turbulent business environment can increase uncertainty and is especially relevant in high-tech compared to low-tech sectors. Firm acquisitions in high-tech industries are more likely to represent opportunities for learning and accessing knowledge-intensive assets such as specialized human resources, innovative technologies and specialized knowledge (Chen and Hennart 2004). The high uncertainty and risk of adverse selection in high-tech industries drive the acquiring firm to pursue a lower level of commitment (Reuer *et al.* 2004). Therefore, we expect EMNEs acquiring firms in high-tech rather than low-tech industries to pursue a lower level of commitment in the target company.

Accordingly, our second set of hypotheses is:

Hypothesis 2a: EMNEs' equity shareholding will be lower in more culturally distant compared to culturally closer target firms.
Hypothesis 2b: EMNEs acquire lower equity shares in target firms operating in unrelated sectors.
Hypothesis 2c: EMNEs' equity shareholding will be lower in acquired high-tech target firms compared to their shareholding in low-tech companies.

Motives and ownership choices

According to the extant literature, firms' ownership choices may be related to the motive and strategies underlying the acquisition as well as the types of activities, strategies and structures of the firms involved (for a survey, see Brouthers and Hennart 2007). Firms with fewer technological capabilities generally undertake knowledge-seeking investments to fill their technology gap through the acquisition of innovative firms and access to their resources (Wesson 2004). Thus, for EMNEs seeking to acquire superior technological capabilities, the local advanced country partner plays a strategic role. Indeed, cooperation with the foreign target company mitigates problems related to the liability of foreignness and cultural differences, and the knowledge gap between the acquiring and target firms (Chen and Hennart 2004). The tacit nature of the knowledge and the highly sophisticated capabilities required in high-tech industries mean that the learning processes of EMNEs need to be supported by the acquired firms. Therefore, if the EMNE's motive for investment is knowledge seeking, we expect the effect of dissimilarity between target and acquiring firm to be stronger, since it will hinder the efficient transfer of knowledge. In this case, the EMNE will be likely to rely on the local partner to acquire knowledge and, thus, will prefer a lower level of commitment in the target company. Our third hypothesis is:

Hypothesis 3: Hypotheses 2a–2c will be more likely to hold if EMNEs invest for knowledge-seeking reasons.

Data

The sample

The empirical analysis is based on acquisitions undertaken by Chinese and Indian companies, in high- and medium-high-tech industries in the 27 European countries in 2003–2011. Data on acquisitions are from EMENDATA, which combines BvD Zephyr and SDC Platinum records and provides deal-level information (e.g. type, date, value, degree of ownership) and general information on the target and acquiring companies (e.g. country, region and city of origin, activities, sectors). The initial sample includes 230 acquisitions: 76 (33 per cent) from China and 154 (67 percent) from India.

Previous studies provide empirical evidence that investments for knowledge-sourcing reasons are particularly relevant in high-tech manufacturing industries (Cloodt *et al.* 2006), and especially in the case of EMNEs investing in advanced economies (Awate *et al.* 2012; Govindarajan and Ramamurti 2011). Therefore, we focus on knowledge-intensive manufacturing acquirers in high- and medium-high-tech sectors, identified on the basis of the Eurostat-OECD (2007) classification (King *et al.* 2008).[2]

The sample excludes: 1) deals undertaken by individual or unknown investors; 2) operations with undisclosed acquirers and/or targets; 3) investments where the acquirer is a sovereign wealth fund (SWF), or the global ultimate owner (GUO) is not from China or India. It also excludes acquisitions for which we have insufficient information to identify the main underlying motive. The final sample includes 170 acquisitions, representing 74 per cent of the initial sample: 53 (31 per cent) undertaken by Chinese firms and 117 (69 per cent) by Indian MNEs. Table 7.1 presents sample characteristics by year and host country. The acquisitions in the sample involve 18 target European countries, among which the UK, Germany and France are the most popular for Chinese and Indian MNEs.

Motives

To classify the main motive for each acquisition, we perform qualitative content analysis to categorize the textual information provided by companies' public announcements. We rely on

Table 7.1 Distribution of the 170 acquisitions by host country and year of investment (no., %)

Host country	2003–2005		2006–2008		2009–2011		Total	
	China	India	China	India	China	India	China	India
Belgium (no.)	0	3	2	3	0	2	2	8
%	0.00	9.37	9.09	5.45	0.00	6.67	3.77	6.84
France (no.)	1	4	4	3	5	3	10	10
%	16.67	12.50	18.18	5.45	20.00	10.00	18.87	8.55
Germany (no.)	2	5	6	12	5	4	13	21
%	33.33	15.62	27.27	21.82	20.00	13.33	24.53	17.95
Italy (no.)	1	0	2	7	3	4	6	11
%	16.67	0.00	9.09	12.73	12.00	13.33	11.32	9.40
Netherlands (no.)	1	2	3	3	4	1	8	6
%	16.67	6.25	13.64	5.45	16.00	3.33	15.09	5.13
Spain (no.)	0	3	1	4	0	2	1	9
%	0.00	9.37	4.54	7.27	0.00	6.67	1.89	7.69
Sweden (no.)	0	1	0	2	3	0	3	3
%	0.00	3.12	0.00	3.64	12.00	0.00	5.66	2.56
UK (no.)	1	10	3	12	0	12	4	34
%	16.67	31.25	13.64	21.82	0.00	40.00	7.55	29.06
Others (no.)	0	4	1	9	5	2	6	15
%	0.00	12.50	4.54	16.36	20.00	6.67	11.32	12.82
Total (no.)	6	32	22	55	25	30	53	117

a deductive category application (Weber 1990) to analyse the text in these announcements in order to identify the main motive underlying each acquisition.

Based on the main FDI motives suggested by Dunning's (1977, 1993) eclectic paradigm, and using an iterative process (feedback loops), we identified market- and strategic-asset-seeking investments, which are the typical types of FDI from emerging to advanced economies (Buckley *et al.* 2007; Ramamurti 2008). We also identified the motive of global legitimacy seeking, which is a quite relevant motive for EMNEs investing in Europe and in advanced countries more generally (Cui and Jiang 2009). We developed explicit definitions, examples and coding rules (Table 7.2) for each deductive category in order to determine unequivocally under what circumstances an announcement can be coded to a certain category (Weber 1990). The qualitative analysis consists of reading, analysing and methodologically assigning a unique category to each announcement.

Following the defined coding rules, two trained researchers carefully read each document to identify the main motive for the investment, and hand-code it. The reliability of the codification process was tested by measuring the level of agreement between coders (Neuendorf 2002) and showed 87 per cent correspondence.

The primary source for public announcements and deal information is LexisNexis, which provides access to billions of searchable documents and records from more than 45,000 legal, news and business sources. We integrated this information with the annual reports and official websites of both acquirer and target firms. Table 7.3 reports the distribution of acquisitions across the three main investment motives, distinguishing between Chinese and Indian MNEs. Total acquisitions are classified as: knowledge seeking 60 (35.29 per cent), market seeking 57 (33.53 per cent) and global legitimacy seeking 53 (31.18 per cent).

Table 7.2 The coding methodology

Category	Definition	Examples	Coding rules
Knowledge-seeking M&A	The acquiring company searches for R&D capacity, innovative products or production processes, design facilities, patent portfolios of local firms and knowledge spillovers provided by the target firm.	'Complementary capabilities between Mahindra & GRD will enhance the product development capabilities, provide a solid European footprint for M&M to leverage technologies & skillsets by harnessing the talent pool of designers and engineers', [Mr Pawan Goenka, President of the Automotive Sector of Mahindra Group] (Mahindra & Mahindra Ltd. acquired G.R. Grafica Ricerca Design SRL in 2008). *Source: Mahindra & Mahindra Ltd. website.*	If at least one of the aspects cited in the definition of *Knowledge-seeking M&A* is mentioned as the main or the only motive of the investment.

(Continued)

Table 7.2 Continued

Market-seeking M&A	The investment is aimed at reaching local or regional markets, often including neighbouring countries. Underlying these types of investments there are trade support reasons, e.g. to access distribution facilities, to facilitate exports, to acquire brand names.	'The acquisition of majority stake in MSI provides immense synergy benefits to both RSB and MSI. RSB, which exports substantial heavy fabrications to Europe, can now have a front-end presence in Europe to consolidate and grow its exports offered by RSB-MSI combine'. [Mr. S.K. Behera, Vice Chairman of RSB Trasmissions India Ltd.] (RSB Transmissions India Ltd. acquired Mechanical Supplies International NV in 2010). *Source: LexisNexis.*	If at least one of the aspects cited in the definition of *Market-seeking M&A* is mentioned as the main or the only motive of the investment.
Global-legitimacy-seeking M&A	The MNE's primary goal in undertaking the acquisition is to become a global player and to gain strategic positions in the global value chain, leveraging the international reputation of the target company. These M&As have a global/international strategic orientation rather than a multidomestic/regional one.	'The acquisition will significantly strengthen the company's position in the global Passenger Car & Chassis Component business and is a step towards attaining global leadership'. [Mr B. N. Kalyani, Chairman and Managing Director of Bharat Forge Ltd.] (Bharat Forge Ltd. acquired CDP Aluminiumtechnik GmbH & Co. in 2004). *Source: Bharat Forge Ltd. website.*	If at least one of the aspects cited in the definition of *Global-legitimacy-seeking M&A* is mentioned as the main or the only motive of the investment.

Table 7.3 Distribution of the 170 acquisitions by main motive of the investment (no., %)

Motive	China	India	Total
Knowledge-seeking (no.)	24	36	60
%	45.28	30.77	35.29
Market-seeking (no.)	16	39	55
%	30.19	33.33	33.53
Global-leg.-seeking (no.)	13	42	55
%	24.53	35.90	31.18
Total	53	117	170

The procedure described above is an application of direct content analysis appropriate when 'existing theory or prior research about a phenomenon that is incomplete would benefit from further description', with the aim 'to validate or extend conceptually a theoretical framework or theory' (Hsieh and Shannon 2005: 1281). Most studies of cross-border investment motives use approaches developed for AMNE contexts, that is, they use host country characteristics to proxy for FDI motives, and categorize FDI in low-cost countries as resource/labour seeking, and FDI in large markets as market seeking. However, Wang et al. (2012) point out that these aggregate measures may be inadequate for understanding how acquisition motives differ from firm to firm. Therefore, in the present analysis we introduce complementary definitions of FDI motives, using firm- and deal-level data to combine traditional FDI explanations with the peculiar characteristics of EMNEs.

Econometric analysis

Dependent variable

The dependent variable is *Share of equity* acquired by the EMNE in the target company. Table 7.4 presents the minimum, maximum, mean and standard deviation of the dependent variable values, distinguishing between Chinese and Indian acquirers. In Table 7.4, full acquisitions are represented by *Share of equity* taking the value 1 (100 per cent); if the dependent variable is lower than 1 (i.e. acquisition of less than 100 per cent of the target firm's equity), this is a partial acquisition. The high incidence of complete ownership is consistent with prior research showing Chinese and Indian firms' preferences for full ownership control over foreign operations (De Beule *et al.* 2014; Sun *et al.* 2012).

Explanatory variables

Knowledge-seeking M&As

The variable *Knowledge seeking* is a dummy that takes the value 1 if the principal motive for the acquisition is access to the technology and knowledge embedded in the target company, and 0 otherwise (i.e. if the acquisition is primarily market seeking or global legitimacy seeking). We showed that 60 out of 170 (35.39 per cent) investments were for knowledge-seeking purposes. Since EMNEs need to cooperate with the local partner to ensure smooth transfer of knowledge and competences, it is likely that they will seek a lower level of commitment in the target company. Therefore, we expect a negative relationship between the dummy *Knowledge seeking* and our dependent variable.

Table 7.4 Distribution of the 170 acquisitions by entry mode (no., %) and share of equity

	China	India	Total
Acquisitions			
Full (no.)	31	87	118
%	58.49	74.36	69.41
Partial (no.)	22	30	52
%	41.51	25.64	30.59
Total (no.)	53	117	170
Share of equity			
Mean	0.81	0.89	0.87
Std Dev.	0.28	0.23	0.25
Min.	0.07	0.10	0.07
Max.	1	1	1

Cultural distance

To measure the cultural distance between China/India and each host country we adopt the traditional index of cultural distance[3] based on Kogut and Singh (1988), which includes the four cultural dimensions of power distance, uncertainty avoidance, masculinity/femininity and individualism, introduced by Hofstede (1980). Thus, cultural distance is defined as:

$$Cultural\ Distance\ (CD)_{jh} = \frac{\sum_{1=1}^{4}\left\{\dfrac{\left(I_{ij}-I_{ih}\right)^2}{V_i}\right\}}{4}$$

where *Cultural distance* $(CD)_{jh}$ is the cultural distance between the home country h and the host country j, Iij is the cultural distance index ith for the jth host country, Iih is the cultural distance index ith for the hth home country, and Vi is the variance of the cultural distance index ith. The data come from Hofstede Centre (http://geert-hofstede.com/the-hofstede-centre.html). Given that higher values of the cultural distance index indicate larger differences between China/India and the host country, we expect a negative correlation between the CD index and the dependent variable.

Relatedness and dissimilarity

To account for whether ownership decisions are affected by dissimilarity between the knowledge bases of the acquiring and target firms (Harrison *et al.* 1991), we include a dummy variable, *Target service sector*, which takes the value of 1 if the primary NACE code of the target firm is in a service sector industry (NACE two-digit Rev.2 45–96 inclusive), and 0 otherwise.[4] In our sample, 28 out of 170 (16.47 per cent) are acquisitions of a service sector target firm operating and 142 (83.53 per cent) are manufacturing sector acquisitions. Data on the primary industry of the target company are from BvD Zephyr and SDC Platinum. Since manufacturing MNEs suffer from higher uncertainty (caused by differences in knowledge bases) if the target company is specialized in services, they will likely commit to lower level of equity than if the target is a manufacturing company (Barkema and Vermeulen 1998). Therefore, we expect a negative relationship between the dummy *Target service sector* and our dependent variable.

Technological intensity of the target company

To account for the technological intensity of the target company, we introduce the dummy variable *Target tech industry*, which takes the value 1 if the target company operates in a high- or medium-high-tech industry according to the Eurostat-OECD (2007) classification, based on

Table 7.5 Distribution of the 170 acquisitions by technology intensity of the target company

Target sector	China	India	Total
High-tech (no.)	38	95	133
%	71.70	81.20	78.24
Low-tech (no.)	15	22	37
%	28.30	18.80	21.76
Total	53	117	170

data provided in BvD Zephyr and SDC Platinum. Table 7.5 shows the distribution of the 170 acquisitions between high- and non-high-tech industries. We expect a negative relationship between the dummy *Target tech industry* and our dependent variable *Share of equity*.

Control variables

Host country variables

To control for market growth in the host country, we introduce the variable *GDP* [gross domestic product] *growth*. According to previous empirical analyses (e.g. Barkema and Vermeulen 1998; Gomes-Casseres 1990), host market growth influences the level of ownership commitment; shared ownership is preferred over full acquisition in host countries showing high market growth. We measure host country GDP growth as host country annual GDP growth rate in the year before the acquisition (based on World Bank Development Indicator data).

The variable *Host cross-border M&As* measures the relative attractiveness of the host country with respect to entry by foreign firms. The international business literature has highlighted that rival companies' presence in a host country is based on a strategy of achieving global market presence, especially in markets regarded as attractive (Hamel and Prahalad 1985). Previous studies suggest also that the relative attractiveness of the host country market may affect the level of commitment in cross-border acquisitions (Chari and Chang 2009; Folta 1998). Thus, following Chari and Chang (2009), we measure *Host cross-border M&As* as the percentage of worldwide cross-border M&As in the target country in the year prior to the focal acquisition. Data are from the UNCTAD Cross-border M&A database.

Industry of the acquiring firm

In order to control for industry-specific effects that might influence the M&A ownership decision, we introduce four sectoral dummies (*Electronics, Machinery* and *Transport*, with *Chemicals* as the benchmark) based on NACE two-digit Rev. 2 20 and 21. In our sample, 60 acquisitions (35.39 per cent) are in the chemical and pharmaceutical industry, 30 acquisitions (17.65 per cent) in the electronic and electrical manufacturing sector, 31 (18.24 per cent) in the machinery industry and 49 (28.82 per cent) in the transport industry. Data on the acquirer's primary industry come from BvD Zephyr and SDC Platinum.

Year dummies

Finally, since we pool data over a 9-year period characterized by strong macroeconomic turbulence, we control for the years of the financial crisis by adding two dummy variables for acquisitions in 2006 or 2007 (*Year t* for t = 2006, 2007). In this way, we account for macroeconomic shocks that might affect the cross-border investment activity. During the financial crisis, there is a general tendency for aggressive takeover of foreign firms by EMNEs, which exploit their liquidity advantages and home country government support, and capitalize on the financial exigencies of – especially advanced country – target firms (Peng 2012).

Model and methodology

To test our hypotheses, we employ the following model:

$$Share\ of\ equity_i = \beta_0 + \beta_1\ Tech\text{-}seeking_i + \beta_2\ Cultural\ distance_i + \beta_3\ Target$$
$$service\ sector_i + \beta_4\ Target\ tech\ industry_i + \beta_5\ Controls + \varepsilon_i$$

where $i = 1, 2, \ldots, 170$ are the acquisition events.

Table 7.6 Descriptive statistics

	Obs.	Mean	Std Dev.	Min.	Max.	Data Source
Share of equity	170	0.87	0.25	0.07	1	BvD Zephyr/SDC
Knowledge seeking	170	0.35	0.48	0	1	LexisNexis
Cultural distance	170	2.35	1.07	0.84	5.32	Hofstede Centre
Target service sector	170	0.16	0.37	0	1	BvD Zephyr/SDC
Target tech industry	170	0.78	0.41	0	1	BvD Zephyr/SDC
GDP growth	170	1.81	2.75	-6.80	8.40	World Bank
Host cross-border M&As	170	0.06	0.07	0	0.21	UNCTAD

Given that our dependent variable is bounded between 0 and 1, we estimate a Tobit regression model, which accounts for both left and right censoring of *Share of equity* (Green 1993). Since some of the deals in the sample (53 observations, 31.18 per cent of the whole sample) are acquisitions made by the same firm, we control for lack of independence between observations. Similar to the approach in Chari and Chang (2009) and Folta and Miller (2002), we use the cluster option which corrects for this problem by computing robust standard errors that account for observations clustered by firms. Table 7.6 provides the descriptive statistics of the dependent and explanatory variables; Table 7.7 presents the correlation matrix. Variance inflation factor rules out multicollinearity problems influencing our results.

RESULTS

Table 7.8 presents the estimated coefficients in our econometric models. Column 1 (Model 1) reports the results of the basic equation model. Note that the variable *Knowledge seeking* has a negative and significant coefficient (at $p<0.05$), showing that EMNEs prefer a lower equity share when investing to acquire knowledge and competences. This confirms Hypothesis 1.

In relation to the characteristics of investors, we analyse the impact of cultural distance. The coefficient of *Cultural distance* is not significant, which does not support Hypothesis 2a. With

Table 7.7 Correlation matrix

	(1)	(2)	(3)	(4)	(5)	(6)	(7)
(1) Share of equity	1						
(2) Knowledge seeking	-0.230	1					
(3) Cultural distance	-0.140	0.226	1				
(4) Target service sector	-0.065	0.061	-0.058	1			
(5) Target tech industry	-0.193	0.203	0.093	-0.304	1		
(6) GDP growth	0.170	-0.172	-0.194	0.122	-0.111	1	
(7) Host cross-border M&As	0.068	-0.026	-0.239	-0.097	0.061	0.045	1

Note: Correlations over ±0.12 significant (p < 0.10)

respect to the impact of dissimilarities in the knowledge base and the relatedness between the target company and the acquirer, on the dependent variable, *Target service sector* is significant (at $p<0.10$) and negatively affects the level of commitment of EMNEs. Thus, according to Hypothesis 2b, dissimilarities in the knowledge base between the acquiring and the target firms lead to a lower level of ownership (Barkema and Vermeulen 1998). For the industry-specific effect, we find that the coefficient of *Target tech industry* is negative and significant (at $p<0.10$). This supports Hypothesis 2c; so the acquiring firm prefers a lower level of ownership if the target firm is specialized in a high-tech industry.

In order to test Hypothesis 3, we split the sample of acquisitions into two sub-samples, distinguishing between knowledge-seeking and other investments (Models 2 and 3, respectively). The results show that target firm- and industry-specific variables have different impacts on the dependent variable if the acquisition is aimed at acquiring knowledge. In line with our expectations, we find that the sign on cultural distance differs between the two acquisition sub-samples. The coefficient of *Cultural distance* is negative in Model 2 but in Model 3 turns positive, although not significant at the conventional level.

Table 7.8 Tobit regression analysis (dep. variable = share of equity)

	Model 1		Knowledge-seeking M&As Model 2		Other M&As Model 3	
Knowledge seeking	-0.290	**				
	(0.113)					
Cultural distance	-0.020		-0.070		0.002	
	(0.058)		(0.083)		(0.075)	
Target service sector	-0.289	*	-0.286	*	-0.253	
	(0.165)		(0.168)		(0.272)	
Target tech industry	-0.233	*	-0.318	*	-0.155	
	(0.140)		(0.190)		(0.200)	
GDP growth	0.061		0.067		0.092	
	(0.060)		(0.063)		(0.087)	
Host cross-border M&As	0.070		-0.088		0.239	**
	(0.065)		(0.076)		(0.119)	
Electronics	-0.070		-0.109		-0.045	
	(0.184)		(0.223)		(0.249)	
Machinery	-0.026		-0.208		0.111	
	(0.168)		(0.206)		(0.279)	
Transport	-0.009		-0.061		-0.108	
	(0.146)		(0.228)		(0.211)	
Year	yes		yes		yes	
Cons	1.680	***	1.427	***	1.726	***
	(0.182)		(0.250)		(0.262)	
No.	170		60		110	
Pseudo R-sq.	0.094		0.097		0.073	

Note: Variables have been standardized. Standard errors are robust after adjusting for clustering by acquirer. Standard errors in parentheses
* $p<0.1$; ** $p<0.05$; *** $p<0.01$

The variables *Target service sector* and *Target tech industry* are negative and significant (at $p<0.1$) only if the acquisition is aimed at gaining knowledge. In other words, if the EMNE acquisition is to access know-how and technical competences embodied in the target firm, then the presence of a local partner is preferred (i.e. the acquirer has a lower level of commitment to the acquired firm) to maximize the opportunities for learning, especially in the case of unrelated knowledge bases.

Among the control variables, the coefficient of *Host cross-border M&As*, that is, the presence of foreign M&As in the host country, is positive and significant ($p<0.05$) only in Model 3, and seems to have no impact on ownership choice for acquisitions aimed at knowledge seeking.

As a robustness check, we test our hypotheses using an alternative econometric specification. We categorize the dependent variable *Share of equity* into three ordered categories (100 per cent, equal to or greater than 100 per cent but below 50 per cent, and below 50 per cent) running a robust Ordered Probit regression. The results show similar behaviour of the explanatory variables, which increases our confidence in the findings.[5]

Conclusions

Acquisitions of European companies by Chinese and Indian MNEs have increased dramatically in the last decade. The literature emphasizes that this activity is aimed mainly at acquiring strategic assets and competences from more advanced companies. However, MNE acquisitions of firms in foreign markets can be based on different strategies and different levels of commitment; they may involve full buy-out, or partial acquisition of the target company and retention of an important role for the local partner. Research shows that this choice depends on firm-, country- and industry-specific factors. This paper contributes by including the acquisition motives and their influence as a moderating factor in the relationship with ownership choice.

This paper contributes to the literature on entry mode by investigating the level of equity and control in cross border acquisitions, a topic that has been largely neglected so far. We also add to the empirical literature on EMNEs' internationalization strategies and work on acquisitions of advanced country firms (e.g. De Beule *et al.* 2014). Our empirical analysis shows that Chinese and Indian MNEs prefer less control if the objective of the acquisition is technological competences rather than a customer base or established brand name. We show also that firm-level and industry-level characteristics have different impacts on the ownership decision depending on the reason for the acquisition. To classify deals according to their main aim, we introduced a novel methodology based on content analysis applied to the information provided in public announcements and company reports. We find that, when acquiring companies in Europe with the aim of accessing technical competences, EMNEs prefer a low level of commitment because of the prospective partner's dissimilar knowledge and highly specific resources.

The study has some limitations that point to opportunities for future research. The major one is the limited number of observations, and the availability of information about the deals, included in the empirical analysis. The problems related to obtaining financial and accounting information about target and acquirer firms reduces the ability to account for relevant firm-specific characteristics such as R&D intensity. Also, although the smaller number of observations allowed hand coding, in larger samples, the procedure could be improved by the use of statistical techniques to identify recurring key words. Another possible limitation is the exclusion of managerial motives in the coding. Further research should examine the applicability of managerial motivations for EMNE acquisitions (for an overview, see Trautwein 1990). Our results could be replicated using alternative measures for cultural distance, although the one applied here is the most frequent in the international business and management literature (Ambos and Hakanson 2014). Shenkar

(2001) points out that most cultural distance indexes and constructs (e.g. Hofstede 1980; Kogut and Singh 1988) oversimplify the relationship between countries, implicitly assuming lack of corporate culture variance (e.g. Hofstede *et al.* 1990). Traditional measures do not assume hetero-geneity among individuals and firms (Zaheer *et al.* 2012), despite empirical results that show that corporate culture can modify the behaviour related to national traditions (Weber *et al.* 1996). This issue is particularly evident in cross-border M&As involving emerging and advanced economies companies. Although we tested the impact of the different motives underlying acquisitions on the ownership decision, future research could investigate other possible moderating effects which might play a role in the entry mode choice. It would be interesting to study how different own-ership strategies affect the innovative performance of the EMNE with respect to initial motive for the investment and the characteristics of the acquiring company. Finally, this empirical exercise could pave the way to future efforts aimed at crafting a conceptual framework within which EMNEs' behaviour and strategies could be better framed and understood.

Notes

1 This paper is an output of the project 'The challenge of globalization: Technology driven foreign direct investment (TFDI) and its implications for the negotiation of International (bi and multilateral) Invest-ment Agreements' funded by the Riksbankens Jubileumsfond.
2 The 2-digit manufacturing industries according to the NACE Rev. 2 classification included in the sam-ple are: pharmaceuticals (20), chemicals (21), computer, electronic and optical products (26), electrical equipment and components (27), machinery and other equipment (28), motor vehicles (29) and other transport equipment (30).
3 Note that, since the effect of distance is a central issue in international management and international business, alternative measures have been suggested. However, and despite some critiques (e.g. Shenkar 2001), the Kogut and Singh index has proved the most popular so far (for a recent focus on the issue of distance in international management, see Special Issue of the *Journal of International Management* on 'The concept of distance in international management research', 2014).
4 Note that, although the concept of relatedness refers to the applicability of the resources and capabilities owned by the company to the new business (Piscitello 2004; Robins and Wiersema 2003), it generally is operationalized by proximity within the SIC-defined system. Thus, although our proxy refers to a rather aggregated industrial classification, it is in line with the measures employed in the literature.
5 The results of this analysis are available from the authors upon request.

References

Ambos, B. and Hakanson L. (2014) 'The concept of distance in international management research', *Journal of International Management*, 20: 1–7.
Anderson, E. and Gatignon, H. (1986) 'Modes of foreign entry: a transaction cost analysis and propositions', *Journal of International Business Studies*, 17: 1–26.
Awate, S., Larsen, M.M. and Mudambi, R. (2012) 'EMNE catch-up strategies in the wind turbine industry: is there a trade-off between output and innovation capabilities?', *Global Strategy Journal*, 2: 205–23.
Barkema, H.G. and Vermeulen, F. (1998) 'International expansion through start-up or acquisition: a learning perspective', *Academy of Management Journal*, 47: 7–26.
Barney, J. (1991) 'Firm resources and sustained competitive advantage', *Journal of Management*, 17: 99–120.
Brouthers, K. and Hennart, J. (2007) 'Boundaries of the firm: insights from international entry mode research', *Journal of Management*, 33: 395–425.
Buckley, P.J., Clegg, J., Cross, A.R., Liu, X., Voss, H. and Zheng, P. (2007) 'The determinants of Chinese outward foreign direct investment', *Journal of International Business Studies*, 38: 499–518.
Cannella, Jr, A.A. and Hambrick, D.C. (1993) 'Effects of executive departures on the performance of acquired firms', *Strategic Management Journal*, 14: 137–52.
Cantwell, J.A. and Mudambi, R. (2011) 'Physical attraction and the geography of knowledge sourcing in multinational enterprises', *Global Strategy Journal*, 1: 206–32.

Chari, M.D.R. and Chang, K. (2009) 'Determinants of the share of equity sought in cross-border acquisitions', *Journal of International Business Studies*, 40: 1277–97.

Chen, S.-F. and Hennart, J.-F. (2004) 'A hostage theory of joint ventures: why do Japanese investors choose partial over full acquisitions to enter the United States?', *Journal of Business Research*, 57: 1126–34.

Child, J. and Rodrigues, S.B. (2005) 'The internationalization of Chinese firms: a case for theoretical extension?', *Management and Organization Review*, 1: 381–410.

Cloodt, M., Hagedoorn, J. and van Kranenburg, H. (2006) 'Mergers and acquisitions: their effect on the innovative performance of companies in high-tech industries', *Research Policy*, 35: 642–54.

Cohen, W.M. and Levinthal, D.A. (1990) 'Absorptive capacity: a new perspective on learning and innovation', *Administrative Science Quarterly*, 35: 128–52.

Cohen, W.M. and Bacdayan, P. (1994) 'Organizational routines are stored as procedural memory: evidence from a laboratory study', *Organization Science*, 5: 554–68.

Chung, W. and Alcacer, J. (2002) 'Knowledge seeking and location choice of foreign direct investment in the United States', *Management Science*, 48: 1534–54.

Cui, L. and Jiang, F. (2009). 'FDI entry mode choice of Chinese firms: a strategic behaviour perspective', *Journal of World Business*, 44: 434–44.

De Beule, F., Elia, S. and Piscitello, L. (2014) 'Entry and access to competences abroad: emerging market firms versus advances market firms', *Journal of International Management*, 20: 137–52.

Deng, P. (2009) 'Why do Chinese firms tend to acquire strategic assets in international expansion?', *Journal of World Business*, 44: 74–84.

Dunning, J.H. (1977) 'Trade, location of economic activity and the MNE: a search for an eclectic approach', in Ohlin, B., Hesselborn, P.O. and Wijkmon, P.M. (eds) *The International Location of Economic Activity*, London: Macmillan.

Dunning, J.H. (1993) *Multinational Enterprises and the Global Economy*, Wokingham: Addison Wesley.

Eurostat-OECD (2007) *Science, Technology and Innovation in Europe*, Eurostat Pocketbooks.

Folta, T.B. (1998) 'Governance and uncertainty: the tradeoff between administrative control and commitment', *Strategic Management Journal*, 19: 1007–28.

Folta, T.B. and Miller, K.D. (2002) 'Real options in equity partnerships', *Strategic Management Journal*, 23: 77–88.

Gammeltoft, P., Barnard, H. and Madhok, A. (2010) 'Emerging multinationals, emerging theory: macro- and micro-level perspectives', *Journal of International Management*, 16: 95–101.

Gomes-Casseres, B. (1990) 'Firm ownership preferences and host government restrictions: an integrated approach', *Journal of International Business*, 21: 1–22.

Govindarajan, V. and Ramamurti, R. (2011) 'Reverse innovation, emerging markets, and global strategy', *Global Strategy Journal*, 1: 191–205.

Green, W.H. (1993) *Econometric Analysis*, 2nd edn, New York: Macmillan.

Hamel, G. and Prahalad, C.K. (1985) 'Do you really have a global strategy', *Harvard Business Review*, 63: 139–48.

Harrison, J.S., Hitt, M.A., Hoskisson, R.E. and Ireland, R.D. (1991) 'Synergies and post-acquisition performance: differences versus similarities in resource allocations', *Journal of Management*, 17: 173–90.

Hennart, J.F and Larimo, J. (1998) 'The impact of culture on the strategy of multinational enterprises: does national origin affect ownership decisions by foreign direct investors into the United States?', *Journal of International Business Studies*, 29: 515–38.

Hofstede, G. (1980) *Culture's Consequences: International Differences in Work-Related Values*, London: Sage Publications.

Hofstede, G., Neuijen, B. Ohayv, D.D. and Sanders, G. (1990) 'Measuring organizational cultures: a qualitative and quantitative study across twenty cases', *Administrative Science Quarterly*, 35: 286–316.

Hsieh, H. and Shannon, S.E. (2005) 'Three approaches to qualitative content analysis', *Qualitative Health Research*, 15: 1277–88.

Jemison, D.B. and Sitkin, S.B. (1986) 'Corporate acquisitions: a process perspective', *Academy of Management Review*, 11: 145–63.

King, D., Slotegraaf, R.J. and Kesner, I. (2008) 'Performance implications of firm resource interactions in the acquisition of R&D-intensive firms', *Organization Science*, 19: 327–40.

Kogut, B. and Singh H. (1988) 'The effect of national culture on the choice of entry mode', *Journal of International Business Studies*, 19: 411–32.

Kogut, B. and Zander, U. (1993) 'Knowledge of the firm, combinative capabilities, and the replication of technology', *Organization Science*, 3: 383–97.

Li, J., Li, Y. and Shapiro, D. (2012) 'Knowledge seeking and outward FDI of emerging market firms: the moderating effect of inward FDI', *Global Strategy Journal*, 2: 277–95.

Luo, Y.D. and Tung, R.L. (2007) 'International expansion of emerging market enterprises: a springboard perspective', *Journal of International Business Studies*, 38: 481–98.

Madhok, A. (1997) 'Cost, value, and foreign market entry mode: the transaction of the firm', *Strategic Management Journal*, 18: 39–61.

Madhok, A. and Keyhani, M. (2012) 'Acquisitions as entrepreneurship: asymmetries, opportunities, and the internationalization of multinationals from emerging economies', *Global Strategy Journal*, 2: 26–40.

Makino, S., Lau, C.M. and Yeh, R.S. (2002) 'Asset-exploitation versus asset-seeking: implication for location choice of foreign direct investment from newly industrialized economies', *Journal of International Business Studies*, 33: 403–21.

Mariotti, S, Piscitello, L. and Elia, S., (2014) 'Local externalities and ownership choices in foreign acquisitions by multinational enterprises', *Economic Geography*, 90: 187–211.

Mathews, J.A. (2006) 'Catch-up strategies and the latecomer effect in industrial development', *New Political Economy*, 11: 313–35.

Narula, R. (2012), 'Do we need different frameworks to explain infant MNEs from developing countries?', *Global Strategy Journal*, 2: 188–204.

Neuendorf, K.A. (2002) *The Content Analysis Guidebook*. Thousand Oaks, CA: Sage.

Peng, M.W. (2012) 'The global strategy of emerging multinationals from China', *Strategic Management Journal*, 2: 97–107.

Piscitello, L. (2004) 'Corporate diversification, coherence and economic performance', *Industrial and Corporate Change*, 13: 757–87.

Ramamurti, R. (2008) *What Have We Learned about Emerging Market MNEs?*, Cambridge: Cambridge University Press.

Ramamurti, R. (2012) 'What is really different about emerging market multinationals?', *Global Strategy Journal*, 2: 41–47.

Ranft, A.L. and Lord, M.D. (2002) 'Acquiring new technologies and capabilities: a grounded model of acquisition implementation', *Organization Science*, 13: 420–41.

Reuer, J.J., Shenkar, O. and Ragozzino, R. (2004) 'Mitigating risk in international mergers and acquisitions: the role of contingent payouts', *Journal of International Business Studies*, 35: 19–32.

Robins, J. and Wiersema, M.F. (2003) 'The measurement of corporate portfolio strategy: analysis of the content validity of related diversification indexes', *Strategic Management Journal*, 24: 39–59.

Rugman, A.M. (2009) 'Theoretical aspects of MNEs from emerging economies' in R. Ramamurti and J. Singh (eds) *Emerging Multinationals in Emerging Markets*, Cambridge: Cambridge University Press.

Rugman, A.M. and Li, J. (2007) 'Will China's multinationals succeed globally or regionally?', *European Management Journal*, 25: 333–43.

Shenkar, O. (2001) 'Cultural distance revisited: towards a more rigorous conceptualization and measurement of cultural differences', *Journal of International Business Studies*, 32: 519–35.

Sun, S.L., Peng, M.W., Ren, B. and Yan, D. (2012) 'A comparative ownership advantage framework for cross-border M&As: the rise of Chinese and Indian MNEs', *Journal of World Business*, 47: 4–16.

Trautwein, F. (1990) Merger motives and merger prescriptions, *Strategic Management Journal*, 11: 283–95.

UNCTAD (2012) *Towards a New Generation of Investment Policies, World Investment Report 2012*, New York and Geneva: United Nations Conference for Trade and Development.

Wang, C., Hong, J., Kafouros, M. and Boateng, A. (2012) 'What drives outward FDI of Chinese firms? Testing the explanatory power of three theoretical frameworks', *International Business Review*, 21: 425–38.

Weber, R.P. (1990) *Basic Content Analysis*, 2nd edn, Newbury Park, CA: Sage.

Weber, Y., Shenkar, O. and Raveh, A. (1996) 'National and corporate cultural fit in mergers and acquisitions: an exploratory study', *Management Science*, 42: 1215–27.

Wesson, T.J. (2004) *Foreign Direct Investment and Competitive Advantage*, Cheltenham: Edward Elgar Publishing.

Williamson, O.E. (1975) *Markets and Hierarchies: Analysis and Antitrust Implications*, New York: The Free Press.

Yildiz, H.E. (2013) 'Not all differences are the same: dual roles of status and cultural distance in sociocultural integration in cross-border M&As', *Journal of International Management*.

Zaheer, S., Schomaker, M.S. and Nachum, L. (2012) 'Distance without direction: restoring credibility to a much-loved construct', *Journal of International Business Studies*, 43: 18–27.

8

Engaged employees in M&A

Illusion or opportunity?

Satu Teerikangas and Liisa Välikangas

Introduction

In this chapter, we approach mergers and acquisitions (M&As) from an engagement lens. Reflecting the assumptions of positive organizational scholarship (Cameron *et al.* 2003; Cameron and Spreitzer 2012), engagement offers a positive take on employee presence and involvement at work (Kahn 1990, Rothbard and Patil 2012). Such a take differs markedly from the reality of many a merger or acquisition, where negative emotionality prevails (Napier 1989; Cartwright and Cooper 1990; Marks and Vansteenskiste 2008). We begin by considering 1) the case for engagement and 2) the performance consequences of an engaged workforce. We then 3) review the theoretical perspectives through which engagement has been approached, discussing their relevance to M&As. This leads us to 4) propose a typology of engagement scenarios in times of M&A, be it by nurturing individual action or by means of organizational support. In light of the many audiences impacting M&As, we finish the chapter with 5) an overview of how differing audiences' engagement dynamics differ in pre- and post-transaction eras. In so doing, our chapter contributes to theorizing on M&As by introducing an engagement lens to employee reactions and involvement during M&As. We also contribute to theorizing on engagement by illustrating the need for engaged employees not only in seemingly static, i.e. normal, work contexts, but also in times of major changes, such as mergers or acquisitions. We argue that, given the radical change in ownership and psychological contract that they represent, M&As offer an arena, wherein the engagement of employees is particularly needed.

The case for engaged employees in times of M&A

The significance of human capital to firm performance spans the history of management. In the present knowledge-based era, where innovativeness and the quality and speed of new ideas have become central to firm survival, human capital arguably takes center stage. In such a context, a firm's competitive advantage has shifted from the efficient management of physical assets to rely on the extent to which it is able to leverage the potential residing in its workforce (Davenport *et al.* 2002). This is reflected in theorizing on the resource-based view of the firm; beyond leveraging tangible, physical resources, the resource-based view of the firm is keen to appreciate how to tap the human potential residing in organizations (Barney and Wright 1998). In the strategic management and strategic human resource management literatures, this resonates with a debate on the significance of a firm's human capital, and its performance implications (Pfeffer 1994; Kor and Leblebici 2005; Wright and Haggerty 2005).

Beyond academic interest, the significance of human capital to firm success has translated into organizations having adopted employee engagement as *the* human resources tool in order to harness the positive energy and enthusiasm of their workforce (Macey and Schneider 2008). Take the example of leading organizations such as Carlsberg, Tata, or Nokia Solutions and Networks—employee engagement is sought and measured. On a broader scale, the emphasis on engaged employees reflects the tenets of positive organizational scholarship, which advocates viewing individuals and organizations from the perspective of their potential, instead of focusing on their weaknesses or negative symptoms, as is the tradition in psychology and organizational psychology (Cameron *et al.* 2003; Cameron 2008; Cameron and Spreitzer 2012).

Despite a corporate emphasis on employee engagement, the reality is that of an employee engagement deficit in many of today's organizations, with engagement levels averaging 30 percent (Schuck 2011). Based on 32,000 respondents, the 2012 *Global Workforce Study* (Towers Watson 2012) warns that only 35 percent of the global workforce is highly engaged. A resource being currently deployed at 35 percent ought to be a serious concern. This explains why Cartwright and Holmes (2006) position the challenge as *regaining* employee engagement, arguing that factors causing a lack of employee engagement have gained an upper hand.

Paralleling corporate interest, employee engagement has gained research interest, particularly since the 2000s (for reviews, see e.g. Schuck and Wollard 2010; Rich *et al.* 2010, Attridge 2009; Maslach *et al.* 2001; Rothbard and Patil 2012). A critical overview of research in this area, however, posits most research being focused on employee engagement in static, or non-transformative, contexts. Whilst change appears to be a defining characteristic of the workplace of the twenty-first century (Hannan and Freeman 1977; Gersick 1991; Brown and Eisenhardt 1997), we appear to be lacking in knowledge about how employees engage in times of major change. Recent findings, though, posit the power of employees' positive emotionality (Avey *et al.* 2008; Huy 2012) and engagement (Sonenshein and Dholakia 2012) in support of strategic change (Golden-Biddle and Mao 2012). Positive emotionality has been found supportive in managing the unexpected (Sutcliffe and Christianson 2012), healing from organizational disruption (Powley 2012), responding to crisis (James and Wooten 2012), and growth following trauma (Maitlis 2012).

In this chapter, we seek to build and extend on this emerging body of knowledge on the role of engagement in times of radical change by focusing on mergers and acquisitions. Though the human dimensions have been identified as having performance consequences for M&As (Larsson and Finkelstein 1999), firms seem to fail in tapping into the positive and generative agency residing in their workforce (Napier 1989; Cartwright and Cooper 1992; Cartwright 2012). We argue that this might be due to the fact that an appreciation of employees actively engaging in times of M&A is lacking. Extant theorizing tends to portray the workforce as a passive recipient of change following M&A (Buono *et al.* 1985; Buono and Bowditch 1989; Haspeslagh and Jemison 1991; Cartwright 2012). Recently, the significance of individual managerial agency following M&A has come to be highlighted, be it as regards acquired firm managers (Graebner 2004), human resource managers (Antila 2006), or acquiring firm integration managers (Teerikangas *et al.* 2011). Beyond an appreciation of individual managerial action, based on extant research, the generative effect of human agency in times of M&A is insufficiently explored. This is the theoretical setting into which our chapter is positioned. Through the lens of engaged employees, we consider the dynamic human agency in times of M&A. This leads us to contribute to theorizing on M&As by introducing an engagement lens to employee reactions and involvement during M&As. Such a take extends our view of active human agency in times of M&A from individual managers to the many employees that make up the M&A arena. In parallel, we contribute to theorizing on engagement by illustrating the need for engaged employees not only in seemingly static, non-transformative, work contexts, but particularly in times of major changes, such as mergers or acquisitions.

Engagement—a theoretical tour

Whilst the term employee engagement is recent, the question "What motivates me?" can be considered central to the managerial agenda. Researchers have had an interest in human motivation since the early twentieth century. In the 1930s, the human relations movement began to draw attention to the human side of the enterprise (Burnes 2009). Since the 1950s, be it in psychology or organizational behavior, work on employee motivation has burgeoned (Miner 2005; Steel and König 2006). Various ways of capturing the motivated employee at work have been sought, ranging from intrinsic vs. extrinsic motivation, employee vs. life satisfaction, work commitment, involvement, participation, and meaningfulness, to the more recent trends of passion (Perttula and Cardon 2012), thriving (Spreitzer *et al.* 2005), fun (Huy 2005), and engagement at work. In this and the following sections, our focus shifts to describing how the study of engagement has evolved and where the field stands at present.

In parallel to the notion of engagement having gained societal and corporate currency, the term is receiving increasing research attention (Macey and Schneider 2008;). Whilst research on engagement emerged in the early 1990s with the work of Kahn (1990, 1992), it was thereafter fed by practitioner interest (see Macey and Schneider 2008). Led by social psychologists and scholars in organizational behavior, since the early twenty-first century, the field has witnessed a burgeoning and rebirth. The study of engagement has been strongest in the areas of applied psychology and sociology, with increasing interest from organization scientists (for reviews, see Shuck 2011; Schuck and Wollard 2010; Rich *et al.* 2010; Attridge 2009; Maslach *et al.* 2001; Rothbard and Patil 2012).

Despite these advances, the field is critiqued for lacking appropriate conceptualizations of what engagement is (Macey and Schneider 2008; Little and Little 2006; Ho *et al.* 2011). Macey and Schneider state: "engagement is a concept with a sparse and diverse theoretical net—the relationships among potential antecedents and consequences of engagement as well as the components of engagement have not been rigorously conceptualized, much less studied" (2008: 3–4). The concept of engagement appears related to cognition, affect, and behavior (Zigarmi *et al.* 2009; Shuck 2011). Also, the relative independence and uniqueness of engagement as a concept and its links to other related concepts has been raised (Hallberg and Schaufeli 2006; Macey and Schneider 2008). Engagement has been argued to differ from job involvement (Hallberg and Schaufeli 2006; Saks 2006), commitment (Hallberg and Schaufeli 2006; Saks 2006;) and workoholism (Bakker *et al.* 2008; Schaufeli *et al.* 2006). Whilst it has been found to differ from job satisfaction, it is also highly related to it (Wefald and Downey 2009). Rich *et al.* (2010) argue that engagement offers a more comprehensive explanation of the relationships with performance than do the related concepts of job involvement, job satisfaction, or intrinsic motivation.

Engagement and performativity

Though difficult to define and capture in academic terms (Mainemelis 2001), engagement appears to matter with respect to individual, team, and corporate performance. The positive performance effects of engagement have received confirmation in a number of studies.

Engagement has been found to be positively related to employee performance (Britt *et al.* 2005; Salanova and Schaufeli 2008). Kahn (1992) observes that engagement results in improved outcome quality and a positive work experience. Engagement has been evidenced to relate negatively to turnover intentions (Schaufeli and Bakker 2004) and positively to job performance, extra-role behavior, good health, and positive work affect (Sonnentag 2003). Engaged individuals produce work that is creative and of high quality, resulting in personal commitment to the outcome and contagious enthusiasm toward others (Teerikangas and Välikangas 2012). Engaged individuals have further been found to experience greater happiness in their lives than non-engaged individuals (Schaufeli *et al.* 2006). Similar positive performance effects have been found as regards cousin concepts such as the meaning of work (Pratt and Ashforth 2003), work as calling (Hall and Chandler 2005), job involvement (Brown and Leigh 1996), and intrinsic motivation (Grant 2008).

Beyond individual-level outcomes, high degrees of engagement impact team creativity (Gilson and Shalley 2004), firm performance, and customer satisfaction (Salanova *et al.* 2005). In terms of corporate performance, a meta-analysis of the Gallup industry database found employee engagement and satisfaction to strongly correlate with employee turnover, customer satisfaction, and safety, and also to correlate with productivity and firm profitability (Harter *et al.* 2002). Recent research posits engagement as a glue binding different organizational levels and units together, shaping firm performance (Ployhart and Moliterno 2011). It would appear that the more one is attuned and emotionally attached to one's job, the better not only one's own, but also one's team's, and, ultimately, the organization's performance.

Paralleling interest in the role of positive emotionality in times of change (Cameron and Spreitzer 2012), Avey *et al.* (2008) find that positive emotions support the engagement of employees in times of organizational change. Marks (2007) argues that engagement is a means to intellectually distance the workforce from the old regime, before energizing them toward the new one. Based on their study of employees' engagement to strategic change, Sonenshein and Dholakia (2012) suggest that not only managers, but also colleagues influence employee reactions during strategic change. These influence mechanisms appear to operate differently. They conclude that everyone bears a role in supporting strategic change. Beyond performance outcomes in static contexts, it appears that engagement bears meaning also in shifting organizational landscapes. In order to further such an appreciation, we turn our attention next onto the perspectives from which engagement has been studied.

Perspectives on engagement and implications for M&As

In defining engagement and its antecedents, a number of approaches can be identified. Despite differences between these approaches to engagement, it is generally agreed that engagement is manifested in a flow of positive emotions, extra-role behaviors, vigor, and energy. Yet, the ways in which these manifestations are defined vary across studies. After reviewing each perspective on engagement, we move onto discussing their implications for M&A, which are summarized in Table 8.1.

Table 8.1 Alternative perspectives to employee engagement and their implications for M&As at personal, managerial, and organizational levels of analysis

Perspectives to engagement Implications for M&As	Perspective 1: Engagement as authenticity	Perspective 2: Engagement as a dyadic process	Perspective 3: Engagement as resources vs. demands	Perspective 4: Multiple foci for engagement
Implications for individuals	The ability to find oneself and one's role in the combined organization. Identity work in relation to the new organization	The ability to find and know one's rhythmic requirements for edging and retreating. Challenge oneself and rest intermittently and regularly. Use digital tools and virtual work smartly in support of such a dyadic process	The ability to manage one's psychological and physical resources to avoid burnout. To know one's limits and manage work-life balance	Consider what are the foci of one's engagement. How can the many foci of engagement act in mutually supportive ways?
Implications for managers	Provide psychological safety in changing situations. Invite engagement rather than control for it.	Provide socio-emotional spaces for challenging people and for recuperation. Design work rhythms to fit individual employee requirements. Manage the intensity of work over time	Balance resources vs. demands in a way that allows calibration as needed.	Accept and support employees' many foci of engagement.
Implications for organizations	Design the organization to suit the employees' needs. Ensure ethical behaviors. Connect isles of engagement to each other.	Design the new organization primarily based on the way employees work (productively/creatively) rather than on the (assumed) requirements of a particular job. Cultivate orchestrated action between highly engaged and less engaged groups of employees in support of engagement contagion.	Set limits to the demands on employees and provide support resources (e.g. mentors). Make resource-scarcity a driver for innovation. Develop organization-wide tools and practices for inviting engagement	Accept and support employees' many foci of engagement.
Underlying literature	Kahn (1990)	Teerikangas and Välikangas (2012)	Schaufeli et al. (2002)	Saks (2006); Macey and Schneider (2008)

Perspective 1: engagement as authenticity

Overview

The seminal academic study on engagement is that of Kahn (1990), who coined the terms personal engagement vs. disengagement at work. Kahn argues that prior literature has taken a static view on a person's fit to one's job, be it in the job involvement, commitment to work, or work alienation literatures. In contrast, Kahn considers engagement from a dynamic, constantly changing lens. Basing himself on Goffman (1961), Maslow (1954), and Alderfer (1972), Kahn defines personal engagement as "the extent to which employees harness themselves in their work roles, i.e. employing and expressing themselves physically, cognitively and emotionally during work role performances" (1990: 701). This is contrasted with personal disengagement, which is likened to automatic or robotic behaviors, effortlessness, and defensive, inexpressive, impersonal, or closed behaviors, i.e. situations wherein one does not fulfill one's role with authenticity (Harter 2002). Kahn (1990) identifies psychological meaningfulness, safety, and availability as enablers of engagement. These factors can be further broken down into psychological, interpersonal, and organizational antecedents. One's psychological availability depends on the degree of physical and emotional energy available for work. Psychological meaningfulness stems from meaningful activity and work interactions. A climate of psychological safety is enabled by the quality of interpersonal interactions at work, group dynamics, management style, and organizational norms (Kahn 1990).

Implications for M&A

Translating Kahn's perspective on personal engagement into an M&A context, the issue is how to maintain one's degree of personal engagement in a changing, shifting situation, where the future is unknown. M&A transactions tend to be paralleled with competitive positioning, uncertainty of one's future employment, worries and protective actions, which are all likely to disable employees' manifestations of authentic behavior (Cartwright 2012; Tienari and Vaara 2012). Such activity discourages personal engagement, given that authenticity is the defining characteristic of personal engagement (Kahn 1990). Kahn's (1990) definition of personal engagement appears to contradict much of the practiced reality in times of M&A.

According to Kahn, securing psychological meaningfulness, safety, and availability amidst changing conditions is critical, if organizations are to enable employee engagement. This translates into actions at the individual, interpersonal, managerial, and organizational levels of analysis. In a merger or acquisition setting, there is thus a role for management in sustaining the conditions for authenticity, hence engagement. Further, how can ethical and fair organizational norms and values be maintained amid a transformation? Beyond managerial and organizational action, Kahn (1990) suggests a role for colleagues in enabling the engagement of others. Positive and trustful interactions help in creating a climate of psychological safety at work. Kahn's findings offer a radical take on M&As and radical change, where interpersonal interactions tend to be characterized by rumor mongering (Cartwright 2012, Ivancevich *et al.* 1987) rather than positive interactions. Finally, the individual employee has a role to bear in supporting one's engagement, be it e.g. by managing one's energy levels or making one's tasks meaningful, even when they are changing. Given the fragility of the engagement experience and its enabling factors, we begin to recognize why achieving personal engagement in normal work contexts, notwithstanding radical transformations, represents a personal and managerial challenge.

Perspective 2: engagement as a dyadic process of edging vs. retreating

Overview

Building on Kahn's (1990) seminal work on personal engagement, a more recent approach posits that, instead of a focus on peak instances only, sustainable, long-term engagement is enabled through a rhythmic, processual dance between edging, consisting in peak states of engagement, and retreating, the need to wind down (Teerikangas and Valikangas 2012, 2014a, 2014b). Given the intensity that peak states represent, engagement is found to be bounded (Teerikangas and Valikangas 2014b).

Engagement appears to peak in "edge" instances (Teerikangas and Valikangas 2012). Such peak experiences exhibit a characteristic of being in a non-space, or at the edge of a cognitive state, hence the term, edging. Such a non-space experience occurs as one stretches toward a challenging goal, as one moves beyond one's habitual daily practices, routines, and boundaries toward unknown, novel, previously untraveled work territory. We consider the edging moment as a ritual transfer from a static, known state toward an unknown one. As long as the future state remains unknown or the situation uncertain, one remains highly engaged (at least within certain limits of time and individual persistence). In essence, these challenging, even wonderful (Carlsen and Sandelands in press), situations require high degrees of cognitive, emotional, and physical vigilance. Such high engagement experiences occur when individuals are engaged in an activity that bears meaning, an element of survival/challenge, and discovery. What these instances of high engagement share is having to be fully alert, vigilant, present (Kahn 1992) in the moment, owing to the inspirational nature of the task (e.g. meaningful work), the intensity of the task (e.g. challenge, survival), or the novelty of the task (e.g. discovery through renewal or learning).

Given the high intensity of these moments, though, they cannot be sustained over long periods of time. For individuals to maintain sustainably high levels of engagement over time, they also need time to retreat. This finding parallels recent work on engagement, where the significance of recovery has been brought to attention (Sonnentag 2003). Teerikangas and Valikangas (2012) argue that such an ongoing dyadic dynamic between edging and retreating is at the core of an individual's personal engagement process. This dyadic tension was found to be characteristic of engagement to the extent that neither full edging, nor continuous retreating, by themselves, are enough to purport high degrees of engagement in the long term. Instead, it is the maintenance and rhythm of this dynamic that enables the sustenance of engagement over time. The dyadic engagement process is supported by engaging physical, socio-emotional, and personal spaces (Teerikangas and Välikangas 2012). Organizations need to consider how physical work contexts, inspiring work interactions, serendipitous work encounters, task autonomy, and meaningful personal ambitions can be accessed as means of encouraging engagement in the workplace.

Implications for M&A

This line of work argues that, in M&A settings, in order for employees to maintain sustained levels of personal engagement, the dyadic process of edging and retreating needs to be respected. Perhaps many a merger or acquisition presents employees with an emphasis on edging only, as a result of which this experience fails to be an engaging one. Where are the opportunities to retreat in times of radical change? Further, is attention paid to engaging physical, socio-emotional, and personal spaces in times of change? As the collective mood veers toward the negative, it becomes harder to sustain an engaging socio-emotional work environment. This means that individuals are left to deal with the change and the resulting cognitive and emotional turmoil with their personal resources only. The lack of socio-emotional resources might explain the employee engagement deficit that is often witnessed in times of radical change.

Perspective 3: engagement as resources vs. demands

Overview

The most empirically tested approach to engagement is one that has its roots in research on burnout (see Maslach and Jackson 1981; Maslach *et al.* 2001), where engagement initially emerged as the conceptual opposite of burnout (Maslach and Leiter 1997; González-Romá *et al.* 2006), though the nature of this relationship remains debated (Schaufeli and Bakker 2004). An individual's psychological relationship to one's job is conceptualized as a continuum between the negative experience of burnout and the positive experience of work engagement (Maslach and Leiter 2008). Work engagement is defined as "a positive, fulfilling, work-related state of mind characterized by vigor, dedication and absorption" (Schaufeli *et al.* 2002: 74).

With its origin in burnout studies, this research stream has developed the "job resources–job demands" model of engagement (Bakker and Demerouti 2007). This is the most empirically tested model in the field (Demerouti *et al.* 2001). The model assumes that each occupation has its own risk factor, defined either as a job resource or a job demand. While job resources (be they organizational, social, or work or task-related) and personal resources (e.g. optimism, efficacy, resilience, self-esteem) create motivation, job demands (whether physical, social, psychological, organizational) create strain. Work engagement results from the ongoing negotiation between job resources and demands. Job resources that are supportive of engagement include social support, feedback, skill variety, autonomy, and opportunities for learning (Bakker and Demerouti 2007). Job demands, on the other hand, related to workload and reorganizations, do not affect engagement but affect burnout by creating exhaustion and cynicism (Bakker *et al.* 2003). The significance of sufficient job resources increases with the demands of the job (Hakanen *et al.* 2005). Instead of being a state to be achieved, engagement is considered as a process requiring constant attention (Maslach and Leiter 1997).

Implications for M&A

This perspective considers engagement from the lens of resources vs. demands. Mergers and acquisitions are here viewed as a demand factor that needs to be balanced against sufficient job and personal resources. This suggests that perhaps M&As demand more than they bring. Under such circumstances, the role of management is to provide a supportive work context (i.e. job resources) and to help employees balance their personal (i.e. psychological, social, and physical) resources in order to avoid burnout and maintain engagement. When this balancing is experienced positively, employees experience sufficient resources.

Taking a critical stance, in this framework, less attention is paid to the possibility of resources being elastic; they will be interpreted and experienced differently, from one person to the next. Moreover, the model ignores the capacity of employees to be creative in their resourcing (Feldman 2004; Sonenshein 2013). Instead of a limiting factor, resource scarcity can be conducive to novel problem solving (Välikangas and Gibbert 2005) or act as a driver for innovative teamwork (Hoegl *et al.* 2008). Notwithstanding, when dealing with human capital resources, there are limits to be observed. Instances of radical change, such as M&As, thus posit an ontological challenge to the job resources–demands model. What kinds of available resources to draw from in order to make the experience of radical change engaging? How to also account for the creativity and elasticity of resources? What kinds of personal resources might individuals draw upon and create?

Perspective 4: multiple foci of engagement

Overview

Some researchers seek to deconstruct engagement. To this end, Saks (2006) distinguishes between job (or work) engagement and organizational engagement. Tyler and Blader (2003) find that group engagement has psychological and behavioral components. Recently, Macey and Schneider (2008) divide engagement into trait (i.e. positive stance to life and work), psychological state (i.e. absorption, pride, alertness), and behavioral engagement (i.e. extra-role behaviors). The model has been subject to a heated debate (see e.g. Macey and Schneider 2008).

Implications for M&A

This perspective reminds us of the complexity of the engagement concept. There are many foci to an employee's engagement. Employees can be engaged with their jobs, their organization, their tasks, or off-work activities. In times of a merger or acquisition, the question is—how to also build engagement toward the M&A transaction and the new owner.

Assuming that contexts of radical change challenge one's experience of engagement, the transferability of engagement across its foci becomes of interest; to what extent is one's engagement in areas outside of work transferable to one's work engagement? Such transfer effects might become particularly salient when securing a high level of engagement in one's work context becomes challenging, as in times of radical change. This might call for seeking engagement beyond the mere work context. Would non-work contexts offer a source for sustainable engagement in times of corporate change? To what extent is engagement a matter of a personal capacity to be positive and the amount of energy available to a person? Where do individuals draw upon their personal resources when the workplace faces turbulence and chaos? How do M&As affect and draw upon these personal resources?

A typology of engagement scenarios in M&As

The above review of perspectives towards engagement suggests that engagement, though differently defined by the scholarly community, is enabled by both personal and organizational resources and resourcing. In the following, we propose a typology of engagement scenarios in times of M&A (Figure 8.1). These scenarios propose that engagement is co-created on the basis of individual employees' actions and the organization's support for engagement. In the following, we consider the implications of these scenarios for engagement in M&As.

Scenario A: low engagement

In the first scenario, the employees in the target firm(s) are disengaged vis-à-vis the M&A transaction. In addition, the practices, structures, and culture of the employing organizations are unsupportive of the employees' engagement. In an M&A setting, low degrees of engagement are expected to make the acquisition particularly vulnerable: few mechanisms to increase employee engagement are readily available.

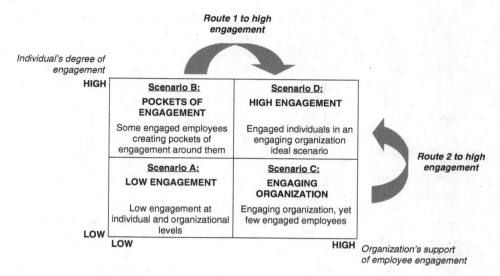

Figure 8.1   Engagement scenarios in M&A

Even if the integration practices would make employees engaged to the deal, this is unlikely to be sustainable, given that the employing organizations' practices are disengaging in themselves. The organization's culture might be unethical or fear-based. There could be elements of workplace bullying. Leadership styles are autocratic and focused on control. Reward systems might not reflect the work conducted. Structures might not provide enough space for autonomous decision-making. In this scenario, we expect employees to fall into the well advertised trap of negative emotional states amid M&As, which may be visible as regards a lack of authenticity, edging-retreating dynamic, and personal creativity in resourcing. The available job resources are perceived as insufficient, and individuals do not leverage their personal resources to make up for this.

Scenario B: pockets of engagement

In the second scenario, some or many individual employees are engaged in their work roles, yet the employing organization has not yet realized its role in supporting its employees in this pursuit. As a result, engaged individuals either 1) exit the organization in due time, as captured in much acquisition research (Walsh 1988; Krug and Nigh 2001), or 2) develop personal adaptation and resourcing strategies to avoid being discouraged by the organization's lack of engagement support mechanisms: they become resiliently engaged.

In so doing, they have potential to create engagement in their immediate organizational vicinity that then, as positivity spirals, enthuses engagement around them (Wrzesniewski 2003; Salanova *et al*. 2010). Pockets of engagement emerge within the organization. This scenario has potentially supportive effects in M&As, provided the isles of engagement can be effectively mobilized to support integration efforts and do not become overwhelmed by the broader lagging sentiment. In this scenario, the capability to engage is strong amongst a handful of individual employees, but weak at the level of the organization. Engagement is thus dependent on the will and persuasive power of particular individuals rather than on organizational mechanisms.

Such a scenario points to the potentially contagious effects of (dis)engagement and has a radical humanistic perspective towards organizations (Burrell and Morgan 1979). It also puts a heavy burden on the individuals, including managers, seeking to engage others. They would need to be able to tap into and resource their surroundings toward engagement. Recent findings on the role of individual managers, whether from the acquired firm (Graebner 2004; Teerikangas 2006) or the acquiring firm sides (Antila 2006; Teerikangas *et al.* 2011) points in this direction. Nevertheless, it remains to be observed whether such activity occurs beyond the managerial level, i.e. those whose role is the "engaging of others." If all organizational actors become engaged in engaging one another, what are the consequences?

Scenario C: engaging organization

In this scenario the individual employee is not engaged, or has lost her engagement owing to the changing circumstances, as in an M&A. However, the organization has realized its role in supporting its employees' engagement; it is seeking to actively engage its employee base. In so doing, it develops and nurtures an organizational-level engagement capability. Managers are engaged and promote the engagement of others. Aspirational goals motivate the workforce, coupled with meaningful rewards. Opportunities for retreating are provided, as in the example of Google offices where food is always close at hand. The organizational culture seeks innovative and entrepreneurial behavior amid a friendly landscape. Workplace interactions are encouraging and inspiring.

In such an organization, employees have the potential to flourish and become engaged if they so wish, yet for some reason (perhaps due to cynicism stemming from poor prior management) the employees have not responded to the engagement call. The employees may, for example, not mobilize their personal resources creatively or do not have an opportunity for edging and retreating.

The organization portrays dormant potential for engagement, provided it can convey credibility and sincerity in its ways of evoking its employees' engagement in the M&A process. Perhaps the shock waves created by a merger or acquisition, challenging and changing as they may be, can also act as a wake-up call prompting engagement. This is a potential managerial tool for enabling an edging-retreating dynamic based on the feelings arising from the radical change, if positively marshaled.

Scenario D: high engagement

In this scenario, high engagement occurs as both individuals are engaged and the employing organization supports these efforts. The microclimate effect (as in scenario B) further enriches the existing organizational engagement efforts, as positive, contagious engagement spirals are created. This results in flourishing individuals who intuitively self-resource for creative outcomes and manage their engagement dynamics. In this scenario, the capability to engage rests both at the level of the individual employee and at the level of the organization. Engagement is co-created in their interactions. Subsequently, high levels of engagement are to be expected. This is the ideal situation for M&As, yet perhaps rare among most acquirers. Companies claimed to excel in their M&A integration practices may fall into this scenario.

Resulting routes to engagement

Going forward, we identify two alternatives routes for management to navigate the four scenarios for enhancing engagement in M&As. Building on Teerikangas and Välikangas (2012), we term the first managerial route, *evocation through individual action and engagement.* This refers to situations wherein a high degree of engagement at the level of employees gradually radiates and transforms toward higher levels of employee engagement across the organization. In M&A situations, the transaction acts as the catalyst to such proactiveness. We claim that in the two high-engagement scenarios (i.e. scenarios B and D), engaged individuals radiate enthusiasm to their surroundings, with these micro behaviors bearing potential for macro-level changes, e.g. causing an engagement-supportive microclimate in the entire organization.

Large organizations could be argued to consist of nests that are to different degrees implicitly engaged, depending on the degrees of personal engagement amidst their leaders and key personnel. This mirrors Losada's work on high-performing teams (Losada 1999; Losada and Heaphy 2004), where positive interactions were found to bear the greatest effect on the degree of member connectivity, and thus team performance. Wrzesniewski (2003) also draws attention to the transfer effects of persons who have a work-as-calling attitude toward the larger social group. The work on emotional contagion (Bartel and Saavedra 2000; Barsade 2002) also attests to such effects.

We term the second route, *evocation through orchestrated action*. This refers to situations wherein high levels of engagement capability in the employing organization, when practiced over time, result in high degrees of employee engagement across the organization. Our suggestion is that, rather than attempting to manage or force-induce engagement in M&As, managers, through their understanding of the micro-level foundations of engagement, should learn to *invite* and enable engagement-supportive conditions. This may require a degree of management innovation (Birkinshaw *et al.* 2008). High engagement is voluntary and fragile. Clearly, if management interventions are used wrongly or superficially, engagement encouragement efforts can contribute to employee cynicism.

Engagement dynamics differ per audience type

The previously presented perspectives bring forth an appreciation of employee engagement as a highly personal and sensitive state of authenticity, presence, and exposure. Whilst our typology offers a lens to the individual and organizational factors shaping engagement levels following M&As, we lack an appreciation of the role-level variation in engagement levels. As engagement is a subjective and personal experience, we can expect different degrees of engagement within a particular transaction, depending on the individual concerned. This parallels models of change management, where individual differences to change have been explored from the lens of personality differences (Cameron and Green 2004). In times of M&A, we argue that not only do personality differences matter, as indicated earlier regarding personal traits and resources, but, further, the timing and degree of one's involvement with the transaction in question matter. This leads us to identify three audiences portraying, respectively, different engagement dynamics.

Engagement dynamics of pre-deal actors

Executives, investors, and consultants engaged in the pre-deal transaction are likely to be engaged—with making the deal! This is an era of excitement; there is limited time, the clock is ticking. A potentially significant deal is to be signed off and closed. The stakes are high, the rewards for those concerned, be they senior executives, investment bankers, or consultants, are potentially significant. Such experiences are captured in a recent study of engagement dynamics in the experience of M&A professionals (Preston 2013; Preston and

Teerikangas 2014). These characterize what we earlier identified as "edging" instances in an engagement process.

There is clear pressure in the pre-deal era to close deals. Such pressure can be attributed to escalating momentum and commitment (Jemison and Sitkin 1986), chief executive hubris (Sudarsanam 2012), and investment bankers pushing deals through in order to secure financial rewards. Working under such intense pressure thus requires skill and intelligence from the acquiring firm's executives to make the right judgment in the face of the information available. This might explain why Happonen (2009) found chief executives to rely on their "gut feeling" amidst the high adrenaline of pre-deal decision-making. If the situation lasts too long, burnout may be near.

Engagement dynamics of post-deal change agents

Managers and consultants engaged in implementing post-deal change are engaged with a different outcome—implementing the change. In contrast to the pre-transaction era, though, the strategic windows in the post-transaction phase are less strict, the outcomes and stakes less tangible, and the immediate rewards not as high. Therefore edging, despite its peaks, may be less intense and harder to sustain over time, occasionally evolving into retreating or disengagement.

For example, despite 30-, 100-, or 300-day plans (Angwin 2004), the completion of post-deal integration cannot be expected to be signed off after a set number of days. It has been shown that integration can last beyond 3 years and all the way to 12 years (Birkinshaw *et al.* 2000; Quah and Young 2005; Barkema and Schijven 2008). The responsibility of the integration team concerns the official integration era, i.e. the first 3, 6, or 12 months post-deal. When this timeline has been reached, integration team members cannot actually sign off on integration; on paper yes; in practice no. Integration is expected to continue over the years to come, without ever reaching a definite end point (Teerikangas and Geraldi 2011).

As a result, the expected outcomes from the integration team are of a less finite nature than for those engaged in closing the transaction. Integration team members are responsible for pushing through change in one or more organizations over the long term. This has been shown to be a difficult task and unlikely to result in finite outcomes, notwithstanding outright success (Haspeslagh and Jemison 1991; Birkinshaw *et al.* 2000). In order to maintain the integration team's engagement levels, tracking progress and measuring success would be critical. Yet, neither is an easy or explicit task.

Finally, the expected (financial) rewards, whilst perhaps interesting, nevertheless do not rival those of pre-acquisition investment bankers and executives. Integration management concerns project and change management, both well known to be difficult endeavors (Burnes 2009; Morris et al. 2012). As a result, the goals, and thus the rewards of integration team members, are not only less explicit and difficult to track, but also harder to reach.

In summary, the implementation task, though engaging for those involved, has a different nature to the pre-deal activity. In an ethnographic study of integration experiences in a university merger, Teerikangas and Tienari (2012) capture the inner experience and turmoil of integration involvement at middle-managerial level. Though the experience has its engaging moments, longer-term resilience is required to maintain high levels of focus throughout the months and years of change that a larger change entails. Resilient engagement is also required, as many pieces of information cannot be disclosed to the wider organizational audience. All the while, workloads remain high, this further challenging a sustainable long-term engagement experience.

Engaging employees

The experience of engagement is of quite a different nature for those less (or not) involved in making the change happen. This is the largely passive audience that has been found to react negatively easily (Napier 1989; Cartwright and Cooper 1990; Marks and Vansteenskiste 2008), yet be prone to positive reactions (Fairfield-Sonn *et al.* 2002; Froese *et al.* 2007; Teerikangas 2012) under more resourceful circumstances. For this audience, radical change, such as M&As, challenges the experience of personal authenticity. This is the audience that has been largely captured by extant research on employee reactions to M&A.

For the average employee who is less involved in implementing the acquisition, not only is there change, but, beyond this, the previous seemingly secure and stable workplace has veered toward fundamental uncertainty. More often than not, the very idea of change brings forth negativity in the organization, if only for a while. Beyond a mere change, mergers and acquisitions represent a violation to one's psychological contract, given that they represent an ownership change. Negative stamina, in parts or islets of the organization, can result in negative emotional contagion (Barsade 2002; Bartel and Saavedra 2000).

Thus, as one's workplace undergoes change, the pillars supportive of engagement, including interpersonal, managerial, and organizational factors, are in temporary turmoil. When one's workplace and psychological contract are under threat, questions such as "How to remain authentic?"; "Who am I as an employee in the new organization, what is my role, my identity?"; "Do I have a future in the merged entity?" abound. Under such circumstances, at least temporarily, the burden and responsibility for engagement comes largely to rest on the individual employee. In other words, the organizational context, undergoing change, is less able to support employees' experiences of engagement, than it might be under normal (static) circumstances. This means that, during the M&A experience, if one seeks to remain motivated, one needs to rely on personal resources, such as personal resilience, optimism, or (non-work) support networks. Some employees may show more resilience than others, again depending on personal traits, the creative resourcing of one's engagement, and available support.

Going forward, this raises intriguing research questions. For one, despite all the uncertainty and lack of organizational support, what explains why some individuals remain engaged over the course of a merger or acquisition? For another, why and how do some employees positively radiate enthusiasm and optimism even in times of radical change? Examples of such behavior are noted at the level of middle managers; motivated target firm managers or acquiring firm integration managers are experienced as motivating others toward the future (Graebner 2004; Teerikangas *et al.* 2011). Going a step further, how many engaging others are required to create an engaged workforce; is there a tip-off point, and if so, what is it? We consider these to be appealing future research themes.

Conclusions

In this chapter, we explored the nature of employee engagement amidst changing conditions such as M&As. By drawing from existing theory and findings, we presented alternative perspectives to appreciating the engagement challenge in M&As and developed a typology of engagement scenarios. Whilst the present chapter calls for future research and practical trials, our findings suggest the following.

Building upon extant literature, we propose alternative perspectives toward engagement in M&As: 1) enabling and supporting authenticity, 2) enabling the dyadic process of edging and retreating in a timely, rhythmic, and socio-emotionally sustainable manner, 3) balancing resources and demands, and 4) considering the many foci of engagement (see Table 8.1).

Acknowledging these perspectives, we suggest some means of enabling engagement in M&As. We premise the consideration of employee engagement on the finding that, when employees see an M&A as an opportunity rather than a threat, they are likely to react more positively to this news (Teerikangas 2012). In the tradition of positive organizational scholarship (Cameron *et al.* 2003), such positive reactions are then likely to further positive, even contagious, spirals, leading to higher degrees of engagement (Bartel and Saavedra 2000; Barsade 2002). The managerial challenge in M&As is hence to leverage individuals who are engaged, islets of engagement, or organizational resources to evoke engagement. Using these levers, the managerial routes to enable higher engagement can be designed based on individual or orchestrated action. Such interventions likely call for nuance and sophistication, as cynicism may easily pre-empt such efforts amid radical change and uncertainty.

Finally, given the nature of the M&A context, we argue that M&As are not arenas for homogeneous displays of engagement; rather our analysis posits that M&As are engagement platforms, wherein a number of actors and audiences, bearing varying stakes and ambitions, portray different dynamics with respect to engagement. This diversity in audience types needs be recognized when discussing engagement in times of radical change.

If persuasively included in the managerial repertoires and scenarios described, employee engagement may not remain the illusion that it often is in M&As today. We advocate considering the different theoretical perspectives presented in this chapter and harnessing them for more nuanced and targeted personal, managerial, and organization action in support of engagement. In part this agenda includes the appreciation of human agency as a resource that is capable of engaging itself and others and creatively resourcing organizational challenges; in part the challenge is that of more supportive managerial action in view of sustainable engagement dynamics. The intensity of M&As tends to invite only edging that may lead to burnout, or retreating that may mean total disengagement, and thus a balanced approach is to be encouraged. In addition, organizations ought to seek to 1) provide a psychological safety net so that individuals do not lose their sense of authenticity amid the uncertainties encountered, 2) balance job demands and resources, 3) encourage the creative resourcing potential of employees, 4) offer socio-emotional spaces that invite engagement dynamics, and 5) appreciate the multiple foci of engagement in that employees differ in their sources of resilience. Managers should tune their capabilities to sensing whether particular employees need more edging or retreating at a particular instance, and time M&A integration activities in such a way that personalized dynamics are possible. Finally, as engagement is contagious, as is disengagement, individual employees matter in their engagement. Each individual's engagement has an impact on others around them. This leads us to ask the reader, "How engaged are you amid change? What is the span of your responsibility in times of change?"

To conclude, the present analysis offers multiple opportunities for future research. To begin with, how do the identified perspectives inform engagement, a central managerial challenge, in M&A? What is the balance of individual, managerial, and organizational resourcing needed in support of employees' engagement? Under what conditions is engagement witnessed during M&A? Beyond M&As, how is engagement manifest in changing organizational conditions? And in what ways are engagement dynamics in times of M&A different from other kinds of change scenarios? Clearly, going forward, intriguing opportunities for research on more nuanced engagement abound in situations of radical and transformative change.

References

Alderfer, C.P. (1972) *Human Needs in Organizational Settings*, New York: Free Press.

Angwin, D. (2004) "Speed in M&A integration: the first 100 days," *European Management Journal*, 22: 418–30.

Antila, E. (2006) "The role of HR managers in international mergers and acquisitions: a multiple case study," *International Journal of Human Resource Management*, 17: 999–1020.

Attridge, M. (2009) "Measuring and managing employee work engagement: a review of the research and business literature," *Journal of Workplace and Behavioural Health*, 24: 383–98.

Avey, J.B., Wernsing, T.S., and Luthans, F. (2008) "Can positive employees help positive organizational change? Impact of psychological capital and emotions on relevant attitudes and behaviors," *The Journal of Applied Behavioral Science*, 44: 48–70.

Bakker, A.B. and Demerouti, E. (2007) "The job demands–resources model: state of the art," *Journal of Managerial Psychology*, 22: 309–28.

Bakker, A.B. and M.P. Leiter (eds.) *Work Engagement: A Handbook of Essential Theory and Research*, New York: Psychology Press.

Bakker, A.B., Demerouti, E., De Boer, E., and Schaufeli, W.B. (2003) "Job demands and job resources as predictors of absence duration and frequency," *Journal of Vocational Behavior*, 62: 341–56.

Bakker, A.B., Schaufeli, W.B., Leiter, M.P., and Taris, T.W. (2008) "Work engagement: an emerging concept in occupational health psychology," *Work and Stress*, 22: 187–200.

Barkema, H.G. and Schijven, M. (2008) "Toward unlocking the full potential of acquisitions: the role of organizational restructuring," *Academy of Management Journal*, 51: 55–77.

Barney, J.B. and Wright, P.M. (1998) "On becoming a strategic partner: the role of human resources in gaining competitive advantage," *Human Resource Management*, 37: 31–46.

Barsade, S.G. (2002) "The ripple effect: emotional contagion and its influence on group behavior," *Administrative Science Quarterly*, 47: 644–75.

Bartel, C.A. and Saavedra, R. (2000) "The collective construction of work group moods," *Administrative Science Quarterly*, 45: 197–231.

Birkinshaw, J., Bresman, H., and Håkanson, L. (2000) "Managing the post-acquisition integration process: how the human integration and task integration processes interact to foster value creation," *Journal of Management Studies*, 37: 395–425.

Birkinshaw, J., Hamel, G., and Mol, M. (2008) "Management innovation," *Academy of Management Review*, 33: 825–45.

Britt, T.W., Castro, C.A., and Adler, A.B. (2005) "Self-engagement, stressors, and health: a longitudinal study," *Personality and Social Psychology Bulletin*, 31: 1475–86.

Brown, S.L. and Eisenhardt, K.M. (1997) "The art of continuous change: linking complexity theory and time-paced evolution in relentlessly shifting organizations," *Administrative Science Quarterly*, 42: 1–34.

Brown, S.P. and Leigh, T.W. (1996) "A new look at psychological climate and its relationship to job involvement, effort and performance," *Journal of Applied Psychology*, 81: 358–68.

Buono, A.F. and Bowditch, J.L. (1989) *The Human Side of Mergers and Acquisitions: Managing Collisions between People, Cultures and Organizations*, London: Jossey-Bass.

Buono, A.F., Bowditch, J.L., and Lewis, J.W. (1985) "When cultures collide: the anatomy of a merger," *Human Relations*, 38: 477–500.

Burnes, B. (2009) *Managing Change*, Harlow: Prentice-Hall.

Burrell, G. and Morgan, G. (1979) *Sociological Paradigms and Organisational Analysis*, Aldershot: Ashgate.

Cameron, E. and Green, M. (2004) *Making Sense of Change Management*, London: Kogan Page.

Cameron, K.S. (2008) "Paradox in positive change," *Journal of Applied Behavioral Science*, 44: 7–24.

Cameron, K.S. and Spreitzer, G. (2012) *The Oxford Handbook of Positive Organizational Scholarship*, Oxford: Oxford University Press.

Cameron, K.S., Dutton, J.E., and Quinn, R.E. (2003) *Positive Organizational Scholarship*, San Francisco: Berrett-Koehler.

Carlsen, A. and Sandelands, L. (2014) "First passion: wonder in organizational inquiry," *Management Learning*, May 20, doi: 10.1177/1350507614533756.

Cartwright, S. and Cooper, C.L. (1990) 'The impact of mergers and acquisitions on people at work: existing research and issues', *British Journal of Management*, 1: 65–76.

Cartwright, S. and Cooper, C.L. (1992). *Managing Mergers, Acquisitions and Strategic Alliances: Integrating People and Cultures*, Oxford: Butterworth-Heinemann.

Cartwright, S. (2012) "Individual response to mergers and acquisitions," in D. Faulkner, S. Teerikangas, and R. Joseph (eds.) *Handbook of Mergers and Acquisitions*, Oxford: Oxford University Press.

Cartwright, S. and Cooper, C.L. (1990) "The impact of mergers and acquisitions on people at work: existing research and issues," *British Journal of Management*, 1: 65–76.

Cartwright, S. and Holmes, N. (2006) "The meaning of work: the challenge of regaining employee engagement and reducing cynicism," *Human Resource Management Review*, 16: 199–208.

Davenport, T.H., Thomas, R.J., and Cantrell, S. (2002) "The mysterious art and science of knowledge-worker performance," *MIT Sloan Management Review*, 44: 23–30.

Demerouti, E., Bakker, A.B., Nachreiner, F., and Schaufeli, W.B. (2001) "The job demands-resources model of burnout," *Journal of Applied Psychology*, 86: 499–512.

Fairfield-Sonn, J.W., Ogilvie, J.R., and DelVecchio, G.A. (2002) "Mergers, acquisitions and long-term employee attitudes," *Journal of Business and Economic Studies*, 8: 1–16.

Feldman, M. (2004) "Resources in emerging structures and processes of change," *Organization Science*, 15(3): 295–309.

Froese, F.J., Pak, Y.S., and Chong, L.C. (2007) "Managing the human side of cross-border acquisitions in South Korea," *Journal of World Business*, 43: 97–108.

Gersick, C.J.G. (1991) "Revolutionary change theories: a multilevel exploration of the punctuated equilibrium paradigm," *Academy of Management Review*, 16: 10–36.

Gilson, L.L. and Shalley, C.E. (2004) "A little creativity goes a long way: an examination of teams' engagement in creative processes," *Journal of Management*, 30: 453–70.

Goffmann, E. (1961) *Encounters: Two Studies in the Sociology of Interaction*, Indianapolis: Bobbs-Merrill Co.

Golden-Biddle, K. and Mao, J. (2012) "Implementing positive change: what makes an organizational change process positive?," in K.S. Cameron and G.S. Spreitzer (eds.) *The Oxford Handbook of Positive Organizational Scholarship*, Oxford: Oxford University Press.

González-Romá, V., Schaufeli, W., Bakker, A., and Lloret, S. (2006) "Burnout and work engagement: independent factors or opposite poles?," *Journal of Vocational Behavior*, 68: 165–74.

Graebner, M.E. (2004) "Momentum and serendipity: how acquired firm leaders create value in the integration of technology firms," *Strategic Management Journal*, 25: 751–77.

Grant, A.M. (2008) "Does intrinsic motivation fuel the prosocial fire? Motivational synergy in predicting persistence, performance, and productivity," *Journal of Applied Psychology*, 93: 48–58.

Hakanen, J.J., Bakker, A.B., and Demerouti, E. (2005) "How dentists cope with their job demands and stay engaged: the moderating role of job resources," *European Journal of Oral Sciences*, 113: 479–87.

Hall, D.T. and Chandler, D.E. (2005) "Psychological success: when the career is a calling," *Journal of Organizational Behavior*, 26: 155–76.

Hallberg, U.E. and Schaufeli, W.B. (2006) "'Same, same, but different'? Can work engagement be empirically separated from job involvement and organizational commitment?," *European Psychologist*, 11: 119–27.

Hannan, M.T. and Freeman, J. (1977) "The population ecology of organizations," *American Journal of Sociology*, 82: 929–64.

Happonen, E. (2009) "The role of pre-deal management in ensuring correct M&A decisions," Master's thesis, Espoo: Helsinki University of Technology.

Harter, S. (2002) "Authenticity," in C.R. Snyder and S.J. Lopez (eds.), *Handbook of Positive Psychology*, Oxford: Oxford University Press.

Harter, J.K., Schmidt, F.L., and Hayes, T.L. (2002) "Business-unit-level relationship between employee satisfaction, employee engagement, and business outcomes: a meta-analysis', *Journal of Applied Psychology*, 87(2): 268–79.

Haspeslagh, P.C. and Jemison, D.B. (1991) *Managing Acquisitions: Creating Value through Corporate Renewal*, New York: The Free Press.

Ho, V., Wong, S. and Lee, C.H. (2011) 'A tale of passion: linking job passion and cognitive engagement to employee work performance', *Journal of Management Studies*, 48(1): 27–47.

Hoegl, M., Gibbert, M., and Mazursky, D. (2008) "Financial constraints in innovation projects: when is less more?," *Research Policy*, 37: 1382–91.

Huy, Q. (2005) "An emotion-based view of strategic renewal," *Advances in Strategic Management*, 22: 3–37.

Huy, Q. (2012) "Strategic change: emotions and strategic change," in K.S. Cameron and G.S. Spreitzer (eds.) *The Oxford Handbook of Positive Organizational Scholarship*, Oxford: Oxford University Press.

Ivancevich, J.M., Schweiger, D.M., and Power, F.R. (1987) "Strategies for managing human resources during mergers and acquisitions," *Human Resource Planning*, 10: 19–35.

James, E.H. and Wooten, L.P. (2012) "Responding to crisis: orientations of positive leadership in times of crisis," in K.S. Cameron and G.S. Spreitzer (eds.) *The Oxford Handbook of Positive Organizational Scholarship*, Oxford: Oxford University Press.

Jemison, D.B. and Sitkin, S.B. (1986) "Corporate acquisitions: a process perspective," *Academy of Management Review*, 11: 145–63.

Kahn, W.A. (1990) "Psychological conditions of personal engagement and disengagement at work," *Academy of Management Journal*, 33: 692–724.

Kahn, W.A. (1992) "To be fully there: psychological presence at work," *Human Relations*, 45: 321–49.

Kor, Y.Y. and Leblebici, H. (2005) "How do interdependencies among human-capital deployment, development and diversification strategies affect firms' financial performance?," *Strategic Management Journal*, 26: 967–85.

Krug, J.A. and Nigh, D. (2001) "Executive perceptions in foreign and domestic acquisitions: an analysis of foreign ownership and its effect on executive fate," *Journal of World Business*, 36: 85–98.

Larsson, R. and Finkelstein, S. (1999) "Integrating strategic, organizational, and human resource perspectives on mergers and acquisitions: a case survey of synergy realization," *Organization Science*, 10: 1–26.

Little, B. and Little, P. (2006) "Employee engagement: conceptual issues," *Journal of Organizational Culture, Communication and Conflict*, 10: 111–20.

Losada, M. (1999) "The complex dynamics of high performance teams," *Mathematical and Computer Modelling*, 30: 179–92.

Losada, M. and Heaphy, E. (2004) "The role of positivity and connectivity in the performance of business teams," *American Behavioral Scientist*, 47: 740–65.

Macey, W.H. and Schneider, B. (2008) "The meaning of employee engagement," *Industrial and Organizational Psychology*, 1: 3–30.

Mainemelis, C. (2001) 'When the muse takes it all: a model for the experience of timelessness in organizations', *Academy of Management Review*, 26(4): 548–65.

Maitlis, S. (2012) "Postraumatic growth: a missed opportunity for positive organizational scholarship," in K.S. Cameron and G.S. Spreitzer (eds.) *The Oxford Handbook of Positive Organizational Scholarship*, Oxford: Oxford University Press.

Marks, M.L. (2007) "A framework for facilitating adaptation to organizational transition," *Journal of Organizational Change Management*, 20: 721–39.

Marks, M.L. and Vansteenskiste, R. (2008) "Preparing for organizational death: proactive HR engagement in an organizational transition," *Human Resource Management*, 47: 809–27.

Maslach, C. and Jackson, S.E. (1981) "The measurement of experienced burnout," *Journal of Occupational Behavior*, 2: 99–113.

Maslach, C. and Leiter, M.P. (1997) *The Truth about Burnout: How Organizations Cause Personal Stress and What To Do about It*, San Francisco, CA: Jossey-Bass.

Maslach, C., and Leiter, M.P. (2008) "Early predictors of job burnout and engagement," *Journal of Applied Psychology*, 93(3): 498–512.

Maslach, C., Schaufeli, W.B., and Leiter, M.P. (2001) "Job burnout," *Annual Review of Psychology*, 52: 397–422.

Maslow, A. (1954) *Motivation and Personality*, New York: Harper and Row.

Miner, J.B. (2005) *Essential Theories of Motivation and Leadership*, New York: M.E. Sharpe.

Morris, P., Söderlund, J., and Pinto, J. (2012) *The Oxford Handbook of Project Management*, Oxford: Oxford University Press.

Napier, N.K. (1989) "Mergers and acquisitions, human resource issues and outcomes: a review and suggested typology," *Journal of Management Studies*, 26: 271–89.

Perttula, K.H. and Cardon, M.S. (2012) "Passion," in K.S. Cameron and G.S. Spreitzer (eds.) *The Oxford Handbook of Positive Organizational Scholarship*, Oxford: Oxford University Press.

Pfeffer, J. (1994) *Competitive Advantage through People: Unleashing the Power of the Work Force*, Boston, MA: Harvard Business School Press.

Ployhart, R.E. and Moliterno, T.P. (2011) "Emergence of the human capital resource: a multilevel model," *Academy of Management Review*, 36: 127–50.

Powley, E.H. (2012) "Healing after trauma—organizational healing: a relational process to handle major disruption," in K.S. Cameron and G.S. Spreitzer (eds.) *The Oxford Handbook of Positive Organizational Scholarship*, Oxford: Oxford University Press.

Pratt, M.G. and Ashforth, B.E. (2003) "Fostering meaningfulness in working and at work," in K. Cameron, J.E. Dutton, and R.E. Quinn (eds.) *Positive Organizational Scholarship*, San Francisco, CA: Berrett-Koehler.

Preston, N. (2013) "Role related dynamics and acquisition performance," Master's thesis, London: University College London.

Preston, N. and Teerikangas, S. (2014) "Shaping individual and organizational performance in M&A through engagement—an explorative study," extended abstract submitted to the 30th Colloquium of the European Group in Organizational Studies.

Quah, P. and Young, S. (2005) "Post-acquisition management: a phases approach for cross-border M&A," *European Management Journal*, 23: 65–75.

Rich, B.L., Lepine, J.A. and Crawford, E.R. (2010) "Job engagement: antecedents and effects on job performance," *Academy of Management Journal*, 53: 617–35.

Rothbard, N.P. and Patil, S.V. (2012) "Work engagement: being there—work engagement and positive organizational scholarship," in K.S. Cameron and G.S. Spreitzer (eds.) *The Oxford Handbook of Positive Organizational Scholarship*, Oxford: Oxford University Press.

Saks, A.M. (2006) "Antecedents and consequences of employee engagement," *Journal of Managerial Psychology*, 21: 600–19.

Salanova, M. and Schaufeli, W.B. (2008) "A cross-national study of work engagement as a mediator between job resources and proactive behavior," *International Journal of Human Resource Management*, 19: 116–31.

Salanova, M., Agut, S., and Peiro, J.M. (2005) "Linking organizational resources and work engagement to employee performance and customer loyalty: the mediation of service climate," *Journal of Applied Psychology*, 90: 1217–27.

Salanova, M., Schaufeli, W.B., Xanthopoulou, D., and Bakker, A.B. (2010) "The gain spirals of resources and work engagement: sustaining positive work life," in A.B. Bakker and M.P. Leiter (eds.) *Work Engagement: A Handbook of Essential Theory and Research*, New York: Psychology Press.

Schaufeli, W.B. and Bakker, A.B. (2004) "Job demands, job resources, and their relationship with burnout and engagement: a multi-sample study," *Journal of Organizational Behavior*, 25: 293–315.

Schaufeli, W.B., Bakker, A.B., and Salanova, M. (2006) "The measurement of engagement with a short questionnaire: a cross-national study," *Educational and Psychological Measurement*, 66: 701–16.

Schaufeli, W.B., Salanova, M., González-Romá, V., and Bakker, A.B. (2002) "The measurement of engagement and burnout: a two sample confirmatory factor analytic approach," *Journal of Happiness Studies*, 3: 71–92.

Schuck, B. (2011) "Four emerging perspectives of employee engagement: an integrative literature review," *Human Resource Development Review*, 10: 304–28.

Shuck, B. and Wollard, K. (2010) "Employee engagement and HRD: a seminal review of the foundations," *Human Resource Development Review*, 9: 89–110.

Sonenshein, S. (2013) "How organizations foster the creative use of resources," *Academy of Management Journal*, 57: 814–48.

Sonenshein, S. and Dholakia, U. (2012) "Explaining employee engagement with strategic change implementation: a meaning-making approach," *Organization Science*, 23: 1–23.

Sonnentag, S. (2003) "Recovery, work engagement, and proactive behavior: a new look at the interface between non-work and work," *Journal of Applied Psychology*, 56: 518–28.

Spreitzer, G., Sutcliffe, K., Dutton, J., Sonenshein, S., and Grant, A.M. (2005) "A socially embedded model of thriving at work," *Organization Science*, 16: 537–49.

Steel, P. and König, C.J. (2006) "Integrating theories of motivation," *Academy of Management Review*, 31: 889–913.

Sudarsanam, S. (2012) "Value creation and value appropriation in M&A deals," in D. Faulkner, S. Teerikangas, and R. Joseph, *Handbook of Mergers and Acquisitions*, Oxford: Oxford University Press.

Sutcliffe, K.M. and Christianson, M.K. (2012) "Managing the unexpected," in K.S. Cameron and G.S. Spreitzer (eds.) *The Oxford Handbook of Positive Organizational Scholarship*, Oxford: Oxford University Press.

Teerikangas, S. (2006) *Silent Forces in Cross-Border Acquisitions: An Integrative Perspective on Post-Acquisition Integration*, Helsinki: Helsinki University of Technology, Institute of Strategy and International Business, Doctoral Dissertation Series, 1/2006.

Teerikangas, S. (2012) "Dynamics of acquired firm pre-acquisition employee reactions," *Journal of Management*, 38: 599–639.

Teerikangas, S. and Geraldi, J. (2011) "Bridging troubled waters: a comparative analysis of the M&A and project literatures," paper presented at the Annual Conference of the European Academy of Management, Tallinn.

Teerikangas, S. and Tienari, J. (2012) "Ambiguities in post-merger integration: a view from within," paper presented at the Annual Colloquium of the European Group of Organization Studies (EGOS), Helsinki.

Teerikangas, S. and Välikangas, L. (2012) "Engaged employees! An actor perspective to innovation," in T. Pitsis, E. Dehlin, and A. Simpson (eds.), *Handbook on Organizational and Management Innovation*, London: Edward Elgar Publishing.

Teerikangas, S. and Välikangas, L. (2014a) "Exploring the dynamic of evoking intuition," in M. Sinclair (ed.), *Handbook of Research Methods in Intuition*, London, UK: Edward Elgar Publishing.

Teerikangas, S. and Välikangas, L. (2014b) "The resourcing of human capital and its malleability in engagement," working paper.

Teerikangas, S., Very, P., and Pisano, V. (2011) "Integration manager's value-capturing roles and acquisition performance," *Human Resource Management*, 50: 651–83.

Tienari, J. and Vaara, E. (2012) "Power and politics in mergers and acquisitions," in D. Faulkner, S. Teerikangas, and R. Joseph, *Handbook of Mergers and Acquisitions*, Oxford: Oxford University Press.

Towers Watson (2012) *Global Workforce Study 2012*.

Tyler, S.L. and Blader, T.R. (2003) "Testing and extending the group engagement model: linkages between social identity, procedural justice, economic outcomes, and extra-role behavior," *Journal of Applied Psychology*, 94: 445–64.

Välikangas, L. and Gibbert, M. (2005) "Constraint-setting strategies for escaping innovation traps," *MIT Sloan Management Review*, 46: 58–66.

Walsh, J.P. (1988) "Top management turnover following mergers and acquisitions," *Strategic Management Journal*, 9: 173–83.

Wefald, A.J. and Downey, R.G. (2009) "Job engagement in organizations: fad, fashion, or folderol?," *Journal of Organizational Behavior*, 30(1), 141–45.

Wright, P.M.W. and Haggerty, J.J. (2005) "Missing variables in theories of strategic human resource management: time, cause and individuals," *Management Revue*, 16: 164–73.

Wrzesniewski, A. (2003) "Finding positive meaning in work," in K. Cameron, J.E. Dutton, and R.E. Quinn (eds.), *Positive Organizational Scholarship*, San Fransisco: Berrett-Koehler.

Zigarmi, D., Nimon, K., Houson, D., Witt, D., and Diehl, J. (2009) "Beyond engagement: toward a framework and operational definition for employee passion," *Human Resource Development Review*, 8: 300–15.

9

M&A and the firm's corporate development portfolio

A call for research integration

Laurence Capron

Introduction

This chapter offers scholars in the field of strategy a perspective from which mergers and acquisitions (M&As) can be viewed within the broader setting of a firm's corporate development portfolio. Mergers and acquisitions can play a significant role in the enhancement or redeployment of a firm's resources and can thus contribute to its survival (Ahuja and Katila 2001; Anand and Singh 1997; Capron 1999; Capron *et al.* 1998; Capron and Guillén 2009; Karim and Mitchell 2000; Graebner and Eisenhartd 2004). However, most research to date has examined M&As in isolation and without accounting for how they might interact with other means of corporate development—such as internal development and alliances.

Scholars have increasingly come to recognize that firms cannot usefully contemplate a particular growth mode in isolation; rather, firms must make integrated resource-sourcing decisions. The objective is to reach an optimal configuration of resource-sourcing modes, an approach referred to as "sourcing multidexterity" (Rothaermel and Alexandre 2009) or as finding a "build–borrow–buy" balance (Capron and Mitchell 2012). The need to take an integrated approach to resource sourcing is especially acute in light of how difficult it can be for business leaders to build a robust corporate development portfolio and reach an optimal configuration of growth modes. Throughout my research and collaboration with companies, I have discovered that many companies either fall into instinctive execution of their favorite growth mode or meet strong internal resistance when attempting to experiment with new modes of growth (Capron and Mitchell 2010, 2012). In short, firms must often mediate the opposing forces of exploitation and exploration.

Thus, the various modes of corporate development cannot be adequately evaluated in isolation because their deployment, resource requirements, and effectiveness are interlinked with those of alternative modes (Capron and Mitchell 2012). I use the term, *corporate development portfolio* in reference to the entire set of modes through which the firm seeks to implement its resource strategy; these include internal innovation projects, alliances, and M&A deals. It is worth remarking that also divestiture, which will not be discussed here, could be seen as part of a firm's corporate development portfolio.

In the rest of this chapter, I draw on a broad set of research traditions in innovation, corporate development, and organizational learning while reviewing literature that is relevant to the notion of considering M&As in the broader context of corporate development and resource sourcing. After a short account of research that addresses the debate over specialization versus variation, I focus on the emerging research stream that deals explicitly with the interplay among various development modes and the concept of a corporate development portfolio. I conclude by outlining the key challenges faced by companies that seek to incorporate M&As into their corporate development portfolio and by identifying avenues for future research.

The corporate development portfolio: specialization or variation?

Extant research focuses mainly on how firms can develop their resources using a particular mode of corporate development: acquisitions (Haleblian and Finkelstein 1999; Zollo and Singh 2004; for a review, see Barkema and Schijven 2008), alliances (Dyer and Singh 1998; Sampson 2005; Kale and Singh 2007; for a review, see Parmigiani and Rivera-Santos 2011), contracts (Argyres and Mayer 2007; Vanneste and Puranam 2010), or internal development (Argote 1999). Some authors have examined how firms can balance their exploitation and exploration needs via a single growth mode, such as internal organization (Benner and Tushman 2003; Greve 2007), alliances (Lavie and Rosenkopf 2006; Rothaermel and Deeds 2004), or acquisitions (Capron and Pistre 2002; Hayward 2002; Laamanen and Keil 2008). However, none of these studies has explored how the firm's overall balance between exploitation and exploration could be achieved by employing different modes of growth.

However, an emerging stream of literature has begun to question whether specializing in one specific type of corporate development is the most effective strategy; this research looks at the tension between specializing in one mode of corporate development versus pursuing a mixture of development modes (Schilling *et al.* 2003). Over time, organizations tend to develop a default approach to obtaining the resources they need. Yet firms that are willing to apply a more varied method may have an advantage—over those that specialize—in seizing a wider range of growth opportunities. Because each corporate development mode fits specific market and resource conditions, it can be argued that careful selection and balance are crucial for firms' survival (Capron and Mitchell 2010, 2012).

Scholars focusing on organizational change regard variation in the firm's activities—that is, incorporating both exploitation and exploration—as beneficial to the firm in the long run (Benner and Tushman 2003; Levinthal and March 1993; March 1991). A preference for exploitation may not be detrimental in the short run (or even in the long run, if the environment is stable), but an exclusive focus on that mode will reduce the organization's ability to uncover opportunities, renew its resources, and respond to changes in the environment (Katila and Ahuja 2002). However, it is difficult to maintain a balance between exploration and exploitation. The pressure to specialize may be especially strong in the short term. This pressure is manifest in the firm's drive for efficiency and conformity, its preference for local search and for accommodating vested interests, and its resistance to conflicting routines (Burgelman 1991; Greve 2007; March 1991). If exploration and exploitation cannot easily coexist, as these considerations suggest, then some form of decoupling is needed. The literature has proposed *organizational decoupling* through the creation of specialized units as well as *temporal decoupling* through alternating among different modes of resource acquisition (Levinthal and March 1993).

Scholars who focus on corporate strategy have applied the notion of decoupling to the formation and renewal of a firm's corporate development portfolio. The implication is that firms specialize in a particular mode of corporate development with a specific goal in mind. In particular, the internal mode is associated with exploitation, and external sourcing is associated with exploration. Under temporal decoupling, the firm switches from one mode to another in order to avoid the bad effects of inertia resulting from intensive internal exploitation and the bad effects of fragmentation stemming from intensive external sourcing (Capron and Mitchell 2012;Vermeulen and Barkema 2001).

Along the same lines, arguments put forth in the dynamic capabilities literature suggest that firms should develop skills in both internal development and external sourcing so that they can renew their resources and thrive over time (Helfat *et al.* 2007). As Agarwal and Helfat (2009) point out, we are beginning to understand how firms undertake such strategic renewal by implementing changes and, more fundamentally, by developing the ability to pursue both internal and external modes of change. Internal development allows a firm to exploit and protect its specific knowledge while coordinating its development activities (Helfat 1994). At the same time, the external sourcing of new resources—through acquisitions, alliances, and purchase contracts—facilitates a firm's guarding against obsolescence and organizational inertia (Rosenkopf and Nerkar 2001;Vermeulen and Barkema 2001). The innovation literature emphasizes that exploiting external knowledge is critical to innovation (Teece *et al.* 1997), and the recognition of this fact has made alliances and acquisitions an integral part of many firms' R&D strategies (Rothaermel and Boeker 2008).

In sum, firms that appropriately select and balance internal development and external sourcing as modes of obtaining new resources can more effectively renew their competitive vitality, thereby gaining a long-term performance advantage (Capron and Mitchell 2009; Hoang and Rothaermel 2010; Lavie 2007).

What do we know so far?

There is an emerging stream of studies that examine the alternation and coordination of building, buying, and partnering (a.k.a. borrowing)—although it should be mentioned that several works across different research fields have previously touched on these issues. Table 9.1 organizes by topic the different studies reviewed in this section.

In their influential work on post-merger integration, Haspeslagh and Jemison (1991) note that acquisitions can drive out internal development when managers emphasize short-term operating results from recent acquisitions at the expense of investing in people or in strategic investment for internal growth. These authors observe that each mode of renewal implies a complementary dose of the other in the sense that "most internal development relies on some acquisition of capabilities. By the same token, even the acquisition of a complete business needs to be made in a developmental perspective if it is to create the most value" (p. 246). This combination of modes generates complementarities but also involves some trade-offs.

In the strategy literature, Hitt *et al.* (1991) find that engaging in M&A strongly affects not only the context in which innovation is framed but also the control mechanisms employed and the design and process of innovation. Given these trade-offs, corporate development modes must be carefully selected.

In the literature on innovation, Arora and Gambardella (1990) examine complementarities between the different external sourcing strategies of major chemical and pharmaceutical firms in biotechnology; these include agreements with other firms and with universities as well as investments in (and acquisitions of) firms based on new technology. The authors find evidence of all types of external sourcing activities, suggesting complementarities among them.

Table 9.1 Research examining the interplay of M&A with other modes

Build Internal development	Buy Mergers and acquisitions	Partner Alliances and licensing
• Haspeslagh and Jemison (1991) • Hitt *et al.* (1991) • Vermeulen and Barkema (2001) • Karim and Mitchell (2000) • Karim (2006) • Arikan and Capron (2013)	• Arora and Gambardella (1990) • Wang and Zajac (2007) • Zollo and Reuer (2010) • Arikan and McGahan (2010) • Van de Vrande (2013)	• Villalonga and McGahan (2005) • Cassiman and Veugelers (2006) • Capron and Mitchell (2009, 2010, 2012) • Rothaermel and Alexandre (2009) • Hagedoorn and Wang (2012) • Stern and Lungeanu (2013) • Bingham *et al.* (2013) • Stettner and Lavie (2014) • Bertrand and Capron (2015)

Although these various contributions are certainly valuable, the overall result is a fragmented perspective of the notion of a corporate development portfolio and the role of M&A within this broader landscape. More recent studies (see Table 9.1) focus explicitly on the interplay between three modes of corporate development: internal development, alliances, and acquisitions. This promising stream of research has so far addressed two main questions. First, does variation in corporate development programs enhance firm survival—and, if so, under what circumstances? Second, how can firms pursue and benefit from concurrent learning processes?

Mode variation, mode complementarities and firm survival

One should not assume that the firm will exhibit variation in its development programs. When it comes to sourcing resources, organizations often make no conscious choice but instead simply employ the mode with which they are most familiar. The outcome of such path dependency is a highly specialized corporate development portfolio, which has been found to undermine firm long-term performance—especially in a high-velocity environment characterized by intensive innovation.

In their pathbreaking study, Vermeulen and Barkema (2001) examine patterns of international expansion—namely, "greenfield" versus acquisition—among 25 large Dutch firms from 1966 to 1994. They find that firms were more likely to survive if they could strike a balance between (on the one hand) exploitation and greenfield activities and (on the other hand) organizational revitalization and acquisition. Hence, successful firms that spent time pursuing acquisitions would tend later to pursue greenfield projects, and vice versa. These findings are in line with the organizational change literature, which posits that firms go through long periods of stability and convergence punctuated by short periods of radical change (Tushman and Romanelli 1985).

In the innovation literature, Cassiman and Veugelers (2006) show that a firm's external knowledge acquisition and own R&D investments are complementary innovation activities that affect its incentive to pursue innovation. An example of this dynamic is that the firm's internal knowledge increases the marginal return to external sourcing strategies. Such interplay is reminiscent of the "absorptive capacity" described by Cohen and Levinthal (1990), who stress the importance of attaining a threshold level of internal knowledge before external resources can be used effectively. At the same time, externally sourced resources may increase the efficiency of a firm's internal development activities.

To examine the key role played by both acquisitions and internal development in business reconfiguration, Karim and Mitchell (2000) track the evolution of 87 product lines and 88 business units in Johnson & Johnson's medical sector from 1975 to 1997. Their study underscores the dual importance of acquisitions and internal development as sources of value and innovation as well as the supporting role of business unit reconfiguration.

Taking an organizational approach, Karim (2006) observes how the business reconfiguration process unfolds within the firm—more specifically, how internal units and acquired units are reconfigured after an acquisition. Using a sample of 250 firms and their units from 1978 to 1997, she finds that acquired units are more likely to be reconfigured than internal units. Moreover, acquired units are reconfigured sooner than internally developed units and are often reconfigured several times. We can thus view acquisitions as malleable components that provide key resources to internal units and provide opportunities for firms to experiment with structure as they strive to create value by reconfiguring acquired targets. Internally developed units, even when integrated with other units, usually retain their modular identity and serve as the firm's foundation.

The underlying message of the evolutionary patterns discerned in the studies cited here is that innovation proceeds from a deep understanding of organizationally embedded routines while undertaking exploratory external search. A necessary component of this process is the ongoing redefinition of both unit boundaries and firm boundaries.

Pulling together the three modes of resource acquisition outlined schematically in Table 9.1, Capron and Mitchell (2009, 2010, 2012) look at the firm's *selection capability* or its ability to match the most appropriate resource-sourcing mode—that is, either "build" (internal development), "borrow" (licensing and alliances), or "buy" (M&A)—with each resource gap that it faces. Their first result (Capron and Mitchell 2009) is that, if the knowledge gap is wide or if the targeted resource conflicts with what is socially accepted within an organization and thus reduces the odds of developing that resource effectively internally, then external sourcing is the best means of acquiring the targeted resource and hence of ensuring the firm's subsequent survival. This finding is consistent with Vermeulen and Barkema's (2001) view of acquisitions as a way to overcome internal inertia. In a study of 162 information and communication technology (ICT) firms, Capron and Mitchell (2012) find a positive relation between the firm's long-term health and its ability to create a portfolio of build–borrow–buy activities.

This notion of selection capability is developed within a practitioner-oriented framework by Capron and Mitchell (2012); that book offers a flowchart—the "resource pathways framework"—dedicated to assessing modes of resource acquisition. Selection capability is viewed as the result of learning from the cycle of identifying resource gaps, selecting the best path to obtain resources, implementing the chosen path, and then realigning and balancing the corporate development portfolio.

Along similar lines, Stettner and Lavie (2014) argue that balancing exploration and exploitation needs *across* modes (internal development, alliances, and acquisitions) is more effective than achieving that balance *within* modes. They posit that balancing exploitation and exploration within each mode undermines firm performance given the existence of conflicting routines, "negative transfer," and limited specialization. Decoupling exploration from exploitation across modes can reduce the interdependence of these two approaches—as well as the cost of maintaining, within each mode, routines that are in conflict—while still allowing the firm to benefit from a simultaneous pursuit of exploration and exploitation. Their analysis of 190 US-based software firms supports this contention by demonstrating that the firm's performance is enhanced by exploring, via externally oriented modes such as acquisitions or alliances, and simultaneously exploiting via internal, organization-based modes.

Shifting the focus to firms that have recently undertaken an initial public offering (IPO), Arikan and Capron (2013) examine the conditions under which M&As increase the hazard of being delisted from the stock exchange. That paper draws on a database of 4,390 IPOs followed over the period from 1988 to 2012, and it finds that M&As can result in two opposite effects. In particular, a firm may be delisted after making too many acquisitions and also after making too few acquisitions. Those IPO'd firms that embark on an aggressive M&A program expose their organization to external and internal turbulence due to substantial changes in scale or structure. Firms pursuing a moderate M&A program enjoy greater organizational stability and are thus less likely to be delisted. Firms that shun M&A are seldom disrupted; however, since their development levels will be relatively low, these firms run the risk of not living up to the market's expectations.

In the innovation literature, Rothaermel and Alexandre (2009) argue that firms with an "ambidextrous" sourcing strategy based on the use of both internal and external sourcing should outperform those that rely on a single sourcing mode. With regard to the technology sourcing of US manufacturing firms, these authors find support for their prediction—especially among firms with a high absorptive capacity.

Exploring further the complex relationship between internal and external R&D strategies, Hagedoorn and Wang (2012) identify when these two strategy types can be viewed as complements or substitutes. They use a 1986 to 2000 panel sample of 83 incumbent pharmaceutical firms to show that the extent of in-house R&D investment, which is characterized by decreasing marginal returns, is a variable that significantly affects the association between internal and external R&D strategies. In particular, internal and external R&D are, respectively, complementary and substitutive strategic options at, respectively, higher and lower levels of in-house R&D investment.

Similarly, Van De Vrande (2013) found a positive relationship between diversity of external sourcing modes (i.e. alliances, joint ventures, minority holdings, and mergers and acquisitions) and firm innovative performance. She develops the notion of a technology-sourcing portfolio, which is close to the notion of a corporate development portfolio.

With a different focal point, i.e. examining conditions under which cross-border acquisitions increase the acquirer's productivity at home, Bertrand and Capron forthcoming) found that *ex post* domestic productivity gains accruing to firms making cross-border acquisitions are greater when acquiring firms make contemporaneous domestic productivity-enhancing investments in conjunction with the acquisition. Their results suggest that cross-border acquisitions and investing in productivity at home are complementary activities.

Balancing the corporate development portfolio and the challenges of concurrent learning

It is clear that balancing exploitation and exploration across modes of development is crucial for a firm's resource renewal and survival, yet challenges arise from the pursuit of such variation in a corporate development portfolio. Such challenges arise from difficulties in concurrently considering and learning multiple modes.

All too often, the inhibiting factor is not a lack of available options but rather the difficulty of considering alternatives (Hamel and Breen 2007). Indeed, it has been shown that having experience with only one development mode is a major factor that prevents firms from considering alternatives. There is ample evidence that, the more experience a firm has with internal development, alliances, or acquisitions, the more likely it is to use that same mode again (Hayward 2002). More recent research has considered how experience with one mode of corporate development can *affect the likelihood* of a firm's using (or not using) other modes and their effectiveness at using multiple modes.

In their study of 9,276 deal announcements—including acquisitions, alliances, and divestitures—made by 86 "Fortune 100" firms in the period from 1990 to 2000, Villalonga and McGahan (2005) find that firms with greater acquisition experience are more likely to choose acquisitions over alliances; however, firms with greater alliance experience were *not* significantly more likely to choose alliances over acquisitions. This result indicates that the spillover effects of experience are asymmetric with respect to different governance forms. Thus governance specialization is much more important for moves toward greater integration than for moves that result in reduced integration. In other words, the knowledge derived from acquiring other firms tends to be specialized to future acquisitions, whereas the knowledge derived from engaging in alliances is more fungible. Experience with alliances yields valuable lessons that can inform both the selection and implementation of future acquisitions, but acquisition experience seems not to inform the firm's future involvement with alliances.

In pursuing this line of investigation, Wang and Zajac (2007) argue that certain aspects of relational capabilities—such as gathering information about external partners, performing financial and cultural due diligence, and negotiating contracts—can be developed from prior experience with either alliances or acquisitions. Drawing on a longitudinal data set from a (1991 to 2000) sample of the largest US firms and focusing on the dyadic characteristics of each inter-firm combination, these authors find that the firms' combined alliance capabilities increased not only the likelihood of allying with each other but also the likelihood of one firm acquiring the other (although the former outcome is more probable). In contrast, it seems that the general knowledge gained from being an acquirer in previous transactions does not encourage firms to engage in an alliance.

Results reported by Villalonga and McGahan (2005) and by Wang and Zajac (2007) point to asymmetric experience spillovers across alliances and acquisitions. This asymmetry is confirmed by Zollo and Reuer (2010), who find that alliance experience has a positive effect on subsequent acquisitions *only* if acquisitions are managed at arm's length; when the target is integrated with the acquirer, negative spillovers are observed.

In their study of acquisitions, alliances, and in-house R&D projects among 30 pharmaceutical firms over the period from 1992 to 2006, Stern and Lungeanu (2013) posit that investments in one mode (e.g. internal development) reflect substantial experience and stable routines for product development that cannot be easily disregarded or altered. Such inertia may in turn divert resources away from alliance and acquisition activities. The authors find that firms pursue their goals by using various R&D means simultaneously and that a firm's experience with one mode of corporate development reduces the likelihood of its using alternative modes.

In their efforts to develop an empirically grounded understanding of how corporate development capabilities can be built in parallel, Bingham *et al.* (2013) employ 20 years of quantitative and qualitative data on Dow Chemical to develop a theoretical framework for explicating the concept of "concurrent learning." They describe how multiple capabilities can be learned concurrently, a process that is facilitated by three key activities: high-level process mapping, backward chaining (codification in reverse chronological order), and portfolio balancing.

In their emphasis on the importance (for firm survival) of alternating corporate development modes, all these studies contribute to our understanding of the role played by M&A in a firm's corporate development portfolio. The research cited here outlines the challenges of combining different modes within an organization to develop a "sourcing multidexterity" that allows it to capture the benefits of variation *without* forgoing opportunities for specialization. It should be noted that firms must develop specialized capabilities if they are to execute effectively a chosen mode of corporate development; as suggested by Arikan and McGahan (2010), this approach is especially important for young firms with initially limited resources for learning multiple modes.

Although Hoang and Rothaermel (2010) do not consider M&A, they do examine the interplay between internal development and other modes of external sourcing such as licensing or alliances. These authors develop an integrative model of organizational learning and propose that competence as regards internal exploration allows firms to leverage their external exploitation experience more fully; in contrast, combining internal and external exploration should have a negative effect on R&D projects. Hoang and Rothaermel (2010) use a data set consisting of 412 R&D biotechnology projects, conducted by large pharmaceutical companies between 1980 and 2000, and find substantial support for their model.

Mulotte *et al.* (2013) study firms that entered the global aircraft industry between 1944 and 2000. The authors posit that, if a firm's market entry relies on product licensing, then that firm will exhibit weaker performance, upon subsequent independent entry, than will firms that undertake independent entry at the outset. The reported performance penalty is increasing in contextual dissimilarity.

Key challenges and future research

Despite the advances made in our appreciation of M&A as a mode of corporate development and of its interplay with alternative modes, we still do not fully understand how firms can best develop a robust ability to form, balance, and (as needed) reconfigure a strong corporate development portfolio. This section outlines three promising avenues for future research, which correspond to three pillars upon which such a capability could be built: 1) integrated sourcing assessment and dealing with intraorganizational impediments, 2) concurrent learning and the fungibility of corporate development capabilities, and 3) portfolio composition and the decoupling of exploitation from exploration.

Integrated sourcing assessment and dealing with intraorganizational impediments

In order to avoid path dependency and overreliance on a dominant mode of corporate development, firms must learn to consider multiple options *before* pursuing a particular mode. In theory, the choice of mode should fit the focal project's resource requirements and forms of governance, but there are several hurdles—which include the firm having limited its experience to one mode only—that can hinder the discipline of discriminating alignment. Although a specialized form of governance enables the firm to achieve more than would otherwise be possible when employing a particular mode, the familiar option may actually be less effective than an alternative one. Experience with just one mode is often associated with calcified processes of decision making and related organizational impediments that prevent firms from making an integrated assessment of different sourcing options.

Such an assessment is more complicated when the organization's decision-making process is fragmented and so a multitude of organizational interests must be placated, which may explain why governance choices are often misaligned with the characteristics of the resource

157

exchange. Recent field studies indicate that the choice of corporate development mode is often more reflective of managers' own interests than of the organization's best interests (Bidwell 2012; Capron and Mitchell 2012). In his study of outsourcing by the IT department of a large financial services firm, Bidwell (2012) emphasizes the value of understanding "make or buy" decisions as an endogenous consequence of the structure in which those decisions take place and not as isolated decisions whose intended benefits are maximized irrespective of their context.

In their field study of resource sourcing in the ICT sector, Capron and Mitchell (2012) document a set of organizational antecedents, including organizational fragmentation and lack of unified incentives among decision makers that lead to suboptimal choices of corporate development modes. For instance, individual incentives are not conducive to sound principles for selecting M&A targets; that is, acquisition team members are often incentivized (for bonus or career reasons) to complete the deal at any cost. In a related study, Dyer *et al.* (2004) report that 76 per cent of the 200 firms they surveyed did not consider—before undertaking their most recent acquisition—the alternative of forming an alliance *even though* 82 per cent of their respondents acknowledged that both alliances and acquisitions were viable means of achieving the firm's growth goals.

All these studies suggest, in the interdisciplinary Carnegie School spirit, promising avenues of research at the intersection of theories on boundaries of the firm and organizational decision making. Existing studies that address the effective sourcing of resources have focused on firms' implementation capability while underemphasizing the importance of selecting the most effective mode and the ways in which certain decision-making contexts can be leveraged to increase that effectiveness.

Concurrent learning and the fungibility of corporate development capabilities

In their efforts to build a strong corporate development portfolio, firms must actively seek learning opportunities in which they can flex their resource development muscles. Thus, firms need to participate in a wide range of activities that include internal projects, internal exploratory environments, contracts, alliances, and major acquisitions.

However, proactively building up the firm's capabilities for multiple modes of corporate development is a process fraught with many challenges. As discussed previously, an organization cannot develop concurrent learning processes without first overcoming the resistance of entrenched groups and leaders. In addition to the hurdles of intraorganizational politics, limitations in size and resource endowments also constrain firms in their efforts to experiment with multiple modes. An organization's size and age typically shape how it gains the necessary experience. Smaller firms will often rely on internal development, contracts, and alliances because it is difficult for them to acquire other firms. In contrast, the challenge for a larger firm, which may well be plagued by ingrained modes of corporate development, is to break out of its historical boundaries before becoming irrevocably trapped within them (Capron and Mitchell 2012).

Once the firm makes an explicit and determined attempt to promote concurrent learning, it must still often face impediments that reflect tensions arising from the trade-off between specialization and variation. It will take time as well as the accumulation of experience with a specific mode before a firm can extract all the benefits from specializing (Arikan and McGahan 2010; Haleblian and Finkelstein 1999). After such capabilities are developed, they constitute sunk costs that justify repeated use of the same mode in order to recoup the learning investment. Much as with any corporate-level decision, adjusting resources to fit the type and volume of corporate development activities is not a frictionless endeavor.

An important aspect of specialized corporate development capabilities is their fungibility. In other words, unless they are transferable to some extent, capabilities may remain unexercised for a certain period of time. Recent studies provide preliminary evidence that experience has limited fungibility across modes. With respect to competitive strategy, the firm must often choose between committing to one mode of corporate development (and thus building related specialized capabilities that are not easily transferred) or committing to a multisourcing strategy (and thereby building less specific yet more fungible corporate development capabilities). An intriguing topic for future research is the firm's choice of which types of corporate development capabilities to develop internally, maintain, redeploy, or abandon.

Portfolio composition and the decoupling of exploitation from exploration

If the firm has established a satisfactory balance between maintaining its current operations and engaging in efforts to renew its sourcing capabilities, then a decision must be reached concerning the relative importance of acquisitions—as opposed to internal development or partnerships—in accumulating, expanding, or redeploying those capabilities. Despite the myriad possible combinations of exploitation and exploration activities across modes, there is one unifying theme: firms that find a mix of corporate development modes that optimally balances their exploitation and exploitation needs will fare better in the long run. However, most organizations have many members who do not see the full picture; hence achieving the optimal mix of modes will seldom be a straightforward process.

In order to deepen our understanding of how best to arrive at the ideal configuration of development modes, we must account for two caveats to the arguments advanced in recent studies. First, one should not simplistically equate either exploration with external sourcing or exploitation with local internal development. Although it may certainly prove fruitful to search beyond the firm's boundaries, innovations can also be developed internally (e.g. through searching within an internal exploratory environment). This means that some firms may be more adept at balancing exploitation and exploration *within* modes while others are better suited to finding such balance *across* modes; still other firms might gain advantages by balancing development styles within *and* across modes. Second, the firm is well advised to monitor the evolving form of whichever development mode is chosen. Some exploratory acquisitions may, over time, transition toward the form of an exploitative internal project (and vice versa). It may likewise be necessary for the chosen corporate development mode to shift toward greater or lesser integration with the mainstream organization; that would have the effect of shifting such development toward more exploratory or exploitative purposes, respectively.

The upshot of these considerations is that implementing the firm's preferred method of "decoupling" its exploitation and exploitation needs will almost always prove to be a challenge. To navigate this balancing act often requires that the firm be able to effect a rapid reconfiguration of their corporate development portfolio upon reviewing the results of past development mode choices. Future research could shed more light on this important line of investigation.

Summary

This aim of this chapter is to widen the scope of scholars in the field of mergers and acquisitions. M&A involves firm growth, but it is only one of multiple paths for firm growth. Clearly, there are opportunities for further research that would extend our knowledge of M&As within the context of a firm's corporate development portfolio and also enable a more nuanced view of how firms can both achieve their exploitation–exploration balance and reach their optimal configuration of growth modes. After all, the M&A mode is but one among many; it complements other modes yet entails trade-offs related to its resource and learning requirements. Acquisitions are relevant when firms face both internal resource limitations as well as failures in the market for resources; yet integrating acquired businesses is a daunting task that might require firms to revisit their sourcing options and consider alternatives such as partial acquisitions, equity-backed joint ventures, or the set-up of an internal exploratory environment (Capron 2013).

Future research work is needed to understand not only when to choose M&A over alternative modes to source new resources and their impact on performance, but also to manage the managerial dynamic processes of building, borrowing, acquiring resources effectively, blending them in an optimal way, and reshuffling and divesting them in a timely manner, without losing sight of the corporate portfolio balance and the difficulties of coordinating, or scaling up or down the corporate functions such as M&As, alliances, licensing, and internal innovation activities.

References

Agarwal, R. and Helfat, C.E. (2009) "Strategic renewal of organizations," *Organization Science*, 20: 281–93.

Ahuja, G. and Katila, R. (2001) "Technological acquisitions and the innovation performance of acquiring firms: A longitudinal study," *Strategic Management Journal*, 22: 197–220.

Anand, J. and Singh, H. (1997) "Asset redeployment, acquisitions and corporate strategy in declining industries," *Strategic Management Journal*, 1: 99–118.

Argote, L. (1999) *Organizational Learning: Creating, Retaining, and Transferring Knowledge*. Kluwer Academic Publishers: Boston, MA.

Argyres, N.S. and. Mayer, K.J. (2007) "Contract design as a firm capability: An integration of learning and transaction cost perspectives," *Academy of Management Review*, 32: 1060–77.

Arikan, A.M. and McGahan, A.M. (2010) "The development of capabilities in new firms," *Strategic Management Journal*, 31: 1–18.

Arikan, A.M. and Capron, L. (2013) "When do internal investment and M&As help or hurt IPOed firm's survival?," paper presented at *2013 AOM Conference*, Orlando, FL.

Arora, A. and Gambardella, A. (1990) "Complementary and external linkages: The strategies of the large firms in biotechnology," *Journal of Industrial Economy*, 3: 361–79.

Barkema, H.G. and Schijven, M. (2008) "How do firms learn to make acquisitions? A review of past research and an agenda for the future," *Journal of Management*, 34: 594–634.

Benner, M.J. and Tushman, M.L. (2003) "Exploitation, exploration, and process management: The productivity dilemma revisited," *Academy of Management Review*, 28: 238–56.

Bertrand, O. and Capron, L. (2015) "Productivity enhancement at home via cross-border acquisitions: The roles of learning and contemporaneous domestic investments," *Strategic Management Journal*, 36: 640–58. http://onlinelibrary.wiley.com/doi/10.1002/smj.2256/pdf.

Bidwell, M. (2012) "Politics and firm boundaries: How organizational structure, group interests and resources affect outsourcing," *Organization Science*, 23: 1622–42.

Bingham, C., Heimeriks. K., Schjiven, M., and Gates, S. (2013). "ConcurrentlLearning: How firms build multiple capabilities in parallel," paper presented at *2013 AOM Conference*, Orlando, FL.

Burgelman, R.A. (1991) "Intraorganizational ecology of strategy making and organizational adaptation: Theory and field research," *Organization Science*, 2: 239–62.

Capron. L. (1999) "The long-term performance of horizontal acquisitions," *Strategic Management Journal*, 20: 987–1018.

Capron, L. (2013) "Cisco's corporate development portfolio: A blend of building, borrowing and buying," *Strategy and Leadership*, 41: 27–30

Capron, L. and Pistre N. (2002) "When do acquirers earn abnormal returns?," *Strategic Management Journal*, 23: 781–94.

Capron, L. and Guillén, M. (2009) "National corporate governance institutions and post-acquisition target reorganization," *Strategic Management Journal*, 30: 803–33.

Capron, L. and Mitchell, W. (2009). "Selection capability: How capability gaps and internal social frictions affect internal and external strategic renewal," *Organization Science*, 20: 294–312.

Capron L. and Mitchell, W. (2010) "Finding the right path." *Harvard Business Review*, 88 (7/8): 102–7.

Capron, L. and Mitchell, W. (2012) *Build, Borrow or Buy: Solving the Growth Dilemma*. Harvard Business Review Press: Boston, MA.

Capron, L., Dussauge P., and Mitchell, W. (1998) "Resource redeployment following horizontal mergers and acquisitions in Europe and North America, 1988–1992," *Strategic Management Journal*, 19: 631–61.

Cassiman, B and Veugelers, R. (2006) "In search of complementarity in innovation strategy: Internal R&D and external knowledge acquisition," *Management Science*, 52: 68–82.

Cohen, W.M. and Levinthal, D. (1990) "Absorptive capacity: A new perspective on learning and innovation," *Administrative Science Quarterly*, 35: 128–52.

Dyer, J.H. and Singh, H. (1998) "The relational view: Cooperative strategy and sources of interorganizational competitive advantage," *Academy of Management Review*, 23: 660–80.

Dyer, J.H., Kale, P., and Singh, H. (2004). "When to ally and when to acquire," *Harvard Business Review*, 82 (7–8): 109–15.

Graebner, M.E. and Eisenhardt, M.K. (2004) "The seller's side of the story: Acquisition as courtship and governance as syndicate in entrepreneurial firms," *Administrative Science Quarterly*, 49: 366–403.

Greve, H.R. (2007) "Exploration and exploitation in product innovation," *Industrial Corporate Change*, 16: 945–75.

Hagedoorn, J. and Wang, N. (2012) "Is there complementarity or substitutability between internal and external R&D strategies?," *Research Policy*, 41: 1072–83.

Haleblian, J. and Finkelstein, S. (1999) "Organizational acquisition experience on acquisition performance: A behavioral learning perspective," *Administrative Science Quarterly*, 44: 29–56.

Hamel, G and Breen, B. (2007) *The Future of Management*. Harvard Business Press: Boston, MA.

Haspeslagh, P.C. and Jemison, D.B. (1991) *Managing acquisitions: Creating value through corporate renewal*. Free Press: New York.

Hayward, M.L.A (2002) "When do firms learn from their acquisition experience? Evidence from 1990 to 1995," *Strategic Management Journal*, 23: 21–39.

Helfat, C.E. (1994) "Evolutionary trajectories in petroleum firm R&D," *Management Science*, 40: 1720–74.

Helfat, C.E., Finkelstein, S., Mitchell, W., Peteraf, M., Singh, H., Teece, D., and Winter, S. (2007) *Dynamic Capabilities: Understanding Strategic Change in Organizations*. Blackwell: London.

Hitt, M.A., Hoskisson, R.E., Ireland, D.R. and Harrison, S.J. (1991). "Effects of acquisitions on R&D inputs and outputs," *Academy of Management Journal*, 34: 693–711.

Hoang, H. and Rothaermel, F. (2010) "Leveraging internal and external experience: Exploration, exploitation, and R&D project performance," *Strategic Management Journal*, 31: 734–58.

Kale, P. and Singh, H. (2007) "Building firm capabilities through learning: The role of the alliance learning process in alliance capability and firm-level alliance success," *Strategic Management Journal*, 28: 981–1000.

Karim, S. (2006) "Modularity in organizational structure: The reconfiguration of internally developed and acquired business units," *Strategic Management Journal*, 27: 799–823

Karim, S. and Mitchell, W. (2000) "Path-dependent and path-breaking change: Reconfiguring business resources following acquisitions in the U.S. medical sector, 1978–1995," *Strategic Management Journal*, 21: 1061–81.

Katila, R., Ahuja, A. (2002) "Something old, something new: A longitudinal study of search behavior and new product introduction," *Academy of Management Journal*, 45: 1183–94.

Laamanen, T. and Keil, T. (2008) "Performance of serial acquirers: Toward an acquisition program perspective," *Strategic Management Journal*, 29: 663–72.

Lavie, D. (2007) "Alliance portfolios and firm performance: A study of value creation and appropriation in the U.S. software industry," *Strategic Management Journal*, 28: 1187–212.

Lavie, D. and Rosenkopf, L. (2006) "Balancing exploitation and exploitation in alliance formation," *Academy of Management Journal*, 49: 797–818.

Levinthal, D. and March, J.G. (1993) "The myopia of learning," *Strategic Management Journal*, 14: 95–112.

March, J.G. (1991) "Exploration and exploitation in organizational learning," *Organization Science*, 2: 71–87.

Mulotte, L. Dussauge, P. and Mitchell, W. (2013) "Does pre-entry licensing undermine the performance of subsequent independent activities? Evidence from the global aerospace industry, 1944–2000," *Strategic Management Journal*, 34: 358–72.

Parmigiani, A. and Rivera-Santos, M (2011) "Clearing a path through the forest: A meta-review of interorganizational relationships," *Journal of Management*, 37: 1108–136.

Rosenkopf, L. and Nerkar, A. (2001) "Beyond local search: Boundary-spanning, exploration, and impact in the optical disc industry," *Strategic Management Journal*, 22: 287–306.

Rothaermel, F.T. and Deeds, D.L. (2004) "Exploration and exploitation alliances in biotechnology: A system of new product development," *Strategic Management Journal*, 25: 201–21.

Rothaermel, F.T. and Boeker, W. (2008) "Old technology meets new technology: Complementarities, similarities, and alliance formation," *Strategic Management Journal*, 29: 47–77.

Rothaermel, F.T. and Alexandre, M.T. (2009) "Ambidexterity in technology sourcing: The moderating role of absorptive capacity," *Organization Science*, 20: 759–80.

Sampson, R. (2005) "Experience effects and collaborative returns in R&D alliances," *Strategic Management Journal*, 26: 1009–31.

Schilling, M., Vidal, P., Ployhart, R., and Marangoni, A. (2003) "Learning by doing something else: Variation, relatedness, and the learning curve," *Management Science*, 49: 39–56.

Stern, I. and Lungeanu, R. (2013) "Cannot study one without the others: An examination of the interdependencies among strategic means," paper presented at *2013 AOM Conference*, Orlando, FL.

Stettner, U. and Lavie, D. (2014) "Ambidexterity under scrutiny: Exploration and exploitation via internal organization, alliances and acquisitions," *Strategic Management Journal*, 35(13), 1903–29.

Stettner, U. and Lavie, D. (2014). Ambidexterity under scrutiny: Exploration and exploitation via internal organization, alliances, and acquisitions. Strategic management journal.

Teece, D.J., Pisano, G. and Shuen, A. (1997) "Dynamic capabilities and strategic management," *Strategic Management Journal*, 18: 509–33.

Tushman, M. and Romanelli, E. (1985) "Organizational evolution: A metamorphosis model of convergence and reorientation," in Cummings, L.L. and Staw, B.M. (eds.), *Research in Organizational Behavior*, 7: 171–222, JAI Press: Greenwich, CT.

Van de Vrande, V. (2013) "Balancing your technology-sourcing portfolio: How sourcing mode diversity enhances innovative performance," *Strategic Management Journal*, 34: 610–21.

Vanneste, B. and Puranam, P. (2010) "Repeated interactions and contractual detail: Identifying the learning effect," *Organization Science*, 21: 186–201.

Vermeulen, F. and Barkema, H. (2001) "Learning through acquisitions," *Academy of Management Journal*, 44: 457–76.

Villalonga, B. and McGahan, A.M. (2005). "The choice among acquisitions, alliances, and divestitures," *Strategic Management Journal*, 26: 1183–208.

Wang, L. and Zajac, E. (2007) "Alliance or acquisition? A dyadic perspective on interfirm resource combinations," *Strategic Management Journal*, 28: 89–105.

Zollo, M. and Singh, H. (2004) "Deliberate learning in corporate acquisitions: Post-acquisition strategies and integration capability in U.S. bank mergers," *Strategic Management Journal*, 25: 1233–56.

Zollo, M. and Reuer, J. (2010) "Experience spillover across corporate development activities," *Organization Science*, 21: 1195–212.

10

The acquisition performance game
A stakeholder approach

Olimpia Meglio

Introduction: a quest for a fresh perspective on acquisition performance

Measuring performance is a central issue for management scholars seeking to gauge the effectiveness of managerial decisions (March and Sutton 1997). Merger and acquisition (henceforth, acquisition) scholars have similarly produced a vast amount of empirical work endeavoring to assess the impact of acquisitions on the acquiring firm performance (e.g. Capron 1999; Cording *et al.* 2008; Fowler and Schmidt 1988). Decades of organizational performance research have yielded a notable lack of consensus about variables, indicators, and metrics (Carton and Hofer 2006; Daily 1994; Venkatraman and Ramanujam 1987). Interpretations of performance have ranged from relatively narrow, focusing on financial aspects as typically deployed by strategic management scholars, to relatively broad, encompassing effectiveness measures as typically employed by organizational scholars. Similarly the study of acquisition performance has resulted in many assessment instruments, including both financial (operational, accounting, and shareholder value) and non-financial (innovation, reputation, and market share) measures as documented in several reviews (e.g., Cording *et al.* 2010; Meglio and Risberg 2011; Zollo and Meier 2008).

The existence of a multitude of measures for acquisition performance explains the difficulties in summarizing results of research through meta-analyses (Datta *et al.* 1992; King *et al.* 2004) and a widespread feeling that we know very little about performance in acquisitions (Bower 2004). The variety of performance measures also signals that acquisition performance is a complex and multidimensional construct (Cording *et al.* 2010; Zollo and Meier 2008) and encourages scholars to reach a better alignment between theory and measures for performance. In this regard, Harrison and Schijven (2015) contend that a better alignment between research questions and measures for acquisition performance can be reached by choosing measures according to the stage of acquisition under investigation.

In this chapter I want to contribute to the ongoing debate about performance measurement by switching our attention from how acquisitions perform to what determines acquisition performance. I achieve this goal by applying the suggestions that Wicker (1985) offers to overcome the limitations that human beings exhibit in research activity, where recurrent thinking prevents adding new knowledge. Specifically, one of the heuristics that Wicker (1985) advises is changing the scale in the analysis of a given topic. In this chapter, I enlarge the domain of acquisition performance by taking into account other stakeholders than shareholders. By doing this, I broaden our knowledge about drivers behind the multiple dimensions of acquisition performance by investigating the influences that internal and external actors exert upon acquisition performance. Studies about mergers and acquisitions have mainly dealt with internal factors (Schriber 2013), with only a few focusing on external actors (see, among the others, Öberg 2008). While current research on acquisition performance is dominated by the acquiring firm's shareholders, corporate social responsibility research shows that other stakeholders deserve recognition (Borglund 2013). Stakeholder theory describes companies as constellations of cooperative and competitive interests possessing intrinsic value (Donaldson and Preston 1995). Including stakeholders in the analysis of acquisition has been recently advanced by Nordic scholars (Anderson *et al.* 2013), who contend that acquisitions put at risk different interests of external and internal stakeholders. By employing a stakeholders' perspective, acquisition performance can be portrayed as a game involving different internal and external actors holding interests that evolve over time. The underlying idea is that it is the stakeholders' relative power that shapes acquisition performance over the acquisition process.

The recognition of the existence of multiple stakeholders exerting influences on performance reinforces the widespread idea that acquisition performance is a multidimensional construct, yet provides a fresh look at this. Developing the multidimensionality of acquisition performance from a stakeholder perspective does justice to the existence of interests and possible influences that different actors hold or exert on performance. Acknowledging that there are several actors having a stake in acquisitions helps to overcome the idea that performance reflects and therefore should be measured using the interests of the acquiring firm only. The acquiring firm is not the only actor involved in acquisitions—several different actors, within or outside the merging companies, have a stake in these deals. Moreover, both the acquiring and the target companies are not monoliths, as they host several different stakeholders whose stakes are put at risk by an acquisition. Identifying stakes and stakeholders within or outside the merging companies elicits different influences on performance. Including stakeholders implies a shift in the focus, from the acquisition or company performance to the analysis of the effects/outcomes of acquisitions on the network of stakeholders involved. Also, the inclusion of stakeholders, along with the analysis of their influences, allows going beyond the simplistic idea of acquisition as a rationally driven process, as it is portrayed in the majority of research and overcomes the prevailing idea that a single performance measure can do justice to the competing, if not conflicting, stakes in an acquisition.

Applying a stakeholder lens to acquisitions

From Freeman (1984) onward, the notion of stakeholder has become central in strategic management literature. Such a theory describes companies as constellations of cooperative and competitive interests possessing intrinsic value (Donaldson and Preston 1995). The idea of different actors or coalitions influencing the conduct of a company was not new, with the idea of dominant coalitions already advanced by Cyert and March (1963) and further developed by Hambrick and Mason (1984) with regard to top management teams. Moreover, in the same period, Mintzberg (1983) discussed the idea of internal and external coalitions and identified configurations of power.

Today, the concept of stakeholder is very popular among management scholars, yet, despite massive research, the question of who stakeholders are remains an open issue. Stakeholder literature offers a variety of definitions of stakeholders—some narrow and some broad—and identifies a set of dimensions to build typologies of stakeholders (Mitchell *et al.* 1997). The notion of stake, which is central to a stakeholder approach, requires distinguishing claimants from influencers. According to Mitchell *et al.* (1997: 859) claimants are "groups that have a legal, moral or presumed claim on the firm," while influencers are "groups that have an ability to influence the firm's behavior, direction, process, or outcomes." From these definitions, it is apparent that the distinction is subtle.

According to Freeman (1984: 46), "a stakeholder in an organization is (by definition) any group or individual who can affect or is affected by the achievement of the organization's objectives." This is a broad definition compared with the narrow one offered by Clarkson (1995), who conceives a stakeholder as being one bearing some risk as a consequence of the investment of capital in the company. This latter view presupposes that resources—and time and attention, in particular—are scarce and that managers are required to focus their attention on bringing those resources to the company.

Besides offering broad or narrow definitions, stakeholder theory scholars have long debated stakeholders' attributes (Mitchell *et al.* 1997). Major attributes are identified in power, legitimacy, and urgency. Taken together, these attributes allow the categorization of stakeholders in terms of importance (see also King 2013). A thorough analysis of them is beyond the scope of this chapter and readers are referred to Donaldson and Preston (1995) or Mitchell *et al.* (1997).

In this chapter, I assume that some individual actors or coalitions are legitimate and powerful claimants of stakes. They are affected by the deal and in turn affect acquisition performance. Relevant stakes are internal or external to the merging companies. Acquisitions radically influence the network of relationships of acquiring and target firms (Halinen *et al.* 1999). In some cases, such influence is based on a contract that links an individual or a company to the acquiring or the merging companies. This is the case with employees, suppliers, or business-to-business customers. Yet, power and, thus, influence can be legitimated by a superior, often collective, interest to protect, as in the case of governmental bodies who may have their say on whether a deal will actually take place. For these reasons, while I recognize the importance of the issues addressed by a narrow definition of stakeholders, I build my analysis on the broad definition that Freeman (1984) offers as it allows me to identify all individuals or groups holding a stake during an acquisition process and detect their influence over acquisition performance.

Building on this definition, an acquisition can be analyzed as a multi-stakeholder deal, with the number of stakeholders magnified over the course of the acquisition process for the simple reason that two companies are involved (Anderson *et al.* 2013). In my discussion, I investigate different stakeholders without explicitly referring to either the acquiring or the target company, even though I recognize that the acquiring and the target companies are almost never in an equal position and that stakes are often divergent.

It is also important to recognize that all stakes are neither alike nor constant. For instance, during the pre-merger phase, top management and companies' owners play a critical role, while the remaining stakeholders are relatively inactive. The announcement of the deal expands the number of stakeholders. Some stakes are instantaneous—the case of investment banks that are interested in getting the transaction fee—while other stakes change over time. This means that some stakeholders may have different goals and are able to exert more or less influence over time.

These considerations drive a process approach to the analysis of the role that stakeholders play during the acquisition process and the power that they exert over acquisition performance (Meglio and Risberg 2010). The definition of process employed here takes a historical developmental perspective and focuses on the sequences of incidents, activities, and actions unfolding over time, taking into account enabling and constraining influences from inner and outer contexts of the firm (Pettigrew 1992). Applied to the analysis of a stakeholder, a process approach

Table 10.1 Internal and external stakeholders in acquisitions: a process perspective

Stakeholder	Pre-acquisition	Closing the deal	Post-acquisition
Internal	Shareholders Top management	Shareholders Top management Unions	Shareholders Top management Middle managers Employees
External	Competitors Investment banks Consulting firms	Competitors Investment banks Consulting firms Government	Suppliers Customers

allows recognition of the importance of several contextual factors shaping the influence of stakeholders on acquisition performance. By way of example, we can refer to the nature of the deal, friendly or hostile, or the degree of relatedness between the merging parties and industries, or the industries involved. In the case of friendly acquisitions, we expect a more positive employees' attitude towards the deal compared with a hostile takeover. In this latter case, we expect that employees may exhibit negative reactions to the acquisition, such as sabotage or an increase in absenteeism. As for the industry, if the deal involves knowledge-intensive firms, scientists will play a key role compared with other employees, as the innovative performance is heavily dependent upon them (Ranft and Lord 2000). These examples are merely illustrative and not exhaustive, as we will see below.

To make sense of the actors holding a stake during an acquisition process, I position each stakeholder along the acquisition process (see Table 10.1). For the sake of clarity, I depict the acquisition process as a linear flow of phases, even though it does not include recursive or alternate paths that actually make up the whole process. Moreover, I distinguish stakeholders as internal or external to the merging companies.

From the table, it emerges that some stakeholders have an influence over the entire process, such as top management teams, while others limit their influence to the post-acquisition phase, such as customers, suppliers, and employees. In the table, I have positioned governmental bodies and unions as influencing the "closing the deal" phase. I recognize that this is a simplistic view, yet it serves to help visualize that these stakeholders exert a narrower influence compared to others. Specifically, unions are generally alerted by the announcement of deals, especially if they are horizontal acquisitions and involve mature industries (i.e. automotive). In these circumstances, they know in advance that the acquisitions will likely include lay-offs.

Having identified the main stakeholders of merging companies, I now move onto the analysis of their stakes and their actual influences upon acquisition performance. Consistent with the distinction between internal and external stakeholder, I will analyze their influences and how they evolve over time separately. The adoption of a process perspective should enable the identification of recursive and alternate paths that influence acquisition performance, and help to overcome the idea of acquisition performance as linear or unitary. With these considerations at hand, I now turn to the analysis of internal and external stakeholders.

Internal stakeholders and acquisition performance measurement

As depicted in Table 10.1, internal stakeholders are mainly shareholders, managers, and employees. Shareholders are legitimated by equity investment. Managers and employees are both legitimated by a contract. Yet, they cannot be treated as homogeneous, as their stakes differ

Table 10.2 Influences of internal stakeholders upon acquisition performance

Internal stakeholder	Stakes	Positive influence on acquisition performance	Negative influence on acquisition performance
Shareholders	Shareholder value	Focus on performance metrics other than market performance	Excessive focus on market performance
Top management	Prestige, pay and career prospects	Achieve synergies	Self-interest choices (financial health and survival)
Middle managers	Career prospects	Constructive role during the integration process	Destructive role during the integration process
Employees	Career prospects	Commitment to the achievement of synergies	Sabotage, lower productivity (also for scientists)
Unions	Employees' interest	Support top management in getting commitment from employees	Strikes

significantly depending on the role they perform and the hierarchical level that they occupy within the companies. I therefore distinguish top managers from middle managers, and line workers are simply referred to as employees. Stakes and influences, positive and negative, are displayed in Table 10.2.

To date, the conventional discourse about acquisitions has emphasized the stake of shareholders over other stakeholders. One can make sense of it by considering that mergers and acquisitions, when announced to external audiences, are generally justified as synergistic or creating value for an acquirer's shareholders (Borglund 2013). The concept of shareholder value gives support and legitimacy to the primacy of shareholders over all other stakeholders (Aglietta 2000). Meanwhile, other stakeholders, although influenced by any deal, are generally neglected by press releases and official speeches. Consistent with this view, companies pursue the best return to their shareholders, and this is indirectly confirmed by empirical research primarily employing market-based measures of acquisition performance (see also Meglio and Risberg 2011). Market-based returns are thus conceived to be the unitary measure for acquisition performance.

The primacy of shareholders is reproduced and reinforced through published research, and it requires reflection on the role that scholars have in shaping acquisition performance measurement. Scholars can be conceived to be influencers or stakeholders in mergers and acquisitions. This latter position is justified by Risberg (2013) in recognizing that researchers have both an interest in and an influence over acquisitions. By their research agenda they contribute to how acquisitions are perceived. Their stake also presents a certain degree of risk: what they risk is not being published, and this in turn influences both career path and pay (Risberg 2013). As findings from the narrative analysis of acquisition performance studies reveal (Meglio and Risberg 2011), there is a prevalence of studies employing market-based measures for acquisition performance. This is in line with the emphasis on the acquiring firm's shareholders as discussed above. The most frequently cited justification for the choice is the search for objectivity. Its use seems to indicate that there is an underlying belief that one type of measure (market-based) is closer to a true performance than other types of measures. The search for objectivity, as an inspiring principle in scholarly research about acquisition performance, has been reaffirmed by referring to past studies. In this regard, scholars, especially those who are US-based, actively contribute to the conventional discourse about acquisition performance that identifies in market-based or accounting measures of performance the prevailing measure of acquisition performance.

Top management teams are considered a dominant coalition within companies (Cyert and March 1963). According to the upper echelon view (Hambrick and Mason 1984), the top management team, with its characteristics, influences the strategic choice of a company and its performance. In the context of acquisitions, the top management team plays a key role during the entire process. Specifically, during the pre-acquisition stage, the top management team pushes the closing of a certain deal on the ground of expected benefits arising from the combination with the target firm. At this stage, the top management team prospectively foresees the attainment of specific synergies, as well as the increase in shareholder value. To avoid self-interest, such as financial health and survival (Donaldson and Lorsch 1983) and a misalignment with shareholders' goals, it is possible to rely on several tools to monitor the top management team's decisions and actions. Stock option pay and executive stock ownership are supposed to have congruent effects in aligning top management interests with those of shareholders, even though some claim that the latter is more effective (Sanders 2001). Other means are internal (senior executives) and external monitors (security analysts, independent outside board members, and activist institutional investors), Wright *et al.* (2002) suggest.

During the post-acquisition stage, it is the duty of top managers to accommodate several other stakeholders in achieving acquisition goals. This "game" is further complicated by changing relations of power among stakeholders. While, during the pre-acquisition stage top management teams from the acquiring firm and the target may have convergent interests (i.e. closing the deal), during the post-acquisition phase they generally have divergent interests. Often an acquisition replaces the top management team of the target company (Walsh 1988 and 1989). The replacement of ineffective management is a frequently advocated rationale for mergers and acquisitions with a disciplinary aim (Walsh and Elwood 1991; Walsh and Kosnik 1993). The replacement of target company managers can be already set during the negotiation phase, in the case of friendly transactions, when golden parachutes are provided to smooth the exit of managers (Hirsch 1987). These costs should be carefully estimated as they influence the overall performance. When the deal is hostile, the exit is imposed top down, and the turmoil is inevitable. In such a case, the magnitude of negative effects on performance is more difficult to predict. Typically, such situations produce both low morale and a decrease in productivity that can lower, or even offset, the envisioned cost synergies.

Middle managers are generally overlooked by existing literature, which is traditionally focused on upper echelons, even though they are responsible for implementing decisions taken by the top management team. Specifically, they are responsible for 22.3 percent of the performance differences among companies, Mollick (2012) contends. Middle managers are generally identified as those two levels below the CEO and one level above line workers and professionals. In acquisitions, there are distinctive middle-management groups that cut across the merging parties. Meyer (2006) outlines how they play an active role during the implementation process as they are responsible for operationalizing the strategic intent. As a result of their position, they heavily shape the dynamic of integration process and therefore acquisition performance. In literature they are often regarded as the primary locus of resistance to change. In such a case, they are seen as adding costs and obstructing information, and their influence is perceived as destructive. They may also play a constructive role, favoring the implementation of required changes, reducing resistance during the implementation process, which in turns depends on their career opportunities as a consequence of the deal. Their stake, that is, their career path, can be put at risk by some contextual factors, such as the nature of the deal (friendly versus hostile) and the degree of relatedness between the merging companies. If the deal is hostile and the acquisition is horizontal, it is very likely that cutting costs to achieve cost synergies will result in many middle managers being let go. In such circumstances, again the internal climate will deteriorate and performance will likely decrease. That many people leave after a deal could be desirable from the acquiring firm's point of view; yet it may also imply losing talented people and their contribution to the performance of the merging companies.

The same line of reasoning applies to *employees*. While they could be considered, at first sight, to be more fungible resources, their fear of being fired implies the disruption of social connections within teams, and a likely reduction in productivity, as a consequence of a lower morale. Scientists, inventors, or knowledge workers provide an exception to this rule as they may affect the performance of high-technology deals. These deals are generally pursued to appropriate and leverage knowledge from the target firm. These goals emphasize the importance of retaining talented people and creating the best conditions to make them productive. Many studies, however, signal how difficult it is to achieve these aims. Ernst and Vitt (2000) show that key inventor productivity slows down after an acquisition. This is explained by the loss of relative standing of key inventors in the acquired company (Paruchuri et al. 2006). Moreover, Kapoor and Lim (2007) find that the productivity of all inventors, regardless of their status, is lower than that of inventors at non-acquired firms.

The description of possible events following an acquisition provided above rests on the assumption that an acquisition is a traumatic event, which disrupt employees' careers. If this scenario materializes, then consequences of all the possible circumstances described so far will likely result in a lower performance. An alternative scenario materializes if the acquisition is welcomed as an opportunity from employees at different hierarchical levels. This may happen in the case of a white knight or when the target is a family business with no second generation within the company willing to replace the founder. In such circumstances, when the survival of the company is at risk, the acquirer is seen positively, and employees are more willing to cooperate. Another possible instance is an acquisition inspired by acquirer diversification. In this case, the need for change within the target company is expected to be low. The assurance about future career prospects should preserve morale and allow cooperative efforts from employees. This reinforces the idea that an acquisition does not in itself assure the achievement of the intended goals. It is essential to carefully understand the stakes of different actors and find the proper strategies to cope with them.

External stakeholders and acquisition performance measurement

In this section, I investigate the role of external stakeholders. Some of them exert a powerful influence over the completion of the deal, such as consulting firms, investment banks, and governmental bodies. Other stakeholders are powerful after the deal is signed, such as suppliers and customers. However, I begin with a largely overlooked group, competitors. As for internal stakeholders, stakes and influences are displayed in Table 10.3.

Competitors are often not regarded as stakeholders in acquisition research, though I find value in including them. Considering competitors as stakeholders enables identifying their stake in a deal and how they may impact acquisition performance. Even though there is no contractual relationship with competitors, a deal can put their competitive position at risk and negatively influence their growth and profitability prospects. These stakes cannot be overlooked as they determine the influence of competitors. Additionally, competitors can take advantage of uncertainty in a deal to poach employees and customers (King 2013). Competitors can also approach

Table 10.3 Influences of external stakeholders upon acquisition performance

External stakeholder	Stakes	Positive influence on acquisition performance	Negative influence on acquisition performance
Consulting firms	Transaction fee	Reduce the time to get the deal approved by governmental bodies	They represent a cost that should be added to the final price
Investment banks	Transaction fee	Fair and reasonable premium price	Too high premium price
Suppliers	Business relationship	Continue business relationship, allowing for cost synergies	Terminate contract
Customers	Business relationship	Continue business relationship, allowing for revenue synergies	Terminate contract
Competitors	Profitability, survival, competitive position	Inactive position, as the industry is a fast-growing one	Make the final price rise up beyond what the target is worth for the acquiring company
Government	Public interest	Financial support for strategic industries (such as defense)	Limit actions that could harm competition and consumers

the government with anti-competitive concerns, with the aim of disrupting a deal, as in the successful attempt by Sprint to disrupt AT&T's merger with T-Mobile USA (Woyke 2011).

During the pre-acquisition phase, the goal of reducing competition is generally a driver for strategic deals, especially in horizontal transactions. Acquisitions are frequently negotiated to reduce competitive pressure in mature or declining industries, or to acquire innovative capabilities or customers of the target firm. Competitors are not passive during the negotiation phase. They are generally alerted from rumors about a possible deal and may react to such rumors. One possible reaction is to take part in the bidding process: when several potential buyers compete for the same target, the price will generally rise. In the short term, the offered price can play a key role in deciding who, among the potential buyers, will win the "bid game," but in the long run it will heavily affect the value creation process and, therefore, acquisition success in a situation called the "winner's curse" (Varaiya and Ferris 1987). If we assume that a deal creates economic value in absolute terms, it is straightforward that the price paid by the buyer to the seller determines their respective share of the value created, with the non-trivial time discrepancy that the seller gets immediately its share whereas the buyer will have to put into practice the synergies that were only prospective in the acquisition plans and are embedded in the valuation of the target (Meglio and Capasso 2012).

Competitors' shareholders may benefit from taking part in the bidding process. Financial economics scholars show how rivals of initial acquisition targets earn abnormal returns due to the increased probability that they will be targets themselves (Song and Walking 2000; Shahrur 2005). These abnormal returns tend to increase, the higher the surprise about the initial acquisition. These dynamics are particularly relevant in the case of horizontal acquisitions.

For the acquiring company, competition for a certain target tends to eliminate all possible bidders' gains that are common to many potential buyers, thus pushing a potential acquirer to abandon the deal (Pablo *et al.* 1996). According to Barney (1988), acquiring firms gain above-normal returns from acquisitions only when private or uniquely valuable synergistic assets are involved. Privacy refers to information about the combination that is not available to potential outside bidders. Uniquely valuable synergy is created when no other combination of firms could produce the same value. If information is not private or if other equally synergistic combinations are possible in the market for corporate control, the target's price will be bid up to a point at which the value from potential synergy is absorbed by the acquisition price. This in turn reinforces the need to effectively manage the integration process.

Investment banks hugely influence whether and how a deal is completed. Executives of both target and bidding firms rely heavily on the advice of investment bankers. Investment banks are supposed to aid the market for corporate control in several ways: they reduce search costs by matching bids and targets, reduce information asymmetries between the parties, and provide technical expertise that could be costly and time consuming to produce internally. Yet, Kesner *et al.* (1994) outline that if investment banks act as agents for both the bidding firm and the target this can create conflicts of interests. Such conflicts of interest may cause bidding companies to bid beyond their financial capacity or pay a price where the target company is not worth buying.

As a result of its peculiar position, an investment bank experiences the so-called negotiator's dilemma, that is, choosing between collaborative tactics that create value for all the parties involved in the deal, and opportunistic tactics that yield even greater value for itself and lower value, or even no value, for the other parties. This generally produces greater premiums paid and puts at risk the achievement of acquisition goals for the acquiring firm. Of course, the position of the acquiring firm is weaker than that of the target, whose shareholders generally benefit from greater premium prices. The importance of reputation when trying to gain further business likely mitigates self-interest by investment banks.

Governmental agencies generally perform the role of regulator. In performing the role of regulator, government agencies may either prevent the deal from actually taking place or actually drive concrete implementation actions that effect stakeholders. Generally, government agencies attempt to assure efficiency and transparency in financial markets so that nobody can exert control over them and to assure fair competition in the marketplace across industries: this means that no competitor can gain, as a consequence of a deal, a dominant position over other competitors, thus protecting consumers from possible abuse of dominant position.

King (2013) outlines how regulatory requirements vary across the globe depending on the countries involved. In the US, for instance, laws require that filings describing both the transaction and the firms involved be submitted to the Federal Trade Commission and the Department of Justice. The decision, after reviewing a transaction, is generally made within 30 days. Acquiring firms often rely on third parties, such as consulting firms, to perform analysis of joint data and provide relevant summaries. Regulatory reviews by other government bodies may also be required before an acquisition can be completed. If the deal involves one company from the European Union (EU), additional reviews might be necessary to ensure that the deal does not harm the competition within the EU. In complying with these requirements, acquiring companies should assess the trade-off between the time needed to have the deal approved (and the impact that a delay produces on the deal) and the incentives paid to consulting firms to accelerate completion.

Central government can also play an active, positive role in promoting a merger or creating more favorable conditions for a merger to take place. This may actually take place if the merger involves a strategic industry, such as the defense industry, where the central government may have an interest other than an economic one to keep control of a certain business. This may also happen when the merger involves both a declining industry and a troubled company. In these circumstances thousands of employees could be at risk and financially helping a consolidation merger could be a way to preserve the employment rate in economic downturn conditions (see for example the merger between FIAT and Chrysler).

Consulting firms represent another important stakeholder in a merger or acquisition and perform roles beyond preparing reviews to submit to regulatory bodies. For example, accounting firms are frequently asked to perform the due diligence, which takes place between the declaration of the initial intent to acquire and the closing of the transaction. Deal closure is contingent on a satisfactory due diligence report. This activity involves a detailed analysis of the condition of the target firm by representatives of the acquiring firm who verify financial records, analyze legal matters and investigate other potential problems. The information obtained during due diligence is generally not publicly available and makes possible a more careful assessment of the value that the transaction might provide.

Since the target has an incentive to make public any positive information, any relevant information uncovered during due diligence is usually unfavorable and should lower the value of the target for the acquirer. If a key goal of this phase is to discover and act on information that may lead to a re-evaluation of the acquisition, due diligence failures occur either when acquirers fail to discover new information that devalues the target firm or, having uncovered it, fail to react in an appropriate manner by revising the price or abandoning a deal (Puranam *et al.* 2006).

After a deal completes, the relationships with suppliers and customers are impacted. These relationships are often long-lasting and they are important stakeholders, though generally neglected. Again financial economics scholars show how horizontal deals may impact the relationships with suppliers and customers. Specifically they focus on gains arising from improved efficiency and anti-competitive collusions, which are not mutually exclusive (Fee and Thomas 2004).

Suppliers are key external stakeholders, as purchasing is strictly related to the cost and quality of the purchased components (Holström 2013). Savings in this function have a direct impact upon corporate profitability and, in an attempt to achieve cost synergies, suppliers to integrating companies will be very likely asked to renegotiate contracts. This may imply reduced/increased volumes, generally lower prices, and compressed lead times. Revising any of these aspects may put the supplier in a difficult position. Empirical evidence about horizontal mergers show that on average suppliers experience significant declines in cash flow margins subsequent to downstream mergers, as a consequence of increased buying power. Fee and Thomas (2004) further contend that purchasing gains for the merging companies depend on the type of suppliers (retained versus terminated) and the industry contexts (concentrated versus fragmented). Suppliers who are terminated after a merger experience significant negative abnormal returns at the merger announcement and significant cash flow reduction after the deal. Moreover, buying power effects are more pronounced when the merging companies operate in relatively concentrated industries.

Of course, suppliers, just like employees, are not all alike. Basically, their relative importance depends on the type of material/service supplied, the existence of alternative suppliers, and ability to switch costs. Taken together, these factors determine the type of relationship between the parties. A deal does not necessarily negatively affect the position of suppliers, yet it certainly adds uncertainty to the relationship with the merging parties and requires the renegotiation of contractual provisions.

Customers, just like suppliers, are key external stakeholders. They have received scant attention in the acquisition-related literature, and this is quite surprising as acquiring customers of the target company is a frequently advocated rationale for pursuing a deal. This is even more important in business-to-business relationships as these customers account for high volumes of sales. In other words, retaining business-to-business customers is of utmost importance during the integration process. Again, financial economics scholars have investigated the effects of horizontal deals on corporate customers. Unlike suppliers, customers seem not to experience negative stock market reactions at the announcement of a deal, or changes in industry-adjusted operating performance following an upstream merger (Fee and Thomas 2004). Acquisitions encompass a broad spectrum of changes that actually cause the dissolution of business relationships with customers. Key personnel leaving a company, dissatisfaction produced by failure to meet customer requirements, bad reputation and financial difficulties of the acquiring company, less favorable business conditions, or product replacement may all be causes for terminating a business relationship (Öberg 2013). This in turn requires careful scrutiny of customers with the goal of reassuring them using customer relationship management strategies to nurture the business relationship with them.

To sum up, business relationships that link the target company to suppliers and customers are not automatically acquired if they are not preserved during the integration process. These relationships have a key impact on performance as they influence costs and revenues of the merging companies.

Discussion

In this chapter, I attempt to provide a fresh perspective to the analysis of acquisition performance and extend the focus of the existing literature beyond the interest of shareholders, specifically those of the acquiring company. This focus is reflected in the prevailing use of market-based measures for acquisition performance in certain academic journals (see Meglio and Risberg 2011). The underlying belief is that acquisitions are neutral events for stakeholders other than shareholders. The conventional portrait of these deals is as a battleground where opposing shareholder groups compete to get the best return, which depends on the price set.

The idea advanced in this chapter builds on the premise that both the merging companies are not monoliths inside and outside their boundaries. Instead, stakeholders can be seen as a network of relationships, internal and external, legitimated by a contract or other interests to protect. Seen in this light, acquisition performance can be analyzed as a game, played by several actors, whose relative power influences outcomes. The nature of the game is contingent upon the stake they hold and how it changes as a consequence of the deal, as illustrated in Tables 10.2 and 10.3. Acknowledging the existence of different stakes recognizes that no single performance measure can actually do justice to all these stakes. This is a new way to conceive the multidimensionality of acquisition performance, which is frequently evoked by scholars, but generally underplayed in theoretical and empirical research.

As anticipated in the introduction, the inclusion of stakeholders goes beyond the idea that mergers and acquisitions are driven solely by rational considerations. As highlighted by literature about integration, mergers and acquisitions are political processes (Vaara 2003). So far, scholars have mainly dealt with internal power struggles without examining their effects on acquisition performance. In this chapter, I have tried to provide a comprehensive assessment of internal and external power dynamics and their influences over performance.

The investigation conducted also has practical implications: acknowledging that acquisition performance is constructed and shaped by the influences of multiple stakeholders that change over time suggests that top management teams should carefully estimate the possible consequences of these influences over performance before the deal is signed. At this stage, it is important that all elements that create costs (during the negotiation and the integration alike) are added to the final price. This is the level against which synergies arising from the deal should be evaluated to determine whether the deal adds value or not. During the post-acquisition phase, it is the integration leader's responsibility to assure collaboration from stakeholders to limit their detrimental influence upon acquisition performance.

References

Aglietta, M. (2000) "Shareholder value and corporate governance: some tricky questions," *Economy and Society*, 29: 146–159.

Anderson, H., Havila, V., and Nilsson, F. (eds.) (2013) *Mergers and acquisitions. The critical role of stakeholders*, New York/Oxon: Routledge.

Barney, J.B. (1988) "Returns to bidding firms in mergers and acquisitions: reconsidering the relatedness hypothesis," *Strategic Management Journal*, 9: 71–78.

Borglund, T. (2013) "The growing importance of corporate social responsibility in mergers and acquisitions, in Anderson, H., Havila, V., and Nilsson, F. (eds.) *Mergers and acquisitions. The critical role of stakeholders*, 17–39, New York/Oxon: Routledge.

Bower, J.L. (2004) "When we study M&A, what are we learning?," in Pablo, A.L. and Javidan, M. (eds.), *Mergers and acquisitions. Creating integrative knowledge*, 235–244, Oxford: Blackwell.

Capron, L. (1999) "The long-term performance of horizontal acquisitions," *Strategic Management Journal*, 20: 987–1018.

Carton, R.B. and Hofer, C.W. (2006) *Measuring organizational performance. Metrics for entrepreneurship in strategic management research*, Cheltenham: Edward Elgar.

Clarkson, M.B.E. (1995) "A stakeholder framework for evaluating corporate social performance," *Academy of Management Review*, 20: 92–117.

Cording, M., Christman, P., and Weigelt, C. (2010) "Measuring theoretically complex constructs: the case of acquisition performance," *Strategic Organization*, 8: 11–41.

Cording, M., Christman, P., and King, D. (2008) "Reducing causal ambiguity in acquisition integration: intermediate goals as mediators of integration decisions and acquisition performance," *Academy of Management Journal*, 51: 744–767.

Cyert, R.M. and March, J.G. (1963) *A behavioral theory of the firm*, Englewood Cliffs, NJ: Prentice Hall.

Daily, C. (1994) "Bankruptcy in strategic studies: past and promise," *Journal of Management*, 20: 263–295.

Datta, D.K., Pinches, G.P., and Narayan, V.K. (1992) "Factors influencing wealth creation from mergers and acquisitions: a meta-analysis," *Strategic Management Journal*, 13: 67–84.

Donaldson, G. and Lorsch, J.W. (1983) *Decision making at the top*, New York: Basic Books.

Donaldson, T. and Preston, L.E. (1995) "The stakeholder theory of the corporation: concepts, evidence and implication," *Academy of Management Review*, 20: 65–91.

Ernst, H. and Vitt, J. (2000) "The influence of corporate acquisitions on the behaviour of key inventors," *R&D Management*, 30: 105–118.

Fee, C.E. and Thomas, S. (2004) "Sources of gains in horizontal mergers: evidences from customer, supplier and rival firms," *Journal of Financial Economics*, 74: 423–460.

Fowler, K.L. and Schmidt, D.R. (1988) "Tender offers, acquisition, and subsequent performance in manufacturing firms," *Academy of Management Journal*, 31: 962–974.

Freeman, R.E. (1984), *Strategic management. A stakeholder approach*, Boston, MA: Pitman.

Halinen, A., Salmi, A., and Havila, V. (1999) "From dyadic change to changing business networks: an analytical framework," *Journal of Management Studies*, 36: 779–794.

Hambrick, D.C. and Mason, P. (1984) "Upper echelons: the organization as a reflection of its top managers," *Academy of Management Review*, 9: 193–206.

Harrison, J. and Schijven, M. (2015) "Event study methodology in the context of M&As: a reorientation," in Risberg, A., King, D.R., and Meglio, O. (eds.) *The Routledge Companion to Mergers and Acquisitions*, Oxon: Routledge.

Hirsch, P. (1987). *Pack your own parachute. How to survive mergers, takeovers and other corporate disasters*, Reading, PA: Addison-Wesley Publishing Company Inc.

Holström, J. (2013) "Supplier relationship at stake in mergers and acquisitions," in Anderson, H., Havila, V., and Nilsson, F. (eds.) *Mergers and acquisitions. The critical role of stakeholders*, 168–184, New York/Oxon: Routledge.

Kapoor, R. and Lim, K. (2007) "The impact of acquisitions on the productivity of inventors at semiconductor firms: a synthesis of knowledge-based and incentive-based perspectives," *Academy of Management Journal*, 50: 1133–1155.

Kesner, I.F., Shapiro, D.L., and Sharma, A. (1994) "Brokering mergers: an agency theory perspective on the role of representatives," *Academy of Management Journal*, 37: 703–721.

King, D.R. (2013) "A phased approach to merger and acquisition integration: tapping experiential learning," in Kannan, V.R. (ed.) *Strategic management in the 21st century*, vol. 2—Corporate Strategy, Santa Barbara: Praeger Press.

King, D.R., Dalton, D.R., Daily, C.M., and Covin, J. (2004) "Meta-analysis of post-acquisition performance: indications of unidentified moderators," *Strategic Management Journal*, 25: 187–200.

March, J.G. and Sutton, R.I. (1997) "Organizational performance as a dependent variable," *Organization Science* 8 (6): 698–706.

Meglio, O. and Capasso, A. (2012) "The evolving role of mergers and acquisitions in competitive strategy research," in Dagnino, G.B. (ed.) *The handbook of competitive strategy research*, 237–263, Cheltenham: Edward Elgar Publishing.

Meglio, O. and Risberg, A. (2011) "The (mis)measurement of M&A performance: a systematic narrative literature review," *Scandinavian Journal of Management*, 27: 418–433.

Meglio, O. and Risberg, A. (2010) "Mergers and acquisitions: time for a methodological rejuvenation of the field?," *Scandinavian Journal of Management*, 26: 87–95.

Meyer, C.B. (2006) "Destructive dynamics of middle management intervention in postmerger processes," *Journal of Applied Behavioral Science*, 42: 397–419.

Mintzberg, H. (1983) *Power in and around organizations*, Englewood Cliffs, NJ: Prentice Hall.

Mitchell, R.K, Agle, B.R., and Wood, D.T. (1997) "Toward a theory of stakeholder identification and salience: defining the principle of who and what really counts," *Academy of Management Review*, 22: 853–886.

Mollick, E. (2012) "People and process, suits and innovators: the role of innovators in firm performance," *Strategic Management Journal*, 33 (9): 1001–1015.

Öberg, C. (2013) "Why do customers dissolve their business relationships with the acquired party following an acquisition?," in Anderson, H., Havila, V., and Nilsson, F. (eds.) *Mergers and acquisitions. The critical role of stakeholders*, 185–202, New York/Oxon: Routledge.

Öberg, C. (2008) "The importance of customers in mergers and acquisitions," Doctoral Thesis 1193, Linköping Studies in Science and Technologies, Linköping University.

Pablo, A., Sitkin, S., and Jemison, D. (1996) "Acquisition decision-making processes: the central role of risk," *Journal of Management*, 22: 723–746.

Paruchuri, S, Nerkar, A., and Hambrick, D.C. (2006) "Acquisition integration and productivity losses in the technical core: disruption of inventors in acquired companies," *Organization Science*, 17: 545–562.

Pettigrew, A.M. (1992) "The character and significance of strategy process," *Strategic Management Journal*, 13: 5–16.

Puranam P., Powell, B.C., and Singh, H. (2006) "Due diligence failure as a signal detection problem," *Strategic Organization*, 4: 319–348.

Ranft, A. and Lord, M. (2000) "Acquiring new knowledge: the role of retaining human capital in acquisition of high-tech firms," *Journal of High Technology Management Research*, 11: 295–319.

Risberg, A. (2013) "The stake of high failure rate in mergers and acquisitions," in Anderson, H., Havila, V., and Nilsson, F. (eds.) *Mergers and acquisitions. The critical role of stakeholders*, 247–266, New York/Oxon: Routledge.

Sanders, G. (2001) "Behavioral responses of CEOs to stock ownership and stock option pay," *Academy of Management Journal*, 44: 477–492.

Schriber, S. (2013) "Managing the influence of external competitive change during integration," in Anderson, H., Havila, V., and Nilsson, F. (eds.) *Mergers and acquisitions. The critical role of stakeholders*, 149–167, New York/Oxon: Routledge.

Shahrur, H. (2005) "Industry structure and horizontal takeovers: analysis of wealth effects on rivals, suppliers and corporate customers," *Journal of Financial Economics*, 74: 61–98.

Song, M.H. and Walkling, R.A. (2000) "Abnormal returns to rivals of acquisition targets: a test of the acquisition probability hypothesis," *Journal of Financial Economics*, 55: 143–171.

Vaara, E. (2003) "Post-acquisition integration as sensemaking: glimpses of ambiguity, confusion, hypocrisy, and politicization," *Journal of Management Studies*, 4: 859–894.

Varaiya, N. and Ferris, K. (1987) "Overpaying in corporate takeovers: the winner's curse," *Financial Analysts Journal*, 43: 64–70.

Venkatraman, V.N. and Ramanujam, V. (1987) "Measurement of business economic performance: an examination of method convergence," *Journal of Management*, 13 (1): 109–123.

Walsh, J.P. (1989) "Doing a deal: mergers and acquisitions negotiations and their impact upon target company top management turnover," *Strategic Management Journal*, 10: 307–332.

Walsh, J.P. (1988) "Top management turnover following acquisitions," *Strategic Management Journal*, 9: 173–183.

Walsh, J.P. and Kosnik, R.D. (1993) "Corporate raiders and their disciplinary role in the market for corporate control," *Academy of Management Journal*, 36: 671–700.

Walsh, J.P. and Ellwood, J.W. (1991) "Mergers, acquisitions and the pruning of managerial deadwood," *Strategic Management Journal*, 12: 201–217.

Wicker, A.W. (1985) "Getting out of our conceptual roots: strategies for expanding conceptual framework," *American Psychologist*, 40: 1094–1103.

Woyke, E. (2011) "Sprint files FCC petition against AT&T/T-Mobile merger," *Forbes*: www.forbes.com/sites/elizabethwoyke/2011/05/31/sprint-files-fcc-petition-against-attt-mobile-merger, retrieved November 2013.

Wright, P., Kroll, M., and Elenkov, D. (2002) "Acquisition returns, increase in firm size and chief executive office compensation: the moderating role of monitoring," *Academy of Management Journal*, 45: 599–608.

Zollo, M. and Meier, D. (2008) "What is M&A performance?," *Academy of Management Perspective*, 22: 55–77.

11

Leadership, power, and collaboration in international mergers and acquisitions

Conflict and resolution

Kathleen Park

Introduction

The global business environment rests on the ongoing formation, renewal, and integration of international investments. Mergers and acquisitions (M&As) represent a foremost form of foreign direct investment and internationalization (Mody 2004). Acquiring firms and assets in other countries effectively contrasts with relatively slower-paced or more limited methods of international expansion such as licensing, exporting, alliances, or greenfields (Bartlett and Beamish 2011). As with other forms of business strategy, internationalization and acquisitions involve the input of strategic leadership (Covin *et al.* 1997; Vaara 2003). The value of top leadership has been sometimes questioned but has been found essential to the forward momentum of firms contingent upon the exploration and exploitation of strategic opportunities suited to the evolving business environment (Wasserman *et al.* 2010). The strategic leadership, context, and actions must fit together.

Global strategy and internationalization draw on a context of companies and countries representing a spectrum of cultures and economic development. Worldwide, family business interests play a crucial role (Palmer and Barber 2001) and operate on a scale from large (e.g. Wal-Mart or Ikea) to small (corner stores). This role intensifies in developing regions, where enterprises in emerging markets and with aspects of family involvement are increasingly contributing to the global economy and the global market for corporate control (Yadong Luo 2011; Yadong Luo and Zhao 2013). With this background in mind (Figure 11.1), the present study explores what are the factors affecting CEO leadership for internationalization from emerging markets, with the internationalization specifically occurring through mergers and acquisitions, and considering aspects of family business. To investigate this research question, this chapter analyzes a case study of a rapidly internationalized and now global business emanating from the Arabian Gulf. The international, multicultural, and resource-rich endowments of this region make it a crucible and a context enabling rapid business globalization in a manner providing insights for the more established and developed Western and Asian economies, as well as the economically developing areas of the world such as in Southeast Asia, Latin America, North and Sub-Saharan Africa, and Eastern Europe.

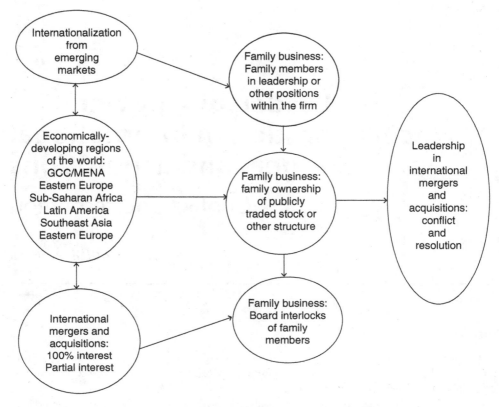

Figure 11.1 Proposed model of the international and family business context

The prevalence of cross-border acquisitions coexists with the frequently problematic nature of these transactions (Hitt *et al.* 2006; Moeller and Schlingemann 2005), motivating the related question, "What are key issues of conflict, resolution, and the deployment of power in the leadership of international mergers and acquisitions?" Specifically this chapter explores international acquisitions from a conflict and resolution perspective of top leadership in a global firm situated in a high-income, rapidly developing emerging market, intersecting with family business. In addition, the analysis brings to the fore the importance of speed and timing in international strategy. Moreover, the chapter emphasizes a methodology employing an in-depth, open-ended, ethnographic style of interviewing within single or multiple case study domains for increasing understanding of these issues.

Background and theory

The theoretical framework for leadership conflicts and resolutions in international acquisitions addresses (1) the centrality of CEO leadership in mergers and acquisitions (Covin *et al.* 1997; Vaara 2003), (2) the counterbalancing of competition and cooperation within and between corporate governance structures (Balmaceda 2009), (3) the importance of family business aspects for key geographic acquisition milieus (Palmer and Barber 2001), (4) the impact of emerging market dynamics (Yadong Luo 2011; Yadong Luo and Zhao 2013) in the global market for

Figure 11.2 Proposed model of influences on leadership in international mergers and acquisitions

corporate control, and (5) the interplay of acquisitions across sovereign borders and gradients of economic development (Hitt *et al.* 2006; Moeller and Schlingemann 2005) (Figure 11.2). These considerations interconnect in such a way that family business multinational corporations (MNCs) in high-growth (emerging) economies are undertaking acquisitions and then rapidly verging on or accomplishing full global engagement (Oviatt and McDougall 1995). Strategic leadership plays a crucial role in engendering a worldwide corporate vision and brokering the acquisitions to achieve this success.

Importance of leadership and management in acquisitions and organizations

The research questions articulated in the introduction highlight the construct of leadership, which occurs throughout an organization, not exclusively in the upper management ranks (Stein 2005). While top leadership decision making and strategic actions guide international M&As (Fendt 2006), the formulation and deployment of these strategic initiatives extends through at least several levels of management to accomplish the designated goals. For instance, the CEO and top management level can instigate corporate-level strategizing (Darling and Fischer 1998), which could involve particular business units, in particular in the implementation of relatively smaller-scale acquisitions. The divisional leadership then becomes heavily involved in enacting the post-acquisition integration or even in running the acquired firm as a distinct subsidiary (Morris and Snell 2011). The middle management in the subsidiaries or business units has frontline responsibilities for handling acquired products and services. Multiple levels of leadership and management work in concert toward effective acquisitions.

It has long been established that mergers and acquisitions are high-risk strategic maneuvers, which often depress value creation (Dewing 1921; Kitching 1967; Livermore 1935). In addition, these transactions carry considerable risks for the leaders of the involved organizations, who can jeopardize their jobs, reputations, and careers in undertaking these expensive, failure-prone, emotion-laden amalgamations (Krug and Shill 2008). Moreover, the transactions present myriad complex challenges to leadership in all phases from inception, through implementation, to assessment of performance (Park 2012). Hence collaboration presumptively assumes vital importance in M&A activity toward increasing the likelihood of favorable outcomes. This collaboration can occur within the focal organization (for instance, within top management teams and throughout the corporate governance) or across organizational boundaries (in interactions between respective CEOs and boards of directors). Power differentials become especially critical in the interpersonal and inter-organizational interactions (Meyer and Altenborg 2008). The greater power does not necessarily rest with the larger, more established firm with higher revenues or with the older, seemingly more respected and entrenched CEO. Rather, the power imbalance could favor the firm with the faster rate of growth, the greater present or prospective profitability, and the larger cash pool. Likewise, the power imbalance could favor a younger, newer, more aggressively forward-looking CEO who has mobilized substantial board and investor support.

Competition, cooperation, and timing in organizational settings

Top management teams are important within organizations for the distribution of power and sharing of leadership responsibilities across various functions, lines of business, and geographic regions. Typically, the top team would consist of the C-level (CEO, COO, CFO, CIO, and so on) executives and sometimes senior vice presidents. Of these executives, the CEO bears the greatest responsibility for conceiving and negotiating large M&A deals (Brown and Sarma 2007). The top management team members can assist in particular with the implementation of the deal (Shanley and Correa 1992). If any of these top team members in addition to the CEO sit on the board of directors as internal members, they can assist with the approval or disapproval of the deal as voted by the board. The external directors on the board can function as liaisons to the proposed acquiring or target firms, in addition to voting to approve or deny deals. The interactions among the CEO, top management team members, and directors form the crux of the leadership power and collaboration issues within an organization. The interactions between the acquiring and target CEOs and the acquiring and target boards constitute the nexus of the power and collaboration dynamics across organizations (Capron and Guillén 2009; Li and Aguilera 2008). In the case at hand, both the intra- and inter-organizational exchanges provide compelling evidence for the importance of the individual and group level leadership factors in acquisitions involving simultaneous family business (Dyer 2003), emerging market (Perkins 2013), and international aspects.

This collaborative framework becomes especially important for international transactions, where the cross-border cooperation should diffuse from the top ranks initially negotiating the deal down through the levels (both managerial and non-managerial) involved in various aspects of implementation. In international acquisitions, issues of both national and organizational culture differences arise. Effective leadership of acquisitions involves effective leadership of cultural issues and differences across organizations (Shearer et al. 2001). National differences could ironically seem less pronounced at top levels where an overlay of elite educational and family backgrounds and global management experience exists, even across various regions of the world (Maclean *et al.* 2006). In the divisional and middle management ranks, as well as at supporting levels, there could be additional need for extensive intercultural learning to facilitate the interactions across borders, yet now within the same company (Keys *et al.* 1993; Schweiger and Goulet 2005).

When addressing the dispersed leadership capabilities and issues throughout a company in the incidence of a merger or acquisition, it also becomes important to bear in mind issues of timing (Angwin 2004). Temporality surfaces in several ways in strategic transactions (Gersick 1994): through elapsed calendar and clock time as calculated in standard units, through relative timing to accomplish milestones and goals so as not to lose momentum established, and through organizational and national cultural time-related norms. Punctuality and efficacy become inter-related to different degrees in different countries—for instance, as commonly portrayed, from the promptness and by-the-minute timing in Germany and to somewhat lesser extents through-out the Western countries, to the more fluid conceptions of "timing" in Latin America and other areas of the globe. Moreover, acquisitions are generally arduous and intensive strategic endeavors, with expectations from investors and observers that the transaction itself and subse-quent results would occur within relatively brief time spans (Hadida and Seifert 2008) and in accordance with related events (Ancona and Chong 1996).

Family business concerns within key geographic acquisition contexts

Extant theoretical and empirical perspectives on emerging multinational companies (E-MNCs) have relatively minimized the importance of family businesses as venues of global strategy in general and international acquisitions strategy in particular (Miller *et al.* 2010). MNCs in emerging economies can be family businesses, and family businesses can become MNCs, and these phenomena merit further research attention. Family MNCs in emerging markets can serve as engines for growth and internationalization from those markets. Acqui-sitions function as a means for not just regional but global expansion into the top tier of industries worldwide (Gaur *et al.* 2013; Gubbi *et al.* 2010).

Family businesses have been recognized as important in the market for corporate control (Filatotchev *et al.* 2007). In nations ranging from frontier economies to fully developed econ-omies, family presence in private and public companies remains at notable levels (Nicholson 2008). The word "emerging" broadly encompasses economies at phases of economic develop-ment from "frontier" to "emerging" to "developing," and the word here applies in that general sense. In these markets, family businesses predominate, including in emerging multinational companies engaging in international acquisition activity (Bhaumik *et al.* 2010). These E-MNCs play both acquiring and target roles in the global market for corporate control. The E-MNC leaders, who may be progenitors or inheritors of family businesses, make deals in markets at all levels of economic development.

Family business MNCs from rapidly expanding economic regions such as the Arabian Gulf have an advantage for this type of expansion because of the natural and financial resources as well as the international networks, affiliations, and opportunities already available. The larger region has become known as the Gulf Cooperation Council (an economic single market especially for the oil-producing countries of the Arabian Gulf), Middle East, and North Africa (hereafter GCC/MENA). This broader region generally shares some religious and cultural char-acteristics as well as economic interests, although not all the countries have the high-income, high-growth aspects that make the Arabian Gulf nations contiguously unique among global emerging markets—in contrast to, for instance, Latin America, Eastern Europe, the Indian subcontinent, and East Asia. Kuwait serves as a focal country for sustainable rapid development in the Gulf, similar to Brazil, Russia, India, and China within their respective regions. In the focal case for the chapter, the E-MNC launched its global growth with the acquisition of a much larger MNC from a developed country, where that MNC had fallen into distressed circumstances, necessitating takeover by private equity and resale to the emerging corporate bidder. The deal thus involved cross-border business considerations as a crucial part of the context.

International dynamics in the global market for corporate control—acquisitions across sovereign borders and gradients of economic development

Cross-border M&As have long interested scholars of strategy, finance, and organizations because of their intrinsic occurrence in a global economy (envisioned by economists in a pure form even before the actual evolution) alongside their often problematic aspects (Park and Vambery 2010). The literature has been equivocal to date on whether the international nature enhances or impedes the performance of the acquisition (Cebenoyan *et al.* 1992; Moeller and Schlingemann 2005). Culture (Björkman *et al.* 2007), goals (Meyer and Altenborg 2008), and expatriation of executives (Hébert *et al.* 2005) can all be instrumental in the success or failure of the deals. Regardless of the unclear aggregate performance, cross-border deals are especially important for continued worldwide economic interconnections and the multilateral flow of assets, goods, and services (Collins *et al.* 2009; Shimizu *et al.* 2004).

Mergers and acquisitions are an essential strategy for the international as well as domestic expansion of companies. The repeated intensive waves of M&A activity from the late nineteenth century through the present represent the popularity of this form of strategy (Harford 2005). Acquisitions can occur across sovereign borders as well as across gradients of economic development and are one of the more advanced modes of foreign direct investment as part of corporate global strategy and internationalization (Mody 2004). Nevertheless, research has decisively shown that most M&A deals fail to generate the desired value or create the intended synergy (Bruner 2002; Selden and Colvin 2003). In spite of the cumulative and collective experience resulting from waves of mergers and acquisitions, the extensive pre-acquisition financial and legal due-diligence, and the large number of scenarios run to simulate expected outcomes in the newly integrated entity, the failure rate of mergers and acquisitions remains around 50–70 percent (Agrawal and Jaffe 2000).

As part of the worldwide economic setting, it is worth emphasizing that international mergers and acquisitions leadership occurs within the general strategic context of global merger waves (Alexandridis *et al.* 2011). Mergers and acquisitions have been demonstrably cyclical over the past century, while the market for corporate control has been largely global for about three decades. As a major method of firm growth and international expansion, mergers and acquisitions provide a potential outlet for the disinvestment of individual family members from family firms while preserving the future of the firm (Alsayrafi 2010; Xiaowei Luo and Chung 2005). In considering such a family business and global strategy overview, it is again important to note the region of the world. Merger markets have typically been considered as: the USA and Canada, Europe, Asia-Pacific, Latin America, Middle East, and Africa (Gomes *et al.* 2011). Clearly variations exist within and among these markets. For the purposes of this chapter, I concentrate on the manifestation and evolution of leadership issues related to international acquisitions emanating from family-owned or family-controlled MNCs from the Arabian Gulf.

Emerging market dynamics in the GCC/MENA, Arabian Gulf and Kuwait

Research focusing on emerging multinationals has been gaining ground. Likewise, research on mergers involving the Middle East and African regions (Gomes *et al.* 2012), or mergers involving family aspects (Allred *et al.* 2005; Davis and Stout 1992; Miller *et al.* 2010; Palmer and Barber 2001; Walsh and Kosnik 1993), has been attaining increased attention. Within the Middle East, key oil-producing countries such as Kuwait, UAE, and Qatar, exert an economic impact disproportionate to their geographic and population size. (Saudi Arabia, in contrast, has both large economic impact and large area size.) Multinational family businesses have also flourished within these countries. With generous resources and successful acquisitions, these businesses have broadened their international platforms. Although a relatively small country in area and population, Kuwait has a high-income, fast-growing economy with five multinational companies ranked on the Forbes Global 2000 lists for 2012–2015. Its national oil company (Kuwait Petroleum Company) and sovereign fund (Kuwait Investment Authority) rank respectively seventh in terms of reserves (Marcopolis 2012) and eighth in assets (KPMG 2013) in the world. Hence the country stands as resource-rich, not merely in oil but also in the type of corporations appropriate for researching issues generalizable for global business relevance. Key family businesses such as Kharafi, Alghanim, Alshaya, AlBahar, Behbehani, Bukhamseen, and Sultan dominate within the region; additional prominent family businesses include Al-Wazzan (Mezzan), Boodai, Al-Zahem, and Marafie (Marcopolis 2012). Such businesses have for the most part remained privately held, with closely guarded financials, and a total of only about 8 percent of GCC family businesses are currently publicly traded, with a total of about 20 percent expressing interest in having an initial public offering (IPO) (Alsayrafi 2010). The increased interest has arisen as the power for capitalization within publicly traded markets becomes more of an imperative and a facilitating factor for international expansion. Whether the firms remain private or opt to become publicly traded, influence and ownership interlocks are common within the top families.

Due to the similarities in economic, demographic, and political structures within the region, the findings become highly relevant to other countries in the Arabian Gulf and to a somewhat lesser extent throughout the GCC/MENA. The findings could also apply to other emerging economic areas and countries, in particular those with rich natural resources, such as in Latin America (Mexico, Brazil, and Venezuela), Africa (Algeria and Nigeria), and Southeast Asia (Malaysia and Indonesia). Moreover, Kuwait as an economically important region of the world has already made huge strides in partnering with Western and non-Western MNCs and organizations in the government and corporate sectors (Forbes 2012).

According to a report from Barclays Wealth Insights (2009), family businesses represent 70 to 90 percent of global gross domestic product (GDP), with the Middle East predominance of family businesses at the upper end of that spectrum. Due to the laws governing inheritance and also due to the typical structure of bequests, the GCC/MENA region has one of the highest occurrences of dynastic wealth in the world (SCAS 2010). This wealth largely occurs through businesses owned, operated, or controlled within the family. Some family businesses have escalated into global enterprises susceptible to worldwide economic effects at the same time that they are vulnerable to internecine conflict, intergenerational tensions, and succession planning issues. Such conflicts are not necessarily the norm in family businesses, but some striking examples have occurred—for instance, in the NewsCorp (UK) tabloid publishing empire, where offspring of the thrice-married, family-oriented Rupert Murdoch have had degrees of disputes and competency struggles. Despite pressures on multiple fronts, family businesses that are MNCs have tremendous potential for coordinated, effective strategic action, drawing on a deeply interrelated shareholding base.

Empirical design, data collection, and analysis

Another key research issue for the case in the chapter involves methodology. To obtain insights into the leadership functions and interactions in M&A activity as a larger research project, a series of interviews have been conducted with pivotal leaders of acquisitions in two regions, (1) North America and (2) Middle East and North Africa area (GCC/MENA). Interviewing as a method enables the collection of data replete with reflections on decision making, successes, struggles, failures, and resolutions. The introspection and retrospection from rich, in-depth, ethnographic-style interviews provide strong complementary or alternative data to survey, archival, or more cursory interview methods. Quantitative data from acquisitions and business databases as well as from corporate sources have been further obtained to enhance insights from the interview-based data.

The empirical evidence for this chapter derives from the study of a large, successful, publicly traded yet family-controlled business in the Arabian Gulf, referred to by the pseudonym, LLC. In the interests of potential generalizability to a range of industries worldwide, the company business does not center on the energy sector. The top leadership reflects a bilingual, multi-cultural and internationally oriented educational, work, and travel background.

Direct observations, documentation, and interviews, all involving the particular company, supplied the three main sources of data for the present part of the study. The observations tended toward the unstructured, arising from the opportunities provided by visits to the company. The documentation derived from a combination of online searching of reputable business sources for the region and also information provided by the company—for instance, on their lines of business, emerging markets presence, and corporate social responsibility program. The online sources included EMIS, the Emerging Markets Information Service; ASMA, the Arab Stock Market Analysis; and Zawya, the Middle East and North Africa business intelligence service of Thomson Reuters. The interviewing relied on a set of 17 open-ended questions to invite in-depth responses and interaction. Similar methodologies have been previously used by Mintzberg (1973) and Carlson (1951) in their now classic studies of managerial work. As the focal company, LLC pursued an intensive acquisitions program over about a 5-year period, then continued with acquisitions at a less fervid pace into the present; each acquisition represented an embedded event or mini-case within the larger case study. The acquisitions were purposely cross-border in scope for acquiring geographically diversified partners, customers, and locations, thereby internationalizing from a business focused on the GCC/MENA region to a services provider to the world.

A total of about 30 hours were spent in interaction with various representatives of the company, including the CEO, a member of the board of the directors, and five managers from assorted business functions. In addition, an array of documentary sources in both English and Arabic were examined with the aid of three native Arabic-speaking research assistants and a cross-cultural consultant. The research assistants functioned also as cultural interpreters and as individuals familiar with the national business environment, customs, and corporate structure of the focal company and country in the Middle East. Two to three cultures—US, UK and Arabian Gulf—are in total represented within each key individual interviewed. From my personal educational and work experience, I had familiarity with the US and UK systems. The research assistants and cross-cultural consultant all had familiarity with two or three systems each. The importance of multiple cultural understandings emerged repeatedly in the segment of the study represented in this chapter, as the focal company successfully functions at a cultural crossroads, having enabled rapid expansion from regional to global presence through acquisitions.

The LLC CEO has native-level English and could be interviewed directly by me for five hours total in three sessions in that language. In addition, there were present at different times two of the bilingual native Arabic-speaking members of the research team, who could provide insights for times when the CEO chatted in Arabic or made particular allusions indigenous to the country and culture. The data were parsed through manual content analysis of repeated phrases and themes throughout the total extended hours of in-depth interview time with all individuals within or related to the company.

Conflict and resolution, leadership decisions going into international mergers and acquisitions from MBA to the present

The empirical analysis broadly involves issues related to conflict between family heritage and individual aspirations, between leadership team objectives and broader shareholder expectations, and between governments and management levels across countries. These three conflict areas are related to specific issues for decision making by the CEO, presented in chronological order of major challenges encountered in his leadership tenure and in the time of his career from receiving his MBA from an elite US business program through the present. I interweave quotes and analysis to provide strategic insights into the development of both the business and the leadership across the past 15 years. The key strategy has involved numerous acquisitions within a relatively short period of time, spanning a full range of ease or difficulty of implementation, while rapidly building a formidably competitive global firm. The CEO himself effectively summarized the experience: "We have been very acquisitive . . . in over 50 acquisitions from 2004 to 2008, we have seen the good, the bad, and the ugly" (all quotes from interviews with the LLC CEO unless otherwise noted).

Issue: to join or not to join the family business

When I came back to [my country in the Arabian Gulf], there were only a couple of options: one was to join the family business which was not very appealing because the family business can be very hierarchical, and not only hierarchical . . . . So I started a firm: it was just me, a secretary, and another guy to start. We focused on privatization because we thought it would be a really big thing at the time, which it was . . . I got the first mandate to do a privatization from the government, to acquire assets which had previously been primarily government-owned and could now be in the private sector.

This tension centers on the divergence that can occur between family heritage and individual aspirations.

At the time of the decision making by the key leader interviewed, he had felt, as he recollected, that the family business would be in many ways too confining. Based on other interviewing for this project, the opinions were expressed that family businesses can provide a great comfort level but can also limit opportunities for both personal and organizational development. Not joining the family business directly meant the opportunity for building a separate business that could still provide service to the family business as an arms-length service provider, and hence make a distinct but still meaningful contribution within a national, regional, and ultimately global network of interactions. Exemplifying the inspiration provided by the successful entrepreneurship of the interviewed leader, the earlier family business in this situation ultimately became publicly traded, unusually for the region, and subsequently built its own platform for international expansion. The conflict centered on what seemed like a separation decision from the family business, and the implicit and explicit strength of those ties. The resolution lay in an independent, transformative venture that turned out to maintain and strengthen intercorporate connections with both the original family business as well as with other internationalizing enterprises.

Issue: to buy or not to buy assets available for privatization

The government had agreed to sell [certain state-owned assets] to groups of investors. There was a loophole in the law that the investors all had to be available on site at the announced time of the auction, but we realized that most of the investors would not be prepared with their valuations. We showed up at the auction and we outbid the other groups. They were authorized to bid [only in small increments]. We actually had no financing to do the deal, but we outbid them. The basic premise for buying the company was the real estate and concessions that they owned, especially the off-balance sheet leases not yet reflected as assets. We determined that [one pivotal concession] alone was worth more than the rest of the company. Our strategy was to have these valuable leases reflected as assets and also further to develop the services side of the business. After bidding and winning and not having any financing to do anything, it was funny that the share price actually doubled and tripled. The way the deal was structured, we had to sell about 50 percent of our shares afterward. It was very easy to do when the share price was already 100 percent–200 percent higher than what we had paid for it.

Not joining the family business directly meant having the opportunity to found a new firm or transform a separate existing firm. The business situation in the country meant that the firm could be relatively quickly launched through the acquisition of previously state-owned assets, with these assets serving as a springboard to additional expansion. The difficulty becomes that the acquisition of state-owned assets does not constitute a long-term viable strategy for growth. In addition, the access to and success in the bidding can result from combinations of factors—funding, expertise, connections, risk, and serendipity—that are difficult to duplicate repeatedly. The analysis of this issue begins with an extended quote on the acquisition of privatized assets to illustrate how the now CEO of LLC identified and followed through on a tremendous opportunity that put the budding public company into such a strong position that the very success became a dilemma for the young leader. His team as well as observers or competitors of the company were uncertain whether he could sustain this success. Capitalizing on the privatization opportunity meant that suddenly he had a sizable public firm to run and the attendant challenges for any such firm and for any young leader newly in such a position. Avoiding the privatization opportunity would have meant many more years to reach the starting point of having a company of a size that could then grow even further through the acquisition of publicly- and privately-owned assets. Acquiring through the third form of ownership, the state, provided the early launch for moving into acquisitions of firms either publicly traded or privately held. The tensions of having an early leadership position and early success have been encountered in the past decades especially in high-technology businesses by entrepreneurs such as Steve Jobs, Bill Gates, Sergei Brin, Larry Page, and Mark Zuckerberg. Each of these individuals has had a different career and life route, and different chances inside and outside their respectively founded companies, for demonstrating competence, stepping relatively into and out of the spotlight and the top leadership position, and continuing to be influential in their chosen arenas. For the soon-to-be LLC CEO, it has been remarkable that he has now had a 15-year unbroken leadership tenure—and, interestingly, he very early on made it a strength and policy of the company to be very much in the vanguard of technological innovations for the industry.

Issue: to lead or not to lead from the start

> There is no way we could have known from day one that we could do this, that we could build a company like this—of this size, scope and profitability—in this amount of time.

This issue centers on the tensions between the leadership team objectives and broader shareholder expectations and interest in the transaction (extending also to shareholders beyond the family).

After the learning experiences and ultimately efficacious privatization acquisitions, the decision very quickly arose as to whether to lead the new venture that would rapidly become the global LLC. At the point of the conflict and decision making, very few people would have envisioned the ensuing fast-paced and profitable internationalization of the firm, or there would perhaps have been greater confidence in the young leader from the start. The newly privatized entity, formed from the acquisition of previously state-owned assets, had the infrastructure, finances, and social capital to move forward swiftly. For our focal leader, the decision also involved whether and how to lead, driven by the desire to be successful within an ethical and sustainable framework reflecting heritage values as well as the multiculturalism intrinsic in a three-country upbringing. This same multiculturalism that could be an asset could be viewed as a drawback by more conservative investors from the country of the founding of the firm. The multiculturalism amounted in essence to drawing on the home country context of a potentially longer-term CEO position, longer-range investment and performance time horizons, and emphasis on expanding into emerging markets, counterbalanced by exposure to and experience with a more Western, developed-market, hard-hitting, aggressive, and even imperialistic acquisitions strategy. Yet the US/EU-style strategy emanating from the GCC/MENA could be executed without being subject to quite the same business practices scrutiny, or financial transparency and disclosure requirements, of a company stock traded on a Western exchange. The conflict centered on counterbalancing leadership styles and corporate objectives from different cultures, on the appropriateness of a decision breaking with family business tradition, and on investor factions with differences stemming from longer-standing factors. The resolution lay in the financial efficacy of the earlier privatization, successful evocation of pivotal family ties through market-driven arms-length business constructs, and clear articulation of the mission and vision for control of the newly privatized venture that would become LLC.

Issue: to expand locally–regionally–globally through key acquisitions or not to expand

> We wanted to grow from our own skill and not just be in a position where we were waiting to see if the government would auction concessions. If you can get those assets, it's great, and we have tried and gotten them, but it's not something you can replicate in other parts of the world—it is a local, not a global strategy. We did some strategizing and figured out that we wanted to focus on services and build a network in the emerging markets and also in developed economies. Part of the strategy to develop that network—now in over 100 countries—was to leverage acquisitions . . . to build a platform for expanding from our founding location to all the places in the world where we are today.

> In the course of acquiring [on average over 10 firms a year for 5 years], we have become a global firm, and more recently we have focused on unifying our brand and growing organically, with the occasional, selected, strategic acquisition. We will be continuing to have more growth, possibly more acquisitions.

This area can involve potential conflict between host country governments and the expanding company leadership, and even between the national interests of two different countries.

This potential conflict area involved identifying the lines of business in which the company would operate in order to have the capabilities for expanding from local to regional to global. The vision for the scope of the company, whether in terms of geography or products and services, influenced the type of acquisitions enacted. Likewise the availability of certain acquisitions could influence the strategic direction of the company. The overarching objective became to expand to a global firm within a framework of essentially related lines of business, which evolved ultimately into four distinct divisions identifiable within a single industry (in other words, not conglomerate-style or unrelated diversification). The basic conflict for the expansion issues was not whether, but how. The "how" involved quickly creating a global meta-network of interlocking competencies within the industry.

> We have created a lot of value by putting together networks spanning the globe, and we did it in fairly short order [within about a 5-year period]. If someone were trying to do that today, it would cost literally billions and billions of dollars.

While favorable for the focal company, the speed of growth through acquisitions would be difficult for another firm to duplicate.

Not only were the cost effectiveness and the speed of the transformation from regional to global startling, but the financials and branding of the company have also been remarkably successful. The "how" therefore also meant defusing any negative feedback or backlash from an aggressive expansion program, which was up to that point unique for a publicly-traded company within the region. The "how" further included pursuing particular regions and countries as part of the initial expansion—in this case, targeting emerging markets previously untapped by the global firms in the industry and consistent with the emerging market heritage of the firm itself. As part of building a global presence, the company [LLC] has also developed and sustained a world-class corporate social responsibility program exhibiting outstanding corporate citizenship in all areas of the world where its services could be of assistance, in situations ranging from local educational initiatives to large-scale disaster relief.

Issue: to rebrand for global marketing strategy or remain with the earlier firm name

> It has definitely been challenging acquiring 50 different company cultures and brands and putting that all together, which leads into one of the main reasons we did our rebranding. We chose to come up with a brand name and logo that was new to everybody, so that everybody had to give something up, and everybody got something in return. We did a lot of research and a lot of thinking to come up with the image, colors and name. We wanted to brand around our unique competencies and to reflect that we put customers at the center of our value proposition. We customize for our customers in a way that really contrasts with our competitors, and we wanted our new corporate brand to express these strengths and capabilities at a high level.

The rebranding or not re-branding question arose as interrelated with the acquisitions strategy, as part of how to assimilate acquired businesses, products, and services. This conflict area captures an essential dilemma in many mergers and acquisitions: to what extent to integrate the target entity and to identify it with the acquiring firm? In this case, LLC had been operating under a highly descriptive, albeit rather cumbersome, name, reminiscent of function rather than the caliber of the company and services. When the company achieved a certain size, scope, and global reach, the CEO had compelling arguments for rebranding to exhibit the enhanced competencies. At the same time, the company originates from a part of the world where history and tradition remain highly important, and therefore the previous name has not entirely disappeared but rather has remained connected to the new name in certain official documentation. It should be noted that subsumed within the conflict areas was the decision whether and where to be publicly quoted. Although indisputably a global firm, the company has opted for listing on essentially regional exchanges. Before the global financial crisis, the firm had road shows in preparation for listing on additional exchanges in major financial centers of the world, but then put those plans on hold. Globalization has meant encountering the inevitable resistance in some form, somewhere, from host country governments. Countering this resistance has required unprecedented dexterity for the company in balancing global transparency with corporate and national privacy concerns, while remaining focused on the corporate objectives.

Discussion and implications

This chapter has addressed CEO leadership in international acquisitions in the context of internationalization from emerging markets. The explication has incorporated family business aspects and broached multiple decision areas as well as issues of multiculturalism and timing. The identified conflict areas (to join or not to join the family business, to buy or not to buy assets available for privatization, to lead or not to lead the privatized business, to expand from regional to global or not, and to rebrand in a global marketing strategy or not) have the potential for resolution with a multifaceted collaborative framework that can encompass dissension while also providing outlets for integrative decision making and actions. The use of power emerges as subtle and inspirational rather than blatantly controlling. Within the family, there can be sharing of responsibilities as well as separation of interests. The structure of voting shares, stock transmission, and intergenerational succession schemes can impede or enhance the flexibility for integration versus implosion, as in the aforementioned example of the NewsCorp empire of the Murdoch family. As further examples, the Hermès family has remained largely united in the face of repeated acquisition attempts by LVMH from 2010 to the present; the Bulgari family business, on the other hand, agreed in 2010 to be acquired by the LVMH conglomerate; the Porsche family battled for years in the second and third generations until guardedly reconciling through the full acquisition of Porsche (founded by Ferdinand Porsche in 1931 and later chaired by his grandson Wolfgang Porsche) by VW (founded in concept by Ferdinand Porsche in 1937, then passing through various levels of government ownership, then later run and chaired by grandson Ferdinand Piëch). In addition, the Porsche and Piëch families have complicated interlocking ownership structures and trusts for their shareholdings in VW (Automotive News Europe 2013). These examples of businesses with family involvement evidence the structural and legal flexibility that can be developed for mutually beneficial and collective strategic action among family members. Even when disagreements inevitably occur and when the time until reconciliation lengthens, shareholding structures can ultimately facilitate more integration than separation of interests. It can also be the case that expensive and time-consuming acquisition offers eventually separate family interests within shareholding structures, for instance as when NewsCorp in 2007

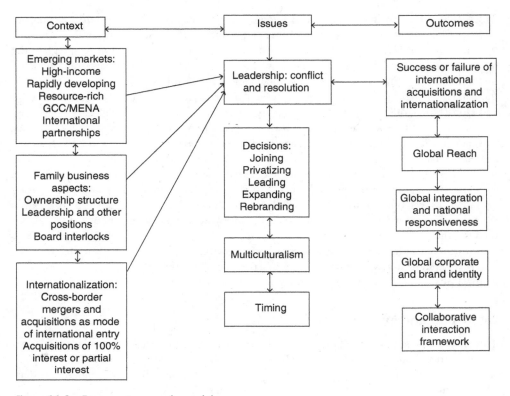

Figure 11.3 Emergent research model

acquired the *Wall Street Journal*, which was originally dominated and still substantially owned and influenced by the Bancroft family in the USA.

Issues of multiculturalism and strategic timing recur in the context of the strategic challenges and collaborative frameworks and can be addressed as integrative aspects leading to identification of implications of this research for research and practice. Figure 11.3 illustrates the emergent research model relating context, issues, and outcomes.

Leadership multiculturalism and corporate internationalization objectives

The individual multiculturalism of the CEO contributes to, reflects, and reinforces the global orientation and intercultural competencies within the company and also the cross-cultural leadership of international M&As. Individual multiculturalism appears to assist with the handling of the cultural intersections of international mergers and acquisitions. Interestingly, the top leadership's multicultural adeptness and personal facility with navigating multiple cultural boundaries coexists with a highly streamlined and intensive approach to the cultural and logistical assimilation of acquired firms.

In a related manner, the initially successful (although financially and logistically ultimately failed) RBS–Santander–Fortis (UK–Spain–Belgium) European banking consortium acquisition of Dutch bank ABN AMRO in 2007–2008 was brokered by an internationally networked, multilingual investment banker coordinating three internationally oriented and ambitious CEOs. The globalization of construction and building materials firm CEMEX from Mexico, then

Latin America, to the rest of the world (1985–present) has been facilitated by the manifold multicultural proficiencies of CEO Lorenzo Zambrano, as has the internationalization of Indian (by heritage) and European (by heritage and current headquartering) steel firm ArcelorMittal (1975–present), led by multicultural savant, CEO Lakshmi Mittal, championing the acquisition of Luxembourg firm Arcelor by his family firm Mittal. These examples emphasize the associations among individual leader, organizational strategy, and mergers and acquisitions successfully accomplished across organizational and cultural boundaries. The three examples also all have aspects of family business heritage, intergenerational leadership transfer, and venturing into new geographies.

Leadership and speed of acquisitions

The issue of timing occurs in at least three ways in the interview-based findings with respect to: 1) longevity of leadership, 2) speed of acquisitions, integration, and overall corporate growth, and 3) pace of decision-making timing as identified by the CEO as a cultural component of acquired firms. The CEO interviewed has led the company for over 15 years and has the backing of the board and shareholders for continued tenure, in essence for as long as the firm remains successful. As compared to publicly traded companies, family businesses in general have the benefits of longer vistas for performance, established leadership for stability, and an enduring sense of identity rooted in history and tradition (Barclays Wealth Insights 2009; Carmeli and Markman 2011). In contrast to widely held conceptions, family businesses do not necessarily suffer unduly from nepotism, greed, or pilfering of the corporate coffers for personal gain (SCAS 2010). The proven longevity and anticipated continuation of the LLC CEO, as well as the listing of the company on non-Western exchanges, mean that the time horizon for strategic formulation, implementation, and outcomes provides greater opportunities for innovation, patience, and persistence. Paradoxically, the present top leadership has exhibited exceptional swiftness in the rate, integration, and success of acquisitions as well as in the overall speed of growth of the company from respected regional contender to global competitor. Thus the juxtaposition of timing effects, from extended leadership longevity to compressed acquisition speed, has inculcated a heightened awareness for the importance of timing as a cultural component in decision making within organizations. The CEO therefore explicitly seeks to understand timing and guidance as two important aspects in the decision-making mechanics of the companies he acquires. Timing has surfaced as a fertile area for increased understanding of intercultural dynamics in international business strategy.

Implications for research and practice

Implications for business practice are for leaders of international acquisitions to have or develop multicultural competencies and to be alert for opportunities for intercultural learning. In addition, leaders of international acquisitions would benefit from an awareness of how each transaction potentially fits within an organizational or corporate strategy for internationalization and expansion. In addition to the individual leadership aptitudes and the firm-level strategy, practice implications exist at the network level of inter-organizational interactions. Top leaders can influence themselves and the organizations they run, but their influence on other organizations (and even on other individuals within their own organization) requires the collaborative approach emergent in the present case. Perhaps the focal organization has already developed an international orientation and deep intercultural learning capabilities, but the leadership should be prepared actively to work with firms being acquired, or firms with which alliances are being formed, to reach beneficial levels of reciprocal strategic and intercultural accord. Reaching those levels could require setting examples and recommending standards and practices for other firms as well as for the focal firm being led.

The linkages among multiculturalism, timing, and acquisition success could be explored further in future research, as could more broadly issues of leadership, internationalization, and acquisitions involving firms from emerging market countries moving into the global business sphere. Suggestions for future research include examining also the array of joining-acquiring-leading-expanding-branding issues identified here and potentially applicable to further companies, countries, and regions. The model of collaborative frameworks for intercultural interactions in international acquisitions could be extended on the basis of similar business environments to cases in other resource-rich nations of economically emerging areas of the world, and it could further be extended for investigating cases in more economically developed regions or in countries less endowed with desired natural resources. In addition, future research could examine leadership-specific issues such as human capital, social capital, acquisition experience, and also subjects such as obscurity-celebrity and confidence-overconfidence. Moreover, sector-specific considerations related to the particular industries of interest, as well as economic and political interconnections for certain industries could be taken into account.

References

Agrawal, A. and Jaffe, J.F. (2000) "The post-merger performance puzzle," in C. Cooper and A. Gregory (eds.) *Advances in Mergers and Acquisitions*, New York: JAI Press: 7–42.

Alexandridis, G., Mavrovitis, C.F., and Travlos, N.G. (2011) "How have M&As changed? Evidence from the sixth merger wave," *European Journal of Finance*, 18: 663–688.

Allred, B.B., Boal, K.B., and Holstein, W.K. (2005) "Corporations as stepfamilies: a new metaphor for explaining the fate of merged and acquired companies," *Academy of Management Executive*, 19(3): 23–37.

Alsayrafi, F. (2010) "The changing face of family business in the Gulf," *Khaleej Times*, 2 February, www.khaleejtimes.com/displayarticlenew.asp?col=&section=opinion&xfile=data/opinion/2010/february/opinion_february9.xml (accessed 2013-10-20).

Ancona, D.G. and Chong, C.-L. (1996) "Entrainment: pace, cycle, and rhythm in organizational behavior," in L.L. Cummings and B.M. Staw (eds.) *Research in Organizational Behavior*, Greenwich, CT: JAI Press: 251–284.

Angwin, D. (2004) "Speed in M&A integration: the first 100 days," *European Management Journal*, 22: 418–430.

Automotive News Europe (2013) "Porsche-Piëch family buys Qatar's 10% stake in VW's majority owner," 6 June, http://europe.autonews.com/article/20130617/ANE/130619890/porsche-piech-family-buys-qatars-10-stake-in-vws-majority-owner#axzz2ot7y28RL (accessed 2013-12-29).

Balmaceda, F. (2009) "Mergers and CEO power," *Journal of Institutional and Theoretical Economics*, 165: 454–486.

Barclays Wealth Insights (2009) "Family business: in safe hands?," *Barclays Wealth in Cooperation with the Economist Intelligence Unit*, Vol. 8, https://wealth.barclays.com/content/dam/bwpublic/global/documents/wealth_management/insights8-family-business-uk.pdf (accessed 2013-10-20).

Bartlett, C. and Beamish, P.W. (2011) *Transnational Management*, 6th edn., New York: McGraw-Hill.

Bhaumik, S.K., Driffield, N., and Pal, S. (2010) "Does ownership structure of emerging-market firms affect their outward FDI? The case of the Indian automotive and pharmaceutical sectors," *Journal of International Business Studies*, 41: 437–450.

Björkman, I., Stahl, G.K., and Vaara, E. (2007) "Cultural differences and capability transfer in cross-border acquisitions: the mediating roles of capability complementarity, absorptive capacity, and social integration," *Journal of International Business Studies*, 38: 658–672.

Brown, R. and Sarma, N. (2007) "CEO overconfidence, CEO dominance and corporate acquisitions," *Journal of Economics and Business*, 59: 358–379.

Bruner, R.F. (2002) "Does M&A pay? A survey of evidence for the decision-maker," *Journal of Applied Finance*, 12: 48–68.

Capron, L. and Guillén, M. (2009) "National corporate governance institutions and post-acquisition target reorganization," *Strategic Management Journal*, 30: 803–833.

Carlson, S. (1951) *Executive Behavior: A Study of the Work Load and the Working Methods of Managing Directors*, Stockholm: Strömberg.

Carmeli, A. and Markman, G.D. (2011) "Capture, governance, and resilience: strategy implications from the history of Rome," *Strategic Management Journal*, 32: 322–341.

Cebenoyan, A.S., Papaioannou, G.J., and Travlos, N.G. (1992) "Foreign takeover activity in the US and wealth effects for target firm shareholders," *Financial Management*, 21: 58–68.

Collins, J.D., Holcomb, T.R., Certo, S.T., Hitt, M.A., and Lester, R.H. (2009) "Learning by doing: cross-border mergers and acquisitions," *Journal of Business Research*, 62: 1329–1334.

Covin, T.J., Kolenko, T.A., Sightler, K.W., and Tudor, R.K. (1997) "Leadership style and post-merger satisfaction," *Journal of Management Development*, 16: 22–34.

Darling, J.R. and Fischer, A.K. (1998) "Developing the management leadership team in a multinational enterprise," *European Business Review*, 98: 100–108.

Davis, G.F. and Stout, S.K. (1992) "Organization theory and the market for corporate control: a dynamic analysis of the characteristics of large takeover targets, 1980–1990," *Administrative Science Quarterly*, 37: 605–633.

Dewing, A.S. (1921) "A statistical test of the success of consolidations," *Quarterly Journal of Economics*, 36: 84–101.

Dyer, W.G., Jr. (2003) "The family: the missing variable in organizational research," *Entrepreneurship: Theory and Practice*, 27: 401–416.

Fendt, J. (2006) "The CEO in Post-Merger Situations: An Emerging Theory on the Management of Multiple Realities," (PhD), Leiden University School of Management, Leiden University.

Filatotchev, I., Strange, R., Piesse, J., and Yung-Chih, L. (2007) "FDI by firms from newly industrialised economies in emerging markets: corporate governance, entry mode and location," *Journal of International Business Studies*, 38: 556–572.

Forbes (2012) "The world's 25 biggest oil companies," 16 July, www.forbes.com/pictures/eejk45elhfg/not-just-the-usual-suspects-3/ (accessed 2013-11-10).

Gaur, A.S., Malhotra, S., and Zhu, P. (2013) "Acquisition announcements and stock market valuations of acquiring firms' rivals: a test of the growth probability hypothesis in China," *Strategic Management Journal*, 34: 215–232.

Gersick, C.J.G. (1994) "Pacing strategic change: the case of a new venture," *Academy of Management Journal*, 37: 9–45.

Gomes, E., Cohen, M., and Mellahi, K. (2011) "When two African cultures collide: a study of interactions between managers in a strategic alliance between two African organizations," *Journal of World Business*, 46: 5–12.

Gomes, E., Angwin, D., Peter, E., and Mellahi, K. (2012) "HRM issues and outcomes in African mergers and acquisitions: a study of the Nigerian banking sector," *International Journal of Human Resource Management*, 23: 2874–2900.

Gubbi, S.R., Aulakh, P.S., Ray, S., Sarkar, M.B., and Chittoor, R. (2010) "Do international acquisitions by emerging-economy firms create shareholder value? The case of Indian firms," *Journal of International Business Studies*, 41: 397–418.

Hadida, A.L. and Seifert, M. (2008) "Strategic decisions in high velocity contexts," in C. Wankel (ed.) *21st Century Management: A Reference Handbook*, Thousand Oaks, CA: Sage Publications.

Harford, J. (2005) "What drives merger waves?," *Journal of Financial Economics*, 77: 529–560.

Hébert, L., Very, P., and Beamish, P.W. (2005) "Expatriation as a bridge over troubled water: a knowledge-based perspective applied to cross-border acquisitions," *Organization Studies*, 26: 1455–1476.

Hitt, M.A., Tihanyi, L., Miller, T., and Connelly, B. (2006) "International diversification: antecedents, moderators, and outcomes," *Journal of Management*, 32: 831–67.

Keys, J.B., Wells, R., and Edge, A. (1993) "International management games: laboratories for performance-based intercultural learning," *Leadership and Organization Development*, 14: 25–31.

Kitching, J. (1967) "Why do mergers miscarry?," *Harvard Business Review*, 45(6): 84–101.

KPMG (2013) "Emerging trends in the sovereign wealth fund landscape," *KPMG Cutting through Complexity*, www.kpmg.com/AE/en/Documents/2013/Emerging_trends_in_the_regional_SWF_landscape.pdf (accessed 2013-10-25).

Krug, J.A. and Shill, W. (2008) "The big exit: executive churn in the wake of M&As," *Journal of Business Strategy*, 29: 15–21.

Li, Y. and Aguilera, R.V. (2008) "Target director turnover in acquisitions: a conceptual framework," *Corporate Governance: An International Review*, 16: 492–503.

Livermore, S. (1935) "The success of industrial mergers," *Quarterly Journal of Economics*, 50: 68–96.

Luo, X. and Chung, C.-N. (2005) "Keeping it all in the family: the role of particularistic relationships in business group performance during institutional transition," *Administrative Science Quarterly*, 50: 404–439.

Luo, Y. (2011) "Strategic responses to perceived corruption in an emerging market: lessons from MNEs investing in China," *Business & Society*, 50: 350–387.

Luo, Y. and Zhao, H. (2013) "Doing business in a transitional society: economic environment and relational political strategy for multinationals," *Business & Society*, 52: 515–549.

Maclean, M., Harvey, C., and Press, J. (2006) *Business Elites and Corporate Governance in France and the UK*, Basingstoke: Palgrave Macmillan.

Marcopolis (2012) "Top 10 companies in Kuwait," online resource specializing in emerging economies, www.marcopolis.net/kuwait-companies.htm (accessed 2013-10-20).

Meyer, C.B. and Altenborg, E. (2008) "Incompatible strategies in international mergers: the failed merger between Telia and Telenor," *Journal of International Business Studies*, 39: 508–525.

Miller, D., Le Breton-Miller, I., and Lester, R.H. (2010) "Family ownership and acquisition behavior in publicly-traded companies," *Strategic Management Journal*, 31: 201–223.

Mintzberg, H. (1973) *The Nature of Managerial Work*, New York: HarperCollins.

Mody, A. (2004) "Is FDI integrating the world economy?," *World Economy*, 27: 1195–1222.

Moeller, S.B. and Schlingemann, F.P. (2005) "Global diversification and bidder gains: a comparison between cross-border and domestic acquisitions," *Journal of Banking and Finance*, 29: 533–564.

Morris, S.S. and Snell, S.A. (2011) "Intellectual capital configurations and organizational capability: an empirical examination of human resource subunits in the multinational enterprise," *Journal of International Business Studies*, 42: 805–827.

Nicholson, N. (2008) "Evolutionary psychology, organizational culture, and the family firm," *Academy of Management Perspectives*, 22(2): 73–84.

Oviatt, B.M. and McDougall, P. (1995) "Global start-ups: entrepreneurs on a worldwide stage," *Academy of Management Executive*, 9(2): 30–43.

Palmer, D. and Barber, B.M. (2001) "Challengers, elites, and owning families: a social class theory of corporate acquisitions in the 1960s," *Administrative Science Quarterly*, 46: 87–120.

Park, K.M. (2012) "Leadership perspectives on the global market for corporate control," in N.J. Delener (ed.) *Service Science Research, Strategy and Innovation: Dynamic Knowledge Management Methods*, Hershey, PA: IGI Global Business Science Reference: 377–399.

Park, K.M. and Vambery, R.G. (2010) "Value creation through international acquisitions in a world of one-way globalization: toward a new paradigm," *International Business & Economics Research Journal*, 9: 1–5.

Perkins, S. (2013) "When does prior experience pay? Institutional experience and the case of the multinational corporation," MIT Sloan Research Paper No. 4986-13, http://ssrn.com/abstract=1088251.

SCAS (2010) "Family-run businesses in the MENA region," www.scasinc.com/scas/family-run-business-in-the-mena-region (accessed 2013-10-20).

Schweiger, D.M. and Goulet, P.K. (2005) "Facilitating acquisition integration through deep-level cultural learning interventions: a longitudinal field experiment," *Organization Studies*, 26: 1477–1499.

Selden, L. and Colvin, G. (2003) "M&A needn't be a loser's game," *Harvard Business Review*, 81: 70–77.

Shanley, M.T. and Correa, M.E. (1992) "Agreement between top management teams and expectations for post acquisition performance," *Strategic Management Journal*, 13: 245–266.

Shearer, C.S., Hames, D.S., and Runge, J.B. (2001) "How CEOs influence organizational culture following acquisitions," *Leadership & Organization Development Journal*, 22: 105–113.

Shimizu, K., Hitt, M.A., Vaidyanath, D., and Pisano, V. (2004) "Theoretical foundations of cross-border mergers and acquisitions: a review of current research and recommendations for the future," *Journal of International Management*, 10: 307–353.

Stein, M. (2005) "The Othello conundrum: the inner contagion of leadership," *Organization Studies*, 26: 1405–1419.

Vaara, E. (2003) "Post-acquisition integration as sensemaking: glimpses of ambiguity, confusion, hypocrisy, and politicization," *Journal of Management Studies*, 40: 859–894.

Walsh, J.P. and Kosnik, R.D. (1993) "Corporate raiders and their disciplinary role in the market for corporate control," *Academy of Management Journal*, 36: 671–700.

Wasserman, N., Nohria, N., and Anand, B. (2010) "When does leadership matter? A contingent opportunities view of CEO leadership," in N. Nohria and R. Khurana (eds.) *Handbook of Leadership Theory and Practice*, Boston, MA: Harvard Business Publishing: 27–64.

Part III
Methodological domain of M&A research

In this section of the book, the chapters address existing methods of study in the M&A field, explore their contributions, and then suggest new ways to study M&As. Further, the methods presented represent different ontologies and epistemologies—from objective positivism, in Chapter 13 by Harrison and Schijven, to a subjective ontology in Chapter 14 by Lund and Tienari that draws from ethnomethodology, symbolic interactionism, Marxist epistemology, and social phenomenology. With this background, the focus of each chapter in this section is briefly summarized.

M&A research has long been dominated by positivistic- or post-positivistic-inspired methods (Meglio and Risberg 2010), though, over the last decade or so, more and more interpretive and social constructionism studies have been published (Yu et al. 2005; e.g. Harwood 2006). Epistemology and methodology are important considerations in research as they determine the knowledge that the research can contribute. This section of the book outlines a more nuanced picture of the recent approaches that researchers are using to learn more about M&A by considering different types of methods and how they contribution to research.

In Chapter 12, Kroon and Rouzies explore the potential and challenge of using mixed methods in M&A research. They suggest that mixed methods could be a way to overcome the methodological conformity where so much M&A research focuses on quantitative methods based on surveys or cross-sectional studies using large databases. Kroon and Rouzies urge scholars to reflect upon the methods they use to gather information and to analyze the data to improve the quality of M&A research. Mixed methods that combine qualitative and quantitative methods and data offer an obvious way to overcome the conformity and limitations of existing research. Though this method offers the potential to study M&As in a variety of ways, benefitting from the different aspects of quantitative and qualitative methods and data, Kroon and Rouzies observe that few M&A studies fully exploit the potential of a mixed method design.

Harrison and Schijven's Chapter 13 examines event study methodology to suggest new ways for using this well-known method in M&A studies. Event studies may be one of the most common methods in the study of M&A performance, but it has also been highly criticized. Harrison and Schijven point out that one of its limitations is its failure to capture processes or cultural and social impacts. They also emphasize the need to redefine and better define the performance construct in event studies. They conclude that event studies could be used as a means to examine investor behavior. For example, they suggest extending event study methodology to include qualitative methods as a way to increase the understanding of investor behavior and decision-making.

In Chapter 14, Lund and Tienari introduce a new method to the M&A field. They point out that M&A research generally tends to view M&As through an abstract and external lens that is ill-suited to gaining an in-depth understanding of employees as they experience the M&A. They suggest institutional ethnography as a promising method for exploring M&A research, especially as a way to overcome objectification and as a way to study culture and identity during M&A integration. Specifically, institutional ethnography offers the possibility to study the everyday experiences of people involved in mergers in new ways. It does so from the standpoint of the problems and issues that employees face in their everyday organizational lives. The method offers a possibility to study the integration process as it takes place.

The next chapter, by Mirc, proposes that M&A should be studied using social network analysis. This method enables capturing the relational aspects of M&A. Mirc states that focusing on relations and social structures as the primary objects of analysis will enhance the understanding of integration processes and their dynamics. Mirc further argues that social network analysis will allow a researcher to go beyond viewing individual and organizational factors as independent settings by adopting a multi-level perspective on M&A integration processes that considers interdependence.

In the section's final chapter, Risberg reviews qualitative and longitudinal M&A research. Risberg finds that qualitative M&A studies provide rigorous, in-depth studies that can clarify relationships in existing theory, as well as generate new theory. Her review shows that qualitative studies researchers often spend extensive time in the field and use multiple sources, enabling them to explain and understand the complexities and the context of M&As.

In summary, a better understanding of M&As requires both asking better questions and using improved methods and perspectives to explore answers. This section introduces the reader to reviews of existing methods, as well as making suggestions for how to rejuvenate the methodological approach to M&A research. For the reader new to or unfamiliar with either qualitative or quantitative methods, it provides a foundation for learning more about M&As.

References

Harwood, I. (2006) "Confidentiality constraints within mergers and acquisitions: Gaining insights through a 'bubble' metaphor," *British Journal of Management*, 1: 347–359.

Meglio, O. and Risberg, A. (2010) "Mergers and acquisitions: Time for a methodological rejuvenation of the field?," *Scandinavian Journal of Management*, 26: 87–95.

Yu, J., Engleman, R.M., and Ven, A.H. Van de (2005) "The integration journey: An attention-based view of the merger and acquisition integration process," *Organization Studies*, 26: 1501–1528.

12

Reflecting on the use of mixed methods in M&A studies

David P. Kroon and Audrey Rouzies

Introduction

In the last decades there has been growing research interest in the factors that influence the success of mergers and acquisitions (hereafter M&As). However, scholars' understanding of M&As is still limited (King *et al.* 2004). Since the mid nineties there has been a steady call for multidisciplinary approaches that would favor a better understanding of M&A integration processes as scholars increasingly see the post-M&A integration phase as critical to realizing the full value of the M&A (Cartwright and Cooper 1995; Larsson and Finkelstein 1999; Pablo 1994). These multidisciplinary approaches are a way to better grasp the complexity of post-M&A integration processes.

In this chapter, we propose a complementary point of view: to better understand M&As, and in particular post-M&A integration processes, researchers should reflect on their methodologies. In other words, questioning the methods used to gather information and to build inferences could be a way to improve the quality of research on M&As. Meglio and Risberg (2010: 88) argue that M&As can be regarded as multi-level, multidisciplinary, and multi-stage phenomena. They also underline that M&A research methods have become standardized and that, if scholars want to advance their understanding of M&As, they must rethink how they produce knowledge in the M&A field in terms of research design and sources of data. Indeed, M&As are multifaceted and complex phenomena (Larsson and Finkelstein 1999) and M&A researchers have to find ways to grasp that complexity in their research design.

One potential route to follow is combining qualitative and quantitative data and methods and to take advantage of that combination. In their review, Cartwright *et al.* (2012) found that only 3.2 percent of the articles dealing with M&As and published in top-tier journals from 1963 to 2009 adopted a mixed methods design. Consequently, we believe that there is room for improvement to rejuvenate the methodological approaches in studying M&As thanks to the use of mixed methods. Our leading research question in this chapter is: How can mixed methods contribute to our understanding of M&As in general and post-merger integration in particular?

In the remainder of this chapter we first explore the potential and contribution of mixed methods by reviewing existing (M&A) studies. Then we provide a reflection of our experience with the use of mixed methods in the investigation of the Air France-KLM merger. Finally, we provide an answer to our research question, discuss our findings, and illustrate some interesting future research opportunities.

Theoretical backdrop

In social sciences, mixed methods research has emerged as an alternative to the dichotomy of qualitative and quantitative traditions (Teddlie and Tashakkori 2009) and can be defined as

> a type of research in which a researcher or a team of researchers combine elements of qual-itative and quantitative approaches (e.g., use of qualitative and quantitative view-points, data collection, analysis, and inference techniques) for the purpose of breadth of understanding or corroboration.
>
> *(Johnson et al. 2007: 123)*

Several authors have proposed mixed methods to overcome the limitations of using mono-methods studies (Jick 1979; Parkhe 1993; Creswell 1994; Tashakkori and Teddlie 2003; Hurmerinta-Peltomäki and Nummela 2006). On the other hand, critics argue that it is epis-temologically difficult to combine qualitative and quantitative methods in one study (Bryman 1988). Therefore, mixed methods scholars propose adopting a pragmatic approach. In other words, methodological choices should be determined by the research question rather than epis-temological and ontological assumptions of a paradigm.

One of the benefits of mixed method research is that we can address both exploratory and confirmatory research questions simultaneously. As M&As can be seen as complex and dynamic research objects, an important advantage of mixed methods is that this research design can clarify, complement, or explore alternative explanations for relationships. Also, in terms of methodolog-ical fit, we believe that mixed methods research is ideally suited for studying M&As (Edmondson and McManus 2007). The M&A literature has surpassed its nascent state but has not reached maturity yet. To give just one example, there is no consensus on what actually constitutes "M&A performance" among M&A scholars and, as a result, scholars attach various labels to the term (Meglio and Risberg 2011; Very, 2011). Although several meta-analyses have been performed (Datta *et al*. 1992; King *et al*. 2004), there is also still no agreement as to what explains "per-formance" in M&As. Given this intermediate state of the research, Edmondson and McManus (2007) argue that it is best to collect both qualitative and quantitative data.

Next to the potential of mixed methods research for studying M&As in general, we believe that the development of mixed methods in post-M&A integration research in particular is necessary in order to gain a multidimensional picture of this complex phenomena. Below, our overview of studies incorporating a mixed method research design also tells us that the so-called "soft factors" (such as knowledge transfer or culture) related to the integration of merged and acquired firms could benefit from mixed methods research. When quantitative findings are enriched with supplemental qualitative data, a more complete and comprehensive picture of the phenomenon of interest can be provided (Eisenhardt 1989), as well as an explanation of the findings generated from the quantitative research (Doyle *et al*. 2009). As we illustrate with our Air France-KLM case study, a qualitative research approach is particularly important if we want to explain aspects of M&As that are not easily quantified, like substantive changes in employees' perceptions during post-M&A integration.

Despite their potential, M&A scholars must be aware of some challenges when they use mixed methods. First of all, mixed methods are not a panacea, and researchers must choose them only when the problem to be addressed requires this type of design and data. Then, it is important to note that mixed methods are a challenging design because of the complexity inherent in collecting, analyzing, mixing, and interpreting quantitative and qualitative data (Plano Clark *et al.* 2008: 381). Even though mixed methods seem to be relevant for the analysis of M&As, they may not be a suitable strategy for all research questions, and researchers must be conscious of some constraints in their utilization. More broadly researchers should base their methodological choices on their research question and the theory they use (see Harrison and Schijven 2015).

A time- and resource-consuming design

Before starting a research project with mixed methods, M&A scholars should carefully antic- ipate the time and resources required to develop the study. Collecting and analyzing both qualitative and quantitative data implies much more time than for a mono-method study. For instance, the researcher has to organize, run and transcribe the interviews while preparing, pre-testing, administrating, and coding the questionnaires. Mixed methods studies may also require more funding than mono-method studies. The increased costs may arise from collect- ing multiple types of data using more resources (such as separate software for quantitative and qualitative analyses) and needing more highly trained assistants who are familiar with the two approaches (Plano Clark *et al.* 2008: 383). The literature on mixed methods proposes several solutions to take full advantage of the mixed design while limiting its drawbacks. The researcher can play with the priority and the stage of implementation of the two methods. One possibility is to develop a dominant-less dominant design where unequal importance is given to the two types of data. In this type of design, time and resources will be, in priority, allocated to one type of data (see Haleblian *et al.* (2006) for an application in an M&A context). Another option is to choose a two-phases design. For instance, the researcher collects qualitative data at time 1 and then quantitative data at time 2 (see Brannen and Peterson 2009 for an application in an M&A context). Consequently, each phase of the data collection is less time consuming and more fea- sible for a mono-method data collection. One must underline that the entire process remains costly in terms of resources and time.

Need for skills

Ideally, researchers should have experience with quantitative and qualitative approaches sepa- rately before combining the two (Plano Clark *et al.* 2008: 382). However, it has been acknowl- edged for a long time that graduate and doctoral training usually prepares the researcher to use one method or another but not to combine methods effectively (Jick 1979). Consequently, M&A scholars should set up teams made of researchers with experience in quantitative designs and others skilled in qualitative designs (such as we illustrate below in our Air France-KLM case study). In this type of team, the members from one approach still need to have some under- standing of the other approach, otherwise important efforts will be required to favor effective collaboration.

Difficult to publish

When it comes to publishing, it has been acknowledged that authors using mixed methods in their articles often struggle to publish in top journals (Hurmerinta-Peltomäki and Nummela 2006). Several reasons can be stressed to explain this situation. First of all, academic journals tend to specialize by methodology, thus encouraging purity of method (Jick 1979). Then, as mixed methods are rather rare and recent in management, there is a need to educate potential reviewers who are usually schooled in one type of method. Finally, the "biggest challenge is describing the complexity of mixed methods studies within the page limits of most journals" (Creswell and Plano Clark 2007: 178). Indeed, mixed methods articles require longer methodology sections. Researchers have to describe the qualitative methodology, the quantitative methodology, present the mixing of the methods, and often justify extensively why it makes sense to use mixed methods to answer the research question raised in the article. It is all the more true in M&A researches where there is usually a need to describe in depth the case of the M&A under study. Plano Clark *et al.* (2008) indicate that mixed methods are accepted in journals as long as the articles are rigorous and communicated in a clear and concise manner. Researchers should describe in detail the procedures for data collection and analysis and also provide a solid justification of why the two types of methods are necessary to answer the research question (see Raukko (2009) for an application in an M&A context).

Validity debate

As mixed methods are still rare in management research, scholars have to thoroughly discuss validity issues when they submit articles using mixed methods. Having collected both quantitative and qualitative data does not in any way ensure validity (Tashakkori and Teddlie 1998; Slonim-Nevo and Nevo 2009). In their *Handbook of Mixed Methods in Social and Behavioral Research*, Tashakkori and Teddlie (2003) lengthily discuss validity issues. In 2006, they proposed an integrative model to assess issues of validity in mixed methods research (Tashakkori and Teddlie 2006). They propose a set of dimensions to assess the quality of the design and another set of dimensions to evaluate the rigor of the interpretation. To analyze the quality of the design, the first dimension is "within-design consistency": the researcher should assess the consistency of the procedures from which the inferences emerged. The second dimension is "design suitability": the researcher should gauge whether the methods are appropriate to address the research question. The third dimension is "design fidelity": the researcher has to evaluate whether the procedure is implemented with quality and rigor. The fourth dimension is "analytic adequacy": the researcher has to judge whether the data analysis techniques are appropriate to address the research question. The second set of dimensions refers to the rigor interpretation when it comes to building inferences thanks to the combination of data. The first dimension is "interpretative agreement." It refers to the consistency of interpretation among the different members of a team or the different persons involved in the interpretation of the data. The second dimension is "interpretative distinctiveness." It refers to the degree to which the inferences are distinctively different from other possible or rival interpretations. The third dimension is "theoretical consistency." In other words, the researcher should evaluate whether the inferences are consistent with the state of knowledge in the field. The fourth dimension is "integrative efficacy": the researcher should assess whether the meta-inference adequately incorporates the inferences from quantitative and from qualitative data/phases of the study.

Taken together, mixed methods research offers a potential way to better understand the complexity of M&As and their processes. However, researchers should be aware of some of the pitfalls in conducting a mixed methods study. In the following section, we illustrate what we can learn from the few mixed methods studies that have been conducted in the M&A field.

The use of mixed methods in the M&A literature

In a contribution, Rouzies (2013) analyzed 450 empirical articles dealing with M&As published in 19 top-tier academic journals between 1963 and 2012. The journals were chosen to maximize the variance in terms of disciplines (finance, human resource management, marketing, organizational behaviour, organizational theory, strategy). Nine papers implementing a mixed methods research design were analyzed.

Buono *et al.* (1985) analyze a merger between two mutual saving banks with a cultural perspective. They propose a case study based on interviews, survey questionnaires, observation data, and archival data. They point out that the combined material "provides a clear picture of the objective and subjective organizational culture and organizational climate profiles . . . in the merger" (Buono *et al.* 1985: 484).

Morosini *et al.* (1998) analyze the effect of national cultural distance on cross-border acquisition performance. The authors indicate that interviews were used "to provide a richer understanding of the mechanisms by which national cultural distance enhanced post-acquisition performance and to confirm the survey results" (Morosini *et al.* 1998: 147).

Bresman *et al.* (1999) focus on knowledge transfer in international acquisitions. They first collected questionnaire data from 42 cases of international acquisitions that they used to test hypotheses about international transfer in acquisitions derived from the literature. Then, they implemented a qualitative phase with 19 interviews leading to detailed case studies of three international acquisitions. For both types of data they collected information at two points in time to examine the patterns of knowledge transfer. The authors justify the use of "multi-method," arguing that "it was clear that one method alone could not satisfactorily answer the questions we were interested in" (Bresman *et al.* 1999: 447).

Birkinshaw *et al.* (2000) analyze task integration and human integration in R&D operations in the integration process of three foreign acquisitions made by Swedish companies. The authors indicate that

> the mix of qualitative and quantitative data allowed us to get rich insights into the integration process as it unfolded as well as some relatively objective measures of the changes that had occurred over the four years between phases of data collection.
>
> *(Birkinshaw et al. 2000: 402)*

Faulkner *et al.* (2002) study human resource management practices adopted by companies from the US, Japan, Germany, and France in the UK companies that they have acquired. The

> research project . . . was carried out both by means of the survey instrument (201 questionnaires), the results from which were subsequently analyzed statistically, and also by means of in-depth interviews (40 interviews). The results of both forms of research were broadly consistent with each other.
>
> *(Faulkner et al. 2002: 110)*

The authors cite quotations from interviews to illustrate statistical results. They emphasize that "the aim of the in-depth interviews is to achieve an element of triangulation in tandem with the statistically analyzed questionnaire" (Faulkner *et al.* 2002: 112).

Dackert *et al.* (2003) study employees' expectations for the merger of the head offices of two public service organizations. A two-stage methodology (Creswell, 1994) was used, combining the repertory grid method with a survey questionnaire. According to the authors, this combination significantly enriched the findings.

Haleblian *et al.* (2006) analyze the combined effect of prior acquisition experience and recent acquisition performance. The authors acknowledge that:

the empirical models built on these large-scale archival data could provide systematic evidence on the hypothesized causal relationships as well as findings with greater generalizability, but we discerned that they might not be able to fully capture the fine-grained, intermediate processes that contribute to the relationships and other context-specific boundary conditions.

(Haleblian et al. 2006: 361)

They further indicate that

because our study was deductive, these qualitative insights were not used to develop theories. Rather, we used these insights to (1) close potential gaps between our theories and empirical models, (2) check the validity of assumptions embedded in our empirical models, (3) incorporate industry-specific boundary conditions or shared assumptions into our study, and (4) help interpret our findings.

(Haleblian et al. 2006: 361)

Brannen and Peterson (2009) illustrate how a multi-method study can be used for multiple applications. The authors used ethnography (comprising fieldwork and participant observation) to illustrate negative individual-level outcomes associated with merger alienation. Then several additional hypotheses were quantitatively tested (by means of a retrospective survey design) as a result of the prevalence of cross-cultural work alienation that some employees had expressed in the ethnographic analysis. Finally, the ethnographic data were re-examined to make sense of unexpected and new quantitative findings. Multi-method triangulation in this study served various research objectives:

to disconfirm cross-cultural work alienation as the general state of the post-acquisition organization; to confirm the substantial success of particular interventions that management implemented to promote cross-cultural integration; to refine our understanding of cross-cultural work alienation at particular hierarchical and functional area pockets of alienation that emerged over time; and to provide a framework for developing a set of measures that cover a broad range of cross-cultural alienation indicators for future studies of post-M&A integration.

(Brannen and Peterson 2009: 485)

The authors used the different methods to their full extent and iteratively developed theory which would not have been possible with a mono-method research design. As they rightfully acknowledge: "Neither method alone would have given the full picture of this post-acquisition experience" (Brannen and Peterson 2009: 485).

Heimeriks *et al.* (2012) analyze underlying mechanisms of deliberate learning in the context of post-acquisition integration. The study is based on a two-pronged research design (Heimeriks *et al.* 2012: 712). They first followed an abductive approach to propose hypotheses thanks to a combination of established arguments from prior research and in-depth qualitative interviews. Then, they tested their hypotheses with quantitative data collected via a questionnaire. The authors indicate that they "combine (1) fine-grained survey data with (2) in-depth qualitative study of integration practices in pursuit of richer insights than either of these two methodologies could yield independently" (Heimeriks *et al.* 2012: 712).

As the M&A literature is not limited to top-tier journals, we have tried to complement Rouzies' survey (2013) by looking for other articles using a mixed methods design in studying M&As. We entered "merger" and/or "acquisition" and "mixed methods" as keywords in search engines such as Ebsco and JStor. Beyond these nine articles published in top-tier journals, we found five articles.

Raukko (2009) in *Baltic Journal of Management* analyzes acquired employees' organizational commitment during the post-acquisition integration with a longitudinal case study. She uses four sequential quantitative surveys at six-month intervals and conducted 58 qualitative interviews in three rounds in between the surveys. Questionnaires were used to measure the levels of organizational commitment, and interviews were run to "obtain a deeper understanding of key persons' commitment following a cross-border acquisition" (Raukko 2009: 340). The interview data "were used to complement the quantitative data and to provide support or explanations and a deeper understanding regarding the quantitative results" (Raukko 2009: 340). The author indicates that method triangulation (qualitative and quantitative data and analysis) was employed to provide stronger analytical generalization (Raukko, 2009: 338).

Angwin and Meadows (2009) in *Long Range Planning* analyze the link between top management type (outsider/insider) and post-acquisition integration strategy (preservation, holding, absorption, or symbiosis). They followed a "medium-grained hybrid method with dual phase (dominant, less dominant) design. A questionnaire was used to survey the acquisition and generate a statistical 'backbone' which was then informed and interpreted by subsequent qualitative interviews" (Angwin and Meadows 2009: 365). In their article, the authors note that a dual method is used "to generalize from our results across a population of acquisitions" (Angwin and Meadows 2009: 364).

Lupina-Wegener *et al.* (2011) in *Journal of Organizational Change and Management* adopt a mixed method approach to study the socio-cultural integration process and to explore potential threats to pre-merger identities in the merger of two European pharmaceutical companies' subsidiaries in Mexico. They collected questionnaires and conducted interviews in order to "triangulate the results and strengthen the construct and internal validity," to "capture the complexity of intra- and inter-group dynamics" and to "initiate new lines of thinking through attention to eventual discrepancies between qualitative and quantitative findings" (Lupina-Wegener *et al.* 2011).

Jardim da Palma *et al.* (2012) in *International Business Research* use a mixed methods design to study a post-acquisition insurance organization. They follow this methodology "to get a detailed comprehension of the dynamics among the identity, image and CEI during an acquisition" (Jardim da Palma *et al.* 2012: 118).

Rouzies and Colman (2012) in *Corporate Reputation Review* examine the role of social interactions on employees' identification after an acquisition. They use a mixed methods longitudinal design collecting both questionnaires and interviews. They indicate that mixed methods "enable a close analysis of employees' identification associated with robust statistical results" and that the combination of qualitative data with quantitative data was used to "provide support and contextualized explanations to quantitative results" (Rouzies and Colman 2012: 147).

Table 12.1 provides an overview of these studies, detailing for each article the research question, the type of data collected, the main findings, and the authors' motivations for using a mixed methods design.

Table 12.1 Overview of M&A studies applying a mixed methods research design

Reference	Journal	Research question(s)	Sources of data	Main findings	Reasons for using mixed methods
Buono, Bowditch, and Lewis (1985)	*Human Relations*	1. What are the effects of organizational culture for the merger process? 2. What are the attitudes and perceptions of organizational members in terms of culture before and after the merger? 3. How does a new organizational culture emerge after a merger? (Morosini *et al.* 1998: 138)	Interviews, questionnaires, observation data and archival data	The cultural shock has a strong impact on employees' perceptions and reactions. The cultural shock is reinforced by the dominance of one partner in the new entity created. Cultural and subjective aspects should not be overlooked during mergers.	The authors indicate that the combined material "provides a clear picture of the objective and subjective organizational culture and organizational climate profiles . . . in the merger" (Buono *et al.* 1985: 484).
Morosini, Shane, and Singh (1998)	*Journal of International Business Studies*	"How does national cultural distance between the acquirers' and targets' countries of origin influence cross-border acquisition performance?" (Morosini *et al.* 1998: 138)	Questionnaires and interviews	"National cultural distance enhances cross-border acquisition performance. Cross-border acquisitions that tended to perform better were those in which the routines and repertoires of the target's country of origin were, on average, more distant than those of the acquirer's. Cross-border acquisitions in more culturally distant countries might provide a mechanism for multinational companies to access diverse routines and repertoires, which have the potential to enhance the combined firm's performance over time." (Morosini *et al.* 1998: 153–54)	The authors indicate that interviews were used "to provide a richer understanding of the mechanisms by which national cultural distance enhanced post-acquisition performance and to confirm the survey results" (Morosini *et al.* 1998: 147).

Bresman et al. (1999)	*Journal of International Business Studies*	1. What are the factors that facilitate knowledge transfer in cases of international acquisition? 2. What does the pattern of international knowledge transfer look like during post-acquisition integration?	Questionnaires and case studies (involving interviews and questionnaires)	"Communication and visits and meetings are significant predictors of technological know-how transfers. In addition to the quantity of knowledge transfer (increases over time) the type of knowledge transfer varies over time. In the early stages, knowledge transfer is mostly one-way from the acquiring to the acquired unit, and typically imposed. In the later stages, knowledge transfer is in both directions and reciprocal transfer is more frequent." (Bresman et al. 1999: 457)	The authors justify the use of "multi-method," arguing that "it was clear than one method alone could not satisfactorily answer the questions we were interested in" (Bresman et al. 1999: 447).
Birkinshaw, Bresman, and Håkanson (2000)	*Journal of Management Studies*	"What is the process through which an acquisition delivers on the value creation sought by the acquiring firm?" (Birkinshaw et al. 2000: 396) *Subsidiary research questions:* "1. What actions are taken over time to manage the task integration process, and what is their impact on the realization of operational synergies?	Interviews, questionnaires and archival and secondary material	"Effective integration is achieved through a two-phase process. In phase one, task integration leads to a satisficing solution that limits the interaction between acquired and acquiring units, while human integration leads to cultural convergence and mutual respect. In phase two, there is renewed task integration built on the success of the human	The authors indicate that "the mix of qualitative and quantitative data allowed us to get rich insights into the integration process as it unfolded as well as some relatively objective measures of the changes that had occurred over the four years between phases of data collection" (Birkinshaw et al. 2000: 402).

(Continued)

Table 12.1 Continued

Reference	Journal	Research question(s)	Sources of data	Main findings	Reasons for using mixed methods
		2. What actions are taken over time to manage the human integration process, and what is their impact on employee satisfaction?		integration that has been achieved, which leads to much greater interdependencies between acquired and acquiring units." (Birkinshaw *et al.* 2000: 395)	
		3. To what extent, and in what ways, do the task integration and human integration processes drive the overall outcome of the acquisition process?" (Birkinshaw *et al.* 2000: 400)			
Faulkner, Pitkethly, and Child (2002)	*International Journal of Human Resource Management*	1. What are the HRM practices in French, German, US, and Japanese companies acquired by UK firms? 2. Is there convergence in international HRM practices?	In-depth interviews and questionnaires	"Different HRM policies are adopted by firms of different nationalities as they attempt to integrate and manage UK-acquired subsidiaries, but there are considerable signs of convergence of practice in certain areas. National differences are still apparent in recruitment, development, and termination practices." (Faulkner *et al.* 2002: 120) "The areas of greatest convergence were in compensation policies." (Faulkner *et al.* 2002: 121)	The authors emphasize that "the aim of the in-depth interviews is to achieve an element of triangulation in tandem with the statistically analyzed questionnaire" (Faulkner *et al.* 2002: 112).

Dackert, Jackson, Brenner, and Johansson (2003)	*Human Relations*	How do members of organizations involved in mergers attach meaning to their own organization, to the other organization, and their expectations of the new organization?	Repertory grid interviews and questionnaires	"The success of the integration process after a merger is critically dependent on how employees of merger partners perceive the culture of the organizations involved and the expectations they have of the new organization." (Dackert et al. 2003: 705)	The authors note that the combination of qualitative and quantitative data significantly enriched the findings.
Haleblian, Kim, and Rajagopalan, (2006)	*Academy of Management Journal*	What are the combined effects of acquisition experience and performance on acquisition behavior? How do experience and performance feedback interact to impact learning outcomes?	Questionnaires and semi-structured interviews	"Both acquisition experience and focal acquisition performance positively influence the likelihood of a firm making a subsequent acquisition. The positive effect of acquisition experience on subsequent acquisition likelihood was even more pronounced when it was accompanied by stronger acquisition performance." (Haleblian et al. 2006: 367)	The authors indicate that "because our study was deductive, these qualitative insights were not used to develop theories. Rather, we used these insights to (1) close potential gaps between our theories and empirical models, (2) check the validity of assumptions embedded in our empirical models, (3) incorporate industry-specific boundary conditions or shared assumptions into our study, and (4) help interpret our findings" (Haleblian et al. 2006: 361).

(Continued)

Table 12.1 Continued

Reference	Journal	Research question(s)	Sources of data	Main findings	Reasons for using mixed methods
Brannen and Peterson (2009)	Journal of International Business Studies	How can we understand both the potential individual-level outcomes from the fallout of poorly managed cross-cultural integration and the intraorganizational mechanisms by which successful integration can be achieved in cross-border M&As?	Ethnography (fieldwork consisting of interviews and participant observation) and questionnaires	Cross-cultural work alienation can limit the overall success of cross-border M&As. However, particular interventions can overcome these negative outcomes and can help to promote successful post-merger integration.	The authors used the different methods to their full extent and iteratively developed theory which would not have been possible with a mono-method research design. As they rightfully acknowledge: "Neither method alone would have given the full picture of this post-acquisition experience." (Brannen and Peterson 2009: 485).
Raukko (2009)	Baltic Journal of Management	"1. How the key employees perceive the organizational changes following an acquisition? 2. How the acquired key employees' organizational commitment evolves during the post-acquisition integration phase? (Raukko 2009: 332)	In-depth interviews and questionnaires	"The results imply that key employees' organizational commitment is complex following an acquisition. Although the results could not determine the causal relationship between organizational change and commitment, the results imply that key persons' organizational commitment is closely linked to the role they had in the organization prior to the acquisition, and how they perceive and experience the post-acquisition integration phase." (Raukko 2009: 346)	The author indicates that method triangulation (qualitative and quantitative data and analysis) was employed to provide stronger analytical generalization (Raukko 2009: 338).

| Angwin and Meadows (2009) | *Long Range Planning* | "1. Which type of top executive, by prior organizational background, is used to manage an acquired company in order to pursue different post-acquisition integration strategies? 2. How does top executive type affect the organizational changes that occur as a result of different integration strategies?" (Angwin and Meadows 2009: 360) | In-depth interviews and questionnaires | "A strong association between top executive type and strategic interdependence is apparent, and the distinction between value capture and value creation is of key importance. The results show substantial variation in the usage of top executive types across a contingency framework. There are also very different change patterns associated with these top executives across and within integration strategies. These variations are likely to confound studies of performance which treat all acquisition integration as homogeneous and assume one type of top executive should be innately superior to the other." (Angwin and Meadows 2009: 380) "Overall this paper has highlighted considerable variation amongst top executive retention across different post-acquisition strategies." (Angwin and Meadows 2009: 382) | The authors note that a dual method is used "to generalize from our results across a population of acquisitions" (Angwin and Meadows 2009: 364). |

(Continued)

Table 12.1 Continued

Reference	Journal	Research question(s)	Sources of data	Main findings	Reasons for using mixed methods
Lupina-Wegener, Schneider, and Van Dick (2011)	Journal of Organizational Change and Management	"The purpose of the paper is to present a study on the socio-cultural integration process in a merger of two European pharmaceutical subsidiaries in Mexico." (Lupina-Wegener et al. 2011: 65) "1. We explore how and in what ways different sub-groups of employees experience the process of socio-cultural integration. 2. Our study tries to explain how perceptions of threat differ at the intra- and inter-group levels. 3. We will investigate how and in what ways threat impacts on the development of a shared identity." (Lupina-Wegener et al. 2011: 67)	In-depth interviews and questionnaires	"Findings indicate that identity of the new organization was largely shared among members of the different subgroups. Though the employees considered their pre-merger identities to be at stake (as demonstrated through the interviews), this experienced threat was not very strongly expressed in the survey. In fact, the subgroups were able to maintain distinctiveness, acknowledge the value added of each group, and had access to resources." (Lupina-Wegener et al. 2011: 65)	The authors indicate that mixed methods were used to "triangulate the results and strengthen the construct and internal validity," to "capture the complexity of intra- and inter-group dynamics," and to "initiate new lines of thinking through attention to eventual discrepancies between qualitative and quantitative findings" (Lupina-et al. 2011: 66).

Heimeriks, Schijven, and Gates (2012)	*Academy of Management Journal*	In the context of post-acquisition integration how can firms strike a balance between the pros and cons of codification in an attempt to optimize their learning?	In-depth interviews and questionnaires	"Successful active acquirers develop higher-order routines—as manifested in complementary sets of concrete organizational practices—that foster ad-hoc problem solving whenever the specific acquisition at hand deviates sufficiently from the norm, thus counteracting the inertial forces brought forth by (zero-order) codified integration routines." (Heimeriks et al. 2012: 719)	The authors indicate that they "combine (1) fine-grained survey data with (2) in-depth qualitative study of integration practices in pursuit of richer insights than either of these two methodologies could yield independently" (Heimeriks et al. 2012: 712).
Jardim da Palma, Lopes, and Soares (2012)	*International Business Research*	"The purpose of our case study is to test the effect of relationship among the identity, image and construed external image of both acquiring and acquired companies on intergroup relations, during the post-acquisition phase." (Jardim da Palma et al. 2012: 116)	Interviews and questionnaires	"The case study of a post-acquisition insurance company showed that the identity was not consistent with the construed external image either for the acquiring or the acquired companies. Consistency between identity and image was found only for the acquiring firm. Our study evidenced that the identity, image and construed external image altogether contribute to a better understanding of intergroup relations than do any of these variables *per se*." (Jardim da Palma et al. 2012: 115)	The authors note that they used mixed methods in order to "to get a detailed comprehension of the dynamics among the identity, image and CEI during an acquisition" (Jardim da Palma Lopes and Soares 2012: 118).

(Continued)

Table 12.1 Continued

Reference	Journal	Research question(s)	Sources of data	Main findings	Reasons for using mixed methods
Rouzies and Colman (2012)	Corporate Reputation Review	"We examine the role of social interactions on identification in the post-acquisition integration process." (Rouzies and Colman 2012: 144)	Interviews and questionnaires	"We show that social interactions influence employees' identification both with the acquirer and with the pre-acquisition unit. We also detail how the role of interaction intensity on identification with the two loci evolves with time. In the qualitative results, we present the situational cues that have favored situated identification." (Rouzies and Colman 2012: 154)	The authors indicate that mixed methods "enable a close analysis of employees' identification associated with robust statistical results" and that the combination of qualitative data with quantitative data was used to "provide support and contextualized explanations to quantitative results" (Rouzies and Colman 2012: 147).

Source: Adapted from Rouzies (2013)

Among the 14 articles presented above, we observe that M&A scholars underline two main arguments to justify their research methodology: the use of mixed methods allows (1) a richer understanding of the phenomenon studied (Birkinshaw *et al.* 2000; Buono *et al.* 1985; Heimeriks *et al.* 2012; Jardim da Palma *et al.* 2012; Morosini *et al.* 1998) and/or (2) a triangulation of data (Angwin and Meadows 2009; Brannen and Peterson 2009; Faulkner *et al.* 2002; Lupina-Wegener *et al.* 2011; Raukko 2009; Rouzies and Colman 2012).

Lupina-Wegener *et al.* (2011) also underline that mixed methods could help to initiate new ideas. They present some results that are in contradiction with the extant literature but they don't explicitly discuss whether these new ideas emerge from the use of mixed methods.

Based on the analysis of the M&A literature, we see that M&A scholars mostly use mixed methods in order to triangulate their data or to complement quantitative findings with qualitative or vice versa. It appears that they do not exploit the full potential of mixed methods offered by the different designs. In the following section, we will present how, in the Air France-KLM case study, we have tried to take advantage of the richness of a mixed methods design. In fact, our experience in examining the Air France-KLM merger tells us that *initiation* studies could raise paradoxes and fresh analysis to thwart US-hegemonized M&A research (Meglio and Risberg 2010).

The Air France-KLM case study

In this section, we discuss in more detail why we believe mixed method research is particularly useful in our case study. We elaborate on our research design and present some of the devices we used to get the collaboration of the companies we studied.

Research design

Our research is based on a longitudinal analysis of the merger between Air France and KLM, two airline companies. Our aim was to capture the complexity of M&As by focusing on post-merger integration processes in general and those dealing with identification and justice in particular. The merger was announced at the end of 2003 and both companies officially merged in May 2004. The case—formally a friendly acquisition—soon became a historical landmark: it was a big merger for the airline industry in terms of the respective size of the companies (turnover 13 + 7 billion euros) and their number of employees (72,000 + 30,000), and, most importantly, the first major international merger in the industry. Our study started shortly after the completion of the merger and covers a period of approximately three-and-a-half years. A formal research protocol was signed in spring 2004 between the authors' respective universities and the two airlines, specifying amongst others what we could study, the parts of the companies that would be involved in the study, the approximate number of interviews to be conducted, and what was expected from us. With regard to the latter: we were to write a report to senior management every six months, reflecting our findings and interpretation of these. It was further agreed that the research team[1] would be allowed to interview a set of employees to gain an in-depth understanding of the post-M&A integration processes and would be allowed to survey a sample of employees on a set of variables.

Although several classifications of mixed methods designs have been developed (Greene *et al.* 1989; Patton 1990; Creswell 1994; Morse 2003; Small 2011), we opted for a longitudinal concurrent design in which we as researchers collected qualitative and quantitative data at the same time over three-and-a-half years. Concerning priority, we gave equal priority to both the quantitative and qualitative data. However, in the different subprojects we put more emphasis on one or the other type of data (as more fully explained below). We collected data at Time 1 (November, 2004) and then every six months ending at Time 6 (February, 2008)[2]. This resulted in a huge dataset comprising 6,415 questionnaires and 682 interviews in the period 2004–08. Our respondents and interviewees represented both Air France and KLM in a cross-section of businesses, functions, and hierarchical levels. In addition, we collected other data sources including a substantial range of documentation, such as published articles, company magazines, internal company documents, and newspaper and magazine reports. Finally, we jumped on every occasion to deepen our knowledge of and increase our involvement in the merging companies by being present at management conventions, regional meetings, and "open days," and talking informally with company representatives at such occasions.

Gaining access and 'relationship-building'

We gained access to the case immediately when the merger plans were announced through direct contact with the CEO of the combined company and he strongly backed our study along the way. This proved to be valuable throughout our study. In the different rounds of data collection we for instance let our survey be accompanied by a letter from the CEO specifying the importance of collaborating and showing the endorsement of the top management committee. We believe that top management support, among other things, also increased the response rates of our survey (around 30 percent for both companies throughout the different rounds of data collection). We met with company representatives who were up in the hierarchy several times. This ultimately led the selection of interviewees to be an iterative process in which we indicated to the contact person for a particular department how many interviews we wanted to conduct, and they proposed a number of names based on criteria like depth of involvement with the merger and variety of experiences. The survey instrument was also developed with contributions from the companies. Notably, the representatives of the airlines played two important roles. First, by organizing a pre-test, they contributed in adapting the 'scholarly rigorous' language into airline-specific vocabularies. Moreover, they were careful to align the language used in the questionnaire with the 'official' language developed by corporate communication services.

Mixed method research as 'rhetorical device'

The Air France-KLM study provided us with the insight that mixed method research is inherently "practical" in the sense that it speaks to practitioners. We observed that mixed methods are more accessible and well accepted by practitioners who perceive more easily the added value of the research. The use of mixed methods also enhances the managerial relevance of the research. Indeed, purely quantitative methods often simplify the M&A context to a set of variables analyzed with secondary data. During a feedback meeting with company representatives in which we illustrated and discussed the results of our questionnaire data a manager for example asked the question: "Could you please provide me with some underlying reasons for these figures? What were people thinking and saying to you?" On the other end, purely qualitative data may appear to practitioners as a subjective analysis of narratives. Another manager with whom we worked for a research project on M&A integration following a mixed methods design told us: "This methodology is more convincing for me and my team than purely qualitative ones because I feel like I can rely on quantitative results and interpret them with the interviews that you've done. I like it" (Rouzies 2013).

214

Purpose of using mixed methods in our case study

We had multiple purposes for combining methods in this case study: triangulation, comple-mentarity, development, initiation, and expansion (see also Greene *et al.* 1989). With trian-gulation we intended to seek convergence, corroboration, or correspondence of results from both the qualitative and quantitative methods (Denzin 1978). Complementarity was used to grasp overlapping but also different facets of a phenomenon, such as those related to iden-tity and identification. Development refers to studies where the first method (being either quantitative or qualitative) is used to "help inform the development of the second method" (Greene *et al.* 1989: 260). For example, we first held a series of qualitative interviews with senior management of Air France-KLM which helped us to refine the wording of the ques-tionnaire used in subsequent phases of data collection. With initiation, we sought to discover paradoxes and contradictions. Our analysis of inconsistent qualitative and quantitative findings and the resulting discussions with senior management favored fresh perspectives and new interpretations on the M&A phenomenon. To give just one example, at the Air France-KLM headquarters our survey results on the perceived satisfaction with the merger did not corre-spond with what people said during the interviews. It seemed that the different departments differed in terms of the extent and speed of integration. Hence, we found that most studies fail to address the complexity of the post-M&A integration phase and offer a one-size-fits-all approach (Schweizer 2005). However, one particular acquisition may look very different to different groups of employees. Finally, with expansion, we sought to extend the breadth and the scope of post-merger integration processes which could help us to give more insight into the multifaceted nature of M&As.

Two practical applications

As discussed in the previous section, mixed methods research has enriched knowledge in the M&A field. The majority of the studies reviewed illustrate that socio-psychological factors related to the integration of merged and acquired firms are especially interesting and fruitful to examine using mixed methods designs. Our case study pays specific attention to two of these factors: identification and justice, which arguably are of particular importance in research on M&A integration processes.

1   As discussed before, one of the benefits of mixed method research is that we can address both exploratory and confirmatory research questions simultaneously. The Air France-KLM study clearly illustrates how a mixed methods research strategy can be applied to the issue of identification in a post-merger integration setting. Applied to an M&A context, an important stream in the identity literature assumes that the 'old' organization continues to exist as an identification target. However, even if the pre-merger organizations continue to exist as entities within the post-merger organization, the organizational identities will change. Moreover, M&As will likely impact how and the extent to which people identify with their occupation. Unfortunately, the organizational identity literature fails to provide a proper empirical description of how employees experience and respond to a threat to their organizational and professional identities. Moreover, we lack insight into the intensity with which people identify with different identification targets during a post-M&A integration process. Finally, we need a better understanding of the consequences of different forms of identity change. In order to understand this, we needed to look in much more detail at

how individual employees make sense of their merger experiences than has been the case in most previous studies.

Our mixed methods research design allowed us to address the confirmatory and exploratory research questions stated above simultaneously. Hence, we used the quantitative survey design to measure how cross-border M&As can intricately influence not only the organizational identity and identifications of employees, but also the relationships between identification targets and types of identifications (confirmatory research question). To answer the more *exploratory* research questions such as: How does the experience of an M&A impact on the organizational identity perceptions of employees? and Can we distinguish different identity responses, and if so, can we understand the factors leading employees to display a particular identity response?, we used our qualitative data in which interviews formed our main source of data. In simpler words, our mixed methods design allowed us to *quantify* the level of employee's identification and to *qualitatively* understand the reasons of the identification. In combination, this mixed method research strategy resulted in and contributed to the articulation of a more complete theory of employee identity responses to strategic organizational change such as an M&A.

2   Another important advantage of mixed methods is that this research design can clarify, complement, or explore alternative explanations for relationships. We illustrate this advantage with our study on justice. Few studies have investigated justice longitudinally as part of organizational change processes such as M&As. Moreover, the justice literature has neither adequately addressed the power that rests with executives as norm setters, nor the various ways in which employees respond to management's justice initiatives (Monin *et al.* 2013). Our survey data illustrate that perceptions of justice change over the course of post-merger integration. For distributive justice, for example, survey results reveal that perceptions of distributive justice are significantly higher at the beginning of the post-M&A phase. By speculating, we could argue that perceptions of fairness may decrease because certain expectations are not met in the course of post-merger integration. However, our qualitative data provided us with stronger inferences. The qualitative results illustrate that, by framing issues in certain ways, (top) management can produce particular context-specific norms of justice that form the basis for subsequent sense making. These discursive norms of justice are subsequently contextualized and consumed and hereby we can better understand whether they 'take hold' or not (and explain the change in justice perceptions as identified in the survey data).[3] In other words, our mixed methods research allows us to build stronger inferences whereby we can complement methodological strengths and off-set weaknesses (see also McGrath 1982; Currall and Towler 2003; Teddlie and Tashakkori 2009; Molina-Azorin 2012).

To sum up, the use of mixed methods in our study of the Air France-KLM merger allowed us to take advantage of all the benefits offered by this research design. First, we observed that mixed methods facilitated relationships with the practitioners and access to the research field. Second, mixed methods permitted us to analyze both exploratory and confirmatory research questions and to subsequently contribute to the literature on organizational identification and organizational justice in a post-M&A integration context. Third, we noted that mixed methods can help M&A scholars to clarify, complement, or explore alternative explanations for relationships. Indeed, mixing methods can help M&A scholars to explore new dimensions and to ask new questions (Hammond 2005). Finally, in today's world, where publication is highly important for researchers, mixed methods studies present a serious advantage: they have a higher scholarly impact compared to mono-method studies (Molina-Azorin 2012).

Conclusion

M&As are often examined differently by scholars with different ontological, epistemological, and philosophical mindsets (Meglio and Risberg 2010). However, as long as researchers come up with well founded arguments regarding their methodological approaches and research designs, there does not seem to be a problem. Yet, the reasons for using a particular study are not always explicitly specified or, worse, recognized by authors. Moreover, in the M&A field there is a strong bias towards particular methods of inquiry. We believe that, in order to produce knowledge and push M&A research further, scholars need to adjust their methodological mindset.

In this chapter, we propose the use of mixed methods as an appropriate research design to overcome the methodological conformity existing in the M&A domain (Meglio and Risberg 2010) and to gain a better understanding of the multifaceted and complex nature of M&As, and in particular the post-M&A integration process. In fact, our study conducted at Air France-KLM illustrates how social-psychological factors such as identity and justice play an important role in a post-M&A setting. In answering our various empirical research questions and providing more insight into these substantive domains, a mixed methods research design was of crucial importance. From a practical side, we also encourage researchers to consider mixed methods as a methodological tool, since practitioners often appreciate and at times favor such a research design.

In addition to our discussion on the advantages of the use of mixed methods designs in the M&A literature, our review of the few mixed methods studies in M&A research illustrates that one can also combine quantitative data with qualitative data to help elaborate a phenomenon and/or qualitative data with quantitative data to provide preliminary tests of relationships (e.g. Jick 1979; Yauch and Steudel 2003). In answering our main research question: How can mixed methods contribute to our understanding of M&As in general and post-merger integration in particular?, we have provided both a theoretical and an empirical ground dealing with issues such as triangulation, complementarity, development, initiation, and expansion. One implication of our findings is that researchers who wish to explore different types of research questions must be methodologically versatile (Edmondson and McManus 2007). Of course, any research project has inherent weaknesses built into its design (Cartwright et al. 2012) but, by using mono-method studies, we are only able to capture a part of the M&A phenomenon. Still, a word of caution is in order here. Mixed methods are not a panacea in M&A research. Indeed, the research question must guide the methodology chosen. For testing narrow and well defined research questions, the study will be better served by using quantitative methods, for instance. Hence, we encourage future research in the M&A field to be specific on the answers to the following questions: Why did you decide to use a mixed methods study? What was the need, purpose, or rationale? Scholars need to be open to both quantitative and qualitative techniques, and they need to develop specific skills, but also a general awareness of when each is most appropriate. In this way, we could expand the types of research questions that will be addressed and thereby also benefit the M&A field. Both the reviewed studies and the Air France-KLM case can be seen as useful examples.

Notes

1 The research team consisted of both qualitative and quantitative researchers.
2 The time period between Time 5 and Time 6 was deliberately longer to enable us to gauge the effects of an important phase of structural integration.
3 For a more elaborate discussion on these qualitative results, we refer to Monin *et al.* (2013).

References

Angwin, D.N. and Meadows, M. (2009) "The choice of insider or outsider top executives in acquired companies," *Long Range Planning*, 42: 359–89.
Birkinshaw, J., Bresman, H., and Håkanson, L. (2000) "Managing the post-acquisition integration process: how the human integration and task integration processes interact to foster value creation," *Journal of Management Studies*, 37: 395–426.
Brannen, M.Y. and Peterson, M.F. (2009) "Merging without alienating: interventions promoting cross-cultural organizational integration and their limitations," *Journal of International Business Studies*, 40(3): 468–89.
Bresman, H., Birkinshaw, J., and Nobel, R. (1999) "International knowledge transfer in acquisitions," *Journal of International Business Studies*, 30(3): 439–62.
Bryman, A. (1988) *Quantity and Quality in Social Research*. London: Routledge.
Buono, A.F., Bowditch, J.L., and Lewis, J.W. (1985) "When cultures collide: the anatomy of a merger," *Human Relations*, 38(5): 477–500.
Cartwright, S. and Cooper, C.L. (1995) "Organizational marriage: 'hard' versus 'soft' issues?," *Personnel Review*, 24(3): 32–42.
Cartwright, S., Teerikangas, S., Rouzies, A., and Wilson-Evered, E. (2012) "Methods in M&A: a look at the past and the future to forge a path forward," *Scandinavian Journal of Management*, 28(2): 95–106.
Creswell, J.W. (1994) *Research Design: Qualitative and Quantitative Approaches*. Thousand Oaks, CA: Sage.
Creswell, J.W. and Plano Clark, V.L. (2007) *Designing and Conducting Mixed Methods Research*. Thousand Oaks, CA: Sage.
Currall, S.C. and Towler, A.J. (2003) "Research methods in management and organizational research: toward integration of qualitative and quantitative techniques," in A. Tashakkori and C. Teddlie (eds.), *Handbook of Mixed Methods in Social and Behavioral Research* (pp. 513–26), Thousand Oaks, CA: Sage.
Dackert, I., Jackson, P.R., Brenner, S-O., and Johansson, C.R. (2003) "Eliciting and analyzing employees' expectations of a merger," *Human Relations*, 56(6): 705–25.
Datta, D.K., Pinches, G.P., and Narayanan, V.K. (1992) "Factors influencing wealth creation from mergers and acquisitions: a meta-analysis," *Strategic Management Journal*, 13: 67–84.
Denzin, N.K. (1978) *The Research Act: A Theoretical Introduction to Sociological Methods*. New York: McGraw-Hill.
Doyle, L., Brady, A.M., and Byrne, G. (2009) "An overview of mixed methods research," *Journal of Research in Nursing*, 14: 175–85.
Edmondson, A.C. and McManus, S.E. (2007) "Methodological fit in management field research," *Academy of Management Review*, 32: 1155–79.
Eisenhardt, K.M. (1989) "Building theories from case study research," *Academy of Management Review*, 14: 532–50.
Faulkner, D., Pitkethly, R., and Child, J. (2002) "International mergers and acquisitions in the UK 1985–94: a comparison of national HRM practices," *International Journal of Human Resource Management*, 13: 106–22.
Greene, J.C., Caracelli, V.J., and Graham, W.F. (1989) "Toward a conceptual framework for mixed-method evaluation design," *Educational Evaluation and Policy Analysis*, 11: 255–74.
Haleblian, J., Kim, J., and Rajagopalan, N (2006) "The influence of acquisition experience and performance on acquisition behaviour: evidence from the US commercial banking industry," *Academy of Management Journal*, 49: 357–70.
Hammond, C. (2005) "The wider benefits of adult learning: an illustration of the advantages of multi-method research," *International Journal of Social Research Methodology*, 8: 239–55.

Harrison, J. and Schijven, M. (2015) Event study methodology in the context of M&A: a reorientation, in Risberg, A., King D.R., and Meglio, O. (eds.), *The Routledge Companion to Mergers and Acquisitions*, Routledge: Oxon.

Heimeriks, K.H., Schijven, M., and Gates, S. (2012) "Manifestations of higher-order routines: the underlying mechanism of deliberate learning in the context of post-acquisition integration," *Academy of Management Journal*, 55: 703–26.

Hurmerinta-Peltomäki, L. and Nummela, N. (2006) "Methods in international business research: a value-added perspective," *Management International Review*, 46: 439–59.

Jardim da Palma, P., Lopes, M.P., and Soares, A.E. (2012) "Relationship among identity, image and construed external image: a missing link on acquisitions," *International Business Research*, 5: 115–30.

Jick, T.D. (1979) "Mixing qualitative and quantitative methods: triangulation in action," *Administrative Science Quarterly*, 24: 602–11.

Johnson, R.B., Onwuegbuzie, A.J., and Turner, A.L. (2007) "Toward a definition of mixed methods research," *Journal of Mixed Methods Research*, 1: 112–33.

King, D., Dalton, D., Daily, C., and Covin, J. (2004) "Meta-analyses of post-acquisition performance: indications of unidentified moderators," *Strategic Management Journal*, 25: 187–200.

Larsson, R. and Finkelstein, S. (1999) "Integrating strategic, organizational and human resources perspectives on mergers and acquisitions: a case survey of synergy realization," *Organization Science*, 10: 1–26.

Lupina-Wegener, A.A., Schneider, S.C., and van Dick, R. (2011) "Different experiences of socio-cultural integration: a European merger in Mexico," *Journal of Organizational Change Management*, 24: 65–89.

McGrath, J.E. (1982) "Dilemmatics: the study of research choices and dilemmas," in J.E. McGrath, J. Martin, and R.A. Kulka (eds.), *Judgement Calls in Research* (pp. 69–102), Beverly Hills, CA: Sage.

Meglio, O. and Risberg, A. (2010) "Mergers and acquisitions: time for a methodological rejuvenation of the field?," *Scandinavian Journal of Management*, 26: 87–95.

Meglio, O. and Risberg, A. (2011) "The (mis)measurement of M&A performance: a systematic narrative literature review," *Scandinavian Journal of Management*, 27: 418–33.

Molina-Azorin, J. (2012) "Mixed methods research in strategic management: impact and applications," *Organizational Research Methods*, 15: 33–56.

Monin, P., Noorderhaven, N.G., Vaara, E., and Kroon, D.P. (2013) "Giving sense to and making sense of justice in post-merger integration," *Academy of Management Journal*, 56: 256–84.

Morosini, P., Shane, S., and Singh, H. (1998) "National cultural distance and cross-border acquisition performance," *Journal of International Business Studies*, 29: 137–58.

Morse, J. (2003) "Principles of mixed methods and multimethod research design," in A. Tashakkori and C. Teddlie (eds.), *Handbook of Mixed Methods in Social and Behavioral Research* (pp. 189–208), Thousand Oaks, CA: Sage.

Pablo, A. (1994) "Determinants of acquisition integration level: a decision making perspective," *Academy of Management Journal*, 37: 803–36.

Parkhe, A. (1993) "'Messy' research, methodological predispositions, and theory development in international joint ventures," *Academy of Management Review*, 18: 227–68.

Patton, M.Q. (1990) *Qualitative Evaluation and Research Methods*. Newbury Park, CA: Sage Publications.

Plano Clark, V., Creswell, J.W., O'Neil Green, D., and Shope, R.J. (2008) "Mixing quantitative and qualitative approaches: an introduction to emergent mixed methods research," in S.N. Hesse-Biber and P. Leavy (eds.), *Handbook of Emergent Methods*, New York: Guilford Press.

Raukko, M. (2009) "Organizational commitment during organizational changes: a longitudinal case study on acquired key employees," *Baltic Journal of Management*, 4: 331–52.

Rouzies, A. (2013) "Mixed methods: a relevant research design to investigate mergers and acquisitions," *Advances in Mergers and Acquisitions*, 12: 193–215.

Rouzies, A. and Colman, H.L. (2012) "Identification processes in post-acquisition integration: the role of social interactions," *Corporate Reputation Review*, 15: 143–57.

Schweizer, L. (2005) "Organizational integration of acquired biotechnology companies into pharmaceutical companies: the need for a hybrid approach," *Academy of Management Journal*, 48: 1051–74.

Slonim-Nevo, V. and Nevo, I. (2009) "Conflicting findings in mixed methods research: an illustration from an Israeli study on immigration," *Journal of Mixed Methods Research*, 3: 109–28.

Small, M.L. (2011) "How to conduct a mixed methods study: recent trends in a rapidly growing literature," *Annual Review of Sociology*, 37: 57–86.

Tashakkori, A. and Teddlie, C. (1998) *Mixed Methodology: Combining Qualitative and Quantitative Approaches.* Thousand Oaks, CA: Sage.

Tashakkori, A. and Teddlie, C. (2003) *Handbook of Mixed-Methods in Social and Behavioral Research.* Thousand Oaks, CA: Sage.

Tashakkori, A. and Teddlie, C. (2006) *Validity Issues in Mixed Methods Research: Calling for an Integrative Framework.* San Francisco, CA: American Educational Research Association.

Teddlie, C. and Tashakkori, A. (2009) *Foundations of Mixed Methods Research. Integrating Quantitative and Qualitative Approaches in the Social and Behavioral Sciences.* Thousand Oaks, CA: Sage.

Very, P. (2011) "Acquisition performance and the 'Quest for the Holy Grail,'" *Scandinavian Journal of Management*, 27: 434–S37.

Yauch, C.A. and Steudel, H.J. (2003) "Complementary use of qualitative and quantitative cultural assessment methods," *Organizational Research Methods*, 6: 465–81.

13

Event-study methodology in the context of M&As

A reorientation

Joseph S. Harrison and Mario Schijven

Introduction

Event-study methodology uses relatively short time frames to assess stock market reactions to discrete events, demonstrated by abnormal stock returns—or the difference between expected and actual stock prices (Cording *et al.* 2010; Haleblian *et al.* 2009). Initially developed in the field of financial economics in the late 1960s (Fama *et al.* 1969), event studies have become a ubiquitous method for measuring the performance effects of mergers and acquisitions (hereafter "M&As" or "acquisitions"). Indeed, while numerous methods have been used to assess the performance effects of acquisitions, reviews and meta-analyses have shown that event studies are the most dominant (Cording *et al.* 2010; Goranova *et al.* 2010; Haleblian *et al.* 2009; King *et al.* 2004).

Despite its prevalence in M&A performance research, scholars hold divergent views on the validity of event-study methodology. While some highlight its ease of use and precision in identifying responses to a particular event (Haleblian *et al.* 2009; McWilliams and Siegel 1997), others argue that, insofar as it is used with the intent to measure actual or objective performance, it is based on overly simplistic assumptions that fail to account for organizational, social, and market complexities (Cording *et al.* 2010; Oler *et al.* 2008; Schijven and Hitt 2012). In this chapter, we provide an overview of event-study methodology, including its underlying assumptions from financial economics, before turning to its limitations through a discussion of the growing body of work—spanning behavioral finance, economic sociology, and social psychology—that has developed an increasingly critical stance toward the methodology. Building on this critique, we then outline various recommendations to improve the application of event-study methodology in M&A performance research. We also argue for a reorientation in the use of event studies, as well as other methodologies in the more general M&A context (i.e. beyond just M&A performance), which opens up unique possibilities for future work and, in particular, for research on the behavioral mechanisms underlying markets and investor decision making.

Event-study methodology: assumptions and critiques

Event-study methodology has been widely used in accounting, finance, and management to measure the performance effects of corporate decisions and events, including acquisitions

(McWilliams and Siegel 1997). Its wide use is based on several key benefits, such as its relative ease of use and the accessibility of market data (McWilliams and Siegel 1997; Oler *et al.* 2008). As primary measures, event studies only require stock market returns for the focal firm(s) and benchmark returns for comparison that are readily available or easily computed based on data from public exchanges (Oler *et al.* 2008). Further, event studies typically use short time frames (i.e. "event windows") so as to minimize "noise" from extraneous variables or events (Cording *et al.* 2010; Haleblian *et al.* 2009; Oler *et al.* 2008), which leads to simpler study designs than other statistical methods and which can greatly alleviate concerns about endogeneity, such as reverse causation and spurious correlation. Overall, event studies are simple to use, widely applicable, and relatively powerful statistically in gauging event-specific market reactions.

At the same time, event-study methodology rests on various assumptions that must be understood and properly applied in order to generate valid findings, and that have been met by harsh criticism across the social sciences. In this section, we highlight the efficient markets hypothesis (EMH) as the primary underlying assumption for the use of event studies in the context of M&As. We outline its origins from financial economics and then discuss various arguments from behavioral finance, economic sociology, and social psychology that challenge the traditional financial economic perspective and the usefulness of event-study methodology as a means of measuring acquisition performance.

Financial economics: the underlying assumptions of event-study methodology

Event-study methodology stems from financial economics and is predicated on a set of assumptions that originated with the efficient markets hypothesis (EMH). In its purest form, the EMH posits that security prices fully reflect all information available to the market. However, as a result of information asymmetry, which reduces the availability of information to market participants, even proponents of event studies admit that this is an "extreme null hypothesis" that is not to be taken literally (Fama 1970). As a consequence, variations of the EMH have been outlined and may be categorized as one of three forms: weak form, semi-strong form, and strong form. In the weak form, prices reflect only historical information; in the semi-strong form, prices adjust to reflect other information that is publicly available besides historical information (e.g. announcements of annual reports, annual earnings, stock splits, new securities); and in the strong form, prices reflect instances in which some investors or groups have monopolistic access to relevant information (i.e. private information) (Fama 1970).

Research on M&A performance has typically used the semi-strong form of the EMH to formulate arguments about the performance effects of acquisitions. Abnormal returns upon (or surrounding) the dates of acquisition announcements are argued to be the best available estimates of the net present value of the merging firms' future cash flows (Haleblian *et al.* 2009) and are therefore used to assess the value created or destroyed by M&As (Cording *et al.* 2010). This argument depends on three underlying assumptions (see Shleifer 2003). First, investors are assumed to value stocks rationally, meaning that stock prices quickly and accurately adjust to new information. Second, to the extent that investors are not rational, irrational decisions surrounding trades are assumed to be made at random, thus neutralizing their overall effect on stock prices. Finally, to the extent that irrational trade is non-random, rational arbitrageurs are assumed to eliminate its influence on stock prices by simultaneously buying up the mispriced stock and shorting a substitute stock, thereby correcting the mispricing. However, these assumptions do not hold in many (perhaps most) settings, which leads to potential issues surrounding the validity of results from event studies, particularly in the context of M&As.

Several alternative perspectives have challenged the theoretical assumptions of efficient markets, including behavioral finance (e.g. Shiller 2003; Shleifer 2003), economic sociology (e.g. Rubtsova *et al.* 2010; Zajac and Westphal 2004), and (albeit more implicitly) social psychology (e.g. Petty and Cacioppo 1986; Petty and Wegener 1999). Each of these perspectives generally considers the EMH to be overly simplistic (e.g. Hirshleifer 2001, Hunter and Coggin 1988), not accounting for the complexities of human judgment and decision making inherent in investor responses. The combination of issues related to the major underlying assumptions indicates serious limitations to the use of event-study methodology in M&A performance research because, if they are violated, empirical results based on the methodology will be biased and imprecise (McWilliams and Siegel 1997). Below, we briefly outline theoretical critiques from each literature and discuss their implications for the use of event-study methodology in M&A performance research.

Behavioral finance: limits to arbitrage and deviations from rationality

The field of behavioral finance emerged in response to market anomalies, which undermine the traditional financial economic perspective (e.g. high trading volumes, high volatility, and stock market bubbles), and suggests that market phenomena can be better understood by relaxing the assumption of investor rationality (Barberis and Thaler 2003; Lawrence *et al.* 2007). Relevant to the use of event studies in M&A performance research, Barberis and Thaler (2003) outline the two major "building blocks" or components of behavioral finance as limits to arbitrage and psychological deviations from rationality. The first component challenges the assumption that mispricing leads to attractive investment opportunities that arbitrageurs will exploit, since arbitrage involves risk and cost. While the EMH assumes that arbitrage offers riskless profits at no cost, behavioral finance argues that risks and costs deter investment in even obviously mispriced securities. For example, limited time and funds as well as the absence of equivalent securities may reduce the ability and/or desire of investors to exploit mispriced securities (Oler *et al.* 2008; Shleifer and Vishny 1997). Consequently, mispricing may remain unchallenged, undermining the efficiency of the market.

The second component of behavioral finance suggests that various psychological constraints reduce investor rationality and, therefore, market efficiency. March and Simon (1958) refer to this phenomenon as bounded rationality, whereby an individual's ability to make rational decisions is constrained by limitations in cognitive capacity—that is, the ability to gather, process, and interpret relevant information. Bounded rationality is further exacerbated by complex situations such as M&As (Oler *et al.* 2008), suggesting that investors will be likely to utilize various heuristics that introduce biases and can lead to suboptimal investment decisions (see Das and Teng 1999; Duhaime and Schwenk 1985; Schwenk 1984, 1985). Examples of these biases include prior hypotheses bias, where individuals continue to make decisions based on previously held beliefs, despite contrary evidence (e.g. Levine 1971; Pruitt 1961; Staw 1976; Wason 1960); confirmatory and contradictory biases, where individuals overestimate the value of confirmatory evidence or undervalue contrary evidence, respectively (Kozielecki 1981); and representativeness bias, where individuals incorrectly associate information with a particular phenomenon (e.g. Steinbruner 1974; Tversky and Kahneman 1974). These and other biases compromise investor rationality and weaken the ability of event-study methodology to reflect the actual value created or destroyed by events like M&As.

A major reason why psychological constraints limit the ability of abnormal returns to reflect actual value creation or destruction is that acquisitions are highly complex. Specifically, while acquisitions may affect multiple areas of the focal firm(s) (Haspeslagh and Jemison

1991), simplifying heuristics fail to account for the widespread and complex effects of M&As. Additionally, research has shown that markets are limited in their ability to predict future value. For example, limiting performance measures to stock market data ignores the effect of M&As over time and on other potentially relevant measures of firm performance, such as accounting measures (King *et al.* 2004). Oler and colleagues (2008: 151) supported this idea in the context of horizontal acquisitions, where they showed that "positive initial market response to an acquisition announcement is contradicted by negative long-run post-acquisition returns, suggesting that the initial response is incorrect and that the error is rectified later." Together, these arguments threaten the assumption of market efficiency underlying event-study methodology and suggest that stock market reactions to M&As are more representative of investor perceptions than actual value creation.

Economic sociology: performativity and the social construction of markets

According to an economic sociological perspective, one of the major critiques of the financial economic approach relates to the performativity of markets. In the social sciences, performativity refers to the idea that scientific theories, models, and statements are "actively engaged in the constitution of the reality [they] describe" (Callon 2007: 10). Economic sociologists describe the performativity of markets by suggesting that economists create and influence markets. MacKenzie (2006: 1) summarizes the concept this way: "To claim that economics is performative is to argue that it *does* things, rather than simply describing (with greater or lesser degrees of accuracy) an external reality that is not affected by economics." In the context of financial markets, this translates into the idea that economists and economic actors (e.g. regulators, traders, and organizations) take an active role in shaping the components of financial markets and the laws regulating them. For example, financial derivatives such as stocks and bonds do not exist outside of the financial market, nor can they operate independently of the rules established to govern their trade (Herrmann-Pillath 2010).

Performativity becomes problematic for the underlying assumptions of event-study methodology because it suggests that financial markets are socially constructed (Samuels 2004) and are therefore subject to the judgments and biases as well as the decisions of (often irrational) economic actors embedded within them. Indeed, while markets may follow natural laws, individuals and organizations *create* those markets, and therefore determine which laws apply. Specific to financial markets, economic sociology suggests that price, volume, and volatility are all affected by networks of social interactions (Granovetter 1985; Preda 2007; White 1981). The distribution and interpretation of information through these networks have serious implications for market efficiency. For example, Zuckerman (2004) showed that earnings announcements for firms in less well defined industries were associated with higher trading volume and price volatility, implying that the market is less efficient at processing information on such firms. Further, Zajac and Westphal (2004) argued that reactions to a particular event, such as stock repurchase plans, are affected by prevailing institutional logics and the degree of acceptance of the event itself. Such logics are likely to bias investment decisions in favor of or against particular companies or events, depending on their legitimacy.

Oler and colleagues (2008: 159) build on this notion by arguing that "a response based on sentiment is more likely to occur when the underlying event is complex or otherwise difficult to understand (i.e. occurs irregularly or has many elements of uncertainty)." Again, given the complexity of acquisitions, institutionally driven investment decisions are even more likely for M&As than for other, less ambiguous events. Further, international acquisitions pose unique problems for event-study methodology because M&As involving multinational corporations or firms headquartered in different countries are often listed on different stock exchanges (Park 2004). Abnormal returns are likely to vary across different exchanges based on institutional logics governing those exchanges in their countries of origin. In combination, and similar to the arguments from behavioral finance, these arguments undermine market efficiency and suggest that abnormal returns reflect investor perceptions of performance, rather than actual acquisition performance.

Social psychology: applying the elaboration likelihood model to financial markets

Similar to the economic sociological perspective, social psychology suggests that individuals tend to behave socially rather than depending solely on economically rational calculations. The basis of this argument lies in theory surrounding the elaboration likelihood model (ELM) developed by Petty and Cacioppo (1986). Initially developed as a way to understand the processes underlying persuasion, the ELM distinguishes between two separate "routes" that individuals can take to make decisions—the central route and the peripheral route (Petty and Cacioppo 1986; Petty and Wegener 1999). While the central route involves first-hand investigation and analysis of relevant information (Petty et al. 2009), the peripheral route relies on an expertise heuristic (e.g. Chaiken 1987). This latter approach is taken when individuals themselves are unable to access necessary information, leading them to assume that those with access to the information will generally make correct decisions (Tormala et al. 2006).

Although the ELM was not initially intended for application to financial markets, Schijven and Hitt (2012) suggest that the distinction between central and peripheral routes has important conceptual implications for the use of event studies, since information asymmetry in financial markets may lead investors to use a peripheral route when making investment decisions. Such a tendency would lead to systematic deviations from rationality, such as listening to rumors or imitating other traders (e.g. Oler et al. 2008; Preda 2007; Shiller et al. 1984), as evidenced by stock market bubbles and other phenomena indicating market inefficiency (Schijven and Hitt 2012). Here again, due to the complex nature of acquisitions, such behavior becomes highly likely. Since acquisitions tend to entail high information asymmetry between managers and investors (Schijven and Hitt 2012), investors are likely to depend on cues from the social environment, including managers, when deciding how to react to an acquisition announcement. As with the other perspectives outlined in this section, then, a social psychological approach suggests limitations to the financial economics perspective and threatens the accuracy of event studies in gauging acquisition performance.

Conclusions from the behavioral perspective of financial markets

Ultimately, behavioral perspectives of financial markets from behavioral finance, economic sociology, and social psychology undermine the basic assumptions of investor rationality underlying the EMH. In the M&A context in particular, which is marked by high complexity and information asymmetry, boundedly rational investors are likely to use individual and social-based heuristics that introduce bias and lead to suboptimal results. As a consequence, depending on investor reactions to gauge the value of M&As becomes problematic. Further, conceptions of markets as performative and evidence of the use of an expertise heuristic in investment decisions hold serious implications for the usefulness and validity of event-study methodology. Overall, while event studies have very apparent benefits, which account for their widespread use, they entail several crucial theoretical limitations that become even more apparent when used to study M&A activity. Given this, we argue that a re-evaluation of event-study methodology—and of the construct of acquisition performance more broadly—is critical to the future of M&A research.

Refining the construct of aquisition performance

The concerns associated with event studies as a method for measuring acquisition performance indicate the need to re-evaluate and refine the construct of acquisition performance. Further, the very nature of acquisitions, as highly complex events that involve various stakeholders and stages, suggests that a single measure cannot capture all of the intricacies of M&A performance for all acquisitions across different stages. As a consequence, some scholars have argued against the use of an overall construct of acquisition performance (see Cording *et al.* 2010; Oler *et al.* 2008; Meglio and Risberg 2011). For instance, Meglio and Risberg (2011: 431) contend:

> Our conclusion is that it is not possible to talk about M&A performance as if it were a universal construct because it is sensitive to and contingent upon contextual conditions. In order to understand what M&A performance is, one must take into consideration the scope conditions as well the conceptualization and operationalization of the construct. The different performance measures tell different stories about performance for different audiences.

We reiterate this argument. Rather than converging on a single definition of acquisition performance, extending the nomological network of M&A performance and more consistently using supplemental or alternative measures (other than abnormal returns) has the potential to increase precision in M&A performance research and broaden our understanding of acquisitions (Cording *et al.* 2010). At the same time, it is critical that researchers choose measures that are aligned with the theoretical dimensions of the particular research question of interest.

We propose that one of the most effective ways to decide on an appropriate measure of acquisition performance is to align the research question of interest with the stage of the acquisition. Table 13.1 outlines four basic stages of an acquisition—selection, transaction, integration, and post-acquisition management (hereafter just "management")—including various activities that may be carried out in each. In general terms, we propose that the selection and transaction stages are associated with the *potential* of the deal to create synergy for the merging firms, while the integration and management stages are associated with the *realization* of that synergistic potential. This distinction parallels that between strategic and organizational fit described elsewhere in the literature (e.g. Barkema and Schijven 2008). Whereas the synergistic potential of an acquisition is based on strategic fit, in terms of resource similarity or complementarity (Harrison *et al.* 1991), the realization of that synergy depends more on organizational fit, or the extent to which the acquired firm is integrated effectively into the acquirer's organization (Haspeslagh and Jemison 1991; Jemison and Sitkin 1986).

Using this conceptualization, we argue that abnormal returns are often appropriate to assess synergistic potential, but alternative measures should be used for later stages in which the realization of that synergy is assessed. In the former case, however, researchers must still subscribe to the EMH, which may have limitations based on some of the issues already described. Therefore, we also propose that researchers consider using alternative measures of acquisition performance even in the early stages of an acquisition in order to properly assess the theoretical constructs related to their research question(s). Below we discuss several specific recommendations to improve upon the operationalization of "performance" in the context of M&As. We begin by outlining various recommendations to improve the use of event studies in M&A performance research, after which we shift our attention to alternative methods and measures (i.e. other than event studies) that should be considered when performing research on M&A performance.

Table 13.1 Acquisition stages and performance

	Stage			
	Selection	Transaction	Integration	Management
Activities	• Identification of targets • Tender offer	• Negotiations • Deal structure and valuation • Completion of deal	• Post-acquisition integration • Knowledge transfer • Systems conversion	• Increased (decreased) economic performance • Increased (decreased) market share • Acquisition survival
	Performance indications *Synergistic potential* *(Strategic fit)*		*Realization of synergistic potential* *(Organizational fit)*	
Examples of appropriate research questions	• What is the potential value of the deal? • What are investor perceptions of the potential value of the deal? • How well aligned are the merging firms in terms of strategic fit? • How do the various characteristics of the deal, firms involved, and/or environment affect the perceived future value of the deal?		• What is the actual value of the deal? • What were the performance effects of the acquisition? • How well are the merging firms aligned in terms of organizational fit? • How did the various characteristics of the deal, firms involved, environment, and/or integration process affect the actual value created by the deal?	

Refining event studies in M&A performance research

The various critiques of event-study methodology in M&A research do not mean that abnormal returns are altogether unsuitable as a measure of M&A performance; rather, they represent limitations to their applicability. In particular, investor irrationality and information asymmetry, which contradict the assumptions of the EMH, suggest that abnormal returns should not be used as an indicator of the actual value created from M&A activity. Instead, such returns should explicitly be interpreted for what they are: investors' perceptions of the *potential value* of the acquisition. This distinction between potential and actual value is evidenced in the extant M&A literature. For example, Oler and colleagues (2008) found inconsistencies between the initial market reaction to horizontal acquisitions and long-run returns: whereas the initial reaction was positive, long-run post-acquisition returns were negative. Based on this information, they concluded that abnormal returns should be treated as a reaction to new information, but not as a measure of actual performance. Using a similar argument, Zollo and Meier (2008) state that researchers using event studies should specify their dependent variable as the "expectation about firm performance" rather than actual performance.

We extend this logic to argue that abnormal returns are valuable insofar as they are used to measure *potential* value or investor behavior. However, abnormal returns do not necessarily help to predict either an acquiring firm's future stock market value or its accounting performance. Returning to the aforementioned concepts of fit, event studies seem relevant to the study of strategic fit, but less relevant to examining issues of organizational fit, or the ability of firms to realize the potential of resource similarities or complementarities through effective integration. This is not to say that investors are unable to differentiate between integration approaches, but that any pre-acquisition assessment of deal value will always represent potential rather than actual value. For instance, if two deals, D1 and D2, have the same potential value in terms of synergy creation, but the acquiring firm in D1 is better equipped to integrate the target than the acquiring firm in D2, investors are likely to assign greater value to D1 than to D2. Despite the ability of investors to differentiate between integrative capabilities, this assessment still represents *potential*, rather than actual, value.[1] It could even be argued that synergistic potential can never be fully realized because of the inability of organizations to perfectly or optimally integrate an acquired firm (Barkema and Schijven 2008). Ultimately, we advise researchers using event studies in the M&A context to frame any findings of significant abnormal returns in terms of expected value or potential performance rather than actual or realized acquisition performance.

Having established that abnormal returns can be used to measure the potential value of an acquisition, the next step in refining event-study methodology in the context of acquisitions is to refine methodological practices related to the design of event studies so as to increase accuracy and statistical conclusion validity. McWilliams and Siegel (1997) provide detailed steps for implementing event studies that are instructive for any researcher using event studies, including those investigating M&As. We refer readers to their paper for detailed descriptions of each step; however, we suggest that those using event-study methodology in the context of M&As pay particular attention to three points: 1) the alignment between theoretical arguments and empirical measures, 2) selection of an appropriate event window, and 3) sampling techniques to increase validity and generalizability.

First, justifying the use of event-study methodology based on the theoretical motivations of the study is critical to the validity of conclusions drawn from this method. Unfortunately, in the management literature, a disconnect often exists between the theoretical construct of interest and the measure used to assess that construct (Cording *et al.* 2010). Increasing the emphasis placed on the alignment between theoretical constructs and their operationalizations will increase the accuracy and generalizability of findings from event studies. Cording and colleagues (2010: 18) suggest one way to accomplish this: "Ideally, researchers would articulate a theoretical link between the explanatory variables being studied and the theoretical domain of their selected acquisition performance measure." Combining this idea with our discussion surrounding the various stages of the acquisition process, we propose that, when the independent variables of interest have to do with potential synergy (e.g. acquirer and target *pre-acquisition* characteristics, such as acquisition experience, acquirer profitability, or target profitability), event-study methodology may be appropriate, whereas, when they have to do with actual value creation (e.g. aspects of integration, such as top management team turnover or transfer of resources), other methodologies or measures should be employed. In the following section, we provide further guidance on this point by suggesting various typologies that could be used to determine appropriate alternatives to abnormal returns as measures of M&A performance, given the theoretical motivations of a particular research study.

Second, choosing an appropriate event window, justifying its length, and then reducing the potential for confounding effects are each critical to generating interpretable results. As a general rule of thumb, when abnormal returns are used to measure reactions to an announcement, a window of three to seven days is generally considered to be appropriate. While shorter windows are common in research (King *et al.* 2004), we urge M&A researchers to be more conservative in their choice of event window. In fact, unless there is good reason to use a shorter window, we suggest that researchers should select a window towards the longer end of this range (i.e. seven days). This is necessary in order to account for the complex nature of acquisitions, since relevant information is not likely to be immediately captured in stock prices. At the same time, ensuring that the chosen window makes sense within the context of the specific acquisition and then controlling for extraneous events that could affect prices within that window are necessary to ensure that any abnormal returns may be reasonably connected to the acquisition. For instance, researchers should use non-equivalent comparison groups of similar firms in the same industry to reduce industry effects. Such controls become particularly important as event windows are increased, since more confounding effects may be introduced, the longer the period of investigation. Care in designing these aspects of the study, then, increases the explanatory power and validity of any significant findings. As a final suggestion related to selecting an event window, researchers could also perform sensitivity analyses, using several different event windows and examining effect sizes and R-squared statistics as a first step towards determining the most appropriate window. Of course, after performing such an analysis, it remains important to be able to justify the event window based on theoretical reasoning.

Finally, as with any methodological design, sampling procedures are an important consideration when designing event studies on M&As, since they affect both the internal and external validity of empirical results. We suggest three common sampling problems that deserve particular attention in the M&A literature. First, while there are recognized subgroups of M&As, most researchers lump acquisitions together in large cross-sections when compiling a sample. Based on a year-long study of M&A activity, Bower (2001: 94) found that "the thousands of deals that academics, consultants, and businesspeople lump together as mergers and acquisitions actually represent very different strategic activities." He summarized these activities into five distinct subgroups based on the rationale for M&A activity (i.e. overcapacity, geographic roll-up, product or market extension, R&D, and industry convergence) and essentially argued that disentangling these types can assist managers in determining whether and how to execute M&As more successfully. In a similar way, accounting for these subgroups in research designs (e.g. through moderation analysis or the use of controls) can assist scholars in clarifying the effects of all kinds of independent variables on acquisition performance and other M&A-related dependent variables. Second, we believe that too many M&A studies use unjustifiably small samples in relation to the sweeping conclusions that they draw. While we admit that it may be difficult to gather data on large samples of acquisitions, using bootstrapping or otherwise increasing the sample size is important for ensuring robust and generalizable results. Third, as with much of the rest of the strategy literature, most M&A studies are limited to public firms in the U.S., which represent just a subset of all M&As. As a result, the existing literature is somewhat limited in its generalizability. The more consistent inclusion of international and/or private M&As would therefore increase the relevance of findings in the M&A literature.

In addition to the steps outlined by McWilliams and Siegel (1997) that we expanded upon above, the complex nature of acquisitions requires additional methodological practices to ensure accurate and generalizable results. For instance, some scholars, particularly in the field of management, argue that accounting measures should be used to supplement abnormal returns when assessing acquisition performance (e.g. Oler *et al.* 2008; Zollo and Meier 2008). While we believe that using multiple measures can have a bolstering effect up to a point, we advise researchers to choose additional measures carefully, so as to ensure consistency with the theoretical question under investigation. If the measures used do not assess the same theoretical construct, they may show contradictory results or otherwise undermine the study. To use multiple measures appropriately, researchers should define whether the measures are being used to describe either *different* theoretical dimensions of the acquisition or various facets of the *same* theoretical construct. Once this is established, multiple measures can add great depth to M&A studies. For example, a researcher may use event-study methodology to assess the strategic fit or synergistic potential of merging firms and compare that measure to an accounting measure (e.g. return on assets) to assess the organizational fit of those firms and the realization of that potential. We will discuss several additional measures that may be implemented as alternatives or supplements to abnormal returns later in this chapter.

As a final suggestion to refine the use of event studies in the broader research on M&A, beyond refining methodological procedures, and consistent with Oler and colleagues (2008), we recommend that researchers strive to answer a wider variety of questions with event-study methodology than have been examined in the past. Although the common implementation of this method has been to measure acquisition performance, we reiterate that short-window event studies should be used to answer more behavioral questions. We will discuss this in greater depth later in this chapter; however, an obvious question based on the inconsistencies found between initial market reactions and long-term market returns would be: When does the market "get it right"? In combination, we believe that these recommendations will simultaneously increase the accuracy and validity of results from event studies and lead to interesting lines of inquiry for future M&A research.

Refining measures of acquisition performance

Shifting the focus from improving the use of event-study methodology in M&A performance research, there are a number of other steps that researchers can take to improve the more general construct of acquisition performance—that is, beyond just abnormal returns. To begin, as touched on earlier, researchers should strive to align the measures they use with the theoretical dimensions of the research question of interest. Acquisition performance is a multidimensional construct with different meanings at different levels of analysis, at different stages, and for different stakeholders. It seems intuitive, then, that different measures should be used to assess acquisition performance within different theoretical contexts.

Past research provides a good foundation for conceptualizing the various aspects of firm performance, in general, as well as M&A performance, specifically, by outlining classification schemes to organize the numerous possible performance measures (e.g. Carton and Hofer 2006; Cording *et al.* 2010; Meglio and Risberg 2011; Venkatraman and Ramanujam 1986; Zollo and Meier 2008). For instance, Cording and colleagues (2010) divide acquisition performance measures into four domains—an announcement effect domain, a long-term stock performance domain, an accounting-based domain, and a managerial self-assessment domain. We refer the reader to their paper for an explanation of the differences between these domains. In general, their analysis suggests that the construct of acquisition performance be expanded to incorporate more than just the value captured by the acquiring firm. Further, these and other typologies are indicative of the ways in which the construct of acquisition performance may be expanded in order to better understand the widespread effects of acquisitions.

One specific way to expand the construct of acquisition performance is to determine which measure of acquisition performance is most relevant based on level of analysis (Meglio and Risberg 2011; Zollo and Meier 2008). For instance, Zollo and Meier (2008) propose a taxonomy of acquisition performance across three levels of analysis—task performance, acquisition performance, and firm performance—in the short term and the long term. According to their taxonomy, the task level relates to the integration process, the transaction level to value creation in terms of cost efficiencies or revenue growth, and the firm level to the performance of the combined entity over and above transaction-level performance. The authors also provide an important warning when they state that "any model of either transaction- or firm-level performance that does not include process-level performance is in danger of being seriously underspecified" (Zollo and Meier 2008: 72). Using measures at the level of analysis and at least one level below, then, is a good practice for ensuring robust results.

Building on the typologies proposed by Cording and colleagues (2010), Zollo and Meier (2008), and others, we outline two alternative conceptualizations of acquisition performance measures as a way to more clearly align the theoretical context of the study with those measures. In doing so, we not only suggest the need for different measures of acquisition performance based on the given theoretical context, but also argue that these measures may be categorized differently depending on the research question of interest. In other words, there is more than one way to conceptualize the taxonomy of acquisition performance measures, and determining which taxonomy fits with a given set of research goals is an important first step towards deciding on an appropriate measure.

First, M&A researchers could benefit from aligning measures of acquisition performance to specific desired outcomes or goals that likely differ from acquisition to acquisition (Bower 2001). While one organization may engage in an acquisition in order to increase market share, another may desire to encourage innovation, and another may seek to vertically integrate operations and cut costs. Therefore, if acquisition performance is only assessed using, say, abnormal returns, empirical analysis of M&As is likely to overlook other important indicators of success. For example, an acquisition may not immediately affect market (or even accounting) returns, but may synergistically improve the generation of new products or services post-acquisition. Given the potential variation in strategic goals, it may often be appropriate to align measures of acquisition performance with the strategic goals of the particular acquisitions under investigation. As a starting point, we propose a simple conceptualization of acquisition performance measures based on three categories of outcomes—economic, strategic, and integrative—which may each be assessed differently depending on the stage of the acquisition (see Table 13.2).

We define economic performance as performance related to the financial or economic benefits of M&As, strategic performance as the method through which economic performance is enhanced or any desired synergies above and beyond pure economic performance, and

Table 13.2 Acquisition performance measures by desired outcome

		Stage	
		Short-term (Selection and transaction)	Long-term (Integration and management)
Outcome	**Economic performance**	• Insider expectations • Advisor expectations • Analyst projections	• Accounting performance • Long-term market returns • Market share
	Strategic performance	• Premium paid • Market reaction (abnormal returns)	• Innovative performance • Brand enhancement/ weakening • Market share
	Integrative performance	• Insider expectations • Advisor expectations	• Acquisition survival • Employee retention • Employee satisfaction levels • Customer retention

integrative performance as the ability of the merging firms to attain a desired level of integration. Of course, these categories are not mutually exclusive. Indeed, as evidenced by the measures we propose for each category, there may be some overlap in theoretical constructs and possible measures to assess those constructs. As a mode for simplifying decision making, we believe that this typology provides a clear way to distinguish between measures, particularly within different stages of the acquisition process. In the short term, each of these benefits can be gauged using survey data of insider (i.e. manager) or advisor (i.e. consultant firm) expectations. In addition, potential economic and strategic performance may be reasonably gauged using abnormal returns, analyst projections, or the premium paid by the acquiring firm. In the long term, the realization of those benefits can be measured using more distinct measures, such as accounting or long-term market data for economic performance; changes in innovation, brand recognition, or any number of other strategic goals for strategic performance; and acquisition survival, or employee or customer retention for integrative performance. Further, multiple measures or categories of measures may be utilized depending on the theoretical contexts so long as those measures are appropriately justified.

Second, researchers may align measures of acquisition performance with the specific stakeholders of interest. Just as goals may differ between acquisitions, performance means different things to different stakeholders. For example, while managers may want to increase economic performance, innovation, and the like, investors may simply want to increase stock returns, and employees may desire more latitude in their job or additional opportunities for growth. Meglio and Risberg (2010: 91) hint at this idea when they state, "M&As are not monolithic and isolated events in organizations as they span long periods of time and affect people both within as well as outside the merging firms." Similarly, Meglio's chapter in this volume demonstrates that acquisitions not only affect shareholder interests, but also put at risk the interests of various other stakeholder groups. According to her perspective, acquisition performance may be conceptualized as a "game" between stakeholders both within and outside the firm with varying levels of relative power and diverse interests, which all have an effect on acquisition outcomes (Meglio, 2015). Using different measures based on the stakeholders involved in the research context, then, also seems relevant to the development of M&A performance research and the construct of acquisition performance. Here again, we provide a starting point for such a taxonomy by conceptualizing acquisition performance for the firm itself as well as across three major groups of stakeholders—management, investors, and other stakeholders—in the short and long term (see Table 13.3).

In this case, the proposed measures are fairly intuitive, based on the interests of the firm or the respective stakeholder; however, care should still be taken to ensure that different measures are used to assess the potential or expected impact versus the actual impact on the firm or each stakeholder. For example, the potential impact of an acquisition on employees may be assessed using surveys gauging turnover intention or satisfaction, while the actual impact may be assessed using actual turnover or satisfaction levels across time. Regardless of the measure of acquisition performance that is used, it is most important for researchers to clearly specify the stakeholders of interest and justify the connection between the measure and the stakeholders' interests.

As a final point of guidance for research assessing the performance effects of M&As, researchers would do well to implement primary data collection techniques in order to assess performance metrics. Research indicates that primary data is seriously underrepresented in work on M&As (Zollo and Meier 2008). The heavy emphasis on archival data limits theory development, since proxy measures are restricted in their ability to explain the "why" behind a particular

Table 13.3 Acquisition performance measures by firm or stakeholder interests

		Stage	
		Short-term (Selection and transaction)	*Long-term (Integration and management)*
	Firm	• Analyst projections • Premium paid	• Accounting performance • Brand enhancement/ weakening • Market share
Stakeholder	**Managers**	• Insider expectations • Advisor expectations	• Goal realization (surveys) • TMT compensation • TMT retention
	Investors	• Market reaction (abnormal returns)	• Long-term market returns
	Other stakeholders	• Employee surveys (e.g. turnover intentions, satisfaction) • Customer reactions (market surveys)	• Employee retention • Employee satisfaction • Customer retention

phenomenon. However, surveying managers, advisors, investors, or other stakeholders could improve the precision of theory related to M&As. For example, since not all acquisitions have the same goals, asking more detailed questions about the degree of realization of particular benefits (e.g. innovative, economic) can help researchers understand which measures are most applicable to a given acquisition.

Acquisitions, event studies, and investor behavior

As an alternative to refining the construct of acquisition performance, M&A research would also benefit by looking at event studies as a means of examining alternative dependent variables, particularly related to investor behavior and financial markets. Krier (2005: 64) provides conceptual motivation for performing such an examination in his statement that "financial markets are remarkably under-conceptualized, more often taken as a starting assumption than as an object of study." Based on the discussion already provided, this is clearly the case in the context of M&As, where financial markets are simply the setting used to examine performance effects of M&As. Yet, using M&As as the empirical setting to examine dependent variables *other* than acquisition performance could greatly enrich the behavioral field of study. In this section, we propose two ways in which using M&As as an empirical setting can enhance behaviorally oriented research—first, by using event studies on M&As to test theories on investor decision-making processes and second, by using qualitative studies on M&As to better understand the mechanisms underlying those processes.

Event studies and investor behavior

Among the most obvious, yet vastly underexplored, behaviorally oriented applications of event-study methodology in the M&A context is the study of investor reactions *for their own sake*, rather than as a "black-box" measure of performance. Investor reactions are the underlying mechanism through which capital markets operate. Prices rise and fall based on investment decisions, which are driven by investor perceptions. Acquisitions provide a convenient setting in which to examine investor decision-making processes because of the causal ambiguity and uncertainty that they entail. Event studies can be helpful in this analysis insofar as abnormal returns are seen for what they are: a measure of stock market reactions that is based on human perception and, as such, offers a glimpse into investors' boundedly rational decision-making processes. For example, Schijven and Hitt (2012) indicate that relaxing the assumption of investor rationality may allow researchers to examine decision-making processes—including perceptions, decisions, and actions—as the dependent variable of interest rather than just the performance outcomes of M&As. The authors submit that such an application could inform future work to integrate a framework classifying categories of signals for investor reactions. Such applications suggest that, while weaknesses in the assumptions underlying event-study methodology may at first appear to be limiting, they may also provide promising avenues for theoretical or philosophical development.

A strong example of the application of event studies in M&A to behavioral research is Louis and Sun (2010). In their study, they use abnormal returns to demonstrate the differential market response to Friday and non-Friday merger announcements—that is, that investors are less attentive to Friday announcements. They further show that, aware of this, managers tend to announce "bad" mergers more consistently on Fridays. While they use event-study methodology in the context of M&As, then, their primary research question and contribution are not associated with acquisition performance, but are strongly related to the behavior of investors and managers. Future research could employ similar methodology to examine a broad range of behavioral-related research questions. Below we discuss four specific possibilities: the accuracy of capital markets in assessing potential value, differences in behavior across investor types, the ability of markets to learn, and market reactions at times other than the announcement date.

First, we have already established that short- and long-term market returns related to M&A activity are often inconsistent. Extending the logic of subjectivity to this phenomenon could lead to various questions examining the accuracy of capital markets. For example, Oler and colleagues (2008) suggest that researchers examine what forces render markets more or less efficient. To answer such questions, we recommend that researchers compare multiple independent event windows (i.e. short vs. long) to determine the conditions under which long-term returns are either consistent or inconsistent with short-term returns. Assessing market returns in this way would be an effective use of the limitations outlined in the behavioral perspective of capital markets and could greatly enhance theory on market efficiency and investor rationality.

Second, previous research has suggested the existence of two broad types of investors—day traders and institutional investors. Day traders are considered inexperienced investors, while institutional investors are considered experienced investors with specific knowledge about the industries in which they invest (List 2004). Institutional investors include investment banks and corporate investors, which pool funds and make large investments in broad portfolios. Past research in behavioral economics suggests that the decision-making processes of these two types of investors vary dramatically. In particular, List (2003, 2004) suggests that, while day traders are irrational, institutional investors tend to make more economically rational decisions. Based on this finding, comparing investor decisions based on the percentage of the company held by institutional investors versus days traders could increase our understanding of the accuracy of market reactions in predicting acquisition value.

Despite what we have said up to this point, if institutional investors are more accurate in their predictions than day traders, market returns surrounding acquisitions may be more reflective of actual acquisition performance for companies owned by larger percentages of institutional investors than for companies owned by larger percentages of day traders. This line of inquiry could add boundary conditions to the EMH, enabling future researchers using event studies to make a stronger case for the validity of their results. At the same time, we argue that even institutional investors will be limited in their ability to predict value-creation potential. Ultimately, we propose that emphasizing differences in decision-making processes between investor groups and what effect those decisions have on driving market outcomes could lead to an intriguing line of inquiry.

Third, research in the M&A context may also develop behavioral theory by observing market trends for various types of acquisitions over time. In particular, it could help researchers develop theory on the ability of markets to learn. Anecdotal evidence from the conglomerate merger waves of the 1960s and 1970s may help to illustrate this point. Event-study methodology showed that diversifying acquisitions were accompanied by positive market reactions during the 1960s and 1970s (Hubbard and Palia 1999; Matsusaka 1993). However, as the long-term effects of diversification were shown to be negligible (Kaplan and Weisbach 1992; Rumelt 1974, 1982; Ravenscraft and Scherer 1987), the market adjusted, and market valuations of diversifying acquisitions in and after the 1980s have been largely negative (e.g. Bhagat *et al.* 1990; Comment and Jarrella 1995; Rhéaume and Bhabra 2008). This example shows the behavioral nature of markets—that is, they are not only socially constructed, but they also learn and adjust over time. Within the context of acquisitions, this phenomenon may lead to additional research questions that have yet to be examined, such as:

- How do investors respond to various types of acquisitions and how has this changed over the past several decades?
- What types of acquisitions are generally perceived as having the most potential?
- In cases where short-term and long-term returns are contradictory, how long does it take the market to react by adjusting to the particular deal or by reacting differently to similar deal announcements?
- Drawing on the idea that day traders and institutional investors tend to make their decisions differently, how might ownership alter the timetable required for the market to learn?

A final application of event-study methodology in the context of M&As that may potentially inform behavioral theory is to study abnormal returns on dates other than the announcement date. To reiterate, while the EMH assumes that investor reactions to an announcement event are complete and unbiased, behavioral theory shows that investors rarely have all of the information they need to make a perfectly rational decision (Barberis and Thaler 2003; Das and Teng 1999; March and Simon 1958). Further, while the EMH suggests that all information surrounding an acquisition is immediately incorporated into the share price on (or surrounding) the announcement date and that there should be no additional response on the completion date, there are solid behavioral reasons to believe that there may often be abnormal returns on dates other than the announcement date. For example, Schijven and King (2013) examine abnormal returns on the completion date and compare them with the initial abnormal returns on the announcement date, arguing that "implementation planning," as measured by the amount of time that elapses between the announcement and completion dates, could have a significant effect on the perceived value of a deal. For example, if the acquirer spends more time "planning," investors may be more optimistic about the chances of the deal to succeed. However, if negotiations drag on too long, perceptions about the deal may become more pessimistic. Other similar questions that could be examined relate to abnormal returns surrounding the completion date, the withdrawal date (for mergers that do not take place), or other dates besides the announcement date to develop a more detailed understanding of investor behavior towards acquisitions and other complex phenomena.

Qualitative research on investor behavior

Aside from event studies, other approaches may be taken in the context of M&As to increase our understanding of investor behavior. As mentioned previously, the use of primary data is seriously underrepresented in the acquisition literature. Further, despite the fact that qualitative or ethnographic research may provide deeper insights into the complexities and ambiguities of acquisitions than quantitative methods (Meglio and Risberg 2010), the vast majority of research on M&A is quantitative (Meglio and Risberg 2011). Researchers rarely use qualitative surveys of managers or advisors to gauge acquisition performance. Even fewer researchers have used primary data on investors, and, at least to our knowledge, no qualitative research has been conducted on how investors actually go about making investment decisions related to M&As. We believe that qualitative research could provide extremely useful insights for the development of theory on investor behavior. We specifically propose two avenues that researchers may take to develop this area: the use of case studies and other qualitative methodologies to examine investor decision processes and the use of "fuzzy set" methodology in M&A research to examine investor behavior.

First, while there is some debate regarding the robustness and generalizability of qualitative methodologies, most researchers seem to agree that qualitative research is eminently useful as a first step towards developing theory (Glaser and Strauss 1965). Indeed, qualitative knowledge often precedes quantitative knowledge (Campbell 1988). As Behrens (1997: 135) notes, "numbers themselves are meaningless unless the data analyst understands the mapping process and the nexus of theory and categorization in which objects under study are conceptualized." Further, as a starting point for inductive processes, a "sample of one (or few)" is justifiable (Mintzberg 2005). Extending these ideas to the present discussion, we believe that qualitative research in the context of M&A could greatly benefit the development of theory, particularly related to the comparatively underdeveloped area of investor behavior.

As previously discussed, M&As provide an excellent setting in which to examine investor behavior because of the high level of uncertainty and complexity associated with acquisitions. Within this context, qualitative research is particularly promising as a way to tease out the processes underlying investor decisions because of its unique ability to capture unobservable phenomena. While we acknowledge that gaining access to qualitative data on investor decision-making processes would be difficult, we believe that the potential knowledge that could be gained from such sources would be well worth the effort. As a practical way to approach this area, we recommend that researchers begin with simple case studies on investor decisions before extending those findings to larger samples of investors—both institutional and day traders. Eisenhardt and Graebner (2007) provide an excellent summary of how to appropriately use case studies or multiple case studies to develop robust theory. They emphasize the importance of "precise language and thoughtful research design: careful justification of theory building, theoretical sampling of cases, interviews that limit informant bias, rich presentation of evidence in tables and appendixes, and clear statement of theoretical arguments" (Eisenhardt and Graebner 2007: 30). We direct the reader to their paper for details on how to generate such research, but reiterate that the proper application of case studies and other qualitative methods in M&A would be useful in answering a broad range of questions related to investor behavior. These include:

- What factors impact the investment decision of different groups?
- What research do investors perform prior to investing and what heuristics are used to judge potential value?
- How do decision-making processes differ among different groups of investors?

Second, in addition to pure qualitative research, fuzzy set methodology also offers opportunities for research in M&A. Fuzzy set theory represents a unique middle ground between qualitative and quantitative methods, overcoming various limitations of each (Ragin 2008). Zadeh (1965) first introduced this methodology to describe mathematical sets with degrees of membership. In contrast to "crisp" sets, which are assessed in binary terms (i.e. either an element belongs to the set, or it does not), fuzzy sets describe situations in which information is incomplete or imprecise and allow for gradation between extremes (Zimmermann 2001). For example, rather than forcing organizations into a binary condition of either "high performing" or "low performing," fuzzy sets would measure the degree of membership in each category. Researchers have used fuzzy set methodologies to deal with complex phenomena across several fields in the social sciences, including the decision sciences, management, political sciences, and sociology (e.g. Amenta *et al.* 1992; Crawford 2012; Cress and Snow 2000; Fiss 2011; Hicks *et al.* 1995; Kogut and Ragin 2006; Krook 2010; Lin *et al.* 2005; Yager and Basson 1975; Vaisey 2007). Associated with decision making, the methodology lends itself well to phenomena related to bounded rationality. Given all that has been presented regarding acquisitions, then, market reactions surrounding M&As seem like a natural context in which to use fuzzy set methodology. Application of the methodology to investor decision making could inform new theory regarding the processes and motivations for investor behavior and, ultimately, broader market reactions and trends.

Summary and conclusions

Event-study methodology has become the dominant method to assess the performance effects of M&As (Cording *et al.* 2010; Goranova *et al.* 2010; Haleblian *et al.* 2009; King *et al.* 2004). Its widespread use is largely due to several key benefits, but also depends on a number of underlying assumptions, which, if they do not apply, may undermine the accuracy and validity of conclusions drawn from such studies. In this chapter, we have outlined these assumptions and their associated limitations, which may present problems for the use of event studies to gauge acquisition performance. We have established that the primary theoretical assumptions stem from the EMH, which, in the semi-strong form, argues that prices adjust to reflect all publicly available information and assumes that investors are rational, trades in the market are made at random, and rational arbitrageurs correct any mispricing that may result from non-random trades (Shleifer 2003). We have also outlined arguments from the growing body of behavioral research—spanning behavioral finance, economic sociology, and social psychology—that criticize the theoretical assumptions of the methodology. In general, these critiques question the assumption of investor rationality and market efficiency and suggest that event studies are more reflective of investor perceptions, or potential value, rather than the actual value created through acquisitions. Drawing on these critiques, we argue for a reorientation in the use of event-study methodology as well as of measures of acquisition performance, beyond abnormal returns.

As an alternative to refining the construct of acquisition performance, we have also discussed the possibility of using event studies as a means of examining alternative dependent variables, particularly related to investor behavior and financial markets, and have explained how extending the examination of acquisitions from event-study methodology to qualitative methods may increase our understanding of investor behavior and decision making. Because of the complex nature of acquisitions, M&As provide an ideal setting in which to analyze investor behavior, regardless of whether that analysis is qualitative or quantitative. Following these suggestions could inform new theory regarding the processes and motivations for investor behavior at the individual as well as the market level.

Ultimately, a reorientation of event-study methodology and refinement of the construct of acquisition performance in general not only has the potential to lead to greater precision in the analysis of acquisition performance, but also opens several intriguing avenues for future research. In particular, the use of M&As as a research setting may provide several exciting possibilities in the analysis of investor behavior and decision making. Additionally, by relaxing the assumptions of investor rationality, the application of event studies in particular could greatly enhance behaviorally oriented theory.

Note

1 We would like to thank an anonymous reviewer for suggesting this insightful example.

References

Amenta, E., Carruthers, B.G., and Zylan, Y. (1992) "A hero for the aged? The Townsend movement, the political mediation model, and US old-age policy, 1934–1950", *American Journal of Sociology*, 98: 308–39.
Barberis, N. and Thaler, R. (2003) "A survey of behavioral finance," in G.M. Constantinides, M. Harris, and R. Stulz (eds.) *Handbook of the Economics of Finance*, Amsterdam: Elsevier.
Barkema, H.G. and Schijven, M. (2008) "Toward unlocking the full potential of acquisitions: The role of organizational restructuring," *Academy of Management Journal*, 51: 696–722.
Behrens, J.T. (1997) "Principles and procedures of exploratory data analysis," *Psychological Methods*, 2: 131–60.
Bhagat, S., Shleifer, A., and Vishny, R.W. (1990) "Hostile takeovers in the 1980s: The return to corporate specialization," *Brookings Papers on Economic Activity*, 1990: 1–72.
Bower, J.L. (2001) "Not all M&As are alike—and that matters," *Harvard Business Review*, 79(3): 92–105.
Callon, M. (2007) "What does it mean to say that economics is performative?," in D. MacKenzie, F. Muniesa, and L. Siu (eds.) *Do Economists Make Markets? On the Performativity of Economics*, Princeton, NJ: Princeton University Press.
Campbell, D.T. (1988) "Descriptive epistemology: Psychological, sociological, and evolutionary," in E.S. Overman (ed.) *Methodology and Epistemology for Social Science: Selected Papers*, Chicago, IL: University of Chicago Press.
Carton, R.B. and Hofer, C.W. (2006) *Measuring Organizational Performance: Metrics for Entrepreneurship in Strategic Management Research*, Cheltenham: Edward Elgar.
Chaiken, S. (1987) "The heuristic model of persuasion," in M.P. Zanna, J.M. Olson, and C.P. Herman (eds.) *Social Influence: The Ontario Symposium*, Hillsdale, NJ: Lawrence Eribaum Associates, Inc.
Comment, R. and Jarrella, G.A. (1995) "Corporate focus and stock returns," *Journal of Financial Economics*, 37: 67–87.
Cording, M., Christmann, P., and Weigelt, C. (2010) "Measuring theoretically complex constructs: The case of acquisition performance," *Strategic Organization*, 8: 11–41.
Crawford, S. (2012) "What is the energy policy-planning network and who dominates it?: A network and QCA analysis of leading energy firms and organizations," *Energy Policy*, 45: 430–39.
Cress, D.M. and Snow, D.A. (2000) "The outcomes of homeless mobilization: The influence of organization, disruption, political mediation, and framing," *American Journal of Sociology*, 105: 1063–104.

Das, T.K. and Teng, B.S. (1999) "Cognitive biases and strategic decision processes: An integrative perspective," *Journal of Management Studies*, 36: 757–78.

Duhaime, I.M. and Schwenk, C.R. (1985) "Conjectures on cognitive simplification in acquisition and divestment decision making," *Academy of Management Review*, 10: 287–95.

Eisenhardt, K.M. and Graebner, M. (2007) "Theory building from cases: Opportunties and challenges," *Academy of Management Journal*, 50: 25–32.

Fama, E.F. (1970) "Efficient capital markets: A review of theory and empirical work," *Journal of Finance*, 25: 383–417.

Fama, E., Fisher, L., Jensen, M., and Roll, R. (1969) "The adjustment of stock prices to new information," *International Economic Review*, 10: 1–28.

Fiss, P.C. (2011) "Building better causal theories: A fuzzy set approach to typologies in organization research," *Academy of Management Journal*, 54: 393–420.

Glaser, B.G., and Strauss, A.L. (1965) "Discovery of substantive theory: A basic strategy underlying qualitative research," *American Behavioral Scientist*, 8: 5–12.

Goranova, M., Dharwadkar, R., and Brandes, P. (2010) "Owners on both sides of the deal: Mergers and acquisitions and overlapping institutional ownership," *Strategic Management Journal*, 31: 1114–35.

Granovetter, M. (1985) "Economic action and social structure: The problem of embeddedness," *American Journal of Sociology*, 91: 481–510.

Haleblian, J., Devers, C.E., Mcnamara, G., Carpenter, M.A., and Davison, R.B. (2009) "Taking stock of what we know about mergers and acquisitions: A review and research agenda," *Journal of Management*, 35: 469–502.

Harrison, J.S., Hitt, M.A., Hoskisson, R.E., and Ireland, R.D. (1991) "Synergies and post-acquisition performance: Differences versus similarities in resource allocations," *Journal of Management*, 17: 173–90.

Haspeslagh, P.C. and Jemison, D.B. (1991) *Managing Acquisitions: Creating Value Through Corporate Renewal*, New York: Free Press.

Herrmann-Pillath, C. (2010) "A neurolinguistic approach to performativity in economics," *Journal of Economic Methodology*, 17: 241–60.

Hicks, A., Misra, J., and Ng, T.N. (1995) "The programmatic emergence of the social security state," *American Sociological Review*, 60: 329–49.

Hirshleifer, D. (2001) "Investor psychology and asset pricing," *Journal of Finance*, 56: 1533–97.

Hubbard, R.G. and Palia, D. (1999) "A reexamination of the conglomerate merger wave in the 1960s: An internal capital markets view," *Journal of Finance*, 54: 1131–52.

Hunter, J.E. and Coggin, T.D. (1988) "Analyst judgment: The efficient market hypothesis versus a psychological theory of human judgment," *Organizational Behavior & Human Decision Processes*, 42: 284–302.

Jemison, D.B. and Sitkin, S.B. (1986) "Corporate acquisitions: A process perspective," *Academy of Management Review*, 11: 145–63.

Kaplan, S.N. and Weisbach, M.S. (1992) "The success of acquisitions: Evidence from divestitures," *Journal of Finance*, 47: 107–38.

King, D.R., Dalton, D.R., Daily, C.M., and Covin, J.G. (2004) "Meta-analyses of post-acquisition performance: Indications of unidentified moderators," *Strategic Management Journal*, 25: 187–200.

Kogut, B. and Ragin, C. (2006) "Exploring complexity when diversity is limited: Institutional complementarity in theories of rule of law and national systems revisited," *European Management Review*, 3: 44–59.

Kozielecki, J. (1981) *Psychological Decision Theory*, Boston, MA: Springer.

Krier, D. (2005) *Speculative Management: Stock Market Power and Corporate Change*, Albany: State University of New York Press.

Krook, M.L. (2010) "Women's representation in parliament: A qualitative comparative analysis," *Political Studies*, 58: 886–908.

Lawrence, E.R., Mccabe, G., and Prakash, A.J. (2007) "Answering financial anomalies: Sentiment-based stock pricing," *Journal of Behavioral Finance*, 8: 161–71.

Levine, M. (1971) "Hypothesis theory and nonlearning despite ideal S-R-reinforcement contingencies," *Psychological Review*, 78: 130–40.

Lin, C., Tan, B., and Hsieh, P.J. (2005) "Application of the fuzzy weighted average in strategic portfolio management," *Decision Sciences*, 36: 489–511.

List, J.A. (2003) "Does market experience eliminate market anomalies?," *The Quarterly Journal of Economics*, 118: 41–71.

List, J.A. (2004) "Neoclassical theory versus prospect theory: Evidence from the marketplace," *Econometrica*, 72: 615–25.

Louis, H. and Sun, A. (2010) "Investor inattention and the market reaction to merger announcements," *Management Science*, 56: 1781–93.

Mackenzie, D. (2006) "Is economics performative? Option theory and the construction of derivatives markets," *Journal of the History of Economic Thought*, 28: 29–55.

McWilliams, A. and Siegel, D. (1997) "Event studies in management research: Theoretical and empirical issues," *Academy of Management Journal*, 40: 626–57.

March, J. and Simon, H.A. (1958) *Organizations*, Oxford: Wiley.

Matsusaka, J.G. (1993) "Takeover motives during the conglomerate merger wave," *RAND Journal of Economics*, 24: 357–79.

Meglio, O. (2015) "The acquistion performance game: a stakeholder approach," in A. Risberg, D.R. King, and O. Meglio (eds.) *The Routledge Companion to Mergers and Acquisitions*, Oxford: Routledge.

Meglio, O., and Risberg, A. (2010). "Mergers and acquisitions—Time for a methodological rejuvenation of the field?," *Scandinavian Journal of Management*, 26: 87–95.

Meglio, O. and Risberg, A. (2011) "The (mis)measurement of M&A performance: A systematic narrative literature review," *Scandinavian Journal of Management*, 27: 418–33.

Mintzberg, H. (2005) "Developing theory about the development of theory," in K.G. Smith and M.A. Hitt (eds.), *Great Minds in Management: The Process of Theory Development*, Oxford: Oxford University Press.

Oler, D.K., Harrison, J.S., and Allen, M.R. (2008) "The danger of misinterpreting short-window event study findings in strategic management research: An empirical illustration using horizontal acquisitions," *Strategic Organization*, 6: 151–84.

Park, N.K. (2004) "A guide to using event study methods in multi-country settings," *Strategic Management Journal*, 25: 655–68.

Petty, R.E. and Cacioppo, J.T. (1986) "The elaboration likelihood model of persuasion," in R.E. Petty and J.T. Cacioppo (eds.), *Communication and Persuasion*, New York: Springer.

Petty, R.E. and Wegener, D.T. (1999) "The elaboration likelihood model: Current status and controversies," in S. Chaiken and Y. Trope (eds.), *Dual-process Theories in Social Psychology*, New York: Guilford Press.

Petty, R., Briñol, P., and Priester, J. (2009) "Mass media attitude change," in J. Bryant and M.B. Oliver (eds.), *Media Effects: Advances in Theory and Research*, New York: Routledge.

Preda, A. (2007) "The sociological approach to financial markets," *Journal of Economic Surveys*, 21: 506–33.

Pruitt, G. (1961) "Informational requirements in making decisions," *The American Journal of Psychology*, 7: 433–39.

Ragin, C.C. (2008) *Redesigning Social Inquiry: Fuzzy Sets and Beyond*, Chicago, IL: University of Chicago Press.

Ravenscraft, D.J. and Scherer, F.M. (1987) *Mergers, Sell-offs, and Economic Efficiency*, Washington, DC: Brookings Institution Press.

Rhéaume, L. and Bhabra, H.S. (2008) "Value creation in information-based industries through convergence: A study of U.S. Mergers and acquisitions between 1993 and 2005," *Information & Management*, 45: 304–11.

Rubtsova, A., Dejordy, R., Glynn, M.A., and Zald, M. (2010) "The social construction of causality: The effects of institutional myths on financial regulation," *Research in the Sociology of Organizations*, 30: 201–44.

Rumelt, R.P. (1974) *Strategy, Structure, and Economic Performance*, Boston, MA: Division of Research, Graduate School of Business Administration, Harvard University.

Rumelt, R.P. (1982) "Diversification strategy and profitability," *Strategic Management Journal*, 3: 359–69.

Samuels, W.J. (2004) "Markets and their social construction," *Social Research*, 71: 357–70.

Schijven, M. and Hitt, M.A. (2012) "The vicarious wisdom of crowds: Toward a behavioral perspective on investor reactions to acquisition announcements," *Strategic Management Journal*, 33: 1247–68.

Schijven, M. and King, D. (2013) "Investors as quasi-advisors to management: Signaling and counter-signaling between acquisition announcement and completion," working paper.

Schwenk, C.R. (1984) "Cognitive simplification processes in strategic decision-making," *Strategic Management Journal*, 5: 111–28.

Schwenk, C.R. (1985) "Management illusions and biases: Their impact on strategic decisions," *Long Range Planning*, 18: 74–80.

Shiller, R.J. (2003) "From efficient markets theory to behavioral finance," *The Journal of Economic Perspectives*, 17: 83–104.

Shiller, R.J., Fischer, S., and Friedman, B.M. (1984) "Stock prices and social dynamics," *Brookings Papers on Economic Activity*, 1984: 457–510.

Shleifer, A. (2003) *Inefficient Markets: An Introduction to Behavioral Finance*, Oxford, UK: Oxford University Press.

Shleifer, A. and Vishny, R.W. (1997) "The limits of arbitrage," *Journal of Finance*, 52: 35–55.

Staw, B.M. (1976) "Knee-deep in the big muddy: A study of escalating commitment to a chosen course of action," *Organizational Behavior & Human Performance*, 16: 27–44.

Steinbruner, J.D. (1974) *The Cybernetic Theory of Decision: New Dimensions of Political Analysis*, Princeton, NJ: Princeton University Press.

Tormala, Z.L., Briñol, P. and Petty, R.E. (2006) "When credibility attacks: The reverse impact of source credibility on persuasion," *Journal of Experimental Social Psychology*, 42: 684–91.

Tversky, A. and Kahneman, D. (1974) "Judgment under uncertainty: Heuristics and biases," *Science*, 185: 1124–31.

Vaisey, S. (2007) "Structure, culture, and community: The search for belonging in 50 urban communes," *American Sociological Review*, 72: 851–73.

Venkatraman, V.N. and Ramanujam, V. (1986), "Measurement of business performance: A comparison of approaches," *Academy of Management Review*, 11: 801–14.

Wason, P.C. (1960) "On the failure to eliminate hypotheses in a conceptual task," *Quarterly Journal of Experimental Psychology*, 12: 129–40.

White, H.C. (1981) "Where do markets come from?," *American Journal of Sociology*, 87: 517–47.

Yager, R. and Basson, D. (1975) "Decision making with fuzzy sets," *Decision Sciences*, 6: 590–600.

Zadeh, L.A. (1965) "Fuzzy sets," *Information and Control*, 8: 338–53.

Zajac, E.J. and Westphal, J.D. (2004) "The social construction of market value: Institutionalization and learning perspectives on stock market reactions," *American Sociological Review*, 69: 433–57.

Zimmermann, H.J. (2001) *Fuzzy Set Theory and Its Applications*, Boston, MA: Springer.

Zollo, M. and Meier, D. (2008) "What Is M&A performance?," *Academy of Management Perspectives*, 22: 55–77.

Zuckerman, E.W. (2004) "Structural incoherence and stock market activity," *American Sociological Review*, 69: 405–32.

14

Institutional ethnography

An alternative way to study M&As

Rebecca Lund and Janne Tienari

Introduction

On the basis of their review of extant research in the field, Olimpia Meglio and Annette Risberg (2010) argue that research on mergers and acquisitions (M&As) is in dire need of methodological rejuvenation. They suggest that real-time, multiple-level longitudinal studies, which employ ethnographic methods such as observations in addition to interviews, are particularly called for. We heed this call by introducing institutional ethnography, developed by Dorothy Smith and her colleagues (2006b), as a promising alternative method of inquiry that enables us to address questions of managing, organizing, and coordinating as well as of politics, power, and resistance in the M&A context in new and meaningful ways.

The study of M&As is dominated by a positivist and functionalist worldview and the use of quantitative methods (Meglio and Risberg 2010). Although extant research also uses qualitative and mixed methods (Cartwright et al. 2012), it can be criticized for viewing its subject matter through an abstract and external lens. The researcher is placed in an analytical role and destined to draw (what appear to be) generalizable conclusions on the basis of transactions and change processes that they have not experienced first-hand as participants or observers (Meglio and Risberg 2010). This kind of research also tends to be overly reliant on the perspectives and perceptions of managerial respondents. This leads to another bias in the study of M&As: a managerial one (Risberg 2001). These critiques are an important step in pinpointing some of the problematic aspects in the field, which we suggest can be in part remedied by institutional ethnography developed by Dorothy Smith and her colleagues.

Employing a different terminology than that of Meglio and Risberg, in institutional ethnography the notion of *objectification* is applied to describe research processes like those that have been found to dominate in scholarly work on M&As. In this chapter, we offer an outline of Smith's critique of objectification, elucidate how institutional ethnography seeks to address it, and point to some problems in M&A studies identified through this lens. Finally, we argue why institutional ethnography, in comparison with other methods of inquiry, is particularly fruitful in the study of mergers and acquisitions.

A critique of objectification

Dorothy Smith developed an extensive critique of the processes of objectification in the field of sociological research. She outlined how, in much research activity, privilege is given to generalizing and standardizing scientific discourses, theoretical concepts, and methods of categorization while making the actual activities and experiences of people an expression of discursive, predetermined, theoretical, and conceptual logic (Smith 1987, 1990a, 1990b, 2004a).

Objectification happens when the researcher removes embodied experiences and activities and replaces them with a fact or phenomenon, thereby losing sight of differences and particularities. Agency is transferred from the experience of subjects to a social phenomenon or category. In M&As this could mean that an expression of frustration with the new merged organization is explained as continued identification with a pre-determined "legacy culture." The account of the research participant is molded to fit a conceptual and theoretical framework and examples are selected to strengthen the theoretical argument. Hence the perspective of the researcher and the theoretical language or discourse activated by her is presented as if it were the perspective of the research subjects (Widerberg 2007; Smith 2004a). Because it disconnects itself from the lived actualities of people, this kind of inquiry tends to reproduce and privilege generalizing and standardizing scientific and theoretical discourse above local positions and the diversity present in the experiences and perspectives of people.

Despite the fact that Dorothy Smith's critique of objectification was developed within and for the context of sociology, parallels can be drawn and the critique extended to M&A studies. Looking at the manner in which the concepts and theories of organizational culture and organizational Identity have been applied and used is a case in point. However, in our view it is important to scrutinize not only the usual suspects—mainstream positivist and functionalist studies—but also the interpretive, social constructionist, and critical approaches to explicate what institutional ethnography can add to the study of M&As.

What is institutional ethnography?

Following the critique of objectification outlined above, it is tempting to expect that in the development of her own method of inquiry Dorothy Smith would aspire to overthrow all processes of theorization. She does not, but she does attempt to challenge conventions of theory development by examining and explicating "how 'abstractions' are put together, with concepts, knowledge, facticity, as socially organized practices" (Smith 1992: 90). Smith is interested in finding out what abstractions *do*: how they organize ways of knowing and doing. And in so doing she shows how we can explicate the conceptual practices of power in research (Smith 1990a).

Institutional ethnography helps us systematically engage with how objectifications organize our everyday lives and explicate how they, when activated, serve the interests of some people while subjugating the interests of others. Objectifying processes happen not only in scholarly research processes but are present in many other textually mediated processes. They could take place for instance in the form of the bureaucratic guidelines and professional concepts used by nurses when they evaluate a patient's health (e.g. Rankin and Campbell 2006); in the forms and concepts used by managers to evaluate their employees with respect to efficiency, attitudes toward work, and the quality of the job performed (e.g. McCoy 1998; Chio 2005; Chio 2008); in ideologies and discourses regarding what it means to an excellent academic (Lund 2012) or a good parent in relation to the schooling of one's children (e.g. Griffith and Smith 2005).

Institutional ethnography has two interconnected objectives: it challenges objectifying research *and* it offers an alternative research practice with which we can explicate objectifying processes as they happen within other institutions. It urges us to explain how such processes organize social relations of inequality, offering some experiences, discourses, practices and interests privilege, while marginalizing and silencing others. Institutional ethnography—a method of inquiry developed by Smith and her colleagues through a "process of discovery" (Smith 1987, 2005; Griffith and Smith 2005)—is characterized not by generalizable theoretical explanations, but rather by the identification of actual social relations. The focus is on how the local activities and experiences of people are hooked into sequences of action and thus involve coordination with other people who are active in other sites at other times. Further, it involves explication of how these relations are textually coordinated.

Standpoints as methodological starting points

In order to pursue the research interests discussed above, Dorothy Smith suggests that we start from a subject position, or a standpoint, within the social relations. From here we can direct attention towards questions or puzzles "'latent' in the actualities of the experienced world" (Smith 1987: 91). They will stand at a particular intersection between actual embodied work, lived experience, particular life situations, and the objectifying artificial reality of the institution that represents and distorts these (Smith 2005: 187). Smith defines work broadly as everything people *do* that takes time and effort when they take part in and produce institutional discourses, processes, and order. This definition of work does not direct our attention to any predefined notion of what counts as work, but rather extends our understanding of work to capture those activities that are not part of the institutional or textual representations.

The discovery of a disjuncture between actual experience/work activities and the virtual institutional reality from a particular standpoint becomes a methodologically significant tool for institutional ethnographers. It does not replace the formulation of research questions, but it directs our research in a manner that exposes and challenges the otherwise taken-for-granted workings of ruling that organize our consciousness and activities. However, starting from the lived experience of people does not mean that we seek to identify their 'true' inner feelings. The experiences are not in themselves the topic of interest, but they are the starting point for spelling out the social and ruling relations of which the institutions are part and which shape them, but that people are often unconscious of (Campbell 2006).

The standpoint epistemology of institutional ethnography is thus aligned with the sense of urgency that a merger, in order to be better understood, should be investigated by mapping it from different viewpoints (Meglio and Risberg 2010). The top management experience is one important standpoint from which to unravel how the social is put together, as his or her work also will be organized within social and ruling relations. But it cannot stand alone. Viewpoints of middle managers, team leaders, and employees in various positions, and perhaps even those of consultants or analysts, could be important sources for the researcher to learn from. Each person is located within the social relations as they unfold in and around M&As, but positioned differently. Various participants will not necessarily experience the process in the same way. Hence, taking a standpoint approach moves us away from the common a priori notion that top managers, due to their position, have a broader view of the organization, whereas middle managers and employees necessarily have a narrower one. Furthermore, within each of these groups there are likely to be diverging standpoints, knowledges, and experiences. In institutional ethnography we consider all perspectives limited, while at the same time playing a crucial role in making the social practice happen.

Taking this approach involves beginning from a given standpoint and continuously return-ing to it when making sense of how the objectifying institutional practices of ruling take place within M&As. Beginning from the point of view of the people whose standpoint we have taken rather than from abstract theory and concepts, we discover how the institutional shapes, downplays, or displaces their experiences; organizes and coordinates their work; places people differently in relation to the effects and outcomes of the M&A; and explicates how people, often unconsciously, take an active part in producing those effects.

Local and translocal practice

Institutional ethnography is a method of inquiry with which we can explicate how everyday life and activities are socially organized and made part of a larger ongoing social coordination. It departs from traditional or dominant forms of ethnography in that it does not confine itself to one local setting. It helps us investigate how local activities are shaped and hooked into trans-local processes—within social and ruling relations—as these exist beyond the immediate local experience. Further, in dominant forms of organizational ethnography the focus of inquiry is on the thick description of *local* practices *within* a particular work organization. While the local practices may be placed in a larger societal context, the two levels are often not brought into extended conversation and hence remain strangely separate as micro, meso, and macro "levels." As institutional ethnographers we explore the institution in order to discover how it organizes and coordinates sequences of action and the work of the people whose standpoint we have taken. Institutions are defined as "clusters of text-mediated relations organized around a specific ruling function" such as higher education or health care (DeVault and McCoy 2006: 17). Such institutions exist in specific *local contexts* and specialize in particular activities and work practices (e.g. researching, teaching, managing, or nursing).

However, local activities are also hooked into and embedded in *translocal* objectifying, stan-dardizing, and generalizing activities and ways-of-knowing. These "translocal" processes are what Dorothy Smith calls ruling relations. They are text-mediated and may be policies, laws, computer tracking systems to hold local workers accountable to central office decisions, or professional, expert, academic, or managerial discourses required in objectification. They typically operate between and across local contexts, ensuring the organization and coordination of activities across spaces and places. In explicating how experiences and activities are coordinated by textu-ally mediated institutional processes we may be able to identify categories that are indifferent to difference and at other times produce categories of difference, which are both significant for the ongoing organization and coordination of efforts to pursue ruling intentions.

Ruling relations is simultaneously a *material* and a *relational* concept. The former, because it points us towards seeing everyday work as embedded in and shaped by texts, discourses, and ide-ologies. The latter, because the standardizing, objectifying, and ruling processes only happen to the extent that people do in fact activate concepts, standards, ways of knowing, and doing—and the texts that convey these—within their particular local context. Institutional ethnography, however, takes into account that the processes within a given local setting cannot be made sense of without placing them in the larger intertextual complex of the ruling relations in which they are embedded and where they participate actively.

Texts as mediators

As indicated above, the text is central in institutional ethnography. As a material replicable arte-fact it is a mediator of the translocal in the given local setting. A material replicable text can be read at different places and different times and by various people. This makes it ethnographically possible to observe when and how the translocal objectifying ruling relations enter into our lives, hold us accountable, and shape our local practices. The process through which the institutional becomes activated locally is revealed (Smith 2005, 2006a: 66).

Certain ways of knowing that originated within *particular* historical, political, and social processes, have over time been "wrested from its original producer" and textualized, and have achieved a position which makes them harder to question and challenge (Smith 2004b, 2004c: 77). While appearing natural, neutral, and objective at a given point in time, these ways of knowing, if activated by people within a given local setting, can operate in an objectifying fashion, shaping, displacing and marginalizing other ways of knowing.

Dorothy Smith regards the relationship between the reader and the text as open-ended and ongoing. Researchers should thus explicate the sequences of action provoked by individuals engaging with particular texts in different places and at different times. Insistence that the text must be an *active and intentional* coordinator constitutes Smith's extension of George Herbert Mead's (1934) theory of symbolic interactionism. Just as the social is constituted relationally between speaker and listener, it is also constituted in the text-reader relationship (Smith 2004d): "When a text is read, watched or heard it brings consciousness into an active relationship with intentions originating beyond the local" (Smith 2001: 164–65). This does not mean that people cannot read, see, or hear these texts differently and that they do not activate and negotiate between different and alternative interpretive practices (Smith 1990b, 2005). What it does mean, however, is that all these interpretive practices have themselves been constituted within a complex of differing social and ruling relations.

As institutional ethnographers we therefore engage in the study of texts on two interconnected levels: by studying, first, the manner in which the text's intention organizes and coordinates the activities and work of actual people in particular contexts as they take up the text, read, interpret, and use it; and second, the manner in which the text itself is part of a larger intertextual complex where higher order texts—formulated elsewhere, at another time—regulate those more specialized texts that enter into our everyday lives and are activated by us (Smith 2006a).

While texts have been important as organizers for centuries, they have assumed an unprecedented role in contemporary capitalist society, in which work organizations are organized to an increasing extent in accordance with neoliberal principles: an abstract scientific economic program or theory—based on a basic belief in individual rationality, deregulation, privatization of public services, free markets, and competition—which has been converted into a political project. Through complex processes the neoliberal program has, however, been de-socialized and de-historized and its status as political denied, being instead positioned as an objective description of reality (Bourdieu, 1998). Neoliberalism constitutes what Smith calls a meta-discourse in contemporary society.

Institutional ethnography is characterized not by offering generalizable theoretical explanations, but rather by outlining the generalizing effects of ruling relations through the identification of actual, often textually coordinated, relationships and activities that define social relations in contemporary capitalist and neoliberal societies. This method stands in opposition to the vast majority of M&A literature and allows us to challenge the forms of objectification that take place in this research (Meglio and Risberg 2010). Various tools for gathering and producing data can be used to make sense of how the social is put together and textually organized. The choice of tools depends on the particular research interests and questions (Smith 2006a). There are examples of institutional ethnographies based on interviews (e.g. Griffith and Smith 1987; Griffith 1995; Weigt 2006; McCoy 2006) as well as participant observation and autoethnography (e.g. Diamond 1995; Diamond 2006; Widerberg 2006; Taber 2010).

Regardless of the tools that one chooses, the objective is to keep the institutions and texts in view from the chosen standpoint. This involves the careful explication of everyday practices—the everyday doings, sayings, and work knowledges—of the research participants, in order to find out where and when the texts and the institutional language enter into their work and what happens when they do. However, in so doing one must attempt to avoid so-called 'institutional capture' when objectifying institutional discourse subsumes or replaces experience. To avoid this, researchers must keep on asking their respondents: What does it mean? From which texts, events, and people did you learn it? How does it work for you?

Explicating objectification in M&A research

Having offered a very brief outline of institutional ethnography, we now turn to literature that has approached M&A through the lenses of organizational culture, identity, and critical inquiry. We show how and why some aspects of these studies are problematic from the perspective of institutional ethnography and offer insights into how they might have been approached differently.

Cultural perspectives on M&A

Since the mid-1980s in particular it has not been uncommon to find organizational culture used by academics and practitioners as an explanation for success and failure in M&A integration (Riad 2005). Despite the fact that there are different framings, methods, and theories ranging from "fit" approaches to more process-oriented ones, they all treat organizational culture as something real and essential for value creation in M&As. In that light, cultural clash, collision, or unsuccessful acculturation are seen to hinder effective integration and stand in the way of value creation (see e.g. Buono et al. 1985; Olie 1994; Teerikangas and Very 2006; Stahl and Voigt 2005). The impact that cultural differences—and their management, or the lack thereof—have on merger performance has attracted a huge amount of research interest, albeit with inconclusive results (Stahl and Voigt, 2005; Teerikangas and Very, 2006; Björkman et al., 2007).

Acculturation, for example, was introduced by Nahavandi and Malekzadeh (1988) as an analytical concept to capture cultural dynamics in merger implementation, distinguishing between different modes of acculturation in different forms of M&A with different strategic objectives. Cross-cultural psychological theories are used by the authors to explain the success or failure of sociocultural and managerial synergy and implementation. The authors adopt a functionalist and managerialist frame from which they build a model of variables, arguing that "the degree of congruence between acquirer and acquired oganizations' preferred modes of acculturation will affect the level of acculturative stress" (Nahavandi and Malekzadeh 1988: 79). They argue that the degree of acculturative stress ultimately depends on the acquirer's approach towards merger implementation and the extent to which cultural diversity is accepted and encouraged. The authors state "that if the members of the acquired organization were forced to change many of their practices and everyday behaviors, the acquirer is likely to be unicultural" (Nahavandi and Malekzadeh 1988: 84).

For the institutional ethnographer, Nahavandi and Malekzadeh's (1988) notions of the culture of acquirer and acquired organizations are strangely abstracted and detached; they somehow exist prior to people's activities. We are left wondering how the cultures came into being, how they were/are (re)produced and ultimately changed and integrated. Organizational members are treated as products determined by their organizational environment; they have clear and consistent preferences on the basis of which they either adapt or resist. Although the model is not a static one—the authors argue for a dynamic, process-oriented understanding of acculturation preferences—it seems that what counts as culture has been prematurely defined and separated from other social relations and practices that hook people into local historical sites and multiple complex ruling relations such as, for example, the organizational technologies and strategies that may shape and influence culture and acculturation. Furthermore, the acquiring and acquired organizations are treated as if they existed in a vacuum. No threads are drawn to the translocal relations and processes of which the organizations are both part and which shape not only the managerial practices and decisions to carry through a merger, but also the practices, positions, experiences, and choices available to the managers and employees. Finally, the managerialist bias of this model means that the focus of the research is on how managers can achieve better control of the merger by means of acculturation. Despite this perspective, the model is treated as interest- and value-free; the standpoint from which it is developed is hidden and thus the ruling relations embedded in it and also within and between the organizations are reproduced as though natural and taken for granted.

A plethora of studies have joined Nahavandi and Malekzadeh (1988) in approaching organizational culture from a functionalist and managerialist perspective. Those that have done so from an interpretive or social constructionist position—arguing against the former's static and essentialist notion of culture, and defining it instead as a result of ongoing negotiation by M&A participants at all levels (Meglio and Risberg 2010)—still seem to share the basic assumption that "organizational culture" can explain merger outcomes, thereby reproducing the theoretical and conceptual objectifying framework of positivist studies.

What strikes us overall is the manner in which the predefined notions, concepts, and theories of organizational culture are used to speak of people's experiences within merging organizations, rather than to *describe* what actually happens to people and how they, more than being produced by their culture, actively constitute it. Culture becomes instead an abstracting lens through which authors collect, organize, and interpret their data. Experiences related to the processes following a merger are analyzed not from the standpoint of the employees and managers, but from the standpoint of a particular conceptualization of organizational culture. We are entered into an objectifying and textually vested discourse where survey questions and answers as well as interview data are molded to suit the theoretical and conceptual lens. Experiences that cannot be expressed through that discourse are marginalized or disappear altogether, and conclusions are drawn in a manner that reproduces the position of organizational culture as an explanatory variable or, in some cases, a root metaphor (cf. Smircich 1983). The same applies to 'national culture,' which has become a popular tool for explaining differences and contradictions in international M&As (Olie, 1994; Calori et al., 1994; Lubatkin et al., 1998).

From the point of view of institutional ethnography, several problematic tendencies can be identified within the stream of cultural research on M&As. One is to apply essentializing assumptions, for example, that your (cultural) stance and vantage point on the merger are determined by your organizational background. This is problematic because it does not consider how organizational members take active part in and are shaped through participation in various social and ruling relations, including relations that are perhaps not formally recognized by the organization (e.g. family relations) or stretch far beyond it (e.g. the neoliberal economic and managerial principles by which organizational activities are organized). From this perspective, people are not viewed as unitary, consistent, or harmonious, but rather as shaped through participation in various social relations, making them full of inconsistencies and always in the process of becoming. Also, differences are relative in the sense that they are informed by the particular 'cultural' comparisons made.

Another related issue is the tendency to categorize people in predetermined social groups, organizations, or nations, creating predetermined dualistic distinctions between who counts as an insider and who as an outsider to a particular category. This can lead both to a lack of sensitivity towards possible overlaps between experiences of people placed in separate categories as well as to differences within categories. Institutional ethnography, by starting from people's actual activities and work-knowledge, moving from there to make sense of the ways in which everyday life is translocally or textually organized, avoids such dichotomies without losing sight of the fact that the translocal relations may look very different depending on the standpoint (within the social and ruling relations) from which they are experienced. Finally, the functionalist bias in much of M&A research, through its quest for variables and mechanisms to explain outcomes, ends up treating culture as something fixed, rather than a result of active, ongoing, and ever developing work-knowledges and social coordination by people in organizations.

To be sure, social constructionist and interpretive approaches in M&A research have sought to address these issues. In such studies, cultural manifestations are not understood to be clearly consistent or inconsistent—neither essentially harmonious nor in conflict—but ambiguous, fragmented, and in flux (Risberg, 1997). From this vantage point, singling out cultural factors that explain merger performance seems a quixotic or even an impossible task (Meglio and Risberg, 2011). Consequently, and following the development of cultural studies on organizations more generally (Weber and Dacin, 2011), research interest in M&A has turned to cultural resources and their mobilization in particular contexts and away from a focus on essential cultural characteristics and their effects on outcome factors such as performance (Vaara and Tienari, 2011).

Cultural studies of M&As have come a long way from the work of Nahavandi and Malekzadeh (1988). Vaara and Tienari's (2011) study of antenarratives or stories-in-the-making in M&As is a case in point. The study takes seriously the ways in which cultural storytelling is not a coherent endeavor but one that draws on various discursive fragments to make sense of the chaotic organizational reality that will define the experiences of organizational members during an M&A process. The authors capture this in the concept of the antenarrative. For an institutional ethnographer, however, the authors, while flagging the discursive and ideological coordination of merger legitimation or resistance—through globalist, nationalist, and Nordic antenarratives respectively—do not provide sufficient insight as to how the coordination happens. The institutional ethnographer would start from actual experience and activities in order to identify how it is negotiated with and shaped by discourses and ideologies that make the social coordination of legitimation and resistance possible.

Furthermore, although Vaara and Tienari (2011) take media and organizational documents into account, it is not clear whether, or how, those texts are in fact used by the organizational members. Explicating which material texts hooked the research participants in different locations into these textual hierarchies and translocal relations would contribute to our understanding of how discursive and ideological social coordination within and across local settings in M&As actually comes about. Taking a concrete standpoint would also allow examination of what types of experience are downplayed in the objectifying textual language and representations of the merger. As it stands, the analysis displays the research participants as characters in the researchers' narrative, a narrative that seem to have been structured around a predefined, antenarrative frame identified in media and organizational documents before the organizational members have been heard.

Despite valuable contributions to cultural studies on M&As, extant research suffers from the basic problem that it does not take the everyday experiences and activities of people as the point of departure and subject of inquiry. The analysis and contributions often remain within texts as the starting point and focus is on the discourses, narratives, or stories within texts, and texts are taken up and scrutinized from the standpoint of other texts by a researcher who speaks and understands the institutional language of those texts. The analysis and critique of power relations, for example, is not grounded in people's actual experiences but rather in discursive, paradigmatic, and theoretical standpoints. From the point of view of the institutional ethnographer, these studies may not be recognizable to the people who are themselves part of the merging organizations, offer insights useful for approaching everyday problematics within them, or offer deeper insights into the *actual* dynamics and social relations in M&As.

Identity perspectives on M&A

Via cultural studies, the processes through which identities and identification are manifest in M&As have been addressed at various levels of analysis. Most often, and similarly to the debate on cultures, this has involved treating managers and employees as groups that make up the different organizations facing the merger (Hogg and Terry, 2000; van Knippenberg et al., 2002). Some grounded, interpretive, real-time, and process-oriented—but arguably still functionalist—studies are a case in point. Clark et al. (2010), focusing on top management in a merger of formerly rival organizations, found that "a transitional identity—an interim sense held by members about what their organizations were becoming—was critical to moving the change process forward" (p. 397). This "transitional" state was found to allow top managers to work toward a new shared organizational identity. Taking a cognitive approach, and studying managerial sensemaking and sensegiving within and between the organizations engaged in a merger process, Clark et al.'s (2010) argument was that a functioning transitional identity needs to be ambiguous enough to allow multiple interpretations of what the merged organization is becoming, but "not so ambiguous as to be threateningly unfamiliar."

In a similar vein, Drori et al. (2013) suggested that what they call boundary negotiation is an engine for "identity creation" in post-merger integration. They argued that this takes place in two stages: first, boundaries are negotiated to leverage and import practices and values of the pre-merger firms and, second, boundaries become blurred as managers build on imported practices and values to impose further systems that define the post-integration firm. Dividing the process into such stages, however, renders invisible how organizational members are actively negotiating at *all times* and that what happens is a result of their participation in and interpretation of work practices. Interpretive practices are in turn shaped by each person's different participation in a complex of social and ruling relations that stretch beyond the organizational context. The institutional ethnographer would look for more clarity as to how these "imported" practices are taken up and activated in a manner that blurs boundaries, and how this process will be experienced differently depending on the standpoint from which it is studied.

Both Clark et al. (2010) and Drori et al. (2013) seem to argue that senior managers are gradually able to leave the past behind and identify with the new merged entity. Despite the fact that both articles display some sensitivity towards the complexities and multi-leveled nature of the merger process and post-merger identity formation, there are some problems from the perspective of the institutional ethnographer. Clark et al. (2010) claim that they apply "grounded theory" in their data analysis. While as a point of departure this approach—which relies, at least initially, on "the informant's own language" and on "naturally" emerging themes—would seem to respond to our call for starting the research from participant experience, it does not go far enough. Within grounded theory it is still in the end up to the researcher to generate the "overarching concepts relevant to the merger process" (Clark et al. 2010: 407–08). From the institutional ethnographer's perspective, what happens in such grounded theory is that the researchers convert their own impressions into concepts or analytical dimensions at the risk of displacing diverging perspectives. The researchers replace the ongoing social organization that produces difference with an interpretive scheme that they have developed. While it is entirely possible for participants to point in other directions with their doings or sayings and thus towards experiences that fall outside the analytical dimensions or scheme, which in this case are "the context of identity destabilization, sources of identity inertia, transitional identity, and enablers of identity change" (Clark et al. 2010: 408), the risk is that whatever is said will be interpreted through these dimensions and that which falls outside the scheme will not be accorded textual representation.

In both Clark et al. (2010) and Drori et al. (2013) the managerial bias entails the risk that organizational identity will be treated as something that exists, it would seem, independently of the people who work to interpret and activate it. Paradoxically, identity exists independently of those who engage in the ongoing social coordination that leads to its (re)production or breakdown. The scheme also excludes how people (be they employees or managers of the merging organizations) are differently positioned in terms of speaking the language of change, integration, and post-merger identity. Finally, while Clark et al. (2010), for example, pay attention to "interorganizational dynamics," the institutional ethnographer would emphasize that these processes and dynamics happen within and across a larger context of social relations and translocally operating ruling relations that shape the change process and, in turn, the positions of the organizations and participants in relation to it.

Further, Maguire and Phillips (2008) introduce the notion of institutional trust in M&As, taking a longitudinal perspective on the subject matter. They focus on how issues of organizational identity and identification contribute to the loss of institutional trust—the trust that members have in their organization—among a group of employees. On the basis of their study, they suggest that this involves two mechanisms. First, the ambiguity surrounding the identity of the newly merged organization can undermine trust. Second, over time, as ambiguity is reduced, those employees who are strongly identified with their legacy organization may continue to experience low institutional trust because they do not identify with the new organization.

In this study we again see the objectifying tendency that renders invisible the experiences and work required of employees to enable organizational identity and identification as well as "institutional trust" in the merger. The problem with Maguire and Phillips's (2008) study from the point of view of the institutional ethnographer is that data generation (interviews and interpretations) is structured around the concepts of identity, identification, and trust. While there is nothing wrong per se with having a directed research interest, the problem is that the authors seem to replace actual doings and sayings with such concepts: making the actual accountable to the discursive, not vice versa. Furthermore, the authors explicitly mention that they have only interviewed and analyzed employees who were identified by the senior managers as having a lack of trust in their organization after the merger (Maguire and Phillips 2008: 381). While seemingly studying institutional trust from the perspective of employees, the problem is that the research design, and what counts as identification and trust, and which work-knowledges are relevant for understanding the organizational problems, comes to be defined by the managers (and the researchers) rather than by the employees, who may or may not experience a disjuncture between their lived experiences and the managerial and institutional representations of them.

In contrast to studies implying that people leave their legacy organization behind to identify with the new merged entity—or, as in Maguire and Phillips's (2008) study, fail to do so—some extant research suggests that a dual process is at play in the merger context. Stakeholders such as managers and employees are argued to *both* cling to the past *and* work for a common future as they struggle to make sense of the unfolding merger (Ailon-Souday and Kunda 2003; Vaara et al. 2003, 2005, 2007; Vaara and Tienari 2011). Identities and identification are depicted in these studies as dynamic, on-going, and negotiated—contingent on the available cultural and discursive resources—rather than as simple either–or questions.

The intriguing ethnography of Ailon-Souday and Kunda (2003) offers a view of how "Israeli national identity" is defined and enacted through "boundary work" by employees and managers in a merger with an American company. This takes place in relation to a common globalized and Americanized identity forced on the organization by the merger. In contrast, the institutional ethnographer might have studied from a particular standpoint how other identities such as gender, class, age, or religion affect the participants' position in relation to the "Israeli national identity," the "boundary work" they do to uphold it, and the particular disjunctures and problematics that they face while doing so. Further, the institutional ethnographer would have looked at the role of texts in hooking the local social relations into translocal objectified social relations. The Americanization of the Israeli organization might have been studied by looking at how it was mediated via the types of organizational texts that create the basis for social coordination and organization, not only of translation, adaptation, and compliance, but also, as in this case, of resistance.

Critical perspectives on M&A

Although mergers and acquisitions may have fundamental implications for societies, communities, and people, explicitly critical analyses of M&As are still scarce. The study of Vaara et al. (2005), focusing on the choice of corporate language as a question of power and politics in an international merger, is an example. The authors used Clegg's (1989) "circuits of power" framework and pointed to the multifaceted implications of corporate language policies in international M&As. Vaara et al. (2005) found that language skills became empowering or disempowering resources in organizational communication; such skills were associated with professional competence and led to the creation of new social networks. Language also became an essential element in the construction of international confrontation. It led to a construction of superiority and inferiority between the counterparts in the merger and reproduced post-colonial identities in the merged organization. The analysis also illustrated how language policies lead to the reification of post- and neocolonial structures of domination.

In the case of Vaara et al.'s (2005) study, the institutional ethnographer may have started explicitly from the standpoint of someone disadvantaged in relation to the new language policy and worked from there to discover how specialized institutional texts related to the corporate language enter into and organize the work of people, thereby creating a form of social organization that locates people differently. Further, these specialized texts would be located more systematically in a larger intertextual hierarchy of ruling relations that have provided some languages with a favorable position in relation to others in the particular local context. While activation of the notion of "post- and neocolonial structures" may be of relevance for understanding these hierarchies and the social organization, the institutional ethnographer would constantly return to relations between people that take place through the webs of practices of which they are part. Speaking of structures has a sterile cling to it. It ignores the fact that structures are not simply out there, but are the outcomes of the ongoing activities of people located in time and space. In institutional ethnography, people would be studied as entangled in post- and neocolonial ruling relations, rather than located in structures.

Drawing from feminist organization theory, in turn, Tienari (2000) studied a domestic merger from a gender perspective. He illustrated how women became marginalized in the merger process and typically ended up in less attractive managerial positions than men. He also showed how the status of feminized management positions declined over time. His study thus brought to the fore how the merger process contributed to the (re)production of gender-based segregation in the new organization. For the institutional ethnographer, Tienari's (2000) study poses some problems in that it starts by identifying and categorizing types of female employees-turned-managers. The risk is that such predefined categorization will obscure internally diverging experiences or, indeed, ignore the convergence of experiences across the defined types. Once again, the actual is held accountable to the theoretical discourse and categorization, while the theoretical discourse is not held accountable to the actual lived experience of people.

Tienari et al. (2005) elaborated on the findings of the earlier study with a focus on a cross-border merger. They explored how male executives explained away the exclusion of women from the top echelons of the organization in processes of internationalization. Among other things, their study brought to the fore how gender intersects with nationality in such processes and how understandings of women's family responsibilities serve as an excuse for excluding them from top management (Calás and Smircich, 1993). From the perspective of institutional ethnography, this study could have taken a step further by trying to make sense of how such segregation, experiences, and explanations are organized by various ideological codes and institutional discourses. These exist and are activated within particular local settings but are often hooked into translocal objectifying ways of knowing and organizing, for example, the nuclear family and motherhood, which may differ across national borders, but also be similar.

Further, Tienari et al.'s (2005) focus was on similarities and differences across the Nordic countries. The Nordic welfare state model, and the laws and regulations put in place to further the dual-earner family model, could be placed within a larger hierarchy of ruling relations related to the EU and OECD that shape and lead to changes within that model. All this may help provide a map of the social and ruling relations that bring about, shape, and legitimate certain practices in organizations. Institutional ethnography is not about finding explanations for the segregation practices per se, but more about providing a form of cartography from which women (in this case), could begin to see how the experience of losing status and being marginalized and excluded is socially organized translocally in ways that are not always plain to see.

Eero Vaara and Janne Tienari—two of the authors—engaged in reflecting upon how they as white middle-aged men established rapport with the male top managers in the interviews, co-producing their accounts and stories. Their colleague Susan Meriläinen, a female feminist professor, provided an outsider's interpretation of Vaara and Tienari's interpretations (Tienari et al. 2005). She challenged their assumptions and interpretations of top managers' talk, and offered an alternative set of assumptions and interpretations. However, the institutional ethnographer might have taken a further step in reflecting upon the 'insider' relation between the two male professors and the top managers. Indeed, not only the sharing of certain social positions—being white middle-class males—may have blinded the researchers to institutional capture (Smith 2005). In addition, although they took a critical approach to gendered managerial practices, Vaara and Tienari's status as professors of business studies makes them highly familiar with the institutional language of business and management. This can make it difficult for them to get beyond the particular language and elicit experience-based descriptions. This arguably applies to Meriläinen who is also a business studies professor. Researchers tend to stay in the world of the professional language they are familiar with, which can then hide the standpoint from which it is spoken and ultimately lead to research that reproduces ruling relations.

Why use institutional ethnography to study M&A?

We argue that institutional ethnography offers a fruitful alternative method of inquiry for research on M&As. Unlike some conventional ethnographic approaches, institutional ethnography does not explicate everyday life and activities in a dualistic fashion that places the particular local setting within a larger macro-context (Marcus 1995). Indeed, creating such a dichotomy is in itself objectifying and hides the manner in which people across various localities work actively to coordinate and concert practices that (re)produce what we recognize as global institutions or what Dorothy Smith calls translocal relations. The translocal ruling relations themselves grow out of particular local social relations, and it is only through work done across various localities that they are (re)produced—and resisted. Smith's theorizations, according to which the text hooks the local into the translocal social relations, makes what are usually ascribed to abstract and objectifying theories about "the system," "the structure," "the patriarchy," "the political," "the economic," "the national," or "the cultural" observable in the local. In its unique way, institutional ethnography challenges the dualism between micro-macro and structure-action, which is often problematic within social sciences.

Although there are certain commonalities, institutional ethnography is not identical to multi-sited ethnography, which also challenges the local-global duality and looks at how such things as material artefacts, metaphors, plots/stories/allegories, biographical narrative structure, and conflicts travel and create cultural formations across multiple sites (Marcus 1995). These two ethnographical approaches hold very different epistemological positions in relation to the question of standpoint and experience. The object of study also differs slightly. Multi-sited ethnography is interested in cultural formations, whereas institutional ethnography focuses more on how work-knowledge—cultural and social practices—is shaped within institutional, objectifying ways of knowing. Institutional ethnography offers a systematic way to understand *how* people connect and take part in sequences of action across sites. Smith's theorization of material, replicable, and active texts is crucial here.

Institutional ethnography begins from a particular standpoint and the issues and problems that originate when experiences are distorted or silenced in the institutional representation of particular experiences or activities (Griffith and Smith 2005) rather than from a standpoint within (objectifying) theory and theoretical discourse. This opens up possibilities for making inquiries that will make a difference in the everyday lives of people. However, institutional ethnography is not identical to participatory action research. Institutional ethnography's particular understanding of power as ruling relations is central to comprehending the difference. In institutional ethnography, the participation of research subjects in defining the research focus is not considered a remedy for the exercise of power in research. From the perspective of institutional ethnography, the participation of subjects does not necessarily make the relation between them and the researchers less asymmetrical (Campbell and Gregor 2004: 68). Also, ideals of equality in the research relations may themselves be an ideological construct, constantly negotiated throughout the research process between researcher and research subjects as well as other research relations and responsibilities, and may at times be unachievable (see e.g. Wolf 1996; Campbell and Gregor 2004; Homanen 2012). However, the two approaches join hands insofar as they consider knowledge to be built from a standpoint and that knowledge production with and for people involves attending to and taking seriously the subject positions and relations between researcher and research participant.

We have spent quite a bit of space in this chapter explaining how institutional ethnography considers the subject as molded within social and ruling relations. But how does institutional ethnography differ from the "Foucauldian" analysis of power and the shaping of subjects? Dorothy Smith has critiqued not Michel Foucault himself, but the many applications of his notion of discourse for ignoring the active subject; that is, for disregarding the subjects who take up, use, and (re)produce the concepts and notions distributed by the discourses. Indeed, Smith makes clear that the notion of discourse, as spelled out by Foucault (1970), is a central aspect of ruling relations. In this regard institutional ethnography does not depart from Foucauldian discourse analysis. It, too, investigates how discourses become naturalized, assume a position of truth so that they cannot easily be contested, and organize the knowledge and activities of people (Riad 2005; Scott 2003).

Institutional ethnography, however, places the subject experience and activity differently than Foucault (1970) who arguably sees experience as something that is *done to us* rather than *by us* in a particular place and at a particular time. As experience is always in the process of becoming, it does not provide a useful entry point for research. We should instead start from an *event* which offers us a glimpse into and a starting point for investigating the taken-for-granted (Raffnsøe, et al. 2009). Unlike in a Foucauldian approach, the focus is not on historical processes that are dominating concepts and "a large scale conversation in and through texts" (DeVault and McCoy 2006). That is, research is not limited to "the exploration of the construction of and relations between discourses and discursive practices . . . that construct the subjectivity [of a given group of individuals]" (Satka and Skehill 2012: 194, 199). Institutional ethnography suggests that our knowledge of the social should be grounded in and begin from the everyday problems, issues, and disjunctures experienced by socially situated people. It holds that we can gain entrance into the taken-for-granted order of things via peoples' experiences of engaging with and activating texts and ruling relations. The disjuncture arises when a particular institutional discourse cannot be used to express an experience and that experience is thereby silenced:

> Speaking from experience speaks from the only site of consciousness—in an individual's own living, and hence as it is, and must be, embedded and active in social relations and organization that are not contained in what people can speak of directly. Experience, as spoken, is always social and always bears its social organization. A sociology for people proposes to explore from experience but goes beyond it, beginning in the living as people can speak of it rather than in the pre-givens of theoretically designed discourse. Discourse itself, and other dimensions of the objectified organization of corporations, government, professions, etc., are themselves understood as being "in the living" and hence investigatable as people's actual practices. . . . This is a social ontology not of meaning but of concerting of activities that actually happen.
>
> *(Smith 2004d: 96–97)*

Institutional ethnography draws explicitly from ethnomethodology, symbolic interactionism, Marxist epistemology, and social phenomenology. Preserving subjects as agents and active participants in the social and ruling relations does not lose sight of divergence and difference. Rather, it becomes the point of departure for making sense of how difference is coordinated and "generates divergence in coordinated human interaction" (Satka and Skehill 2012: 199). Importantly, institutional ethnography not only allows for investigating M&As in real-time from multiple perspectives (Meglio and Risberg 2010), but also demands that the researcher *take sides* in the study—it is an explicitly political mode of inquiry (Campbell and Gregor 2004; Smith 2005) that is in our view direly needed in studying M&As.

Conclusion

In this chapter, we have responded to Meglio and Risberg's (2010) call for methodological rejuvenation of M&A studies. We have offered institutional ethnography, developed by Dorothy Smith and her colleagues, as an alternative method of inquiry for M&A research and suggested that it avoids the pitfalls of objectification and thereby provides an opportunity to appreciate the everyday experience of people in merging organizations in new ways. Meglio and Risberg (2010) argue that the study of M&As has been dominated by objectifying approaches that are overtly reliant on the abstracted accounts of managerial respondents. Their criticism is targeted in particular at positivist, functionalist, and managerialist studies of M&As. We argue that interpretive and social constructionist M&A research also relies on abstract language based on organizational texts to describe the complex processes of merging. At the same time, these studies draw from particular theories and concepts (and not others) that provide the lens through which data are produced, interpreted, and analyzed. As a result the dominant position of particular objectifying theoretical frameworks, and the assumptions on which they are based, are reproduced and remain unchallenged in making sense of M&A.

Institutional ethnography provides a method of inquiry by which we can *challenge the processes of objectification as they happen* within research. It also allows us to explicate objectifying processes as they take place in institutions and in organizational contexts, such as those in and around an M&A. It does this by suggesting that we begin our inquiry not from objectifying and abstract theories, but from a standpoint in the everyday life of people, and specifically from the problems and issues faced by people who stand at a particular intersection between actual embodied everyday work, lived experience, particular life situations, and the objectifying reality of the institution that represents and distorts these. From those problematics and disjunctures we move to understand how everyday experience is shaped within social relations, how those social relations are hooked into local activities and practices as they happen and are shaped by translocal ruling relations through people's engagement with various forms of material, replicable, and active texts.

In sum, institutional ethnography can offer M&A scholars a fruitful vantage point from which to focus on how certain ways of knowing and doing achieve an unchallengeable and unquestionable position; how these ways of knowing in everyday activities are sometimes dominant and at other times resisted; how these ways of knowing and doing work for some people and not for others and thereby come to organize patterns of inclusion and exclusion; and how the texts (and the discourses, ideologies, institutional logics, etc., conveyed by them) that organize employees and managers and hold them accountable lose sight of actual everyday work activities and with what consequences.

References

Ailon-Souday G. and Kunda, G. (2003) "The local selves of global workers: The social construction of national identity in the face of organizational globalization," *Organization Studies*, 24: 1073–96.

Björkman, I., Stahl, G., and Vaara, E. (2007) "Impact of cultural differences on capability transfer in acquisitions: The mediating roles of capability complementarity, absorptive capacity, and social integration," *Journal of International Business Studies*, 38: 658–72.

Bourdieu, P. (1998) "The essence of neoliberalism," *Le Monde Diplomatique*, 8 December.

Buono, A.F., Bowditch, J.L., and Lewis, J.W. (1985) "When cultures collide: The anatomy of a merger," *Human Relations*, 38: 477–500.

Calás, M. and Smircich, L. (1993) "Dangerous liaisons: The 'feminine-in-management' meets 'globalization,'" *Business Horizons*, March–April: 73–83.

Calori, R., Lubatkin, M., and Véry, P. (1994) "Control mechanisms in cross-border acquisitions: An international comparison," *Organization Studies*, 15: 361–79.

Campbell, M.L. (2006) "Institutional ethnography and experience as data," in Smith, D. (ed.), *Institutional Ethnography as Practice*, New York: Rowman & Littlefield Publishers.

Campbell, M.L. and Gregor, F. (2004) *Mapping Social Relations: A Primer in Doing Institutional Ethnography*, Lanham, MD: AltaMira Press.

Cartwright, S., Teerikangas, S., Rouzies, R., and Evered-Wilson, E. (2012) "Methods in M&A: A look at the past, and the future, to forge a path forward," *Scandinavian Journal of Management*, 28: 95–106.

Chio, V.C. (2005) *Malaysia and the Development Process: Globalization, Knowledge Transfers and Postcolonial Dilemmas*, New York: Routledge.

Chio, V.C. (2008) "Transfers, training and inscriptions: The production of modern market citizens in Malaysia," *Critical Perspectives on International Business*, 4: 166–88.

Clark, S.M., Gioia, D.A., Ketchen, D.J., and Thomas, J.B. (2010) "Transitional identity as a facilitator of organizational identity change during a merger," *Administrative Science Quarterly*, 55: 397–438.

Clegg, S.R. (1989) *Frameworks of Power*, London: Sage.

DeVault, M.L. and McCoy, L. (2006) "Institutional ethnography: Using interviews to investigate ruling relations," in Smith, D. (ed.), *Institutional Ethnography as Practice*, New York: Rowman & Littlefield Publishers.

Diamond, T. (1995) *Making Gray Gold: Narratives of Nursing Home Care*, Chicago, IL: University of Chicago Press.

Diamond, T. (2006) "Where did you get that fur coat, Fern? Participant observation in institutional ethnography," in Smith, D. (ed.), *Institutional Ethnography as Practice*, Oxford: Rowman & Littlefield Publishers.

Drori, I., Wrzesniewski, A., and Ellis, S. (2013) "One out of many? Boundary negotiation and identity formation in postmerger integration," *Organization Science*, 24: 1717–41.

Foucault, M. (1970) *The Order of Things: An Archeology of the Human Sciences*, London: Tavistock.

Griffith, A. (1995) "Multiculturalism as ideology: A textual analysis," in Campbell, M. and Manicom, A. (eds.), *Knowledge, Experience and Ruling Relations: Studies in the Social Organization of Knowledge*, Toronto: University of Toronto Press.

Griffith, A. and Smith, D. (1987) "Constructing cultural knowledge: Mothering as discourse," in Gaskell, J. and McLaren, A. (eds.), *Women and Education: A Canadian Perspective*, Calgary: Detselig.

Griffith, A. and Smith, D. (2005) *Mothering for Schooling (Critical Social Thought)*, New York: Routledge.

Hogg, M.A. and Terry, D.J. (2000) "Social identity and self-categorization processes in organizational contexts," *Academy of Management Review*, 25: 121–40.

Homanen, R. (2012) "Reflecting on work practices: Possibilities for dialogue and collaborative knowledge production in institutional ethnography," in Phillips, L., Kristiansen, M., Vehviläinen, M., and Gunnarsson, E. (eds.) *Knowledge and Power in Collaborative Research: A Reflexive Approach*, London: Routledge.

Lubatkin, M., Calori, R., Véry, P., and Veiga, J. (1998) "Managing mergers across borders: A two nation test of nationally bound administrative heritage," *Organization Science*, 9: 670–84.

Lund, R. (2012) "Publishing to become an 'ideal academic': An institutional ethnography and feminist critique," *Scandinavian Journal of Management*, 28: 218–28.

Maguire, S. and Phillips, N. (2008) "'Citibankers' at Citigroup: A study of the loss of institutional trust after a merger," *Journal of Management Studies*, 45: 372–401.

Marcus, G.E. (1995) "Ethnography in/of the world system: The emergence of multi-sited ethnography," *Annual Review of Anthropology*, 24: 95–117.

McCoy, L. (1998) "Producing 'what the deans know': cost accounting and the restructuring of postsecondary education," *Human Studies*, 21: 395–418.

McCoy, L. (2006) "Keeping the institution in view: Working with interview accounts of everyday experience," in Smith, D. (ed.), *Institutional Ethnography as Practice*, Oxford: Rowman & Littlefield Publishers.

Mead, G.H. (1934) *Mind, Self and Society: From the Standpoint of a Social Behaviorist*, Chicago, IL: Chicago University Press.

Meglio, O. and Risberg, A. (2010) "Mergers and acquisitions—time for a methodological rejuvenation of the field?," *Scandinavian Journal of Management*, 26: 87–95.

Meglio, O. and Risberg, A. (2011) "The (mis)measurement of M&A performance—a systematic narrative literature review," *Scandinavian Journal of Management*, 27: 418–33.

Nahavandi, A. and A.R. Malekzadeh (1988) "Acculturation in mergers and acquisitions," *Academy of Management Review*, 13: 79–90.

Olie, R. (1994) "Shades of culture and institutions in international mergers," *Organization Studies*, 15: 381–405.

Raffnsøe, S., Gudman-Høyer, M., and Thaning, M. (2009) *Foucault*, Gylling: Narayana Press.

Rankin, J. and Campbell, M. (2006) *Managing to Nurse: Inside Canada's Health Care Reform*, Toronto: University of Toronto Press.

Riad, S. (2005) "The power of 'organizational culture' as a discursive formation in merger integration," *Organization Studies*, 26: 1529–54.

Risberg, A. (1997) "Ambiguity and communication in cross-cultural acquisitions: Towards a conceptual framework," *Leadership & Organization Development Journal*, 18: 257–66.

Risberg, A. (2001) "Employee experiences of acquisitions," *Journal of World Business*, 36: 58–84.

Satka, M.E. and Skehill, C. (2012) "Michel Foucault and Dorothy Smith in case file research: Strange bed-fellows or complementary thinkers?," *Qualitative Social Work*, 11: 191–205.

Scott, D. (2003) "Culture in political theory," *Political Theory*, 31: 92–115.

Smircich, L. (1983) "Concepts of culture and organizational analysis," *Administrative Science Quarterly*, 28: 339–58.

Smith, D. (1987) *The Everyday World as Problematic: A Feminist Sociology*, Boston. MA: North Eastern University Press.

Smith, D. (1990a) *The Conceptual Practices of Power: A Feminist Sociology of Knowledge*, Boston, MA: North Eastern University Press.

Smith, D. (1990b) *Texts, Facts and Femininity: Exploring the Relations of Ruling*, London: Routledge.

Smith, D. (1992) "Sociology from women's experience: A reaffirmation," *Sociology Theory*, 10(1): 88–98.

Smith, D. (2001) "Texts and the ontology of organizations and institutions," *Studies in Cultures, Organizations and Societies*, 7: 159–98.

Smith, D. (2004a) "Feminist reflections on the political economy," in Smith, D. (ed.), *Writing the Social: Critique, Theory and Investigations*, Toronto: Toronto University Press.

Smith, D. (2004b) "Ideology, science and social relation: A reinterpretation of Marx's epistemology," *European Journal of Social Theory*, 7: 445–62.

Smith, D. (2004c) "The ruling relations," in *Writing the Social: Critique, Theory and Investigations*, Toronto: Toronto University Press, 73–95.

Smith, D. (2004d) "Telling the truth after postmodernism," in *Writing the Social: Critique, Theory and Investigations*, Toronto: Toronto University Press.

Smith, D. (2005) *Institutional Ethnography: A Sociology for People*, Oxford: AltaMira Press.

Smith, D. (2006a) "Incorporating texts into ethnographic practice," in Smith, D. (ed.), *Institutional Ethnography as Practice*, Oxford: Rowman & Littlefield Publishers.

Smith, D. (ed.) (2006b) *Institutional Ethnography as Practice*, Oxford: Rowman & Littlefield Publishers.

Stahl, G. and Voigt, A. (2005) "Do cultural differences matter in mergers and acquisitions? A tentative model and examination," *Organization Science*, 19: 160–76.

Stahl, G. and Voigt, A. (2005). "Impact of cultural differences on merger and acquisition performance: A critical research review and an integrative model." *Advances in Mergers and Acquisitions*, 4: 51–82.

Taber, N. (2010) "Institutional ethnography, autoethnography, and narrative: An argument for incorporating multiple methodologies," *Qualitative Research*, 10: 5–25.

Teerikangas, S. and Very, P. (2006) "The culture-performance relationship in M&A: From yes/no to how," *British Journal of Management*, 17: S31–S48.

Tienari, J. (2000) "Gender segregation in the making of a merger," *Scandinavian Journal of Management*, 16:111–44.

Tienari, J., Vaara, E., and Meriläinen, S. (2005) "Yhteisyyden rakentuminen haastattelussa," in Ruusuvuori, J. and Tiittula, L. (eds.), *Haastattelu: Tutkimus, tilanteet ja vuorovaikutus*, trans. *Construction of Togetherness in Interviews*, Tampere, Finland: Vastapaino.

Vaara, E. and Tienari, J. (2011) "On the narrative construction of MNCs: An antenarrative analysis of legitimation and resistance in a cross-border merger," *Organization Science*, 22: 370–90.

Vaara, E., Tienari, J., and Säntti, R. (2003) "The international match: Metaphors as vehicles of social identity-building in cross-border mergers," *Human Relations*, 56: 419–52.

Vaara, E., Tienari, J. and Irrmann, O. (2007) "Crafting an inter-national identity: The Nordea case," in Lerpold, Lin, Ravasi, Davide, van Rekom, Johan, and Soenen, Guillaume (eds.), *Organizational Identity in Practice*, London: Routledge.

Vaara, E., Tienari, J., Piekkari, R., and Säntti, R. (2005) "Language and the circuits of power in a merging multinational corporation," *Journal of Management Studies*, 42: 595–623.

van Knippenberg, D., van Knippenberg, B., Monden, L., and De Lima, F. (2002) "Organizational identification after a merger: A social identity perspective," *British Journal of Social Psychology*, 41: 233–52.

Weber, K. and Dacin, T. (2011) "The cultural construction of organizational life," *Organization Science*, 22: 286–98.

Weigt, J. (2006) "Compromises to carework: The social organization of mothers' experiences in the low-wage labor market after welfare reform," *Social Problems*, 53: 332–51.

Widerberg, K. (2007) "Institusjonell etnografi—en ny mulighet for kvalitativ forskning?," *Sociologi i dag*, 37: 7–28.

Widerberg, K. (2006) "Tiredness in the light of institutional ethnography," *Sociologisk Forskning*, 3: 74–82.

Wolf, D. (1996) *Feminist Dilemmas in Fieldwork*, Colorado: Westview Press Inc.

15

Merging networks

Contributions and challenges of social network analysis to study mergers and acquisitions

Nicola Mirc

Introduction

Centuries of merger and acquisition (M&A) research have allowed the development of a fairly wide-ranging understanding of organizational and managerial issues to consider and overcome when implementing a merger or acquisition. Scholars have investigated pre- and post-acquisition processes, identifying numerous factors critical to M&A performance (see Gomes *et al.* 2013 for a review). In the pre-acquisition phase, research has attempted to identify factors influencing acquisition decision-making and target selection processes. In the post-acquisition phase, the pivotal role of effective management of the integration process has become a widely accepted fact. In this regard, scholarly work has underlined the importance of considering employee reactions and commitment to, and identification with, the merged entity; cultural, strategic, and organizational compatibilities or discrepancies between acquisition partners; and further managerial decision-making on the targeting, pace and scope of integration (see Mirc 2013 for a review).

What remains far less extensively addressed is the actual state and evolution of relationships between merger partners, or between the acquiring and the acquired firms. However, the development of such relations – whether as work collaborations, means of knowledge and information transfer, the sharing of client accounts or simply reporting or hierarchical dependencies – appears crucial for effective implementation and value creation.

By the same token, it is not only the development of relations between the merging entities or organizational members that merits in-depth consideration, but also the evolution of relationships with the firms' environment. The study of business networks and network organization has become increasingly popular in management research. Looking more closely into the way that M&As may impact – or be impacted by – the structure of the business or industry network in which they take place seems therefore not only a natural but also an indispensable step.

In this chapter, I address how the method of social network analysis (SNA) enables the study of M&As from this relational, network-based perspective. By focusing on structures and patterns of relationships, SNA indeed appears a fruitful means of addressing the emergence of, and change in, inter- and intra-organizational relations in the course of M&As. I will start by introducing the method and then present studies that have used SNA to study M&As, focusing on their contributions, and on avenues for future research with this method. I then discuss the methodological challenges and limitations of SNA in the context of M&A research.

The social network approach

SNA is fundamentally about revealing relationship patterns between actors. Actors in social settings are connected through relationships that, taken together, constitute a social network. This network is social by nature, since it relies fundamentally on interactions between its parts. The primary objective of SNA is to study the properties of these relationships and of the social structure they build. In this regard, SNA is not limited to being a method or a tool, but can also be considered as deriving from a complete theoretical paradigm relating to the network as a whole system. It assumes that social structures and individual interactions are fundamentally interdependent (White 1992; Wasserman and Faust 1994; Burt 1992, 2005; see Wellman 1988 for a review of the evolution of the field). On one hand, actors' interactions are the constitutive forces through which social structure emerges. On the other hand, the social structure in which they occur has a constraining effect, so that actors are not entirely free in the way they behave and interact with each other. In other words, SNA considers that social structure emerges only from – and exists only through – the social relations that occur between the parts of the network (be they individuals, groups, firms, countries etc.), but that the way in which these parts behave and relate to each other is shaped by the structure of all relationships that form the network.

The focus is thus primarily on relationships – rather than on categorical attributes that regroup units (such as age, gender etc.) – and the way that they are structurally embedded (Granovetter 1973; Uzzi 1997). Methodologically speaking, the unit of analysis is accordingly the relationship between two actors, and not the individual actor. The type of relations (or ties) can be various, including any kind of connection that might relate two different actors. Applied to the organizational context, relationships under study can be formal or informal, internal or external, and work-related or extra-professional. Examples include business relations, hierarchical relations, work collaborations, group affiliation, communication, information exchange, kin or friendship and relations with clients, providers and competitors.

The body of social network research in management science is substantial and steadily growing (see, for instance, Borgatti and Foster 2003 for an overview). Scholars have created a sound understanding of network patterns and effects at both the intra- and the inter-organizational levels. Organizational network research has investigated various topics, which Brass et al. (2004) – in their excellent review – regroup into three different levels: interpersonal networks, inter-unit networks and inter-organizational networks. For each level, scholars are engaged in analysing the antecedents and consequences of network structures and actor relationships.

Identified drivers of interpersonal networks are, for instance, similarities between actors in terms of age, sex, education, prestige or social class (Carley 1991; Ibarra 1993; McPherson et al. 2001) – or proximity in the organizational structure induced by geographical proximity or task relatedness (Burkhardt and Brass 1990; Borgatti and Cross 2003). Interpersonal networks have been found to impact on actors' similarity in attitudes, job hunting, job satisfaction, performance and turnover (e.g. Granovetter 1973; Ibarra 1992; Krackhardt and Porter 1985; Mehra et al. 2001; Morrison 2002).

Research on inter-unit networks points out antecedents such as functional ties or organizational structures and processes as playing a significant role (Tsai 2002). Structural patterns of inter-unit networks have further been associated with performance and innovation capacities.

Units with high internal density, for instance, have been found to perform better, whereas strong ties between units promote the sharing of complex knowledge and innovativeness (e.g. Hansen 1999; Reagans and Zuckerman 2001).

Research on the antecedents of inter-organizational networks has addressed motives for firm cooperation, learning effects and the role of trust (e.g. Galaskiewicz 1985; Ebers 1997; Powell et al. 1996; Zaheer et al. 1998). On the outcome side, scholars note imitative practices, innovativeness, firm survival and performance (e.g. Ahuja 2000; Shan et al. 1994; Uzzi 1997).

Studying M&As as merging networks

The focus on relationships as the central object of analysis appears particularly relevant for the study of inter-organizational encounters, such as alliances and M&As, where the development of relationships between firms is the primary objective. Whereas alliance research has made much use of SNA as the focal method of investigation, this is less so in the field of M&As. Nonetheless, SNA has much to offer here. In this paper, I present M&A scholarly work using SNA, and give examples of possible avenues of future research where SNA could provide a fertile means of developing new perspectives and knowledge. The aim is to provide some examples for illustration, not to develop an exhaustive overview of all possible fields of application. The section is organized in three parts, addressing different stages and perspectives on M&A processes. I will start with the pre-acquisition phase and move to the post-acquisition phase, discussing two different levels: the environmental business level and the organizational level.

Influence of pre-acquisition networks on acquisition decision-making

The pre-acquisition phase and antecedents to M&A decision-making have been a prominent topic under study, notably in the field of strategy research (see, for instance, Gomes et al. 2013 for a review). One key issue addressed here is the selection of the target by the acquiring company. Scholars have pointed out various factors affecting decision-making at that stage, emphasizing economic and financial explanations above all. In these studies, acquisition decision-making is generally considered to be a rather atomistic process, occurring within the top management of the acquiring firm in a discrete manner. An alternative perspective is to think of acquisition decision-making as embedded in a much larger social and economic context, paced by how the acquiring form relates to its environment. Firms are not isolated but relational entities, subject to opportunities and constraints in their networks (Uzzi 1997).

This perspective has notably been adopted by Yang et al. (2011a, 2011b), studying the influence of network relations on M&A patterns in China and the United States. In their study, the authors explore the impact of the acquiring firm's network on the likelihood of its acquiring former alliance partners. They find strong support for the importance of relational drivers in acquisition decision-making. This shows that alliance partners who share central brokerage positions in their industry network are more likely to join in the course of an acquisition, notably if partners prioritized exploratory shared learning over 'mere' resource exploitation during the alliance. By studying behavioural factors (form of alliance learning) and relational factors (network embeddedness) as interdependent settings, the authors propose a complementary underexplored explanation of acquisition drivers.

Similarly, Vanhaverbeke et al. (2002) use a network approach to identify relational factors that impact on the decision as to whether to acquire, or to form an alliance with, a given firm. They find that prior direct ties between firms within their industry network promote subsequent acquisitions, whereas indirect ties favour the formation of strategic alliances. Further, they find that a firm's network position influences whether it will acquire or be acquired. Those firms that are more centrally located in the network of inter-firm alliances are more likely to be acquirers, whereas the more peripheral firms tend to be acquired.

The recognition of the importance of relationships in the formation of acquisitions is also at the center of Haunschild's (1993) and Beckman and Haunschild's (2002) work on interlocking directorates. The authors explore the question of whether the network of an acquirer – through the 'interlocks' it shares with other firms – has an influence on the acquisition-making process. Haunschild (1993) finds notable evidence that firms are submitted to normative and informational influences from their network partners that make them adopt an acquisition strategy based on imitation. Beckman and Haunschild (2002) analyse the effect of diversity of network partners and of their experience on the price paid for an acquisition. They point out that the more the network of a firm is heterogeneous in terms of acquisition experience and firm size, the more the focal firm is likely to pay less for an acquisition and to show higher levels of acquisition performance. Palmer *et al.* (1993) also found an association between interlocks and firms' participation in M&As.

Influences exerted by a firm's network do, however, concern not only direct business partners but also third parties involved in the acquisition process, such as consulting firms and investment banks – a topic that has recently been investigated by several (though not SNA-based) studies (Holburn and Vanden Bergh 2014; Huang *et al.* 2014). Using a social network approach, Sleptsov *et al.* (2013) study, in this regard, the influence of relationships with what they call 'information brokers' – intermediaries on acquisition decision-making. They find that relationships with multiple investment banks enhance the quality of acquisition-related information and, subsequently, acquisition performance. Firms who relied on exclusive ties with the same investment bank showed less positive performance outcomes, leading the authors to conclude that competition among external actors enhances the quality of the information and the service they provided.

From a completely different angle, D'Aveni and Kesner (1993) adopt the perspective of the target firm and study how social networks shared by executives of both firms shape target managers' motivation to respond to tender offers. They find that target managers tend to respond positively when they perceive their internal relations to be less prestigious than those developed by managers in the acquiring firm and when both firms share external connections to the same prestigious organizations externally.

So far, SNA-based studies on pre-acquisition processes have provided original insights into relational factors affecting acquisition decision-making and target selection processes. They focus on relationships such as alliance partnerships, interlocking directorates and links with external parties. Deepening these research findings with complementary studies would be an interesting endeavour. The influence of interlocking directorates, for instance, is much studied by social network scholars concerned with identifying the effects of board-of-director composition on managerial strategies in various respects (Mizruchi 1996). Boards of directors are significant because a firm's directors often sit on the boards of other firms, creating privileged inter-firm relationships that promote sharing of market information, management practices and personal contacts. They can thus be expected to play a significant role in acquisition decision-making processes; this topic still needs to be fully exploited. By the same token, scholarly comprehension of the role of external parties involved in acquisition processes – such as governments, banks and consulting firms – could be enhanced by analysing their linkage to, and influence on, the acquiring firm's acquisition strategy. Further, other types of business relations might be studied with the approach, for instance influential ties with suppliers or customers in vertical deals.

Effects of M&As on industry structures and relations with the environment

A second fertile ground for applying a social network approach to M&A research constitutes the study of effects of M&As on the business environment. In a similar way to the relational perspective developed in the previous section, which considers firms not as atomistic but as relational entities that are influenced by the networks that they are part of, SNA here aims to address the consequences of acquisitions on these very networks after a deal has been closed. This concerns industry structures as well as the direct and indirect relationships that the acquiring and acquired firms, or merged firms, hold with their environment.

Such an attempt has been made by several marketing scholars, such as Lusch *et al.* (2011), who apply SNA to investigate the impacts of M&A on the business network and, in particular, on customer relations. They observe the detrimental effects of horizontal business combinations of suppliers on downstream channel customers, decreasing their satisfaction and enhancing their likelihood of switching. Similarly, adopting an industrial marketing perspective, Anderson *et al.* (2000, 2001) address the changes in relationships with customers and suppliers induced by an acquisition. They advance the idea that management can have only limited control on the evolution of such relationships, notably because they are socially constructed and fundamentally interactive. The lack of control stems from the dyadic nature of these business ties: their existence and persistence are based on the behaviour of both parties, which is further influenced by each party's other relationships (i.e. its network).

In a working paper, Anderson *et al.* (2003: 2) underline the importance of considering:

> organisations as ongoing processes consisting of human interaction. This approach reveals that any merger or acquisition is not one clear-cut process, but consists of many ongoing, interfering sub-processes both within and between organisations. . . . Our key message is to show that connectedness in time and context, is important, and we also propose an approach, which enables its consideration.

The authors advocate adopting a social network approach to understanding M&As as contextually bounded. As they argue (Anderson *et al.* 2003: 3), M&A failure is often the result of a neglected analysis of the impact of M&As on external exchange relations:

> Although an acquisition mainly influences the dyadic relationship between the merging parties (e.g. through integration processes), this confined change often becomes connected change and changes spread in the network. A key issue for development is how actors perceive changes in the dyad and the network effects.

In a similar vein, Spedale *et al.* (2007) study factors that affect the target firm's network after an acquisition, drawing on the concept of embeddedness (Uzzi 1997). They find that acquirers' attempts to build close relationships with the target result in the dissolution or deterioration of strong ties that the target has maintained with external market actors before the acquisition. Arguing that M&A research traditionally focuses on the parent–target dyad, the authors propose focusing more straightforwardly on the impacts of acquisitions on external relationships and networks. Spedale *et al.* (2007: 1172) state that 'acquisitions are discontinuous events in the life of an organization and generate significant uncertainty and ambiguity in all its aspects, including the relational. They represent, therefore, an ideal setting for the study of network relationships and their dynamics.'

Öberg (2012) and Öberg *et al.* (2007) adopt a different approach and discuss shifts of network pictures, i.e. the way in which actors in the firm perceive changes in the firm's relationships after the deal. They show how pre-acquisition networks might radically change due to the acquisition, thus challenging managers to drastically change their perceived network picture in time.

Additional research into impacts on relationships with customers and suppliers, notably in specific industries, is required. Also, investigating M&A-induced changes to the relationships with other types of actors – such as governments, competitors and alliance partners – through a social network approach would enhance our comprehension of business environment-related factors that impact on M&A performance.

Effects of M&As on internal relations, and the evolution of ties between merger or acquisition partners

A third area of contribution of SNA concerns the study of post-acquisition integration processes. Notably, at the organizational level, SNA enables new light to be shed on integrative dynamics, apprehending them in their very essence, i.e. as emergent links between merging organizations through which resources, processes and structures can be combined. It puts the emphasis on the emergence of relationships between two entities and their members that allow synergy and integration to materialize. Moreover, from a social network perspective, post-acquisition organizational integration and its outcome can be considered inherent to the emergence of social relations between units of both firms that allow the establishment of linkages through which value is to be created. Social relations between both units appear as the main mechanisms through which resources and competencies can be shared and transferred. In other words, post-acquisition integration is – from a social network perspective – essentially rooted in the social relations and interactions that emerge between actors (individuals and units) of both firms.

During recent years, some first studies have used a social network approach to disentangle the role and evolution of social relations between acquirer and target during the post-acquisition period. In this way, Briscoe and Tsai (2011) investigate to what extent and under what conditions collaborations between partners in a law firm developed during the post-acquisition process, and so promoted integration and value creation. In particular, they study the practice of client-sharing between lawyers of the acquirer and of the two acquired law firms. They find that the characteristics of the personal network as it existed before the acquisition have a strong influence on individuals' willingness to share clients with the acquisition partner's lawyers. The authors found that individuals who collaborated strongly with others before the acquisition engaged more in collaborations with the acquisition partner, thus greatly promoting integration between the two firms. At the same time, however, their level of intra-unit collaboration decreased, so detracting from integration.

Another study, carried out by Allatta and Singh (2011), looks at the evolution of communication patterns between employees during the three years after acquisition. They observe that the period immediately following the acquisition is characterized by an increased level of communication between members of the two firms, especially if their tasks are interdependent, but that the level decreases afterwards. Employees rapidly turn back to their original communication routines, a phenomenon that the authors explain in terms of individuals' perception that there is less need to communicate with members of the acquisition partner once they have obtained information and got to know each other (and so have developed a common ground).

In a working paper, Allatta *et al.* (2010) address more closely the influence of homophily (i.e. the tendency of individuals to associate and bond with similar others) on the evolution of communication patterns after the acquisition. Their findings show that homophily has an important impact in this situation, in that individuals tend to communicate with those who share similar attributes. One dominant attribute here is company affiliation, i.e. communication flows better between individuals of the same company (who share a common history and culture) than between those of the target and the acquirer companies. Whereas such within-company homophily can be a significant barrier to post-acquisition integration, the authors also find evidence for the existence of what they refer to as 'cross-cutting circles'. These, in contrast, have a positive effect on integration: homophily based on common job group (same functional domain) and on common managerial status attenuated company-based homophily and, importantly, promoted communication across both companies – and so promoted post-acquisition integration.

My own research (Mirc 2012, 2014) on post-acquisition collaborative practices in a consultancy firm provides additional insights, relating to some of the points made by the above studies. Taking snapshots of the collaboration networks between the two firms and for each single firm (the acquisition being a symbiotic one, preserving both entities) at several points in time (before and after the acquisition), I find that group cohesion significantly hinders integration. In the acquiring firm in particular, where the internal collaboration networks were dense and cohesive (with individuals regularly collaborating with many others), individuals were much less disposed to engage in collaborations with those from the acquired firm. Homophily was actually strengthened here by the cohesiveness of the network, and thus had a strong negative impact on integration. The analysis of relationships that did emerge between employees from both firms pointed towards there being a small number of actors who engaged in such inter-firm collaborations much more extensively than others. Together with Very (Mirc and Very forthcoming), I term these individuals 'acquisition brokers', i.e. individuals who act as key people in the integration process by strongly promoting, through their relationships, cross-firm ties and integrative practices. In terms of structural characteristics, these individuals occupy particularly central positions and brokerage roles in their focal firm's network, suggesting tendencies to preferential attachment (i.e. relating preferably to prominent others). This partly mirrors the findings by Briscoe and Tsai (2011). In our study, however, these central positions were maintained and even reinforced during the post-acquisition period, suggesting effects of prestige and power gained through their integration-brokerage activities.

The identification of individuals who act at the intersection of the merging firms, and thus drive forward organizational integration, is indeed an exciting field of study that SNA enables us to explore. It sheds new light on important topics such as key people, leadership and integration managers (e.g. Angwin and Meadows 2009; Ashkenas and Francis 2000; Teerikangas et al. 2011). As Angwin and Meadows (2009) note, the choice of the leader who will be driving organizational integration is critical. A more substantial knowledge of the relational profiles of such leaders could be a means of enhancing our understanding of the way this leadership is exerted and made effective.

In a similar vein, an analysis of network effects of the departure of individuals after the acquisition could complement studies on the effects of top management turnover (TMT). Findings remain contradictory, with some scholars suggesting that TMT has a negative effect on performance (Cannella and Hambrick 1993; Krishnan et al. 1997) and others suggesting that it has a positive one (Anslinger et al. 1996). Analysing the effects of TMT more locally (in terms of network positions and flows) by focusing on specific individuals might help inform this debate.

The analysis of flows inside networks can further be of interest in investigating knowledge transfer or communication processes. Many scholars have identified effective knowledge transfer as being critical in post-acquisition integration (e.g. Ranft and Lord 2000; Puranam et al. 2006). However, there is limited knowledge on the actual processes through which knowledge is transferred in M&As (exceptions being Empson 2001 and Greenberg and Guinan 2004). SNA allows the knowledge flow to be traced in a very direct way and enables the role and functioning of informal networks in the process to be grasped (Ranft and Lord 2000); this topic has received significant attention by SNA scholars (e.g. Cross *et al.* 2001; Cross *et al.* 2002). By the same token, focusing on individual contributions in post-acquisition innovation processes through a network lens potentially provides new insights into relational attributes (such as social status and centrality) that have been found to play influential roles (Paruchuri *et al.* 2006). As I have attempted to demonstrate, many possible contributions of applying SNA to M&A research are conceivable. While I have listed only a few, many other potential areas of investigation are certainly possible. A growing number of studies has started to exploit this potential, and has provided new perspectives on pre-acquisition and post-acquisition processes.

While having proved to be a powerful tool, regarding not only M&A studies also but inter-organizational research in general, SNA also presents some challenges and limitations. Reviewing general requirements for data collection and processing, I will address some of these challenges in the context of M&A research. Readers who wish to go further are invited to consult one of the numerous SNA manuals dedicated to in-depth discussions of methodological implications (e.g. Borgatti *et al.* 2013; Scott 2013; Wasserman and Faust 1994).

Methodological challenges and limits

Network data can be collected from either primary or secondary sources through different means such as questionnaires, archival records, interviews and observations. As the relationships being studied can be of various types, the main issue concerns building a research design. This should allow the gathering of data that provides information about the relationship between actors and not only about the actor as an individual (for example, in terms of attributes, opinions or behaviour – as in standard questionnaires used in social science).

One method regularly used to gather primary data is the network survey. Network surveys ask actors directly about the relationships they are involved in. Two different methods are commonly used in this regard. The first provides the respondents with a list of all members of the network being studied, asking them to indicate all the people they are themselves connected to (according to the type of relationship specified for each question – see, for instance, Mirc 2012). This technique has the advantage that it diminishes the risk of a bias induced by memory issues, but necessitates that the researcher is able to establish the boundaries of the network (i.e. which actors are to be considered part of the network studied, and which are excluded) and that the sample does not exceed a certain size (which would make the process of sifting through the names too laborious). If a sample cannot be determined with sufficient certainty or the sample is too large, an alternative technique is the so-called 'roster' format, or 'free recall' approach. Here, no complete list of potential actors is provided, but respondents are asked to name a certain number of people to whom they relate (see, for instance, studies carried out by Friedkin (1984) and Moore (1979) on community elites).

Secondary data can be obtained through archives or databases. In their study on post-acquisition collaborative practices in a law firm, Briscoe and Tsai (2011) develop a research design based on company records of billable hours. These records, available for each partner, provide information about who worked with whom on a given case (or project) for each year. Company records of personnel data and evaluations from partners were also used. Allatta and Singh (2011) and Allatta *et al.* (2010) use a different approach, using email logs to collect relational data. Over a period of approximately three years, the researchers extracted email logs from all employees every four months. This data provided them with information on who exchanges emails with whom, to what extent and during which period. In addition, actor–attribute data was collected regarding the division they worked in, their job title, their job group and their age, gender and length of employment.

Contrary to the use of secondary data as used in these two examples, a certain bias has to be acknowledged when collecting primary data through network surveys. As data is provided directly by actors, the observed network might be said to be more subjective, in that it reflects the network as it exists in the minds of the actors involved. This is not the case when making use of accounting data or formalized records on particular practices (such as email logs). However, what might be considered here is the overall purpose pursued by the research design. The study may be aimed at revealing structural properties and constraints, and the way these influence actors' actions and attitudes (for instance, whether actors tend to relate to similar others). If we consider that actors' behaviour is determined by the way that they evaluate their environment, the fact that the network reflects not an objective but a perceived reality is then of great interest. In addition, many types of relationships – especially informal ones – might not be easily detectable in archives or databases. Gathering data directly from the actors involved might thus be the only option to obtain network records.

A second challenge of SNA is that the method requires complete data. For a given population, or at least the defined sample, relational data for each actor is needed in order to be able to analyse network structures in a reliable way. This means that the researcher has to be able to collect data on the relationships of every member of the network. Each piece of missing information risks distorting analysis of the overall network structure in a significant way. For instance, if data on an important network broker is missing, analysis might be strongly biased. This methodological constraint is a major drawback of network studies; it is minimized when company records are used, assuming that these are complete. Surveys, on the other hand, necessitate a very high (if not exhaustive) response rate, which can be difficult to obtain. In the situation of a merger or acquisition – where people are preoccupied with their own employment, career development and additional work load brought about by reorganization – respondents might be reluctant or too busy to provide information on their relationships with colleagues. This problem is amplified in longitudinal research settings, where individuals are repeatedly asked to respond to a survey. In addition, employees might leave the firm between two observation periods, which enhances the risks of missing data. Further, people might tend to overstate their network position, the latter being tightly linked to representations of power and influence in an organization. As M&As may induce uncertainties about potential lay-offs or future career development, employees might thus 'embellish' the representation of their network and report relationships that make them look more powerful or influential than is actually the case.

These considerations bring us to point out an important limitation to SNA when carried out in a strictly structural manner. A rigid focus on structural dynamics does not allow proper analysis of M&A processes, especially organizational ones. In other words, research that highlights only the transformation of social networks in structural terms would not be sufficient. It might be usefully coupled with other non-structural data, such as qualitative interviews, in order to be able to develop a comprehensive picture of integrative processes. Simply to highlight network properties at one or more points in time does not enhance our understanding of what drives individuals or organizations from one state to the other. For instance, factors such as culture or identification cannot be grasped through relational data. On topics where human interactions and representations are important, it is therefore vital to combine structural with non-structural data in order to highlight the actual processes and factors explaining the observed shifts at the structural level.

Conclusion

The aim of this chapter was to discuss the potential contributions of SNA to the study of M&As. As I argued – and demonstrated using existing literature – SNA allows M&As to be approached as contextual and relational phenomena, where relationships between firms, groups and individuals influence pre- and post-acquisition processes. M&As are fundamentally about linking two organizations, and their assets, processes and people. SNA enables the explicit highlighting of the patterns, emergence and evolution of such inter-organizational links.

In the field of M&A research, SNA has been applied in different ways. Three bodies of research can be distinguished. The first concerns the study of the impact of a firm's network on M&A decision-making and target selection, putting the emphasis on the influence of pre-acquisition relationships and external parties. The second line of research focuses on the post-acquisition phase, and tries to comprehend the effects of M&As on firms' business networks. Recently, a third line of research has emerged, using SNA to address organizational integration dynamics. The purpose is to disentangle the effects on firms' internal ties, notably between individuals of both firms, and the way that these ties evolve during the integration process. Nonetheless, relatively few studies on M&A processes have made use of SNA, although there are many possible avenues for future research.

On an industry or business level, SNA enables more direct exploration of the impacts of a firm's network on acquisition decision-making on the one hand, and of the impacts of M&As on the firm's business environment on the other, highlighting changes in relationships with suppliers, clients and competitors that have so far been only partly explored. The study of business networks and network organization has indeed become increasingly popular in management research. Looking more closely at how M&As may impact, or be impacted by, the structure of the business or industry network in which they take place seems, therefore, not only a natural but also an indispensable step.

At the organizational level, changes to organizational processes and inter-individual relationships in each firm induced by M&As can be analysed in a more tangible way. SNA allows group processes to be revealed in a very concrete way, highlighting phenomena such as cooperative practices, knowledge exchange and the role of key people. Many other topics are conceivable, such as the evolution of hierarchical relationships, information channels, work processes, financial flows, the effects of top management and employee turnover. Also, in research concerned with the role of trust, culture sharing, identification processes and employees' resistance to change, the relational approach might be a fruitful means to understand these issues from a different perspective. For instance, how do cultural differences translate into group segmentation/group cohesion? How do relationships of trust develop and how do they influence the emergence of inter-organizational links? And how do network structures influence employees' identification processes?

SNA allows researchers to go beyond the focus on individual or organizational factors as two independent settings. The network approach – which considers individual behaviour and structural properties as fundamentally interdependent – offers a multi-level perspective on M&A integration processes, enabling researchers to address interactions between individual factors at the micro level, and organizational factors at the macro level (Angwin and Vaara 2005; Mirc 2012).

Of course, SNA presents challenges and limitations in terms of the constraints imposed on data collection and processing. The necessity of collecting complete data sets is notably a significant barrier, which might be especially important in the context of M&A research. But as shown by the related studies, this barrier is possible to overcome. Scholars maintain the call for more comprehensive studies and explicitly point out that a focus on connectivity between merging organizations could be a means to achieving this endeavor (Angwin and Vaara 2005). Although challenging, studying M&A through the lens of SNA constitutes a promising and captivating ground to respond to that call.

References

Ahuja, G. (2000) 'Collaboration networks, structural holes, and innovation: a longitudinal study', *Administrative Science Quarterly*, 45: 425–55.

Allatta, J. and Singh, H. (2011) 'Evolving communication patterns in response to an acquisition event', *Strategic Management Journal*, 32: 1099–118.

Allatta, J., Iyengar, R. and Van den Bulte, C. (2010) 'Social network dynamics after a corporate acquisition', *Academy of Management Annual Meeting*, Montreal.

Anderson, H., Havila, V. and Salmi, A. (2001) 'Can you buy a business relationship? On the importance of customer and supplier relationships in acquisitions', *Industrial Marketing Management*, 30: 575–86.

Anderson, H., Andersson, P., Havila, A. and Salmi, A. (2000) 'Business network dynamics and M&As: structural and processual connectedness', *16th IMP Conference*, Bath, 7–9 September.

Anderson, H., Andersson, P., Salmi, A., Halinen-Kaila, A., Havila, V., Holström, J. and Vaara, E. (2003) 'M&A processes in business networks: managing connectedness', Work-in-progress paper submitted to the *19th Annual IMP Conference*, Lugano, 4–6 September.

Angwin, D.N. and Vaara, E. (2005), Introduction to the special issue, 'Connectivity in merging organizations: beyond traditional cultural perspective', *Organization Studies*, 26: 1445–53.

Angwin, D.N. and Meadows, M. (2009) 'The choice of insider or outsider top executives in acquired companies', *Long Range Planning*, 42: 359–89.

Anslinger, P.L., Copeland, T.E. and Thomas, E. (1996) 'Growth through acquisitions: a fresh look', *Harvard Business Review*, 74: 126–33.

Ashkenas, R.N. and Francis, S.C. (2000) 'Integration managers: special leaders for special times', *Harvard Business Review*, 78: 108–16.

Beckman, C.M. and Haunschild, P.R. (2002) 'Network learning: the effects of partners' heterogeneity of experience on corporate acquisitions', *Administrative Science Quarterly*, 47: 92–124.

Borgatti, S.P. and Cross, R. (2003) 'A relational view of information seeking and learning in social networks', *Management Science*, 49: 432–45.

Borgatti, S.P. and Foster, P.C. (2003), 'The network paradigm in organizational research: a review and typology', *Journal of Management*, 29: 991–1013.

Borgatti, S.P., Everett, M.G. and Johnson, J.C. (2013) *Analyzing Social Networks*, London: Sage Publications.

Brass, D.J., Galaskiewicz, J., Greve, H.R., and Tsai, W. (2004), 'Taking stock of networks and organizations: a multilevel perspective', *Academy of Management Journal*, 47: 795–817.

Briscoe, F. and Tsai, W. (2011) 'Overcoming relational inertia: how organizational members respond to acquisition events in a law firm', *Administrative Science Quarterly*, 56: 408–40.

Burkhardt, M.E. and Brass, D.J. (1990) 'Changing patterns or patterns of change: the effects of a change in technology on social network structure and power', *Administrative Science Quarterly*, 35: 104–27.

Burt, R.S. (1992) *Structural Holes: The Social Structure of Competition*, Cambridge, MA: Harvard University Press.

Burt, R.S. (2005) *Brokerage and Closure: An Introduction to Social Capital*, Oxford: Oxford University Press.

Cannella, D.C. and Hambrick, A.A. (1993) 'Relative standing: a framework for understanding departures of acquired executives', *Academy of Management Journal*, 36: 733–62.

Carley K. (1991) 'A theory of group stability', *American Sociological Review*, 56: 331–54.

Cross, R., Borgatti, S.P. and Parker, A. (2002) 'Making invisible work visible: using social network analysis to support strategic collaboration', *California Management Review*, 44: 25–46.

Cross, R., Parker, A., Prusak, L. and Borgatti, S.P. (2001) 'Knowing what we know: supporting knowledge creation and sharing in social networks', *Organizational Dynamics*, 30: 100–20.

D'Aveni, R.A. and Kesner, I.F. (1993) 'Top managerial prestige, power and tender offer response: a study of elite social networks and target firm cooperation during takeovers', *Organization Science*, 4: 123–51.

Ebers, M. (1997) 'Explaining inter-organizational network formation', in Ebers, M. (ed.), *The Formation of Inter-organizational Networks*: 3–40, Oxford: Oxford University Press.

Empson, L. (2001) 'Fear of exploitation and fear of contamination: impediments to knowledge transfer in mergers between professional service firms', *Human Relations*, 54, 839–62.

Friedkin, N.E. (1984) 'Structural cohesion and equivalence explanations of social homogeneity', *Sociological Methods and Research*, 12: 236–61.

Galaskiewicz, J. (1985) 'Interorganizational relations', in Turner, R. and Short, J. (eds), *Annual Review of Sociology*, vol.11: 281–304, Palo Alto, CA: Annual Reviews.

Gomes, E., Angwin, D.N., Weber, Y., and Tarba, S.Y. (2013) 'Critical success factors through the mergers and acquisitions process: revealing pre- and post-M&A connections for improved performance', *Thunderbird International Business Review*, 55: 13–35.

Granovetter, M. (1973) 'The strength of weak ties', *American Journal of Sociology*, 78: 1360–80.

Greenberg, D. and Guinan, P.J. (2004) 'Mergers and acquisitions in technology-intensive industries: the emergent process of knowledge transfer', in Pablo, A. and Javidan, M. (eds), *Mergers and Acquisitions: Creating Integrative Knowledge*, Oxford: Blackwell Publishing.

Hansen, M.T. (1999) 'The search-transfer problem: the role of weak ties in sharing knowledge across organization subunits', *Administrative Science Quarterly*, 44: 82–111.

Haunschild, P.R. (1993) 'Interorganizational imitation: the impact of interlocks on corporate acquisition activity', *Administrative Science Quarterly*, 38: 564–92.

Holburn, G.L.F. and Van den Bergh, R. (2014) 'Integrated market and nonmarket strategies: political campaign contributions around merger and acquisition events in the energy sector', *Strategic Management Journal*, 35: 450–60.

Huang, Q., Jiang, F., Lie, E. and Yang, K. (2014) 'The role of investment banker directors in M&A', *Journal of Financial Economics*, 112: 269–86.

Ibarra, H. (1992) 'Homophily and differential returns: sex differences in network structures and access in an advertising firm', *Administrative Science Quarterly*, 37: 422–47.

Ibarra, H. (1993) 'Personal networks of women and minorities in management: a conceptual framework', *Academy of Management Review*, 18: 56–87.

Krackhardt, D. and Porter, L.W. (1985) 'When friends leave: a structural analysis of the relationship between turnover and stayers' attitude', *Administrative Science Quarterly*, 30: 242–61.

Krishnan, H.A., Miller, A. and Judge, W.Q. (1997) 'Diversification and top management team complementarity: is performance improved by merging similar or dissimilar teams?', *Strategic Management Journal*, 18: 361–74.

Lusch, R.F., Brown, J.R. and O'Brien, M. (2011) 'Protecting relational assets: a pre and post field study of a horizontal business combination', *Journal of the Academy of Marketing Science*, 39: 175–97.

McPherson, M., Smith-Lovin, L. and Cook, J. (2001) 'Birds of a feather: homophily in social networks', *Annual Review of Sociology*, 27: 415–44.

Mehra, A., Kilduff, M. and Brass, D.J. (2001) 'The social networks of high and low self-monitors: implications for workplace performance', *Administrative Science Quarterly*, 46: 121–46.

Mirc, N. (2012) 'Connecting the micro and macro-level: proposition of a research design to study post-acquisition synergies through a social network approach', *Scandinavian Journal of Management*, 28: 121–35.

Mirc, N. (2013) 'Human impacts on the performance of mergers and acquisitions', in Cooper and Finkelstein (eds), *Advances in Mergers & Acquisitions*, 12: 1–31, Bingley: Emerald Group Publishing Limited.

Mirc, N. (2014) 'Network evolution after a corporate acquisition: the role of network cohesion and acquisition brokers on post-acquisition integration', *European Academy of Management*, Valencia, Spain, 4–6 June 2014.

Mirc, N. and Very, P. (forthcoming) 'Acquisition brokers as resource to ensure acquisition integration', in Larimo, J. and Nummela, N. (eds), *Edward Elgar Handbook on Strategic Alliance and Network Research*, Cheltenham: Edward Elgar..

Mizruchi, M. (1996) 'What do interlocks do? An analysis, critique, and assessment of research on interlocking directorates', in Hagan, J. and Cook, K.S. (eds), *Annual Review of Sociology*, vol.22: 271–98, Palo Alto, CA: Annual Reviews.

Morrison, E.W. (2002) 'Newcomers' relationships: the role of social network ties during socialization', *Academy of Management Journal*, 45: 1149–60.

Moore, M. (1979) 'The structure of a national elite network', *American Sociological Review*, 44: 673–92.

Öberg, C. (2012) 'Using network pictures to study inter-organisational encounters', *Scandinavian Journal of Management*, 28: 136–48.

Öberg, C., Henneberg, S. and Mouzas, S. (2007) 'Changing network pictures: evidence from mergers and acquisitions', *Industrial Marketing Management*, 36: 926–40.

Palmer, D., Jennings, P.D. and Zhou, X. (1993) 'Late adoption of the multidivisional form by large US corporations: institutional, political, and economic accounts', *Administrative Science Quarterly*, 38: 100–31.

Paruchuri, S., Nerkar, A. and Hambrick, D. (2006) 'Acquisition integration and productivity losses in the technical core: disruption of inventors in acquired companies', *Organization Science*, 17: 545–62.

Powell, W.W., Koput, K. and Smith-Doerr, L. (1996) 'Inter-organizational collaboration and the locus of innovation; networks of learning in biotechnology', *Administrative Science Quarterly*, 41: 116–45.

Puranam, P., Singh, H. and Zollo, M. (2006) 'Organizing for innovation: managing the coordination–autonomy dilemma in technology acquisitions', *Academy of Management Journal*, 49: 263–80.

Ranft, A.L., and Lord, M.D. (2000) 'Acquiring new knowledge: the role of retaining human capital in acquisitions of high-tech firms', *Journal of High Technology Management Research*, 11: 295–319.

Reagens, R. and Zuckerman, E.W. (2001) 'Networks, diversity, and productivity: the social capital of corporate R&D teams', *Organization Science*, 12: 268–92.

Scott, J. (2013) *Social Network Analysis*, London: Sage Publications.

Shan, W., Walker, G. and Kogut, B. (1994) 'Interfirm cooperation and startup innovation in the biotechnology industry', *Strategic Management Journal*, 15: 387–94.

Sleptsov, A., Anand, J. and Vasudeva, G. (2013) 'Relational configurations with information intermediaries: the effect of firm-investment bank ties on expected acquisition performance', *Strategic Management Journal*, 34: 957–77.

Spedale, S., Van den Bosch, F. and Volberda, H. (2007) 'Preservation versus dissolution of the target firm's embedded ties in acquisitions', *Organization Studies*, 28: 1169–96.

Teerikangas, S., Very, P. and Pisano, V. (2011), 'Integration managers' value-capturing roles and acquisition performance,' *Human Resource Management*, 50: 651–83.

Tsai, W. (2002) 'Social capital, strategic relatedness, and the formation of intra-organizational linkages', *Strategic Management Journal*, 21: 925–39.

Uzzi, B. (1997) 'Social structure and competition in interfirm networks: the paradox of embeddedness', *Administrative Science Quarterly*, 42: 35–67.

Vanhaverbeke, W., Duysters, G. and Noorderhaven, N. (2002) 'External technology sourcing through alliances or acquisitions: an analysis of the application-specific integrated circuits industry', *Organization Science*, 13: 714–33.

Wasserman, S. and Faust, K. (1994) *Social Network Analysis: Methods and Applications*, Cambridge: Cambridge University Press.

Wellman, B. (1988) 'Structural analysis: from method and metaphor to theory and substance', in Wellman and Berkowitz (eds), *Social Structures: A Network Approach*, 19–61, Cambridge: Cambridge University Press.

White, H. (1992) *Identity and Control: A Structural Theory of Social Action*, Princeton, NJ: Princeton University Press.

Yang, H., Lin, Z. and Peng, M. (2011a) 'Behind acquisitions of alliance partners: exploratory learning and network embeddedness', *Academy of Management Journal*, 54: 1069–80.

Yang, H., Sun, S.L., Lin, Z., and Peng, M. (2011b) 'Behind M&As in China and the United States: networks, learning and institutions', *Asia Pacific Journal of Management*, 28: 239–55.

Zaheer, A., McEvily, B. and Perrone, V. (1998) 'Does trust matter? Exploring the effects of inter-organizational and interpersonal trust on performance', *Organization Science*, 9: 141–59.

16

Qualitative and longitudinal studies of mergers and acquisitions

A reflection of methods in use

Annette Risberg

Since the early 2000s there has been an increased focus on methods in studies of mergers and acquisitions. In 2009, a symposium on qualitative methods in merger and acquisition studies was held at the Academy of Management conference. In 2012, Susan Cartwright, Satu Teerikangas, Audrey Rouzies, and Elizabeth Wilson-Evered edited a special issue of *Scandinavian Journal of Management* with a focus on method in what they called inter-organizational encounters (Cartwright *et al.* 2012), and in 2010 Meglio and I (Meglio and Risberg 2010) called for a wider use of qualitative and longitudinal methods in the study of mergers and acquisitions.

The use of qualitative methods in merger and acquisition research is, however, not new. Many scholars have done qualitative studies, or mixed methods since the 1980s (see Kroon and Rouzies' Chapter 12 in this book). For example, in the legendary study on *The Human Side of Mergers and Acquisitions*, Buono and Bowditch (1989) mixed qualitative and quantitative data. Côté *et al.* (1999) used interviews as a method in a longitudinal study of acquisition strategy and dominant logic. Risberg's (2003) study on employee experiences in acquisitions was mainly based on interviews, as was Vaara's (2003) study on success and failure narratives in post–merger integration and Ullrich *et al.*'s study (2005) on social identity in a merger. Qualitative methods are also apt for longitudinal studies as these methods allow the researcher to spend more time in the merging organizations and to return to the merged entity on multiple occasions for longer periods of time.

A commonly used statement among merger and acquisition researchers is that findings from qualitative empirical studies are "anecdotal" (e.g. Lubatkin *et al.* 1999; Chakrabarti *et al.* 2009). Nothing could be more wrong, as the articles reviewed for this chapter will show. Qualitative studies tend to have rigorous data collection and methods of analysis. In this chapter, I explore the qualitative methods used in merger and acquisition studies. I will pay extra attention to the temporal aspect of the research design: if the study is longitudinal or not. I will also describe the varieties of data collection methods, sources, and analysis methods used under the broad term 'qualitative methods.' While doing so, I will reflect on what phenomena qualitative or longitudinal studies can capture from the merger and acquisition process compared to other methods. The aim is to paint a more extensive and more nuanced picture of qualitative methods in the studies of mergers and acquisitions.

The articles reviewed in this chapter are selected from 11 management journals (*Academy of Management Journal, Administrative Science Quarterly (ASQ), British Journal of Management, Human Relations, Journal of Management, Journal of Management Studies, Management Science, Strategic Management Journal, Organization Science, Organization Studies*, and *Scandinavian Journal of Management*). A research assistant did the literature search, with instructions to use the following selection criteria: the article shall be on mergers and acquisitions, based on field material, should use qualitative methods, and be published between 1970 and 2014. A total of 32 articles were selected for review. The selected articles may not be all-inclusive, but they suit the goal of this chapter by offering a good overview of qualitative and longitudinal research of mergers and acquisitions.

Qualitative research methods

Qualitative methods is an umbrella term for a number of research methods where the aim is to gain a more in-depth understanding of what is studied. The term covers "an array of interpretive techniques which seek to describe, decode, translate, and otherwise come to terms with the meaning, not the frequency, of certain more or less naturally occurring phenomena in the social world" as Van Maanen (1979a: 520) wrote in the editorial for an *ASQ* special issue on qualitative methods. It has roots in the so-called Chicago School in the 1920s and 1930s (e.g. Whyte 1943) and anthropological studies that emphasize the importance of qualitative inquiry for the study of human group life (see Denzin and Lincoln 2003).

These research traditions have been brought into the studies of organizations and are often categorized as inductive studies (cf. Alvesson and Kärreman 2011). Inductive research emphasizes the building of theory from data, not testing existing theories. Langley and Abdallah (2011) identify two distinctive templates for conducting qualitative research. One template aims at nomothetic theory building and is developed from Eisenhardt's (1989) now classic article on theory building as well as her research that followed that article. The other template aims at building process models and developing novel concepts and builds on Gioia's work on organizational processes (see for example Corley and Gioia 2004). I will here call them the nomothetic template and the process template.

The nomothetic template tends to be followed rather rigorously by its adherents. For example, Eisenhardt (1989) describes how the analysis of case studies requires an iterative process where the researcher moves back and forth between data and literature. Theory is developed through the intimate contact that the research has with the empirical material, and two important steps in the process are the within-case analysis and search for cross-case patterns (Eisenhardt 1989). This template builds on a post-positivist epistemology.

Like much other theory building in qualitative research, the second template is inspired by Glaser and Strauss's (1967) work on grounded theory, as well as by Van Maanen (1979a, 1979b) and Lincoln and Guba (1985). For example, Corley and Gioia (2004) describe carefully how through in-vivo coding they identify first-order concepts that are close to the field, then merge them into second-order themes that are more abstract and theoretical, to end up with fewer aggregated dimensions. The process template builds on interpretive epistemology and is located in traditions of interpretivism, hermeneutics, or social constructionism (for example see Schwandt 2003 for a more detailed description). It makes sense to have these two templates in mind while reading qualitative merger and acquisition research as most research can easily be located in one or the other template as you will notice when different research is described below. Langley and Abdallah (2011) describe the differences between research based on the two templates in the following way: research using the nomothetic template searches for facts and aims to develop theory in the form of testable propositions; research using the process template searches for informants' understanding of organizational events and aims to capture and model informants' meanings.

The palette of methods to collect empirical data in qualitative research is varied and includes case study, personal experience, life story, interview, artifacts, observations (participant or not), historic or archival material, visual texts, among others. The commonalities among the collected materials are that the data describes routines and problematic moments and meanings in individual or groups' lives (Denzin and Lincoln 2003). As mergers and acquisitions are events that often interrupt individuals' meanings about the organization and tend to be experienced by the members of the organization to be, if not problematic, at least uncertain, qualitative methods lend themselves well to the study of such events.

Qualitative methods in merger and acquisition research

In merger and acquisition research, case study is probably the most common method. Data can be collected in many ways, but structured or semi-structured interviewing is without doubt most commonly used. However, the menu of methods is more extensive, and one can also add participant observation, unstructured interviews, and text or discourse analysis as suitable for investigating what is going on in merger and acquisition processes. Many studies do not rely on a single method but use several of these methods. For example, it is common to analyze company documents, external sources, and media texts as a complement to interviews (Schweizer 2005) or to combine interviews and observations with archival material (Monin *et al.* 2013). Some use mixed methods, such as Heimeriks *et al.* (2012), who combined interviews with a survey, or Larsson and Finkelstein (1999), who used secondary sources (other researchers' qualitative case descriptions) to codify and analyze quantitatively in a so-called case survey method.

The aim with most qualitative studies is to gain an in-depth understanding of aspects of the merger and acquisition process that are more difficult to capture with quantitative methods. If this is also combined with longitudinal data collection, the merger can be followed over a longer period of time to observe how the organization and its members change over time, how the employees' reactions change over time, or what the long-term impact may be on individuals, groups, or the whole organization, to mention a few possible angles. But many researchers do not stop at rich descriptions. Most also build theory from the analysis using the Eisenhardt (1989) analysis method, process-oriented analysis methods (as in the Gioia template), grounded theory (Glaser and Strauss 1967), or other appropriate rigorous methods. Let us see what methods the scholars actually use when they do qualitative studies of mergers and acquisitions.

Case studies

Most case studies tend to be qualitative and some may even view qualitative studies as equivalent with case studies. In the papers reviewed for this chapter, all but Heimeriks *et al.* (2012) conducted case studies. Case study is probably the method most suitable to get rich and in-depth data about organizational processes (Graebner and Eisenhardt 2004).

Hitt *et al.* (1998) argue that an inductive case study method is needed in merger and acquisition research to develop a more comprehensive theoretical explanation for acquisition outcomes. According to Hitt *et al.* (1998:94), the more common hypothesis-testing approach is limited in achieving this as it "by definition, places boundaries (constraints) on what can be learned from a project. Large sample hypothesis-testing research often makes only an incremental contribution to theory." Hitt *et al.* claim that this type of research is limited to building on existing theory in order to get published, and they also claim that these traditional methods tend to constrain the researcher to minor extensions of current understanding.

Merger and acquisition researchers use single as well as multiple case studies in their research. Graebner and Eisenhardt (2004) and Graebner (2009) argue that multiple case studies are more generalizable and better grounded than single case studies. Vaara *et al.* (2005), on the other hand, argue for a single case study, as it provides rich ethnographic material. (Their different views can be related to the two different templates mentioned earlier.) There is a tendency that the fewer cases in the study, the more data sources are used. More cases do not necessarily have to be better, just different. An advantage with multiple cases in a study is that one can make cross-case comparisons and find patterns across the different cases. A disadvantage is that the researcher tends to use fewer sources and interview fewer informants per case. In their study, Graebner and Eisenhardt carried out, for example, over 80 interviews, but in 12 different cases, meaning that on average they interviewed about seven informants in each case. Vaara *et al.*, on the other hand, conducted 53 interviews in just one case. Together with other data collected, they could make a rich and in-depth case description as well as analysis. Research using single or few case studies cannot generalize to a larger population as a statistical law or a universal law as one does in natural studies. And this is not the objective with the study. What qualitative researchers do is to abstract their findings and relate the findings to existing theories (Mayring 2007) or to build new theories, for example, as in grounded theory (Glaser and Strauss 1967). Mayring (2007) provides a good overview of different types of generalization in qualitative as well as quantitative research for any interested reader.

Researchers conducting case studies of mergers and acquisition aim to generate rich and complex explanations, understanding, and knowledge. Vaara (2003), for example, aims to examine decision making in post-acquisition integration from a sense-making perspective, whereas Mantere *et al.* (2012) aim to understand the failure to return to a pre-merger strategy after a canceled merger effort and can trace the failure to contradiction in symbolic change management. Lander and Kooning (2013) in turn explore trust development in the context of an international merger negotiation. These are only a few examples of what case studies lend themselves to but they illustrate that qualitative case studies are apt to explore complex organizational merger and acquisition phenomena that can hardly be measured and definitely not captured by, for example, cross-sectional analysis. Furthermore, in line with what Hitt *et al.* (1998) point out, this method lends itself well to introducing new theoretical explanations and even to building new theory, just as Eisenhardt and Graebner (2007) and Eisenhardt (1989) propose. An advantage with the case study method is that the sources may be extensive. For example, the researcher can gather a large number of interviews and other multiple sources (e.g. archive data, media) for data triangulation. Below I will outline the most commonly used sources found in the review of qualitative merger and acquisition research.

Interviews

Interviewing is a basic mode of inquiry for explaining and understanding human beings.

> The purpose of in-depth interviewing is not to get answers to questions, not to test hypotheses, and not to 'evaluate' as the term is normally used. At the root of in-depth interviewing is an interest in understanding the experience of other people and the meaning they make of that experience.
>
> *(Seidman 1998: 3)*

As mergers and acquisitions are initiated, managed, and affected by, as well as affecting, human beings, interviewing is appropriate to understanding how such events unfold from the point of view of the people who are part of the events. Seidman (1998, citing Bertaux 1981) writes that those who urge social scientists to imitate the natural sciences seem to ignore one basic difference between the subjects of inquiry in the natural sciences and those in the social sciences: in the social sciences, the subjects of inquiry can talk and think. When given a chance to talk freely, people know a lot about what is going on.

Interviewing is by far the most commonly used data collection method in qualitative merger and acquisition research. Of the 32 articles reviewed for this book chapter, the interview was a data collecting method in 27 articles. Most of those conducted semi-structured interviews to allow the informants to elaborate on their answers and the interviewer to ask follow-up questions. Vaara et al. (2005: 604), for example, aim for "a 'story telling' approach with the use of a semi-structured interview guide." Vince (2006), on the other hand, conducted unstructured interviews, but with a focus on certain themes.

Interviews are conducted when the researchers are interested in the informants' own experiences of the merger and acquisition process, or aim to get as many different perspectives of what happened as possible. Having said that, most studies rely on what is called 'key informants' (e.g. Meyer 2001) or 'key actors' (e.g. Vaara 2002), who often represent the top echelons of the organizational hierarchy. The choice of informants is of course driven by the research question and focus of the study. For example Zueva-Owens et al. (2012) explored the discursive frames that employees use to form their cultural evaluations in acquired companies, and therefore they interviewed 65 employees at all hierarchical levels in three acquired firms. Graebner (2004), on the other hand, wanted to examine the role of acquired managers in creating value; thus she interviewed 60 company leaders in eight cases plus investors. All of these studies used semi- or unstructured interviews except Meyer and Lieb-Dóczy (2003), who used structured interviews (however, they do not argue for their choice of interview method).

Interviewing is a method well suited for gaining a deeper understanding of the experiences of people involved in mergers and acquisitions, and provides a possibility to gain an in-depth and rich understanding of the phenomena studied. Such understanding can help to explain mergers and acquisitions, how they unfold, how they affect the organization and its members, or explain merger and acquisition outcomes. Interviews are often combined with other collecting methods such as observation.

Observation

One way to gain in-depth understanding is to observe what is going on by being present in the organization and participating in organizational activities such as specific events or meetings. A notion behind this method is to observe people in a 'natural' setting, although it may be difficult as the people under study often are aware that they are being observed (Alvesson and Kärreman 2011). This may be a reason why merger and acquisition scholars often choose to observe meetings (e.g. Yu et al. 2005; Monin et al. 2013) or other events. The advantage is that this type of ethnographic method allows the researcher to follow the merger and acquisition process over a longer period of time, but also that she or he will gain a close rapport with the organizational members and can follow the development and unfolding of the integration process. To do participative research does not mean that the researcher must be present in the organization on a daily basis. There are different ways to organize the observations: one could spend time in the organization in periods with some time in between these periods; one could observe specific events and meetings; or one could choose to spend time in the organization over a longer period of time, but only once or twice a week, or on a daily basis. The list could be longer, and it is only the research question at hand, the imagination of the researcher, and the access to the company that will set limits to how observations can be organized.

Clark et al. (2010) had rather unique access to their case as they spent a total of 11 months at the site doing participative observation. The data collection started two months before the merger and continued nine months after. This data collection method gave them the opportunity to observe the emergence of a transitional identity and how this identity facilitated the new shared organizational identity change. Leroy and Ramanantsoa (1997) conducted on-site observation over an eight-month period. This allowed one of the researchers to become immersed in the research context to explore cognitive and behavioral aspects of organizational learning. In addition, they conducted 103 interviews. These methods provide the researchers with rich, nuanced, and in-depth data.

A unique study in this context is Yu et al.'s (2005) ethnographic study of an integration process. The research team observed bi-weekly senior management meetings over a period of eight years. This allowed the research team to follow the creation of the new organization – a large healthcare system – in real time. The research design led to findings about what senior managers pay attention to during an integration process and allowed the researchers to identify patterns in events and issues. Such findings are valuable in understanding how integrations unfold and how and what to pay attention to when planning integration. They also provide explanations for merger and acquisitions outcomes.

Another way to do participant observation is to include an employee of the organization under study in the research team. This was done in Meyer and Altenborg (2007), a study on a Norwegian telecommunication merger, where Altenborg was a manager employed by one of the merging companies. As such, she participated extensively in meetings and had access to key merger documents. A similar method was used in Vaara et al. (2005), where one of the authors was employed as a manager in personnel development and as such had a unique opportunity to observe how employees of the two merging firms reacted to the merger. He was also involved in integration activities. Such access provides a kind of in-depth knowledge that can never be gained by a researcher. Having the other researchers of the team critically analyzing the data balances the risk of biased data. In most studies, participant observation is combined with other data collection methods such as interviews, archival data, or external sources.

Archival data

Archival and other internal company material is often used to complement interviews. Such material can be valuable in order to reconstruct the merger and acquisition process, to understand what decisions have been made (meeting protocols), or what information has been given to employees (news bulletins, intranet). Riad (2005) theorizes organizational culture as a discursive formation, and to reach this theorization she combined multiple sources among which was "document collection, both internal (including emails, minutes of all the meetings, newsletters, press releases and integration plans) and external (Parliamentary debates and media articles)" (Riad 2005: 1537). The archival data functions, in this case, as a supplement to interviews and observations in order to understand the context or to receive further information. Its use can also serve as a control of information retrieved from other sources.

Though most studies use archival data as a complement, Hitt et al. (1998) rely solely on archive material, external secondary sources, and media texts. They conducted a longitudinal study so that they collected published material on 24 acquisitions (48 firms) for a seven-year period (three years prior, the year of the acquisition, and three years after, for each case). In addition to the external secondary sources, the research team also examined annual reports for the merged firms for the year of the acquisition. Based on this secondary qualitative material, they identified attributes of successful and unsuccessful acquisitions.

Many scholars mention how they triangulate the interview data with archival data. Clark *et al.* (2010), for example, rely on multiple resources (archival material, pilot interviews, telephone interviews, participant observations –11 months – and interviews), and they describe how they used archival documents as a secondary data source to provide "insights into the context and storyline of the merger process" (2010: 407). Leroy and Ramanantsoa (1997) also describe how they use a "principle of triangulation by using more than one source of information." Harwood (2006), relying on multiple sources such as interviews, observation, secondary data, and research dairies, argues for triangulation as a way to provide construct validity and minimize the potential for bias.

Archival data is often used in order to complement or check the validity of other data sources such as interviews and observations. Archive data are often easy to access, and with the increased use of intranets and social media in companies, the data may be massive. Another increasingly common source is media coverage of mergers and acquisitions.

Media texts

If the merger and acquisition studied includes large and well-known companies, the media coverage can be extensive. Media texts have become more and more common to use to analyze merger and acquisition discourses. While many studies use media texts as a complement to internal sources (Olie 1994; Hitt *et al.* 1998; Vaara 2002; Schweizer 2005; Vaara *et al.* 2005; Maguire and Phillips 2008; Lander and Kooning 2013), several recent studies have been conducted based solely on media texts on specific mergers and acquisitions (e.g. Hellgren *et al.* 2002; Risberg *et al.* 2003; Riad and Vaara 2011). I will focus on the latter in this section. Riad and Vaara (2011) focus on the role of language in international mergers and acquisitions and aim to identify different types of national metonymy to illustrate how these are used to construct national cultural differences in accounts of mergers and acquisitions. To accomplish this, they analyzed 1,075 media accounts on two different cases (Lenovo-IBM PCD and InBev-Anheuser Busch). The analysis was abductive, identifying metonyms, but also frequency and functions of the same, where recorded.

Hellgren *et al.* (2002) studied discursive practices in the AstraZenec merger by collecting media texts from Swedish and British newspapers. Departing from the notion that media coverage has an impact on organizational change as mergers and acquisitions are performed in a wider social and societal context than just the organization, they found that sense making and sense giving in relation to the merger is to some extent taking place in and through the media. The analysis was made in two steps: first a content analysis was made, and later a critical discourse analysis. They found that discourses of winner or loser of the merger and a nationalistic discourse were dominant.

The use of media text, as mentioned here, provides a new perspective on mergers and acquisitions where one is not only studying what is going on inside the merging organization or measuring the market reactions to the merger. By studying media discourses, the researcher puts the merger and acquisition in a broader social context, acknowledging that merger and acquisition outcomes are affected by internal as well as external activities and discourses.

Analysis methodology

In qualitative research, not only should the data be collected in a qualitative manner but also the analysis must be conducted according to a qualitative method. These methods vary, and I will here mention some used in the reviewed articles.

A commonly used method is inductive, when the researcher uses an iterative process by going back and forth between the data and the literature (e.g. Birkinshaw *et al.* 2000). Birkinshaw *et al.* did a longitudinal study of managing the integration process using mixed methods. The conducted analysis allowed them to understand the causal processes underlying the integration processes, and the result was how human integration and task integration processes interact to advance value creation. An inductive analysis can be combined with different approaches: something that Kitchener (2002) did in his study of merging health centers. He combined the inductive analysis with a narrative approach, looking for patterns and themes in the field material that he compared to patterns and themes found in literature.

Grounded theory is also commonly used, for example, by Greenwood *et al.* (1994) in their study of merging service firms. They explain their methodology as "a form of grounded theory, which builds an understanding of the setting and events from accounts and impressions provided by participants, but organized in terms of preparatory ideas and propositions" (Greenwood *et al.* 1994: 243). The method led to, in their own words, theoretical understanding of the merger process.

A thematic analysis is probably the most common method in qualitative research, no matter if it is called narrative, grounded, discourse, or anything else. The researcher can start identifying patterns of themes from the field material directly or one can identify themes from the literature (e.g. Lander and Kooning 2013) that one uses to analyze the field material. The most common processes are iterative (e.g. Graebner 2009) or abductive (e.g. Riad and Vaara 2011; Monin *et al.* 2013), where the researcher goes back and forth between the field material and the literature. One way to structure the analysis is to start with first-order categories, which are categories close to the field. These are then collapsed into second-order categories, which are closer to categories found in existing theory, and this is where theorizing starts (cf. the process template, described above). Often the researcher ends with merging the second-order categories into aggregated dimensions, which is a more abstract level of theorizing. As Van Maanen (1979b: 540) describes it, "[p]ut simply, first-order concepts are the 'facts' of an ethnographic investigation and the second-order concepts are the 'theories' an analyst uses to organize and explain these facts."

Mantere *et al.* (2012) provide a detailed description of their analysis, grounded theory, but also close to what Eisenhardt (1989) describes in her article on building theory from case studies. Mantere *et al.*'s (2012) analysis was made in three rounds, beginning with a fine-grained reading of the data, a practice called microanalysis. They wrote a detailed case description based on the microanalysis. In the second analysis round, they began to theorize by coding the detailed description resulting in the first-order categories. In the third analysis round, they did axial coding, which is a practice of structuring the data into theoretical categories and more general aggregated dimensions (second-order themes and aggregated dimensions). A software program was used to do the coding.

Such detailed descriptions of the analysis (see also Clark *et al.* 2010; Monin *et al.* 2013) shows how rigorous qualitative research is and also that it can be generalizable when it results in theorizing. It is far from anecdotal stories about mergers and acquisitions but is based on well-established meticulous methods.

Longitudinal aspects of qualitative merger and acquisition research

Many but not all qualitative studies are also longitudinal in one way or the other. Even though we all know what longitudinal means, how it is actually practiced differs. A longitudinal study can be historical, it can be in real time for a long period of time, or it can be in terms of a number of interview rounds during a longer period of time.

Côté *et al.* (1999) did a historical case study based on in-depth retrospective interviews. Their justification for this method is: "because growth by acquisition occurs over very long periods, making observation in real time impractical, a historical approach was used here" (Côté *et al.* 1999: 922). Whether a study is retrospective or not is often dependent upon the type of access that the researcher gets to the merger and acquisition. A merger or acquisition is rarely publicly known before it actually takes place and it is therefore difficult to gain real-time access for the researcher. In addition, many companies do not want an outsider to be in the organization during a sensitive period such as an integration process. This is probably a reason why in some real-time merger and acquisition studies the researcher has also acted as a merger and acquisition consultant (e.g. Vaara 2003; Meyer and Altenborg 2007).

Monin *et al.* (2013) is a longitudinal real-time analysis of a friendly acquisition. The researchers gained access immediately after the announcements of the acquisition plans and followed the integration process for five years. Interviews were conducted every six months for about four years. This research design allowed the research team to analyze sense giving and sense making over time.

Birkinshaw *et al.* (2000), using mixed methods, collected data at two points in time: during year zero and year four after the acquisition took place. At the two points in time, interviews were made with key individuals on both sides of the acquisition.

Leroy and Ramanantsoa (1997) spent eight months on the site following the merger process closely. During this long stay in the field, the researcher conducted interviews and observed, and sometimes participated in, workshops, merger committees, and executive committees. This long and close contact with the field resulted in explaining how mergers provide opportunities for organizational learning and what the managerial implications are.

The advantage with longitudinal studies is that one can follow the merger or acquisition and the integration process over time to see the development and what changes take place in the organization. One can also observe changes in attitudes, sense making, experiences, and learning among organizational members over time. Another advantage is that the researcher gains in-depth knowledge and understanding of the merging organization and its members, which can lead to better informed analysis, interpretations, and explanations of the processes.

Conclusion

This review of merger and acquisition studies using a qualitative method reveals that many different types of data collection and analysis methods can be found under this umbrella term. Most important, it shows that qualitative research is theory-generating research which enables the researcher to add new theory through new knowledge and new perspectives to existing merger and acquisition theory. Qualitative methods and longitudinal studies provide opportunities to study complex phenomena that cannot be captured by one-dimensional variables and simple frequencies, or that cannot be explained by correlations. These methods can instead be used for fine-grained, in-depth, informed, and rich descriptions, understandings, and explanations of what happens in an organization and to its members during a merger or an acquisition. Simply put, qualitative methods can help the merger and acquisition research community to further the knowledge and theorizing about mergers and acquisitions.

References

Alvesson, M. and Kärreman, D. (2011) *Qualitative Research and Theory Development*. London, UK: Sage Publications, Ltd.

Birkinshaw, J., Bresman, H., and Håkanson, L. (2000) "Managing the post-acquisition integration process: how the human integration and task integration processes interact to foster value creation," *Journal of Management Studies*, 37: 395–425.

Buono, A.F. and Bowditch, J.L. (1989) *The Human Side of Mergers and Acquisitions*. San Francisco, CA: Jossey-Bass.

Cartwright, S., Teerikangas, S., Rouzies, A., and Wilson-Evered, E. (2012) "Methods in M&A: a look at the past and the future to forge a path forward," *Scandinavian Journal of Management*, 28: 95–106.

Chakrabarti, R., Gupta-Mukherjee, S., and Jayaraman, N. (2009) "Mars–Venus marriages: culture and cross-border M&A," *Journal of International Business Studies*, 40: 216–36.

Clark, S.M., Gioia, D.A., Ketchen, J., David J., and Thomas, J.B. (2010) "Transitional identity as a facilitator of organizational identity change during a merger," *Administrative Science Quarterly*, 55: 397–438.

Corley, K.G. and Gioia, D.A. (2004) "Identity ambiguity and change in the wake of a corporate spin-off," *Administrative Science Quarterly*, 49: 173–208.

Côté, L., Langley, A., and Pasquero, J. (1999) "Acquisition strategy and dominant logic in an engineering firm," *Journal of Management Studies*, 36: 919–52.

Denzin, N.K. and Lincoln, Y.A. (2003) "Introduction: the discipline and practice of qualitative research," in N.K. Denzin and Y.A. Lincoln, (eds.), *The Landscape of Qualitative Research: Theories and Issues*. Thousand Oaks, CA: Sage Publications, Inc.

Eisenhardt, K.M. (1989) "Building theories from case study research," *Academy of Management Review*, 14: 532–50.

Eisenhardt, K.M. and Graebner, M.E. (2007) "Theory building from cases: opportunities and challenges," *Academy of Management Journal*, 50: 25–32.

Glaser, B.G. and Strauss, A. (1967) *The Discovery of Grounded Theory: Strategies for Qualitative Research*. Chicago, IL: Aldine Publishing Co.

Graebner, M.E. (2004) "Momentum and serendipity: how acquired leaders create value in the integration of technology firms," *Strategic Management Journal*, 25: 751–77.

Graebner, M.E. (2009) "Caveat venditor: trust asymmetries in acquisitions of entrepreneurial firms," *Academy of Management Journal*, 52: 435–72.

Graebner, M.E. and Eisenhardt, K.M. (2004) "The seller's side of the story: acquisition as courtship and governance as syndicate in entrepreneurial firms," *Administrative Science Quarterly*, 49: 366–403.

Greenwood, R., Hinings, C.R., and Brown, J. (1994) "Merging professional service firms," *Organization Science*, 5: 239–57.

Harwood, I. (2006) "Confidentiality constraints within mergers and acquisitions: gaining insights through a 'bubble' metaphor," *British Journal of Management*, 17: 347–59.

Heimeriks, K.H., Schijven, M., and Gates, S. (2012) "Manifestations of higher-order routines: the underlying mechanisms of deliberate learning in the context of postacquisition integration," *Academy of Management Journal*, 55: 703–26.

Hellgren, B., Löwstedt, J., Puttonen, L., Tienari, J., Vaara, E., and Werr, A. (2002) "How issues become (re)constructed in the media: discursive practices in the AstraZeneca merger," *British Journal of Management*, 13: 123–40

Hitt, M., Harrison, J., Ireland, R.D., and Best, A. (1998) "Attributes of successful and unsuccessful acquisitions of us firms," *British Journal of Management*, 9: 91–114.

Kitchener, M. (2002) "Mobilizing the logic of managerialism in professional fields: the case of academic health centre mergers," *Organization Studies*, 23: 391–420

Lander, M.W. and Kooning, L. (2013) "Boarding the aircraft: trust development amongst negotiators of a complex merger," *Journal of Management Studies*, 50: 1–30.

Langley, A. and Abdallah, C. (2011) "Templates and turns in qualitative studies of strategy and management," in D.J. Ketchen and D.D. Bergh, (eds.), *Research Methodology in Strategy and Management*. Bingley: Emerald Group Publishing.

Larsson, R. and Finkelstein, S. (1999) "Integrating strategic, organizational, and human resource perspectives on mergers and acquisitions: a case survey of synergy realization," *Organization Science*, 10: 1–26.

Leroy, F. and Ramanantsoa, B. (1997) "The cognitive and behavioral dimensions of organizational learning in a merger: an empirical study," *Journal of Management Studies*, 34: 871–94.

Lincoln, Y.S. and Guba, E. (1985) *Naturalistic Enquiry*, Beverly Hills, CA: Sage Publications.

Lubatkin, M., Schweiger, D., and Weber, Y. (1999) "Top management turnover in related M&A's: an additional test of the theory of relative standing," *Journal of Management*, 25: 55–73.

Van Maanen, J. (1979a) "Reclaiming qualitative methods for organizational research: a preface," *Administrative Science Quarterly*, 24: 520–26.

Van Maanen, J. (1979b) "The fact of fiction in organizational ethnography," *Administrative Science Quarterly*, 24: 539–50.

Maguire, S. and Phillips, N. (2008) "'Citibankers' at Citigroup: a study of the loss of institutional trust after a merger," *Journal of Management Studies*, 4: 372–401.

Mantere, S., Schildt, H.A., and A. Sillince, J.A. (2012) "Reversal of strategic change," *Academy of Management Journal*, 55: 173–96.

Mayring, P. (2007) "On generalization in qualitatively oriented research," *Forum Qualitative Sozialforschung / Forum: Qualitative Social Research*, 8(3).

Meglio, O. and Risberg, A. (2010) "Mergers and acquisitions: time for a methodological rejuvenation of the field?," *Scandinavian Journal of Management*, 26: 87–95.

Meyer, C.B. (2001) "Allocation processes in mergers and acquisitions: an organizational justice perspective," *British Journal of Management*, 12: 47–66

Meyer, K.E. and Lieb-Dóczy, E. (2003) "Post-acquisition restructuring as evolutionary process," *Journal of Management Studies*, 40: 459–82.

Meyer, C.B., and Altenborg, E. (2007) "The disintegrating effects of equality: a study of a failed international merger," *British Journal of Management*, 18: 257–71.

Monin, P., Noorderhaven, N., Vaara, E., and Kroon, D. (2013) "Giving sense to and making sense of justice in postmerger integration," *Academy of Management Journal*, 56: 256–84.

Olie, R. (1994) "Shades of culture and institutions in international mergers," *Organization Studies*, 15: 381–405

Riad, S. (2005) "The power of 'organizational culture' as a discursive formation in merger integration," *Organization Studies*, 26:1529–54.

Riad, S. and Vaara, E. (2011) "Varieties of national metonymy in media accounts of international mergers and acquisitions," *Journal of Management Studies*, 48: 737–71.

Risberg, A. (2003) "Shared and multiple realities in acquisitions: an empirically based critique of merger and acquistion literature," *Nordiske Organisasjonsstudier*, 5: 58–82.

Risberg, A., Tienari, J., and Vaara, E. (2003) "Making sense of a transnational merger: media texts and the (re)construction of power relations," *Culture & Organization*, 9: 121–37.

Schwandt, T.A. (2003) "Three epistemological stances for qualitative inquiry: interpretivism, hermeneutics, and social constructionism," in N.K. Denzin and Y.A. Lincoln, (eds.), *The Landscape of Qualitative Research: Theories and Issues*. Thousand Oaks, CA: Sage Publications, Inc.

Schweizer, L. (2005) "Organizational integration of acquired biotechnology companies into pharmaceutical companies: the need for a hybrid approach," *Academy of Management Journal*, 48: 1051–74.

Seidman, I. (1998) *Interviewing as Qualitative Research. A Guide for Researchers in Education and the Social Sciences*, 2nd edn. New York and London: Teachers College Press.

Ullrich, J., Wieseke, J., and Van Dick, R. (2005) "Continuity and change in mergers and acquisitions: a social identity case study of a German industrial merger," *Journal of Management Studies*, 42: 1549–69.

Vaara, E. (2002) "On the discursive construction of success/failure in narratives of post-merger integration," *Organization Studies*, 23: 211–48.

Vaara, E. (2003) "Post-acquisition integration as sensemaking: glimpses of ambiguity, confusion, hypocrisy, and politicization," *Journal of Management Studies*, 40: 859–94.

Vaara, E., Tienari, J., Piekkari, R., and Säntti, R. (2005) "Language and the circuits of power in a merging multinational corporation," *Journal of Management Studies*, 42: 595–623.

Vince, R. (2006) "Being taken over: managers' emotions and rationalizations during a company takeover," *Journal of Management Studies*, 43: 343–65.

Whyte, W.F. (1943/1993) *Street Corner Society*. 4th edn. Chicago, IL: The University of Chicago Press.

Yu, J., Engleman, R.M., and Van de Ven, A.H. (2005) "The integration journey: an attention-based view of the merger and acquisition integration process," *Organization Studies*, 26: 1501–28.

Zueva-Owens, A., Fotaki, M., and Ghauri, P. (2012) "Cultural evaluations in acquired companies: focusing on subjectivities," *British Journal of Management*, 23: 272–90.

Part IV

Conceptual domain
of M&A research

The fourth and final section of the book addresses key concepts used in merger and acquisition (M&A) research. In this section, we have challenged chapter authors to rethink commonly used key concepts and maybe even introduce new concepts borrowed from neighboring fields. We believe that, by using and discussing key concepts in new and different ways, it may contribute to new explanations and understandings of M&As.

In the first contribution in the section, Chapter 17, Grant, Frimanson, and Nilsson take a fresh look at the notion of M&A processes by reviewing how they have been studied empirically, especially using qualitative methods. They aim to outline what is empirically known from process research. Based on their review of top journal articles, they identify five process categories and reflect on what one can learn about M&A processes from these categories. In doing so, they contribute to the understanding of M&As as processes.

In Chapter 18, DeGhetto, Ro, Lamont, and Ranft take a closer look at how the pre-deal process affects anticipatory justice and post-deal integration. Their contribution is theoretical and blends justice theory with acquisition research to point out how important "first impressions" in the pre-deal phase are for later phases of the acquisition process. They propose that anticipatory justice is central to the acquisition integration process to facilitate target employee engagement and improved acquisition outcomes.

In the next chapter, Schriber also offers a theoretical contribution by introducing a competitive dynamics perspective on the value potential from M&A. Schriber points out that little attention has been paid to external competitive change in the environment following an acquisition. This lack of attention contrasts with the motive for many M&As to increase the competitiveness for the merging firms. He argues that complementarity among the merging firms in regard to the external environment may contribute to increased post-M&A value.

In Chapter 20, Bauer reviews current studies on speed of integration in M&As to establish what the research community currently knows about the relationship of integration speed with M&As. He argues that, despite its importance, M&A research has little focus on integration speed beyond the discussion of fast or slow integration. He also identifies a limitation in existing research on acquisition speed, namely its not using a relative measure that captures both the amount and rate of change. Bauer points to the need to broaden research on integration speed, and he identifies three areas to address with future research.

Organizational identity and threats to this identity are discussed in Chapter 21 by Lupina–Wegener, Karamustafa, and Schneider. Identity has gained increased interest in the M&A literature as researchers recognize that creating a shared identity is important for successful M&A outcomes. Lupina–Wegener, Karamustafa, and Schneider propose that shared identity can be difficult to develop when the employees of the merging firms experience identity threat. Drawing upon acculturation and social identity theories, the authors develop a typology of identity threats and discuss how certain identity threats may trigger collective reactions. Their approach may help managers plan the integration and achieve a shared organizational identity.

Chapter 22, by Rothermel and Bauer, suggests that corporate brands are heavily affected by M&A activities; yet the impact of brands remains largely unexplored in M&A and marketing research. As an intangible asset, brands are vulnerable to changes in stakeholder perceptions during M&As. By reviewing existing literature, they outline a typology of branding choices and associated opportunities and threats that managers can use to guide branding decisions during M&As.

In summary, M&As, both as a phenomenon and as a topic of study, represent a journey. Better understanding M&As requires both filling in details for lines of research already explored, as well as exploring uncharted areas. The chapters of this section are intended to represent established as well as emerging areas of M&A research, and they all explore M&As in new ways, either by filling in details about well-known areas or by entering unexplored territory. As editors of the book, serving as your guides along the chapters, we hope that the notions, theories, and models presented here and in the other sections of the book will sustain you in your journey in understanding M&As.

17

Mergers and acquisitions as multitude of processes
A review of qualitative research

Michael Grant, Lars Frimanson and Fredrik Nilsson

Introduction

A conventional idea in merger and acquisition (M&A) research is that M&A phenomena can be thought of as a linear process (Risberg 1999; Calipha *et al.* 2010). This idea is evident from two terms commonly used to describe M&A processes: the pre-merger phase and the post-merger phase (cf. Shrivastava 1986). Events and actions in the pre-merger phase typically relate to antecedents of M&A and transaction activities such as due diligence, valuation and negotiations. Post-merger events and actions often address integration and restructuring issues. These events and actions are complex because M&A phenomena involve several stakeholders who have different and sometimes changing expectations and motives (Anderson *et al.* 2013). Moreover, each M&A process involves unique cultural, organizational and social dimensions (Meglio and Risberg 2010). This makes it difficult to build a generic M&A process theory (Cartwright *et al.* 2012), tempting us to suggest that theorizing based on a single research tradition will never help us understand all the empirical complexities of M&A processes.

Process is conceptually important because it can help M&A researchers provide explanations of observed sequences of events or actions (Van de Ven and Poole 2005; Langley *et al.* 2013) and to construct understandings of how people experience being part of and (re)create meaning around M&A processes (Meglio and Risberg 2010). Jemison and Sitkin (1986) introduced process as a perspective in M&A research to provide a conceptual alternative to the rational choice perspective. Subsequently, calls for process research were heard, often accompanied by a formulated need for qualitative research to better uncover what is going on in different M&A phases (Haspeslagh and Jemison 1991; Pablo and Javidan 2004; Cartwright and Schoenberg 2006; Risberg 2006; Meglio and Risberg 2010; Cartwright *et al.* 2012; Faulkner *et al.* 2012). A growing body of qualitative literature on M&A processes has been emerging ever since, using a broad variety of theoretical perspectives to address an increasing range of complex pre-merger and post-merger issues, as well as outcomes[1] of M&A processes. In the past decade or so, this research has developed theoretically, and many empirical papers now make it to top-rated academic journals. Yet, no systematic knowledge exists on what is empirically known from qualitative process research and therefore we ask: What do these papers research empirically about M&A processes?

The purpose of this chapter is to answer this question by conducting a review of qualitative M&A process research published between 2001 and 2010 in top journals. Building on a detailed examination of the empirical substance of process in this research, we identify five process categories, reflect thematically on the insights made from the studies in each process category and suggest potential avenues for further M&A process research.

Method

We define *qualitative M&A process research* in two steps: 1) the research reports some empirical sequence of M&A events or actions and 2) the research reports retrospective and/or prospective qualitative data. Papers meeting these two criteria are included in our review, including quantitative research also reporting qualitative data. M&A processes involve many empirical phenomena, and these have been linked to a range of different theoretical perspectives. For our purposes, however, we examine the empirical substance of process in this research. Process categories developed by us are, accordingly, based on our interpretations of process data reported by authors. We focus on qualitative data because it 'emphasizes qualities of entities – the processes and meanings that occur naturally' (Gephart 2004: 455), rather than on pre-designed conceptions of entities and relations between them.

We aim to provide a broad review of qualitative M&A process research of high academic standards, covering several fields related to business and management studies. These considerations led us to select all journals in the top two quality categories (4* and 4) on the 2010 list published by the Association of Business Schools, resulting in a sample of 94 journals covering 20 fields. The fields of *Business ethics and governance* and *Management development and education* were excluded because they lacked top-two quality journals. The 2001–2010 period was chosen at the onset to analyse the current state of qualitative M&A process research. Hence, the review does not include the latest qualitative studies. However, we believe that this caveat does not change the overall analysis and message provided in the chapter.

We want to provide a broad review of empirical M&A processes and therefore reject the idea of an acquisition as a transaction in a market for corporate control, simply because it is an idea that fails to recognize all the complex and interlinked events and actions that can make up M&A processes. In the 94 selected journals, we ran an abstract search for the keywords *merger, merge, acquisition, divest* and *divestment*, including their plural forms. We searched the terms, divest and divestment because we wanted to include pre-merger processes influencing acquisitions. Studies of divestments not leading to acquisitions were excluded.

The first author read each title and abstract to identify if a paper could potentially be classified as an M&A study. If an abstract did not give clear guidance, the paper was read partly or entirely. For each journal search, the same author recorded the search date, name of database, number of hits and number of M&A papers per keyword. All references were saved in EndNote software. For each journal, the search record, the EndNote reference list and all the papers in full were saved in a binder distributed to all authors for initial analyses. In total, 476 papers were identified as M&A studies.

The first author then read sections describing method and data in all papers to identify qualitative process studies. All authors discussed uncertain cases to form a joint decision. A general principle was to initially include studies that were ambiguous as to whether they could be identified as qualitative M&A process studies. Thus, the studies identified are not only based on qualitative research, and they do not only research M&A processes. However, they all report retrospective and/or prospective qualitative data of some sequence of M&A events or actions. As shown in Table 17.1, we identified 51 empirical papers as qualitative process studies.

Table 17.1 Number of identified qualitative M&A process papers, total M&A papers and journals covered across fields on the 2010 list published by the Association of Business Schools (ABS)

Sub-field	Qualitative process studies	Total M&A studies	Number of journals
General management[2]	18	91	7
Organization studies	15	40	4
HR and employment studies	4	6	4
Social science	4	19	12
Business history	4	4	1
International business and area studies	3	30	1
Accountancy	1	18	5
Psychology	1	8	16
Strategic management	1	55	1
Economics	0	34	17
Entrepreneurship and small business management	0	9	2
Finance	0	139	5
Information management	0	0	2
Innovation	0	1	1
Marketing	0	9	5
Operations research and management science	0	9	4
Operations technology and management	0	1	1
Public sector management	0	2	3
Sector studies	0	1	1
Tourism and hospitality management	0	0	2
TOTAL ABS LIST 4 AND 4*	51	476	94

Partly assisted by fellow authors, the first author scrutinized the 51 studies and recorded, in a 1–2 page document, abstract, research question, research design, type of organizations and time period studied, research method, type of data, level of analysis, theoretical perspective, research tradition and main findings. Together, the authors then tried to identify overall categories by iteratively searching for empirical process patterns. This iterative search continued for approximately 2 years. Joint discussions were used to form tentative categorizations to be tested. The first author analysed the main findings in each paper by reading our records and original papers to identify how empirical sequences of events or actions fitted the proposed categories. Test results were discussed, uncertain cases re-analysed after a joint read of the original papers and our records refined. Some initial categorization schemes changed completely. After two or three iterations, some categories emerged as reasonably stable and were kept. Others required a few more iterations to stabilize. Ultimately, the empirical substance in these papers was condensed into five process categories. Based on this categorization, the first author explicated several potential underlying themes within each process category. Subsequently, the second author reviewed all records and original papers to identify overlaps between potential themes and suggest mergers of these to finalize the coding of themes. Finally, all authors discussed the final themes and agreed upon the categorization shown in Table 17.2.[3]

Table 17.2 Process characterization of qualitative, empirical merger and acquisition research published between 2001 and 2010 in 4*- and 4-rated journals according to the 2010 list published by the Association of Business Schools

Processes	Themes	References	Empirical context	Level of analysis	Research tradition
Environmental	Institutional forces	Thornton, P.H. 2001	Acquisitions, higher education and publishing market, US, 1958–1990	Societal	Positivistic
		Wood, S. 2001	Acquisitions and divestments, department store industry, US, 1998	Societal and organizational	Positivistic
		Kitchener, M. 2002	Merger (failed), academic healthcare centres, US, 1995–2000	Societal and organizational	Critical
		Cheffins, B.R. 2004	Mergers in UK, late 1950s until early 1970s	Societal	Positivistic
		Lu, Q. 2010	Acquisitions, banks, UK–US, 1978–1980	Societal and organizational	Positivistic
		Mtar, M. 2010	Acquisitions, 3 cases, manufacturing, construction, water distribution, FR–UK for all cases, late 1980s to late 1990s	Organizational	Positivistic
	Stakeholder relationships	Wallis, E. and J. Winterton 2001	Acquisition (privatization), 4 collieries by RJB Mining from British Coal, UK, 1994	Organizational	Positivistic
		Hellgren, B., J. Löwstedt, L. Puttonen, J. Tienari, E. Vaara and A. Werr 2002	Merger of equals, pharmaceutical, SE–UK, 1998–1999	Societal	Interpretive
		Savage, L. 2004	Merger, a public and a private hospital, US, 1994–1996	Organizational (inter-organizational)	Positivistic
		Kim, S.-J. 2006	Acquisitions, agriculture, US–KR, 1998–1999	Societal and organizational	Positivistic
		Vaara, E., J. Tienari and J. Laurila 2006	Merger of equals, pulp and paper, SE–FI, 1998	Societal	Critical
		Spedale, S., F.A.J. Van Den Bosch and H.W. Volberda 2007	Acquisitions, 2 cases, electronic global distribution services and food, 1 domestic transaction in US, 1 cross border in Europe, time periods not available	Organizational (inter-organizational)	Positivistic
Long-term development		Cheffins, B.R. 2004	Mergers in UK, late 1950s until early 1970s	Societal	Positivistic
		Higgins, D.M. and S. Toms 2006	Acquisitions, textile, UK, 1950–1990	Societal and organizational	Positivistic
		Meyer, K.E. 2006	Acquisitions and divestments (globalization), manufacturing, DK–other countries, 1989–2005	Organizational	Positivistic
		Jones, G. and P. Miskell 2007	Acquisitions, ice-cream and tea businesses, UK/ NL–other countries, 1920–1990	Organizational	Positivistic

	Reference	Description	Level	Paradigm
Coordination	Meyer, C. B. 2001	Merger and hostile acquisition, financial services, NO, 1989–1994 and 1991–1995	Organizational	Positivistic
Influencing drivers	Ranft, A. L. and M. D. Lord 2002	Acquisitions, 7 cases, high tech, US, until 3 years after acquisitions were completed	Organizational	Positivistic
	Schweizer, L. 2005	Acquisitions, 5 cases, pharmaceutical and biotech industries, US, 2 cases, DE–US, 2 cases, CH–US, 1995–1999	Organizational	Positivistic
	Bresman, H., J. Birkinshaw and R. Nobel 2010	Acquisitions, 3 cases, industrial companies, CH–US, SE–UK, SE–US, 1988–1996	Organizational	Positivistic
	Vaara, E. and P. Monin 2010	Merger (failed), biological diagnostic and pharmaceutical companies, FR, 2000–2002	Societal and organizational	Interpretive
Improbabilities	Empson, L. 2001	Acquisitions, 3 cases, professional services, UK, 2 cases 1–3 years post-closing, 1 case 4–6 years post-closing	Individual	Positivistic
	Morris, T., J. Storey, A. Wilkinson and Cressey, P. 2001	Merger, 3 unions, UK, 1998–1999	Organizational	Positivistic
	Fulop, N., G. Protopsaltis, A. King, P. Allen, A. Hutchings and C. Normand 2005	9 mergers, healthcare providers, UK, 1999–2002	Organizational and group	Positivistic
	Keller, B. 2005	Merger, 5 unions, DE, 2001	Organizational (inter-organizational)	Positivistic
	Harwood, I. 2006	Acquisition, pharmaceutical, UK, time period not available	Group	Positivistic
	Meyer, C. B. and E. Altenborg 2007	Merger of equals (failed), telecom, SE–NO, 1999	Organizational	Positivistic
	Meyer, C. B. and E. Altenborg 2008	Merger of equals (failed), telecom, SE–NO, 1999	Organizational	Positivistic

(Continued)

Table 17.2 Continued

Processes	Themes	References	Empirical context	Level of analysis	Research tradition
Leader	Difficulties of change	Denis, J.-L., L. Lamothe and A. Langley 2001	2 mergers (1 failed), hospitals, CA, 1994–1998	Organizational and group	Positivistic
		Yu, J., R.M. Engleman and A.H. Van de Ven 2005	Large healthcare system created by a merger and several acquisitions, focal unit clinic group with 50 clinics, US, 1994–2002	Organizational and group	Positivistic
		Kavanagh, M.H. and N.M. Ashkanasy 2006	Mergers between universities and colleges, 3 cases, AU, 6-year study	Organizational and group	Positivistic
	Unexpected actions	Denis, J.-L., L. Lamothe and A. Langley 2001	2 mergers (1 failed), hospitals, CA, 1994–1998	Organizational and group	Positivistic
		Yu, J., R.M. Engleman and A.H. Van de Ven 2005	Large healthcare system created by a merger and several acquisitions, focal unit clinic group with 50 clinics, US, 1994–2002	Organizational and group	Positivistic
		Ng, W. and C. De Cock 2002	Hostile takeover, construction companies, SG, 2-year time period studied	Individual	Interpretive
		Graebner, M.E. 2004	Acquisitions/divestments, 8 cases, technology entrepreneurial companies, acquired US, acquirer not stated, 1999–2000	Individual	Positivistic
		Graebner, M.E. and K.M. Eisenhardt 2004	Divestments, 12 cases (incl. 4 which did not sell), technology entrepreneurial companies, acquired US, acquirer not stated, 1999–2000	Individual	Positivistic
	Importance of sellers	Graebner, M.E. 2004	Acquisitions/divestments, 8 cases, technology entrepreneurial companies, acquired US, acquirer not stated, 1999–2000	Individual	Positivistic
		Graebner, M.E. and K.M. Eisenhardt 2004	Divestments, 12 cases (incl. 4 which did not sell), technology entrepreneurial companies, acquired US, acquirer not stated, 1999–2000	Individual	Positivistic
		Graebner, M.E. 2009	Acquisitions/divestments, 12 cases (incl. 4 which did not sell), technology entrepreneurial companies, acquired US, acquirer not stated, 1999–2000	Individual	Positivistic

Employee	Alienation	Marks, M.L. and R. Vansteenkiste 2008	Divestment, a global spirit and wine group sold in parts to 2 competitors, seller FR, buyer not stated, 2000–2002	Group	Positivistic
		Brannen, M.Y. and M.F. Peterson 2009	Acquisition, paper converting plant, JP–US, 1986–1991	Individual	Positivistic
	Discursive practices	Vaara, E. 2002	Cross-border acquisitions and mergers, 8 cases, various industries (e.g. cranes, electrical engineering, computers, banks), all cases FI–SE, 1984–1997	Individual	Interpretive
		Ford, J. and N. Harding 2003	Merger, 2 healthcare organizations, country not available, 6-year study	Individual	Critical
		Vaara, E. 2003	Acquisitions, a large furniture manufacturer acquiring 3 smaller ones, FI–SE, 1996–2000	Individual	Critical
		Riad, S. 2005	Merger, 3 government organizations, NZ, 8-month study	Group	Critical
		Vaara, E., J. Tienari, R. Piekkari and R. Säntti 2005	Merger, Nordbanken (SE) and Merita (FI), financial services industry, 1998–2000	Group and individual	Critical
		Llewellyn, S. 2007	Merger, pharmaceutical companies, SE–UK, 2001–2002	Group	Positivistic
Identity	Identity change	Dackert, I., P.R. Jackson, S.-O. Brenner and C.R. Johansson 2003	Merger, 2 public service organizations, SE, 9–2 months before merger	Organizational	Positivistic
		Ullrich, J., J. Wieseke and R. Van Dick 2005	Merger, 2 large global industrial organizations, DE, 2000–2001	Organizational	Interpretive
		Clark, S.M., D.A. Gioia, D.J. Ketchen, and J.B. Thomas 2010	Merger, 2 formerly rival hospitals, US, 11-month period	Organizational	Interpretive
		van Vuuren, M., P. Beelen and M.D.T. de Jong 2010	Merger, 2 universities, ZA, collected data on pre- and post-merger, time period not stated	Organizational	Interpretive

(Continued)

Table 17.2 Continued

Processes	Themes	References	Empirical context	Level of analysis	Research tradition
	Identity differentiation	Ailon-Souday, G. and G. Kunda 2003	Acquisition, high tech, IL–US, 1998	Individual	Critical
		Dackert, I., P. R. Jackson, S.-O. Brenner and C. R. Johansson 2003	Merger, 2 public service organizations, SE, 9–2 months before merger	Organizational	Positivistic
		Vaara, E., J. Tienari and R. Säntti 2003	Merger, Nordbanken (SE) and Merita (FI), financial services industry, 1999–2000	Individual	Critical
		Clark, S. M., D. A. Gioia, D. J. Ketchen, and J. B. Thomas 2010	Merger, 2 hospitals, formerly rivals, US, 11-month period	Organizational	Interpretive
		van Vuuren, M., P. Beelen and M. D. T. de Jong 2010	Merger, 2 universities, ZA, collected data on pre- and post-merger, time period not stated	Organizational	Interpretive
	Unpredictability of identity change	Empson, L. 2004	Acquisition, accounting firms (a global and a mid-sized), UK, followed the process during 3 years post acquisition	Organizational and group	Interpretive
		Brown, A.D. and M. Humphreys 2006	Merger, 2 colleges, UK, 2002–2003	Group	Critical
		Maguire, S. and N. Phillips 2008	Merger, Citicorp and Travellers, financial services industry, US, 1999–2001	Group	Interpretive
		van Vuuren, M., P. Beelen and M. D. T. de Jong 2010	Merger, 2 universities, ZA, collected data on pre- and post-merger, time period not stated	Organizational	Interpretive

Results

Table 17.2 provides an overview of 51 identified studies according to empirical context, level of analysis and research tradition, and how 13 themes were characterized by five different process categories: environmental, coordination, leader, employee and identity processes.

The studies reviewed exhibit some general characteristics. One is that they are based on different research traditions. For example, there are several positivistic studies, some of which include normative statements such as how to integrate biotech companies into pharmaceutical companies (Schweizer 2005); interpretive studies showing how individuals construct irrational characteristics which make organizational integration difficult (Vaara 2003); and critical studies describing how the term organizational culture is constructed through discourse and used to manage conflicts between merging organizations (Riad 2005).

The studies span different levels of analysis. For example, Empson (2001) explores how and why individuals oppose knowledge transfer in mergers between professional service organizations. Harwood (2006) studies how groups use confidentiality agreements during integration. Ranft and Lord (2002) investigate knowledge and capability transfer between organizations in high-tech acquisitions. The societal level is present in several studies. One example is Hellgren et al. (2002) analysing how media (re)construct issues such as division of ownership and choice of top executives. There are also studies spanning several levels of analysis, for example, Kitchener (2002) studying how M&A became institutionalized in US healthcare as a managerial innovation or myth.

Another observation is that each study has its own temporal characteristic (cf. Langley et al. 2013). The length of processes and when they start or end are often difficult to determine. Studies of individuals' emotions or identity change have no clear start or end (Ford and Harding 2003; Vaara et al. 2003). It can be equally difficult to determine when integration processes end, as is exemplified by an ethnographic study of a merger in the healthcare sector in which the integration process was still in progress after eight years (Yu et al. 2005). Other examples include a study of institutional change between 1958 and 1990 in the publishing industry and its impact on acquisitions (Thornton 2001), and historical studies of how acquisitions contribute to long-term development across decades (Higgins and Toms 2006; Jones and Miskell 2007). A contrasting example is a study of corporate culture seminars revealing how people experience being part of a merger, spanning only a few days (Vaara et al. 2003).

In line with previous research (Meglio and Risberg 2011; Very 2011),[4] our review shows that there exist many different types of outcomes following an M&A process. Examples of outcomes are how industrial relations are affected (Wallis and Winterton 2001), how transfer of technologies and capabilities is achieved (Ranft and Lord 2002), how choice of language policy affects power relations (Vaara et al. 2005) or how organizational identity changes (Empson 2004). In some cases, however, it does not seem meaningful to talk about outcome, at least not in the more traditional sense. Examples include how media construct winners and losers in mergers (Hellgren et al. 2002), trust and deception between buyers and sellers (Graebner 2009), emotional processes in mergers (Ford and Harding 2003) or how employees perceive their own and the expected merged organization before a merger (Dackert et al. 2003).

In summary, the studies reviewed exhibit considerable variation regarding research traditions, levels of analysis, temporal characteristics and outcomes. The image that emerges is that M&As are anything but a process made up of a pre-merger phase and a post-merger phase. In the following section we present general characteristics of the five identified M&A process categories. We discuss how the identified themes within each category may add to our knowledge of M&A phenomena. Finally, we discuss how this multitude of processes can develop our understanding of M&As and how future research can benefit from these insights.

Environmental processes

M&As are not only related to processes within acquiring and acquired organizations. Processes in organizational environments can also shape and be shaped by M&As, sometimes over several decades and several transactions. Environmental processes relate to three identified themes:[5] institutional forces (6), stakeholder relationships (6) and long-term development (4).

Environmental process research enables us to comprehend the potency of institutional forces for M&A events and actions. Wood (2001) shows how an acquisition-based portfolio-restructuring strategy was affected by anti-competitive regulation. The company studied acquired a competitor to block other competitors from acquiring it and gaining market share. In order to pre-empt regulatory action, the acquirer divested part of its business. This exemplifies how regulation may link acquisition decisions to divestment decisions. Cheffins (2004) illustrates how regulation influenced merger activities in Britain during the late 1950s to the early 1970s. He argues that anti-competitive regulation fostered the discontinuation of cartel-like arrangements in favour of mergers, leading to a British merger wave, resulting in larger companies and a separation of ownership and control. Similarly, Lu (2010) shows how the acquisition of a US bank by a foreign bank was impacted by differences in federal and state policies, and thus different legislations, leading to uncertainty as to whether the transaction would be concluded, delays and increased acquirer costs.

The apolitical imagery of M&A is challenged by environmental process research that illustrates couplings between institutional logics and M&A. A study by Thornton (2001), for instance, discusses how a change in institutional logic in the publishing market – from editorial logic to market logic – increased the risk of being acquired for companies not adapting their strategy and structure to the new market logic. Similarly, Kitchener (2002) explains how political choices in healthcare caused a shift from professionalism to a market-managerial logic. Executive board members of academic healthcare centres, business press and management consultants uncritically adopted a standard of the 'merger-is-effective' myth. This led to a merger between two healthcare centres that, subsequently, was discontinued. Moreover, Kitchener (2002) gives emphasis to the role of managerial agency, describing how managers select innovations from a menu of legitimized M&A options that change over time. This leads to the question of institutional forces as drivers of M&As and what settings, e.g. type of industry or organization, can lead to a similar and uncritical use of M&As. Finally, Mtar (2010) demonstrates how the implementation of French national management systems into UK acquisition practices was affected by institutional distance, power dependency and market structure.

A second theme in environmental process research relates to stakeholder relationships. A number of studies show how M&A attracts media attention, which is commonly used by management to convey their messages. For example, Hellgren *et al.* (2002) argue that media create winners and losers around issues, often by uncritically drawing on nationalistic perspectives. Likewise, Vaara *et al.* (2006) show how the media legitimate what is happening in M&A processes by a largely uncritical use of communication originating from top managers. These studies exemplify how the media (re)construct meaning around M&A issues such as ownership, composition of top management, head office location and staff reduction, which in turn influence merged organizations and their employees. Likewise, Savage (2004) shows in a merger between two hospitals how a local union influenced negotiations by mobilizing local and national communities and unions through the media, resulting in terms that protected healthcare quality and work conditions.

In a different context, Wallis and Winterton (2001) demonstrate, in the sale and privatization of British coal, how union relationships were impacted at different pits. The outcome varied between pits, depending on whether the government required the buyer to keep existing regulation or not. Moreover, development of customer and supplier relationships can also be important for integration of acquirer and acquired organizations. The research by Spedale *et al.* (2007) shows how relationships to customers and suppliers in a target firm changes during integration. Some relationships were terminated, others changed character, from including social attachment to purely commercial relationships. Also, in an acquisition of a South Korean agricultural company by a US company, Kim (2006) describes how a local, multinational competitor unpredictably appealed to nationalist sentiments through the media and other channels to negatively influence the acquired company and gain market shares, also making the acquired company lose its state subsidies.

The final theme of environmental process research concerns long-term development. Understanding M&A outcomes as consequences of single, isolated transactions is, for example, very different from viewing M&As as a set of steps for corporate renewal across decades. The studies by Higgins and Toms (2006), Meyer (2006), and Jones and Miskell (2007) demonstrate how organizations use M&A in building strong global businesses through several acquisitions and divestments over decades. Capabilities of these organizations and their competitive position have been strengthened over time through M&A opportunities in unique organizational environments (cf. Haspeslagh and Jemison 1991). Historical studies in particular include detailed accounts of how this is achieved. For example, Jones and Miskell (2007) illustrate how acquired complementary assets in the form of detailed local knowledge added value for Unilever in building a global ice cream business over 40 years and a global tea business over 60 years. In the latter case, strategy changed over time because of acquisitions adding long-term value from emerging business opportunities rather than from a planned serial acquisition programme (cf. Haspeslagh and Jemison 1991; Laamanen and Keil 2008).

The conventional short-term view of M&A is further challenged by studies showing how influencing factors change over time. Meyer (2006) gives an example of how several factors influence acquisitions and divestments. In two Danish companies the process of focusing product portfolios by divestments and that of going global by acquisitions were mainly driven externally by evolution in the industry, liberalization of the institutional environment and financial markets, and internally by top management. Similarly, in a historical study by Cheffins (2004), the influence of competitive regulation, managerial skills and economies of scale on M&A decisions was dynamic across time, as well as across countries.

Coordination processes

The coordination category includes processes related to coordination inside acquiring and acquired organizations. We identified two themes: influencing drivers (5) and improbabilities (7).

Coordination process research has augmented our understanding of drivers influencing coordination issues rendered by M&As. Studies by Bresman *et al.* (2010), Ranft and Lord (2002) and Schweizer (2005) reveal how multiple short- and long-term motives lead to differences in how integration is coordinated. For example, a short-term motive can be to improve market position rapidly by absorbing new products or patents, whilst a long-term motive can be to access know-how supporting long-term growth (Schweizer 2005). The former motive calls for instant integration; the latter requires gradual, long-term integration to foster socialization between acquirer and acquired organizations. Articulated knowledge such as patents is explicit, making knowledge transfer more or less a unidirectional activity between one and three years after a finalized acquisition, with limited personal interaction, sometimes even imposed upon acquired organizations (Bresman *et al.* 2010). Socially embedded knowledge such as know-how is tacit, making knowledge transfer a complex bidirectional activity that needs to involve several people over long periods of time, often between three and five years (Bresman *et al.* 2010; Ranft and Lord 2002).

In studying allocation processes, Meyer (2001) explains how choice of distributive and procedural justice mediates the effect of multiple M&A motives on perceptions of fairness and usefulness of allocation approaches, and the moderating roles of differential power relations and ambiguity in such allocation processes. In contrast, drawing on the interpretative research tradition, Vaara and Monin (2010) explore the role of discursive legitimation of merger motives, by the media and the merger parties, in coordination processes. As integration of merged organizations proceeded, lack of a realized synergy potential (i.e. technologies, products and practices) led to de-legitimation of original merger motives and legitimation of merger break-up.

Coordination process research also attests to the improbability of purposeful and predictable coordination efforts following M&As. A study by Empson (2001), for example, elegantly shows how employee perceptions can differ between acquirer and acquired organization and hinder integration. Some stakeholders perceived certain knowledge as being explicit, others as tacit, whereby knowledge sharing was impeded. Similarly, Meyer and Altenborg (2007), in a study of a cross-border merger, show how differences in perceptions of fairness in allocating functions and positions can lead to social disintegration when governance structures paralyse top manager decision-making. In a merger between three unions, Morris *et al.* (2001) demonstrate how it was dependent on intensive leader negotiation efforts, convergence of organizational structures and values, and a demonstrable equal power balance. In another study, Meyer and Altenborg (2008) explain that the merger parties had complementary assets and, hence, a strategic fit, whereas management subsequently exhibited divergent views on how these resources should be deployed.

In a German context, Keller (2005) studies consequences of a merger between five unions, finding that outcomes are ambiguous regarding realization of synergies and membership development. One interpretation that he suggests is that the merger was driven by a merger wave and not by an analysis of the future. Fulop *et al.* (2005) show how delays in appointing middle managers in public sector organizations affect integration of subordinate healthcare units. Because a due process needs to be demonstrated, integration took longer than in private sector mergers. Finally, Harwood (2006) shows how confidentiality agreements create space to develop scenarios and contingency plans for integration, while these at the same time changed the power balance and trust between those inside and outside the agreements.

Leader processes

Leader process research illustrates that M&As put high demands on leaders in both acquiring and acquired organizations. We identified three partly overlapping themes in leader process research: difficulties of change (3), unexpected actions (5) and importance of sellers (3).

Leader process research highlights that it can be difficult for leaders to accommodate change in merged organizations. This is illustrated by three merger studies of pluralistic organizations, i.e. organizations that have diffuse power structures and divergent objectives. For instance, in a five-year study of mergers between hospitals, Denis *et al.* (2001) observed that change required simultaneous coupling between three hierarchical levels in the merged organization: the board, management and subordinate employees. This coupling was difficult to maintain, however, resulting in a long and sporadic change process. Yu *et al.* (2005) analysed what managers direct their attention to during a post-merger integration. They observed that management spent most attention on administrative matters. It took five years before the initial purpose of the merger – patient care – came into focus, and the change process was still underway after eight years. Similarly, in three case studies Kavanagh and Ashkanasy (2006) show that organizational change takes a long time. In one of the mergers no significant change could be observed after a six-year integration process. The authors argue that the pace of change is important for gaining employee acceptance and that an incremental change approach increases the prospects of obtaining employee acceptance and decreases the risk of employee resistance.

The rational choice perspective of M&A is confronted by leader process research that illustrates the need for leaders to engage in unexpected action. For example, Yu *et al.* (2005) conclude that interactions within a larger medical healthcare system were seen as irrational by senior managers, demonstrated by the emergence of unexpected behaviour during the integration process. In a narrative analysis of a hostile takeover, Ng and De Cock (2002) reveal how the chairman of the target company used storytelling skills to carve out a powerful position to serve his own purposes. Leaders may also take on different roles in M&As. Graebner (2004), for instance, explains how leaders of acquired firms may support the creation of value in the implementation of acquisitions, and Denis *et al.* (2001) show the importance of collective leadership to achieve organizational change. Moreover, Graebner and Eisenhardt (2004) articulate in detail how leaders and board members in an interdependent partnership acted as sellers of their firms through courtship behaviour. These studies exemplify that individual leaders, or groups of leaders, can have multiple and different roles in M&A processes.

In contrast to early M&A process perspectives (Jemison and Sitkin 1986; Haspeslagh and Jemison 1991), leader process research demonstrates the importance of the seller side in understanding M&A. Rather than assuming that it is owners who decide whom to sell to, and that owners sell to the highest bidder in a market for corporate control, Graebner presents evidence that is contradictory to these views in three studies. For instance, Graebner and Eisenhardt (2004) identify three factors – strategic hurdles, personal motivation and attraction of buyers – influencing when and to whom leaders sell their firms, and it is not necessarily to the highest bidder. They characterize acquisition processes as strongly dependent on social exchange. Similarly, Graebner (2009) explores how trust and deception develop between leaders of sellers and buyers during acquisition and integration of businesses, pointing to the importance of analysing both sellers and buyers to understand pre-merger action. Finally, Graebner (2004) shows how leaders from acquired organizations manage integration processes through lines of cross-organizational responsibilities. As a result, resource reconfiguration opportunities were identified unexpectedly and created serendipitous value.

Employee processes

Employee process research highlights M&A issues of individuals and groups who are not leaders and do not involve identity. We discerned two themes of research relating employee reactions to power and politics: alienation (2) and discursive practices (6).

Employee process research suggests that employee processes may start well before transactions take place. Following the announcement of a possible sale three years ahead of the actual transaction, for instance, Marks and Vansteenkiste (2008) describe how a human resource team worked proactively to manage employees in the transition from a healthy and vibrant workplace to an uncertain future characterized by changing employee opinions, relocation efforts and many potential layoffs. The study demonstrates that restricting M&A research to the acquirer's perspective will not only restrict our understanding of pre-transaction events and actions but also the role of those in post-transaction phases. Brannen and Peterson (2009) argue that work alienation may lead to unrealized integration goals, such as technology transfer and knowledge sharing. Pockets of alienation were identified in the post-merger phase, and the authors suggest that interventions such as visiting acquirers' home country or transfer of acquirer supervisors may help overcome such group-level alienation.

Employee process research also enables us to understand the role of discursive practices. In a cross-border merger, for instance, Vaara et al. (2005) show how employees with skills in the selected corporate language became empowered at the expense of those without skills. Similarly, Riad (2005) traced how knowledge of organizational culture forms discourse and beliefs about truths, which served to enable or resist integration and legitimatize managerial intervention. Likewise, in a multiple case study by Vaara (2002), four types of discourse were identified to play different roles when managers (re)constructed justifications of their own actions and responsibilities, which at times also required managers to change discourse depending on power structures and political circumstances. Vaara (2003) shows how cross-border integration decisions, involving powerful middle managers, were characterized by language, and cultural and social differences. This created ambiguity, cultural confusion, organizational hypocrisy and politicization of integration issues and, hence, irrational integration decision-making. In studying a merger integration team, Llewellyn (2007) explores how team members constituted themselves as agents of change. She discerned four types of agential roles that enabled them to draw on certain knowledge, rules, powers and resources to manage an integration process. Finally, in a narrative analysis, Ford and Harding (2003) explore depowered managers' talk about their emotions in response to critical leader communications during an integration of two healthcare organizations. These studies demonstrate the many roles that use of talk and text may have for M&A events and actions.

Identity processes

Identity process research problematizes the constitution of identity change by characterizing it as a product of on-going constructive or interpretative acts to create meaning around M&A. We identified three themes of identity process research: identity change (4), identity differentiation (5) and the unpredictability of identity change (4).

Identity process research illustrates that identity change may start well ahead of transactions and continue during integration of organizations. Ullrich et al. (2005), for instance, show that absence of employees' sense of continuity for organizational identity in a recently merged industrial organization was eroded by the pre-existence of two strong and different organizational cultures in place before the merger. This affected post-merger interpretations of top management's symbolic actions, producing uncertainty for employees around, for example, their personal and the company's future. Clark et al. (2010) illustrate similar pre-merger destabilization of organizational identity. When a possible merger between two rival healthcare organizations became known, they reveal how two top management teams crafted a transitional identity that served as an interim identity bridge; it was ambiguous enough to enable members to disconnect from the old identities and start working toward creating a new and shared identity. Similarly, Dackert et al. (2003) examined employees informed up to nine months in advance of a merger between two public organizations. They argue that integration was critically dependent on how people perceive culture in the two organizations involved and on what expectations they have of the new organization before the transaction. Pre-merger events and actions, again, are important for understanding M&A identity change processes, and there is evidence in other studies to show this to some extent (e.g. van Vuuren et al. 2010). These processes start when the possibility of transactions becomes known, again highlighting the importance of developing our understanding of pre-merger processes.

In addition, identity process research displays differentiated constructions of meaning around identity changes in M&A. For example, Vaara et al. (2003) analyse strong emotional responses by employees using nationalistic stereotypes to describe 'us' and 'them' in a cross-border merger. They illustrate how employees used metaphors to build social identity through cognitive, emotional and political constructions of superiority and inferiority. Likewise, also in a cross-border acquisition, Ailon-Souday and Kunda (2003) argue that national identity is a symbolic resource that enabled employees of the acquiring organization to struggle for local separateness (national identity as boundary) and global status (national identity as organizational merit) through us-and-them constructions such as 'we Israelis' and 'the Americans'. Similar forms of us-and-them constructions and in-group favouritism can be found in other identity process studies (e.g. Dackert et al. 2003; Clark et al. 2010; van Vuuren et al. 2010). A common aspect of identity differentiation studies is an observed prevalence of expectations in both merger parties that one party will dominate the merger and that this will lead to limited changes for the dominant party and radical changes for the submissive party.

Related to the notion of identity differentiation in identity process research is an element of the unpredictability of identity change. For instance, in a study of a merger between a traditionally 'white' and a traditionally 'black' university in South Africa, van Vuuren et al. (2010) show how both groups of employees shifted identity from being organizational members and instead started to identify themselves with the academic profession. Surprisingly, academics from both groups claimed to be the dominant group. Also, Maguire and Phillips (2008) describe in a merger between two financial companies how a group of employees did not identify themselves with the identity narrative of the merged organization, leading to an unexpected loss of institutional trust. Similarly, Brown and Humphreys (2006) show how a group of employees were able to locate place as a discursive resource to defend their version of organizational identity. In an acquisition in the accounting industry, Empson (2004) illustrates in detail the complex ways in which organizational identity change can be related to professional identity change. Because different change processes took place within different groups of the organizations involved, distinctively different professional identities coexisted within different functional parts of the merged organization. A complex interplay followed during a three-year integration process between professional identities, managers' aspirations for organizational image and organizational members' changing conceptualizations of their professional identities. This produced an uncertain and evolving notion of organizational identity, manifest in de-identification and re-identification action.

Concluding discussion and future research

Previous M&A process research emphasizes 'the acquisition process itself' (Jemison and Sitkin 1986: 145) with a pre- and post-merger phase resulting in some outcome (e.g. Mace and Montgomery 1962; Jemison and Sitkin 1986; Haspeslagh and Jemison 1991). This review provides reasons to question this view. We argue that M&As instead should be regarded as a multitude of environmental, coordination, leadership, employee and identity processes. Hereafter, we discuss in more detail the results of the review and how these relate to the traditional pre-merger–post-merger view of M&A processes. By doing that we will be able to show that the empirical accounts do not really reflect the conventional idea of M&A as a linear process with two distinct phases and an outcome.

The review shows, surprisingly, that only three studies focus on transaction activities (Graebner and Eisenhardt 2004; Graebner 2009; Vaara and Monin 2010). A reason for the lack of studies in this regard is most probably the difficulty of obtaining access to material for the study of this important phase. Therefore, more effort must be put into convincing companies of the advantages of taking part in such studies and by doing so helping to enhance our understanding of M&A processes. The lack of studies on transaction activities could also be a result of researchers finding the conventional view on M&A processes as overly simplistic and that the distinction of the pre- and post-merger phase is arbitrary. For example, several studies of leaders, employees and identity reveal that activities related to how integration processes unfold start at the moment people become aware of a possible sale. In some cases such changes can begin several years prior to a transaction. One of these studies discusses how roles within organizations, employee perceptions and opinions of a sale change during the process (Marks and Vansteenkiste 2008). Dackert *et al.* (2003) analyse how employees of two merger parties perceive the culture of the organizations involved and the expectations they have of the new organization, starting nine months before the merger. Also, the study by Graebner (2009) shows how differences in trust between sellers and buyers in the negotiation phase can lead to deception in the integration of organizations. All in all, we argue that dividing M&A into these very distinct (and few) phases restricts our way of understanding M&A phenomena and especially how integration processes evolve.

Turning to M&A outcome we can conclude that earlier research has emphasized financial performance and has had a strong focus on the acquirer (e.g. Haspeslagh and Jemison 1991; Cartwright and Schoenberg 2006; Haleblian *et al.* 2009; Meglio and Risberg 2010, 2011). The review shows that outcome is a difficult construct to operationalize and measure. One example is environmental processes which affect the outcome for several different stakeholders and their relationships with the acquiring and/or acquired company, such as industrial relations (Wallis and Winterton 2001), public healthcare and employment conditions (Savage 2004), competitors (Kim 2006) and customers and suppliers (Spedale *et al.* 2007). Environmental process studies also show the difficulty in analysing acquisitions as single events in the development of firms. One example is the study by Wood (2001), which describes how a company, for regulatory reasons, was forced to divest parts of its business to be allowed to acquire a retail chain. Similarly, the historical studies by Higgins and Toms (2006) and Jones and Miskell (2007) show how global businesses are built through several acquisitions and divestments over long periods of time. To understand such lengthy processes, we need to expand our view of outcome as a single activity to embrace a view of outcome as a result of long-term change for corporate development. Coordination process research also includes examples of different types of outcomes such as transfer of knowledge (Ranft and Lord 2002; Bresman *et al.* 2010), use of confidentiality agreements (Harwood 2006) and fairness in allocation of functions and positions (Meyer 2001; Meyer and Altenborg 2007). Leader process research gives examples of outcomes of organizational change (Denis *et al.* 2001) and value creation in which leaders of acquired firms have important roles (Graebner 2004). Employee and identity process research describes outcomes that include individual emotions (Ford and Harding 2003), power effects of the choice of language policy (Vaara *et al.* 2005), organizational identity change (Empson 2004) and institutional trust (Maguire and Phillips 2008). This research helps to deepen our understanding of the many different outcomes that are the result of M&As. It also helps us to understand that the outcome is affected by a multitude of processes rather than events and actions that can be clearly related to the pre- and/or post-merger phases.

In summary, this chapter shows that it is questionable if a division into pre- and post-merger phases is helpful for understanding processes in acquiring and acquired organizations, leading to acquisition and eventually integration. The chapter shows that this division tends to restrict our way of surveying and understanding these phenomena. We will therefore provide some final examples of how viewing M&A as a multitude of processes can remedy this shortcoming and offer some recommendations for future research directions.

First, the review shows that, in the few papers that exist, transaction activities and events are typically studied from the perspective of the acquirer. Adding the seller would bring in the 'other side', challenging earlier views based on a passive seller only focused on maximizing the price (Graebner and Eisenhardt 2004). Research in this area could be highly rewarding and increase our understanding of issues and activities in post-merger phases as well as related outcomes. Second, studying M&A processes means that we need to understand when and how they start and how long we want to study them. For example, employee and identity processes can start as soon as employees become aware of a possible M&A (Dackert et al. 2003). Processes of organizational change can be long, and the review includes examples of processes still continuing after more than eight years (Yu et al. 2005). In future research the temporal aspects of M&A processes should be highlighted, especially why a certain period of study is chosen and when outcomes should be measured (Meglio and Risberg 2011). Third, by adding a longer time perspective in future research, processes of multiple M&As can be studied as a means of long-term corporate renewal (Wood 2001; Higgins and Toms 2006; Meyer 2006; Jones and Miskell 2007). Outcomes of these transactions should be assessed jointly and not as outcomes of single transactions. Finally, in most previous studies outcome has dealt with the performance of acquirers (Haleblian et al. 2009; Meglio and Risberg 2010, 2011). In future research studies of a multitude of processes can enhance our ability to talk about outcomes for many processes, involving several organizations and actors. Examples are environmental processes with outcomes such as how relationships with customers and suppliers affect acquisitions or, in structural processes, how the transfer of knowledge succeeds (e.g. Spedale et al. 2007).

These overall conclusions and directions for future research show that the conventional idea of M&As as a linear process – commonly described as pre-merger and post-merger phases leading to some outcome – is genuinely problematic. M&A phenomena are much more complex, consisting of a multitude of processes. These processes relate to the environment, structures and people: in other words, research areas that attract attention also in the fields of strategy and organization studies. We can also conclude that the field of M&A process research is still not a mature research area. Therefore it is not surprising that the field has a rather heterogenic character – albeit dominated by a positivist research tradition – in which the different studies and results indicate a low level of integration. The literature review and the presentation of the results show this. Even though we do not believe that there will ever exist a single, generic M&A process theory, we would like to encourage more research aiming at consolidating the field. This literature review is a first and obviously insufficient step towards a higher degree of consolidation. A second step in this endeavour could be to create an alternative process model to the one presented by Jemison and Sitkin (1986) more than 25 years ago. This would, without doubt, be a much welcomed contribution to M&A process research.

Acknowledgement

This paper was presented at the Nordic Academy of Management Conference, August 20–24, 2011, Stockholm; The European Group for Organizational Studies, July 2–7, 2012, Helsinki; and Behavioural Finance and Cross Border Investments & Acquisition, 21–22 June, 2012, Behavioural Finance Working Group / M&A Research Centre, Cass Business School, London. We would like thank the participants at these conferences, as well as the members of the Accounting Group, Department of Business Studies, Uppsala University, for valuable comments.

Notes

1 We do not consider the outcome in itself to be a process, even though the evaluation of the pre- and the post-merger phases typically has process characteristics (cf. Anderson 2013).
2 We exclude *Harvard Business Review* because papers published in it do not meet scientific publication standards (e.g. methods used are not disclosed).
3 Some papers are attributed to more than one theme within a category but not across categories.
4 These authors use the term, performance instead of outcome. Meglio and Risberg (2011) discuss market performance, accounting performance, operational performance and overall performance.
5 The number of papers attributed to each theme is indicated in brackets.

References

Ailon-Souday, G. and Kunda, G. (2003) 'The local selves of global workers: the social construction of national identity in the face of organizational globalization', *Organization Studies*, 24: 1073–96.
Anderson, H. (2013) 'Reflection on the critical role of stakeholders in mergers and acquisitions', in H. Anderson, V. Havila and F. Nilsson (eds) *Mergers and Acquisitions: The Critical Role of Stakeholders*, New York: Routledge, pp. 269–80.
Anderson, H., Havila, V. and Nilsson, F. (2013) *Mergers and Acquisitions: The Critical Role of Stakeholders*, New York: Routledge.
Brannen, M.Y. and Peterson, M.F. (2009) 'Merging without alienating: interventions promoting cross-cultural organizational integration and their limitations', *Journal of International Business Studies*, 40: 468–89.
Bresman, H., Birkinshaw, J. and Nobel, R. (2010) 'Knowledge transfer in international acquisitions', *Journal of International Business Studies*, 41: 5–20.
Brown, A.D. and Humphreys, M. (2006) 'Organizational identity and place: a discursive exploration of hegemony and resistance', *Journal of Management Studies*, 43: 231–57.
Calipha, R., Tarba, S. and Brock, D. (2010) 'Mergers and acquisitions: a review of phases, motives, and success factors', *Advances in Mergers and Acquisitions*, 9: 1–24.
Cartwright, S. and Schoenberg, R. (2006) 'Thirty years of mergers and acquisitions research: recent advances and future opportunities', *British Journal of Management*, 17: S1–S5.
Cartwright, S., Teerikangas, S., Rouzies, A. and Wilson-Evered, E. (2012) 'Methods in M&A: a look at the past and the future to forge a path forward', *Scandinavian Journal of Management*, 28: 95–106.
Cheffins, B.R. (2004) 'Mergers and the evolution of patterns of corporate ownership and control: the British experience', *Business History*, 46: 256–84.
Clark, S.M., Gioia, D.M., Ketchen, D.J. and Thomas, J.B. (2010) 'Transitional identity as a facilitator of organizational identity change during a merger', *Administrative Science Quarterly*, 55: 397–438.
Dackert, I., Jackson, P.R., Brenner, S.-O. and Johansson, C.R. (2003) 'Eliciting and analysing employees' expectations of a merger', *Human Relations*, 56: 705–25.
Denis, J.-L., Lamothe, L. and Langley, A. (2001) 'The dynamics of collective leadership and strategic change in pluralistic organizations', *Academy of Management Journal*, 44: 809–37.
Empson, L. (2001) 'Fear of exploitation and fear of contamination: impediments to knowledge transfer in mergers between professional service firms', *Human Relations*, 54: 839–62.
Empson, L. (2004) 'Organizational identity change: managerial regulation and member identification in an accounting firm acquisition', *Accounting, Organizations & Society*, 29: 759–81.
Faulkner, D., Teerikangas, S. and Joseph, R.J. (2012) *The Handbook of Mergers and Acquisitions*, Oxford: Oxford University Press.
Ford, J. and Harding, N. (2003) 'Invoking Satan or the ethics of the employment contract', *Journal of Management Studies*, 40: 1131–50.
Fulop, N., Protopsaltis, G., King, A., Allen, P., Hutchings, A. and Normand, C. (2005) 'Changing organisations: a study of the context and processes of mergers of health care providers in England', *Social Science and Medicine*, 60: 119–30.
Gephart, R.P. (2004) 'From the editors: qualitative research and the Academy of Management Journal', *Academy of Management Journal*, 47: 454–62.
Graebner, M.E. (2004) 'Momentum and serendipity: how acquired leaders create value in the integration of technology firms', *Strategic Management Journal*, 25: 751–77.
Graebner, M.E. (2009) 'Caveat venditor: trust assymetries in acquisitions of entrepreneurial firms', *Academy of Management Journal*, 52: 435–72.

Graebner, M.E. and Eisenhardt, K.M. (2004) 'The seller's side of the story: acquisition as courtship and governance as syndicate in entrepreneurial firms', *Administrative Science Quarterly*, 49: 366–403.

Haleblian, J., Devers, C.E., McNamara, G., Carpenter, M.A. and Davison, R.B. (2009) 'Taking stock of what we know about mergers and acquisitions: a review and research agenda', *Journal of Management*, 35: 469–502.

Harwood, I. (2006) 'Confidentiality constraints within mergers and acquisitions: gaining insights through a "bubble" metaphor', *British Journal of Management*, 17: 347–59.

Haspeslagh, P. and Jemison, D.E. (1991) *Managing Acquisitions: Creating Value for Corporate Renewal*, New York: Free Press.

Hellgren, B., Löwstedt, J., Puttonen, L., Tienari, J., Vaara, E. and Werr, A. (2002) 'How issues become (re) constructed in the media: discursive practices in the AstraZeneca merger', *British Journal of Management*, 13: 123–40.

Higgins, D.M. and Toms, S. (2006) 'Financial institutions and corporate strategy: David Alliance and the transformation of British textiles, c.1950–c.1990', *Business History*, 48: 453–78.

Jemison, D.B. and Sitkin, S.B. (1986) 'Corporate acquisitions: a process perspective', *Academy of Management Review*, 11: 145–63.

Jones, G. and Miskell, P. (2007) 'Acquisitions and firm growth: creating Unilever's ice cream and tea business', *Business History*, 49: 8–28.

Kavanagh, M.H. and Ashkanasy, N.M. (2006) 'The impact of leadership and change management strategy on organizational culture and individual acceptance of change during a merger', *British Journal of Management*, 17: S81–S103.

Keller, B. (2005) 'Union formation through merger: the case of Ver.di in Germany', *British Journal of Industrial Relations*, 43: 209–32.

Kim, S.-J. (2006) 'Networks, scale, and transnational corporations: the case of the South Korean seed industry', *Economic Geography*, 82: 317–38.

Kitchener, M. (2002) 'Mobilizing the logic of managerialism in professional fields: the case of academic health centre mergers', *Organization Studies*, 23: 391–420.

Laamanen, T. and Keil, T. (2008) 'Performance of serial acquirers: toward an acquisition program perspective', *Strategic Management Journal*, 29: 663–72.

Langley, A., Smallman, C., Tsoukas, H. and Van de Ven, A. (2013) 'Process studies of change in organization and management: unveiling temporality, activity, and flow', *Academy of Management Journal*, 56: 1–13.

Llewellyn, S. (2007) 'Introducing the agents', *Organization Studies*, 28: 133–53.

Lu, Q. (2010) 'The US Government dual banking regulation levels, transaction costs and HSBC's strategy in acquiring Marine Midland Banks, Inc., 1978–80', *Business History*, 52: 955–77.

Mace, M.L. and Montgomery, G.G. (1962) *Management Problems of Corporate Acquisitions*. Boston: Harvard University, Graduate School of Business and Administration.

Maguire, S. and Phillips, N. (2008.) '"Citibankers" at Citigroup: a study of the loss of institutional trust after a merger', *Journal of Management Studies*, 45: 372–401.

Marks, M.L. and Vansteenkiste, R. (2008) 'Preparing for organizational death: proactive HR engagement in an organizational transition', *Human Resource Management*, 47: 809–27.

Meglio, O. and Risberg, A. (2010) 'Mergers and acquisitions: time for a methodological rejuvenation of the field?', *Scandinavian Journal of Management*, 26: 87–95.

Meglio, O. and Risberg, A. (2011) 'The (mis)measurement of M&A performance: a systematic narrative literature review', *Scandinavian Journal of Management*, 27: 418–33.

Meyer, C.B. (2001) 'Allocation processes in mergers and acquisitions: an organizational justice perspective', *British Journal of Management*, 12: 47–66.

Meyer, C.B. and Altenborg, E. (2007) 'The disintegrating effects of equality: a study of a failed international merger', *British Journal of Management*, 18: 257–71.

Meyer, C.B. and Altenborg, E. (2008) 'Incompatible strategies in international mergers: the failed merger between Telia and Telenor', *Journal of International Business Studies*, 39: 508–25.

Meyer, K.E. (2006) 'Globalfocusing: from domestic conglomerates to global specialists', *Journal of Management Studies*, 43: 1109–44.

Morris, T., Storey, J., Wilkinson, A. and Cressey, P. (2001) 'Industry change and union mergers in British retail finance', *British Journal of Industrial Relations*, 39: 237–56.

Mtar, M. (2010) 'Institutional, industry and power effects on integration in cross-border acquisitions', *Organization Studies*, 31: 1099–127.

Ng, W. and De Cock, C. (2002) 'Battle in the boardroom: a discursive perspective', *Journal of Management Studies*, 39: 23–49.

Pablo, A.L. and Javidan, M. (2004) *Mergers and Acquisitions: Creating Integrative Knowledge*, Malden, MA: Blackwell Publishing

Ranft, A.L. and Lord, M.D. (2002) 'Acquiring new technologies and capabilities: a grounded model of acquisition implementation', *Organization Science*, 13: 420–41.

Riad, S. (2005) 'The power of 'organizational culture' as a discursive formation in merger integration', *Organization Studies*, 26: 1529–54.

Risberg, A. (1999) *Ambiguities Thereafter: An Interpretive Approach to Acquisitions*, Malmö: Lund University Press.

Risberg, A. (2006) *Mergers and Acquisitions: A Critical Reader*, London: Routledge.

Savage, L. (2004) 'Public sector unions shaping hospital privatization: the creation of Boston medical center', *Environment and Planning A*, 36: 547–68.

Schweizer, L. (2005) 'Organizational integration of acquired biotechnology companies into pharmaceutical companies: the need for a hybrid approach', *Academy of Management Journal*, 48: 1051–74.

Shrivastava, P. (1986) 'Postmerger integration', *The Journal of Business Strategy*, 7: 65–76.

Spedale, S., Van Den Bosch, F.A.J. and Volberda, H.W. (2007) 'Preservation and dissolution of the target firm's embedded ties in acquisitions', *Organization Studies*, 28: 1169–96.

Thornton, P.H. (2001) 'Personal versus market logics of control: a historically contingent theory of the risk of acquisition', *Organization Science*, 12: 294–311.

Ullrich, J., Wieseke, J. and Van Dick, R. (2005) 'Continuity and change in mergers and acquisitions: a social identity case study of a German industrial merger', *Journal of Management Studies*, 42: 1549–69.

Vaara, E. (2002) 'On the discursive construction of success/failure in narratives of post-merger integration', *Organization Studies*, 23: 211–48.

Vaara, E. (2003) 'Post-acquisition integration as sensemaking: glimpses of ambiguity, confusion, hypocrisy, and politicization', *Journal of Management Studies*, 40: 859–94.

Vaara, E. and Monin, P. (2010) 'A recursive perspective on discursive legitimation and organizational action in mergers and acquisitions', *Organization Science*, 21: 3–22.

Vaara, E., Tienari, J. and Säntti, R. (2003) 'The international match: metaphors as vehicles of social identity-building in cross-border mergers', *Human Relations*, 56: 419–51.

Vaara, E., Tienari, J. and Laurila, J. (2006) 'Pulp and paper fiction: on the discursive legitimation of global industrial restructuring', *Organization Studies*, 27: 789–813.

Vaara, E., Tienari, J., Piekkari, R. and Säntti, R. (2005) 'Language and the circuits of power in a merging multinational corporation', *Journal of Management Studies*, 42: 595–623.

Van de Ven, A.H. and Poole, M.S. (2005) 'Alternative approaches for studying organizational change', *Organization Studies*, 26: 1377–404.

van Vuuren, M., Beelen, P. and de Jong, M.D.T. (2010) 'Speaking of dominance, status differences, and identification: making sense of a merger', *Journal of Occupational & Organizational Psychology*, 83: 627–43.

Very, P. (2011) 'Acquisition performance and the "quest for the Holy Grail"', *Scandinavian Journal of Management*, 27: 434–37.

Wallis, E. and Winterton, J. (2001) 'Industrial relations in privatized UK mining: a contingency strategy?', *British Journal of Industrial Relations*, 39: 565–83.

Wood, S. (2001) 'Regulatory constrained portfolio restructuring: the US department store industry in the 1990s', *Environment and Planning A*, 33: 1279–304.

Yu, J., Engleman, R.M. and Van de Ven, A.H. (2005) 'The integration journey: an attention-based view of the merger and acquisition integration process', *Organization Studies*, 26: 1501–28.

18

Antecedents of anticipatory justice among acquired firm employees

Kaitlyn DeGhetto, Sangbum Ro, Bruce T. Lamont, and Annette L. Ranft

Introduction

In business interactions, first impressions are crucial. While you can't stop people from making snap decisions—the human brain is hardwired in this way as a prehistoric survival mechanism—you can understand how to make those decisions work in your favor.

Forbes, 2011

Despite the prevalence of acquisitions, we know that the majority (between 70 percent and 90 percent) end in failure (Christensen *et al.* 2011). In an effort to help mitigate failures and enhance the chances of successful outcomes, scholars have emphasized the importance of managing the acquisition integration process (e.g. Cording *et al.* 2008; Ellis *et al.* 2009; Haspeslagh and Jemison 1991; Ranft and Lord 2002). Specifically, effectively managing the acquisition process starting from an early stage, such as due diligence and negotiations, is important to secure employee engagement during the integration phase (Jemison and Sitkin 1986) which in turn can lead to value creation (Birkinshaw *et al.* 2000). While it has long been posited that the quality of the due diligence, or pre-deal, phase has important effects on the later stages of the acquisition process, little systematic theoretical work has clarified how the pre-deal process actually sets the stage for employee engagement during the integration process. Thus, the purpose of our study is to highlight the importance of "first impressions" in the acquisition process.

Acquisition pre-deal processes vary, including the templates used, overall complexity, time frame allotted, and employees involved. Despite these differences, all acquisition processes include a pre-deal phase, more than just the top executives become aware of the pending deal to varying degrees, and all acquirers have the opportunity to manage the pre-deal process to their advantage. Drawing on anticipatory justice theory and supporting evidence, we posit that the first impression made by the acquiring firm, positive or negative, will become salient in the minds of target firm managers and employees as they enter the integration process. Further, these initial perceptions are difficult to change and will continue to influence future perceptions.

In this chapter, anticipatory justice refers to "expectations regarding whether one will (or will not) experience justice in the context of some future event" (Rodell and Colquitt 2009: 989; Shapiro and Kirkman 2001) as it relates to target employee justice expectations in the integration process. Drawing on acquisition process research, we identify certain process characteristics that the acquiring firm can develop and implement during the pre-deal phase to increase the likelihood of target employee anticipatory justice which should in turn lead to their engagement and a smoother and more successful integration process. Also, by blending both acquisition research and justice theory, we elaborate our model by including factors likely to moderate the effects of the pre-deal process characteristics on anticipatory justice.

In sum, the proposed model allows us to speculate about the path-dependent acquisition process that will unfold depending upon actions taken during the pre-deal phase and the justice intentions of the acquirer's top managers. In the following sections, we 1) describe various pre-deal processes and highlight several practical examples; 2) introduce and describe the concept of anticipatory justice; 3) elaborate on our conceptual model and develop propositions; and 4) conclude with a discussion of the main contributions, implications, and opportunities for future research.

Pre-deal processes: practical insights

Although the pre-deal phase varies from acquisition to acquisition, it is an important aspect of every acquisition process. Part of the variation in pre-deal processes is due to the acquirer's past experiences and templates used to guide the due diligence process, but variation may also be due to the characteristics of the acquisition itself (Marks and Mirvis 2010). Due to the noted differences in acquisition processes, target employees become aware of the pending acquisition during the pre-deal to varying degrees and, in turn, begin to form perceptions about the forthcoming acquisition. Below, we discuss several reasons why pre-deal processes vary and provide practical examples that highlight circumstances when target employees throughout the firm became aware of the prospective acquisition prior to the deal being finalized.

Merger size is one reason that pre-deal processes differ. A merger between two large firms is more complicated and takes longer than a merger between firms in which at least one firm involved in the deal is small (Ellis et al. 2009). For example, the merger between Mellon Financial Corporation and The Bank of New York resulted in the "largest securities services and asset management firm" in the world (Taliaferro et al. 2009: 2). Thus, it took several years and substantial efforts from a wide-range of employees from both firms during the pre-deal (Taliaferro et al. 2009).

The extent of intended integration is also directly related to the complexity of the acquisition process and length of the pre-deal phase. Partial integration may only affect a few functional areas of the combined firms, whereas full integration will likely result in substantial changes for both firms across all departments (Haspeslagh and Jemison 1991). The complexity of full integration requires more thorough investigation and complete analysis to be conducted prior to the closing of a deal, typically requiring a prolonged, comprehensive pre-deal process that may involve more employees throughout the firm (Haspeslagh and Jemison 1991; Marks and Mirvis 2010).

Beyond intended integration, ownership structure can also impact the acquisition process. In their case study of Starbro Manufacturing, a family-owned firm acquired by BGD Industries, Mickelson and Worley (2003) indicated that family-owned firms may have unique motives, deal requirements, and processes. Differences may occur because emotions and identities are closely tied to the company, all affected family members must approve the deal, and family members demand to be included within the combined firm. Also, Capron and Shen (2007) described how acquiring a publicly held versus a privately held firm will lead to differences in the availability of information during the pre-deal process in terms of both quality and quantity. They proposed that acquiring firms will incur greater search costs when purchasing a privately held firm due to a lack of transparent information.

Further, certain regulatory environments and associated laws introduce additional hurdles and restrictions for mergers and acquisitions that can significantly extend the pre-deal process (Capron and Guillen 2009). Indeed, Dikova et al. (2010) found that the institutional environment and the institutional distance between the acquiring and target firms' home nations impacts the completion rates and timeliness of cross-border acquisitions. These scholars emphasized that differences in antitrust laws or national legal systems (civil vs. common law) may complicate acquisition processes.

The cross-border acquisition between DuPont (US-based) and Danisco (Denmark-based) is a prime example of how the regulatory environment within a given nation can significantly impact the length of the pre-deal process. Although an arguably friendly acquisition from the firms' perspectives, this particular deal was stalled because Danish law requires tender from 90 percent of shareholders and multiple countries had to approve the acquisition (Kullman 2012). Another time-intensive merger occurred between Sirius Satellite Radio Inc. and XM Satellite Radio Holding Inc. for regulatory reasons. The deal was announced 16 months prior to its full approval by the US Federal Communication Commission (*Forbes* 2008), and ample media attention surrounded this merger during the pre-deal process. In these instances, regulatory requirements extended the pre-deal phase, increasing the number of employees from both sides who were aware of and potentially involved in the deal.

Also, many acquisitions occur after the firms have worked together in partnership arrangements. Ultimately, prior business relationships impact pre-deal processes and target employees' perceptions because the acquisition is not the first time that the two firms' employees have worked together. For example, Google Inc. acquired wind energy company Makani Power in May 2013. However, Google's relationship with Makani Power, and investment in the company, dates back to 2006 (*Yahoo Finance* 2013), indicating that the two firms developed a long-term collaborative relationship prior to the pre-deal phase. In addition, DuPont and Danisco were involved in joint ventures prior to DuPont's acquisition of Danisco. These prior partnership arrangements are important because they establish a base of trust that will subsequently transfer into the pre-deal phase (Gulati 1995, Zaheer et al. 1998). Prior research has noted the benefits of two firms first engaging in lower-risk projects in order to temper feelings of vulnerability and increase trust (McCarter et al. 2011), Further, gaining a preview of the other firm during alliances relates to higher performance outcomes (Porrini 2004). Thus, if the target and acquiring firms have a record of prior collaborative relationships, the pre-deal phase may create less uncertainty for the target firm employees and result in greater value creation for stakeholders.

Regardless of the degree of active participation by target employees or aforementioned variations in the pre-deal process, target employees may hear about the pending deal through their supervisors, peers, the media, or simply rumors in the industry (Scheweiger and DeNisi 1991). Prior research indicates that discourse and framing techniques used by the media and executives have a substantial impact on how mergers and acquisitions are perceived by various stakeholder groups (Risberg et al. 2003; Vaara and Tienari 2002; Vaara et al. 2003). Thus, executives should recognize the importance of the pre-deal phase and begin to manage perceptions as early as possible.

These practical examples illustrate that 1) pre-deal processes vary depending upon the circumstances and 2) there are instances when employees at all levels are aware of the pending deal, even if not directly involved. Regardless of the reasons for the varying pre-deal processes, we posit that it is likely that these differences will differentially shape the target firm participants' expectations of fair treatment and, in turn, their receptivity toward change and engagement after the deal is complete.

Anticipatory justice

Anticipatory justice versus experienced justice

Anticipatory justice describes the phenomenon of how individuals form expectations that justice will be carried out in the future based on past justice episodes (Shapiro and Kirkman 2001). In turn, individuals become more receptive to forthcoming changes or other critical decisions that affect them (Cropanzano and Ambrose 2001; Rodell and Colquitt 2009; Shapiro and Kirkman 2001). Prior studies show that anticipatory justice is conceptually and empirically distinct from "experienced" justice, the typical foci of the justice and M&A literature (Bell *et al.* 2006; Colquitt *et al.* 2001; Rodell and Colquitt 2009). Simply put, anticipatory justice is an antecedent to experienced justice (Rodell and Colquitt 2009). Individuals are biased in that there is a tendency to unknowingly focus on new information that supports prior beliefs (Jonas *et al.* 2001; Nickerson 1998). Thus, perceptions of what is experienced (i.e. experience justice) are at least partially a result of what is expected, or anticipated (Shapiro and Kirkman 2001). For these reasons, the concept of anticipatory justice is important to consider separately from experienced justice. However, to our knowledge, the concept of anticipatory justice has yet to be considered in M&A research.

Anticipatory justice in acquisitions

In the acquisition context, target employees' anticipatory justice formed during the pre-deal phase equates to their beliefs about how they will be treated by the acquirer during the integration phase (Shapiro and Kirkman 2001). This is important because how individuals expect to be treated generally mirrors their "reality," or the justice they perceive, within a future event. Once an individual forms anticipatory justice from a current or past event, it impacts the cognitive frame applied to evaluate relevant future events (Rodell and Colquitt 2009; Shapiro and Kirkman 1999). In turn, individuals will be more or less receptive to forthcoming changes or other critical decisions that affect them (Rodell and Colquitt 2009). Anticipating justice will result in target employees' acceptance of the change and motivation to engage in productive behavior and positive feelings at the onset of the integration process (Bell *et al.* 2006; Rodell and Colquitt 2009). By contrast, anticipatory injustice likely results in dysfunctional behavior (Shapiro and Kirkman 1999; Shapiro and Kirkman 2001; Sinetar 1981).

Two aspects of anticipatory justice should be noted. First, fairness judgments do not involve thorough consideration of all relevant information. In explaining how fairness judgments are formed, Lind (2001) posited that, at the outset of new relationships, individuals use readily available information to form expectations about future fairness. Research indicates that individuals take a cognitive shortcut by relying on the first available information or impression (Bell *et al.* 2006). These findings highlight the importance of first impressions in the acquisition process, and acquiring firm managers should emphasize pre-deal processes that shape anticipatory justice. Indeed, a negative first impression of anticipatory injustice is costly and difficult to change. For example, Lind *et al.* (1998) found that employees who experienced injustice early in their interaction with supervisors were more likely to view their supervisors' future actions as unfair. Other studies found that anticipatory injustice is significantly related to employees' resistance to change, turnover, withdrawal of commitment, and defiance of leadership authority (Greenberg 1990; Shapiro and Kirkman 1999).

Second, anticipatory justice is heightened when there is a high level of uncertainty in the environment (Shapiro and Kirkman 2001). Justice formation occurs during a substantial change in the organizational context such as leadership change, acquisitions, or major restructuring because these events create a sense of uncertainty and insecurity among employees. The positive relationship between uncertainty and formation of justice has been empirically examined in a number of studies (Dutton and Duncan 1987; Rodell and Colquitt 2009; Shapiro and Kirkman 2001; Weick 1995). In particular, Shapiro and Kirkman (1999) found that employees, when faced with substantial organizational changes, engage in sense making and try to predict subsequent outcomes based on their expectations in order to deal with uncertainty and insecurity. Anticipating how one will be treated in the future, in this case during acquisition integration, helps individuals cope with anxiety and uncertainty (Bell *et al.* 2006).

We believe that the concept of anticipatory justice has important implications for the acquisition process, particularly the pre-deal process. During the pre-deal process, new relationships are starting to form, change and uncertainty are substantially high, and there are opportunities for acquiring firm managers to develop positive (or negative) first impressions. Further, within this context, justice expectations are likely to be informed by salient preceding events. As such, anticipatory justice formed during the pre-deal process sets the stage for employees' receptiveness and participation at the beginning of the integration process, in which most value from the acquisition is created.

Conceptual development

With this chapter, we propose that anticipatory justice is central to the acquisition integration process to facilitate target employee engagement. In the following section, we develop several propositions surrounding the theoretical model depicted in Figure 18.1.

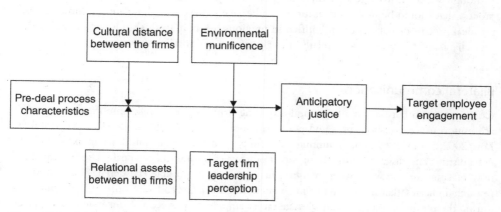

Figure 18.1   Anticipatory justice in the M&A pre-deal processs

Pre-deal process characteristics

Previous studies have found that target firm employee engagement during the integration phase is critical to integration efforts and the future success of the newly combined firm (e.g. Ellis *et al.* 2009; Graebner 2004; Ranft and Lord 2000). Many of these studies also emphasized the importance of perceived justice as a precondition for employee engagement. Employees become more receptive to changes and actively participate in the integration process when they perceive justice. While a number of studies have looked at the antecedents and consequences of perceived, or experienced, justice during the integration phase (e.g. Ellis *et al.* 2009; Lipponen *et al.* 2004; Meyer 2001; Steensma and van Milligen 2003), no known research has explicitly addressed what can be done during the pre-deal phase to enhance employees' senses of justice, expectations, and resulting employee receptiveness to change.

Anticipatory justice has important implications for acquisition research because of the situational contexts that acquisitions create. That is, acquisitions tend to create a high level of uncertainty, anxiety, and even fear among members of both firms involved, but especially for target firm employees (Bastien 1987; Jemison and Sitkin 1986; Schweiger and DeNisi 1991). Scholars have gone as far as equating mergers and acquisitions to "major life changes" for employees (Sinetar 1981: 863). A proactive involvement and fair treatment of target managers and employees in the pre-deal phase is essential for affecting employees' construction of anticipatory justice and, in turn, employee engagement.

Noteworthy organizational change events, such as acquisitions, provide an opportunity for managers to engage in sense-giving processes (Søderberg 2003). This is because existing mental models used for sense making are no longer useful and must be adjusted to understand the new organization (Weick 1995). If the acquiring firm managers understand this, they can take actions to support the adoption of a preferred schema (Søderberg 2003). Prior studies found that discourse used in the pre-deal process can play a substantial role in framing how the acquisition is perceived (Risberg *et al.* 2003; Søderberg 2003; Vaara *et al.* 2003; Vaara and Tienari 2002). By taking a lead role in guiding and managing the organizational change event, target firm executives can influence how lower-level employees interpret the upcoming change (Kanter *et al.* 1992). Thus, we believe that implementing key pre-deal processes can lead to anticipatory justice rather than injustice. Specifically, we discuss the following pre-deal process characteristics: 1) bilateral communication, 2) range of participants, 3) comprehensiveness, and 4) consistency. Although we acknowledge that there are still other characteristics or aspects of the pre-deal process that should be evaluated in future studies, we believe that these are the most pertinent pre-deal process characteristics identified in previous research. In this study, we posit that these four characteristics will directly relate to target employees' anticipatory justice.

Bilateral communication

Communication between the target and acquiring firm employees is an important aspect of the acquisition process, in both pre- and post-acquisition phases (Allatta and Singh 2011; Ranft and Lord 2002; Searby 1969). The mounting uncertainty created by the acquisition context and heightened distrust and dissatisfaction among target employees during the pre-deal phase requires a rich flow of communication between merging firms as early as possible (Bastien 1987). Indeed, past research indicates that, by engaging in frequent, high-quality and one-on-one communication during the pre-deal, managers can alleviate target employees' anxiety and uncertainty and prevent them from developing negative biases about the forthcoming changes (Schweiger and DeNisi 1991; Sinetar 1981). Further, target employees perceive the acquiring firm as increasingly "trustworthy, honest, and caring" if realistic communication about post-acquisition plans is provided (Schweiger and DeNisi 1991: 128). In their experimental study, Schweiger and DeNisi (1991) found that open, realistic communication by managers mitigates dysfunctional feelings and attitudes among employees created by merger announcements.

Lander and Kooning (2013) observed in the merger between Air France and KLM that close cooperation and open communication between the two companies early in the pre-deal process contributed to long-lasting positive views and attitudes during later stages of the pre-deal. They also observed that the anticipation and trust that was first developed among top managers of both firms quickly trickled down to lower-level employees affecting their beliefs about future changes. Alternatively, when communication quality is poor or incongruent, target employees rely on rumors and gossip to cope with uncertainty, which may damage anticipatory justice and generate negative expectations about the upcoming integration procedures (Bastien 1987). In sum, if bilateral communication exists during the pre-deal process, target employees are likely to feel more comfortable with the idea of the pending acquisition and anticipate the same amount of communication and justice in the future.

Range of participants

In many acquisitions, top managers fail to realize that they need to work closely with functional managers for input and place themselves in charge of the entire integration planning (Haspeslagh and Jemison 1991). However, it may also be important to engage a wide range of participants during the pre-deal, while still trying to minimize interruption of the normal operations. Target employees' participation in the pre-deal process can help them to cope with the pending changes (Amiot et al. 2006). Also, getting initial input from employees affected by and responsible for the integration efforts is useful in identifying potential integration issues as early as possible. Further, involving more participants may increase overall commitment to the post-acquisition firm and the likelihood of anticipatory justice among target employees (Jemison and Sitkin 1986).

Organizational change, oftentimes substantial, is inevitable in most acquisitions (Searby 1969). This change will trigger a sense-making process for the target firm employees which is impacted by perceptions of justice (Monin et al. 2013). For many employees, the fact that they are invited into the pre-deal planning and due diligence process can raise their justice expectations by signaling that 1) they will be treated with respect after the acquisition, 2) they may be a part of the decision-making process in the future, and 3) they will be provided with accurate and quality information. Indeed, the opportunity to have a voice in the pre-deal process increases feelings of value, respect, and belonging for the target employees (Steensma and van Milligen 2003).

The merger between Mellon Financial Corporation and The Bank of New York is a good example of the importance of developing a sense of justice during the pre-deal phase by involving managers and employees from both parties in the deal (Taliaferro et al. 2009). After the CEOs agreed to pursue a merger between the two institutions, they quickly organized a merger committee comprised of approximately an equal number of top managers from both firms. This equal representation signaled to the employees of both firms that they would be treated with fairness and respect in the future. In addition to the merger committee comprised of top managers, the two firms also established a merger task committee comprised of operational-level leaders from both firms. The members of the merger task committee were selected based not only on subject-matter expertise but also on reputation for people-driven personalities. The primary responsibility of the merger task committee was to provide task-specific expertise to managers, but they were also expected to facilitate the communication and collaboration among the employees at the operational level. This case illustrates how firms can leverage a wide range of participation for overall efficiency and reduced feelings of uncertainty. Further, if involved in the acquisition process during the pre-deal phase, target employees may begin to identify with the "new" organization and feel a sense of common group membership with the acquiring firm employees (Lipponen *et al.* 2004).

Comprehensiveness

Acquisition scholars argue that an effective integration plan should be thorough and comprehensive (Haspeslagh and Jemison 1991; Jemison and Sitkin 1986). A comprehensive integration plan not only serves as a good road map but also as an agent in reducing anxiety for both target firm top managers and employees which in turn will enhance positive expectations about the future changes. However, even prior to the integration phase, acquiring firm managers can influence anticipatory justice by recognizing the importance of a comprehensive pre-deal process. Despite the time pressures that often accompany an acquisition, acquiring firm managers should start early and take time to fully understand firm differences, including conflicting values and managerial styles (Datta 1991; Hitt *et al.* 2001).

For example, in the merger between Mellon Financial Corporation and The Bank of New York, the merger committee conducted a thorough cultural analysis in which similarities and dissimilarities in values and management styles were clearly identified and solutions for reconciliation were devised (Taliaferro *et al.* 2009). The early detection of the potential conflicts due to the cultural differences not only helped both firms to generate a more realistic plan for the integration, but also served to reduce employees' uncertainty and anxiety by signaling that the firms would amicably work together rather than forcefully infuse one system into the other (Taliaferro *et al.* 2009).

Often, target employees have their own distinct social identity, which can add value to the future acquisition if appropriately understood and maintained (Colman and Lunnan 2011). If the acquiring firm managers work with target firm employees during the pre-deal to gain a comprehensive understanding of the idiosyncrasies of the target firm, employees may expect to receive the same levels of respect, consideration, and collaboration during the future integration process. Therefore, comprehensive pre-deal planning provides both the target firm top managers and employees with information regarding what to expect once integration starts, thereby positively influencing justice expectations.

Consistency

Due to the uncertainty created by acquisitions, target firm top managers and employees demand consistency in decisions and plans made regarding the acquisition. This can be traced to the sense-giving and sense-making processes (Gioia and Chittipeddi 1991; Weick 1995). Decisions and plans made during the pre-deal provide information to be used for sense-giving and sense-making purposes (Monin *et al.* 2013) and, when facing crucial changes in both firm structure and identity, the target firm members try to make sense out of all the upcoming changes from the available information. Ambiguity, on the other hand, may limit employees' abilities to deal with and make sense out of the upcoming change (Sinetar 1981). It is important to note that there are likely multiple "realities" or interpretations of the acquisition depending upon the position held within the target firm, involvement within the acquisition process, and amount of details provided by upper management (Risberg 2001; Risberg 2003). Effective and consistent communication surrounding the motives, goals, and objectives of the pending acquisition may help deter employees from anticipating the worst case scenario and, in turn, disengaging or leaving the company (Risberg 2001).

Indeed, researchers have identified consistency as an important aspect of organizational justice (Arino and Ring 2010; Kim and Mauborgne 1991). When decision-making processes are consistent, the decisions are perceived to be fair. When consistency is perceived in decisions and plans made by the top managers during the pre-deal, anticipatory justice will form. Even if they do not like the outcome, target employees will feel the process used to get there was just (Marks and Mirvis 2010). In contrast, inconsistency in decisions leads to feelings of deception, deprivation, and unfair procedures (Kahneman 1992). As such, if information obtained during the pre-deal is inconsistent, target employees may develop low expectations about future information quality or accuracy and develop anticipatory injustice.

In sum, there are certain pre-deal process characteristics that can result in anticipatory justice when properly implemented during early phases of the acquisition process. Formally stated:

> Proposition 1: Pre-deal process characteristics, including bilateral communication, a wide range of participants, comprehensiveness, and consistency are positively related to anticipatory justice.

Moderators

In addition to the expected main effects between pre-deal process characteristics and anticipatory justice, it is important to highlight several moderators of these main effects. Certain events that occur prior to or concurrent with the pre-deal process may impact the overall importance of implementing the aforementioned pre-deal process characteristics. Further, due to the proposed moderating effects, target employees may rely more or less on justice cues from the acquiring firm during the pre-deal process. The moderators considered in this chapter include, 1) cultural distance, 2) previously developed relational assets, 3) prior justice experiences within the acquired firm, and 4) environmental munificence.

Cross-border acquisitions: cultural distance

Despite the added complexity due to institutional differences such as cultural distance, cross-border acquisitions are increasingly common across the globe (cf. Bertrand and Betschinger 2012; Bertrand and Zitouna 2008; Hitt et al. 2001). In particular, differences in national culture, defined as shared values, social norms, and beliefs within a given nation (Hofstede, 1983), can result in language barriers, conflicting values, diverse business practices, methods of communication, etc. (Ghemawat 2001; Johanson and Vahlne 1977). We believe that cultural distance is an important aspect of the pre-deal phase because target employees may rely on salient differences in national culture to make sense of the deal.

Although lower-level employees may be involved in certain aspects of the deal, top executives are usually the ones more actively engaged in every aspect of the pre-deal process (Jemison and Sitkin 1986). Due to different levels of involvement, information asymmetry typically exists between top executives managing the deal and lower-level employees, leaving lower-level employees more uncertain about the pending deal when compared with top executives. For these reasons, deal specifics are bypassed, and public, readily available information, such as national culture, plays a role in shaping target employees' expectations about the pending acquisition.

M&A scholars have researched the impact that culture has on integration and subsequent performance (Calori et al. 1994; Chatterjee et al. 1992; Datta 1991; Marks 1982; Morosini et al.

1998; Olie 1990). While some studies conclude that differences in culture hinder integration efforts and diminish returns to shareholders (Datta and Puia 1995), others find positive effects (Morosini *et al.* 1998). However, these differences, if understood, can be managed to the combined firm's advantage (Reus and Lamont 2009). Indeed, if properly managed, cultural distance between the acquiring and target firm may ultimately result in positive outcomes through new learning occurring across traditional domestic boundaries (e.g. Chakrabarti *et al.* 2009; Slangen 2006; Reus and Lamont 2009).

Considering the mixed results found in the literature, culture is a complex phenomenon (Teerikangas and Very 2006) that is often conceptualized as a double-edged sword (Stahl and Voigt 2008). Although there is some disagreement on whether and how culture impacts performance, there is general consensus that effort should be taken by managers to understand cultural differences from the earliest stages of the acquisition process (Cartwright and Cooper 1993; Teerikangas and Very 2006). This is because cognitive biases stemming from national culture are difficult to change and impact how individuals view the world (Berger and Luckmann 1967). Indeed, past research shows that national culture is deeply rooted in history and relates to target employees' identities, sense-making processes, and "us versus them" stereotypes (Vaara *et al.* 2003). When these in-group biases form and the acquiring firm is perceived as a threat, stereotypes can drive distrust, hostility, stress, turnover, and lack of engagement that impact sociocultural integration (Cartwright and Cooper 1993; Datta and Puia 1995; Stahl and Voigt 2008).

For these reasons, we propose that national cultural distance may impact the proposed main effects between pre-deal process characteristics and anticipatory justice. Due to stereotypes related to national culture (Vaara *et al.* 2003), cultural distance may heighten target firm employees' sensitivity to justice cues in the pre-deal process and increase skepticism about the future acquisition. The breakdown in target employees' existing sense-making processes (Søderberg 2003; Weick 1995) provides an increased need for the acquiring firm executives to engage in specific pre-deal processes that promote anticipatory justice. For these reasons, we posit that cultural distance may strengthen the proposed relationship between pre-deal process characteristics and formation of anticipatory justice.

> Proposition 2: Cultural distance moderates the relationship between pre-deal process characteristics and anticipatory justice such that with larger cultural distance the relationships become stronger.

Relational assets between the firms

Relational assets refer to previous cooperative relationships between the two firms. Regardless of the acquiring firm's motives for shifting from cooperative arrangements to acquisition, prior collaborative interactions may affect acquisition planning and integration processes by predetermining the level of established trust (Gulati 1995; Rousseau *et al.* 1998).

According to past research, alliances and joint ventures provide a platform to build trust between partners through frequent interactions (Zaheer *et al.* 1998). Thus, the more familiar the acquirer and target firms are with one another due to past collaborative relationships, the more likely that trust exists between the two parties (Gulati 1995). McCarter *et al.* (2011) described how smaller wins and pilot projects between two firms can lead to reduced perceptions of vulnerability and increased trust during subsequent, larger-scale collaborative relationships. The DuPont-Danisco acquisition, previously discussed, is a primary example. Key employees from the acquirer (DuPont) and the target (Danisco) were familiar with one another before the formal negotiation and due diligence processes began, and they had a previously established base of trust between them (Gulati 1995, Kullman 2012).

Individuals form anticipatory justice from first impressions or initial salient events. However, a history of repeated interactions between the acquiring and target firms will affect anticipatory justice. This is because the target firm employees form general opinions about the acquirer from past work relationships. When previous interactions (prior to the pre-deal phase) between the acquirer and target are positive overall and trusting relationships are developed, target employees will pay less attention to justice cues and pre-deal process characteristics. Therefore, relational assets between the two firms tend to weaken the effect of the pre-deal process characteristics on the formation of anticipatory justice.

Proposition 3: Previously developed relational assets between the target and acquiring firm moderate the relationship between pre-deal process characteristics and anticipatory justice such that with increased relational assets between the two firms the relationships become weaker.

Target firm leadership perception

Employees activate their mental structure and stereotypes about prior leaders when developing evaluation and attitudes toward new leaders (Ritter and Lord 2007). Similarly, Rodell and Colquitt (2009) found that employees' general perceptions about employee-leadership relationships predetermine the perceived anticipatory justice during a major organizational change. Within the acquisition context, target employees' perceptions about the current leadership are likely to bias their ideas about the leadership of the future combined firm. Target employees' perceptions of the current leadership not only determine their perceptions of the future leadership but also affect how they interpret the acquiring firm's pre-deal efforts. Biases about the future combined leadership may lead individuals to interpret new information in such a way that it confirms existing biases, even furthering these biases (Tversky and Kahneman 1974).

Due to this confirming behavior, target employees with negative perceptions about the current leadership will likely develop a skeptical view of the pre-deal efforts by the acquiring firm. For example, bilateral communication efforts may be viewed as commandeering and monitoring, a wide range of participation may be viewed as interruption or more work, and comprehensiveness may be viewed as being forceful. With a negative bias about the new future leadership, the pre-deal procedural cues are reminders that they are being transferred from one poor employee-management relationship to another. Related to this idea, Welsh et al. (1993) found that providing a participative management opportunity to Russian employees did not increase their task performance. Based on historical events, these employees believed their voices would be ignored by management, and previously developed biases were difficult to change. Therefore, we propose that, when target employees have a poor perception of the current management, pre-deal process characteristics will be negatively related to the formation of anticipatory justice.

Alternatively, if the target employees have trusting relationships with the current leadership, it will be much easier for top managers of the acquiring firm to shape their anticipatory justice during the pre-deal phase. Target employees' inclination to confirm their positive feelings toward the future leadership will lead them to view the acquiring firms' pre-deal efforts in a positive way. Specifically, we posit that, when target employees' perceptions of current leadership are positive, the pre-deal process characteristics will increasingly be related to anticipatory justice.

Proposition 4:Target employees' relationships with their current management moderate the relationship between pre-deal process characteristics and anticipatory justice. Specifically, if perceptions of the current leadership are negative, the pre-deal process characteristics will weaken the relationships; by contrast, if perceptions of the current leadership are positive, the pre-deal process characteristics will strengthen the relationships.

Environmental munificence

Extant research indicates that target employee turnover rates are typically high post-acquisition (Walsh 1988). Generally, this trend increases the need for acquiring firm managers to implement pre-deal process characteristics that shape anticipatory justice, in an effort to engage and retain key target employees. However, the relationship between pre-deal process characteristics and anticipatory justice may also be affected by uncontrollable conditions within the external environment. Especially relevant in this context is environmental munificence (Dess and Beard 1984). Munificence refers to the carrying capacity of the environment and the availability of resources for industry prosperity and growth, which also impacts employment opportunities and unemployment rates (Dess and Beard 1984; Castrogiovanni 1991; Castrogiovanni 2002).

Environmental munificence may affect target firm employees' abilities to obtain alternative employment if dissatisfied with the pending acquisition. For example, according to the Bureau of Labor Statistics (2012), due to the recent economic recession, the unemployment rate in the United States rose from 5 percent in December 2007 to 10 percent in October 2009, the highest rate since 1982. Looking beyond these average trends, certain demographic groups, industries, states, and countries were, and continue to be, more affected by macro-economic trends. Although these environmental conditions are uncontrollable, they do impact opportunities that are available to target employees. Due to the difficulties associated with obtaining any form of alternative employment when environmental munificence is declining, target employees will place less emphasis on ascertaining whether or not the pending acquisition will relate to just treatment in the future based on pre-deal process characteristics. Alternatively, when the environment is munificent and target employees have alternative options for employment, they will be more sensitive to justice cues during the pre-deal process. This is because there are ample opportunities for employment, and if target employees are unhappy or anticipate injustice based on the pre-deal process, they may resign and seek alternative employment options. Therefore, we posit that environmental munificence positively moderates the expected main effect between pre-deal process characteristics and anticipatory justice.

Proposition 5: Environmental munificence moderates the relationship between pre-deal process characteristics and anticipatory justice such that with environmental munificence the relationships become stronger.

Discussion

The proposed model and propositions developed in this chapter allow us to clarify how the pre-deal process affects anticipatory justice perceptions among target firm employees and their receptivity and support of the changes to follow after the deal is consummated. As a result, we make several contributions to the M&A literature.

First, extant research integrating justice theory with acquisition process research has focused on experienced justice during the integration phase. We employed anticipatory justice to emphasize the importance of justice formation through first impressions during the pre-deal process, which has been largely overlooked in previous M&A process literature. Pre-deal processes and the number of employees aware of the deal differ for many reasons, including regulatory environments, ownership structures, media attention, prior business relationships, overall complexity, and the time frame allotted. Despite these differences, closer evaluation of several practical examples provides evidence that there are circumstances that mandate time-intensive pre-deal processes. Further, there are circumstances that result in employees throughout the organization becoming aware of the deal prior to final closing. Thus, we believe that there are opportunities to manage justice perceptions earlier in the acquisition process. If acquiring firm executives take steps to shape anticipatory justice during the pre-deal phase, target employees will develop positive perceptions surrounding the acquisition.

Second, our conceptual model delineates the myriad pre-deal factors likely in play that shape the perceptions of anticipatory justice among employees of the target firm. Specifically, we highlighted bilateral communication, range of participants involved, comprehensiveness, and consistency as common pre-deal process characteristics that may help to shape anticipatory justice. Further, we suggested key moderators that will likely affect the relationship between pre-deal process characteristics and anticipatory justice. By identifying specific antecedents and moderators to anticipatory justice, we hope to provide guidance to practitioners and a research platform for scholars.

Finally, we discussed how anticipatory justice can lead to employee engagement at the beginning of the integration phase. Although not yet integrated with the M&A literature, prior justice studies found that anticipatory justice is a distinct construct from experienced justice (e.g. Rodell and Colquitt 2009). Anticipatory justice is an important predictor of justice that is experienced in some future event, as well as overall employee engagement (Shapiro and Kirkman 2001). Based on prior findings linking anticipatory justice, experienced justice, and engagement (Bell et al. 2006; Rodell and Colquitt 2009; Shapiro and Kirkman 1999; Shapiro and Kirkman 2001), we believe that there are opportunities to manage justice perceptions earlier in the acquisition process. In turn, anticipatory justice will result in target employees' positive perceptions surrounding the acquisition and a desire to engage and add value in the newly combined organization. Where target employee support is required for realizing value from a particular deal, the effects on value creation are likely to be substantial (Ranft and Lord 2000).

This work has several limitations that we would like to acknowledge, but these limitations also open up opportunities for future research. First, we did not theoretically consider the dimensionality of anticipatory justice. Specific dimensions, including procedural, informational, interpersonal, and/or distributive justice, may be more or less important in the pre-deal phase. These dimensions can be considered under the umbrella of experienced justice or anticipatory justice. Again, anticipatory justice is a distinct concept from experienced justice, and certain dimensions of anticipatory justice may predict certain dimensions of experienced justice. Prior empirical studies, outside of the M&A literature, have taken steps to test these relationships (e.g. Rodell and Colquitt 2009). In this chapter, we work to introduce the concept of anticipatory justice and theorize how it may be integrated within the existing M&A literature. However, going forward, we encourage researchers to evaluate how different types of anticipatory justice developed during the pre-deal phase relate to different types of experienced justice during the integration phase.

Second, we encourage researchers to explore the empirical relationships between pre-deal process characteristics and the various dimensions of anticipatory justice in the merger and acquisition context. For example, a wide-range of participation may be more relevant to procedural anticipatory justice than to the other types of justice, whereas comprehensiveness may be more closely related to informational anticipatory justice. Finally, we considered several key moderators and pre-deal process characteristics within our conceptual model. However, there are likely additional variables that should be included in the future. For instance, outcome favorability expectations have been examined in past anticipatory justice studies (Rodell and Colquitt 2009) and may potentially have an effect on the proposed relationships.

In conclusion, our intent was to highlight the importance of the pre-deal phase in shaping justice expectations in target firms. We hope we have succeeded in outlining useful avenues for future research on this underrepresented, but potentially important, factor in explaining employee engagement among target employees in the integration process.

References

Allatta, J.T. and Singh H. (2011) "Evolving communication patterns in response to an acquisition event," *Strategic Management Journal*, 32: 1099–118.

Amiot, C., Terry, D., Jimmieson, N., and Callan, V. (2006) "A longitudinal investigation of coping processes during a merger: implications for job satisfaction and organizational identification," *Journal of Management*, 32: 552–74.

Arino, A. and Ring, P.S. (2010) "The role of fairness in alliance formation," *Strategic Management Journal*, 31: 1054–87.

Bastien, D.T. (1987) "Common patterns of behavior and communication in corporate mergers and acquisitions," *Human Resource Management*, 26: 1–17.

Bell, B.S., Wiechmann, D., and Ryan, A.M. (2006) "Consequences of organizational justice expectations in a selection system," *Journal of Applied Psychology*, 91: 455–66.

Berger, P.L. and Luckman, T. (1967) *The social construction of reality: a treatise in the sociology of knowledge.* Garden City, NY: Anchor Books.

Bertrand, O. and Zitouna, H. (2008) "Domestic versus cross-border acquisitions: which impact on target firm's performance?," *Applied Economics*, 40: 2221–38.

Bertrand, O. and Betschinger, M. (2012) "Performance of domestic and cross-border acquisitions: empirical evidence from Russian acquirers," *Journal of Comparative Economics*, 40: 413–37.

Birkinshaw, J., Bresman, H.L., and H{ar}kanson, L. (2000) "Managing the post-acquisition integration process: how the human integration and task integration processes interact to foster value creation," *Journal of Management Studies*, 37: 395–424.

Bureau of Labor Statistics (2012) "Spotlight on statistics: the recession of 2007–2009," February. Available at: www.bls.gov/spotlight/2012/recession/pdf/recession_bls_spotlight.pdf (accessed August 15 2013).

Calori, R., Lubatkin M., and Very P. (1994) "Control mechanisms in cross-border acquisitions: an international comparison," *Organization Studies*, 15: 361–79.

Capron, L. and Shen, J.-C. (2007) "Acquisitions of private vs. public firms: private information, target selection, and acquirer returns," *Strategic Management Journal*, 28: 891–911.

Capron, L. and Guillen, M. (2009) "National corporate governance institutions and post-acquisition target reorganization," *Strategic Management Journal*, 30: 803–33.

Cartwright, S. and Cooper, C.L. (1993) "The role of culture compatibility in successful organizational marriage," *Academy of Management Executive*, 7: 57–70.

Castrogiovanni, G.J. (1991) "Environmental munificence: a theoretical assessment," *Academy of Management Review*, 16: 542–65.

Castrogiovanni, G.J. (2002) "Organization task environments: have they changed fundamentally over time?," *Journal of Management*, 28: 129–50.

Chakrabarti, R., Gupta-Mukherjee, S., and Jayaraman, N. (2009) "Mars-Venus marriages: culture and cross-border M&A," *Journal of International Business Studies*, 40: 216–37.

Chatterjee, S., Lubatkin, M., Schweiger, D.M., and Weber, Y. (1992) "Cultural differences and shareholder value in related mergers: linking equity and human capital," *Strategic Management Journal*, 13: 319–34.

Christensen, C.M., Alton, R., Rising, C., and Waldeck, A. (2011) "The big idea: the new M&A playbook," *Harvard Business Review*, 89: 48–57.

Colman, H.L. and Lunnan, R. (2011) "Organizational identification and serendipitous value creation in post-acquisition integration," *Journal of Management*, 37: 839–60.

Colquitt, J.A., Conlon D.E., Wesson M.J., Porter C.O.L.H., and Ng K.Y. (2001) "Justice at the millennium: a meta-analytic review of 25 years of organizational justice research," *Journal of Applied Psychology*, 86: 425–45.

Cording, M., Christmann, P., and King, D.R. (2008) "Reducing causal ambiguity in acquisition integration: intermediate goals as mediators of integration decisions and acquisition performance," *Academy of Management Journal*, 51: 744–67.

Cropanzano R. and Ambrose, M.L. (2001) "Procedural and distributive justice are more similar than you think: a monistic perspective and a research agenda," in Greenberg, J.S. and Cropanzano, R. (eds.) *Advances in organizational justice*. Stanford, CA: Stanford University Press.

Datta, D.K. (1991) "Organizational fit and acquisition performance: effects of post-acquisition integration," *Strategic Management Journal*, 12: 281–97.

Datta, D.K. and Puia, G. (1995) "Cross-border acquisitions: an examination of the influence of relatedness and cultural fit on shareholder value creation in U.S. acquiring firms," *Management International Review*, 35: 337–59.

Dess, G.G. and Beard D.W. (1984) "Dimensions of organizational task environments," *Administrative Science Quarterly*, 29: 52–73.

Dikova, D., Sahib, P.R., and van Witteloostuijn, A. (2010) "Cross border acquisition abandonment and completion: the effect of institutional differences and organizational learning in the international business service industry, 1981–2001," *Journal of International Business Studies*, 41: 223–45.

Dutton, J.E. and Duncan, R.B. (1987) "The influence of the strategic planning process on strategic change," *Strategic Management Journal*, 8: 103–16.

Ellis, K.M., Reus, T.H., and Lamont, B.T. (2009) "The effects of procedural and informational justice in the integration of related acquisitions," *Strategic Management Journal*, 30: 137–61.

Forbes (2008) "FCC approves XM-Sirius merger; 3–2 vote." Available at: www.forbes.com/2008/07/25/fcc-approves-xm-sirius-merger-tech-cx_pco_0725paidcontent.html (accessed August 6 2013).

Forbes (2011) "Seven seconds to make a first impression." Available at: www.forbes.com/sites/carolkinseygoman/2011/02/13/seven-seconds-to-make-a-first-impression (accessed August 6 2013).

Ghemawat, P. (2001) "Distance still matters: the hard reality of global expansion," *Harvard Business Review*, 79: 137–47.

Gioia, D.A. and Chittipeddi, K. (1991) "Sensemaking and sensegiving in strategic change initiation," *Strategic Management Journal*, 12: 433–48.

Graebner, M.E. (2004) "Momentum and serendipity: how acquired leaders create value in the integration of technology firms," *Strategic Management Journal*, 25: 751–77.

Greenberg, J. (1990) "Organizational justice: yesterday, today, and tomorrow," *Journal of Management*, 16: 399–432.

Gulati, R. (1995) "Does familiarity breed trust? The implications of repeated ties for contractual choice in alliances," *Academy of Management Journal*, 38: 85–112.

Haspeslagh, P.C. and Jemison, D.B. (1991) *Managing acquisitions: creating value through corporate renewal*. New York: Free Press.

Hitt, M.A., Ireland, R.D., and Harrison, J.S. (2001) "Mergers and acquisitions: a value creating or value destroying strategy," in Hitt, M.A., Freeman R.E., and Harrison J.S. (eds.) *Blackwell handbook of strategic management*. Malden, MA: Blackwell Publishing.

Hofstede, G. (1983) "The cultural relativity of organizational practices and theories," *Journal of International Business Studies*, 14: 1983: 75–89.

Jemison, D.B. and Sitkin, S.B. (1986) "Corporate acquisitions: a process perspective," *Academy of Management Review*, 11: 145–63.

Johanson, J. and Vahlne, J.E. (1977) "The internationalization process of the firm: a model of knowledge development and increasing foreign market commitments," *Journal of International Business Studies*, 8: 23–32.

Jonas, E., Schulz-Hardt, S., Frey, D., and Thelen, N. (2001) "Confirmation bias in sequential information search after preliminary decisions: an expansion of dissonance theoretical research on selective exposure to information," *Journal of Personality and Social Psychology*, 80: 557–71.

Kahneman, D. (1992) "Reference points, anchors, norms, and mixed feelings," *Organizational Behavior and Human Decision Processes*, 51: 296–312.

Kanter, R.M., Stein, B.A., and Jick, T.D. (1992) *The challenge of organizational change: how companies experience it and leaders guide it*. New York: The Free Press.

Kim, W.C. and Mauborgne, R.A. (1991) "Implementing global strategies: the role of procedural justice," *Strategic Management Journal*, 12: 125–43.

Kullman, E. (2012) "DuPont's CEO on executing a complex cross-border acquisition," *Harvard Business Review*, July–August: 1–5.

Lander, M.W. and Kooning, L. (2013) "Boarding the aircraft: trust development amongst negotiators of a complex merger," *Journal of Management Studies*, 50: 1–30.

Lind, E.A. (2001) "Fairness heuristic theory: justice judgments as pivotal cognitions in organizational relations," in Greenberg, J.S. and Cropanzano, R. (eds.) *Advances in organizational justice*. Stanford, CA: Stanford University Press.

Lind, E.A., Kray, L., and Thompson, L. (1998) "The social construction of injustice: fairness judgments in response to own and others' unfair treatment by authorities," *Organizational Behavior and Human Decision Processes*, 75: 1–22.

Lipponen, J., Olkkonen, M.E., and Moilanen, M. (2004) "Perceived procedural justice and employee responses to an organizational merger," *European Journal of Work and Organizational Psychology*, 13: 391–413.

McCarter, M.W., Mahoney, J.T., and Northcraft, G.B. (2011) "Testing the waters: using collective real options to manage the social dilemma of strategic alliances," *Academy of Management Review*, 36: 621–40.

Marks, M.L. (1982) "Merging human resources: a review of current research," *Mergers and Acquisitions*, 17(2): 38–44.

Marks, M.L. and Mirvis, P.H. (2010) *Joining forces: making one plus one equal three in mergers, acquisitions, and alliances*. San Francisco, CA: Jossey-Bass.

Meyer, C.B. (2001) "Allocation processes in mergers and acquisitions: an organizational justice perspective," *British Journal of Management*, 12: 47–66.

Mickelson, R.E. and Worley, C. (2003) "Acquiring a family firm: a case study," *Family Business Review*, 16: 251–68.

Monin, P., Noorderhaven, N., Vaara, E., and Kroon, D. (2013) "Giving sense to and making sense of justice in postmerger integration," *Academy of Management Journal*, 56: 256–84.

Morosini, P., Shane, S., and Singh, H. (1998) "National cultural distance and cross-border acquisition performance," *Journal of International Business Studies*, 29: 137–58.

Nickerson, R.S. (1998) "Confirmation bias: a ubiquitous phenomenon in many guises," *Review of General Psychology*, 2: 175–220.

Olie, R. (1990) "Culture and integration problems in international mergers and acquisitions," *European Management Journal*, 8: 206–15.

Porrini, P. (2004) "Can a previous alliance between an acquirer and a target affect acquisition performance?," *Journal of Management*, 30: 545–62.

Ranft, A.L. and Lord, M.D. (2000) "Acquiring new knowledge: the role of retaining human capital in acquisitions of high-tech firms," *The Journal of High Technology Management Research*, 11: 295–319.

Ranft, A.L. and Lord, M.D. (2002) "Acquiring new technologies and capabilities: a grounded model of acquisition implementation," *Organization Science*, 13: 420–41.

Reus, T.H. and Lamont, B.T. (2009) "The double-edged sword of cultural distance in international acquisitions," *Journal of International Business Studies*, 40: 1298–316.

Risberg, A. (2001) "Employee experiences of acquisition processes," *Journal of World Business*, 36: 58–84.

Risberg, A. (2003) "Notions of shared and multiple realities in acquisitions: unfolding and critiquing dominating notions of acquisitions," *Nordiske Organisasjonsstudier*, 5: 58–82.

Risberg, A., Tienari, J., and Vaara, E. (2003) "Making sense of a transnational merger: media texts and the (re)construction of power relations," *Culture & Organization*, 9: 121–37.

Ritter, B.A. and Lord, R.G. (2007). "The impact of previous leaders on the evaluation of new leaders: an alternative to prototype matching," *Journal of Applied Psychology*, 92: 1683–95.

Rodell, J.B. and Colquitt, J.A. (2009) "Looking ahead in times of uncertainty: the role of anticipatory justice in an organizational change context," *Journal of Applied Psychology*, 94: 989–1002.

Rousseau, D.M., Sitkin, S., Burt, R.S., and Camerer, C. (1998) "Not so different after all: a cross-discipline view of trust," *Academy of Management Review*, 23: 393–404.

Schweiger, D.M. and DeNisi, A.S. (1991) "Communication with employees following a merger: a longitudinal field experiment," *Academy of Management Journal*, 34: 110–35.

Searby, F.W. (1969) "Control postmerger change," *Harvard Business Review* September–October: 4ff.

Shapiro, D.L. and Kirkman, B.L. (1999) "Employees' reaction to the change to work teams: the influence of "anticipatory" injustice," *Journal of Organizational Change Management*, 12: 51–67.

Shapiro, D.L. and Kirkman, B.L. (2001) "Anticipatory injustice: the consequences of expecting injustice in the workplace," in Greenberg, J.S. and Cropanzano, R. (eds.) *Advances in organizational justice*. Stanford, CA: Stanford University Press.

Sinetar M. (1981) Mergers, morale, and productivity, *Personnel Journal*, 60: 863–67.

Slangen, A.H.L. (2006) "National cultural distance and initial foreign acquisition performance: the moderating effect of integration," *Journal of World Business*, 41: 161–70.

Søderberg, A.-M., (2003) "Sensegiving and sensmaking in integration," in Czarniawska, B. and Gagliardi, P. (eds.). *Narratives we organize by: narrative approaches in organization studies*. Philadelphia, PA: John Benjamins.

Stahl, GK. and Voigt, A. (2008) "Do cultural differences matter in mergers and acquisitions? A tentative model and examination," *Organization Science*, 19: 160–76.

Steensma, H. and van Milligen, F. (2003) "Bases of power, procedural justice outcomes of mergers: the push and pull factors of influence tactics," *Journal of Collective Negotiations*, 30: 113–34.

Taliaferro, R., Rose, C., and Lane, D. (2009) "Merger of equals: the integration of Mellon Financial and The Bank of New York (A)," *Harvard Business School Case*, 210-016: 1–26. (Revised February 2010.)

Teerikangas, S. and Very, P. (Mar2006 Supplement) "The culture–performance relationship in M&A: from yes/no to how," *British Journal of Management*, 17: S31–S48.

Tversky, A. and Kahneman, D. (1974) "Judgment under uncertainty: heuristics and biases," *Science*, 185: 1124–31.

Vaara, E. and Tienari, J. (2002). "Justification, legitimization and naturalization of mergers and acquisitions: a critical discourse analysis of media texts," *Organization*, 9: 275–304.

Vaara, E., Risberg, A., Søderberg, A.-M., and Tienari, J. (2003) "The construction of national stereotypes in a merging multinational," in Søderberg, A.-M. and Vaara, E. (eds.) *Merging across borders: people, cultures and politics*. Copenhagen, Denmark: Copenhagen Business School Press.

Walsh, J.P. (1988) "Top management turnover following mergers and acquisitions," *Strategic Management Journal*, 9: 173–83.

Weick, K.E. (1995) *Sensemaking in organizations*. Thousand Oaks, CA: Sage Publications.

Welsh, D.H., Luthans, F., and Sommer, S.M. (1993) "Managing Russian factory workers: the impact of US-based behavioral and participative techniques," *Academy of Management Journal*, 36: 58–79.

Yahoo Finance (2013) "Google acquires Makani Power." Available at: http://finance.yahoo.com/news/google-acquires-makani-power-125002039.html (accessed August 6 2013).

Zaheer, A., McEvily, B., and Perrone, V. (1998) "Does trust matter? Exploring the effects of interorganizational and interpersonal trust on performance," *Organization Science*, 9: 141–59.

19

Toward a competitive dynamics perspective on value potential in M&A

Svante Schriber

Introduction

Mergers and acquisitions (M&As) are often described as vehicles to achieve strategic growth and increase firm profitability. Combining the resources and markets of previously separate firms can increase the competitiveness of participating firms. M&As are typically used for accessing new customers (Lee and Lieberman 2010), technologies (Makri *et al.* 2010), or lower production costs (Hitt *et al.* 1998). To the extent that such additions are valuable in combination with previously controlled assets, this can allow firms participating in M&As to strengthen their competitiveness in relation to their environments.

A central challenge when considering M&As is assessing the future value potential. Although future gains are difficult to predict in virtually any strategic decision, the importance of this prediction is accentuated in M&As. In comparison to other growth modes, such as organic growth, joint ventures, or strategic alliances, which typically involve only limited parts of a focal organization and where financial resources can be added incrementally (Hagedorn and Duysters 2002), M&As offer ownership of an already existing organization with "lumpy" resources all at once. Since M&As involve upfront payment with financial benefits typically realized years later, future gains depend on avoiding overpayment. Indeed, overpayment is a common explanation for why M&As fail (Sirower 1997; Singh and Montgomery 1987; Datta *et al.* 1992), making the assessment of value potential central to M&A research.

Strategic management research on M&As is mainly concerned with identifying potential value and target selection. The dominant approach is to use stock market reactions as a measure of the potential value that strategic decision makers are pursuing over the long term. Since the value potential is specific to a particular combination of firms, this research typically aims at identifying and developing generally applicable theoretical constructs of an M&A's value, reflecting assessment criteria available to strategic decision makers at the time of the transaction. These constructs thereby are central to identifying M&As that are likely to lead to higher performance, and they guide the design of studies, what data is gathered, and the analysis.

Since the theoretical concepts of value potential take such a prominent role in strategic management research on M&As, their ability to reflect real values has received considerable research attention. For instance, Porter (1985: 318) criticizes how value potential has been discussed in research, seeing much of the discussion focused on what creates value in M&As as incomplete conceptualizations or "fuzzy notions of fit." In a similar vein, others have criticized particular measures such as the common use of industry codes to assess fit (St. John and Harrison 1999; Miller *et al.* 2010; Neffke and Henning 2013). While these views have highlighted issues relating to the internal precision of how value potential is conceptualized, there are other issues that need attention.

This chapter complements the above developments by bringing to the fore a tendency in research to emphasize the initial relation between the firms involved in M&As, while the relation to the competitive environment is largely disregarded. In particular, this chapter proposes that current research on value potentials largely overlooks M&As as competitive moves that are likely to be parts in ongoing jostling. In contrast, this chapter views M&As as responses as well as causes to competitive retaliation evolving over time, which makes initial plans of the acquirer unlikely to fully materialize. The internal relation is of central importance for the synergistic benefits that can be achieved, but it is in relation to the environment that achieved improvements (e.g. operating efficiency) should be measured. For example, are results below industry average? Do they present a competitive advantage? Or are they perhaps even irrelevant? Since the value that is available to the involved firms from such improvements is often realized years after the transaction, relevant measures of value potential should reflect the situation at the time of realization rather than that at the time of the transaction. This puts the searchlight on external dynamism in the period after M&A, which can severely alter the value that can be extracted from M&As, and, in cases where such external dynamism is not sufficiently reflected theoretically, studies risk giving incomplete or obsolete pictures of value potential in M&As.

This chapter has the goal of guiding future M&A research by suggesting a competitive dynamics perspective on value potential in M&As. Specifically, this chapter examines the theoretical constructs most commonly used to depict value potential. If these theoretical constructs for value potentials are not adjusted to better include dynamism, many of the conclusions drawn about M&A performance risk relying on overly optimistic, or even erroneous, foundations. Embracing a more dynamic and competitive perspective in M&A research can inform both research and practice, and contribute to improving explanations of the high failure rate in M&As that is so often observed in research (Datta *et al.* 1992; King *et al.* 2004; Moeller *et al.* 2005).

Next, I turn to presenting the most common theoretical constructs used in M&A performance studies in the strategic management field, showing that this research is biased towards studying conditions that reflect some, but not all, of the factors relevant for the value that is created. Thereafter I turn to present an alternative perspective that can better reflect value potential. I then point to how some existing research on M&As can be reinterpreted and complemented. The last section of this chapter summarizes the theoretical conclusions along with advice to practitioners.

Conditions for value creation in M&As

M&As are often seen as a means of achieving increased competiveness, and thereby increasing performance of the involved firms. Academic research has given much attention to performance of M&As from various perspectives. Much of financial economics research has aimed at answering whether M&As generally create value or not (Moeller *et al.* 2005) and how these values are distributed between buyers and sellers (Bulow and Klemperer 2009). In parallel, thriving research is concerned specifically with identifying the reasons for performance differences between M&As. A great deal of effort has been invested in strategic management literature to identify deal characteristics with an influence on M&A performance (Datta *et al.* 1992;

King *et al.* 2004; Hitt *et al.* 1998; Pehrsson 2006; Gantumur and Stephan 2012). Central to these studies is the view that performance depends on the degree to which the initial conditions of M&As offer increased performance and on the extent to which these are taken advantage of. This leads to two analytically distinct but related challenges to strategic decision makers wishing to increase the likelihood of success in M&As.

A first challenge relates to assessing value potential—the known and unknown but not yet realized combinatory effects derived from the M&A. This requires making long-term projections of future cash flows. Since acquiring managers often have only limited information about the target firm, correct assessments of the size, type, and organizational location of these synergies is typically characterized by substantial uncertainty (Coff 1999; Puranam *et al.* 2006). Second, an insight from organizational studies now broadly embraced in M&A research is that much, if not most, value creation in M&As is contingent on organizational integration (Haspeslagh and Jemison 1991; Lubatkin *et al.* 1998). This process requires skillful management to achieve intended effects, while avoiding a wide range of interrelated organizational challenges involving organizational culture (Vaara *et al.* 2012), power and resistance (Meyer and Altenborg 2007), and perceptions of justice among employees (Ellis *et al.*, 2009) that potentially impact the outcome of M&As (Teerikangas 2010). Organizational dynamism between the involved firms is difficult to predict and it makes initial value potential assessments less accurate.

While these two challenges are partly interrelated, strategic management research mainly has attributed such organizational dynamism to M&As comprising certain properties. Generally speaking, M&As combining firms with similar resources can benefit from firmer and closer integration, compared to firms where part of the goal is to draw on concepts unique to the target firm (Haspeslagh and Jemison 1991). Further, M&As with large overlaps have been found to lead to greater anxiety over job loss, in turn associated with employee resistance (Larsson and Finkelstein 1999). While the dynamism in the post-M&A phase that plays out between the involved firms (Datta 1991) and the effects of M&As on rivals (Clougherty and Duso 2009; Keil *et al.* 2013) is receiving increasing attention, less interest has been devoted to how dynamism in relation to the external business environment affects M&A performance. This is most visible in how value potentials are conceptualized. Therefore, I now turn to a critical discussion of the most dominating approaches to studying value potential in M&As.

Common constructs for value potential

Strategic management research on M&As promising above-average value creation primarily has focused on types of transactions. M&As combine firms, resources, and processes developed over time and in specific circumstances, making each transaction unique (Bower 2001; Lubatkin 1987). In adopting the decision-making perspective of top managers typical to the wider strategic management research stream (Spender 2001) and attempting to draw general conclusions about performance, this research typically approaches transactions as falling within types or categories. In so doing, research typically draws on and develops constructs condensing characteristics regarded as central to the value potential which are then compared with performance measures.

One common approach to classifying M&As is to draw on theoretical frameworks. A framework that has been influential is provided by the Federal Trade Commission (FTC) (cf. Lubatkin 1983). It classifies transactions involving firms in the same product market as "horizontal"; cases with production or distribution overlaps as "product extension"; cases where similar products are sold on different geographical markets as "market extension"; those when the merger involved a prior customer relation as "vertical"; and cases when none of the conditions apply as "conglomerate." Similar yet more directly involved in assessing value potentials is the framework suggested by Shelton (1988). It classifies transactions as "similar," when firms serve the same customers with the same products; "related-supplementary," when new customers are reached; "related-complementary," when new products are added; and "unrelated," when none of the conditions apply.[1]

Although Shelton (1988) does not define customer overlap geographically (instead, she uses the extent to which both firms serve consumer, industrial, professional, and government customers), both frameworks are comparable and representative for much of the frameworks drawn upon in M&A research.

A more frequent approach to depicting value potential in M&As involves drawing on two distinct yet interrelated theoretical constructs—strategic fit and relatedness. These concepts are used both together and/or separately. Sometimes relatedness is regarded as the operationalization of strategic fit. For instance, Nupponen (1995) operationalizes strategic fit using three subcategories: relatedness being one, overlap of business processes and market power the others. However, relatedness is often used alone (Salter and Weinhold 1979) or interchangeably with fit (Kim and Finkelstein 2009). Taken together, these concepts not only permeate the thinking of theoretical frameworks such as Shelton's (1988), but have also come to dominate much of the theoretical debate regarding value potential in M&As by being used in several influential studies (e.g., Anand and Singh 1997; Brush 1996; Finkelstein and Haleblian 2002; Fowler and Schmidt 1989; Harrison *et al.* 1991; Homburg and Bucerius 2006; Lien and Klein 2006; Miller *et al.* 2010; Seth 1990; Gary 2005; Singh and Montgomery 1987; St. John and Harrison 1999).

The concept of strategic fit, borrowed from the general strategic management literature, denotes the benefits of combining firms through M&As. More formally, Jemison and Sitkin (1986: 146) define the term as "the degree to which the target firm augments or complements the parent's strategy and thus makes identifiable contributions to the financial and non-financial goals of the parent." The second concept, relatedness, typically is thought of as the degree of sameness or difference between firms involved in M&As and defined as "the strategic similarity and the strategic complementarity of operations of the joining firms" (Larsson and Finkelstein 1999: 6).

There are several reasons why these two concepts have taken center stage in research on value potentials in M&As. One trait making them useful in a strategic management context is that they address the scope of the firm, arguably the central issue to strategic decision making. Historically, strategies for increasing firm competitiveness through M&As have swung from favoring conglomerate M&As, bringing essentially different firms together during the 1960s (Shleifer and Vishny 1991), to a focus on core competencies and similarities beginning in the 1980s (Prahalad and Hamel 1990), and then to a renewed interest in appropriating essentially different and typically hard to develop capabilities through M&As (Makri *et al.* 2010). Another explanation for the popularity of these concepts is that they are familiar to and generally accepted in much of the research on M&As, offering a foundation for continued academic discussions. It is hardly surprising then that they have come to influence much of the thinking in M&A research.

While having contributed to the progress in M&A research, the dominance of these constructs has left important aspects of value potentials in M&As unattended. The term 'strategy' in both definitions is used in the broad strategic management research to represent how a firm is able to compete based on its resource endowments (Barney 1991), capabilities (Amit and Schoemaker 1993), and position in the industry (Porter 1980) sharing an emphasis on the relation between the firm and its environment (Ansoff 1965). Accordingly, both definitions thereby could be expected to enlighten research regarding how and how much M&As contribute to the competitiveness of the involved firms in relation to their environment. However, while currently dominating theoretical constructs focus on one central dimension in the understanding of value potential in M&As, they also risk limiting theory by downplaying another dimension.

The focus and limits in current theoretical constructs

A characteristic common to the frameworks commonly used as well as to the constructs of strategic fit and relatedness is their emphasis on the relation *between* the involved firms while leaving little room for exogenous, external change. Even if there is steady progress in how value potentials are conceptualized, they still draw heavily on the degree of similarity between the involved firms. Most commonly, studies drawing on both constructs typically measure the overlap between the involved firms, their resources, and markets. Davis and Thomas (1993) argue that the degree of similarity typically is assessed in one of two ways. The first is judgmental, where the researcher classifies a deal as related or not (e.g. Rumelt 1986). Similarly, St. John and Harrison (1999) classify similarities in the raw materials, product and process technology, and resource conversion process and then let colleagues grade these according to SIC (Standard Industrial Classification) codes.

The second, more common approach is called mechanistic and it involves comparing similarities between the SIC code classifications of the involved firms. Whereas some, such as Bruton *et al.* (1994), use a broader two-digit level overlap, others increase the level of detail by drawing on the three- or four-digit similarities between the SIC codes of the involved firms (Finkelstein and Haleblian 2002; Miller *et al.* 2010; Oler *et al.* 2008). Davis and Thomas (1993) point to three problems common to the use of SIC codes: 1) that this measures product market similarities only, while potentially leaving capabilities unaccounted for; 2) that vertical relations are typically not included; and 3) that all similarities are assumed to provide the same value potential. Lien and Klein (2006) develop a related, yet distinct, line of thought when they criticize SIC code comparisons for not being truly continuous and for being likely to overestimate value potential, arguing for the need to improve the ways in which relatedness is measured.

Kim and Finkelstein (2009), similar to Larsson and Finkelstein (1999), argue that strategic fit not only depends on similarities but on complementarities between the involved firms, especially when capabilities allow the acquiring firm to benefit from these complementarities. Zaheer *et al.* (2011) make an important point in establishing that, beyond the potential positive effects of similarities, differences between the firms can be either complementary or lacking effect on performance, thus requiring more attention to measures of the types of complementarities involved in M&As. Similar to Finkelstein and Haleblian (2002), who point to negative synergies, this contributes to increasing the level of detail of these constructs. Others have made similar points, arguing that the measures typically used for relatedness risk being too aggregate to fully reflect value potential. Instead, it is suggested, value potential in transactions involving firms operating in more than one industry is better reflected by using multiple SIC codes (Finkelstein and Haleblian 2002). Further, Makri *et al.* (2010) combine measures of similarity and complementarity for technology (using patent overlap) and science (drawing on research communities and science disciplines), thus contributing to furthering the internal precision of the constructs of value potential.

Despite progress, the current use of the strategic fit and relatedness terms means that much of what can be expected to change beyond the control of managers in the involved firms is assessed using a measure essentially comparing the degree of similarity *between* firms. Also markets that, intuitively, could be seen as largely influenced by other forces and hence exogenously dynamic are typically measured as the degree of overlap. The reader might recall that Shelton (1988) probed value potential by comparing whether both firms served similar customer types. Homburg and Bucerius (2006) operationalize the concept of "external relatedness" as the level to which customers and markets of the involved firms are the same. Kim and Finkelstein's (2009) study of complementarity in acquisitions in the US banking industry measured the extent to which the involved firms had branches in the same geographical area before the transaction, as did Ramaswamy (1997) in the same industry. Common for these studies is that it is not the market conditions as such, but rather whether they are served by both firms or not, that is captured.

This tendency of conceptualizing value potential as the degree of similarity is visible also in some formal definitions in this stream of research. For instance, relatedness, defined by Rumelt (1986: 11) as "common skills, resources, markets, production technologies, distribution systems, and purposes between the combined firms," is similar, indeed, to how strategic fit is conceptualized by Pablo et al. (1996: 728), namely as "similarity or complementarity of core organizational competencies." Thus, in contrast to the definitions provided by Jemison and Sitkin (1986) and Larsson and Finkelstein (1999) referred to earlier, the definitions suggested by Rumelt (1986) and Pablo et al. (1996) seem geared solely toward the internal relation between the involved firms without any relation to the strategy or strategic or competitive situation.

The consequence is that a firm's relation to the external environment, often at the center of the strategic fit concept in strategic management literature (e.g. Ansoff 1965), in M&A research is collapsed into a degree of similarity between the involved firms before the transaction. Even important steps to develop a more fine-grained view of the overlap (St. John and Harrison 1999; Makri et al. 2010) miss the fundamental point of validity of what is included in the measure once the transaction has taken place. This means that industry dynamism, maturity, technical complexity, or level of rivalry is excluded from the conceptualizations of value potential. For instance, Zollo and Meier (2008) find that virtually no attention is given to whether customers are retained or not following M&As.

In summary, value potential in M&As is commonly conceptualized as a degree of similarity between the involved firms at the time of M&A, rather than how a transaction alters the relation between the involved firms and their competitive environment. This makes value predictions vulnerable to dynamism in the environment. In industries that are either sufficiently stable or benevolent for business conditions to remain predictable, or where the various organizational actors do not attempt to benefit at the expense of each other, this concern remains of minor importance. However, in situations that are unpredictable and where the profit distribution in the industry is contested, this concern is more important. If not reflected in theoretical constructs, external changes risk making value potential measures based on the degree of initial internal similarity obsolete. Current constructs, I argue, can fruitfully be accompanied by more attention to what can be thought of as competitive dynamism external to M&As. In the following, I sketch some reasons why such a competitive dynamism following the announcement of M&As might be relevant for strategic management literature, before outlining some consequences from adopting a competitive dynamics perspective for the broader M&A research.

Toward a competitive dynamics perspective on M&As

Complementing current research conceptions of value potential with a competitive dynamics perspective requires viewing M&As as inherently intertwined with ongoing change within and between industries. Typically, research on competitive dynamics has focused on firm dyads (Baum and Korn 1999; Chen et al. 2007). Assuming dyadic competitive relations are central for firm behavior, but also regarding these as embedded in the general dynamism in the relevant business environment, has consequences for theories on M&As. M&As viewed as adjustments to past and expected change will be more likely in dynamic environments and will also spark further external change. It follows that the effects of an M&A should be considered in relation to its competitive environment (Clougherty and Duso 2009) and with the environment changes effecting value potential. Taking such a competitive dynamics perspective leads to the conclusion that an understanding of value potential also requires understanding whether and how the external environment can change.

There are several reasons why value potential in M&As could change after the announcement. The societal, economic, legal, or other conditions in which M&As are initiated to create increased competitiveness rarely are completely stable. Research has convincingly shown that it can take up to seven (Birkinshaw *et al.* 2000) or even 12 years to fully realize the benefits from M&As (Barkema and Schijven 2008), leaving industry conditions ample time to change. While the level of dynamics differs between industries (e.g. Nadkarni and Narayanan 2007), an increasing number of industries are undergoing fundamental and rapid change (D'Aveni 1994; Brown and Eisenhardt 1997), which increases the likelihood that the external environment will alter during M&A processes. In addition, M&As are more likely to take place under dynamic environmental conditions compared to when environments are more stable (Heeley *et al.* 2006), increasing the likelihood that M&As are followed by dynamism.

While the risk of such general change is inherent in business, there are reasons to assume that M&As might be especially exposed to dynamism. Taking a strategic management perspective typically involves regarding M&As as a means to increase competitiveness against an often hostile environment. While some transactions can turn out to be "checkmate M&As" that provide participating management with nearly complete control of the relevant business environment, many M&s are instead likely to be followed by a deliberate response from the environment. Research on inter-firm rivalry has found competitive retaliation to be more likely against strategic moves that are visible and perceived as a threat (Chen 1996). M&As are often more visible compared to more routine investments (Oler *et al.* 2008), and M&As are often announced publicly along with their specific aims (Sirower and Lipin 2003). Further, M&As that are truly competitive will likely be perceived as threats. The time it typically takes to realize synergies (Larsson and Finkelstein 1999) offers competitors and other industry participants the opportunity to retaliate by approaching the same markets as a competitor (Turner *et al.* 2010; Steenkamp *et al.* 2005) or responding with M&As (Keil *et al.* 2013). It is not surprising, therefore, that external industry participants such as competitors have been found to actively attempt interfering with the realization of those effects, thus reducing the value that can be extracted compared to those initially anticipated (Schriber 2012).

The above discussion suggests that general change as well as retaliatory response directed specifically against M&As can alter the environments and hence the possibilities for M&As to create value. Such dynamism falls outside of the current use of strategic fit and relatedness in M&A research. It therefore appears fruitful to adjust measures of value potential to include a larger measure of external dynamism. One means of doing so is to adopt a perspective on M&As in general, and on value potentials in particular, that can be thought of as dynamic and competitive. While sketched only briefly above, a first step toward explicating a competitive dynamics perspective on M&As suggests a need to shift the emphasis in M&A research. The potential in such a perspective is illustrated in its ability to extend understanding of M&As through reinterpreting existing research findings and opening paths to new ones in several streams of M&A research.

Consequences for M&A research

Some consequences of applying such a competitive dynamics perspective on past as well as future research can be outlined. For instance, it is possible to interpret the findings from M&A performance research in light of the above discussion. Studies of M&A performance measures have pointed to the diverging results between differences in short- and long-term performance (e.g. Zollo and Meier 2008). For instance, King *et al.* (2004) found positive abnormal returns turning negative on average 22 days after M&A announcements. One reason put forward by Lubatkin *et al.* (1997) is that initial positive market expectations of M&A performance tend to fall when information gradually increases awareness of the organizational challenges of integration. The perspective proposed here adds to such internal reasons for performance change and points also to external explanations. For instance, retaliatory reactions from external industry actors in the period following M&As (Schriber 2012) would seem consistent with such performance patterns, since market awareness of such responses are likely to increase in the days following a focal transaction.

A dynamic competitive perspective also could contribute to theories on performance differences between types of M&A. For instance, Kim and Finkelstein (2009) found that M&As involving new market entry were associated with lower performance than those staying in the same market, which is also consistent with the findings of Shelton (1988) and Lubatkin *et al.* (1997). This is interpreted by Kim and Finkelstein (2009) as the integration of new markets requiring partly new managerial capabilities. A competitive dynamics perspective could add that entering new markets through M&As not only involves the challenge of integrating the resources, business model, culture, and reporting systems of another firm (Datta *et al.* 1992). It also includes entering a market with a potentially very different competitive context (e.g. Barney and Zajac 1994), requiring new organizational capabilities to make sense of and handle a new competitive environment (Porac *et al.* 2011). While this argument is consistent with the overall findings of Kim and Finkelstein (2009), pointing to the influence of a dynamic competitive environment adds to the explanations of M&A performance. Strategic management research might benefit from including the acquirer's degree of familiarity with the competitive situation of the target firm. For instance, it is likely that unrelated M&As bring different external hurdles to value creation than related ones.

For instance, constructs of value potential could benefit from reflecting change in the general business conditions in the industry, such as deregulation or the opening of new geographical markets that alter the conditions under which M&As can create value (Meyer and Lieb-Dozcy 2003). Other shifts include changes in customer preferences or economic disturbances leading to further M&A activity in the industry (Trautwein 1990). Whereas external change can increase the value of existing or create new value potentials, they also can leave firms participating in M&As worse off than competitors: reductions of slack following M&As can leave the involved firms less able to respond to sudden and unexpected increases in demand (Gary 2005).

A competitive dynamics perspective also holds potential for expanding the scope of research focusing on the integration process. As noted earlier, the integration process is rarely explicitly in focus in strategic management studies but often acknowledged as central for whether value creation occurs or not. A consequence of taking a competitive dynamics perspective is that it allows regarding employee interpretations of the organizational processes as part of a larger context. This means complementing the current emphasis on the role of management for how the integration process evolves with factors outside the involved organizations. For instance, media representations of the transaction (Riad *et al.* 2012) might form employee perceptions of their own situation. In addition, negative perceptions of the integration that can lead to increased employee turnover (Lubatkin *et al.* 1999) also can be put in context in that employee turnover can be expected to increase with the availability of alternative job offers. In sum, a dynamic competitive perspective suggests that constructs for value potential fruitfully could include factors in the environment to reflect employee interpretations of M&As, perhaps such as in M&As in high-tech acquisitions, where employee motivation is often argued to be of special importance for value creation (Ranft and Lord 2002; Schweizer 2005).

Conclusions

Much M&A research revolves around identifying M&As that create value. Studies typically take their starting point in the view that managers select, or should select, targets depending on the size of the available value potential and the likelihood that it can be realized. While the idea that the internal integration process between the involved firms is complex and often hampered by unexpected turbulence has gained ground in research, *external* dynamism in the environment affecting the post-M&A phase so far has been largely overlooked. Examining research using the dominating theoretical constructs for value potential, this chapter has argued that current research does not sufficiently acknowledge that M&As are likely to face unintended, general change, as well as meet intentional efforts by competitors or other external industry actors perceiving a risk of losing in relative competitiveness.

While some M&As take place in stable and predictable industries, and others might turn out to be "checkmate M&As," providing participating firms with control over the industry, this seems far from a general rule. In contrast to several approaches in general strategic management that stress the need to reflect dynamism in theories (e.g. Farjoun 2002; Helfat *et al.* 2007; Porter 1991), current research on value potential in M&A studies seems a target of Spender's (2001: 29) criticism that "the pivotal notion of fit seems an incomprehensible hang-over from microeconomic equilibrium theory." In line with what I labeled a competitive dynamic perspective on M&As, this chapter has emphasized that the gains available in M&As depend on how well the two firms complement each other in relation to the external environment, which likely is not stable.

The ambition of this chapter has been to outline future M&A research by suggesting a competitive dynamics perspective on value potential in M&As. Extending initial steps in this direction (Keil *et al.* 2013; Schriber 2012), this chapter suggests that, while *ex ante* comparisons of similarities or complementarities of the involved firms are likely to remain central for value potential assessments, lack of attention to changes in the environment risks making such predictions incomplete or even obsolete. This means that traditional approaches might be less valid in dynamic and competitive environments, and that the perspective proposed here can complement existing research on M&A performance. This relates to the point made by King *et al.* (2004: 197) who, in finding little evidence for the concepts typically used to predict value potential, claim that researchers "simply may not be looking at the 'right' set of variables as predictors of post-acquisition performance." In this sense, this chapter concludes that adding a contingency component reflecting the main characteristics of the relevant industry or industries in which the M&As take place is a potential avenue for developing existing concepts for value potential, in turn furthering the theoretical understanding of M&A performance. The competitive dynamics perspective proposed here is a first step in this direction and bears potential for opening a much needed theoretical discussion regarding the currently dominating concepts for value potential; for re-interpreting current research findings; and for directing future finance, strategic management, and integration research.

Practitioners can benefit from assessing the benefits available in M&As through the lens of a competitive dynamics perspective. Conclusions from this chapter complement, rather than contest, the importance of resource overlaps and the internal challenges facing integration managers identified in earlier research. But since initial overlaps are likely to give only a partial picture of the benefits available in the post-M&A period in dynamic and competitive industries, practitioners can benefit from placing more emphasis on a structured approach to addressing the likelihood and effects of changing circumstances on the foundations of identified benefits. Beyond assessing the effects from a strategic go–no-go or valuation perspective, managers responsible for and involved in the integration process need to remain open to the chance that integration level and efforts should be reassessed in relation to an ever evolving competitive environment. Since management attention typically is drawn to the internal organizations during M&A integration (Larsson and Finkelstein 1999), managers might need to keep a certain amount of attention on the external environment during integration.

Note

1 The FTC collected and reported data for larger mergers for 1948–1979.

References

Amit, R. and Schoemaker, P.J H. (1993) "Strategic assets and organizational rent," *Strategic Management Journal*, 14: 33–46.

Anand, J. and Singh, H. (1997) "Asset redeployment, acquisitions and corporate strategy in declining industries," *Strategic Management Journal*, 18: 99–118.

Ansoff, I.H. (1965) *Corporate Strategy: An Analytic Approach to Business Policy for Growth and Expansion*. New York: McGraw-Hill Book Company.

Barkema, H.G. and Schijven, M. (2008) "Toward unlocking the full potential of acquisitions: the role of organizational restructuring," *Academy of Management Journal*, 51: 696–722.

Barney, J.B. (1991) "Firm resources and sustained competitive advantage," *Journal of Management*, 17: 99–120.

Barney, J.B. and Zajac, E.J. (1994) "Competitive organizational behavior: toward an organizationally-based theory of competitive advantage," *Strategic Management Journal*, 15: 5–9.

Baum, J.A.C. and Korn, H.J. (1999) "Dynamics of dyadic competitive interaction," *Strategic Management Journal*, 20: 251–78.

Birkinshaw, J., Bresman, H., and Håkanson, L. (2000) "Managing the post-acquisition integration process: how the human integration and task integration processes interact to foster value creation," *Journal of Management Studies*, 37: 395–425.

Bower, J.L. (2001) "Not all M&As are alike – and that matters," *Harvard Business Review*, 79: 93–101.

Brown, S.L. and Eisenhardt, K.M. (1997) "The art of continuous change: linking complexity theory and time-paced evolution in relentlessly shifting organizations," *Administrative Science Quarterly*, 42: 1–34.

Brush, T.H. (1996) "Predicted change in operational synergy and post-acquisition performance of acquired businesses," *Strategic Management Journal*, 17: 1–24.

Bruton, G.D., Oviatt B.M., and White, M.A. (1994) "Performance of acquisitions of distressed firms," *Academy of Management Journal*, 37: 972–89.

Bulow, J. and P. Klemperer (2009) "Why do sellers (usually) prefer auctions?," *American Economic Review*, 99: 1544–75.

Chen, M.J. (1996) "Competitor analysis and interfirm rivalry: toward a theoretical integration," *The Academy of Management Review*, 21: 100–34.

Chen, M.J., Su, K.H., and Tsai, W.P. (2007) "Competitive tension: the awareness-motivation-capability perspective," *Academy of Management Journal*, 50: 101–18.

Clougherty, J.A. and Duso, T. (2009) "The impact of horizontal mergers on rivals: gains to being left outside a merger," *Journal of Management Studies*, 46: 1365–95.

Coff, R.W. (1999) "How buyers cope with uncertainty when acquiring firms in knowledge-intensive industries: caveat emptor," *Organization Science*, 10: 144–61.

Datta, D.K. (1991) "Organizational fit and acquisition performance: effects of post-acquisition integration," *Strategic Management Journal*, 12: 281–97.

Datta, D.K., Pinches, G.E., and Narayanan, V.K. (1992) "Factors influencing wealth creation from mergers and acquisitions: a meta-analysis," *Strategic Management Journal*, 13: 67–84.

D'Aveni, G.S. (1994) *Hypercompetition: Managing the Dynamics of Strategic Manoeuvring*. New York: The Free Press.

Davis, R. and Thomas, L.G. (1993) "Direct estimation of synergy: a new approach to the diversity-performance debate," *Management Science*, 39: 1334–46.

Ellis, K.M., Reus, T.H., and Lamont, B.T. (2009) "The effects of procedural and informational justice in the integration of related acquisitions," *Strategic Management Journal*, 30: 137–61.

Farjoun, M. (2002) "Towards an organic perspective on strategy," *Strategic Management Journal*, 23: 561–94.

Finkelstein, S. and Haleblian, J. (2002) "Understanding acquisition performance: the role of transfer effects," *Organization Science*, 13: 36–47.

Fowler, K.L. and Schmidt, D.R. (1989) "Determinants of tender offer post-acquisition financial performance," *Strategic Management Journal*, 10: 339–50.

Gantumur, T. and Stephan, A. (2012) "Mergers and acquisitions and innovation performance in the telecommunications equipment industry," *Industrial and Corporate Change*, 21: 277–314.

Gary, S.M. (2005) "Implementation strategy and performance outcomes in related diversification," *Strategic Management Journal*, 26: 643–64.

Hagedorn, J. and Duysters, G. (2002) "External sources of innovative capabilities: the preference for strategic alliances or mergers and acquisitions," *Journal of Management Studies*, 39: 167–88.

Harrison, J.S., Hitt, M.A., Hoskisson, R.E., and Ireland, D.R. (1991) "Synergies and post-acquisition performance: differences versus similarities in resource allocations," *Journal of Management*, 17: 173–90.

Haspeslagh, P.C. and Jemison, D.B. (1991) *Managing Acquisitions: Creating Value through Corporate Renewal*. New York: Free Press.

Heeley, M.B., King, D.R., and Covin, J.G. (2006) "Effects of firm R&D investment and environment on acquisition likelihood," *Journal of Management Studies*, 43: 1513–35.

Helfat, C.E., Finkelstein, S., Mitchell, W., Peteraf, M.A., Singh, H., Teece, D.J., and Winter, S.G. (2007) *Dynamic Capabilities: Understanding Strategic Change in Organizations*. Malden, MA: Blackwell Publishing.

Hitt, M., Harrison, J., Ireland, D.R., and Best, A. (1998) "Attributes of successful and unsuccessful acquisitions of US firms," *British Journal of Management*, 9: 91–114.

Homburg, C. and Bucerius, M. (2006) "Is speed of integration really a success factor of mergers and acquisitions? An analysis of the role of internal and external relatedness," *Strategic Management Journal*, 27: 347–67.

Jemison, D.B. and Sitkin, S.B. (1986) "Acquisitions: the process can be a problem," *Harvard Business Review*, March–April: 107–16.

Keil, T., Laamanen, T., and McGrath, R.G. (2013) "Is a counterattack the best defense? Competitive dynamics through acquisitions," *Long Range Planning*, 46: 195–215.

Kim, J.-Y.J. and Finkelstein, S. (2009) "The effects of strategic and market complementarity on acquisition performance: evidence from the U.S. commercial banking industry 1989–2001," *Strategic Management Journal*, 30: 617–46.

King, D.R., Dalton, D.R., Daily, C.M., and Covin, J.G. (2004) "Meta-analyses of post-acquisition performance: indications of unidentified moderators," *Strategic Management Journal*, 25: 187–200.

Larsson, R. and Finkelstein, S. (1999) "Integrating strategic, organizational, and human resource perspectives on mergers and acquisitions: a case study of synergy realization," *Organization Science*, 10: 1–26.

Lee, G.K. and Lieberman, M.B. (2010) "Acquisition vs. internal development as modes of market entry," *Strategic Management Journal*, 31: 140–58.

Lien, L.B. and Klein, P.G. (2006) "Relatedness and acquirer performance," in C.L. Cooper and S. Finkelstein (eds.), *Advances in Mergers and Acquisitions*, 5: 9–23. Amsterdam: JAI.

Lubatkin, M. (1983) "Mergers and the performance of the acquiring firm," *Academy of Management Review*, 8: 218–25.

Lubatkin, M. (1987) "Merger strategies and stockholder value," *Strategic Management Journal*, 8: 39–53.

Lubatkin, M., Srinivasan, N., and Merchant, H. (1997) "Merger strategies and shareholder value during times of relaxed antitrust enforcement: the case of large mergers during the 1980s," *Journal of Management*, 23: 59–81.

Lubatkin, M., Schweiger, D.M., and Weber, Y. (1999) "Top management turnover in related M&A's: an additional test of the theory of relative standing," *Journal of Management*, 25: 55–73.

Lubatkin, M., Calori, R., Very, P., and Veiga, J.F. (1998) "Managing mergers and acquisitions across borders: a two-nation exploration of a nationally bound administrative heritage," *Organization Science*, 9: 670–84.

Makri, M., Hitt, M.A., and Lane, P.J. (2010) "Complementary technologies, knowledge relatedness, and invention outcomes in high technology mergers and acquisitions," *Strategic Management Journal*, 31: 602–28.

Meyer, C.B. and Altenborg, E. (2007) "The disintegrating effects of equality: a study of a failed international merger," *British Journal of Management*, 18: 257–71.

Meyer, K.E. and Lieb-Dozcy, E. (2003) "Post-acquisition restructuring as evolutionary process," *Journal of Management*, 40: 459–82.

Miller, D., Le Breton-Miller, I., and Lester, R.H. (2010) "Family ownership and acquisition behavior in publicly-traded companies," *Strategic Management Journal*, 31: 201–23.

Moeller, S.B., Schlingemann, F.P., and Stulz, R.M. (2005) "Wealth destruction on a massive scale? A study of acquiring firm returns in the recent merger wave," *The Journal of Finance*, 40: 757–82.

Nadkarni, S. and Narayanan, V.K. (2007) "The evolution of collective strategy frames in high- and low-velocity industries," *Organization Science*, 18: 688–710.

Neffke, F. and Henning, M. (2013) "Skill relatedness and firm diversification," *Strategic Management Journal*, 34: 297–316.

Nupponen, P. (1995) "Post-Acquisition Performance: Combination, Management, and Performance Measurement in Horizontal Integration." Doctoral thesis. Helsinki School of Economics and Business Administration.

Oler, D.K., Harrison, J.S., and Allen, M.R. (2008) "The danger of misinterpreting short-window event study findings in strategic management research: an empirical illustration using horizontal acquisitions," *Strategic Organization*, 6: 151–84.

Pablo, A.L., Sitkin, S.B., and Jemison, D.B. (1996) "Acquisition decision-making processes: the central role of risk," *Journal of Management*, 22: 723–46.

Pehrsson, A. (2006) "Business relatedness and performance: a study of managerial perceptions," *Strategic Management Journal*, 27: 265–82.

Porac, J.F., Thomas, H., and Baden-Fuller, C. (2011) "Competitive groups as cognitive communities: the case of Scottish knitwear manufacturers revisited," *Journal of Management Studies*, 48: 646–64.

Porter, M.E. (1980) *Competitive Strategy: Techniques for Analyzing Industries and Competitors*. New York: The Free Press.

Porter, M.E. (1985) *Competitive Advantage: Creating and Sustaining Superior Performance*. New York: The Free Press.

Porter, M.E. (1991) "Towards a dynamic theory of strategy," *Strategic Management Journal*, 12: 95–117.

Prahalad, C.K. and Hamel, G. (1990) "The core competence of the corporation," *Harvard Business Review*, 68: 79–91.

Puranam, P., Powell, B.C., and Singh, H. (2006) "Due diligence failure as a signal detection problem," *Strategic Organization*, 4: 319–48.

Ramaswamy, K. (1997) "The performance impact of strategic similarity in horizontal mergers: evidence from the US banking industry," *Academy of Management Journal*, 40: 697–715.

Ranft, A.L. and Lord, M.D. (2002) "Acquiring new technologies and capabilities: a grounded model of acquisition implementation," *Organization Science*, 13: 420–41.

Riad, S., Vaara, E., and Zhang, N. (2012) "The intertextual production of international relations in mergers and acquisitions," *Organization Studies*, 33: 121–48.

Rumelt, R.P. (1986) *Strategy, Structure, and Economic Performance* (2nd edn). Boston, MA: Harvard University Press.

Salter, M.S. and Weinhold, W.A. (1979) *Diversification through Acquisition: Strategies for Creating Economic Value*. New York: The Free Press.

Schriber, S. (2012) "Managing the influence of external competitive change during integration," in Anderson, H., Havila, V., and Nilsson, (eds.), *Mergers and Acquisitions: The Critical Role of Stakeholders*. New York and Abingdon: Routledge.

Schweizer, L. (2005) "Organizational integration of acquired biotechnology companies into pharmaceutical companies: the need for a hybrid approach," *Academy of Management Journal*, 48: 1052–74.

Seth, A. (1990) "Sources of value creation in acquisitions: an empirical investigation," *Strategic Management Journal*, 11: 431–46.

Shelton, L.M. (1988) "Strategic business fits and corporate acquisition: empirical evidence," *Strategic Management Journal*, 9: 279–287.

Shleifer, A. and Vishny, R.W. (1991) "Takeovers in the '60s and the '80s: evidence and implications," *Strategic Management Journal*, 12: 51–59.

Singh, H. and Montgomery, C.A. (1987) "Corporate acquisition strategies and economic performance," *Strategic Management Journal*, 8: 377–86.

Sirower, M.L. (1997) *The Synergy Trap: How Companies Lose the Acquisition Game*. New York: The Free Press.

Sirower, M.L. and Lipin, S. (2003) "Investor communications: new rules for M&A success," *Financial Executive*, 19: 26–30.

Spender, J.C. (2001) "Business policy and strategy as a professional field," in Volberda, H.W. and Elfring, T. (eds.), *Rethinking Strategy*. London: Sage Publications.

Steenkamp, J.-B.E.M., Nijs, V.R., Hanssens, D.M., and Dekimpe, M.G. (2005) "Competitive reactions to advertising and promotion attacks," *Marketing Science*, 24: 35–54.

St. John, C.H. and Harrison, J.S. (1999) "Manufacturing-based relatedness, synergy, and coordination," *Strategic Management Journal*, 20: 129–45.

Teerikangas, S. (2010) "Dynamics of acquired firm pre-acquisition employee reactions," *Journal of Management*, 38: 599–639.

Trautwein, F. (1990) "Merger motives and merger prescriptions," *Strategic Management Journal*, 11: 283–95.

Turner, S.F., Mitchell, W., and Bettis, R.A. (2010) "Responding to rivals and complements: how market concentration shapes generational product innovation strategy," *Organization Science*, 21: 854–72.

Vaara, E., Sarala, R., Sahl, G.K., and Björkman, I. (2012) "The impact of organizational and national cultural differences on social conflict and knowledge transfer in international acquisitions," *Journal of Management* Studies, 49: 1–27.

Zaheer, A., Castañer, X., and Souder, D. (2011) "Synergy sources, target autonomy, and integration in acquisitions," *Journal of Management*, 39: 604–32.

Zollo, M. and Meier, D. (2008) "What is M&A performance?," *Academy of Management Perspectives*, 22: 55–77.

20

A literature review and a suggested future research agenda on speed of integration in M&A

Taking stock of what we know

Florian Bauer

Introduction

Mergers and acquisitions (M&As) have been a prominent topic in academic management literature and practice for decades (Cartwright and Schoenberg 2006). During the peak of the last mergers and acquisitions wave in 2007, the volume of the market for corporate control reached 4.83 trillion US dollars. Due to the current economic and financial crisis, the volume has decreased to 1.78 trillion US dollars in 2011 (according to Bloomberg). Despite the enormous amount of research in the field of M&As, the average success rates of M&As are quite low (Capasso and Meglio 2005). Failure rates between 40 and 60 percent are usually reported (Bagchi and Rao 1992; Cartwright and Cooper 1995), and some researchers state that they are even higher at between 70 and 90 percent (Christensen *et al.* 2011). Since the 1970s, the M&A phenomenon has been studied through several theoretical lenses (Birkinshaw *et al.* 2000; Haspeslagh and Jemison 1991). Financial studies still dominate current M&A research, but additional research streams have developed (Cartwright and Schoenberg 2006).

In strategic management, research is mainly concerned with pre-merger attitudes of buying and target companies (Phersson 2006; Stimpert and Duhaime 1997; Singh and Montgomery 1987). Scholars point out that some kind of strategic fit is beneficial for value creation in terms of efficiency-based and enhancement-based synergies (Larsson and Finkelstein 1999). Other researchers investigate empirically the influence of acquisition experience on M&A performance (Halebian and Finkelstein 1999; Barkema *et al.* 1996). Up to now, the results on acquisition experience are a mixed blessing (King *et al.* 2004). There is also growing recognition of the importance of cultural factors (Very *et al.* 1997; Sarkar *et al.* 2001; Aw and Chatterjee 2004), human resource-related issues (Kavanagh and Askanasy 2006; Buchholtz *et al.* 2003; Colquitt *et al.* 2001), and M&A integration (Capron and Pistre 2002; Puranam *et al.* 2009; Paruchuri *et al.* 2006; Birkinshaw *et al.* 2000). A more derivate angle is the so-called process school or perspective (Haspeslagh and Jemison 1991), which is concerned with more operative topics in M&A integration (Birkinshaw *et al.* 2000; Bragado 1992; Jemison and Sitkin 1986).

Interestingly, there is significant agreement on the importance of integration, as value creation in M&As takes place in the integration phase (Haspeslagh and Jemison 1991), but there are fundamentally different assumptions concerning the ideal speed of integration. Speed of integration describes the time from deal closing until the end of the integration process, when the desired degree of integration is reached (Cording *et al.* 2008; Homburg and Bucerius 2006). Even though speed is cited to have an enormous importance from a practical perspective (Schlaepfer *et al.* 2008), only limited academic research has been done on this topic (Homburg and Bucerius 2006; Angwin 2004; Schweiger and Goulet 2005; Homburg and Bucerius 2005; Ranft and Lord 2002; Olie 1994; Inkpen *et al.* 2000). Homburg and Bucerius (2006) state in their study that speed of integration is a broadly neglected topic in academic M&A research even though speed of integration is usually recognized to have an enormous impact on M&A outcome (Homburg and Bucerius 2005; Homburg and Bucerius 2006; Angwin 2004; Ranft and Lord 2002).

Against this background, I discuss the topic of speed with regard to several problem areas in this paper. In the first section of my literature review on speed, I discuss the performance effects of speed. In the second section, I begin to analyze factors that have influence on speed of integration, and, in the third section, I compare and analyze already empirically tested measurement models. On the basis of my literature review and the definition of the problem areas in research on speed of integration, I conclude with a future research agenda.

The speed-performance relationship

In business practice and research, there is growing recognition of the importance to speed up operations for building competitive advantages. The issue of speed affects many strategic perspectives like new product development speed, time-based competition, first mover advantages, and many more (Kessler and Chakrabarti 1996). The main idea of the speed-oriented literature is that firms can generate first-mover or pioneering advantages (Lieberman and Montgomery 1988). Nonetheless, the usage of speed-based advantages affects all organizational facets as speed could be beneficial or detrimental in terms of increasing profits while at the same time cutting costs or lowering market risk (Page 1993). Consequently, it is worth exploring whether speed is also an important issue in M&As. In this section, I review the speed-performance relationship, discuss why speed of integration is decisive for M&A outcomes, and provide some empirical evidence from academic research.

In business practice, there is a common sense perspective on the positive effects of speed of integration on M&A performance (Homburg and Bucerius 2006). In a practitioner-oriented study by Schlaepfer *et al.* (2008), 50 percent of the surveyed companies have planned to finalize the integration process within the first seven months. Nearly 40 percent of the companies in their sample mentioned that integration was not fast enough. These results—that speed is positively correlated with M&A performance—are affirmed in similar research, and it seems that the discussion on the topic of speed is in line with the credo of Chase (1998: 3) that there are "three things that matter the most here, and they are speed, speed, speed (Chase 1998)."

Proposed performance effects

Angwin (2004) demonstrates several arguments in his article as to why a high speed of integration is beneficial for the M&A outcome. He states that fast integration leads to faster returns on investment, less uncertainty among employees and instability in the organization, retaining enthusiasm among stakeholders, bigger effects of early actions, reduced exposure to uncertainties from the external environment, and less time available to competitors to respond (Angwin 2004). Along with these arguments, Buono and Bowditch (2003) point out that speed is relevant in terms of resource reconfiguration and synergy realization. Meanwhile, there are some researchers who stress the beneficial effects of a slow integration.

It is argued that slow integration fosters mutual understanding of employees and the willingness to learn from each other (Buono and Bowditch 2003). As the acculturation process starts with understanding and reconciliation of differences (Nahavandi and Malekzadeh 1988), the arguments for slow integration become even more crucial. But speed of acculturation is not only a topic of slow integration, as it is a process that can be managed to some extent (Schweiger and Goulet 2005; Empson 2004). Other scholars argue that trust-building needs time, but in the end it fosters the realization of financial performance. Therefore, a high speed would have detrimental consequences for value creation (Bijlsma-Frankema 2004). Even though all of these arguments appear intuitive, in a practical study only 33 percent of the participants agreed with possible negative consequences of a fast integration speed (Gerds and Schewe 2004; see also Schlaepfer et al. 2008). These conflicting underlying arguments are in line with the first-mover literature that suggests that speed is a decisive factor, even though speed has advantages and disadvantages (Lieberman and Montgomery 1988).

Empirical results on the speed-performance relationship

Consistent with diversified theoretical arguments on integration speed, the empirical results for the relationship of speed of integration on performance remain ambiguous. Table 20.1 illustrates the major empirical results on speed of integration published after 2000, and I briefly discuss the findings of each study.

Birkinshaw et al. (2000) separate integration in task and cultural integration and state: "they can probably occur at different times" (p. 399). As a result of their multiple case study, they come to the conclusion that the integration of human aspects leads to a shared identity and to mutual respect, which are essential for achieving knowledge transfer and combination synergies (Birkinshaw et al. 2000). In the next study on the topic, Ranft and Lord (2002) infer that managers usually connect learning with communication and speed (Ranft and Lord 2002). Similarly, Gates and Very (2003) conclude that "once an appropriate atmosphere has been created, the acquirer can focus on the 'capability transfer' stage" (p. 170).

Schlünzen and Jöns (2003) investigated speed of integration with expert interviews and concluded that there is a "window of opportunity" which is crucial for uncertainty avoidance (employees and customers) and trust building. Consistent with the idea of a limited window, Angwin (2004) concluded that the long-term performance (more than 3 years after closing) is better for those companies that integrated faster (Angwin 2004). Still, after conducting a qualitative study, Bijlsma-Frankema (2004) concludes that slow integration has beneficial effects on post M&A performance as trust-building needs time. After conducting a quantitative study, Cording et al. (2008) discovered a positive effect on internal reorganization and, therefore, an indirect positive effect of speed of integration on market expansion. Contrary to the fast vs. slow debate, Schweiger and Goulet (2005) argue that integration is a manageable process and that a fast and successful M&A integration requires an understanding of cultural differences.

In a cross-sectional study on marketing integration in M&As with a sample size of 232 managers from acquiring firms, Homburg and Bucerius (2005) found a significantly positive relationship of speed of integration and market-related performance after the acquisition. Even though they state that speed can have negative performance effects, they reason that fast integration limits customer uncertainty and, therefore, fosters market-related performance (Homburg and Bucerius 2005). Meanwhile, another study on marketing related issues and M&As found empirical evidence for the hypothesis that slow integration is valuable for sustainable resource reduction, but the proposed significant relationship to absolute M&A performance was not confirmed (Wille et al. 2011).

Table 20.1 Literature on the speed-performance relationship

Authors	Topic	Method	Speed Measure	Outcomes
Birkinshaw et al. (2000)	Cultural and task integration	Multiple case study on three Swedish acquisitions	Qualitative study, no measures used	• Task and cultural integration can be finished at different times. • Cultural integration is necessary for closer task integration. • A shared identity and mutual trust are prerequisites of closer task integration and thus synergy realization.
Ranft and Lord (2002)	Acquisition implementation	Seven in-depth cases of high technology acquisitions	Qualitative study, no measures used	• Speed of integration is a key dimension of implementation. • Speed of integration/ implementation is closely connected with learning. • Speed of integration/ implementation is connected with communication.
Gates and Very (2003)	Performance measures of M&A integration	53 Fortune 500 and Europe 500 transactions and 20 in-depth interviews with managers	No measures used	• Speed is a critical decision in the integration process. • Speed is the time horizon for the expected value creation. • Speed of integration is an often used operative measure
Schlünzen and Jöns (2003)	Relationship of meaning and performance with integration speed	In depth interviews with 20 managers	Qualitative study, no measures used	• 95% of managers perceive speed of integration as an important success factor. • Speed of integration cannot be analyzed in isolation. • A high integration speed avoids uncertainty among employees and customers.
Angwin (2004)	Speed and performance	70 UK transactions that took place between April 1991 and March 1993	Single item	• Perceptions of success will diminish over time. • Curvilinear relationship with integration success elapses over time. • Early actions lead to better long-term performance.

Study	Topic	Sample/Method	Measurement	Findings
Bijlsma-Frankema (2004)	Speed versus carefulness	Qualitative research with 9 managers from a Dutch multinational engineering company	Qualitative study, no measures used	• Quick changes can avoid troubles with employees. • Trust building needs time but is beneficial in the long run. • A focus on the quick achievement is counterproductive for target employee commitment.
Cording et al. (2008)	The effect of integration speed on internal reorganization	129 horizontal transactions in the US that took place between 1997 and 2001	Single item measure	• Speed is beneficial for internal reorganization. • The direct effect on market expansion is fully mediated by internal reorganization.
Schweiger and Goulet (2005)	Cultural learning and acquisition integration	Longitudinal field experiment in 6 manufacturing plants, survey at 3 different time points	Not measured	• Speed of acculturation is not an undirected evolution, it is a manageable process. • Cultural understanding and the reconciliation of cultural differences enhances speed and M&A success.
Homburg and Bucerius (2005)	Speed of marketing integration and M&A outcome moderated by firm and market-/industry-level variables	232 horizontal transactions in the German-speaking part of Europe that took place between 1996 and 1999	Measured with 8 (marketing-related) items on a 5-point scale ranging from longer than 24 months to less than 6 months	• Marketing integration speed is beneficial for market-related performance due to the fact that customer uncertainty is limited. • But: agreement on the fact that speed can have negative effects, too (was not tested in the study).
Wille et al. (2011)	Corporate brand management in M&A	72 transactions described by M&A consultants and experts in the German-speaking part of Europe that took place between 2004 and 2008	Single item measurement	• A higher degree of integration reduces the speed of integration. • Speed of integration has no significant effect on M&A performance. • A slower speed of integration leads to greater resource reduction.

(Continued)

Table 20.1 Continued

Authors	Topic	Method	Speed Measure	Outcomes
Homburg and Bucerius (2006)	Speed of integration and M&A success moderated by internal and external relatedness	232 horizontal transactions in the German speaking part of Europe that took place between 1996 and 1999	Measured with 8 (marketing-related) items on a 5-point scale ranging from longer than 24 months to less than 6 months	• The speed-performance relationship is dependent on relatedness. • Speed is beneficial with low external and high internal relatedness. • Speed is detrimental with high external and low internal relatedness.
Morag and Barakonyi (2009)	Speed of integration and M&A integration success	Case study research	No quantitative measure	• Speed is a success factor. • Speed depends on the main reason of the acquisition, the type of acquisition (domestic or cross-border), the characteristics of the involved firms, and the integration approach.
Bauer and Matzler (2014)	The effect of integration speed on M&A success	106 transactions in the German-speaking part of Europe that took place between January 2005 and April 2008	Measured with 4 items; due to a lack of reliability, 2 items had to be deleted	• There is no significant effect from integration speed on M&A success. • Speed is determined by strategic complementarity, cultural compatibility and the degree of integration.

In a different study on speed of integration, Homburg and Bucerius (2006) found—depending on the circumstances—several relationships between speed of integration and performance. The shape of the relationship ranges from significant positive over significant negative to non-significant, depending on internal and market relatedness (Homburg and Bucerius 2006). In a similar vein, Morag and Barakonyi (2009) argue, after conducting case study research, that speed is a decisive factor for M&A performance but that the beneficial or detrimental effects of speed of integration depend on motives, transaction types, and the characteristics of the involved firms. Finally, the most recent study on speed of integration and performance found no significant relationship at all (Bauer and Matzler 2014).

In summary, there is no clear evidence whether speed of integration has a positive, a negative, or no effect on M&A outcomes. Further, there are two detrimental theoretically opposite perspectives on speed of integration. Therefore, it is no wonder that researchers highlight the dilemma presented in the choice between careful integration and speed of integration (Gadiesh *et al.* 2003; Bijlsma-Frankema 2004; Bragado 1992). The question that remains is whether it is simply a choice between "speed over elegance" or if other influencing or deterministic factors have to be considered. For example, Kessler and Chakrabarti (1996) analyzed innovation speed literature and tried to uncover conditions under which speed is beneficial and to elaborate contextual factors as well as antecedents in a conceptual model. However, a conceptual framework does not exist for integration speed literature even though it would benefit future research.

Factors influencing speed of integration

As already pointed out in the previous section, speed of integration cannot be analyzed in isolation as it depends on several factors. In the following paragraphs, I will demonstrate and organize potential factors that influence speed of integration.

Contextual factors

Contextual factors strongly influence speed of integration, but these factors may not be an integral part of the actual M&A process. By now, researchers often argue for fast or slow integration while ignoring that, to some extent, it is not only the buying companies' free choice of how to integrate. For example, in Austria and Germany there are several legal regulations concerning tax, business or labor law (e.g. § 3ff AVRAG; § 613a BGB; §221 UGB; § 267 HGB; § 244ff UGB; § 290ff HGB) that serve as pacemakers for speed of integration. National law is an important contextual factor for reorganization. Capron and Guillén analyzed 253 acquisitions with targets in 27 countries with regards to labor rights and shareholder rights. While a high level of shareholder rights is beneficial for reorganization, the opposite is the case for countries with strict labor law (Capron and Guillén 2009). Next to inner-organizational issues like negative emotions etc., they argue that the legal framework is decisive for employees exerting their power (Capron and Guillén 2009).

Another important contextual factor is institutional distance. It influences strategies and behavior (Kostova 1999, Gaur and Lu 2007) and by extension the implementation of a transaction. In a recent study on 106 transactions, Bauer and Matzler (2014) found empirical evidence that, with a high regulative distance of target and buyer country, when the buyer country is better developed, the need for integration increases, while in the opposite situation the effect changes. To conclude, firms are not completely free in their decisions regarding integration and, therefore, not free with regard to speed of integration. National legal requirements as well as institutional differences affect speed of integration.

M&A motives

According to Christensen *et al.* (2011) there are only two main motives as to why firms engage in M&As. If the strategic aim of the M&As is to boost the buying companies' performance, deep and fast integration would be beneficial, while if the aim is reinventing the business model, deep and fast integration would be detrimental (Christensen *et al.* 2011). Bragg (2009) differentiates three types of motives, namely strategic, financial, and managerial motives and argues that they differ from target to buyer. If the motive of the transaction is to increase the existing market share or the production capacity, firms are usually seeking for synergy of total addition. In those cases, the value chains are nearly identical and a deep integration is necessary to eliminate redundant resources and to use the increased market share. Thus, integration and integration management, as well as speed, are decisive for the increase in ratability (Krüger and Müller-Stewens 1994).

If the motive of the transaction is the reduction of cyclicality, and a firm acquires a company outside their industry (Bragg 2009), a complete integration is not necessary as value creation does not derive from cost savings or the elimination of redundant resources. In those cases, the integration of financial, controlling, or managerial information systems is enough. Considering the financial motive of liquidation, where a firm acquires an under-evaluated target with the intention of liquidation (Longenecker *et al.* 2006), integration will not take place. To sum up, integration, integration management, and speed of integration are strongly dependent on the strategic, financial, or managerial intention of the acquisition.

Pre-merger issues

Next to contextual factors, there are M&A process-inherent factors that influence the speed of integration. Homburg and Bucerius (2006) argue that the beneficial as well as the detrimental value creation mechanisms of speed of integration depend on the pre-merger issues of internal and external relatedness, while external relatedness refers to aspects outside the merging organizations (e.g. target markets, market positioning) and internal relatedness focuses on the firm's management styles. Their cross-sectional study with 232 managers from the acquiring firms gives clear evidence that a high speed of integration is most beneficial with a low external and a high internal relatedness, while it is detrimental with low internal and high external relatedness (Homburg and Bucerius 2006). Another study on strategic complementarity provides empirical evidence that strategic complementarities foster speed of integration, while cultural compatibility lowers it (Bauer and Matzler 2014). The authors of this study argue that cultural compatibility is an indicator for "common ground" and, therefore, informal coordination mechanisms are highly relevant for integration even though they are not as controllable and manageable as top-down integration processes. With this common ground effect, the need for structural integration decreases (Puranam *et al.* 2009) and, therefore, a high speed of integration is not necessary. Beyond those two studies, our knowledge on pre-merger influences on speed of integration is rather low. Next to pre-merger issues, I want to emphasize that value creation takes place after the acquisition (Haspeslagh and Jemison 1991). Therefore, post-merger issues—which will be discussed in the next section—are highly relevant for deciding whether high speed is beneficial or detrimental.

Merger issues

Even though speed of integration starts on the day that a deal closes, the merger phase has a strong impact on the implementation strategy, the organization of integration, and, thus, on integration speed (Jemison and Sitkin 1986). Intuitively, it makes sense to argue that the longer the due diligence and the negotiation phases are, the more careful the acquisition planning and more efficient the implementation process. Nonetheless, firms are usually not free in making the time decision, as regulatory reviews or the need for secrecy impact due diligence length. Saorín-Iborra (2008) analyzed the determinants of time pressure in the merging phase, like the need for secrecy; a high level of time pressure can shorten the time available and lead to non-thoroughly thought-out decisions for the integration phase. The anticipated result of shortened planning would be inefficient integration speed, though it could be argued that there are beneficial effects such as uncertainty avoidance among employees. Again, this suggests a dilemma. On the other hand, a long time frame would allow for thorough planning, but on the other hand it can lead, due to a lack of information, to rumors (in the media or in the organization) which can lead to organizational resistance (Schweiger et al. 1987). These negative effects can again lead to inefficient integration and, thus, to an unsuitable integration speed.

Post-merger issues

As with pre-merger issues, our knowledge on the interdependencies of post-merger issues and speed of integration are rather limited. Interestingly, the only two quantitative studies (to the best of my knowledge) on the relationship of the degree of integration and speed of integration provide us with diverging results. While one study gives empirical evidence that a high degree of marketing integration lowers the speed of integration (Wille et al. 2011), another study shows a positive effect from degree of integration and speed of integration. The empirical results of the second study lead to the conclusion that firms that seek a high degree of integration in production and marketing try to finish the integration as fast as possible (Bauer and Matzler 2014). Meanwhile, a study by Cording et al. (2008) included both constructs, but they do not test the relationship between them. The correlation matrix they provide in their paper shows a low correlation (0.03) between the two constructs (Cording et al. 2008), which leads us to the conclusion that there is no statistically significant relationship between degree of integration and speed of integration. Likewise, Homburg and Bucerius (2005) do not test the relationship between degree of integration and speed of integration. Nonetheless, their correlation matrix indicates a stronger relationship, as the correlation, with 0.273, is quite high. With a result of 0.304, the correlation for customer orientation of integration is even higher (Homburg and Bucerius 2005).

Another important issue is integration management itself. The early installation of an integration management team which consists of representatives from buyer and target company, as well as active communication from the announcement day onwards, is cited to be important (Vester 2002). Employees should learn about the transaction from responsible persons in the organization rather than from the daily press to avoid uncertainty and anxiety (Schweiger and Denisi 1991). Even though communication is a central task of an organization, Schweiger et al. (1987) concluded, after 166 in-depth interviews, that only a few managers were able to minimize negative consequences on their subordinates. Thus, active management is an important issue to avoid resistance and other negative effects that influence speed of integration. Decisions concerning the integration of an acquired company should be met fast and with respect to possible psychological traumata (Schweiger et al. 1987). Early decisions regarding the integration can help to avoid uncertainty and, therefore, work as a trigger for efficient integration.

Other, possible influencing factors

Next to contextual factors, pre-merger issues, motives, merger issues, and post-merger issues, speed of integration depends on factors such as kind of transaction, relative size of target, and branch growth. A recent study provides some insights into the dependencies of those—normally used as control variables—factors. Therefore, speed can be much higher with conglomerate transactions than with horizontal ones. Firms seek faster integration with bigger targets than with smaller ones, and branch growth negatively influences the speed of integration. That means that companies in a fast growing business do not integrate as fast as companies in a stable or decreasing business (Bauer and Matzler 2014). Inkpen *et al.* (2000) found empirical evidence in a case study which shows that geographic proximity influences speed of integration. With an increasing distance of target and buyer, speed of integration is slowed down.

As the literature review on all influencing factors shows, there are effects that enormously influence speed of integration, but up to now the amount of academic research as well as the gained knowledge on these issues are rather limited.

Measurement of speed of integration

A third problem area in research related to speed of integration has to do with measurement. Most practically and scientifically oriented studies provide us with a single-item measurement of speed of integration (Schlaepfer *et al.* 2008; Wille *et al.* 2011; Cording *et al.* 2008). Due to the fact that integration is a multi-level process (Shrivastava 1986) it is questionable if integration can be conducted on all levels with the same speed (Olie 1994; Ranft and Lord 2002). Just to name an example, financial or controlling issues can usually be integrated much faster than cultures or organizational structures. Therefore, single-item measurement seems not to be applicable for analyzing speed of integration. Nonetheless, multiple-item measures, on the other hand, provide us with some reliability problems. Homburg and Bucerius (2006) operationalized their latent variable "speed of integration" with eight items. The individual item reliabilities have a range from 0.4 to 0.76 (Homburg and Bucerius 2006). Even though the reported values reach the recommended threshold of 0.4 (Bagozzi and Baumgartner 1994), the low reliability values could be a serious concern. In the above-described study of Bauer and Matzler (2014), a very similar problem occurred. Their originally planned measurement model consisting of four items did not work out, as loadings of two items were too low and one was not even significant. As loadings are correlations, they should share more than 50 percent variance with their underlying construct, which means that the squared correlation should exceed a value of 0.5, loadings below 0.5 or 0.4 should be dropped, and items with low reliabilities "must be interpreted with caution" (Hulland 1999: 199).

Therefore, I propose that, by now, research has not covered the complexity of speed of integration in stable and solid measurement models. Hulland (1999) names three reasons for low loadings of items (poor wording, inappropriate items, or the improper contextual transfer of items), from which the consequences are low reliability, poor content validity, and non-generalizability. To sum up, the literature review on measurement of speed of integration shows a deficit in conceptual work on scale development.

Developing a future research agenda

As the literature review showed, the academic work on speed of integration in M&As is rather limited except for a few quantitative (Angwin 2004; Homburg and Bucerius 2005; Homburg and Bucerius 2006; Bauer and Matzler 2014; Wille *et al.* 2011; Bragado 1992) and qualitative (Bijlsma-Frankema 2004; Olie 1994; Inkpen *et al.* 2000) studies. It becomes clear that the question of speed over elegance is too simplistic, as I was able to identify three areas of problems in current research:

1 the speed-performance relationship
2 factors influencing speed of integration
3 measurement of speed of integration

In this section, I want to demonstrate how the above-described problems in research could be solved. Finally, I try to design a future research agenda.

Speed-performance relationship

There seems to be more than a "one-path" relationship from speed to performance, as acquisition performance itself is a theoretically complex construct which consists of numerous dimensions and, thus, research is faced with the dilemma of the trade-off between precision and generalizability (Cording *et al.* 2010). Next to considerations like "value for whom" and "assessed by whom," one needs to consider the time period that makes the effects of speed open to research. With regard to integration and integration performance, event study measures do not seem to be applicable as it is stated that the completion of an integration process needs three to five years (Homburg and Bucerius 2005; Zollo and Meier 2008). But to imply that speed has only long-term effects does not help us in understanding the phenomenon. To measure the effects of early actions, such as communication to avoid uncertainty or the loss of talents or early decisions that foster the integration process (Vester 2002," Schweiger *et al.* 1987), a single performance measure seems too limited.

A different approach was chosen by Cording *et al.* (2008). They implemented an intermediate step to M&A success with their measurement of internal reorganization. In addition to internal reorganization, which has a positive effect on the M&A outcome (Cording *et al.* 2008), there are other underlying possible value-creating mechanisms. As possible value-creating mechanisms are described theoretically (Angwin 2004; Homburg and Bucerius 2006), I am wondering why they have not been empirically tested. The mechanisms for value creation—faster exploitation of synergies, reduced uncertainty among employees (Angwin 2004) and customers (Homburg and Bucerius 2006), or the advantage of the early enthusiasm stage (Angwin 2004)—are empirically underdeveloped. Additionally, transactions and speed of integration have different effects on different stakeholders, which all have different interests (King and Taylor 2012). While quick decisions and security are important for employees and can help to avoid increased turnover (Schweiger *et al.* 1987), firms need to consider quality disruptions that occur due to fast integration (King and Taylor 2012). This suggests that other major stakeholders such as customers, advisors, lenders, vendors, and government regulators may have different perceptions of integration speed.

As the M&A outcome is not uni-dimensionally captureable, I would propose a broader framework for value creation mechanisms and performance indicators. The implementation of some measures would provide us with valuable insights into the value-creating or -destroying effects of speed of integration. Moreover, it would make intuitive sense to broaden the group of respondents. Most quantitative studies addressed acquiring CEOs and they ignore employees, customers, retailers, suppliers, lenders, or shareholder perspectives. Even though CEOs from the acquiring firms seem to be most knowledgeable about the transaction and the integration process (Datta 1991), their rating correlates highly with objective success measures (Datta 1991; Homburg and Bucerius 2005). I argue that a multiple set of measures is necessary to assess the performance mechanisms of speed of integration. This would help us in gaining a better and a deeper understanding of the speed-performance relationship and the underlying value creation mechanisms.

Factors influencing speed of integration

The literature review demonstrates that our knowledge is rather limited. As the state of the art on empirical work demonstrates, those factors have an enormous impact on speed of integration. Following those empirical results, I conclude that first, there are more, up to now unexamined, influencing factors and second, that a multi-dimensional framework is needed to gain a better understanding of those influencing factors. Third, the interdependencies of pre-merger issues and post-merger issues should be investigated. This postulation is not new in M&A research (King *et al.* 2004) but research on those interdependencies remains limited. To analyze antecedents of intergation, speed could be valuable to understand the concept itself better. Next to triggers of speed such as motives or strategic, financial, or managerial intentions, there are some uninvestigated decelerators of speed of integration.

In line with the study of Capron and Guillén (2009), one could easily argue that labor law affects speed of integration, as a stricter labor law hinders the internal reorganization. Further, the literature review demonstrates that speed is not always beneficial or detrimental; rather, it depends on the context. In their study on speed of integration and the moderating role of external and internal relatedness, Homburg and Bucerius (2006) conclude that there are many more moderating effects than just fit. They argue that, for example, ingrained cultures or acquisition experience could moderate the relationship (Homburg and Bucerius 2006). Building on transfer theory or experimental learning, one could argue that acquisition experience moderates the relationship from speed to performance. The taking of more factors into consideration would lead to better and more reliable managerial implications than just "integrate as fast as possible". The question of "speed over elegance" could become obsolete when research uncovers the antecedents and conditions when integration speed is beneficial or detrimental. Nonetheless, the implementation of too many influencing factors would make research difficult. For measuring and testing the role of speed, a clear industry focus or the concentration on a specific type of acquisition (e.g. solely horizontal domestic deals) could serve as a starting point as this would lead to a reducion of the complexity of influencing factors.

Measurement of speed of integration

The results of the applied measurement modes provide us with a mixed blessing. As the review of quantitative papers indicate, single item measurement appears unable to capture a multi-sided construct (Schlaepfer *et al.* 2008) like speed of integration because several organizational levels should be taken into account (Shrivastava 1986). Nonetheless, theoretically well developed measurement models provide us with inconclusive results concerning their reliability (Homburg and Bucerius, 2006) or the scope of the measurement concept (two items deleted in Bauer and Matzler's (2014) measurement model).

One thing I am missing in research on speed of integration is that speed is usually used as a term that sets two aspects into a relationship to each other (like "miles per hour"). The application of a relative speed measure is quite common in new product development (NPD) speed literature, where duration is compared with other reference units like competitors, schedule deviations, or the fastest feasible duration (Goktan and Miles 2011; Akgün and Lynn 2002; Kessler and Bierly 2002). Nonetheless, in current M&A research, speed is usually measured in absolute terms with questions like, "approximately how long did the integration process take?" (Cording *et al.* 2008: 761). Thus, I think that a new approach could solve the problem of statistical reliability as well as the content-related problems in research. A simple comparison of the duration measure does not allow for an inter-firm comparison, as the duration is dependent on influencing factors. Recent research on NPD speed shows the strength of relative measurement concepts due to the comparability with e.g. competitors (Carbonell *et al.* 2009). In the case of M&As, the degree of integration could be a possible relation to assess a "relative speed measurement" even though there would be some inherent problems with the relation as the degree of integration is dependent on other factors. For example, firms that show a high strategic and cultural fit could reach a high degree of integration with much less change and effort than organizations with a low or no fit. Therefore, I propose that the perceived level of change could serve as a better reference unit for a relative speed of integration measure. Coming back to the example, those firms that provide a high strategic and cultural fit have a low level of perceived change, while this level is much higher for firms that have none or just a low level of fit. Thus, with the same "absolute" integration speed (duration), the "relative speed measurement" would provide us with quite different results as it would be lower for those firms with a high fit and higher for firms with a low fit, as "absolute speed" stays equal. Still, a recent meta-analytic review on NPD speed gave empirical evidence that the results of a relative and an absolute speed measure do not significantly differ (Chen *et al.* 2010).

I want to mention that, consistent with existing arguments, several areas of integration should be considered (Shrivastava 1986; Birkinshaw *et al.* 2000) and, therefore, several levels of relative speed. Research divides integration into task and human integration (Birkinshaw *et al.* 2000). For sharing resources or transferring capabilities, task integration is essential (Buono and Bowditch 2003; Angwin 2004), while, for employee satisfaction and a shared identity, human integration is necessary (Birkinshaw *et al.* 2000, Olie 1994). Even though task and human integration are conceptually different areas, their interdependencies should not be disregarded. Birkinshaw *et al.* (2000) argue that faster human integration fosters a shared identity and mutual trust among employees, and these are a basis for closer task integration. If we assessed speed with a relative measure and on different areas or activities, we could broaden our understanding of speed itself. Furthermore, it would be useful to implement a question, "where did the change occur?" and use it as a control variable.

As the explanations on the three problem areas of speed of integration in M&As have shown, it is an interesting future research field. The topic is very relevant for M&A practice. Therefore, academic research should better fill the gap between bargain and the demand for conceptual implications. This conceptual paper offers insights into possible future research agendas. In the next section, I will draw a conclusion for future academic empircal and conceptual work.

Conclusion

As my analysis has shown, there is only very limited academic research on speed of integration. While most of the papers offer valuable insights, there are three problem areas in this research, which I propose to be solved in future. Figure 20.1 displays the central topics and issues of the three problem areas and gives insights into possible solutions and future research areas.

Of course, an integrated comprehensive research framework would be favorable, but as the relationships between the factors are very complex, future research should try to integrate just a few aspects into one model rather than developing an overly complex model. After a certain number of empirical studies, a meta-analytic review could then strengthen the theoretically assumed and empirically investigated relationships on a higher level of analysis.

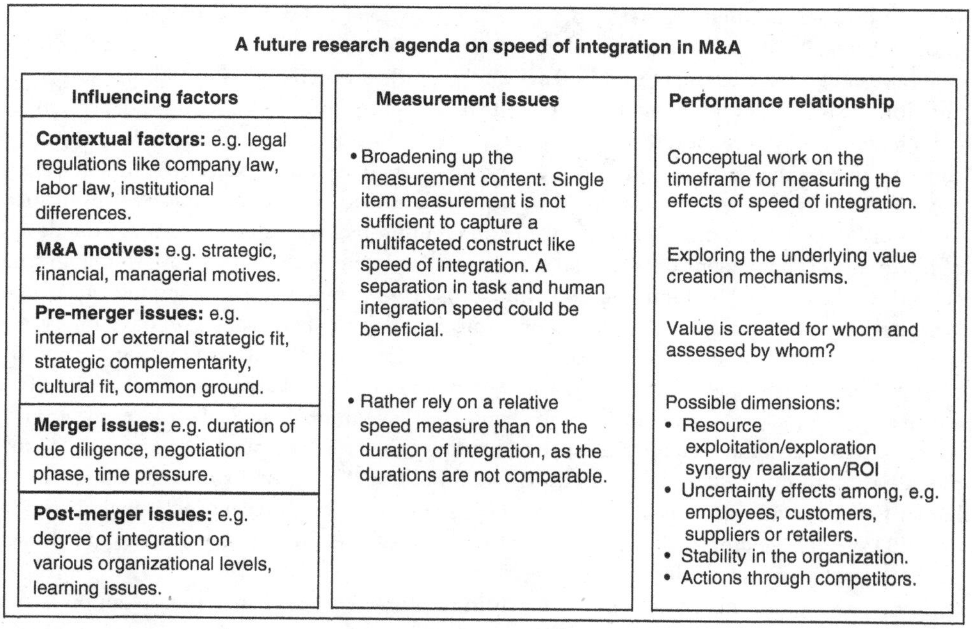

Figure 20.1 Conceptual framework for future research

References

Akgün, A. and Lynn, G. (2002) "New product development team improvisation and speed-to-market: an extended model," *European Journal of Innovation Management*, 5: 117–29.

Angwin, D. (2004) "Speed in M&A integration: the first 100 days," *European Management Journal*, 22: 418–30.

AVRAG—Austrian law amending the labor contract law.

Aw, M.S.B. and Chatterjee, R.A. (2004) "The performance of UK firms acquiring large cross-border and domestic takeover targets," *Applied Financial Economics*, 14: 337–49.

Bagchi, P. and Rao, R.P. (1992) "Decision making in mergers: an application of the analyic hierarchy process," *Managerial Decision Economics*, 13: 91–99.

Bagozzi, R.P. and Baumgartner, H. (1994) "The evaluation of structural equation models and hypothesis testing," in: Bagozzi, R.P. (ed.) *Principles of Marketing Research*. Cambridge: Blackwell Publishers.

Barkema, H.G., Bell, J.H.J., and Pennings, J.M. (1996) "Foreign entry, cultural barriers, and learning," *Strategic Management Journal*, 17: 151–66.

Bauer, F. and Matzler, K. (2014) "Antecedents of M&A success: the role of strategic complementarity, cultural fit, and degree and speed of integration," *Strategic Management Journal*, 35: 269–91.

BGB—Austrian Civil Code.

Bijlsma-Frankema, K. (2004) "Dilemmas of managerial control in post-acquisition processes," *Journal of Managerial Psychology*, 19: 252–68.

Birkinshaw, J., Bresman, H., and Håkanson, L. (2000) "Managing the post acquisition integration process: how human integration and task integration processes interact to foster value creation," *Journal of Management Studies*, 37: 365–425.

Bragado, J.F. (1992) "Setting the correct speed for postmerger integration," *M&A Europe*, 5: 24–31.

Bragg, S.M. (2009) *Mergers & Acquisitions: A Condensed Practitioner's Guide*. New Jersey: John Wiley & Sons.

Buchholtz, A.K., Ribbens, B.A., and Houle, I.T. (2003) "The role of human capital in postacquisition CEO departure," *Academy of Management Journal*, 46: 506–14.

Buono, A.F. and Bowditch, J.L. (2003) *The Human Side of Mergers and Acquisitions: Managing Collisions between People, Cultures and Organizations*. Washington, DC: Beard Books.

Capasso, A. and Meglio, O. (2005) "Knowledge transfer in mergers and acquisitions: how frequent acquirers learn to manage the integration process," in Capasso, A., Dagnino, G.B., and Lanza, A. *Strategic*

Capabilities and Knowledge Transfer within and between Organizations. Northampton, MA., Cheltenham: Edgar Elgar.

Capron, L. and Pistre, N. (2002) "When do acquirers earn abnormal returns?," *Strategic Management Journal*, 23: 294–312.

Capron, L. and Guillén, M. (2009) "National corporate governance institutions and post-acquisition target reorganization," *Strategic Management Journal*, 30: 803–33.

Carbonell, P., Rodríguez-Escudero, A., and Pujari, D. (2009) "Customer involvement in new service development: an examination of antecedents and outcomes," *Journal of Product Innovation Management*, 26: 536–50.

Cartwright, S. and Cooper, G.L. (1995) "Organizational marriage: 'hard' versus 'soft' issues?," *Personnel Review*, 24: 31–42.

Cartwright, S. and Schoenberg, R. (2006) "Thirty years of mergers and acquisitions research: recent advances and future opportunities," *British Journal of Management*, 17: 1–5.

Chase, B. (1998) "National city's latest mergers put premium on fast execution," *American Banker*, 163(230): 3–4.

Chen, J., Damanpour, F., and Reilly, R. (2010) "Understanding antecedents of new product development speed: a meta-analysis," *Journal of Operations Management*, 28: 17–33.

Christensen, C.M., Alton, R., Rising, C., and Waldeck, A. (2011) "The new M&A playbook," *Harvard Business Review*, March: 48–57.

Colquitt, J.A., Wesson, M.J., Porter, C.O.L.H., and Yee, K.N. (2001) "Justice at the millennium: a meta-analytic review of 25 years of organizational justice research," *Journal of Applied Psychology*, 86: 425–45.

Cording, M., Christman, P., and King, D.R. (2008) "Reducing causal ambiguity in acquisition integration: intermediate goals as mediators of integration decision and acquisition performance," *Academy of Management Journal*, 51: 744–67.

Cording, M., Christmann, P., and Weigelt, C. (2010) "Measuring theoretically complex constructs: the case of acquisition performance," *Strategic Organization*, 8: 11–41.

Datta, D.K. (1991) "Organizational fit and acquisition performance: effects on post acquisition integration," *Strategic Management Journal*, 12: 281–97.

Empson, L. (2004) "Organizational identity change: managerial regulation and member identification in an accounting firm acquisition," *Accounting, Organizations and Society*, 29: 759–81.

Gadiesh, O., Ormiston, C., and Rovit, S. (2003) "Achieving an M&A's strategic goals at maximum speed for maximum value," *Strategy & Leadership*, 31: 35–41.

Gates, S. and Very, P. (2003) "Measuring performance during M&A integration," *Long Range Planning*, 36: 167–85.

Gaur, A. and Lu, J. (2007) "Ownership strategies and survival of foreign subsidiaries: impacts of institutional distance and experience," *Journal of Management*, 33: 84–110.

Gerds, J. and Schewe, G. (2004) *Post Merger Integration: Unternehmenserfolg durch Integration Excellence*, Berlin, Heidelberg, New York: Springer.

Goktan, A. and Miles, G. (2011) "Innovation speed and radicalness: are they inversely related?," *Management Decision*, 49: 533–47.

Halebian, J. and Finkelstein, S. (1999) "The influence of organizational acquisition experience on acquisition performance: a behavioural learning perspective," *Administrative Science Quarterly*, 44: 29–56.

Haspeslagh, P.C. and Jemison, D.B. (1991) *Managing Acquisitions*. New York: Free Press.

HGB—German Commercial Code.

Homburg, C. and Bucerius, M. (2005) "A marketing perspective on mergers and acquisitions: how marketing integration affects postmerger performance," *Journal of Marketing*, 69: 96–113.

Homburg, C. and Bucerius, M. (2006) "Is speed of integration really a success factor of mergers and acquisitions? An analysis of the role of internal and external relatedness," *Strategic Management Journal*, 27: 347–67.

Hulland, J. (1999) "Use of partial least squares (PLS) in strategic management research: a review of four recent studies," *Strategic Management Journal*, 20: 195–204.

Inkpen, A.C., Sundaram, A.K., and Rockwood, K. (2000) "Cross-border acquisitions of U.S. technology assets," *California Management Review*, 42: 50–71.

Jemison, D.B. and Sitkin, S.B. (1986) "Corporate acquisitions: a process perspective," *The Academy of Management Review*, 11: 145–63.

Kavanagh, M.H. and Askanasy, N.M. (2006) "The impact of leadership and change management strategy on organizational culture and individual acceptance of change during a merger," *British Journal of Management*, 17: 81–103.

Kessler, E.H. and Chakrabarti, A.K. (1996) "Innovation speed: a conceptual model of context, antecedents and outcomes," *Academy of Management Journal*, 21: 1143–91.

Kessler, E.H. and Bierly, P. (2002) "Is faster really better? An empirical test of the implications of innovation speed," *IEEE Transactions on Engineering Management*, 49: 2–12.

King, D.R. and Taylor, R. (2012) "Beyond the numbers: seven stakeholders to consider in improving acquisition outcomes," *Graziadio Business Review*, 15: 1–5.

King, D.R., Dalton, D.R., Daily, C.M., and Covin, J.G. (2004) "Meta-analyses of post-acquisition performance: indications of unidentified moderators," *Strategic Management Journal*, 25: 187–200.

Kostova, T. (1999) "Transnational transfer of strategic organizational practices: a contextual perspective," *Academy of Management Review*, 24: 308–24.

Krüger, W. and Müller-Stewens, G. (1994) "Matching acquisition policy and integration style, " in Korgh von, G., Sinatra, A., and Singh, H. (eds.) *The Management of Corporate Acquisitions: International Perspectives*. Houndmills, Basingstoke: The Macmillan Press.

Larsson, R. and Finkelstein, S. (1999) "Integrating strategic, organizational, and human resource perspectives on mergers and acquisitions: a case survey of synergy realization," *Organizational Science*, 10: 1–26.

Lieberman, M.B. and Montgomery, D.B. (1988) "First mover advantages," *Strategic Management Journal*, 9: 41–58.

Longenecker, J., Moore, C., Petty, W., and Palich, L. (2006) *Small Business Management: An Entrepreneurial Emphasis,* 13th edn. Mason, OH: South-Western.

Morag, O. and Barakonyi, K. (2009) "The influence of speed of integration on M&A integration success," *Vezetèstudomàny*, 11: 55–59.

Nahavandi, A. and Malekzadeh, A.R. (1988) "Acculturation in mergers and acquisitions," *Academy of Management Review*, 13: 79–90.

Olie, R. (1994) "Shades of culture and institutions in international mergers," *Organization Studies*, 15: 381–405.

Page, A.L. (1993) "Assessing new product development practices and performance: establishing crucial norms," *Journal of Product Innovation Management*, 10: 273–90.

Paruchuri, S., Nerkar, A., and Hambrick, D.C. (2006) "Acquisition integration and productivity losses in the technical core: disruption of inventors in acquired companies," *Organization Science*, 17: 545–62.

Phersson, A. (2006) "Business relatedness and performance: a study of managerial perceptions," *Strategic Management Journal*, 27: 265–82.

Puranam, P., Singh, H., and Chaudhuri, S. (2009) "Integrating acquired capabilities: when structural integration is (un)necessary," *Organization Sience*, 20: 313–28.

Ranft, A.L. and Lord, M.D. (2002) "Acquiring new technologies and capabilities: a grounded model of acquisition implementation," *Organization Science*, 13: 420–41.

Saorín-Iborra, M.C. (2008) "Time pressure in acquisition negotiations: its determinants and effects on parties' negotiation behaviour choice," *International Business Review*, 17: 285–309.

Sarkar, M.B., Echambadi, R., Cavusgil, T.S., and Aulakh, P.S. (2001) "The influence of complementarity, compatibility, and relationship capital on alliance performance," *Journal of the Academy of Marketing Science*, 29: 358–73.

Schlaepfer, R.C., di Paola, S., Kupiers, R.W., Brauchli-Rohrer, B., Marti, A., Brun, P., and Baldinger, G. (2008) "How can leadership make a difference: an integration survey," *PWC*: 1–16.

Schlünzen, U. and Jöns, I. (2003) "Die Bedeutung und Gestaltung der Integrationsgeschwindigkeit bei Fusionen und Akquisitionen," *Mannheimer Beiträge zur Wirtschafts- und Organisationspsychologie*, 1: 3–9.

Schweiger, D. and Denisi, A. (1991) "Communications with employees following a merger: a longitudinal field experiement," *Academy of Management Journal*, 34: 110–35.

Schweiger, D.M. and Goulet, P.K. (2005) "Facilitating acquisition integration through deep-level cultural learning interventions: a longitudinal field experiment," *Organization Studies*, 26: 1477–99.

Schweiger, D.M., Ivancevich, J.M., and Power, F.R. (1987) "Executive actions for managing human resources before and after acquisition," *Academy of Management Executive*, 1: 127–38.

Shrivastava, P. (1986) "Postmerger integration," *The Journal of Business Strategy*, 7: 65–76.

Singh, H. and Montgomery, C.A. (1987) "Corporate acquisition strategies and economic performance," *Strategic Management Journal*, 8: 377–86.

Stimpert, J.L. and Duhaime, I.M. (1997) "In the eyes of the beholder: conceptualizations of relatedness held by managers of large diversified firms," *Strategic Management Journal*, 18: 111–25.

UGB—Austrian Commercial Code.

Very, P., Lubatkin, M., Calori, R., and Veiga, J. (1997) "Relative standing and the performance of recently acquired European firms," *Strategic Management Journal*, 18: 593–614.

Vester, J. (2002) "Lessons learned about integrating acquisitions," *Research Technology Management*, 45: 33–41.

Wille, C., Bauer, F., and Anslinger, T. (2011) "Corporate brand management bei mergers and acquisitions," in Wollersheim, J. and Barthel, E. (eds.) *Forum Mergers & Acquisitions 2011*, Wiesbaden: Gabler.

Zollo, M. and Meier, D. (2008) "What is M&A performance?," *Academy of Management Perspectives*, August: 55–77.

21

Causes and consequences of different types of identity threat

Perceived legitimacy of decisions in M&As

Anna A. Lupina-Wegener, Güldem Karamustafa, and Susan C. Schneider

Introduction

Both academics and practitioners have argued that developing a shared identity is important for the success of mergers and acquisitions (M&As) (van Dick *et al.* 2006; Millward and Kyriakidou 2004; van Dick 2004). Thus, literature mostly focuses on development of a shared identity, which is seen to be crucial in achieving a positive outcome of M&As. However, research findings also indicate that developing a shared identity can be problematic if the identities of the merging organizations are threatened (Terry and Callan 1998).

Identity threat often occurs as a result of disruptive organizational events, such as major strategic change or restructuring, that challenge collective self-perceptions of "who we are" and members' beliefs about what is central to and distinctive about their organization (Ravasi and Schultz 2006). Indeed, in the context of M&As, employees may wonder about "who we were" and "who we will be" in the post-merger organization. Research has demonstrated that developing a shared identity becomes problematic when employees experience identity threat (Millward and Kyriakidou 2004) and subsequently engage in collective efforts to preserve their distinctive values as well as their self-esteem and sense of continuity. Yet the causes and consequences of identity threat and the multi-faceted and complex nature of threat (Albert and Whetten 1985) have not been examined in great depth by M&A scholars. It remains unresearched what causes employees to experience identity threat and, furthermore, what types of threat may be experienced and what employees' subsequent reactions to these threats might be. Addressing this research gap may help integration agents reduce identity threat in order to move forward and help to develop a shared identity and achieve a positive outcome of the integration process.

In this chapter, we will draw upon acculturation and social identity theories. Acculturation theory provides the basis for understanding the causes of identity threat in M&As (Buono *et al.* 1985; Marks and Mirvis 2011b; Nahavandi and Malekzadeh 1988). Social identity theory (SIT) explains different types of threat and subsequent collective employees' reactions (Albert and Whetten 1985; Branscombe *et al.* 1999; Hogg and Terry 2000). Building on these two theoretical approaches to M&As, we propose a typology of identity threat and a model wherein employees' perceived legitimacy of implementation decisions can trigger a particular type of identity threat and subsequent collective reactions to reduce that threat. As a result, we believe that this chapter will provide a more nuanced understanding of identity threat and employees' subsequent reactions during socio-cultural integration process by recognizing that identity threat can be experienced for different reasons with particular reactions. The typology and model presented can have major practical implications that can provide guidance to the integration managers as well as employees going through the merger.

The chapter is structured as follows. First, we review studies of identity threat in M&A literature and present the two theoretical approaches to socio-cultural integration in M&As as the basis for understanding the causes and consequences of different types of identity threats. Afterwards, we introduce the typology wherein the perceived legitimacy of integration decisions can generate different types of identity threat. We further proceed with a model of the causes and consequences of different types of identity threat as well as efforts to reduce that threat. Finally, we conclude with recommendations for managerial practice.

Identity threat in M&A studies

The majority of M&A research has focused on the post-merger integration process, defined as "a guided process to implementing organizational change, affecting mainly the acquired unit(s), and ultimately the parties involved, with the aim of aligning the new unit(s) with the desired strategic direction" (Teerikangas and Joseph 2012: 342). In this chapter we focus more specifically on socio-cultural integration (Stahl and Voigt 2008), wherein formerly separate (often competing) groups need to work together and exchange knowledge. Developing a shared identity is considered to be crucial for a successful outcome (Lupina-Wegener *et al.* 2011; Teerikangas and Very 2006; Ullrich *et al.* 2005; van Knippenberg *et al.* 2002). Shared identity is typically conceptualized as both content—perception of a common ingroup identity (Gaertner *et al.* 1993)—and process—degree of identification with the new organization (van Dick *et al.* 2006; cf. Haslam *et al.* 2003 for conceptualization of shared identity in terms of *content* and *process*). However, threat to pre-merger identities has been found to create intergroup dynamics, which may interfere with developing a shared identity (Gleibs *et al.* 2008; Terry and Callan 1998; van Dijk and van Dick 2009).

Although the general notion of identity threat has been well established in M&A research, the causes and consequences are less understood as theoretical and methodological issues prevail. First, from a theoretical standpoint, existing research adopts a definition that does not allow different types of identity threat to be captured, for example in reference to human resource (HR) practices that may pose a "threat to positive identity" (Smith *et al.* 2012) or employees' resistance to change as threat to change agent's identity (van Dijk and van Dick 2009). Rather, identity threat needs to be considered as a multidimensional construct. We conceptualize identity threat, building on Albert and Whetten (1985) and Branscombe *et al.* (1999), according to whom three types of identity threat may be experienced by organizational members: value threat, distinctiveness threat, and continuity threat.

Value threat may be experienced when employees perceive that their competencies and capacities are not appreciated in the post-merger organization. Specifically, they may experience their pre-merger identity to be less valued than the pre-merger identity of the outgroup (Gleibs *et al.* 2010). This perceived underestimation of self-esteem constitutes value threat.

Distinctiveness threat refers to employees' perceived loss of a previously well defined pre-merger identity allowing differentiation from significant others (Brewer 1991). Pre-merger groups experience distinctiveness threat when, "What makes us different from the outgroup?" is no longer clear (Gioia *et al.* 2010). Indeed, ingroup members seek to emphasize differences from outgroup members (Tajfel and Turner 1979). And thus, the integration of pre-merger groups risks challenging the essence of group distinctiveness (Branscombe *et al.* 1999).

Continuity threat is related to the broken stability of pre-merger identity over time. M&A research reveals that employees have a need to perceive continuity not only between present and past (van Knippenberg *et al.* 2002) but also between present and future (Clark *et al.* 2010; Lupina-Wegener *et al.* 2014; Ullrich *et al.* 2005). This perceived lack of continuity between pre- and post-merger organization and post-merger organization in the early stage and its future identity constitutes continuity threat.

Second, from a methodological standpoint, identity threat in M&As was chiefly operationalized and measured as individuals' appraisal of the stressfulness of the event as compared with other stressful situations experienced (Terry and O'Brien 2001), their sense of uncertainty (Terry and Callan 1998), or the degree of perceived continuity between pre- and post-merger identity (Bartels *et al.* 2009; van Dick *et al.* 2006). These approaches are problematic because operationalizing threat as stress confounds the experience with the reaction. Also, these measures neither capture the specific causes nor the types of threat possible.

Summing up, past M&A research has not drawn enough attention to these three distinctive types of threat and particular reactions of employees, which may follow. Indeed, with social identity, scholars reveal that different collective reactions (ingroup bias, trust) might be observed under a specific type of threat (Smurda *et al.* 2006; Voci 2006). Consequently, there is a need to provide a more differentiated understanding of specific types of identity threat that may emerge in socio-cultural integration. We present the two theoretical perspectives on the socio-cultural integration process in order to identify antecedents to three types of identity threat and employees' possible subsequent reactions.

Two perspectives on socio-cultural integration and implications for identity threat

Socio-cultural integration has predominantly been studied based on two theoretical perspectives, acculturation theory (Berry 1980) and social identity theory (Tajfel and Turner 1979). While these two theoretical perspectives are similar in their focus on the outcome, they approach the socio-cultural integration process focusing on different levels of analysis. More specifically, the acculturation perspective focuses on cultural change and autonomy decrease (organizational level) and subsequent employee reactions (e.g. stress) and resistance (Buono *et al.* 1985; Marks and Mirvis 2011b), while the social identity perspective addresses threats to pre-merger identities (organizational level) and subsequent intergroup dynamics (Terry and Callan 1998; Terry and O'Brien 2001).

Socio-cultural integration from the acculturation theory perspective

Derived from anthropology, acculturation is defined as cultural changes resulting from the contact between two groups with distinctive cultures (Berry 1980). In the context of mergers and acquisitions, different modes of socio-cultural integration have been identified: "blending" or "integration"—taking the best of each and developing a new culture and practices; "separation"—retaining distinct identities; and "assimilation," where one party adopts all or part of the other's culture (Schweiger *et al.* 1993).

The different approaches are considered to be a function of the motive behind the decision to acquire and the degree of synergies expected (Haspeslagh and Jemison 1991; Shrivastava 1986) or "combination potential" (Larsson and Finkelstein 1999). Consequently, the level of change in pre-merger cultures and the degree of autonomy decrease may vary according to the socio-cultural integration approach taken. For example, if synergies are sought, managerial interventions will be designed for a high level of operational integration. This may lead to many changes to well established norms and patterns of behavior (i.e. culture) that have evolved over time prior to the merger (Barth 2006) in order to ensure value creation (Haspeslagh and Jemison 1991). Furthermore, to enhance synergies or to gain better control, managerial interventions may reduce freedom of choice and action, resulting in a decrease in autonomy of the pre-merger organizations (Datta and Grant 1990; Eilam and Shamir 2005; Hambrick and Cannella 1993). Thus, integration decisions regarding staffing, rewards and benefits, and systems and procedures signal the extent to which pre-merger culture change and decrease in autonomy can be expected. Efforts to reduce stress and enhance social integration through HR practices, communication, and social controls are encouraged (Larsson and Lubatkin 2001; Schweiger and Denisi 1991).

And indeed, success or failure of the integration process is often attributed to employees' anxiety reactions to cultural change and loss of autonomy (Marks and Mirvis 2011a). Past research also points out that the compatibility of the integration mode between merging groups might help enhance positive M&A outcomes (Nahavandi and Malekzadeh 1988). Thus, employees might prefer to merge with a company that has an attractive culture (Cartwright and Cooper 1993) or may opt for an integration mode that minimizes change (Giessner et al. 2006; Gleibs et al. 2013). As a result, the more that cultural change is imposed and the more that autonomy decreases, the more pre-merger identity may be called into question, posing a threat to pre-merger identity (Fiol et al. 1998). Overall, scholars examining socio-cultural integration from an acculturation theory perspective provide the basis for understanding the causes of identity threat in M&As.

Social identity approach to socio-cultural integration

M&A research based on social identity theory (Tajfel and Turner 1979) seeks to explain employees' collective reactions to the socio-cultural integration process wherein pre-merger identities are threatened. SIT addresses social behavior, wherein individuals are not acting on the basis of their personal identities but as members of their group(s) in relation to members of other groups. Personal identity, "How am I different from him/her?," becomes less salient particularly when there is intergroup contact, as is the case with M&As. In parallel, self-categorization theory (Turner 1985; Turner et al. 1987) underlines that various social identities for self-categorization are available to an individual at a particular time (Brewer 1991). Individuals may choose to identify with groups that provide a distinctive and positive identity in order to enhance self-esteem (Tajfel and Turner 1979) as well as to reduce uncertainty (Hogg and Terry 2000). This can result in intergroup dynamics wherein group members tend to engage in ingroup favoritism and outgroup discrimination (Terry and Callan 1998, Terry and O'Brien 2001, van Dijk and van Dick 2009).

While developing a shared identity is considered to be necessary for successful M&A outcomes, much of the prior research adopting a social identity approach has sought to determine how intergroup dynamics in terms of power asymmetries on the one hand and boundary permeability on the other hand may affect merger outcomes (Hogg and Terry 2000; Lupina-Wegener et al. 2011; Terry et al. 2001; Terry and O'Brien 2001). Power asymmetries refer to the distribution of influence of pre-merger organizations in the integration process, i.e. whether one merger partner is dominant over the other (as is typically the case in acquisitions) versus "mergers of equals" (Meyer and Altenborg 2007). On the other hand, boundary permeability is defined as a possibility of mobility within the new organization or having access to resources in terms of rewards, development opportunities, informal networks, and career progress (Santos and

Eisenhardt 2005). Merging groups' perceptions regarding implementation decisions may create intergroup dynamics about power asymmetries as well as boundary permeability. Employees may experience identity threat when the implementation decision is perceived as illegitimate, and subsequently merging organizations do not agree on who dominates and on who is a new ingroup and who is not (cf. Gleibs *et al.* 2013; Giessner *et al.* 2006 for a legitimacy of integration patterns).

The implications for identity threat are twofold. First, adopting an acculturation theory perspective we identify that employees' perceptions of the legitimacy of implementation decisions with regard to loss of autonomy and change in culture can generate identity threat. Second, following social identity theory, we suggest that employees collectively react to identity threat as efforts to redress the perceived illegitimacy through identity work. In light of existing theoretical perspectives and M&A research, we now present a typology that differentiates specific types of identity threat and subsequent collective reactions.

Typology of identity threat

Building on past research embedded in acculturation and social identity theories, the typology developed here identifies distinct types of threat during socio-cultural integration that may be experienced by the employees regardless of the "officially proclaimed" implementation approach (Gleibs *et al.* 2013; Lupina-Wegener *et al.* 2011). Furthermore, based on SIT, three types of identity threat will be experienced as a function of the perceived legitimacy of implementation decisions in two dimensions, autonomy decrease and change as identified by the acculturation theory. The typology presented in Figure 21.1 discusses each type of threat as it may be experienced with regard to the experienced legitimacy of implementation decisions.

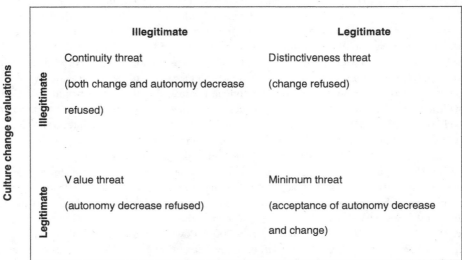

Figure 21.1 Typology of pre-merger identity threat based on employees' evaluation of the implementation decisions

Continuity threat is related to the enduring nature of identity. In the seminal paper by Albert and Whetten (1985), continuity threat is discussed in terms of stability over time and further extended by Rousseau (1998), underlining the necessity of maintaining a sense of continuity rather than sameness. In M&As, such continuity can be put at stake when both autonomy decrease and culture change are experienced as illegitimate. Indeed, in some circumstances, members of merging organizations might seek to preserve pre-merger culture and to maintain autonomy in terms of impact on building the post-merger organization. If a desired implementation decision is not coherent with an actually implemented one, continuity threat will be apparent. An example would be the case of an acquisition of a successful start-up by an established, bureaucratic holding with strongly established procedures and systems, wherein the acquirer imposes their ways of doing business on the acquired firm. Then, a move from a relatively small structure to a business unit position in a large conglomerate might imply an important loss of "who they were" before the acquisition, and fears for survival in the post-merger organization may increase for the members. This can result in employees feeling disoriented given the loss of the former identity—"who we were"—and the lack of a clear vision of "who we are going to be." As a result, employees may increase their complaints or may be demotivated from engaging in the integration process.

Distinctiveness threat refers to the perceived loss of a previously well-defined identity as compared to a significant outgroup (Jetten and Hutchison 2011; Stahl *et al.* 2011). In M&As, such distinctiveness threat might emerge when an implementation decision aims at culture change and reducing differences between two merging organizations. Indeed, in some circumstances, group members may resist attempts to be assimilated into the culture of the acquirer, and any efforts to change cultures might then be considered as illegitimate. At the same time, employees might consider their loss of autonomy as appropriate, as for example in circumstances of rescue from bankruptcy.

Value threat is experienced when employees feel that their competencies and capacities are not appreciated in the post-merger organization. Indeed, in some circumstances, group members might welcome change in culture, but they may seek to maintain autonomy. This might be the case in a "reverse takeover" or in a "best-of-both" integration wherein changes are introduced to both acquired and acquiring groups. Thus, an acquirer might agree to introduce changes to their pre-merger culture if the culture of the acquired organization is more attractive and is believed to contribute to the performance of the post-merger organization. While change might be welcomed, concerned group members seek to have an influence on how the post-merger organization is constructed. If an actual implementation decision is not coherent with a desired one, a decrease of autonomy might be perceived to challenge positive pre-merger group perceptions and, thus, lead to value threat. Interestingly, a qualitative study conducted by Smith *et al.* (2012: 318) reveals how value threat might emerge. Indeed, HR practices imposed by the dominant organization might lead to threat to positive identity so that "the HR practices appear as an aggression that demands a response."

The typology helps to understand employees' reaction under identity threat in relation to their experiences of autonomy decrease and culture change. Employees' reactions under identity threat were one of the emerging themes of a case study conducted by one of the authors. The case study explored how capabilities develop during a post-merger integration process, relying on interviews and archival data as primary data sources. The methodology of the study is presented elsewhere in detail (cf. Karamustafa *et al.* 2013; Castañer *et al.* 2013). In the following section, we present the case study to illustrate how different types of threat can be observed during the socio-cultural integration process.

Identity threats: a case example

A German multinational corporation (MNC) (MarsCo) was acquired by an American MNC (SunCo), a global player in the consumer goods industry. MarsCo was acquired with the objective of growth in the beauty sector both in retail and professional sales channels. MarsCo's different business units were considered to be a strategic fit given the product lines and presence in different geographic locations. In particular, the unique capability of MarsCo's core business in the professional sales channel was an important motive behind the acquisition.

Acquisition implementation: After the acquisition announcement, integration plans were delayed due to the regulatory differences in the respective institutional context. While Mars-Co's management was maintained, MarsCo and SunCo employees had limited contact until the conflict was resolved. Almost a year after the acquisition announcement, MarsCo's smallest business that sold products through retailers was absorbed into SunCo's much larger business that had a strong presence in the retail channel. In the meantime, the decision to implement SunCo's structure into MarsCo's largest business (the core business that possessed the unique capability) was taken, during which MarsCo's second business was integrated into SunCo's similar and equivalently sized business. The combination of this second similar business had high synergy potential; thus, the integration approach formally adopted was a "best of both," where the contributions of members of both organizations were jointly considered. Meanwhile, the integration at MarsCo's core business was further delayed by SunCo's acquisition of another American company, VenusCo, that was ten times larger than MarsCo.

A year after implementing SunCo's structure at MarsCo's core business, its top manager was replaced by a SunCo executive. In contrast to SunCo's more centralized organization with many detailed processes and systems, MarsCo had a decentralized structure where the country organizations enjoyed autonomy with their own resources. The country organizations were then placed under a new structure putting an additional layer between the country managers and the head of the business unit, thus limiting their autonomy. Once the resources were secured from the SunCo corporate offices, an integration team was put in place to complete the remaining integration. In the final step, harmonization of systems and HR processes took place along with functional integration, leading to a complete absorption within roughly three years.

Identity threats: The acquisition triggered identity threats for MarsCo's employees. Indeed, MarsCo was a European, family company, highly decentralized and much smaller compared to SunCo, an American publicly owned, highly centralized, global multi-business company. Mars-Co's employees worried that MarsCo's pre-merger identity, highly influenced by its core business established by the founding family, would not be appreciated and maintained at SunCo, due to very different national and organizational cultures. Many MarsCo employees were wondering how much their traditional way of doing business as a family company in the professional sector, for example being very relationship oriented, would be retained and drive the future of the business. Thus, continuity threat was apparent among MarsCo's employees, particularly during the initial stages. MarsCo's employees highlighted MarsCo's long-standing heritage and expertise built over years.

The differences became more apparent once employees started to work together, confronting MarsCo employees with the SunCo culture. The more that SunCo processes and systems were implemented, the more SunCo culture was introduced. SunCo employees promoted their structured approach, their processes and systems, as well as their global presence and success in the market. However, MarsCo's employees did not consider SunCo's highly centralized and process-oriented structures appropriate for MarsCo's core business, given that they were designed for doing business in the retail channel. Being a family company encouraged strong relationships and loyalty within the company as well as with their customers. Speed and entrepreneurial spirit were considered to be distinctive features that had made MarsCo successful in the past. As a result, MarsCo's employees experienced distinctiveness threat and engaged in ingroup favoring comparisons through differentiation on the basis of how the business is conducted.

Decisions taken to create a more centralized organization further limited MarsCo's autonomy in its core business. Although MarsCo's employees accepted that MarsCo would not be the same as before the acquisition, reflecting on the fact that they were a family company acquired by a large multinational (cultural change legitimate), they considered that their decreased autonomy at the core business was illegitimate given that MarsCo's unique capability at the core business was the motive of the acquisition. Also, limiting the autonomy of MarsCo's country organizations was not only hampering their relationship with their customers but also reducing the speed in responding to market needs. They complained that their implicit knowledge of the business was not appreciated within SunCo. Moreover, MarsCo's employees did not feel that their capabilities were being valued in a business that was different from most of the other SunCo businesses. As a result, they felt that they were in a disadvantageous position compared to employees in other SunCo businesses in terms of career progression at SunCo. This constituted a value threat to MarsCo's employees, which created passive resistance to SunCo's dominance in determining the future of MarsCo's core business. Particularly, employees reacted to ensure a legitimate level of autonomy by status-related comparisons.

In summary, the case reveals the presence of three different types of identity threat based on the perceived legitimacy of integration decisions as well as collective reactions such as resistance and intensified intergroup conflicts. In the SunCo–MarsCo case, continuity threat was prevalent as both culture change and autonomy decrease were considered illegitimate, especially following the acquisition announcement. Stress, anxiety, and fear were apparent among MarsCo's employees, who sought to maintain the continuity between the pre-merger and post-merger organization. When the autonomy at MarsCo's core business was somewhat maintained following implementation delay due to the institutional context, efforts to change MarsCo's existing processes and systems lead to distinctiveness threat among MarsCo employees. As a result, ingroup favoritism and outgroup derogation increased, and MarsCo employees sought to preserve their pre-merger identity, increasing their opposition to the changes being introduced. The decrease in autonomy in MarsCo's core business, for example in the country organizations, led to value threat. MarsCo's employees resisted the increased influence of SunCo through defensive reactions such as questioning the decisions and making status-related comparisons.

Model of employees' collective reactions to identity threat

In this section, we introduce a model of employees' collective reactions to different types of identity threat. Indeed, a comparative case study by Courpasson et al. (2012) found that employees' resistance can actually influence top management's decisions and produce eventual change. Organizational members attempt to make sense of the consequences of change, and how they act on their observations in turn generates further changes (Stensaker and Langley 2010). Hence, it is apparent that the unfolding socio-cultural integration process is influenced by both employees' evaluations of the legitimacy of the implementation decisions and their subsequent collective reactions that in turn may create pressures to modify the implementation decision. Figure 21.2 illustrates that first implementation decisions can result in perceptions of culture change and decrease of autonomy. The extent to which these are considered by employees to be illegitimate results in specific identity threats such as continuity, distinctiveness, and value threats, as depicted in the typology of identity threat (Figure 21.1). Second, employees will collectively

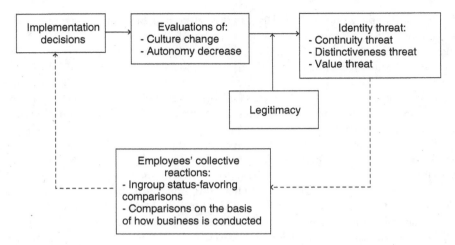

Figure 21.2   Process model of identity threat

react to restore legitimate levels of autonomy decrease or culture change and, thus, to reduce threat. Specifically, they may engage in intergroup comparisons in order to preserve self-esteem, distinctiveness, and continuity in the post-merger organization. However, collective reactions and subsequent group dynamics will differ depending on the type of threat experienced.

Employees who experience value threat might try to restore legitimate levels of autonomy through status-related comparisons such as seeking visibility in executive positions. Particularly, they may react by trying to engage more actively in the integration process, demonstrating specific skills and knowledge that are valued. Members of the acquired organization may seek to maintain their value by bringing forward their contribution that was initially appealing for the acquirer and therefore was the motive for the acquisition, as in the case of MarsCo. Summing up, in the case of value threat, employees react to ensure a legitimate level of autonomy by status-related comparisons.

Employees who experience distinctiveness threat will seek to preserve their differences in the way the business was done prior to the merger. They may promote the effectiveness in management processes and procedures or friendliness in the work climate in the pre-merger organization. Such efforts to reassert pre-merger identity and, thus, restore distinctiveness (Van Leeuwen *et al.* 2003) can exacerbate intergroup conflict through ingroup favoritism and outgroup derogation (Stahl *et al.* 2011). Summing up, in the case of distinctiveness threat, employees react to ensure a legitimate level of culture change by differentiating themselves on the basis of how the business is conducted.

When employees experience continuity threat, they will recall the past and make past-related descriptions in terms of intra-group (nostalgia) and at the same time make ingroup-favoring comparisons to be carried into the future organization (Iyer and Jetten 2011). As in the case of MarsCo, employees may bring forward the long-standing heritage and past success. In other words, restoring autonomy and minimizing change take place through attempts to preserve the past "reality" intact. Summing up, in the case of continuity threat, employees react to preserve both the pre-merger autonomy and pre-merger culture by strong past-orientated comparisons on the basis of status and also on how the business is conducted.

Integration leaders, or change agents, may respond to employees' collective reactions by modifying the integration decision and deploying interventions to increase employees' evaluations of the legitimacy of autonomy decrease and culture change. However, change agents tend not to respond to employees' collective reactions, if perceived as resistance. If employees' reactions threaten the identity of managers in charge (van Dijk and van Dick 2009), they may in turn also respond with resistance. Thus, instead of addressing employees' concerns regarding identity threat, management may become more controlling, thus further limiting autonomy and imposing culture change. Indeed, the latest research suggests that employees' collective reactions such as ingroup favoritism and outgroup derogation might be reactions to identity threat and recognized as efforts to reduce it (Courpasson et al. 2012). Therefore, modification of the implementation decision might be necessary. Indeed, there is a growing body of literature on employee voice—focusing on helping managers understand employee concerns and helping employees know that managers will hear their voiced concerns (Wilkinson and Fay 2011).

Specifically, we propose that implementation decisions may be redesigned or managerial interventions may be deployed to address the type of threat that corresponds to the experiences of groups. In cases of value threat, staffing plans may need to be made carefully, for example, assigning acquired leaders to manage the change process. As a result, integration leaders can reduce identity threat by acknowledging the unique contribution of each group and their status in the new organization. Employees may actively seek to maintain autonomy to restore positive identity and a positive self-image through defensive reactions or resistance and thus limit identification with the post-merger organization (Stahl et al. 2011). When distinctiveness threat is salient, integration managers may consider designing interventions not only to recognize differences in pre-merger identities but also to focus on how differences might be utilized as an asset to the new organization, which in turn can reduce distinctiveness threat. When members experience continuity threat, even intentions to combine the "best of both" might not reduce the threat. Rather, the past has to be acknowledged and embraced by keeping the artifacts alive so as to make clear links between the past, present, and future.

Summing up, and as indicated in Figure 21.2, employees may react to reduce identity threat and to restore a legitimate level of autonomy decrease and culture change, which in turn may pose a threat to other groups within the organization and which might produce further threats and subsequent reactions. Thus, we argue that modifying integration decisions, taking into account the degree of autonomy decrease or culture change, might be necessary and that the employee perceptions of their legitimacy can decrease the experience of identity threat. However, failure to identify what causes threats and, thus, modifying implementation decisions in the wrong dimension (i.e. autonomy or culture change) can reinforce the experience of identity threat.

Conclusions

In this paper, we contribute to existing M&A research by considering the dynamic interaction of employees' perceptions of the legitimacy of culture change or autonomy decrease in implementation decisions and the subsequent reactions to reduce identity threat. Based on the two most referenced approaches to the integration process—acculturation and social identity theories—we argue that employees' evaluation of the implementation decision in terms of culture change and decrease in autonomy can result in threat to identities. However, the degree to which culture change and decrease in autonomy is evaluated as legitimate results in three different types of identity threat: continuity, distinctiveness, and value. We provide a typology of identity threat based on the evaluation of legitimacy of culture change and autonomy decrease. The differentiation of threat types allows a more nuanced understanding of employees' reactions and a better appreciation of the impact of implementation decisions. Thus, incorporating insights from two theoretical approaches to socio-cultural integration helps to understand how the socio-cultural integration process unfolds in ways that are more or less intended, with outcomes that are more or less hoped for. Furthermore, it is important to mention that different types of threat and the dynamic process presented in this chapter are not limited to M&As but may be observed in other contexts of major strategic change. Thus, we contribute to the literature regarding identity dynamics in strategic organizational change by studying how employees' evaluation of the implementation decision may create identity threat, employee reactions, and the dynamic interactions at multiple levels of analysis—organizational, group, and individual. By exploring these actions and reactions, managers and employees can be helped to better navigate these events and thus enhance the likelihood of achieving the hoped for outcomes.

References

Albert, S. and Whetten, D.A. (1985) "Organizational identity," in L.L. Cummings and B.M. Staw (eds.), *Research in Organizational Behavior*, Greenwich, CT; London: JAI Press, 7: 263–95.

Bartels, J., Pruyn, A., and de Jong, M. (2009) "Employee identification before and after an internal merger: a longitudinal analysis," *Journal of Occupational and Organizational Psychology*, 82: 113–28.

Barth, B. (2006) "Rivera wants Spinks WBA champ issues challenge," *Telegram & Gazette*, D.1–D1. Worcester, MA.

Berry, J.W. (1980) "Acculturation as varieties of adaptation," in A.M. Padilla (ed.), *Acculturation: Theory, and Some New Findings*, Boulder, CO: Westview.

Branscombe, N.R., Ellemers, N., Spears, R., and Doosje, B. (1999) *The Context and Content of Social Identity Threat*, Oxford: Blackwell Science.

Brewer, M.B. (1991) "The social self: on being the same and different at the same time," *Personality and Social Psychology Bulletin*, 17: 475–82.

Buono, A.F., Bowditch, J.L., and Lewis, J.W. (1985) "When cultures collide: the anatomy of a merger," *Human Relations*, 38: 477–500.

Cartwright, S. and Cooper, C.L. (1993) "The psychological impact of merger and acquisition on the individual: a study of building society managers," *Human Relations*, 46: 327–47.

Castañer, X., Karamustafa, G., and Davis, J.D. (2013) "Why are acquirers unable to learn from the target even when they want to?," paper presented at the *Strategic Management Society* conference, Atlanta, GA, September.

Clark, S.M., Gioia, D.A., Ketchen, D.J., and Thomas, J.B. (2010) "Transitional identity as a facilitator of organizational identity change during a merger," *Administrative Science Quarterly*, 55: 397–438.

Courpasson, D., Dany, F., and Clegg, S. (2012) "Resisters at work: generating productive resistance in the workplace," *Organization Science*, 23: 801–19.

Datta, D.K. and Grant, J.H. (1990) "Relationship between type of acquisition, the autonomy given to the acquired firm and acquisition success: an empirical analysis," *Journal of Management*, 16: 29–44.

Eilam, G. and Shamir, B. (2005) "Organizational change and self-concept threats: a theoretical perspective and a case study," *The Journal of Applied Behavioral Science*, 41: 399–421.

Fiol, C.M., Hatch, M.J., and Golden-Biddle, K. (1998) "Organizational culture and identity: what's the difference anyway?," in P.G.D. Whetten (ed.), *Identity in Organizations: Building Theory through Conversations*, Thousand Oaks, CA: Sage.

Gaertner, S.L., Dovidio, J.F., Anastasio, P.A., Bachman, B.A., and Rust, M.C. (1993) "The common ingroup identity model: recategorization and the reduction of intergroup bias," *European Review of Social Psychology*, 4: 1–26.

Giessner, S.R., Viki, G.T., Otten, S., Terry, D.J., and Täuber, S. (2006) "The challenge of merging: merger patterns, premerger status, and merger support," *Personality and Social Psychology Bulletin*, 32: 339–52.

Gioia, D.A., Price, K.N., Hamilton, A.L., and Thomas, J.B. (2010) "Forging an identity: an insider-outsider study of processes involved in the formation of organizational identity," *Administrative Science Quarterly*, 55: 1–46.

Gleibs, I.H., Mummendey, A., and Noack, P. (2008) "Predictors of change in postmerger identification during a merger process: a longitudinal study," *Journal of Personality and Social Psychology*, 95: 1095–112.

Gleibs, I.H., Noack, P., and Mummendey, A. (2010) "We are still better than them: a longitudinal field study of ingroup favouritism during a merger," *European Journal of Social Psychology*, 40: 819–36.

Gleibs, I.H., Täuber, S., Viki, G.T., and Giessner, S.R. (2013) "When what we get is not what we want: the role of implemented versus desired merger patterns in support for mergers," *Social Psychology*, 44: 177–90.

Hambrick, D.C. and Cannella, A.A. (1993) "Relative standing: a framework for understanding departures of acquired executives," *Academy of Management Journal*, 36: 733–62.

Haslam, S.A., Postmes, T., and Ellemers, N. (2003) "More than a metaphor: organizational identity makes organizational life possible," *British Journal of Management*, 14: 357–69.

Haspeslagh, P.C. and Jemison, D.B. (1991) *Managing Acquisitions: Creating Value through Corporate Renewal*, New York: Free Press.

Hogg, M.A. and Terry, D.J. (2000) "Social identity and self-categorization processes in organizational contexts," *Academy of Management Review*, 25: 121–40.

Iyer, A. and Jetten, J. (2011) "What's left behind: identity continuity moderates the effect of nostalgia on well-being and life choices," *Journal of Personality and Social Psychology*, 101: 94–108.

Jetten, J. and Hutchison, P. (2011) "When groups have a lot to lose: historical continuity enhances resistance to a merger," *European Journal of Social Psychology*, 41: 335–43.

Karamustafa, G., Schneider, S.C., and Davis, J.D. (2013) "Unpacking the dynamics of the post-merger integration process: interaction between identities, interpretations, emotions and the role of language," paper presented at the *Academy of International Business conference*, Istanbul, Turkey, July.

Larsson, R. and Finkelstein, S. (1999) "Integrating strategic, organizational, and human resource perspectives on mergers and acquisitions: a case survey of synergy realization," *Organization Science*, 10: 1–26.

Larsson, R. and Lubatkin, M. (2001) "Achieving acculturation in mergers and acquisitions: an international case survey," *Human Relations*, 54: 1573–607.

Lupina-Wegener, A.A., Schneider, S.C., and van Dick, R. (2011) "Different experiences of socio-cultural integration: a European merger in Mexico," *Journal of Organizational Change Management*, 24: 65–89.

Lupina-Wegener, A.A., Drzensky, F., Ullrich, J., and van Dick, R. (2014) "Focusing on the bright tomorrow? A longitudinal study of organizational identification and projected continuity in a corporate merger," *British Journal of Social Psychology*, 53: 752–72.

Marks, M.L. and Mirvis, P.H. (2011a) "A framework for the human resources role in managing culture in mergers and acquisitions," *Human Resource Management*, 50: 859–77.

Marks, M.L. and Mirvis, P.H. (2011b) "Merge ahead: a research agenda to increase merger and acquisition success," *Journal of Business and Psychology*, 26: 161–68.

Meyer, C.B. and Altenborg, E. (2007) "The disintegrating effects of equality: a study of a failed international merger," *British Journal of Management*, 18: 235–52.

Millward, L. and Kyriakidou, O. (2004) "Linking pre- and post-merger identities through the concept of career," *Career Development International*, 9: 12–27.

Nahavandi, A. and Malekzadeh, A.R. (1988) "Acculturation in mergers and acquisitions," *Academy of Management Review*, 13: 79–90.

Ravasi, D. and Schultz, M. (2006) "Responding to organizational identity threats: exploring the role of organizational culture," *Academy of Management Journal*, 49: 433–58.

Rousseau, D. (1998) "Invited essay," *Journal of Organizational Behavior (1986–1998)*, 19: 217–33.

Santos, F.M., and Eisenhardt, K.M. (2005) "Organizational boundaries and theories of organization," *Organization Science*, 16: 491–508.

Schweiger, D.M. and Denisi, A.S. (1991) "Communication with employees following a merger: a longitudinal field experiment," *Academy of Management Journal*, 34: 110–35.

Schweiger, D.M., Csiszar, E.N., and Napier, N.K. (1993) "Implementing international mergers and acquisitions," *Human Resource Planning*, 16: 53–70.

Shrivastava, P. (1986) "Postmerger integration," *Journal of Business Strategy*, 7: 65–76.

Smith, L.G.E., Amiot, C.E., Callan, V.J., Terry, D.J., and Smith, J.R. (2012) "Getting new staff to stay: the mediating role of organizational identification," *British Journal of Management*, 23: 45–64.

Smurda, J.D., Wittig, M.A., and Gokalp, G. (2006) "Effects of threat to a valued social identity on implict self-esteem and discrimination," *Group Processes and Intergroup Relations*, 9: 181–97.

Stahl, G.K. and Voigt, A. (2008) "Do cultural differences matter in mergers and acquisitions? A tentative model and examination," *Organization Science*, 19: 160–76, 186.

Stahl, G.K., Larsson, R., Kremershof, I., and Sitkin, S.B. (2011) "Trust dynamics in acquisitions: a case survey," *Human Resource Management*, 50: 575–603.

Stensaker, I. and Langley, A. (2010) "Change management choices and change trajectories in a multidivisional firm," *British Journal of Management*, 21: 7–27.

Tajfel, H. and Turner, J.C. (1979) "An integrative theory of intergroup conflict," in W.G. Austin, and S. Worchel (eds.), *The Social Psychology of Intergroup Relations*, Monterey, CA: Brooks/Cole.

Teerikangas, S. and Very, P. (2006) "The culture-performance relationship in M&A: from yes/no to how," *British Journal of Management*, 17: 31–48.

Teerikangas, S. and Joseph, R. (2012) "Post-deal integration: an overview," in D. Faulkner, S. Teerikangas, and R. Joseph (eds.) *The Handbook of Mergers and Acquisitions*, Oxford: Oxford University Press.

Terry, D.J. and Callan, V.J. (1998) "Ingroup bias in response to an organizational merger," *Group Dynamics: Theory, Research, and Practice*, 2: 67–81.

Terry, D.J. and O'Brien, A.T. (2001) "Status, legitimacy, and ingroup bias in the context of an organizational merger," *Group Processes and Intergroup Relations*, 4: 271–89.

Terry, D.J., Carey, C.J., and Callan, V.J. (2001) "Employee adjustment to an organizational merger: an intergroup perspective," *Personality and Social Psychology Bulletin*, 27: 267–80.

Turner, J.C. (1985) "Social categorization and the self-concept: a social cognitive theory of group behavior," in E.J. Lawler (ed.) *Advances in Group Processes*, Greenwich: JAI Press.

Turner, J.C., Hogg, M.A., Oakes, P.J., Reicher, S.D., and Wetherell, M.S. (1987) *Rediscovering the Social Group: A Self-Categorization Theory*, Oxford: Basil Blackwell.

Ullrich, J., Wieseke, J., and van Dick, R. (2005) "Continuity and change in mergers and acquisitions: a social identity case study of a German industrial merger," *The Journal of Management Studies*, 42: 1549–69.

van Dick, R. (2004) "My job is my castle: identification in organizational contexts," in C.L. Cooper, and I.T. Robertson (eds.) *International Review of Industrial and Organizational Psychology*, Chichester: Wiley.

van Dijk, R., and van Dick, R. (2009) "Navigating organizational change: change leaders, employee resistance and work-based identities," *Journal of Change Management*, 9: 143–63.

van Dick, R., Ullrich, J., and Tissington, P.A. (2006) "Working under a black cloud: how to sustain organizational identification after a merger," *British Journal of Management*, 17: 69–79.

van Knippenberg, D., van Knippenberg, B., Monden, L., and de Lima, F. (2002) "Organizational identification after a merger: a social identity perspective," *British Journal of Social Psychology*, 41: 233–52.

Van Leeuwen, E., van Knippenberg, D., and Ellemers, N. (2003) "Continuing and changing group identities: the effects of merging on social identification and ingroup bias," *Personality and Social Psychology Bulletin*, 29: 679–90.

Voci, A. (2006) "The link between identification and in-group favouritism: effects of threat to social identity and trust-related emotions," *British Journal of Social Psychology*, 45: 265–84.

Wilkinson, A. and Fay, C. (2011) "New times for employee voice?," *Human Resource Management*, 50: 65–74.

22

Branding in mergers and acquisitions

Current research and contingent research questions

Marcella Rothermel and Florian Bauer

Introduction

Brands are valuable and strategic intangible assets of firms, and there is a general agreement in marketing literature that they are key mechanisms for value creation (Madden *et al.* 2006; Srivastava *et al.* 1998). A study of Interbrand, an American global branding consultancy, reveals that organizations generate earnings from brand assets and tangible assets, as well as other intangible assets (Perrier 1997). Out of these different assets, the brand earnings can have a share of up to 70 percent, depending on the market (Lindemann 2003). The brand-building process requires constant efforts in marketing and advertising activities, and the creation of positive consumer associations is a long-term investment (Rossiter and Percy 1997). Due to the great meaning of brands (Homburg and Bucerius 2005), many companies are willing to pay high prices when acquiring brands, and the value paid for them can range from 1 percent to 50 percent of the total deal value (Bahadir *et al.* 2008). In mergers and acquisitions (henceforth: M&As), the redeployment of brands, which are complex organizational intangible assets, is difficult (Capron 1999), even though the target firm's legitimacy for products and technology can be enhanced when acquired by a firm with a strong brand (Wernerfelt 1984). With research and development (R&D)-intensive targets, the post-acquisition interaction of the target's specific resources and the acquirer's brand and marketing resources can enhance the acquisition performance (King *et al.* 2008). Nonetheless, many firms try to avoid the high risks of new product and brand development and instead they acquire firms with established brands for corporate development purposes (Capron 1999; Mahajan *et al.* 1994). Further, as brand building needs time and the transfer of brands across borders is difficult, the acquisition of local brands is often a key element in the internationalization strategies of firms (Anand and Delios 2002).

However, it seems that the retaining of brand equity is a difficult task. According to the study of Jaju *et al.* (2006), the redeployment of corporate brands leads to a loss of perceived consumer brand equity—no matter which brand integration strategy is chosen. This finding leads to the question: How can the loss of brand equity be minimized? And beyond minimizing the loss of brand equity, managers should, rather, think about how to leverage the brand. Following Lamb-kin and Muzellec (2010), the management of brand equity in M&As requires the identification and measurement of differences of the merging corporate brands before the deal as well as the management of the transfer between the two merging entities after the deal. Their study reveals that consumer perceptions about the acquirer can influence the perception of new products of the target company. In summary, the acquisition of brands provides access to new resources. In order to keep or to enlarge this value, it is important to retain and redeploy the equity of all involved corporate brands and to leverage it among the merging entities (Capron 1999).

Despite the undisputed value of brands, during M&As these aspects are often paid less attention—from a practical, theoretical, and empirical point of view (Jaju *et al.* 2006). Ettenson and Knowles (2006) state that decisions regarding the target brand are—among all M&A-related decisions—the mandatory ones, even though they are often given little attention. Further, during acquisitions, firms tend to ignore brand matters and, rather, concentrate on strategic and financial issues (Jaju *et al.* 2006; Kumar and Blomqvist 2004), and brand equity is commonly given consideration after operational and financial concerns (Hise 1991; Hitt *et al.* 1990; Homburg and Bucerius 2005; Kumar and Blomqvist 2004; Mazur 2000).

Even though brands and communication during M&As enjoy more and more attention in both literature and research (Balmer and Dinnie 1999; Bahadir *et al.* 2008; Jaju *et al.* 2006; Melewar and Harold 2000), our knowledge and understanding of branding issues in M&As, apart from marketing considerations, is limited (Homburg and Bucerius 2006; Jaju *et al.* 2006). Summarizing existing research, one can learn that branding in M&As primarily faces three challenges: 1) keeping the focus on brand management during a transaction, 2) retaining brand values, and 3) considering the perspective of all stakeholders.

In this chapter, we provide a comprehensive view of corporate branding in M&As by addressing theoretical and managerial issues to identify opportunities for future research. This chapter is structured as follows: First, we have outlined the basic underlying theories that have been used for researching branding in M&As; second, we have striven to present brand management during the M&A process; and third, we have dicussed possibilities for future research.

Theoretical underpinnings for studying the phenomenon

Motives behind the branding strategy of merging entities primarily originate from company and individual interests. On the one hand, scholars argue that changes in brand names are based on strategic decisions in order to extend the scope of business (Basu 2006; Berry 1975; Rock and Rock 1990; Seth 1990; Steiner 1975). On the other hand, theorists state that acquisition behavior and decision making during acquisitions is based on the selfishness and opportunistic behavior of managers. Consequently, changes in brand names during acquisitions are an expression of the managers' power and a demonstration of their sphere of influence (Yunker 1983). Nonetheless, increased reliance on corporate governance mechanisms—used as a countermeasure for managerial opportunism—has not led to decreasing M&A activity (King *et al.* 2004); thus, we believe that managerial opportunism is not decisive for decision making prior to and during acquisitions as regards branding. Based on the understanding of Jaju *et al.* (2006 p: 208) that "from a pragmatic viewpoint, a newly merged company should prefer a branding strategy that maximizes the equity associated with the new organization," we will now present various theories that underpin research on branding-related issues, decisions, and strategies of merging entities.

In general, research in the field of M&As can be classified into four core schools of thought that reduce the complexity of the research field: the financial-economics school, the strategic school, the organizational-behavior school, and the process perspective (Birkinshaw *et al.* 2000;

Haspeslagh and Jemison 1991). As brands are valuable strategic assets, we subsume branding during acquisitions within the strategic school. Here, the market-based view and the resource-based view are essential theoretical underpinnings for studying M&As (Birkinshaw *et al.* 2000; Wirtz 2003). Nonetheless, with regard to branding, only the resource-based view seems to be an applicable theoretical underpinning for research.

The market-based view assumes resource homogeneity among firms as well as resource mobility. The major assumption of this paradigm is that entering into attractive industries through cost leadership or differentiation enables the creation of a sustainable position (Porter 1987). Linking this to M&As, firms positioned in an industry with low average profitability can positively influence their situations by extending their own capacity (cost leadership) or acquiring special products/services for differentiation purposes. Still, this view falls short with regard to brands, as brands can be seen as firm-specific resources that are developed over time and that are not easily transferable (Capron and Hulland 1999). The above-mentioned underlying assumptions of resource mobility and homogeneity do not provide a theoretical framework for investigating branding during acquisitions.

Resource-based view

The resource-based view assumes that companies differentiate themselves from each other in terms of resources which are not mobile but rather bounded to a firm (Penrose 1959). As the internal development of new resources is difficult due to intellectual capabilities and time (Singh and Montgomery 1987), firms are forced to acquire entire businesses and resources in order to obtain new resources (Barney 1991; Capron *et al.* 1998). M&As provide companies with the opportunity to get access to target firm-specific resources in order to link these with existing ones (Ahuja and Katila 2001). Thus, the aim of M&As from a resource-based viewpoint can be seen as the access to new resources and their reconfiguration, since own resources are limited (Colombo *et al.* 2007). Brands are seen as rare, non-imitable, path-dependent, and sticky resources (Bergen *et al.* 1996). Consequently, the resource-based view can act as a theoretical underpinning for branding and M&As.

Nevertheless, we argue that an exclusive strategic thought is not completely sufficient, as M&As go beyond resources and their interaction. Instead, we think that an organizational theory has to be taken into consideration to handle the effects of corporate brands in M&As properly. In the following, we draw attention to the stakeholder theory, where we debate the applicability of the underlying phenomenon.

Stakeholder theory

Next to consumers and the investment community, brands are often a key element of corporate cultures and, thus, closely tied to the routines and the systems of organizations (Capron 1999). Scholars argue that firms have to consider, beside customers, responses of other stakeholders to the corporate brand (Roper and Davies 2007). In line with theory, studies have shown that stakeholders may be treated as separate target groups for corporate branding because different stakeholders have different perspectives (Fiedler and Krichgeorg 2007; Roper and Davies 2007) and interests (King and Taylor 2012).

In fact, in M&As it is a difficult task to develop a corporate image that is welcomed by all involved stakeholders (Brown *et al.* 2006). Customers—as well as other stakeholders—expect honesty from companies, and managers should acknowledge customer-related issues in decision making during M&As (Gundersen and Meyn 2014). Uncertainty among customers, employees, and the investment community plays a decisive role in M&As. From an external point of view, this uncertainty can have negative effects on the service portfolio (Urban and Pratt 2000) and even lead to a loss of trust among the stakeholders (Homburg and Bucerius 2006), as managerial energy is often absorbed by internal issues, which can lead managers to neglect external tasks (Hitt *et al.* 1990). This decline can, for example, cause customers to question their future relationship with the merging firms, leading to defection to competitors (Reichheld and Henske 1991). From an internal point of view, the identification with brands by employees plays an important role for stability in the organization (Hieronimus 2006), as the building of trust and loyalty requires established values (Basu 2006). These basic values could be disrupted through improper branding decisions. Nonetheless, branding-related decisions can be used by executives as a key element to communicate the new vision of the acquired entity and to send compulsive and reliable signals inside and outside the organization to work against uncertainty (Ettenson and Knowles 2006).

According to the stakeholder theory, firms should strive for a balanced relationship with external and internal stakeholders simultaneously. Thus, regardless of which brand integration strategy is chosen, the redeployment of corporate brands must face the consequences for consumers and investors, while simultaneously ensuring that the identification of employees with the redeployed brand is positive (Jaju *et al.* 2006). Consequently, stakeholder theory could act as a theoretical underpinning for studying M&As, as M&As affect a broad variety of stakeholders with different interests (King and Taylor 2012). In the following section, we want to demonstrate the effects of brand management during the M&A process.

Brand management in mergers and acquisitions

Scholars frequently claim that brand considerations do not play a major role in the management of M&As, and that managers postpone these considerations to a later time as more urgent topics, like operational and financial matters, are handled first (Hitt *et al.* 1990; Knudsen *et al.* 1997; Kumar and Blomqvist 2004; Mazur 2000). This is in line with the study by Ettenson and Knowles (2006), who state, "rebranding becomes part of a post-acquisition cleanup in which the driving question for marketing executives is, 'How are we now going to make this deal work?'" (p. 40). Balmer and Dinnie (1999) argue that a lack of focus on corporate branding is one major reason why many mergers fail to reach expected outcomes.

Against this background, we argue that the effects and consequences of branding decisions in M&As are not only a post-merger issue but rather concern the entire M&A process. Brand analysis as well as branding-related decisions must be met during all stages, as the consequences of branding often occur at a later point in time. In the following section, we want to give an overview on relevant branding issues during M&As with regard to the M&A phases.

Pre-merger issues: the fit between the merging corporate brands

In recent decades, numerous researchers have sought to explain the success or failure of M&As on the basis of some kind of strategic match between the merging entities (Chatterjee 1986; Lubatkin 1987; Seth 1990; Swaminathan *et al.* 2008). This strategic match has been conceptualized in different ways. First, industry relatedness is applied as an indicator for related or unrelated M&As, depending on how close the core businesses of the merging entities are (Kang and Sakai 2001). Following this logic, horizontal and vertical transactions are more likely to be related, whereas conglomerates are unrelated (Ramaswamy 1997). It is argued that related M&As are more likely to create value or to increase performance, first, by being more efficient due to economies of scale and second, due to a greater market share (Chatterjee 1986; Datta *et al.* 1992;

Kim and Finkelstein 2009; Lubatkin 1983; Pilar Socorro 2004; Ramaswamy 1997; Shelton 1988; Singh and Montgomery 1987). Even though the empirical results on relatedness are not univocal, in general it can be said that relatedness has a positive effect on the performance of the acquiring firm (Capon *et al.* 1988; Datta *et al.* 1992; Kusewitt 1985).

Second, similarities in resources between an acquirer and target firm have received serious attention from researchers as crucial factors for success or failure in acquisitions (Hitt *et al.* 1998; Larsson and Finkelstein 1999; Ramaswamy 1997; Walker 2000). According to Karim and Mitchell (2000), similarities in resources enable firms not only to eliminate redundant resources but also to offer possibilities for an expansion of resources due to the interaction of resources. Additionally, as dissimilarities urge conflicts (Lubatkin 1983; Salter and Weinhold 1979) particularly in decision making during post-merger integration (Swaminathan *et al.* 2008), similarities can be a beneficial source for effective integration. Consequently, the similarity in resources is seen as an indicator for synergy potential (Meyer and Altenborg 2008).

Even though strategic fit has been broadly operationalized in terms of product markets, resources, and/or supply chain-related issues (Pehrsson 2006; Stimpert and Duhaime 1997), brand fit in M&As has been largely overlooked as branding research mainly investigates the brand phenomenon under stable conditions (Bahadir *et al.* 2008). However, M&As are a disruptive event for firms and they do not only affect the organizations but also customers, employees, and investors (King and Taylor 2012; Mizik *et al.* 2011). A very similar situation occurs during brand extensions, where firms try to transfer the reputation of a brand onto a new/or another product category (Dacin and Smith 1994). In the brand extension literature, brand fit has received serious attention from researchers (Bottomley and Holden 2001; Park *et al.* 1991) and is investigated in terms of similarity in product characteristics, brand concepts or brand logos (Bottomly and Holden 2001; Keller and Lehmann 2006; Park *et al.* 1991). There is empirical evidence that consumer evaluations are best when there is a fit between the brands and the products (Park *et al.* 1991), while greater variances lower these (Dacin and Smith 1994). Bridging this logic to M&As, one could assume that brand fit is an indicator for consumer responses to acquisitions and is therefore decisive for market-related performance. Furthermore, as brands are valuable resources, a high brand fit can be seen as an indicator for a potential resource interaction and, therefore, for synergy after the acquisition. By now there is only little empirical evidence, but the study of Jaju *et al.* (2006) reveals that similar brand attitudes lead to the least changes in consumer brand equity and Bauer *et al.* (2012) found empirical evidence that high brand relatedness positively influences the market performance after M&As.

Post-merger issues

As industry relatedness and resource similarity, and brand fit or relatedness can only be seen as an indicator for synergy, the leveraging of these synergies can only be undertaken in post-merger integration. This is in line with Haspeslagh and Jemison (1991) holding that value creation in M&As is a post-merger integration issue. Thus, we have chosen to focus on branding issues during post-merger integration, namely the branding decisions and the integration of resources.

Branding decisions

Fundamentally, Lambkin and Muzellec (2010) argue that branding decisions should ideally be driven by marketing considerations in order to communicate the new strategic focus to all stakeholders and to generate synergies from brand equities of all involved firms. Branding in

Table 22.1 Corporate brand integration strategies after an M&A

Acquirer corporate brand	Target corporate brand	
	Retained	*Not retained*
Retained	*Multi-brand* (e.g. Procter & Gamble + Gillette = Procter & Gamble; Gillette) *Hybrid brand* (e.g. Molson + Adolph Coors = Molson Coors)	*Target dominance brand* (e.g. Chemical Banking Corporation + Chase Manhattan Corporation = Chase)
Not retained	*Acquirer dominance brand* (e.g. Hewlett-Packard + Compaq = Hewlett-Packard)	*New brand* (e.g. Ciba-Geigy + Sandoz = Novartis)

Source: own elaboration according to Brockdorff and Kernstock (2001); examples provided by Jaju *et al.* (2006)

M&As initially raises the question about how brand is defined. Classical branding literature offers plenty of different definitions. Based on the more general brand definition of the American Marketing Association (AMA), Muzellec and Lambkin (2006 p. 805) state that

> a possible characterization of rebranding is therefore the creation of a new name, term, symbol, design or a combination of them for an established brand with the intention of developing a differentiated (new) position in the mind of stakeholders and competitors.

Depending on how brand is defined, there are multiple strategies for redeploying corporate brands in M&As. If one defines corporate brands simply as names, there are five basic strategies for the new entity: multi-brand, hybrid brand, acquirer dominance brand, target dominance brand, and new brand strategy (see Table 22.1). These strategies are differentiated from each other depending on whether the involved corporate brands are retained or not (Ettenson and Knowles 2006; Jaju *et al.* 2006; Vu *et al.* 2009).

As Table 22.1 shows, the multi-brand strategy retains the corporate brand names of the merging entities in its original form. Similar to this is the hybrid brand strategy, which retains the corporate brand names of the merging entities and combines them for the new entity. The dominance strategy retains only one corporate brand for the new entity. In the acquirer dominance strategy the new entity only retains the acquirer corporate brand, whereas in the target dominance strategy the new entity only retains the target corporate brand. The new brand strategy does not retain any corporate brand; all involved brands are deleted and a new corporate brand is created for the merging entity. Basically, all strategies contain opportunities and threats, which are summarized in Table 22.2.

Recent studies underline that the five basic brand integration strategies, (multi-brand, hybrid brand, acquirer dominance brand, target dominance brand, and new brand) rarely exist in their pure forms in practice. Instead, extended versions of the basic corporate brand options are present. For instance, Jaju *et al.* (2006) further distinguish whether the acquirer or target corporate name is placed first. Thus, in case of the hybrid strategy, the target corporate brand may be placed first (e.g. Farnell + Premier Industrial = Premier Farnell PLC). In their study, Ettenson and Knowles (2006) identified several modifications (extension of basic brand integration strategies) when defining corporate brands as a name and logo. For example, around 3 percent of 207 studied mergers applied the hybrid brand integration strategy in its pure form (retention of

Table 22.2 Corporate brand opportunities and threats in M&A

Integration strategy	Opportunities	Threats
Multi brand	• No destruction of brand value (retaining of all corporate brands) • Maximization of market-coverage	• High maintaining costs (due to remaining of all corporate names) • Low synergy potential
Hybrid brand	• No destruction of brand value (retaining of all corporate brands) • Simplicity of implementation	• Low synergy potential (often similar positioning)
Dominance brand	• Realization of synergies (e.g. within the marketing-mix) • Transfer of positive image attributes the new entity • Simplicity of implementation (simply not retaining the unpopular brand)	• Destruction of brand value (retaining only one corporate brand) • Uncertainty among stakeholders (on behalf of the not retained brand)
New brand	• Launch of a new brand that perfectly fits to internal and external requirements • Exclusion of negative brand equity (symbolization of a new beginning)	• Destruction of corporate brand values (due to deletion of existing ones) • Huge establishment costs (creation and communication of new corporate brand) • Uncertainty among stakeholders (esp. customers, employees, and investors) • Challenge to embed the new corporate brand into customer's memory (due to often saturated and competitive markets)

corporate brand name and logo in a combined way). Around 5 percent of all transactions implemented this approach in a modified way by additionally changing the symbol of the acquiring company, while the identity elements of the target company were kept. Another further example is provided in a study by Machado *et al.* (2012), revealing that in a case of a merger which involves two strong brands, consumers may eventually prefer alternatives that preserve elements of both. Putting the basic corporate brand integration strategies and their redefined versions together, it seems that potential threats of the five basic options may be minimized when other aspects of a brand (e.g. logo) are part of the redeployment.

Resource interaction and integration

After M&As, the resources of acquirer and target firms can be combined to create a competitive advantage of the newly combined entity (Capron and Hulland 1999). For the desired resource interaction or combination, a certain level of integration is necessary. If brands are poorly managed in post-merger integration, synergies might fail to materialize (Basu 2006) and employee and customer relationships degrade (Ettenson and Knowles 2006). Thus, the acquirer needs a well-handled brand integration management in order to retain and enhance the relationships with customers (Ettenson and Knowles 2006; Kumar and Blomqvist 2004), employees, and investors, since these are the key stakeholders during a transaction (Ettenson and Knowles 2006). Consequently, a clear brand strategy formulation and integration can be seen as an important marketing, as well as organizational, task during M&As (Balmer and Dinnie 1999; Brooks *et al.* 2005; Melewar 2001). Branding strategies developed during M&As need to consider resource interactions.

An acquirer's brand, if it is a well recognized brand, can complement target products or markets. These spillover effects can be used without the brand value dwindling (King *et al.* 2008; Slotegraaf *et al.* 2003). King *et al.* (2008) found empirical evidence for a positive interaction effect of an acquirer's marketing and the target´s research and development resources. Even though not all resources can be redeployed equally due to their organizational complexity, Capron and Hulland (1999) found empirical evidence that the redeployment of brands from target to acquirer affects the geographic coverage as well as the market share in a negative way, while redeployment in the other direction has beneficial effects for both.

Against the positive considerations of integration, Homburg and Bucerius (2005) argue that extensive marketing integration has, on the one hand, positive effects on cost savings as the number of brands, for instance, can be reduced but, on the other hand, it has detrimental effects on market-related performance due to negative customer evaluations and the absorption of managerial energy by internal reorganization issues.

In summary, scholars claim that paying attention to brands in M&As is essential in order to generate value after the deal (e.g. Ettenson and Knowles 2006). Managers should neither ignore the corporate brands by keeping them without any changes (Basu 2006), nor should they pay too much attention to the corporate brands as that might lead to a contentious business (Ettenson and Knowles 2006).

Discussion

The previous sections have shown that corporate branding in M&As is an essential but largely unexplored topic. From the prior review, we now identify future research areas, beginning with the enlargement of theoretical underpinnings that might help to address knowledge gaps (corporate branding issues in particular) and research gaps (corporate branding issues in their entirety).

Enlarging theoretical underpinnings

In general, research in the field of mergers and acquisitions can be classified into four core schools of thought that reduce the complexity of the research field: the financial-economics school; the strategic school; the organizational-behavior school; and the process perspective (Birkinshaw *et al.* 2000; Haspelsagh and Jemison, 1991). The previous section has shown that, by now, research in the field of corporate branding in mergers and acquisitions uses the underlying assumptions of the resource-based view and the stakeholder theory. In the following, we present specified forms of these approaches, namely the dynamic capabilities view and the social identity theory, which might explain the redeployment of corporate brands in a better way.

Dynamic capabilities view

The dynamic capabilities view (e.g. Eisenhardt and Martin 2000; Teece *et al.* 1997) advances the resource-based view of the firm (e.g. Barney 1991; Wernerfelt 1984) and it may improve insights on M&A brand management. Using the definition of Helfat *et al.* (2007), dynamic capabilities involve "the capacity of an organization to purposefully create, extend or modify its resource base" (p. 1). Following Teece (2007), dynamic capabilities comprise the processes of reconfiguration, leveraging, learning, and integration. Therefore, this might be a possible approach to face the redeployment of corporate brands in a comprehensive way. Brands can be observed during an entire transaction process: reconfiguration—transformation and recombination of assets and resources (in this case: corporate brand integration); leveraging—the replication of a process or system (in this case: brand extensions); learning—the task to perform more effectively and efficiently (in this case: potential post-merger brand adaptions); and integration—the coordination of assets and resources (in this case: brand architecture).

Social identity theory

Beside the stakeholder theory, social identity theory, derived from psychology, could be another relevant theoretical framework to explain the effects of different brand integration strategies in M&As. Mergers and acquisitions can be seen as market disruptions as they are "major events occurring in the market that threaten customer-brand relationships" (Lam *et al.* 2010 p. 128). As customer-brand identification, according to social identity theory, is defined as the overlap of the personal identities of brands and consumers (Bhattacharya and Sen 2004), we argue that social identity theory could be a powerful framework to explain .the effects of branding in M&As. The effects of changes in the existing brand concepts, namely brand switching or decreasing brand loyalty, can be explained with this theory.

Addressing knowledge gaps: corporate branding issues in particular

The previous section has shown that the redeployment of corporate brands is, by now, rather drafted than explored in a detailed way. Within every single stage of a merger or acquisition process there occur specific questions that leave space for further research. In particular the timing and communication of corporate brand implementation, as well as the inclusion of stakeholder perspectives, seem to be promising research areas—especially for qualitative approaches.

Timing and communication of corporate brand implementation

Even though literature suggests specific brand integration strategies after M&As, our knowledge about the operational implementation of the new corporate brand is quite limited. According to Liedtke (1994), the implementation of a corporate brand can happen in two ways: abrupt change or incremental transition. An abrupt change can appear with or without an explanation for stakeholders. An incremental transition can be applied by changing over or using a two-step approach. Drawing from those statements, Esch *et al.* (2006) argue that a dominant brand strategy, for instance, might benefit from an abrupt change when the brand integration strategy is used as repositioning. Meanwhile, the use of the dominant brand strategy for original brands with similar target groups induces a changeover, i.e. brand elements are incrementally changed over time.

To the best of our knowledge, research has not consistently addressed the timing of corporate brand implementation. This might be an interesting gap to close since the timing and the speed of integration seems to be an important factor for the success of an M&A. For instance, the study of Homburg and Bucerius (2006) reveals that the speed of marketing integration positively influences the market-related performance of an aquistion. They argue that fast integration decreases uncertainty among customers (Homburg and Bucerius 2005). Based on that argument, a potential future research question might be: How does the timing and the speed of implementation of the brand integration strategy affect the M&A outcome (e.g. financial brand equity)? Further, as uncertainty is a crucial factor when focusing on the stakeholder (Ettenson and Knowles 2006), it raises the question: How does the timing and the speed of corporate brand implementation increase or decrease uncertainty among stakeholders?

Additionally, communication of the new corporate brand is closely connected to this phenomenon. Stakeholder communication is one area that is named as a major reason for the failure of an M&A (Balmer and Dinnie 1999; Krishnan *et al.* 2007). Following Lambkin and Muzellec (2010), branding decisions should be based on marketing considerations in order to communicate the new strategic focus in a bettter way. However, our knowledge with regard to communication to stakeholders in the area of corporate branding in M&As is rather limited. This gap may be closed via quantitative studies, adressing questions like: What type of operational communication is suitable for different corporate brand integration strategies?

Inclusion of multiple stakeholder perceptions

Successfully managing the redeployment of corporate brands in M&As requires the understanding of how the different interest groups perceive certain brand modifications (Brown *et al.* 2006; Jaju *et al.* 2006). Consumers and investors as external stakeholders, in particular, as well as employees as internal stakeholders, play a major role here (Wirtz 2003; Ettenson and Knowles 2006). Existing research primarily addresses consumers (e.g. Jaju *et al.* 2006; Machado *et al.* 2012), and therefore future research might be concerned with the question: How does the redeployment of corporate brands in mergers and acquisitions affect other interest groups?

We also recommend distinguishing between acquirer and target stakeholders. This separation gains importance with "mergers of unequals". Ettenson and Knowles (2006) illustrate in detail how an acquirer as well as a target stakeholder might react to corporate brand changes, revealing that these reactions differ from each other. We assume that a more specific understanding of target stakeholders will improve our understanding of branding in M&As.

Moreover, literature reveals that corporate brand integration should be based on a company's valuable interests (Basu 2006; Berry 1975; Rock and Rock 1990; Seth 1990; Steiner 1975) such as access to new resources and not on the vested interests of individual managers (Yunker 1983). The study of Bauer *et al.* (2012) concludes that antecedents and determinants of the chosen brand integration strategy are still undetected. Thus, in order to avoid negative stakeholder reactions after an M&A, it seems that knowledge of the expectations of each interest group before a deal is a promising approach. Following the study of Jaju *et al.* (2006), consumer judgments on the fit of the merging corporate brands are an important factor for decision making. In this area, there are fundamental questions to address, such as: What is decision making based upon when redeploying corporate brands?, Who is in general included in corporate brand decision making?, or Which interest groups should be included in order to rebrand in a successful way?

Addressing research gaps: corporate branding issues in their entirety

As previously mentioned, the redeployment of corporate brands is, by now, rather drafted than explored in a detailed way. Thus, a comprehensive view is so far described in a relatively complete manner and there exist studies that face corporate branding in a comprehensive way. However, their results are quite limited and might have their origin in insufficient measurements and/or a lack of included corporate frameworks. In the following, these issues are described in more detail.

Redefining measurements

Addressing the fit between the merging corporate brands, existing studies have used the measure of relatedness (Bauer *et al.* 2012; Wille *et al.* 2011). Another aspect is the complementarity between the merging entities. The central assumption of the complementarity concept is that similarities might generate potential after a transaction but complementarities in resources do the same by reconstructing (Capasso and Meglio 2005; Kim and Finkelstein 2009). This party argues that a high complementarity between the acquirer and target firm is more valuable (Harrison *et al.* 1991; Hitt *et al.* 1998; Larsson and Finkelstein 1999). Building on existing literature, Kim and Finkelstein (2009) define complementarity "as occurring when merging firms have different resources, capabilities, and/or strategies that can potentially be combined or reconfigured to create value that did not exist in either firm before the acquisition" (p. 619).

Empirical studies reveal that complementarity is a crucial factor in transactions (Kim and Finkelstein 2009). Complementarities between merging alliances reveal that complementarities have a positive influence on the post-merger performance (Krishnan *et al.* 1999, Lambe *et al.* 2002). Specifically addressing acquisitions, complementarities are identified as a crucial factor for generating synergies, whereas a high degree of integration pushes this effect (Larsson and Finkelstein 1999). Strategic complementarities have—especially with a less strategic focus—a positive influence on performance (Kim and Finkelstein 2009). This also addresses complementarities in resources which have a huge influence on success (Hitt *et al.* 1998). Differences have no significant negative influence on the post-merger performance; however, marketing activities and the structure of customers have a huge influence on success (Ramaswamy 1997).

Putting everything together, one can learn that both the similarities and complementarities seem to be a promising concept. Since it is really difficult to strictly differentiate between similarities and complementarities, it might be interesting to use the broader term 'fit' as a combination of both. Following the advice of Lambkin and Muzellec (2010), branding decisions ideally should be driven by marketing considerations in order to communicate the new strategic focus to all stakeholders and to generate synergies from brand equities of all involved firms. Thus, the central element of the pre-merger phase is probably the 'marketing fit' which might be further distinguished between an external and internal view, since such a differentiation enables clearer results, as prior studies have shown (Homburg and Bucerius 2006). Putting everything together, these redefined measurements might end up in the following research question: "How does the internal and external marketing fit influence the integration of corporate brands?"

Using the individual consumer as a unit of analysis, the performance of the merging entities has been measured so far with consumer-related brand equity (Jaju *et al.* 2006; Lee *et al.* 2011); taking the acquiring firm as a base, the overall performance of the merger or acquisition was used (Bauer *et al.* 2012; Wille *et al.* 2011). The latter approach might be redefined into market-related success, since the content is within the marketing area. Thus a possible research question could be "How do the corporate brand options influence the market-related success of mergers and acquisitions?"

Inclusion of the corporate strategy

An additional field of decision making involves the organizational integration approach, which depends on the need for strategic interdependence and organizational autonomy (Haspelsagh and Jemison 1991). A related aspect is the aim of M&As, which impacts corporate branding. For instance, Basu (2006) finds that the redeployment of corporate brands depends on the type of M&A (e.g. an industry convergence suggests a new brand option). The qualitative study by Vu *et al.* (2010) of horizontal transactions reveals that multi- and dominant brand strategies are connected with cost-saving objectives, while the hybrid and new brand integration strategies aim at growth. This poses the questions: "How is the redeployment of corporate brands related to the integration approach of the organization?" and "How do the different classifications (horizontal, vertical, and conglomerate) of M&As influence the redeployment of corporate brands?"

Conclusion

Making corporate branding-related evaluations and decisions prior to, during and after M&As is an essential management task. Although firms are willing to pay high prices to acquire corporate brands, literature reveals that these efforts are often undermined by a lack of corporate brand management during the entire process, which makes it difficult to retain brand values and meet stakeholder expectations. In prior research, these hurdles are explored in a relatively limited way. While the pre-merger evaluation of brands in M&A research is broadly ignored, the brand extension literature could deliver valuable insights, basic arguments, and methods to study the brand phenomenon in M&As. The arguments for a beneficial effect of brand fit or relatedness can be drawn from more positive customer evaluations, a better interaction of brand resources, and easier integration, as employees strongly identify themselves with the brand. Another major gap exists in the field of brand integration strategies. Apart from the different basic brand integration strategies, there is little empirical evidence of their effects on different stakeholders. A third stream prompting future research is the interaction and complementing effects of the resource brand. We recommend research in these fields, especially in terms of timing, speed, and communication of corporate brand integration. Further, the integration of a broader stakeholder perspective as well as the link of branding issues with corporate strategy could serve as a valuable future research area. In closing, we highlight the importance of an increased focus on brands in M&As that considers multiple stakeholders and new theoretical perspectives.

References

Ahuja, G. and Katila, R. (2001) "Technological acquisitions and the innovative performance of acquiring firms: a longitudinal study," *Strategic Management Journal*, 22: 197–220.

Anand, J. and Delios, A. (2002) "Absolute and relative resources as determinants of international acquisitions," *Strategic Management Journal*, 23: 119–34.

Bahadir, C.S., Bharadwaj, S.G., and Srivastava, R.K. (2008) "Financial value of brands in mergers and acquisitions: is value in the eye of the beholder?," *Journal of Marketing*, 72: 49–64.

Balmer, J.M. and Dinnie, K. (1999) "Corporate identity and corporate communications: an antidote to merger madness," *Corporate Communications: An International Journal*, 4: 182–94.

Barney, J. (1991) "Firm resources and sustained competitive advantage," *Journal of Management*, 17: 99–120.

Basu, K. (2006) "Merging brands after mergers," *California Management Review*, 48: 28–40.

Bauer, F.A., Matzler, K., and Wille, C. (2012) "Integrating brand and marketing perspectives in M&A," *Problems and Perspectives in Management*, 10: 57–70.

Bergen, M., Dutta, S., and Shugan, S.M. (1996) "Branded variants: a retail perspective," *Journal of Marketing Research*, 33(February): 9–19.

Berry, C.H. (1975) *Corporate Growth and Diversification*, Princeton, NJ: Princeton University Press.

Bhattacharya, C.B. and Sen, S. (2004) "Doing better at doing good: when, why, and how consumers respond to corporate social initiatives," *California Management Review*, 47: 9–24.

Birkinshaw, J., Bresman, H., and Håkanson, L. (2000) "Managing the post-acquisition integration process: how the human integration and task integration processes interact to foster value creation," *Journal of Management Studies*, 37: 365–425.

Bottomley, P.A. and Holden, S.J.S. (2001) "Do we really know how consumers evaluate brand extensions? Empirical generalizations based on secondary analysis of eight studies," *Journal of Marketing Research*, 38: 494–500.

Brockdorff, B. and Kernstock, J. (2001) "Brand integration management—Erfolgreiche Markenführung bei Mergers and Acquisitions," *Thexis*, 4: 54–9.

Brooks, M.R., Rosson, P.J., and Grassman, H.I. (2005) "Influences on post-M&A corporate visual indentity choices," *Corporate Reputation Review*, 8: 136–44.

Brown, T.J., Pratt, G., and Whetten, D.A. (2006) "Identity, intended image, constructed image, and reputation: an interdisciplinary framework and suggested terminology," *Journal of the Academy of Marketing Science*, 34: 99–106.

Capasso, A. and Meglio, O. (2005) "Knowledge transfer in mergers and acquisitions: how frequent acquirers learn to manage integration process," in Capasso, A., Dagnino, G.B., and Lanza, A. (eds.) *Strategic Capabilities and Knowledge Transfer Within and Between Organizations*, Cheltenham: Edward Elgar Publishing.

Capon, N., Farley, J.U., and Martin, L.E. (1988) "Corporate diversity and economic performance: the impact of market specialization," *Strategic Management Journal*, 9: 61–74.

Capron, L. (1999) "The long-term performance of horizontal acquisitions," *Strategic Management Journal*, 20: 987–1018.

Capron, L. and Hulland, J. (1999) "Redeployment of brands, sales forces, and general marketing management expertise following horizontal acquisitions: a resource-based view," *The Journal of Marketing*, 63: 41–54.

Capron, L., Dussauge, P., and Mitchell, W. (1998) "Resource redeployment following horizontal acquisitions in Europe and North America, 1988–1992," *Strategic Management Journal*, 19: 631–61.

Chatterjee, S. (1986) "Types of synergy and economic value: the impact of acquisitions on merging and rival firms," *Strategic Management Journal*, 7: 119–39.

Colombo, G., Conca, V., Boungiorno, M., and Gnan, L. (2007) "Integrating cross-border acquisitions: a process-oriented approach," *Long Range Planning*, 40: 202–22.

Dacin, P.A. and Smith, D.C. (1994). "The effect of brand portfolio characteristics on consumer evaluations of brand extensions," *Journal of Marketing Research*, 31: 229–42.

Datta, D.K., Pinches, G.E., and Narayanan, V.K. (1992) "Factors influencing wealth creation from mergers and acquisitions: a meta-analysis," *Strategic Management Journal*, 13: 67–84.

Eisenhardt, K.M. and Martin, J.A. (2000). "Dynamic capabilities: What are they?," *Strategic Management Journal*, 21(10–11): 1105–21.

Esch, F.-R., Brockdorff, B., Langner, T., and Tomczak, T. (2006) "Corporate Brands bei Mergers and Acquisitions gestalten," in Esch, F.-R., Tomczak, T., Kernstock, J., and Langner, T. (eds.) *Corporate Brand Management. Marken als Anker Strategischer Führung von Unternehmen*, 2nd edn., Wiesbaden: Gabler Verlag.

Ettenson, R. and Knowles, J. (2006) "Merging the brands and branding the merger," *MITSloan Management Review*, 47: 39–49.

Fiedler, L. and Krichgeorg, M. (2007) "The role concept in corporate branding and stakeholder management considered: Are stakeholder groups really different?," *Corporate Reputation Review*, 10: 177–88.

Gundersen, G.A. and Meyn, M. (2014) "Brand attitude change and acquisition attitude: an experimental study of U.S. consumers in an M&A setting," Master Thesis, MSC Oslo.

Harrison, J.S., Hitt, M.H., Hoskisson, R.E., and Ireland, D.R. (1991). "Synergies and post-acquisition performance: Differences versus similarities in resource allocations," *Journal of Management*, 17(March): 173–190.

Haspelsagh, P.C. and Jemison, D.B. (1991) *Managing Acquisitions: Creating Value Through Corporate Renewal*, 1st edn., New York: Free Press.

Helfat, C.E., Finkelstein, S., Mitchell, W., Peteraf, M., Singh, H., Teece, D., Winter, S., and Maritan, C. (2007) "Dynamic capabilities and organizational processes," in *Dynamic Capabilities: Understanding Strategic Change in Organizations*, Blackwell, London.

Hieronimus, F. (2006) "Marketintypenstrategieansätze: Markenstrategische Ansätze bei Unternehmensfu-sionen," in Wirtz, B.W. (ed.) *Handbuch Mergers & Acquisitions Management*, Wiesbaden: Gabler Verlag.

Hise, R.T. (1991) "Evaluating marketing assets in mergers and acquisitions," *Journal of Business Strategy*, 12: 46–51.

Hitt, M.A., Hoskission, R.E., and Ireland, R.D. (1990) "Mergers and acquisitions and managerial commitment in innovation in M-form firms," *Strategic Management Journal*, 11: 29–47.

Hitt, M.A., Harrison, J., Ireland, D.R., and Best, A. (1998) "Attributes of successful and unsuccessful acqui-sitions," *British Journal of Management*, 9: 91–114.

Homburg, C. and Bucerius, M. (2005) "A marketing perspective on mergers and acquisitions: how market-ing integration affects postmerger performance," *Journal of Marketing*, 69: 96–113.

Homburg, C. and Bucerius, M. (2006) "Is speed of integration really a success factor of mergers and acquisitions? An analysis of the role of internal and external relatedness," *Strategic Management Journal*, 27: 347–67.

Jaju, A., Joiner, C., and Reddy, K. (2006) "Consumer evaluation of corporate brand redeployments," *Journal of the Academy of Marketing Science*, 34: 206–15.

Kang, N.-H. and Sakai, K. (2001) *New Patterns of Industrial Globalisation: Cross-Border Mergers and Acquisitions and Strategic Alliances*, Paris: Oraganisation for Economic Co-operation and Development.

Karim, S. and Mitchell, W. (2000) "Path-dependent and path-breaking change: reconfiguring business resources following acquisitions in the U.S. medical sector, 1978–1995," *Strategic Management Journal*, 21: 1061–81.

Keller, K.L. and Lehmann, D.R. (2006) "Brands and branding: research findings and future priorities," *Marketing Science*, 2: 740–59.

Kim, J.-Y.J. and Finkelstein, S. (2009) "The effects of strategic and market complementarity on acquisition performance: evidence from the U.S. commercial banking industry, 1989–2001," *Strategic Management Journal*, 30: 617–46.

King, D.R. and Taylor, R. (2012) "Beyond the numbers: seven stakeholders to consider in improving acqui-sition outcomes," *Graziadio Business Review*, 15.

King, D.R. Slotegraaf, R. and Kesner, I. (2008) "Performance implications of firm resource interactions in the acquisition of R&D-intensive firms," *Organization Science*, 19: 327–40.

King, D.R., Dalton, D.R., Daily, C.M., and Covin, J.G. (2004) "Meta-analyses of post-acquisition perfor-mance: indications of unidentified moderators," *Strategic Management Journal*, 25: 187–200.

Knudsen, T.R., Finskud, L., Törnblom, R., and Hogna, E. (1997) "Brand consolidation makes a lot of eco-nomic sense," *The McKinsey Quarterly*, 4: 189–93.

Krishnan, H.A., Hitt, M.A., and Park, D. (2007) "Acquisition premiums, subsequent workforce reductions and post-acquisition performance," *Journal of Management Studies*, 44: 709–32.

Krishnan, H.A., Miller, A., and Judge, W.Q. (1999) "Diversification and top management team complemen-tarity: is performance improved by merging similar or dissimilar teams?," *Strategic Management Journal*, 18: 361–74.

Kumar, S. and Blomqvist, K.H. (2004) "Mergers and acquistions: making brand equity a key factor in M&A decision-making," *Strategy & Leadership*, 32: 20–7.

Kusewitt, J.B. (1985) "An exploratory study of strategic acquisition factors relating to performance," *Strategic Management Journal*, 6: 151–69.

Lam, S.K., Ahearne, M., Hu, Y., and Schillewaert, N. (2010) "Resistance to brand switching when a radically new brand is introduced: a social identity theory perspective," *Journal of Marketing*, 74: 128–46.

Lambe, C.J., Spekman, R.E., and Hunt, S.D. (2002) "Alliance competence, resources, and alliance success: conceptualization, measurement, and initial test," *Journal of the Academy of Marketing Science*, 30: 141–58.

Lambkin, M.C. and Muzellec, L. (2010) "Leveraging brand equity in business-to-business mergers and acquisitions," *Industrial Marketing Management*, 39: 1234–39.

Larsson, R. and Finkelstein, S. (1999) "Integrating strategic, organizational, and human resource perspec-tives on mergers and acquisitions: a case survey of synergy realization," *Organizational Science*, 10: 1–26.

Lee, H.-M., Lee, C.-C., and Wu, C.-C. (2011) "Brand image strategy affects brand equity after M&A," *European Journal of Marketing*, 45: 1091–111.

Liedtke, A. (1994) "Der Wechsel des Markennamens," in Bruhn, M. (ed.) *Handbuch Markenartikel*, Stuttgart: Schäffer-Poeschel.

Lindemann, J. (2003) "Brand valuation," in Clifton, R. and Simmons, J. (ed.) *Brands and Branding*, London: The Economist.

Lubatkin, M. (1983) "Mergers and the performance of the acquiring firm," *The Academy of Management Review*, 8: 218–25.

Lubatkin, M. (1987) "Merger strategies and stockholder value," *Strategic Management Journal*, 8: 39–53.

Machado, J.C., Vacas-de-Carvalho, L., Costa, P., and de Lencastre, P. (2012) "Brand mergers: examining consumers responses to name and logo design," *Journal of Product & Brand Management*, 21: 418–27.

Madden, T., Fehle, F. and Fournier, S., 2006 "Brands matter: an empirical demonstration of the creation of shareholder value through branding," *Journal of the Academy of Marketing Science*, 34: 224–35.

Mahajan, V., Vithala, R.R., and Rajendra, K.S. (1994) "An approach to assess the importance of brand equity in acquisition decisions," *Journal of Product Innovation Management*, 11: 221–35.

Mazur, L. (2000) "When brands and cultures clash," *Marketing Intelligence & Planning*, 22–3.

Melewar, T.C. (2001) "Measuring visual identity: a multi-construct study," *Corporate Communications: An International Journal*, 6: 36–43.

Melewar, T.C. and Harold, J. (2000) "The role of corporate identity systems in merger and acquisitions activity," *Journal of General Management*, 26: 17–31.

Meyer, C.B. and Altenborg, E. (2008) "Incompatible strategies in international mergers: the failed merger between Telia and Telenor," *Journal of International Business Studies*, 39: 508–25.

Mizik, N., Knowles, J. and Dinner, I. (2011) "Value implications of corporate branding in mergers," *Social Science Research Network Working Papers*, University of Washington and University of North Carolina, Chapel Hill.

Muzellec, L. and Lambkin, M. (2006) "Corporate rebranding: destroying, transferring or creating brand equity?," *European Journal of Marketing*, 40: 803–24.

Park, C.W., McCarthy, M.S., and Milberg, S.J. (1991) "The effects of direct and associative brand extension strategies on consumer response to brand extensions," *Advances in Consumer Research*, 20: 28–33.

Penrose, E. (1959) *The Theory of the Growth of the Firm*, New York: Oxford University Press.

Perrier, R. (1997) *Brand Valuation*, London: Premier Books.

Pehrsson, A. (2006) "Business relatedness and performance: a study of managerial perceptions," *Strategic Management Journal*, 27: 265–82.

Pilar Socorro, M. (2004) "Mergers and the importance of fitting well," *Economic Letters*, 82: 269–74.

Porter, M.E. (1987) "From competitive advantage to corporate strategy," *Harvard Business Review*, 56: 28–46.

Ramaswamy, K. (1997) "The performance impact of strategic similarity in horizontal mergers: evidence from the U.S. banking industry," *Academy of Management Journal*, 40: 697–715.

Reichheld, F.F. and Henske, B. (1991) "The only sure method of recouping merger premiums," *Journal of Retail Banking*, 8: 9–17.

Rock, L. and Rock, R.H. (1990) *Corporate Restructuring*, New York: McGraw-Hill.

Roper, S. and Davies, G. (2007) "The corporate brand: dealing with multiple stakeholders," *Journal of Marketing Management*, 23: 75–90.

Rossiter, J.R. and Percy, L. (1997) *Advertising, Communications and Promotion Management*, 2nd edn., New York: McGraw-Hill Book Company.

Salter, M.S. and Weinhold, W.A. (1979) *Diversification Through Acquisition: Strategies for Creating Economic Value*, New York: Free Press.

Seth, A. (1990) "Value creation in acquisitions: a re-examination of performance issues," *Strategic Management Journal*, 11: 99–115.

Shelton, L.M. (1988) "Strategic business fits and corporate acquisition: empirical evidence," *Strategic Management Journal*, 9: 279–87.

Singh, H. and Montgomery, C.A. (1987) "Corporate acquisition strategies and economic performance," *Strategic Management Journal*, 8: 377–86.

Slotegraaf, R.J., Moorman, C., and Inman, J.J. (2003) "The role of firm resources in returns to market deployment," *Journal of Marketing Research*, 40(3): 295–309.

Srivastava, R.K., Shervani, T.A., and Fahey, L. (1998) "Market-based assets and shareholder value: a framework for analysis," *Journal of Marketing*, 62: 2–18.

Steiner, P.O. (1975) *Mergers: Motives, Effects and Policies*, Ann Arbor, MI: University of Michigan Press.

Stimpert, J.L. and Duhaime, M. (1997) "In the eyes of the beholder: conceptualizations of relatedness held by managers of large diversified firms," *Strategic Management Journal*, 18: 111–25.

Swaminathan, V., Murshed, F., and Hulland, J. (2008) "Value creation following merger and acquisition announcements: the role of strategic emphasis alignment," *Journal of Marketing Research*, 45: 33–47.

Teece, D.J. (2007) "Explicating dynamic capabilities: the nature and microfoundations of (sustainable) enterprise performance," *Strategic Management Journal*, 28(13): 1319–50.

Teece, D., Pisano, G., and Shuen, A. (1997) "Dynamic capabilities and strategic management," *Strategic Management Journal*, 18: 509–33.

Urban, D.J. and Pratt, M.D. (2000) "Perceptions of banking services in the wave of bank mergers," *Journal of Services Marketing*, 14: 118–31.

Vu, D.A., Shi, Y., and Gregory, M. (2010) "Brand and product integration in horizontal mergers and acquisitions," *European Journal of International Management*, 4: 79–113.

Vu, D.A., Shi, Y., and Hanby, T. (2009) "Strategic framework for brand integration in horizontal mergers and acquisitions," *Journal of Technology Management in China*, 4: 26–52.

Walker, M.M. (2000) "Corporate takeovers, strategic objectives, and acquiring-firm stakeholder wealth," *Financial Management*, 17: 1233–44.

Wernerfelt, B. (1984) "A resource-based view of the firm," *Strategic Management Journal*, 5: 171–80.

Wernerfelt, B. (1988) "Umbrella branding as a signal of new product quality," *Rand Journal of Economics*, 19: 458–66.

Wille, C., Bauer, F.A., and Anslinger, T. (2011) "Corporate brand management bei mergers and acquisitions: Problemfelder und Erfolgsfaktoren," in Wollersheim, J. and Barthel, E. (eds.) *Forum Mergers & Acquisitions 2011*, Wiesbaden: Gabler.

Wirtz, B.W. (2003) *Mergers and Acquisitions Management—Strategie und Organisation von Unternehmenszusammenschlüssen*, Wiesbaden.

Yunker, J.A. (1983) *Integrating Acquisitions: Making Corporate Marriages Work*, New York: Praeger.

Conclusion
Deconstructing M&A research – paradigm progress

Amy L. Pablo

Introduction

In 2002, a conference on mergers and acquisitions (M&As) (called the M&A Summit 2002) was held in Calgary, Alberta, Canada attracting scholars from around the world. At that time, we observed that there was a divergence between conventional academic wisdom and executive practice, and we recognized that existing research on M&As provided only a limited and insufficient understanding of this important phenomenon. While the construct is multidimensional and cross-disciplinary, most of the research was single-discipline and one-dimensional producing only a partial understanding of the phenomenon. A volume produced from that conference was published in 2004 (Pablo and Javidan 2004). That volume contained six parts, those being M&A Performance, M&A Strategy, Merger Implementation and Integration, M&A Knowledge Transfer and Learning, Culture and Leadership in M&As, and Research in M&As. The intent of the conference and resulting volume was throwing down a gauntlet to future M&A researchers by pointing out the need for better paradigm development, more attention to operationalization and measurement of key constructs, and importantly more multidisciplinary research utilizing methodologies that can capture the dynamics of the phenomenon under study.

The relevance of M&A clearly remains. In the 2000s, we saw what some have called a renaissance in merger and acquisition activity (Harding *et al.* 2013). In fact, at the beginning of that period we saw about 37,000 global M&A transactions with a value of about $3.5 trillion (Pablo and Javidan 2004). Those figures continued to grow until we saw a peak in 2007 when they surpassed 40,000 transactions valued at $4.6 trillion, but the global fiscal crisis brought that trend to a grinding halt. In the sobering light of the morning after, companies began to reconsider their use of this inorganic growth strategy more carefully, assessing the impact on their company's performance, and the whys of it. Given the high failure rates of M&As (estimated by some to be around 50 percent), one CEO opined: "In the end, M&A is a flawed process, invented by brokers, lawyers and super-sized, ego-based CEOs" (Baxter 2004, p. 1). Following the sea-change in activity levels after 2007, we began to see a more measured attraction to acquisitions.

Flash forward to today, and it is worth noting that in 2014 M&A activity is rivaling 2007 levels (Davis 2014), but the complexion of deals is a little bit different this time around. In fact, if you look at the deals being made, you'll see that the activity is not so geopolitically centric around the developed world (North America and Europe). By 2013, worldwide, M&As of more than 36,800 deals valued at $2.4 trillion were announced, with emerging-market companies taking a strong position in the deal-making race (accounting for one-quarter of M&A transactions); about 60 percent come from what are known as the BRIC countries (Brazil, Russia, India and China; Thomson Reuters 2013). The current companion volume takes the step of examining how the complexion of M&As is shifting. For example, the growing role of international acquisitions is considered in Chapters 7 and 11. The result is an increased recognition of the need to consider multiple perspectives in M&A research as the complexity of the phenomenon of interest continues to evolve. In sum, now is an appropriate time to assess where M&A research is at and where it needs to go.

What we have learned

In this present volume, approximately a decade after the M&A summit and associated volume, we address new areas to add a little more definition to the question of what exactly we are studying, how we are studying it, and to what purpose. In that quest, we delineate work relating to the Substantive domain of merger and acquisition research, the Contextual domain of merger and acquisition research, the Methodological domain of merger and acquisition research, and the Conceptual domain of merger and acquisition research. This addresses concerns expressed in the 2004 volume of M&A research that prior research was not cross-disciplinary or provided only a partial understanding of M&A (Pablo and Javidan 2004). In the 22 preceding chapters, we cover topics that focus on how M&As help firms to effect intentions relating to contextual needs presented by their changing environment, further develop M&A capabilities as needed and as required within their context, impact stakeholders such as employees and powerbrokers, and create new social networks and processes needing identification and further empirical research. Here, we set the stage for detailing what has occurred in the past ten years, and the broader picture of what we have learned, continue to learn, and need to learn more about. In the following paragraphs, I summarize a handful of topics that continue to be relevant.

M&A performance

Most observers of the M&A markets use shareholder return as the measure of deal success: it's easy to determine and it is easily understood. Thus, we have many researchers using event study methodology as a tool to measure the value-creating (or -destroying) effects of M&A. Some of the problems with this measure are that it is ex-ante, archaic, simplistic, uninterested, and uninformed. In other words, it is before anything happens to the combining organizations. It shows a blind faith in the financial markets, it doesn't take into account any of the difficulties an acquirer will encounter on this most difficult route, scholars don't want to invest the time and energy it takes to really understand the ex-post outcome, and they don't know how to isolate the impact of the deal. Thus, here we call for a more deliberate choice of measures and/or the use of multiple performance measures to enable rethinking what acquisition performance actually means, getting down to the level of investor behavior and decision making beyond the assumption of total rationality in the transaction. In fact, in Chapter 13 in the current book, we make a call for reorientation in the measurement of acquisition performance. Further, here we suggest the potential importance of managers' staying cognizant of changes outside the box of just their focal acquisition situation (i.e. put it in context: What's going on in the environment?).

Finally, when we look at what senior executives actually use to determine acquisition success, these are factors that take time to become known. Only 5 percent say 6 months or less, and the majority say 1 year plus after the deal is completed. However, they do check how integration is going more quickly and regularly after the deal is done (*Intelligent Mergers* 2009). In other words, performance is not measured with either a single measure or at a single point in time.

Integration and synergies

In a review of M&As during the 2000s, models of M&A management that result in above normal total shareholder returns depended on the entire M&A process (Harding *et al.* 2013). Specifically, they found that repeatable models of successful acquirers include not only that they find, analyze, and execute the transaction, but, once the deal is done, they integrate the two companies. The importance of integration is receiving increased acceptance by executives. For example, in Bain & Company surveys between 2002 and 2012, integration challenges fell from the number one reason for disappointing M&A outcomes to number six (Harding *et al.* 2013). This reflects that successful acquirers devote more time, money, and attention to integration of the companies.

As explained by Pablo (1994), integration is the making of changes in the functional activity arrangements, organizational structures and systems, and cultures of the combining organizations to facilitate their consolidation into a functioning whole. The degree of change is dependent on what synergies are required to reinforce the corporate strategy behind making the merger/acquisition. Further, during the period of the 2000s researchers found that materiality mattered where the cumulative value of M&As amounted to a major percentage of the firm's market capitalization, such that the acquisition would command a more appropriate level of managerial attention and corporate resources. The impact of integration and associated issues reflected during integration are covered in Chapters 3, 15, 18, 20, and 21. Next, aspects of a paradigm for how to enact M&As for more profitable growth are outlined.

Strategic value

As shown in Chapters 1 and 5, M&As provide a way to acquire capabilities and pursue dynamic capabilities. Dynamic capabilities as described by Eisenhardt and Martin (2000) involve strategic organizational routines that enable firms to achieve new resource configurations or facilitate positive growth and development. To the extent that corporate growth is a valid strategic goal, M&As are a valid way to achieve them inorganically, potentially changing the organization in a beneficial direction along the way. In Chapter 5 of this volume, the authors describe M&As as a dynamic capability and describe how they involve a multi-layered temporally dependent process requiring multiple organizational mechanisms to ultimately result in a successful acquisition outcome. In that qualitative study, multinational companies were studied as a new venue for understanding the breakdown of how the acquisition capability is built from the ground up through organizational parts combining in processes and culminating in an acquisition capability which is dynamic enough to be used to reconfigure the organization on an as-needed basis.

In Chapter 9, M&As are looked at within their role in the whole corporate development portfolio where decisions are made about how to meet the organizational objective of growth. Developed routines lead organizations to choose between either exploiting a known growth strategy or exploring new avenues to gain resources (i.e. provide fuel for the engine of growth). The author examines the performance advantages that can be gained through appropriate selection and balancing of modes of growth, specifically building (organic growth/internal development), buying (mergers and acquisitions), or partnering (alliances and leasing), but also recognizes the different managerial challenges of each. The author suggests that more research is needed to better understand the impact of the chosen corporate development portfolio not only on firm survival, and also, taking a contingency view, under what circumstances what kinds of effects it will have, and what learnings can be gained by each.

Importance of learning

An example of a dynamic capability is an organization's ability to learn new practices or routines. Learning is a dynamic process that combines experimentation and repetition in a non-linear process aimed at improving both organizational efficiency and effectiveness (Eisenhardt and Martin 2000). An example of a dynamic capability is an organization's ability to learn new practices or routines. Learning is a dynamic process that combines experimentation and repetition in a non-linear process aimed at improving both organizational efficiency and effectiveness (Eisenhardt and Martin 2000). In the case of an acquisition capability, there must be continued codification of the knowledge held and assignment of managerial responsibility for intraorganizational transfer to key functional members of an acquisition team. As acquisitions are complex, with many dimensions influencing their outcomes, a number of studies have shown that at best 50 percent of acquisitions are successful. Thus it is that we see amongst the most successful M&As firms that have codified their acquisition activities. This is reinforced in the next section where some of the more and less successful M&As since the turn of the century are reviewed.

Continued lessons

Dramatic examples of success and failure continue to persist in M&As, and reviewing successful acquirers and specific deals that exemplify success and failure demonstrates that practice can continue to improve, while also highlighting areas for research.

Best M&As

Berkshire Hathaway (BRK) has made a reputation for being a successful serial acquirer. Probably because the acquisition process is so complicated and difficult, "serial acquirers" appear to be more successful with M&As than occasional acquirers (Douma and Schreuder 2013). Under the leadership of Warren Buffett, operating as a holding company, BRK acquisitions have been made solely for the purpose of gaining a controlling interest in another company, not for managing its ongoing operations, achieving synergy, or blending. Thus, integration is not a central issue for the success of these acquisitions. Financed largely by BRK's ongoing insurance firm holdings, Warren Buffett (CEO) has been able to spread the risk of his M&A investments widely. Considered to be the most successful investor of the twentieth century, he in fact is noted for his value-investing philosophy and his own personal frugality. In a famous quote from Buffett, he said: "Price is what you pay. Value is what you get" (Berger 2014). This is an apt description of the difference between market price (i.e. the price that the market requires to effect a transaction) and intrinsic value (i.e. the intrinsic worth of a business, which is a function of cash flow to be generated by the acquired business, which in turn is a function of core operations, expected synergies, integration success, and other factors).

In fact, BRK has set forth a stringent set of criteria for making business acquisitions, as follows:

1   large purchases (at least $75 million of pre-tax earnings unless the business will fit into one of their existing units);
2   demonstrated consistent earning power (future expectations are of no interest to them, nor are "turn-around" situations);
3   businesses earning good returns on equity while employing little or no debt;
4   management in place (they can't supply it);
5   simple businesses (if there's lots of technology, they won't understand it);
6   an offering price (they don't want to waste their or the seller's time bargaining).

This acquisition capability was used to great success in the 2000s, enabling BRK to complete what is considered to be their fabulous five. They represent Berkshire's largest non-insurance businesses and they are in a wide variety of industries including wind energy for electricity generation (MidAmerican Energy), coal transportation for electricity production (BNSF Railway), an Israeli metal-working company (Iscar), a tank car maker (Marmon Group), and a controlling interest in a chemical maker for $9 billion in cash in 2011 (Lubrizol). Buffett expanded that coverage into yet another industry, spreading his risk even further through his 2013 acquisition of Heinz for $28 billion in partnership with 3G capital. The lessons from BRK appear to be recognized by other businesses. For example, Cisco is another successful serial acquirer that has established criteria for acquisitions (Bunnell 2000), and acquisitions by firms in emerging markets involve less integration (Kale *et al.* 2009).

Another successful acquisition from 2008 that bears a more industry-specific strategic tone is the acquisition of Anheuser Busch by InBev. In fact, InBev resulted from a merger between the Belgian company Interbrew and the Brazilian brewer AmBev in 2004. The brewing industry world-wide has recently experienced consolidation, reflecting increased M&A activity, transforming the global beer industry. The Anheuser Busch InBev combination created the global leader in beer and one of the world's top five consumer products companies. In this case, a thorough integration of these two firms (taking nearly 3 years) was essential to realize necessary cost savings and synergies. Integration allowed them to realize over $250 million in cost savings and expected synergies of $2.25 billion even in the face of the global recession. The result was the world's largest brewer with 22 percent of global market share and 50 percent of US market share. This transaction also prompted the creation of even more consolidation in the brewing industry (e.g. Miller Coors and Molson Coors) through joint-ventures. This highlights the importance of competitor responses to acquisitions that is introduced in Chapter 19, but has largely not been considered by research.

Worst M&As

The $360 million AOL-Time Warner merger in 2000 was hailed at the time as a dream marriage of the old and new media. However, it quickly fizzled and became widely regarded as the deal that came to define the dot.com era. This was, at the time of the merger, considered to be evidence that the old and new media were converging, with internet companies doing the buying and the old media (including properties like Time, People, Fortune, Warner entertainment, HBO and CNN) doing the selling. Moving from old to new media can be seen as a journey in technology, and acquisition as a method of adaptation. In the buy-versus-build question, Time Warner thought that it had found a ready-made solution to its lack of internal digital capabilities in its suitor AOL, which had resources to burn. What went so wrong?

First, there's the question of the cultures of the two organizations, being vastly different (the conventional and long-established representative of the print media world versus the innovative and liberating dot-com of the internet world). Normally, as a company matures from a startup to a more established company, the company culture changes. Additionally, as the environment in which the company operates (the laws, regulations, business climate, etc.) changes, the company culture also evolves. These changes may be positive, or they may not. The changes in company culture may be intended, but often they are unintended. They may be major changes or minor ones. The company culture will change, and it is important to be aware of the changes. Cultural conflict between AOL Time Warner reflected that the cultures were the products of companies at different levels of maturity and apparently different prospects for the future (Quinn 2009; Ray 2012). AOL and Time Warner essentially were two different societies at war with one another. Readers interested in related ideas can read Chapters 11, 14 and 21.

Second, even though they may try to, and pretend to work together, another issue at the heart of firms that can cause problems is managerial hubris. The AOL and Time Warner CEOs had to realize that there were differences, but they thought they could overcome not only the differences between their firms but also the inherent philosophical and age differences between the two. The result was an internal firm environment of essentially survival of the fittest, while the external environment around them was going through a foundational upheaval. Life as these people knew it was essentially being transformed. This wasn't just a merger of two businesses, or just related versus unrelated businesses trying to become one—this was a merger of necessity. Both of these companies were in the media business, but one of the parties to the merger (AOL) was being tremendously overvalued by investors who believed in its potential, while the other (Time Warner) had a proud past with dim prospects on its own. Again, this suggests that the competitive context of an acquisition is important; some of these issues are discussed in Chapters 12, 17 and 18.

Third, societal change compounded the problems of cultural issues and managerial hubris to contribute to the failure of AOL and Time Warner. As noted by McGeorge Bundy, an advisor to President Kennedy, "There is no safety in unlimited technological hubris" (Bundy 1987). Much like Alexander the Great, the CEOs of AOL and Time Warner considered themselves to be the gods of the media world, one which was denoted by promise, hope, efficiency, and speed, and the other by a consistent stable of performers. In the campaign for success in the battles of the old and new media, these CEOs wanted to claim their place in history. As with Alexander the Great, the reason for their exploits were not political but personal. Their quests, though of great genius, were made out of pure hubris. Like Alexander, they acted as if they were the sons of a god, because since early on the stock market had told them so. Their quests were for recognition by others but most of all by themselves. They each believed that they had made their places in history. According to Case from AOL, "This is a historic moment in which new media has truly come of age"; and, according to Levin of Time Warner, the Internet had begun to create "unprecedented and instantaneous access to every form of media and unleash immense possibilities for economic growth, human understanding and creative expression" (Arango, 2010). Little did they know it, but the dot-com bubble was about to burst, causing investors to abandon a problematic corporate combination like rats leaving a sinking ship. Again, the competitive environment of acquisitions is discussed in Chapter 19.

In the end, old and new media were not just of different cultures, they were different species that were inherently at war. Although they were both media companies, it was more a matter of how they operated or firm values. Firm values influence how a deal is done. In the case of AOL Time Warner, differences in values led to integration never taking place. Further, cultural conflict resulted from business units working against each other, reflecting a lack of trust between the two that was constant and manifested harmful organizational practices. Unfortunately, similar cases of cultural clashes and hubris persist in acquisitions that destroy value, as demonstrated by the DaimlerChrysler merger (Krug *et al.* 2014).

Paradigm progress

With this new companion, the gauntlet thrown down approximately a decade ago has been taken up to substantively contribute to the development of M&A paradigms. Paradigm development is a theory or a group of ideas about how something should be done, made, or thought about. Beyond simply shifting between paradigms, progress likely depends on an interplay of paradigms that recognizes and contrasts perspectives to improve understanding (Schultz and Hatch 1996). Herein, we have included works that give more attention to operationalization and measurement of key constructs (i.e. Chapter 13) and, importantly, more multidisciplinary research utilizing multiple methodologies that can capture the dynamics of the phenomenon under study. For example, Chapter 14 outlines the application of institutional ethnography as a method for studying M&A.

Going forward, greater interplay of paradigms could facilitate reconciliation of the larger M&A phenomenon with different subgroups focused on technology, emerging markets, family firms, and so on. Further, comparison of perspectives focused within firms (i.e. capabilities) and external perspectives (i.e. competitive dynamics) could provide useful insights. M&As defy simple stereotyping, with the implication that research needs to evolve to consider emerging practices and offer insights to improve managerial practice. This means that there is a greater requirement for researchers to identify and examine current M&A practices. While there is absolutely a need for additional study, we believe that we have contributed substantially to M&A research and practice.

References

Arango, T. (2010) "How the AOL–Time Warner merger went so wrong," New York Times: www.nytimes.com/2010/01/11/business/media/11merger.html?p&_r=0. Accessed May 1, 2014.

Baxter, E. (2004) "Should we brace ourselves for another era of M&A value destruction?," Harvard Business School Working Knowledge, 5 April: http://hbswk.hbs.edu/item/4037.html.

Berger, R. (2014) "5 lessons every investor should learn from Warren Buffet," Forbes, March 19: www.forbes.com/sites/robertberger/2014/03/19/5-key-takeaways-from-buffetts-2013-letter-to-shareholders.

Bundy, M. (1987) "A world without nuclear arms?," New York Times, April 5: www.nytimes.com/1987/04/05/magazine/symposium-a-world-without-nuclear-arms-arms-control-not-competition.html. Accessed April 30, 2014.

Bunnell, D. (2000) *Making the Cisco connection: The real story behind the real internet superpower.* John Wiley & Sons: New York.

Davis, A. (2014) "No slowdown in sight for 2014's M&A frenzy," Forbes, June 24: www.forbes.com/sites/alexadavis/2014/06/24/no-slowdown-in-sight-for-2014s-ma-frenzy. Accessed June 25, 2014.

Douma, S. and Schreuder, H. (2013) *Economic approaches to organizations,* 4th edn. p. 306. Pearson Education: Essex.

Eisenhardt, K. and Martin, J. (2000) "Dynamic capabilities: What are they?" *Strategic Management Journal,* 21: 1105–21.

Harding, D., Shankar, S., and Jackson, R. (2013) "The renaissance in mergers and acquisitions: The surprising lessons of the 2000s," Bain & Company: www.bain.com/Images/BAIN_BRIEF_The_renaissance_in_mergers_and_acquisitions.pdf. Accessed April 30, 2014.

Intelligent Mergers. (2009) "Measuring M&A deal success": http://intelligentmergers.com/2009/12/17/measuring-ma-deal-success/. Accessed May 1, 2014.

Kale, P., Singh, H., and Raman, A. (2009) "Don't integrate your acquisitions, partner with them," *Harvard Business Review,* 87(12): 109–15.

Krug, J., Wright, P., and Kroll, M. (2014) "Top management turnover following mergers and acquisitions: Solid research to date but much to be learned," *Academy of Management Perspectives*, 28: 147–63.

Pablo, A. (1994) "Determinants of acquisition integration level: A decision-making perspective," *Academy of Management Journal*, 37: 803–36.

Pablo, A. and Javidan, M. (2004) *Mergers and acquisitions: Creating integrative knowledge.* Blackwell Publishing: Oxford.

Quinn, J. (2009) "Final farewell to worst deal in history—AOL-Time Warner," *The Telegraph*: www.telegraph.co.uk/finance/newsbysector/mediatechnologyandtelecoms/media/6622875/Final-farewell-to-worst-deal-in-history-AOL-Time-Warner.html. Accessed April 30, 2014.

Ray, S. (2012) "Cultural dimension analysis of AOL-Time Warner merger," *Journal of Applied Library and Information Science*, 1: 39–41.

Schultz, M. and Hatch, M. (1996) "Living with multiple paradigms: The case of paradigm interplay in organizational culture studies, *Academy of Management Review*, 21: 529–57.

Thomson Reuters. (2013) "Preliminary mergers and acquisitions review": http://share.thomsonreuters.com/pr_us/Prelim_MA_Financial4Q13_Review.pdf. Accessed: April 15, 2014.

Index